IRISH FOOTBALL HANDBOOK
1994-95

Dave Galvin   Gerry Desmond

"Irish Football At Your Fingertips"

Red Card Publications
Cork

Red Card Publications
P.O. Box 10, Eglinton Street, Cork.
Republic of Ireland

© 1994 Dave Galvin & Gerry Desmond

All rights reserved. No part of this publication may be reproduced, stored in a retrieval system, electronic, mechanical, photocopying, recording or otherwise, without the prior permission in writing of the authors.

British Library Cataloguing-in-Publication Data.
A catalogue record of this book is available from the British Library.

ISBN 0 9517987 3 1

Front Cover: Main Photo	**Viva Aldo!** John Aldridge scores a vital goal against the Mexicans in Orlando (EOH)
2nd Photo	**Untangled** Peter Eccles Captain of Champions Shamrock Rovers emerges with the ball as Ken De Mange (Bohemians) feels the pain. (The Star)
Inside Back Cover:	**Football can be fun too!** Things get a little heated on the sidelines in Orlando. (EOH)
Back Cover:	**Gone Fishing!** Roberto Baggio and Jack Charlton looking a little glum at the Giants Stadium. (EOH)

Typeset, printed and bound in the Republic of Ireland
by
Litho Press Co., Midleton, Co. Cork.

DEDICATIONS

Gerry: For *Peter*, the Villan, completely addicted; for *Ellen* who, at 17 months, knows a good goal when she sees one; especially for *Theresa* who has suffered because of it all.
And for
Ritchie Barrett, whose crossbar was my earliest transportation to away games: I haven't forgotten, cuz!

Dave: To my darling wife *Mary* and our eldest sons *Stephen* and *Paul*, whose patience and understanding in the face of this obsession remains unfailing, and to our brilliant new arrival *Kevin*, naturally the highlight of the season.

SPECIAL APPRECIATION

We would particularly like to thank the following for their contribution to the fourth edition of the *Irish Football Handbook*, **The Star** team, especially *Paul Cooke, Fintan Gavigan, Paul Lennon* and *Stephen Finn* and our good friends *Eddie O'Hare* and *Tony Sheehan* for whom nothing is too much trouble.

Thanks also to *Seán Connolly* (F.A.I.) and *Eamonn Morris* (F.A.I. National League) for their kind permission to reproduce the fixtures which remain the property of

The Football Association of Ireland
and
F.A.I. National League

ACKNOWLEDGEMENTS

We would like to express our sincere gratitude to the following people for their help in making the "Irish Football Handbook 1994/95" a reality, and trust we have omitted no relevant names.

Norma Ahern (Midleton), Ebor Benson, John Botos, Frank Boylan (St. Patrick's Athletic), George Briggs (L.F.A.), Seán Brodie (L.F.A.I.), Finbarr Buckley, Nora Buckley, Denis Burke (Bus Eireann), Kieran Burke, Stephen Burke (Bohemians), Michael Butler (Waterford Utd.), Charlie Cahill (L.S.L), Des Casey (National League), Paul Clifford (Monaghan Utd.), Seán Connolly (F.A.I.), Finbarr Constant (Irish Oxygen Co.), Paul Cooke (The Star), Cork City Supporters Club Committee, Willie Cotter, Finbarr Crowley (Cork Communications), Donal Crowther (Bohemians), Donal Cullen, Ian Curristan (Finn Harps), Tony Daly, Seán Dempsey (Longford Town), Joan Desmond, Ken Desmond, Rose Desmond, Theresa Desmond, Breda Devereux, Francis Devine (Howth Celtic), Pat Dolan (St. Patrick's Athletic), Paul Doolan (Shamrock Rovers), Michael Duffy (Bray Wanderers), Angela Duggan, Pat Duggan, Noelle Feeney, Christy Fenlon, Stephen Finn (The Star), Brendan and Deirdre Flanagan, Eamonn Flanagan (Derry City), Donie Forde (M.F.A.), Ian Friary (Monaghan United), Deirdre Galvin, Derry Galvin, Kitty Galvin, Mary Galvin, Michael Galvin, Pat Galvin, Philip Galvin, Robbie Galvin, Seán Galvin, Steve Galvin, Tim Galvin, Tim Galvin (Snr.), Noel Gannon (Athlone Town), Fintan Gavigan (The Star), Michael Geasley (Cobh Ramblers), Bill George, Marshall Gillespie, Mary Ginty (Longford Town), Mick Gleeson (Cherry Orchard), George Guest (Galway United), Paul Hamilton (Sligo Rovers), Tina Healy, Ray Hennessy (Cork City), Chris Herlihy (Cork City), Declan Hughes (U.C.D.), Tom Humphries (Irish Times), Charlie Hurley (Drogheda United), Irish Football Programme Club Committee (John Holmes, Shay Kett, Pat O'Callaghan, Henry Randle, Fergus Reid), Mandy Johnston (F.A.I.), Gerry Juhel (St. James's Gate), Dermot Kelly (Imperial Hotel), Pat Kelly (Galway United), Billy Kenny (Cork City), Eamonn Kirwan, Michael Kirwan (Shelbourne), Thomas Lawless (Bohemians), Paul Lennon (The Star), Brendan Loughran (Drogheda United), Pat McAuliffe (R.T.E.), Gail McEvoy (Leinster Ladies League), Stephen McLoughlin (Castlebar), Jimmy Magee (R.T.E.), Frank Martin, Ulrich Matheja (Kicker Sportmagazin), Joe Molloy (Sligo Rovers), Eamonn Morris (National League), John Moynihan, Peter Mulhall (St. James's Gate), Betty Murphy, Edward Murphy (Ford (Ireland) Ltd.), Jim Murphy (M.S.L./M.F.A.), Richard Murphy, Ray Nixon (Dundalk), Barney O'Brien, Paul O'Brien (Galway United), Bill O'Callaghan (Litho Press), Dave O'Connell (Cork Examiner), Tony O'Donoghue (R.T.E.), Andrew O'Dowd (Longford Town), Imelda O'Hanlon (Munster Ladies League), John "The Man" O'Leary, Sonny O'Reilly, Mark Phelan, Jim Rhatigan (Kilkenny City), Gerry Rice (Dundalk), Frank Riordan, Catherine Ryan, Michael Ryan, Seán Ryan (Sunday Independent), Tony Sheehan (National League), Tony Shinnors (Limerick), Oliver Slattery, Noel Spillane (Cork Examiner), Aidan Stanley (R.T.E.), Anne Twomey, Mary Twomey, Trevor Welch (Cork Communications).

CONTENTS

First and Record League Goalscorers	1
League of Ireland Membership	2
Club Directory	3
Where they played/L.O.I. Grounds	73
Comings and Goings	76
International Review (including Ireland at USA '94 and full Statistics 1993/94)	78
Ladies Soccer 1993-94	99
Republic of Ireland First 150 Line-Ups	100
Republic of Ireland International Players 1926-1975	106
B, U-23 & U-21 Results & Line-Ups	109
U.E.F.A. U16 Championship Finals 1994	119
The Copa Independencia do Brasil / International Flashback	125
European Review and Statistics 1993-94	137
L.O.I. Clubs in Europe 1957-1994	146
Athlone Town v A.C. Milan / European Flashback	154
The Championship Review	162
First Division Championship Review	166
League Tables & Statistics 1993-1994	168
L.O.I. Hotshots	176
100 Club and Current Top Scorers	178
F.A.I. Cup Review & Statistics 1994	180
Non-League Clubs in F.A.I. Cup 1922-1994	188
League Cup Review & Statistics 1993-94	205
Previous League Cup Finals	208
Non-League Clubs in the League Cup 1976-1994	210
First Division Shield	212
Leinster Senior Cup	216
Munster Senior Cup	221
President's Cup	230
Non-League Provincial Tables & Intermediate Cup	232
Everpresents	238
Player Directory	239
Awards	268
Transfer Trail	272
Final Positions last Ten Seasons	275
Friendly Scene	276
Northern Ireland 1993-94	279
Fixtures	281
Bibliography, Sources, Photo credits	286

BUS ÉIREANN

Ireland's National Bus Company at Your Service

"Expressway"	Nationwide Network of Services
"Supabus"	To Britain and the Continent
"Breakaways"	Mini-Breaks-Including Accommodation and Travel
Summer Day Tours	To all Scenic Areas
Family Tickets on all Services	Covering 2 Adults and 3 Children (U16)
Rambler Tickets	Valid for 3, 8, or 15 Days
Midweek Travel	Return Tickets at Single Fares - Tues/Wed/Thurs.
Return Tickets	Now Valid for One Month

Information

Cork: 021 - 508188
Tralee: 066 - 23566
Killarney: 064 - 34777
Dublin: 01 - 8366111

Limerick: 061 - 313333
Galway: 091 - 62000
Waterford: 051 - 79000

FOREWORD

Welcome to the 1994-95 edition of the Irish Football Handbook published in association with The Star. Now in its fourth year, the Irish Football Handbook is firmly established as the authoritative record on the game in Ireland.

The Star is delighted to join forces with authors Gerry Desmond and Dave Galvin in this year's edition. In the past three years the authors have each spent hundreds of hours in researching facts and figures about the game in this country.

While the exploits of Jack Charlton's side in two World Cup finals and the Euro '88 finals have accordingly grabbed the headlines in recent years, the domestic game has also grown stronger through the upgrade of facilities and installation of floodlights.

It is fitting that the Irish Football Handbook has also gone from strength to strength in that time. This edition adds new features for the reader's enjoyment while updating the vital club and player sections.

Have Many Hours of Happy Reading!

Paul Lennon
Soccer Correspondent, The Star

Where'd the ball go?
Eoin Mullen (Shamrock Rovers) on ground, scores against Bohemians (The Star)

Wunderbar!
Gary Kelly celebrates his goal against Germany in Hannover   (The Star)

INTRODUCTION

Better late than never! is an old adage and we hope you will find our late arrival worthwhile as we welcome you to the fourth *Irish Football Handbook*.

The Handbook has grown annually, improving production quality while expanding scope and content. This, of course, remains a hobby for us yet we feel the end result bears favourable comparison with equivalent yearbooks in other countries produced by professional publishing houses and enjoying a large market base. We are thrilled ours is perceived as the authoritative work on the game in the Republic of Ireland. Two non-football people are primarily responsible for the Handbooks existence – *Mary* and *Theresa* – whose tolerance of our obsession is above and beyond the call of matrimonial duty.

A new step this year has been the introduction of a full-colour cover, a direct result of *The Star's* welcome involvement. The response from Paul Cooke, Paul Lennon and the team at Ireland's brightest daily when we routinely approached them for an advert was more enthusiastic than we could have hoped for. Since that initial contact *The Star* has had every facet of the Handbook as a genuine concern, supplying many superb photographs, publicising it's existence and generally wanting it to succeed. Having long admired their commitment to all levels of Irish football – the International team, the National League and junior soccer all rank in the paper's colourful sports coverage – we are naturally delighted to have *The Star* associated with the *Irish Football Handbook*. Many thanks to the Pauls, Stephen Finn and Fintan Gavigan for all their help and support.

To all our other advertisers, besides our thanks for your generous support the certain knowledge that without your help the Handbook would still be confined to our notebooks.

Tony Sheehan, press officer for the National League has, as always, been a paragon of assistance, encouragement and kindness while *Mandy Johnston* at the FAI has been a real gem. Everybody on the acknowledgements list is deserving of a sincere "thank you," all the help received has made our task much easier. We are particularly indebted to *Marshall Gillespie* who came up with urgent solutions to our problems at short notice.

It has been an eventful year for all connected with Irish football, culminating in the marvellous spectacle of USA 94. The general feeling of disappointment felt after Ireland's elimination perhaps best sums up how far the team has progressed though some irresponsible journalism, suggesting Ireland were good enough to win the tournament, no doubt led many astray. It is obvious, however, that merely taking part is now no longer enough for many of the Green Army. People now expect The Lads to make an impact at the top level.

The FAI quite successfully hosted its first ever international tournament when the UEFA U-16 finals were run-off as April turned to May with 32 games at 13 venues around the country. Hopefully the good organisation on show will attract further finals in the future.

Significant changes are afoot in the home game, particularly with the much heralded amalgamation of the FAI and National League which should see matters improve domestically and form a vital platform for the future of Irish football. The floodlighting and upgrading of league grounds continues with now only a handful of venues to go before the programme is complete. Clubs now have the flexibility to compete with counter attractions and, with a little top brass initiative, a further boost could be given by introducing an all-Ireland floodlit competition particularly as the threat of paramilitary violence has been removed. Soccer, the global communicator, should be able to offer the hand of friendship from one end of this small island to the other.

The increase in representative games is another positive step on the home scene with the return of inter-league fixtures against the Welsh and Irish Leagues and also top club sides such as IFK Gothenburg visiting our shores. It is disappointing, however, that National League players still cannot break into Maurice Setters' U-21 side, yet are selected almost immediately on joining an English club.

On the league front, the controversial top six / bottom six split has been scrapped after a two-year trial period. It was a bold experiment which had it's advocates but the dissenters finally prevailed and we have returned to a traditional format once again though three points for a win has been retained. This years championship looks wide open and the increase in title candidates can only be a good thing.

Losing a guaranteed berth in the Champions' Cup has been bad for the image of the league but in many ways this is the result of decades in which no priority planning was given to our participation in UEFA competitions. We still await a national initiative to restore our champion teams to Europe's premier club tournament.

Finally, we would like to wish you an enjoyable 1994-95 and hope it is a good year for Irish football.

Oh Ray, Oh Ray, Oh Ray!
Houghton celebrates after scoring the most famous goal of the Charlton era (The Star)

EXPLANATORY NOTES

(a) Due to the constantly changing nature of the **Club Directory Section**, particularly in respect of club personnel, it should be noted that all information is correct at time of going to press. All club records are correct to end of 1993-94.

(b) The **Club Directory** contains full line-ups for all clubs for season 1993-94. This information was compiled from as many sources as possible including newspapers, magazines, match programmes, club consultation, foreign libraries and so on. Every effort has been made to obtain this information from the clubs themselves. Unfortunately, as some clubs again failed to reply and in the absence of reliable club programme information, in certain cases accuracy is solely dependant on newspaper reports.
It should also be noted that the positions given in the line-up sequences are those calculated on Monday morning after a full series of weekend matches and not those which may appear in the press after Friday or Saturday evening games.

(c) In the **Competitions Section** a name appearing in brackets indicates a substitute appearance and immediately follows the player replaced.

(d) Where included, figures in brackets in results sequences refer to half-time scores.

(e) All Derry City information in the Club Directory refers to the clubs League of Ireland membership only.

SYMBOLS

Club Directory: Under the heading "Points In a Season" a single asterisk (*) appears before any entry for season 1981/82 as the points system was changed to 4 for an away win, 3 for a home win, 2 for an away draw and 1 for a home draw. A double asterisk (**) before any entry for season 1982/83 signifies another experimental points system, re-introduced last season, of 3 for a win and 1 for a draw. In every other season the League of Ireland has operated the traditional 2 points per win and 1 point for a draw.
Under the heading "League Appearances 1993/94" any number following the plus symbol (+) indicates substitute appearances. For example, 6 + 3 means 6 appearances plus 3 further appearances as substitute.
In the Line-Ups sequences any numeral (1, 2, 3 etc.) after a players name represents goals scored by the player in that particular game. The symbol • after a player denotes the player was substituted by number 12. Similarly, the symbol # indicates replacement by number 13.

An own goal (OG) in the extreme right hand column signifies the team has benefitted from an opponents error.

It should be particularly noted that the numbers 1-13 do not necessarily represent those worn by players in any given match.

In "The Republic of Ireland first 150 Line-Ups" the symbols used are exactly the same as those employed for the line-up sequences in the Player Directory.

In "The Republic of Ireland International Players 1926-1975" the format used is best illustrated by the following example.

Eglington Tommy (Shamrock Rovers) 1946[2], (Everton) 1946[3]-55   **(24)**

With the year quoted being a calender year, this indicates that Tommy won the first two of his caps with **Shamrock Rovers** in 1946, i.e. **(1946[2])**. He then transferred to Everton where his next cap again in 1946 i.e. **(1946[3])** and indeed all his subsequent honours right up to 1955 i.e. **(-55)** were won with the Goodison Park outfit. In all Tommy Eglinton won twenty four **(24)** caps with the Republic of Ireland.

In the **Republic of Ireland "B,"** U-23 and U-21 appearances section an asterisk (*) indicates a goal scored in a particular game. The number of asterisks corresponds to the number of goals scored.

In the **Player Directory** every effort has been made to present uniform information on roughly 500 players who made at least one L.O.I. appearance last season 1993-94.

Explanation of the format used in the **Player Directory** is best illustrated by the following example:

MURPHY, John b. Cork 29 Feb. 1967
Jan. '93   Tramore Ath to Cobh Ramblers
               COBH RAMBLERS v Shamrock Rovers (4-0) 2G, 20 Jan '93
1992/93   Cobh Ramblers   17 + 3 (6)
1993/94   Cobh Ramblers   1 + 1 (1)
Mar. '94   Waterford United (L)   4 + 1 (1)

Line 1   Gives the players basic biographical details;
Line 2   Gives signing date and source club prior to L.O.I. debut or, where such details are unconfirmed, earliest known transfer between L.O.I. clubs.
Line 3   L.O.I. debut details
         Remaining information refers to playing record from season 1992/93 i.e. number of appearances plus substitute appearances with goals scored in brackets
         (L) indicates a loan transfer.
         It should be particularly noted that the appearances/goals statistics included in the section cover the past three seasons only while many players' careers obviously pre-date this starting point.

The remaining format of the Irish Football Handbook should be easy enough to follow for any soccer fan though perhaps an explanation of the Shield may be necessary. As this competition is now solely confined to First Division clubs it has been treated as a separate competition, namely, the First Division Shield.

Current Clubs' First and Record League Goalscorers

	1st Scorer	Opponents	Venue			Record Scorer		Total
					Game No.			
Athlone Town	John Sweeney	v St. James's Gate	Athlone Sportsground	16 Sep. '22	(1-3)	1	Michael O'Connor	107
Bohemians	Frank Haine	v YMCA	Dalymount Park	17 Sep. '21	(5-0)	1	Turlough O'Connor	120
Bray Wanderers	Martin Nugent	v Newcastle United	The Desmesne	27 Oct. '85	(3-0)	2	John Ryan	32
Cobh Ramblers	Frank O'Neill	v Monaghan United	St. Colman's Park	20 Oct. '85	(2-1)	1	Terry Kearns	31
Cork City	Bobby Woodruff	v Waterford United	Flower Lodge	22 Sep. '84	(3-1)	2	Pat Morley	72
Derry City	Kevin Mahon	v Emfa	Buckley Park	20 Oct. '85	(1-1)	1	Jonathan Speak	70
Drogheda United[1]	Mick McElroy	v Cork Hibernians	Lourdes Stadium	10 Nov. '63	(2-2)	1	Damien Byrne	47
Dundalk	Joe Quinn[2]	v Fordsons	Ballinlough	21 Aug. '26	(1-2)	1	Joey Donnelly	69
Finn Harps	Brendan Bradley	v Cork Hibernians	Finn Park	5 Oct. '69	(3-1)	1	Brendan Bradley	181
Galway United[3]	Eamonn Deacy	v Thurles Town	Greyhound Stadium	2 Oct. '77	(1-0)	6	Paul McGee	74
Home Farm	Frank Devlin	v Dundalk	Oriel Park	8 Oct. '72	(1-0)	1	Frank Devlin	30
Kilkenny City[4]	Jimmy Leahy	v Derry City	Buckley Park	20 Oct. '85	(1-1)	1	John Kelly	23
Limerick[5]	Gary Hulmes	v Shelbourne	Markets Field	6 Nov. '83	(1-1)	1	Tommy Gaynor	35
Longford Town	Tony O'Kelly	v Shamrock Rovers	Milltown	23 Sep. '84	(1-6)	2	Richie Parsons	26
Monaghan United	Seamus Finnegan	v Cobh Ramblers	St. Colman's Park	20 Oct. '85	(1-2)	1	Jim Barr	23
St. James's Gate	Bill O'Shea	v Dublin United	St. James's Park	17 Sep. '21	(5-1)	1	Paddy Bradshaw	68
St. Patrick's Athletic	Johnny Coyle	v Drumcondra	Milltown	18 Nov. '51	(1-2)	1	Shay Gibbons	108
Shamrock Rovers	Bob Fullam	v Pioneers	Strand Road	23 Sep. '22	(5-1)	2	Paddy Ambrose	109
Shelbourne	Canning[6]	v Frankfort	Richmond Road	17 Sep. '21	(4-0)	1	Eric Barber	126
Sligo Rovers	Gerard McDaid	v St. James's Gate	Showgrounds	28 Oct. '34	(2-3)	1	Johnny Armstrong	85
U.C.D.	Fintan Drury	v Home Farm	Tolka Park	23 Sep. '79	(1-0)	3	Darren O'Brien	46
Waterford United	Mick Madigan	v Shelbourne	Harold's Cross	3 Oct. '82	(2-5)	1	Michael Bennett	49

Notes:
1. Played as Drogheda
2. Some sources credit Frank Brady with an own goal.
3. Played as Galway Rovers.
4. Played as Emfa
5. Played as Limerick City
6. Christian name unknown.

LEAGUE OF IRELAND MEMBERSHIP
1921/22 - 1993/94

73	*Bohemians*	1921/22-1993/94
72	*Shamrock Rvs*	1922/23-1993/94
71	*Shelbourne*	1921/22-1933/34
		1936/37-1993/94
68	*Dundalk*	1926/27-1993/94
51	Sligo Rovers	1934/35-1939/40
		1948/49-1961/62
		1963/64-1993/94
46	Limerick/	
	Limerick Utd.	1937/38-1982/83
46	Waterford	1930/31-1931/32
		1934/35-1940/41
		1945/46-1981/82
44	Drumcondra	1928/29-1971/72
43	*St. Pat's Ath.*	1951/52-1993/94
31	Athlone Town	1922/23-1927/28
		1969/70-1993/94
30	Drogheda/	
	Drogheda Utd.	1963/64-1993/94
28	Evergreen Utd./	
	Cork Celtic	1951/52-1978/79
27	St. James's Gate	1921/22-1943/44
		1990/91-1993/94
25	*Finn Harps*	1969/70-1993/94
21	*Home Farm*	1972/73-1993/94
19	Bray Unknowns	1924/25-1942/43
19	Cork Hibernians	1957/58-1975/76
17	Galway Rvs/	
	Galway Utd.	1977/78-1993/94
16	Brideville	1925/26-1931/32
		1935/36-1942/43
		1944/45
15	*UCD*	1979/80-1993/94
14	Transport	1948/49-1961/62
12	*Waterford Utd.*	1982/83-1993/94
11	Jacobs	1921/22-1931/32
11	*Limerick City/*	
	Limerick	1983/84-1993/94
10	Cork United	1939/40-1948/49
10	*Cork City*	1984/85-1993/94
10	*Longford Town*	1984/85-1993/94
9	*Bray Wanderers*	1985/86-1993/94
9	*Cobh Ramblers*	1985/86-1993/94
9	Cork Athletic	1948/49-1956/57
9	*Derry City*	1985/86-1993/94
9	Emfa/	
	Kilkenny City	1985/86-1993/94
9	*Monaghan Utd*	1985/86-1993/94
8	Cork	1930/31-1937/38
7	Dolphin	1930/31-1936/37
6	Albert Rovers/	
	Cork Albert/	
	Cork United	1976/77-1981/82
6	Fordsons	1924/25-1929/30
5	Newcastle Utd/	
	Newcastlewest	1985/86-1989/90
5	Thurles Town	1977/78-1981/82
4	Pioneers	1922/23-1925/26
2	Brooklyn	1923/24-1924/25
2	Cork Bohemians	1932/33-1933/34
2	Cork City	1938/39-1939/40
2	Dublin Utd.	1921/22-1922/23
2	Midland Ath.	1922/23-1923/24
2	Olympia	1921/22-1922/23
2	Shelbourne Utd	1922/23-1923/24
1	Frankfort	1921/22
1	Rathmines Ath	1922/23
1	Reds Utd.	1935/36
1	YMCA	1921/22

Note: Due to the high number of name changes by League of Ireland clubs it should be noted that in several cases clubs of the same name are separate entities, for example Cork City (1938) and Cork City (1984); Cork United (1940) and Cork United (1980's) and the current Limerick F.C. and Limerick (1937). For presentation purposes clubs which collapsed in mid-season are considered members for that full season. Clubs in **bold** are current League members.

Athlone Town   Premier Div.

Founded: 1887
Home: St. Mel's Park, Athlone, Co. Westmeath. Tel. (0902) 78323
Capacity: 7,000; 200 seated
Previous Grounds: Sportsground   (1922/23 & 1925/26)
                    Ranelagh Grds.   (1926/27 & 1927/28)
Nickname: "Town"
Colours: Blue & Black striped shirts, Black shorts.
2nd Colours: White shirts and shorts.
Manager: Michael O'Connor   Succeeded: Pat Devlin (May 1992)
President: John Keena
Chairman: Paddy McCaul
Secretary: Jack McKervey, 7 St. Francis Tce., Athlone.
            Tel. Home: (0902) 75268; Office: (0902) 92156; Fax. (0902) 93107

Honours/Best Performances:

League of Ireland Champions	:	1980/81, 1982/83	(2)
First Division Champions	:	1987/88	(1)
F.A.I. Cup Winners	:	1924	(1)
League Cup Winners	:	1979/80, 1981/82, 1982/83	(3)
League of Ireland Shield	:	Runners-up 1922/23, 1970/71	
Leinster Cup Winners	:	1969/70, 1987/88, 1991/92	(3)
Dublin City Cup	:	Runners-up 1975/76	
Presidents Cup Winners	:	1983/84	(1)
Tyler Cup Winners	:	1979/80	(1)

League Career:
Elected 1922 as League extended to 12 Clubs. Resigned end 1927/28.
Rejoined with Finn Harps 1969. Relegated end 1986/87. Promoted end 1987/88. Relegated end 1991/92. Promoted end 1993/94

European Appearances: 3

Champions Cup:	1981/82	v	K.B. Copenhagen	2 - 2,	1 - 1
	1983/84	v	Standard Liege	2 - 3,	2 - 8
U.E.F.A. Cup:	1975/76	v	Valerengen	3 - 1,	1 - 1
		v	A.C. Milan	0 - 0,	0 - 3

Record League Victory:

Home	:	8 - 0	v	Thurles Town	29 Sep. 1981
Away	:	5 - 0	v	Thurles Town	03 Oct. 1978
			v	U.C.D.	15 Sep. 1979
			v	Finn Harps	16 Sep. 1984

Record League Defeat:

Home	:	2 - 7	v	Shelbourne	15 Nov. 1927
Away	:	0 - 7	v	Finn Harps	07 Nov. 1971

Most League Goals
(Match)   4:   Michael O'Connor v Finn Harps 4 - 2 (A) 28 Apr. 1982
(Season) 23:   Eugene Davis 1980/81
(Career) 107:   Michael O'Connor 1979/80 - 1986/87 & 1989/90 - 1993/94

Points in a Season:
Most	:	51	1980/81	(30 games)
		65**	1982/83	(26 games)
		67*	1981/82	(30 games)
Least	:	5	1927/28	(18 games)

Goals Scored in a Season:
Most	:	70	1981/82	(30 games)
Least	:	15	1927/28	(18 games)

League Appearances 1993/94:
27 Frank Darby, David Dowling, Chris Malone, 26 Conor Frawley, Val Keenan, Barry Murphy, 25 Paul Brady, Tommy Keane, 24 Anthony Keenan, 16+5 Donal Golden, 5+15 Michael O'Connor, 14+3 Johnny Morris-Burke, 5+5 Rod De-Khors, 8+1 P.J. O'Connell, 4+5 Frank O'Connell, 4+1 Dermot Lennon, 2+3 Gordon Brett, 3 Shane Curran, 2 Tom Fallon, 1 Keith Reynolds, 0+1 Ian Kiernan.
Players Used: 21

IRISH OXYGEN
CORK

Suppliers in Munster to all Engineering, Education, Construction, Motor & Agricultural Industry.

Oxygen, Acetylene, Argon, Carbondioxide, Nitrogen, Welding Mixes, special gases - in fact any gas you need.

Any size from the requirements of heavy engineering industry to that of the small one-man repair shop.

For full detail for your welding or cutting jobs
Please phone us at (021) 541821

**Irish Oxygen Company Limited
Waterfall Road, Cork.**

Phone 021 541821

Athlone Town 1993/94

Date	V	Opposition	Score	Pos	1	2	3	4	5	6	7	8	9	10	11	12	13
19 Sep	A	St. James's Gate	2-0	-	Curran	Malone	Darby	Murphy	V. Keenan	Brady	Morris-Burke	Frawley[1]	Golden[1]	Dowling[1]	Keane	O'Connor	
26 Sep	H	Kilkenny City	0-0	1st	Curran	Malone	Darby	Murphy	V. Keenan	Brady	Lennon	Frawley	Golden[#]	Dowling	Keane[*]	O'Connor	Kiernan
3 Oct	A	U.C.D.	1-0	1st	A. Keenan	Malone	Darby[1]	F. O'Connell	V. Keenan	Brady	Brett	Frawley	Golden[*1]	Dowling[1]	Keane	Golden	
10 Oct	H	Home Farm	2-2	1st	A. Keenan	Malone	Darby	Murphy	V. Keenan	Brady	Brett	Frawley	Golden[1]	Dowling[1]	Keane[#]	Golden	Lennon
17 Oct	A	Longford Town	0-0	2nd	A. Keenan	Malone	Darby	Murphy	V. Keenan	Brady	F. O'Connell	Frawley	O'Connor	Dowling	Keane[#]	Golden	
24 Oct	H	Bray Wanderers	1-1	2nd	A. Keenan	Malone	Darby	Murphy	V. Keenan	Brady[*]	F. O'Connell	Frawley[1]	O'Connor[*]	Dowling[1]	Keane	Brett	
31 Oct	H	Sligo Rovers	2-1	1st	A. Keenan	Malone	Darby	Murphy	V. Keenan	Brady[*]	Lennon[1]	Frawley[1]	O'Connor[*]	Dowling[1]	Keane[1]	Brett	F. O'Connell
7 Nov	A	Waterford United	1-1	2nd	Curran	Malone	Darby	Murphy	V. Keenan	Frawley[*]	Lennon	Golden	O'Connor[#]	Dowling[1]	Keane[1]	F. O'Connell	
14 Nov	H	Finn Harps	2-2	2nd	A. Keenan	Malone[1]	Darby	Murphy	V. Keenan	Frawley[*]	Morris-Burke[*]	Golden	Brady	Dowling[1]	Keane	Morris-Burke	
21 Nov	H	Finn Harps	1-0	1st	A. Keenan	Malone[*]	Darby[1]	Murphy	V. Keenan	Frawley[2]	Morris-Burke[*]	Golden	Brady	Dowling	Keane	Brett	
28 Nov	A	St. James's Gate	3-1	1st	A. Keenan	Malone	Darby	Murphy	V. Keenan	Frawley[1]	Morris-Burke[*]	Golden[1]	Brady[1]	Dowling	Keane[1]	O'Connor	
5 Dec	H	Kilkenny City	3-1	1st	A. Keenan	Malone	Darby	Murphy	V. Keenan	Frawley	Morris-Burke[*]	Golden[1]	Brady	Dowling[1]	Keane[1]	De-Khors	O'Connor
12 Dec	H	U.C.D.	2-0	1st	A. Keenan	Malone	Darby[*]	Murphy	De-Khors	Frawley	Morris-Burke	Golden[*]	Brady	Dowling[1]	Keane[*1]	F. O'Connell	O'Connor
19 Dec	H	Home Farm	1-1	1st	A. Keenan	Malone	Darby	Murphy	V. Keenan	Frawley	F. O'Connell[*]	Golden[*]	Brady	Dowling[1]	Keane[#1]	F. O'Connell	O'Connor[1]
26 Dec	H	Longford Town	2-1	1st	A. Keenan	Malone	Darby	Murphy	V. Keenan	Frawley	Morris-Burke	Golden	Brady	Dowling[1]	Keane[1]	O'Connor	F. O'Connell
2 Jan	A	Bray Wanderers	0-0	1st	A. Keenan	Malone	Darby	Murphy	V. Keenan	Frawley	Morris-Burke	Keane[*]	Brady	Dowling	Keane[#]	Brett	O'Connor
8 Jan	A	Sligo Rovers	2-2	1st	A. Keenan	Malone[*]	Darby[1]	Murphy	V. Keenan	Frawley	Morris-Burke[#]	Keane[*]	Brady[1]	Dowling	Fallon	F. O'Connell	O'Connor[1]
15 Jan	H	Waterford United	1-0	1st	A. Keenan	Malone[*]	Darby[1]	Murphy[1]	V. Keenan	Frawley	Morris-Burke[#]	Keane[*]	Brady	Dowling[*]	P.J. O'Connell	De-Khors	O'Connor
23 Jan	H	St. James's Gate	2-3	1st	A. Keenan	Malone	Darby	Murphy[1]	V. Keenan	Frawley	O'Connor	Keane[*]	Brady	Dowling	P.J. O'Connell	O'Connor	
28 Jan	H	Kilkenny City	0-0	2nd	A. Keenan	Malone[*]	Darby	Murphy	V. Keenan	Frawley	Morris-Burke	Keane[*]	Brady	Dowling	P.J. O'Connell	Morris-Burke	De-Khors
13 Feb	A	U.C.D.	1-1	2nd	A. Keenan	Malone	Darby	Murphy	V. Keenan	Frawley	De-Khors	Keane[*]	Brady[1]	Dowling	P.J. O'Connell	Golden	O'Connor
20 Feb	H	Home Farm	2-0	1st	A. Keenan	Malone	Darby	Murphy	V. Keenan	Frawley	De-Khors	Keane	Brady[1]	Dowling	P.J. O'Connell[1]	Golden[1]	
6 Mar	A	Longford Town	0-0	2nd	A. Keenan	Malone	Darby	Murphy	V. Keenan	Frawley	De-Khors	Keane	Brady	Dowling	P.J. O'Connell	O'Connor	
11 Mar	H	Bray Wanderers	0-0	2nd	A. Keenan	Malone[*]	Darby	Murphy	V. Keenan	Frawley	Morris-Burke	Keane	Brady	Dowling	P.J. O'Connell	Golden	Morris-Burke
16 Mar	H	Sligo Rovers	0-2	2nd	A. Keenan	Malone	Darby	Murphy	V. Keenan	Frawley	Morris-Burke	Keane[*]	Brady	Dowling	P.J. O'Connell	O'Connor	De-Khors
27 Mar	A	Waterford United	1-0	2nd	A. Keenan	Malone	Darby	Murphy	V. Keenan	Frawley	Morris-Burke	Keane	Brady	Dowling[*]	Golden[1]	P.J. O'Connell	
2 Apr	A	Finn Harps	0-1	2nd	A. Keenan	Malone	Darby	Murphy	V. Keenan	Frawley	Morris-Burke	De-Khors	Reynolds	Dowling	P.J. O'Connell	O'Connor	

5

Bohemians   Premier Div.

Founded: 1890
Home: Dalymount Park, Phibsborough, Dublin 7,
      Tel. (01) 8680923; Fax. (01) 8681022
Capacity: 25,000
Nickname: "Gypsies"
Colours: Red & Black striped shirts, Black shorts
2nd Colours: White shirts, Black shorts
Manager: Turlough O'Connor   Succeeded: Eamonn Gregg (Dec. 1993)
Asst. Manager: Larry Corbally (Dec. 1992)
President: Tony O'Connell
Secretary: Donal Crowther, 44 Woodbine Drive, Raheny, Dublin 5.
           Tel. Home: (01) 8480387; (088) 564119

Honours:

League of Ireland Champions	: 1923/24, 1927/28, 1929/30, 1933/34, 1935/36, 1974/75, 1977/78,	(7)
F.A.I. Cup Winners	: 1928, 1935, 1970, 1976, 1992	(5)
League Cup Winners	: 1974/75, 1978/79	(2)
League of Ireland Shield Winners	: 1923/24, 1927/28, 1928/29, 1933/34, 1938/39, 1939/40	(6)
Dublin City Cup Winners	: 1935/36	(1)
Leinster Cup Winners	: 1893/94, 1894/95, 1895/96, 1896/97, 1897/98, 1898/99, 1901/02, 1902/03, 1904/05, 1906/07, 1909/10, 1910/11, 1911/12, 1914/15, 1915/16, 1925/26, 1927/28, 1939/40, 1946/47, 1965/66, 1966/67, 1972/73, 1974/75, 1975/76, 1978/79, 1979/80, 1983/84, 1985/86, 1988/89, 1992/93	(30)
Top Four Winners	: 1971/72	(1)
Presidents Cup Winners	: 1965/66, 1967/68, 1974/575, 1975/75, 1976/77, 1977/78, 1978/79, 1982/83	(8)
Inter-City Cup Winners	: 1944/45	(1)
I.F.A. Cup Winners	: 1908	(1)

League Career:
Founder member in 1921. Everpresent, Premier Division 1985/86 to date.
Re-elected end: 1932/33, 43/44, 44/45, 45/46, 47/48, 48/49, 49/50, 52/53, 56/57, 58/59, 59/60, 60/61, 62/63, 63/64, 67/68, 68/69, (16 Times)

Players Capped (ROI): 20
First : Harry Cannon &
         Jack McCarthy   v Italy   (A) 21 Mar. 1926
Last   : Barry Murphy   v Uruguay (H) 23 Apr. 1986
Most   : Eamonn Gregg (8) 1978/81

Players Capped (NI) 16

First	:	J.C. Fitzpatrick	v	England (H) 07 Mar. 1896
Last	:	Johnny McMahon	v	Scotland (A) 16 Sep. 1933
Most	:	Harold Sloan (8)		1903/09

European Appearances: 13

Champions Cup:	1975/76	v	Glasgow Rangers,	1 - 1,	1 - 4
	1978/79	v	Omonia Nicosia,	1 - 0,	1 - 2
		v	Dynamo Dresden,	0 - 0,	0 - 6
Cup Winners Cup:	1970/71	v	Gottwaldov,	1 - 2,	2 - 2
	1976/77	v	Esbjerg,	2 - 1,	1 - 0
		v	Slask Wroclaw,	0 - 1,	0 - 3
	1992/93	v	Steaua Bucharest,	0 - 0,	0 - 4
U.E.F.A. Cup:	1972/73	v	I.F.C. Cologne,	0 - 3,	1 - 2
	1974/75	v	S.V. Hamburg	0 - 1,	0 - 3
	1977/78	v	Newcastle United	0 - 0,	0 - 4
	1979/80	v	Sporting Lisbon,	0 - 0,	0 - 2
	1984/85	v	Glasgow Rangers,	3 - 2,	0 - 2
	1985/86	v	Dundee United,	2 - 5,	2 - 2
	1987/88	v	Aberdeen,	0 - 0,	0 - 1
	1993/94	v	Girondins de Bordeaux	0 - 1,	0 - 5

Record League Victory:

Home	:	8 - 0	v	Olympia	18 Dec. 1922
Away	:	8 - 0	v	Home Farm	05 Feb. 1978

Record League Defeat:

Home	:	0 - 6	v	Shelbourne	08 Jan. 1949
Away	:	0 - 7	v	Shamrock Rovers	05 Feb. 1955

Most League Goals:

(Match) 4

G. Cooke	v	Olympia	8 - 0 (H)	22 Nov. 1922
Fred Horlacher	v	Jacobs	5 - 1 (H)	16 Jan. 1932
Johnny McMahon	v	St. James's Gate	5 - 6 (A)	05 Nov. 1932
Frank Fullen	v	Cork	7 - 2 (A)	23 Jan. 1938
Bobby Smith	v	Bray Unknowns	4 - 0 (H)	27 Dec. 1941
Mick O'Flanagan	v	Limerick	6 - 0 (H)	01 Feb. 1947
Matt Foster	v	Cork Athletic	4 - 4 (A)	03 Apr. 1955
Turlough O'Connor	v	Cork Celtic	7 - 0 (H)	14 Oct. 1973
Terry Flanagan	v	St. Patrick's Athletic	7 - 0 (H)	04 Apr. 1974
Joe Salmon	v	Waterford	7 - 3 (H)	15 Jan. 1978
Turlough O'Connor	v	Home Farm	8 - 0 (A)	05 Feb. 1978

(Season) 24: Turlough O'Connor 1977/78
(Career) 120: Turlough O'Connor 1964/65 - 1965/66 & 1972/73 - 1978/79

Points in a Season:
Most	:	46	1987/88	(38 games) (includes play-offs)
		72*	1981/82	(30 games)
Least	:	05	1959/60	(22 games)

Goals Scored in a Season:
Most	:	74	1977/78	(30 games)
Least	:	15	1959/60	(22 games)

League Appearances 1993/94:
31 Tony O'Connor, 30 Robbie Best, 29 Maurice O'Driscoll, 23+2 Donal Broughan, 21+2 Tony Cousins, 20+2 Dave Tilson, 13+9 Tommy Fitzgerald, 17+4 Jim Crawford, 20 Pat Fenlon, 18+2 Tommy Byrne, 14+6 Howard King, 19 Mick Moody, 18+1 Ken De Mange, 17 Dave Henderson, 15+2 John Connolly, 15+1 Paul Whelan, 13+1 Liam Dunne, 7 Wayne Cooney, Pat Kelch, 2+4 Thomas Lawless, 2 Mark Devlin, 0+2 Stephen Brazil, 1 Ken Blood, 0+1 Declan Geoghegan.
Players Used: 24

League Goalscorers 1993/94
8 Tony Cousins, 5 Dave Tilson, 4 Pat Fenlon, 2 Wayne Cooney, Liam Dunne, Tommy Fitzgerald, Tony O'Connor, ogs. 1 Donal Broughan, Ken Blood, Jim Crawford, Ken De Mange, Howard King, Mick Moody, Maurice O'Driscoll.
Total: 34

Pas De Deux!
Tommy Fitzgerald (Bohemians) skips past his Bordeaux opponent Zinedine Zidane
(The Star)

Bohemians 1993/94

Date	V	Opposition	Score	Pos	1	2	3	4	5	6	7	8	9	10	11	12	13
20 Aug	H	Galway United	3-0	-	Henderson	Broughan	Keith	Moody	O'Driscoll	Dunne	Devlin*	O'Connor	Fitzgerald	Fenton[1]	Tilson[2]	Crawford	King
26 Aug	A	St. Patrick's Ath.	0-0	1st	Henderson	Crawford	Keith	Moody	O'Driscoll	Dunne	Best	O'Connor	Fitzgerald	Fenton	Tilson	Crawford	King
29 Aug	H	Monaghan United	0-0	2nd	Henderson	Crawford#	Keith	Moody	Devlin*	Dunne	Best	O'Connor	Fitzgerald	Fenton	Tilson	Geoghegan	King
5 Sep	A	Cork City	0-2	3rd	Henderson	King	Keith	Moody	O'Driscoll	Dunne	Best	O'Connor*	Fitzgerald	Fenton[1]	Tilson	Fitzgerald	
11 Sep	A	Drogheda United	4-0	3rd	Henderson*	T. Byrne	Keith	Moody	Cousins*[1]	Dunne[1]	Best	O'Connor[1]	Cousins*[1]	Fenton[1]	Tilson	Fitzgerald	
18 Sep	H	Derry City	2-0	2nd	Henderson	T. Byrne	Keith	Moody	O'Driscoll	Dunne[1]	Best	O'Connor	Fitzgerald*	Fenton[1]	Connolly	Fitzgerald	
26 Sep	H	Shamrock Rovers	1-2	4th	Connolly	T. Byrne	Kelch	Moody[1]	O'Driscoll	Dunne	Best*	O'Connor	Fitzgerald*	Fenton	Tilson	Cousins	Broughan
3 Oct	A	Limerick	1-0	4th	Henderson	T. Byrne	Broughan*	Moody[1]	O'Driscoll	Cousins	Best#	O'Connor	Fitzgerald*	Fenton	Tilson*	Dunne	Crawford
10 Oct	A	Cobh Ramblers	0-0	3rd	Henderson	T. Byrne	Broughan	Moody	O'Driscoll	Cousins	Best	O'Connor	Dunne	Fenton	King[1]	King	
15 Oct	H	Shelbourne	1-0	3rd	Henderson	T. Byrne	Broughan	Moody	O'Driscoll	Cousins[1]	Best	O'Connor	Dunne	Fenton	Tilson*	Fitzgerald	
24 Oct	A	Dundalk	1-1	3rd	Henderson	Tilson*	Broughan	Moody	O'Driscoll	Cousins[1]	Best	O'Connor	Dunne	Fenton[1]	King		
29 Oct	H	Galway United	1-0	3rd	Henderson	T. Byrne	Broughan*	Crawford	O'Driscoll	Cousins	Best	O'Connor	Fitzgerald	Fenton	King	Fitzgerald	
7 Nov	A	Galway United	1-1	3rd	Henderson	T. Byrne	Broughan	De-Mange	O'Driscoll	Cousins	Best	O'Connor	Dunne	Fenton	King*	Fitzgerald	
14 Nov	H	Monaghan United	0-0	2nd	Henderson	T. Byrne	Broughan[1]	De-Mange	O'Driscoll	King	Best	O'Connor	Fitzgerald[2]	Fenton	Whelan*	Crawford	King
21 Nov	A	Cork City	3-4	5th	Henderson	T. Byrne	Crawford	De-Mange[1]	O'Driscoll	King#	Best	O'Connor*	Fitzgerald	Fenton	Broughan*	Connolly	Tilson
26 Nov	H	Drogheda United	0-1	5th	Connolly	T. Byrne	Whelan	De-Mange	O'Driscoll	Cousins*[1]	Best	O'Connor	Tilson[1]	Fenton	Broughan	Tilson	Cousins
5 Dec	A	Derry City	0-3	6th	Connolly	T. Byrne	Crawford	De-Mange	King	Cousins	Best	O'Connor	Tilson[1]	Fenton*	Broughan	Fitzgerald	
12 Dec	H	Shamrock Rovers	2-0	6th	Connolly	T. Byrne	Crawford	De-Mange	O'Driscoll[1]	Cousins*[1]	Best	O'Connor[1]	Tilson	Fenton*	Whelan	Fitzgerald	
17 Dec	A	Limerick	0-3	6th	Connolly	T. Byrne	Crawford[1]	De-Mange*	O'Driscoll[1]	Cousins*	Best	O'Connor*	Tilson	Fenton*	Broughan	King	
2 Jan	H	Cobh Ramblers	2-0	5th	Connolly	T. Byrne	Crawford[1]	De-Mange	O'Driscoll	Cousins*	Best	O'Connor[1]	Tilson	Fenton*	Broughan	Fitzgerald	
9 Jan	A	Shelbourne	1-2	5th	Connolly	Fitzgerald	Crawford[1]	Cooney	O'Driscoll	Cousins	Best	O'Connor	Tilson[1]	Fenton*	Broughan	Whelan	
16 Jan	H	Galway United	2-0	5th	Connolly	Fitzgerald	Crawford[1]	Cooney	O'Driscoll	Cousins	Best	O'Connor*	Tilson[1]	Fenton	Broughan	King	
21 Jan	H	Shelbourne	1-3	5th	Henderson	Fitzgerald	Crawford*	Cooney	O'Driscoll	Cousins	Best	O'Connor	Tilson[1]	Whelan	Broughan	Fitzgerald	
30 Jan	A	Shamrock Rovers	2-1	5th	Henderson	Fitzgerald*	Crawford[1]	Cousins*	O'Driscoll	Moody	Best	De-Mange	Tilson*	Whelan	Broughan	King	De-Mange
13 Feb	A	Derry City	0-4	5th	Connolly	Fitzgerald*	Crawford	Cousins*	Cooney	Moody	Best	De-Mange	Tilson[1]	Whelan	O'Connor	T. Byrne	Broughan
20 Feb	A	Derry City	1-1	5th	Connolly	T. Byrne	Crawford	King	Cooney*[1]	Moody	Best	De-Mange	Tilson*	Whelan	O'Connor	Lawless	
6 Mar	H	Shamrock Rovers	1-2	5th	Connolly	Broughan[1]	Crawford	Tilson	Cooney	Moody	Best	De-Mange	O'Driscoll	Whelan	O'Connor	Lawless	
11 Mar	A	Shelbourne	2-0	5th	Connolly	Broughan*	Crawford	Tilson	Cooney[2]	Moody	Best	De-Mange	O'Driscoll	Whelan	O'Connor	Lawless	Brazil
16 Mar	A	Galway United	0-1	5th	Connolly	Broughan*	Crawford#	King	Cooney	Moody	Best	De-Mange	O'Driscoll	Whelan	O'Connor	Cousins	
27 Mar	H	Cork City	1-3	5th	Connolly	Lawless	Crawford*	King	Cooney[1]	Moody	Best	De-Mange	O'Driscoll	Whelan	O'Connor	Dunne	
2 Apr	H	Derry City	1-3	6th	Connolly	Broughan	Lawless	King	Cousins	Moody	Blood[1]	De-Mange	O'Driscoll	Whelan	O'Connor	Brazil	

Bray Wanderers   First Div.

Founded: 1942
Home: Carlisle Ground, Bray, Co. Wicklow, Tel. (01) 2828214
Nickname: "Seasiders"
Colours: Green & White striped shirts, White shorts
2nd Colours: Green shirts, White shorts
Manager: John Holmes   Succeeded: Pat Devlin (Dec 1990)
Chairman: Eddie Cox
Secretary: John O'Brien, Phoenix House, Newcourt Road, Bray, Co. Wicklow
           Tel. (01) 2861685

Honours/Best Performances:

Championship	:	8th 1986/87, 1991/92
First Division Champions	:	1985/86 (1)
F.A.I. Cup Winners	:	1990 (1)
League Cup	:	Quarter Finals 1985/86, 1986/87
Leinster Cup	:	Finalists 1988/89, 1989/90
Presidents Cup	:	Finalists 1989/90, 1990/91

League Career:
Elected to new First Division 1985. Promoted end 1985/86. Relegated end 1987/88. Promoted end 1990/91. Relegated end 1992/93. Re-elected end 1993/94.

European Appearances: 1
Cup Winners Cup: 1990/91   v   Trabzonspor   1 - 1, 0 - 2

Record League Victory:

Home	:	4 - 0	v	Longford Town	17 Sep. 1989
Away	:	3 - 0	v	Newcastle United	27 Oct. 1985
			v	Cobh Ramblers	17 Nov. 1985
			v	Longford Town	01 Jan. 1986
			v	Monaghan United	09 Oct. 1988
			v	Finn Harps	30 Oct. 1988
			v	Monaghan United	28 Jan. 1990
			v	Home Farm	27 Feb. 1991
			v	Monaghan United	24 Mar. 1991

Record League Defeat:

Home	:	0 - 5	v	Shamrock Rovers	13 Dec. 1992
Away	:	1 - 7	v	Shamrock Rovers	08 Jan. 1988

Most League Goals:
(Match): No Bray player has scored more than twice in any League match.
(Season) 16:   John Ryan 1989/90
(Career) 32:   John Ryan 1988/89 to 1990/91

Points in a Season:
Most : 35 1989/90 (27 games)
Least : 17 1986/87 (22 games)

Goals Scored in a Season:
Most : 41 1988/89 & 1989/90 (27 games)
Least : 17 1991/92 (33 games)
        17 1993/94 (27 games)

League Appearances 1993/94:
27 Alan Smith, Gavin Teehan, 23 Pat O'Brien, 22+1 Adrian Cairns, 21+1 Conor Best, 20+1 Dermot Judge, 20 Maurice Farrell, 17 Josh Moran, 12+5 Derek Smith, 15+1 Anto Kennedy, 12+4 Philip Gormley, 9+5 Brian Honan, 11+1 Ronnie Allen, Martin Nugent, 10+1 Colm Kelly, 10 Colm Phillips, 5+5 Stephen Brien, 8 Stephen Horan, 7+1 Robert Coyle, 5+2 Alan Noctor, 2+2 Eddie Meaney, 3 Ian Douglas, 0+3 Shane Wall.
Players Used: 23

League Goalscorers 1993/94:
5 Conor Best, 4 Brian Honan, 3 Alan Smith, 1 Ian Douglas, Philip Gormley, Dermot Judge, Martin Nugent, Derek Smith.
Total: 17

All time League of Ireland goalscorers 1985 - 1994
32 John Ryan, **27** Martin Nugent, **16** Kieron Cooper, **15** Mick Doohan, Derek Gough, Alan Smith, **13** Eugene Davis, Kevin Reynolds, **10** Jason Byrne, **8** Richie Parsons, **6** Dermot Judge, Tommy McDermott, David O'Brien, **5** Conor Best, Joe Lawless, **4** Brian Honan, Jim Mahon, Anthony McKeever, **3** Cormac Breslin, John Finnegan, Eddie Gormley, Dave Kealy, Stephen O'Reilly, Colm Tresson, **2** Trevor Coleman, Paul Cullen, Des Kavanagh, Andy Lynch, Clem McAuley, Anto Whelan, **1** Brian Callaghan, Greg Coleman, Derek Corcoran, Pat Devlin, Ian Douglas, Derek Gilroy, Phillip Gormley, Brian McEvoy, Derek Mullhall, Terry Murphy, Colm Notaro, Joe O'Flaherty, Colm Phillips, Noel Reid, Derek Smith: **8** Opponents
Total: **257**   Games: **246**   Average per game: **1.04**

Captain Courageous
Skipper Andy Townsend surveys the damage   (EOH)

Bray Wanderers 1993/94

Date	V	Opposition	Scr	Pos	1	2	3	4	5	6	7	8	9	10	11	12	13
19 Sep	A	Longford Town	0-1	-	Moran	Cairns	Teehan	Judge	Noctor	Phillips	Nugent	A. Smith	Best	Douglas[1]	Coyle*	Meaney	
26 Sep	H	Home Farm	1-0	6th	Moran	Cairns	Teehan	Judge	Allen	Phillips	Nugent	A. Smith	Best*	Douglas[1]	Meaney*	Noctor	Meaney
3 Oct	A	Finn Harps	1-2	8th	Moran	Cairns	Teehan	Farrell	Allen	Phillips	Nugent	A. Smith[1]	Best*	Douglas	Coyle*	Noctor	
10 Oct	H	U.C.D.	0-2	9th	Moran	Cairns	Teehan	Farrell	Allen	Phillips*	Nugent	A. Smith	Best	Judge	Noctor	Honan	
17 Oct	H	St. James's Gate	0-0	9th	Moran	Cairns	Teehan	P. O'Brien	Allen	Honan*	Meaney*	A. Smith	Best	Judge	Noctor	Wall	
24 Oct	A	Athlone Town	1-1	9th	Moran	Cairns	Teehan	P. O'Brien	Allen	Honan[1]	Farrell	A. Smith[1]	Best	Judge	Noctor*		
31 Oct	H	Waterford United	1-1	10th	Moran	Cairns*	Teehan	P. O'Brien	Allen	Honan*[1]	Farrell	A. Smith	Best	Judge	D. Smith	Wall	Kennedy
7 Nov	A	Sligo Rovers	1-1	10th	Moran	Cairns	Teehan	P. O'Brien	Allen	Nugent[1]	Farrell	A. Smith	Best	Judge	D. Smith		
14 Nov	A	Kilkenny City	1-1	10th	Moran	Cairns	Teehan	P. O'Brien	Allen*	Nugent	Farrell	A. Smith	Best[1]	Judge	D. Smith	Honan	
21 Nov	H	Kilkenny City	1-1	10th	Moran*	Cairns	Teehan	P. O'Brien	Allen	Nugent	Farrell	A. Smith	Best[1]	Judge	D. Smith[1]	Kelly	
28 Nov	H	Longford Town	2-1	7th	Kelly	Kennedy	Teehan	P. O'Brien	Allen	Gormley	Farrell	A. Smith	Best[1]	Judge[1]	S. Brien		
5 Dec	A	Home Farm	2-3	8th	Kelly	Kennedy	Teehan	P. O'Brien	D. Smith	Gormley	Farrell	A. Smith	Best*	Judge	S. Brien*	Cairns	Nugent
12 Dec	H	Finn Harps	0-4	9th	Kelly	Kennedy	Teehan	P. O'Brien	D. Smith*	Nugent	Farrell	A. Smith	Best[2]	Judge	Phillips	Gormley[1]	Allen
19 Dec	A	U.C.D.	2-1	9th	Kelly	Kennedy	Teehan	P. O'Brien	D. Smith	Nugent	Cairns	A. Smith	Best	Judge	Phillips	Gormley[1]	
27 Dec	H	St. James's Gate	1-1	8th	Kelly	Kennedy	Teehan	P. O'Brien	D. Smith*	Nugent	Cairns	A. Smith	Best*	Gormley	Phillips	Honan	
2 Jan	H	Athlone Town	0-0	9th	Kelly	Kennedy	Teehan	P. O'Brien	D. Smith*	Nugent*	Cairns	A. Smith	Best*	Farrell	Phillips	Brien	Gormley
16 Jan	H	Sligo Rovers	0-3	9th	Moran	Kennedy	Teehan	P. O'Brien	Gormley	Nugent*	Cairns	A. Smith[1]	Best	Farrell	Phillips	Honan	D. Smith
23 Jan	A	Longford Town	1-1	9th	Moran	Kennedy	Teehan	P. O'Brien	Gormley[1]	D. Smith*	Cairns	A. Smith	Best	Farrell	Horan	Honan	S. Brien
30 Jan	H	Home Farm	0-0	9th	Moran	Kennedy	Teehan	P. O'Brien	Gormley*	D. Smith	Judge	A. Smith	Best*	Farrell	Horan	Gormley	S. Brien
13 Feb	A	Finn Harps	0-1	9th	Kelly	Phillips	Teehan	P. O'Brien	Honan*	D. Smith*	Judge	A. Smith	Cairns	Coyle*	Horan	Best	S. Brien
6 Mar	H	St. James's Gate	0-0	9th	Moran	Kennedy	Teehan	P. O'Brien	Gormley	Best*	Judge	A. Smith	Cairns	Farrell	Horan	D. Smith	S. Brien
11 Mar	A	Athlone Town	0-0	9th	Kelly	Kennedy	Teehan	P. O'Brien	Gormley*	Coyle	Judge	A. Smith	Cairns	Farrell	Horan		
17 Mar	H	Waterford United	0-0	9th	Moran	Kennedy	Teehan	P. O'Brien	Gormley*	Coyle	Judge	A. Smith	Cairns	Farrell	Horan	D. Smith	
20 Mar	A	Waterford United	0-0	9th	Moran	S. Brien	Teehan	P. O'Brien	Honan[1]	Coyle	Kennedy	A. Smith	Cairns*	Farrell	Horan	D. Smith	
26 Mar	A	Sligo Rovers	0-1	9th	Kelly	S. Brien	Teehan	P. O'Brien	Honan[1]	Coyle	Kennedy	A. Smith	Cairns*	Gormley*	Horan	Judge	
31 Mar	H	U.C.D.	1-0	9th	Kelly	S. Brien	Teehan	P. O'Brien	Honan[1]	Coyle	Kennedy	A. Smith	Cairns*	Gormley	Horan	D. Smith	Coyle
3 Apr	A	Kilkenny City	1-1	9th	Kelly	Farrell	Teehan	P. O'Brien	Honan[1]	Judge	Kennedy*	A. Smith	Cairns*	Gormley	Horan		

Cobh Ramblers   Premier Div.

Founded: 1922
Home: St. Colmans Park, Cobh, Co. Cork. Tel. (021) 812371/813078
Nickname: "Ramblers" or "The Rams"
Colours: Claret & Blue
Manager: George Mellerick   Succeeded: Liam McMahon (Feb. 1991)
Asst. Manager: Noel Keane
President: David Stack
Chairman: John O'Rourke
Secretary: Danny Cronin, 5 Coolamber Ave., Cobh, Co Cork
           Tel. Home: (021) 811412; Office: (021) 378011 Ext. 1113; Fax. (021) 811412

Honours/Best Performances:

Championship	:	10th 1993/94
First Division	:	Runners-up 1987/88, 1992/93
F.A.I. Cup	:	Semi-Final *1982/83
League Cup	:	Semi-Final *1976/77
Munster Cup Winners	:	*1924/25, *1943/44, *1978/79, *1982/83 (4)

* as a non-League club

League Career:

Elected to new First Division 1985. Promoted end 1987/88. Relegated end 1988/89. Promoted end 1992/93.

Record League Victory:

Home: 5 - 0   v   Home Farm   17 Mar. 1991
Away: 5 - 0   v   St. Patrick's Athletic   26 Mar. 1994

Record League Defeat:

Home: 2 - 5   v   Derry City   13 Nov. 1988
Away: 0 - 5   v   Derry City   06 Nov. 1988

Most League Goals:

(Match)   3   Eric Hogan v Home Farm 5 - 0 (H) 17 Mar. 1991
(Season): 13   Terry Kearns 1989/90
(Career): 31   Terry Kearns 1987/88 to 1989/90

Points in a Season:

Most	:	38	1987/88	(27 games)
Least	:	15	1985/86 & 1986/87	(18 games)

Goals Scored in a Season

Most	:	41	1987/88	(27 games)
Least	:	14	1985/86	(18 games)

League Appearances 1993/94

34 Stephen Henderson, Packie Kelly, Ken O'Rourke, 31 Jason Lynch, 30+1 Paul Bannon, 27 Seán Francis, 22+5 Brendan O'Callaghan, 23+2 Philip Long, 21+4 Anthony Kenneally, 20+4 Kevin Kelly, 18+3 Tommy Cregoe, 5+7 John O'Rourke, 6+5 Damien Martin, 9+1 Alan O'Neill, 8+2 Gary O'Sullivan, 5+4 Patsy Freyne, 8 Warren Patmore, 7 James Connor, 5+2 Mark Devlin, 0+6 Austin O'Connor, 5 Pat O'Toole, Brett Smith, 0+5 Eric Hogan, 4 Pat Byrne, Danny Chapman, John Peacock, 2 Steve Benton, Jason Kaminsky, 1 Shane Greene, 0+1 Pat Duggan.
Players Used: 30

League Goalscorers 1993/94:

9 Seán Francis, 5 Ken O'Rourke, 4 Alan O'Neill, 3 Paul Bannon, Warren Patmore, 2 Gary O'Sullivan, 1 James Connor, Mark Devlin, Packie Kelly, Anthony Kenneally, Jason Lynch, Brendan O'Callaghan, John O'Rourke, o.g.
Total: 34

All time League of Ireland goalscorers 1985 - 1994
31 Terry Kearns, 20 Eddie O'Halloran, 18 Bob Donovan, 14 Seán Francis, 11 Brendan O'Callaghan, 10 Fergus McDaid, Ken O'Rourke, 9 Paul Newe, 8 Colman Mulcahy, Alan O'Neill, 7 Tom McCarthy, Damien Martin, 6 Paul Crowley, Patsy Freyne, 5 Niall Abbott, Darren Fenton, Derek Grace, Kieran Myers, Michael O'Leary, Eric Hogan, Wimmie Van Wijnen, 4 Packie Kelly, David O'Connor, John O'Rourke, Niall O'Rourke, 3 Paul Bannon, Paul Cashin, Seán Hegarty, Kevin Kearney, Anthony Kenneally, Jason Lynch, Tony Neiland, Frank O'Neill, Warren Patmore, 2 Pat Cleary, Denis Keane, Pascal Keane, Conor McCarthy, Kieran Nagle, Gary O'Sullivan, Peter Piggott, George Wilshaw, 1 James Connor, Gordon Cowpar, Mark Devlin, Roy Keane, Andy King, Johnny Mullane, Ken O'Neill, Martin Reid, Anthony Sibanda: 7 Opponents
Total: 275   Games: 238   Average per game: 1.16

Last Chance Saloon!
The Cobh Ramblers team which beat Finn Harps three-nil to retain their place in the Premier Division   (M.G.)

Cobh Ramblers 1993/94

Date	V	Opposition	Score	Pos	1	2	3	4	5	6	7	8	9	10	11	12	13
21 Aug	A	Derry City	0-2	-	Henderson	P. Kelly	Long	Lynch	Bannon	Cregoe*	K. O'Rourke	O'Callaghan	Freyne	K. Kelly*	Duggan	J. O'Rourke
25 Aug	H	Limerick	0-0	11th	Henderson	P. Kelly	Long	Lynch	Bannon	Martin	Cregoe*	K. O'Rourke	O'Callaghan	K. Kelly	Kennealy	J. O'Rourke
29 Aug	A	Shelbourne	1-1	11th	Henderson	P. Kelly	Long	Lynch	Bannon	Connor	Patmore*	K. O'Rourke	O'Callaghan	Kaminsky*	Freyne	Martin
5 Sep	H	Dundalk	2-0	5th	Henderson	P. Kelly	Cregoe	Lynch	Bannon	Chapman	Patmore[1]	K. O'Rourke	O'Callaghan	Freyne	Hogan	K. Kelly
12 Sep	H	Galway United	0-2	8th	Henderson	P. Kelly	Cregoe	Lynch	Bannon	Chapman	Patmore	K. O'Rourke	O'Callaghan	Connor	K. Kelly	Kennealy
18 Sep	A	St. Patrick's Ath.	1-1	8th	Henderson	P. Kelly	Long	Lynch[1]	Bannon	Francis	Patmore	K. O'Rourke	O'Callaghan	Kennealy*	Connor[1]	Hogan
26 Sep	H	Monaghan United	2-0	6th	Henderson	P. Kelly	Long	Lynch	Bannon	Francis	Patmore	K. Kelly[1]	O'Callaghan[1]*	Kennealy*	Connor[1]	O'Callaghan
3 Oct	A	Cork City	0-2	6th	Henderson	P. Kelly	Long	Lynch	Bannon	Francis	Patmore	K. O'Rourke	K. Kelly	Freyne	Martin	Cregoe
10 Oct	H	Bohemians	0-0	8th	Henderson	P. Kelly	Long	Martin	Bannon[1]	Francis	Patmore[1]	K. O'Rourke	O'Callaghan	Freyne	Connor	
16 Oct	A	Drogheda United	3-1	7th	Henderson	P. Kelly	Lynch	Martin	Bannon	Francis	Long	K. O'Rourke	O'Callaghan[1]	Devlin[1]	Freyne	
24 Oct	H	Shamrock Rovers	1-3	7th	Henderson	P. Kelly	Lynch	Kennealy	Bannon	Francis	Long	K. O'Rourke	O'Callaghan	Freyne	Benton*	
31 Oct	A	Shamrock Rovers	0-3	8th	Henderson	P. Kelly	Lynch	Martin	Bannon	Francis[1]	Long	K. O'Rourke	Peacock*	Devlin[1]	Freyne	Hogan
7 Nov	H	Derry City	1-3	10th	Henderson	P. Kelly	Lynch	Martin	Kennealy[1]	Francis[2]	Long	K. O'Rourke	Peacock	Smith	Devlin	Kennealy
14 Nov	A	Limerick	5-1	10th	Henderson	P. Kelly	Lynch	Bannon	Kennealy[1]	Francis[1]	Long	K. O'Rourke	Peacock*	Smith	Hogan	J. O'Rourke
19 Nov	H	Shelbourne	0-1	10th	Henderson	P. Kelly	Lynch	Bannon	Kennealy	Francis	Devlin	K. O'Rourke	Smith	J. O'Rourke	Martin	Devlin
28 Nov	A	Dundalk	0-2	10th	Henderson	P. Kelly	Lynch	Bannon	Kennealy	Francis	Long	K. O'Rourke	Smith	J. O'Rourke	Martin	Hogan
5 Dec	A	Galway United	0-4	10th	Henderson	P. Kelly	Lynch*	Bannon*	Kennealy	Francis*	Greene	K. O'Rourke	O'Callaghan	Smith	K. Kelly	Martin
12 Dec	H	St. Patrick's Ath.	0-1	10th	Henderson	P. Kelly	Lynch	K. Kelly[1]	Kennealy*	Francis	Long	K. O'Rourke	O'Callaghan	Byrne	J. O'Rourke	
19 Dec	A	Monaghan United	1-2	10th	Henderson	P. Kelly	Lynch	K. Kelly	Kennealy*	Francis[2]	Cregoe	K. O'Rourke	O'Callaghan	O'Toole	Long	
26 Dec	H	Cork City	2-1	10th	Henderson	P. Kelly	Lynch	K. Kelly	Kennealy*	Francis[1]	Cregoe	K. O'Rourke	Bannon	Byrne	O'Toole	J. O'Rourke
2 Jan	A	Bohemians	0-2	10th	Henderson	P. Kelly	Lynch	K. Kelly	Kennealy*	Francis[1]	Cregoe	K. O'Rourke	Bannon*	O'Toole	Long	
9 Jan	H	Drogheda United	1-2	10th	Henderson	P. Kelly	Lynch	K. Kelly	Long	Francis*	Cregoe	K. O'Rourke	Bannon	O'Toole	O'Callaghan	Kennealy
16 Jan	A	Monaghan United	1-1	10th	Henderson	P. Kelly	K. Kelly	Kennealy	Long	Francis	Cregoe	K. O'Rourke	Bannon*	O'Toole	O'Callaghan	
23 Jan	A	Dundalk	0-0	10th	Henderson	P. Kelly	Lynch	K. Kelly	Kennealy*	Francis	Cregoe	K. O'Rourke	Bannon	O'Sullivan	O'Neill	O'Connor
30 Jan	A	Limerick	1-0	10th	Henderson	P. Kelly	Long	Kennealy	Bannon	Francis	Cregoe	K. O'Rourke	Bannon	O'Sullivan*[1]	K. Kelly	
13 Feb	A	Drogheda United	1-2	10th	Henderson	P. Kelly	Lynch	O'Neill	Kennealy	Francis	Cregoe	K. O'Rourke	Bannon	O'Sullivan	K. Kelly	O'Connor
20 Feb	H	St. Patrick's Ath.	0-1	10th	Henderson	P. Kelly	Lynch	O'Neill[1]	Kennealy	Francis	Cregoe	K. O'Rourke	Bannon	O'Sullivan	O'Callaghan	
6 Mar	H	Limerick	0-0	11th	Henderson	P. Kelly	Lynch	O'Neill	Kennealy*	Francis	Patmore	K. O'Rourke	Bannon	O'Sullivan	O'Callaghan	O'Connor
13 Mar	H	Dundalk	1-1	11th	Henderson	P. Kelly	K. Kelly	O'Neill	Bannon	Francis	Patmore	K. O'Rourke	Bannon	O'Sullivan*	O'Callaghan	
17 Mar	H	Monaghan United	1-2	11th	Henderson	P. Kelly	K. Kelly	O'Neill[1]	Cregoe	Francis	Patmore	K. O'Rourke	Bannon	O'Sullivan	O'Gallaghan*	Cregoe
26 Mar	A	St. Patrick's Ath.	5-0	10th	Henderson	P. Kelly	K. Kelly	O'Neill[2]	Cregoe	Francis[2]	Patmore	K. O'Rourke	Bannon	O'Sullivan	Kennealy	
3 Apr	A	Drogheda United	1-0	10th	Henderson	P. Kelly	K. Kelly	O'Neill*	Lynch	Francis	K. O'Rourke	K. O'Rourke	Bannon	Kennealy	O'Callaghan	
9 Apr	H	Finn Harps	0-1	P/O	Henderson	P. Kelly	K. Kelly	O'Neill*	Lynch	Francis	K. O'Rourke	K. O'Rourke	Bannon	O'Sullivan	O'Sullivan	
16 Apr	H	Finn Harps	3-0	P/O	Henderson	P. Kelly	K. Kelly	Lynch	Kennealy	Francis*[1]	Long	K. O'Rourke	Bannon	J. O'Rourke	O'Connor	

Cork City   Premier Div.

Founded: 1984
Home: Bishopstown, Cork. (021) 344613;312522; Fax. (021) 313354
Capacity: 13,000; 3,000 seated
Previous Grounds: Flower Lodge   (1984/85 - 1985/86),
                  Turner's Cross (1986/87 - 1991/92)
Nickname: "City"
Colours: Green, White and Red striped shirts, Green shorts
2nd Colours: All black
Manager: Damien Richardson Succeeded: Noel O'Mahony (Jul. 1993)
Asst. Manager: Alek Ludzik
Chairman: Pat O'Donovan
Secretary: John O'Donovan, 15 Sandymount Ave., Glasheen Road, Cork. Tel. (021) 542375
Ass. Secretary: Aisling O'Leary, Tel. (021) 344613

Honours/Best Performances:

League of Ireland Champions	:	1992/93	(1)
F.A.I. Cup	:	Runners-up 1989, 1992	
League Cup Winners	:	1987/88	(1)
Munster Cup Winners	:	1987/88, 1989/90, 1990/91, 1991/92	
		1992/93, 1993/94	(6)

League Career:
Elected with Longford Town 1984. Premier Division 1985/86 to date.

European Appearances: 3

Champions Cup	1993/94	v	Cwmbran Town	2 - 1, 2 - 3
		v	Galatasaray	0 - 1, 1 - 2
Cup Winners Cup	1989/90	v	Torpedo Moscow	0 - 1, 0 - 5
U.E.F.A. Cup	1991/92	v	Bayern Munich	1 - 1, 0 - 2

Record League Victory:

Home:	4 - 0	v	Galway United	29 Jan. 1989	
		v	Shelbourne	15 Apr. 1990	
		v	Dundalk	08 Dec. 1991	
Away:	7 - 1	v	Limerick	26 Sep. 1993	

Record League Defeat:

Home:	0 - 4	v	Sligo Rovers	31 Mar. 1985
Away:	2 - 7	v	Derry City	27 Sep. 1987

Most League Goals:

(Match)	3:	John Caulfield v Sligo Rovers	3 - 2 (H)	23 Nov. 1986
		Pat Morley v Drogheda United	3 - 1 (A)	05 Jan. 1992
		John Caulfield v St. Pat's Ath.	4 - 2 (A)	19 Jan. 1992
(Season)	20:	Pat Morley 1992/93		
(Career)	72:	Pat Morley 1989/90 - 1993/94		

Points in a Season:
Most	:	50	1990/91	(33 games)
		59 **	1993/94	(32 games)
Least	:	18	1985/86	(22 games)

Goals Scored in a Season:
Most	:	60	1993/94	(32 games)
Least	:	23	1985/86	(22 games)

League Appearances 1993/94
32 Declan Daly, Stephen Napier, 31 Pat Morley, 28+3 Liam Murphy, 25+5 John Caulfield, 29 Phil Harrington, 27+2 Tommy Gaynor, 24+5 Johnny Glynn, 27 Fergus O'Donoghue, 25+1 Anthony Buckley, 24+1 Dave Barry, 14+3 Declan Hyde, 9+7 Cormac Cotter, 9 Justin Phillips, 6+3 Declan Roche, 5 Paul Hague, 3+1 Alex Ludzik, 2+2 Tony Eeles, 0+3 Billy Woods, 0+1 Stuart Ashton.
Players Used: 20

League Goalscorers 1993/94:
15 Pat Morley, 11 Tommy Gaynor, 9 John Caulfield, 7 John Glynn, 6 Dave Barry, 4 Anthony Buckley, 2 Declan Hyde, Declan Roche, og's 1 Stephen Napier, Justin Phillips.
Total: 60

All time League of Ireland goalscorers 1984 - 1994
72 Pat Morley, 71 John Caulfield, 45 Dave Barry, 14 Johnny Glynn, 13 Patsy Freyne, 11 Tommy Gaynor, 9 Paul Bannon, Eamonn O'Keeffe, Declan Roche, 8 Philip Long, Kieran Nagle, 7 Paddy Hughes, Declan Hyde, 6 Paul Bowdren, Ian Hennessey, Liam Murphy, Bobby Woodruff, 5 Cormac Cotter, Pat 'Ginger' Healy, Dave Waters, 4 Ivan Aherne, Anthony Buckley, Kevin Kearney, Donal Madden, Kevin Nugent, Anto Whelan, 3 Denis Allen, Paul Armstrong, Mike Mellon, Kieran Myers, Fergus O'Donoghue, 2 Len Downey, Liam Keane, Gerry McCabe, Stephen Napier, 1 Dave Bleasdale, John Butler, Mick Conroy, Declan Daly, Norman Fry, Jim Leahy, Terry McDermott, Dave Morley, Tony Neiland, Jim Nodwell, Dave O'Connor, Mick "Slap" O'Keeffe, Trevor Parr, Justin Phillips:
10 Opponents
Total: 393   Games: 309   Average per game: 1.27

Chop Suat
Euro action as Cormac Cotter tackles Suat of Galatasaray   (E.O.H)

Cork City 1993/94

Date	V	Opposition	Score	Pos	1	2	3	4	5	6	7	8	9	10	11	12	13
22 Aug	H	Monaghan United	1-0	-	Harrington	Daly	Napier	O'Donoghue	Hague	Buckley	Roche*	Hyde*	Glynn	Gaynor	Caulfield	Murphy	Cotter
25 Aug	A	Galway United	0-0	4th	Ludzik	Daly	Napier	O'Donoghue	Hague	Buckley	Roche	Murphy	Morley	Gaynor	Caulfield	Cotter	
29 Aug	A	Derry City	1-0	1st	Harrington	Daly	Napier	O'Donoghue*	Hague	Hyde	Roche	Murphy	Morley[1]	Glynn	Caulfield	Murphy	Cotter
5 Sep	H	Bohemians	2-0	1st	Harrington	Daly	Napier*	O'Donoghue	Hague	Hyde	Buckley	Gaynor	Morley[1]	Glynn*	Caulfield[1]	Murphy	
12 Sep	A	Shamrock Rovers	0-3	2nd	Harrington	Daly	Napier	O'Donoghue	Hague	Hyde	Buckley	Gaynor	Morley	Glynn*	Caulfield[1]	Barry	
19 Sep	H	Drogheda United	1-1	3rd	Harrington	Daly	Napier	O'Donoghue*	Cotter	Hyde	Buckley*	Gaynor	Morley[1]	Barry[1]	Glynn	Murphy	Glynn[1]
26 Sep	A	Limerick	7-1	2nd	Harrington	Daly	Napier	Murphy	Cotter	Hyde[1]	Buckley[1]*	Gaynor[2]	Morley	Barry[1]	Glynn	Caulfield	Roche[1]
3 Oct	H	Cobh Ramblers	2-0	1st	Harrington	Daly	Napier	Murphy	O'Donoghue*	Hyde*	Caulfield	Gaynor	Morley	Barry	Glynn	Roche	Cotter
8 Oct	A	Shelbourne	1-0	1st	Harrington	Daly	Napier	Murphy	Cotter*	Buckley	Caulfield	Gaynor	Morley	Barry	Roche	Woods	
17 Oct	H	Dundalk	0-1	2nd	Harrington*	Daly	Napier	Murphy	Cotter*	Buckley	Caulfield*	Gaynor	Morley	Barry	Glynn	Ludzik	Ashton
24 Oct	A	St Patrick's Ath	4-3	2nd	Harrington	Daly	Napier	Murphy	Cotter	Buckley	Hyde	Gaynor	Morley[1]	Barry[1]	Glynn[1]	Caulfield	Roche[1]
31 Oct	H	St Patrick's Ath	1-1	2nd	Ludzik	Daly	Napier[1]	Murphy	Cotter	Buckley	O'Donoghue	Gaynor	Morley	Roche*	Glynn[1]	Woods	
7 Nov	A	Monaghan United	1-2	2nd	Ludzik	Daly	Napier	Murphy	Eeles	Buckley	O'Donoghue	Gaynor	Morley	Caulfield	Glynn*	Caulfield	
14 Nov	H	Galway United	1-2	3rd	Harrington	Daly	Napier	Murphy	Eeles	Buckley[1]	O'Donoghue	Gaynor	Morley	Barry[1]	Glynn*	Caulfield	Cotter
21 Nov	H	Derry City	1-0	2nd	Harrington	Daly	Napier	Murphy	Caulfield[1]	Phillips	O'Donoghue	Gaynor	Morley	Barry#2	Glynn*	Buckley	Eeles
26 Nov	A	Bohemians	4-3	2nd	Harrington	Daly	Napier	Murphy	Caulfield	Phillips	O'Donoghue	Gaynor[1]	Morley[1]	Barry*[1]	Buckley	Glynn	Woods
5 Dec	H	Shamrock Rovers	2-2	2nd	Harrington	Daly	Napier	Murphy	Caulfield[1]	Phillips	O'Donoghue	Gaynor#2	Morley[2]	Barry	Glynn	Hyde	
12 Dec	A	Drogheda United	5-0	2nd	Harrington	Daly	Napier	Murphy	Caulfield[1]	Phillips	O'Donoghue	Gaynor	Morley[1]	Barry*[1]	O'Donoghue	Hyde	
19 Dec	H	Limerick	3-0	2nd	Harrington	Daly	Napier	Murphy	Caulfield[1]	Phillips	Buckley	Gaynor	Morley[1]	Barry[1]	Glynn*	Glynn	
26 Dec	H	Cobh Ramblers	1-2	2nd	Harrington	Daly	Napier	Murphy	Caulfield[1]	Phillips	Buckley	Gaynor	Morley[1]	Barry	Glynn	Hyde	
9 Jan	A	Dundalk	2-2	2nd	Harrington	Daly	Napier	Murphy	Caulfield[1]	Phillips	Buckley*	Gaynor	Morley[2]	Barry	O'Donoghue	Glynn	
16 Jan	A	Shelbourne	1-1	2nd	Harrington	Daly	Napier	Murphy	Caulfield[1]	Phillips	Buckley*	Gaynor	Morley	Barry	O'Donoghue	Glynn	
23 Jan	H	Derry City	4-2	2nd	Harrington	Daly	Napier	Murphy	Caulfield[1]	Phillips	Buckley	Gaynor	Morley	Barry	O'Donoghue	Cotter	
30 Jan	A	Galway United	1-0	2nd	Harrington	Daly	Napier	Murphy	Caulfield[1]	Glynn	Hyde*	Gaynor	Morley	Barry	O'Donoghue	Hyde	
13 Feb	H	Shamrock Rovers	2-1	1st	Harrington	Daly	Napier	Murphy	Caulfield[1]	Glynn[2]	Buckley	Phillips*	Morley	Barry	O'Donoghue	Hyde	
20 Feb	A	Bohemians	1-1	1st	Harrington	Daly	Napier	Murphy	Caulfield[1]	Glynn*	Buckley	Hyde	Morley[1]	Barry	O'Donoghue	Gaynor	
6 Mar	A	Galway United	2-0	1st	Harrington	Daly	Napier	Murphy	Caulfield[1]	Glynn	Buckley	Cotter	Morley[1]	Gaynor	O'Donoghue	Gaynor	
13 Mar	A	Derry City	2-3	2nd	Harrington	Daly	Napier	Murphy	Caulfield	Glynn	Buckley*	Cotter	Morley	Barry[1]	O'Donoghue	Gaynor	
17 Mar	H	Shelbourne	1-1	2nd	Harrington	Daly	Napier	Murphy	Caulfield	Glynn[1]	Gaynor[1]	Hyde	Morley	Barry	O'Donoghue		
20 Mar	H	Shelbourne	3-1	2nd	Harrington	Daly	Napier	Murphy	Buckley*	Glynn*	Gaynor	Hyde[1]	Morley[1]	Barry	O'Donoghue		
27 Mar	H	Bohemians	3-1	2nd	Harrington	Daly	Napier	Murphy	Buckley*	Glynn[1]	Gaynor	Hyde[1]	Morley[1]	Barry	O'Donoghue		
3 Apr	A	Shamrock Rovers	0-2	2nd	Harrington	Daly	Napier	Murphy		Glynn	Gaynor	Hyde	Morley	Barry	O'Donoghue	Caulfield	Cotter

18

Derry City   Premier Div.

Founded: 1928
Home: Brandywell Stadium, Lone Moore Road, Derry,
      (080504) 262276
Office: 12 Queen Street, Derry BT48 7EF. Tel. (080504) 374542
Nickname: "Candystripes"
Colours: Red & White striped shirts, Black shorts
2nd Colours: Purple shirts, Black shorts
Manager: Tony O'Doherty: Succeeded: Roy Coyle (Sep. 1993)
President: Phil Coulter
Chairman: Paul Diamond
Secretary: Kevin Friel, 3 Greenlaw Drive, Ballymagorey, Strabane.
         Tel. Home: (080504) 884363; Office: (080504) 382076; Fax. (080504) 383755

Honours:

League of Ireland Champions	:	1988/89	(1)
First Division Champions	:	1986/87	(1)
F.A.I. Cup Winners	:	1989	(1)
League Cup Winners	:	1988/89, 1990/91, 1991/92, 1993/94	(4)
First Division Shield Winners	:	1986/87	(1)
Irish League Winners	:	1964/65	(1)
I.F.A. Cup Winners	:	1949, 1954, 1964	(3)

League Career:
Members of the Irish League 1929-1972. Elected to the First Division 1985. Promoted end 1986/87. Premier Division 1987/88 to date.

European Apearances: 6

Champions:	*1965/66	v	Lyn Oslo	5 - 1, 3 - 5
		v	Anderlecht	Scr, 0 - 9
	1989/90	v	Benfica	1 - 2, 0 - 4
E.C.W.C.	*1964/65	v	Steaua Bucharest	0 - 2, 0 - 3
	1988/89	v	Cardiff City	0 - 0, 0 - 4
U.E.F.A. Cup	1990/91	v	Vitesse Arnhem	0 - 1, 0 - 0
	1992/93	v	Vitesse Arnhem	1 - 2, 0 - 3

* As an Irish League club

Players Capped (ROI): 1

First	:	Jimmy Kelly	v	Holland	(A)	08 May 1932
Last	:	Jimmy Kelly	v	Luxembourg	(A)	09 May 1936
Most	:	Jimmy Kelly (4)	1932/36			

Players Capped (NI): 5

First	:	Jimmy Kelly & S.R. Russell	v	England	(H)	17 Oct. 1931
Last	:	Liam Coyle	v	Chile	(H)	26 May 1989
Most	:	Jimmy Kelly (11)	1931/37			

19

Record League Victory:
Home : 9 - 1 v Galway United   08 Oct. 1989
Away : 6 - 0 v Galway United   27 Dec. 1989

Record League Defeat:
Home : 1 - 4 v Dundalk   12 Sep. 1993
               v Shelbourne   28 Nov. 1993
Away : 1 - 5 v Longford Town   12 Jan. 1986

Most League Goals:
(Match) 6: Jonathan Speak v Sligo Rovers 7 - 2 (A) 24 Apr. 1988
(Season) 24: Jonathan Speak 1987/88
(Career) 70: Jonathan Speak 1987/88 to 1991/92

Points in a Season:
Most : 53   1988/89   (33 games)
Least : 22   1985/86   (18 games)

Goals Scored in a Season
Most : 72   1989/90   (33 games)
Least : 26   1992/93   (32 games)

League Appearances 1993/94:
32 Dermot O'Neill, 31 Paul Curran, 28 Peter Hutton, 27 Paul McLaughlin, 24 Stuart Gauld, 23 Liam Coyle, 11+10 Barry Ryan, 20 Paul Kinnaird, Pascal Vaudequin, 16+3 Kevin McKeever, 17+1 Joe Lawless, 16+1 Donal O'Brien, 12+1 Neil McNab, 8+1 Scott McGarvey, John Sayers, 6+3 Mark Ennis, 8 Paul Carlyle, 5+3 Gary Heaney, 4+4 John McGarvey, 7 Gary Lennox, 2+4 Liam Curran, 5 Paul Lemon, 4 Luther Blissett, Mike Smith, 3 Adrian Doherty, Willie Wilson, 2 John McElroy, Noel Murray, Steve Williams, 1+1 Ralph Milne, Mark Nixon, 0+2 Brian McCarron, Emmett McIntyre, 0+1 Ian McConnell.
Players Used: 34

League Goalscorers 1993/94:
8 Liam Coyle, 6 Peter Hutton, 4 Joe Lawless, 3 Stuart Gauld, Donal O'Brien, 2 Paul Curran, Paul Kinnaird, Barry Ryan, 1 Luther Blissett, Adrian Doherty, Mark Ennis, Gary Heaney, Kevin McKeever, Paul McLaughlin, o.g.
Total: 37

All time League of Ireland goalscorers 1985 - 1994
69 Jonathan Speak, **31** Stuart Gauld, Alex Krstic, **27** Owen Da-Gama, **25** Liam Coyle, **24** Felix Healy, Donal O'Brien, **18** Paul Doolin, **17** Paul Carlyle, **15** Paul Curran, **13** John Coady, **8** Kevin Mahon, **7** Dessie Gorman, Peter Hutton, Noel Larkin, Mick Neville, **6** John Cunningham, Paul Hegarty, Noel King, Greg Kearney, **5** Joe Hanrahan, Jack Keay, Nelson Da Silva, Pascal Vaudequin, **4** Brendan Bradley, Joe Lawless, **3** John Bacon, Mark Ennis, John McDaid, Paul McLaughlin, Kevin O'Neill, **2** Frank Devlin, Paul Kinnaird, Barry McCreadie, Paul Mooney, Barry Ryan, Jeremy Smith, Alan Sunderland, Paul Trainor, Paul Whelan, **1** Paul Dixon, Adrian Doherty, Luther Blissett, Alan Harrison, Gary Heaney, Martin McCann, Tony McCarthy, Liam McDermott, Ray McGuinness, Jim McKechnie, Kevin McKeever, Paul McLaughlin, John Mannion, John Quigg: **11** Opponents
Total: **440** Games: **265** Average per game: **1.66**

Derry City 1993/94

Date	V	Opposition	Score	Pos	1	2	3	4	5	6	7	8	9	10	11	12	13
21 Aug	H	Cobh Ramblers	2-0	-	O'Neill	Hutton	McLaughlin	Lennox	P. Curran	Gauld	Doherty[1]	Carlyle	Ryan[*]	Coyle[1]	Sayers	Ennis	
26 Aug	A	Monaghan United	1-1	2nd	O'Neill	Hutton	McLaughlin	Lennox	P. Curran	Gauld	Nixon[*]	Carlyle	Ennis	Coyle[1]	Sayers	McCarron	
29 Aug	H	Cork City	0-1	4th	O'Neill	Hutton	McLaughlin	Lennox	P. Curran	Gauld	Doherty[*]	Carlyle	Ennis[*]	Coyle	Sayers[#]	Nixon	McCarron
5 Sep	A	Shelbourne	0-2	6th	O'Neill	Hutton	McLaughlin	Lennox	P. Curran	Gauld	Doherty	Carlyle	Ennis	Coyle	Lemon	McConnell	
12 Sep	A	Dundalk	1-4	9th	O'Neill	Hutton	McLaughlin	Lennox	P. Curran	Gauld	Smith[*]	Carlyle	Coyle[#1]	Coyle[*]	Lemon	Ryan	J. McGarvey
18 Sep	A	Bohemians	0-2	12th	O'Neill	Hutton	McLaughlin	Lennox	P. Curran	Wilson	Smith[*]	J. McGarvey	Ennis	Coyle[#]	Lemon	Ryan	Ennis
26 Sep	H	Drogheda United	1-1	12th	O'Neill	Hutton	McLaughlin	Lennox	P. Curran[1]	Wilson	Smith[*]	S. McGarvey	Murray	Coyle[#]	Lemon	Ryan	
3 Oct	A	St. Patrick's Ath.	0-0	11th	O'Neill	Hutton	McLaughlin	Carlyle	P. Curran	Wilson	Smith[*]	S. McGarvey	Murray	Coyle	Lemon	Ryan	Ennis
10 Oct	H	Shamrock Rovers	0-0	11th	O'Neill	Hutton	McLaughlin	Carlyle	P. Curran	Williams	J. McGarvey[*]	S. McGarvey	Ennis	Coyle	Ryan		
17 Oct	A	Galway United	1-2	11th	O'Neill	Hutton	McLaughlin	Carlyle	P. Curran	Williams[*]	J. McGarvey[#]	S. McGarvey	McNab	Kinnaird	Blissett[1]	Ennis	
24 Oct	H	Limerick	0-0	11th	O'Neill	Hutton	McLaughlin	Gauld[1]	P. Curran	Coyle	Ryan	S. McGarvey	McNab	Kinnaird	Blissett	Milne	
31 Oct	H	Limerick	1-0	10th	O'Neill	Vaudequin	McLaughlin	Gauld[1]	P. Curran	Lawless	Ryan	S. McGarvey	McNab	Milne[#]	Blissett	J. McGarvey	L. Curran
7 Nov	A	Monaghan United	3-1	9th	O'Neill	Hutton	McLaughlin	Gauld	P. Curran	Lawless	Hutton[2]	S. McGarvey	McNab	Kinnaird	Blissett[#]	McKeever	Ryan[1]
14 Nov	H	Cork City	1-0	8th	O'Neill	Hutton	McLaughlin	Gauld	P. Curran	Lawless	Hutton[1]	S. McGarvey[*]	McNab	Coyle	Blissett	McKeever	Ryan
21 Nov	A	Shelbourne	0-1	8th	O'Neill	Vaudequin	McLaughlin	Gauld	P. Curran	Ryan[*]	Hutton	McKeever[1]	McNab	Coyle	Coyle	S. McGarvey	
28 Nov	H	Dundalk	1-4	8th	O'Neill	Vaudequin	P. Curran	O'Brien	Lawless	Hutton[*]	McKeever[*]	McNab	Kinnaird	Coyle	J. McGarvey		
5 Dec	H	Bohemians	2-2	8th	O'Neill	Vaudequin	P. Curran	O'Brien	Lawless	Gauld	Hutton	S. McGarvey[*]	McNab	Kinnaird	Coyle[3]	S. McGarvey	
12 Dec	A	Drogheda United	3-0	8th	O'Neill	Vaudequin	P. Curran	O'Brien	Lawless	Gauld	Hutton	McKeever	McNab	Kinnaird	Coyle	McKeever	
19 Dec	A	St. Patrick's Ath.	1-0	8th	O'Neill	McKeever	P. Curran	O'Brien	Lawless	Gauld	Hutton[1]	McLaughlin[1]	McNab	Kinnaird	Coyle[1]		
27 Dec	H	Shamrock Rovers	2-0	7th	O'Neill	McKeever	P. Curran	Vaudequin	Lawless	Gauld	Hutton	McLaughlin	McNab	Kinnaird	Coyle[1]	O'Brien	
2 Jan	H	Galway United	1-0	6th	O'Neill	McKeever	P. Curran	Vaudequin	Lawless	Gauld	Hutton	McLaughlin[*]	O'Brien[*]	Kinnaird[*]	Coyle	McNab	Ryan
9 Jan	A	Shamrock Rovers	0-0	6th	O'Neill	McKeever	P. Curran[1]	Vaudequin	Lawless	Gauld	McLaughlin	O'Brien[*]	Kinnaird[*]	Coyle	Heaney		
16 Jan	H	Cork City	1-0	5th	O'Neill	McKeever	P. Curran[1]	Vaudequin	Sayers	Gauld	Ryan	Lawless[#]	O'Brien	Kinnaird[1]	Coyle[*1]	Ryan	Heaney
23 Jan	A	Shelbourne	2-4	6th	O'Neill	McKeever	P. Curran	Vaudequin	Sayers	Gauld	Heaney[*]	Ryan	O'Brien[1]	Kinnaird[1]	Coyle	J. Curran	
28 Jan	A	Bohemians	1-1	6th	O'Neill	McKeever	P. Curran	Vaudequin	Sayers[#]	Gauld	Hutton[*]	Coyle	O'Brien[2]	Kinnaird[*1]	McLaughlin	Lawless	Ryan
13 Feb	H	Shelbourne	4-0	5th	O'Neill	McKeever	P. Curran	Vaudequin	Lawless	Gauld[*]	Hutton	Coyle	O'Brien	Kinnaird	McLaughlin	Heaney	Sayers
5 Mar	H	Cork City	3-2	4th	O'Neill	McKeever[*]	P. Curran	Vaudequin	Lawless[*]	Gauld[2]	Hutton	Sayers	O'Brien	Kinnaird	McLaughlin	L. Curran	J. McGarvey
13 Mar	A	Shamrock Rovers	0-3	4th	O'Neill	McKeever[*]	P. Curran	Vaudequin	Lawless[1]	Gauld	Hutton	Heaney	O'Brien	Kinnaird[#]	McLaughlin	L. Curran	Ryan
17 Mar	H	Galway United	1-1	4th	O'Neill	McKeever	P. Curran	Vaudequin	Lawless[1]	Gauld	Hutton	Heaney	O'Brien	Ryan[1]	McLaughlin	McIntyre	J. McGarvey
24 Mar	A	Bohemians	3-1	4th	O'Neill	McKeever	P. Curran	Vaudequin	Lawless[2]	McElroy	Hutton	Heaney[*]	O'Brien[*]	Ryan	Kinnaird	L. Curran	

Drogheda United First Div.

Founded: 1919
Former Name: Drogheda
Home: United Park, Windmill Road, Drogheda, Co. Louth, (041) 37432
Capacity: 5,000; 400 seated
Previous Ground: Lourdes Stadium (1963/64 - 1978/79)
Nickname: "United"
Colours: Maroon & Blue
2nd Colours: Red & Black stripes, Black shorts
Manager: Jim McLaughlin Succeeded: Pat Devlin (Dec. 1993)
Asst. Manager: Noel White
President: Charlie Hurley
Chairman: Vincent Hoey
Secretary: Mr. Charlie Hurley, 38 Hillview, Rathmullen, Drogheda, Co. Louth. Tel. Home: (041) 30190; Fax. (041) 30190
Admin. Secretary: Anna McKenna, George's Street, Drogheda. Tel. (041) 31843

Honours/Best Performances:

Championship	: Runners-up 1982/83	
First Division Champions	: 1988/89, 1990/91	(2)
F.A.I. Cup	: Runners-up 1970/71, 1975/76	
League Cup Winners	: 1983/84	(1)
League of Ireland Shield	: Finalists 1971/72	
First Division Shield Winners	: 1990/91	(1)
Leinster Cup	: Runners-up 1982/83, 1985/86	
Tyler Cup	: Finalists 1979/80	

League Career:

Elected with Sligo Rovers 1963. Re-elected 65/66, 70/71, 72/73 (3 times). Relegated end 1984/85. Promoted end 1988/89. Relegated end 1989/90. Promoted end 1990/91. Relegated end 1993/94.

European Appearances: 1

U.E.F.A. Cup : 1983/84 v Tottenham Hotspur 0 - 6, 0 - 8

Players Capped (ROI): 3

First : Mick Meagan v Scotland (H) 21 Sep. 1969
Last : Jerome Clarke & Cathal Muckian v Poland (A) 12 Apr. 1978

Record League Victory:

Home : 6 - 1 v Sligo Rovers 20 Sep. 1972
         v Thurles Town 04 Apr. 1982
Away : 7 - 1 v Finn Harps 24 Apr. 1977

Record League Defeat:
Home   : 0 - 7 v   Shamrock Rovers   08 Jan. 1984
Away   : 1 - 8 v   Cork Hibernians   30 Jan. 1972

Most League Goals:
(Match) 3:
Pat Cruise	v	Waterford	4 - 3 (H)	15 Jan. 1967
Pat Cullen	v	Drumcondra	4 - 1 (H)	14 Nov. 1971
Denis Stephenson	v	Waterford	4 - 2 (H)	24 Nov. 1974
Greg McElroy	v	Finn Harps	4 - 4 (A)	12 Jan. 1975
Cathal Muckian	v	Cork Celtic	6 - 3 (H)	03 Oct. 1976
Damien Byrne	v	Finn Harps	7 - 1 (A)	24 Apr. 1977
Martin Kerr	v	Thurles Town	6 - 1 (H)	04 Apr. 1982
Martin Murray	v	St. Pat's. Ath	5 - 1 (H)	31 Oct. 1982
Mick Fairclough	v	Waterford	4 - 2 (H)	07 Oct. 1984
Paddy Dillon	v	Longford Town	6 - 2 (H)	27 Jan. 1985

(Season) 21:   Cathal Muckian 1977/78
(Career) 47:   Damien Byrne 1974/75 to 1982/83

Points in a Season:
Most	:	42	1978/79	(30 games)
		49**	1982/83	(26 games)
Least	:	05	1965/66	(22 games)

Goals Scored in a Season:
Most	:	60	1978/79	(30 games)
Least	:	15	1965/66	(22 games)

League Appearances 1993/94:
32 John Ryan, Colm Tresson, 28+2 John Carroll, 22+5 Trevor Crolly, 27 Mick Shelley, 23+2 Paul McLaughlin, 19+6 Dave Connell, 20+3 Noel Reid, 19+3 Joe Reynolds, 21 Seán Byrne, Jim Grace, 17 Barry Kehoe, 11+4 Ian Douglas, 14 Barry O'Connor, 11+2 Eddie Gormley, 11 Alan Kane, 6+3 Mick Kinsella, 7+1 Lee King, 3+2 Albert Murphy, 4 Paul Trainor, 2+1 Neil Poutch, 2 David Staunton, 0+2 Mick Power, Alan Weldrick, 0+1 Glenn Kealy..
Players Used: 25

League Goalscorers 1993/94:
7 Lee King, 5 Barry O'Connor, 4 John Ryan, 2 Trevor Crolly, Noel Reid, 1 Seán Byrne, Dave Connell, Ian Douglas, Barry Kehoe, Paul Trainor, Colm Tresson.
Total: 26

Do you want the inside track on League of Ireland Football?
then read **Oliver Slattery**
in the **Avondhu**
every Thursday

Drogheda United 1993/94

Date	V	Opposition	Score	Pos	1	2	3	4	5	6	7	8	9	10	11	12	13
22 Aug	H	St Patrick's Ath.	1-1	-	Kane	Tresson•	Reynolds	Reid	Carroll	Connell#	Murphy	Crolly	Ryan	O'Connor	Gormley	Power	Weldrick
26 Aug	A	Dundalk	1-0	3rd	Grace	Tresson	Reynolds	Reid	Carroll	Shelley	Murphy•	Crolly•	Ryan	O'Connor	Gormley	Kinsella	
29 Aug	H	Galway United	1-4	7th	Grace	Tresson#	Reynolds	Reid	Connell¹	Shelley	Kinsella	Crolly	Ryan	O'Connor	Gormley	Weldrick	Power
5 Sep	A	Monaghan United	0-1	7th	Grace	Tresson	Reynolds	Reid	Connell	Carroll	McLaughlin	Crolly#	Ryan	O'Connor	Gormley•	Murphy	
12 Sep	H	Bohemians	0-4	10th	Grace	Tresson	Reynolds	Reid¹	Connell	Carroll	Shelley	Kinsella	Ryan	O'Connor	Gormley•	McLaughlin	Murphy
19 Sep	A	Cork City	1-1	10th	Grace	Tresson•	Reynolds	Reid	Connell	Carroll	Shelley	Kinsella	Ryan	O'Connor¹	McLaughlin		
26 Sep	A	Derry City	1-1	10th	Grace	Tresson•	Reynolds	Reid	Connell	Carroll	Shelley	Kinsella	Ryan¹	O'Connor¹	Murphy#	Crolly	Poutch
1 Oct	H	Shamrock Rovers	2-1	8th	Grace	Tresson	Reynolds	Reid	Connell	Carroll	Shelley	Kinsella	Ryan¹	O'Connor	Crolly¹	Gormley	
10 Oct	A	Limerick	1-1	9th	Grace	Tresson	Reynolds	Reid	Connell	Carroll	Shelley•	Kinsella#	Ryan¹	O'Connor	Crolly	Gormley	McLaughlin
16 Oct	H	Cobh Ramblers	1-3	10th	Grace	Tresson	Reynolds	Reid	Connell	Carroll	McLaughlin	Gormley	Ryan	O'Connor	Crolly		
24 Oct	H	Shelbourne	0-1	10th	Grace	Tresson	Reynolds	Reid	Connell	Carroll	McLaughlin	Gormley	Ryan	O'Connor²	Crolly		
29 Oct	H	St Patrick's Ath	2-2	11th	Kane	Tresson¹	Byrne	Poutch#	Connell#	Shelley	McLaughlin	Gormley	Ryan	O'Connor	Crolly	Carroll	Kealy
7 Nov	A	Dundalk	1-4	11th	Kane	Tresson	Byrne	Poutch#	Connell¹	Shelley	McLaughlin	Gormley	Ryan	O'Connor	Crolly	Carroll	Kinsella
21 Nov	H	Galway United	0-3	11th	Kane	Tresson	Byrne	Reid	Connell	Carroll	McLaughlin	Gormley	Ryan	O'Connor	Crolly		
26 Nov	A	Monaghan United	1-4	12th	Kane	Tresson	Byrne	Reid	Kehoe	Carroll	McLaughlin	Gormley•	Ryan•	Reynolds	Crolly		
5 Dec	A	Bohemians	1-0	11th	Grace	Tresson	Byrne	Connell	Kehoe#	Carroll	McLaughlin	Shelley	Ryan	Reynolds	Douglas	Douglas¹	Crolly
12 Dec	H	Cork City	0-5	11th	Grace	Tresson	Byrne	Connell	Kehoe•	Carroll	McLaughlin	Shelley	Ryan	Reynolds	Douglas	Reid	Crolly
19 Dec	H	Derry City	0-1	11th	Grace	Tresson	Byrne	Connell	Kehoe	Carroll	McLaughlin	Shelley	Ryan	Reynolds	Douglas	Kinsella	
27 Dec	A	Shamrock Rovers	0-2	12th	Grace	Tresson	Byrne	Connell•	Kehoe	Carroll•	McLaughlin	Shelley	Ryan	Reynolds	Douglas	Crolly	
2 Jan	H	Limerick	0-2	12th	Grace	Tresson	Byrne	Crolly	Kehoe	Carroll	McLaughlin	Shelley	Ryan•	Reynolds	Douglas	Connell	
9 Jan	A	Cobh Ramblers	2-1	12th	Grace	Tresson	Byrne	Crolly	Kehoe	Carroll	McLaughlin	Shelley	Ryan¹	Trainor¹	Douglas•	Connell	
14 Jan	H	Limerick	0-2	12th	Grace	Tresson	Byrne	Crolly	Kehoe	Carroll	McLaughlin	Shelley#	Ryan	Trainor	Douglas•	Connell	Reynolds
23 Jan	H	Limerick	0-1	12th	Grace	Tresson	Byrne	Crolly¹	Kehoe	Carroll	McLaughlin	Shelley#	Ryan	Trainor	Douglas•	Connell	
28 Jan	H	St Patrick's Ath.	2-0	12th	Grace	Tresson	Byrne	Crolly•	Kehoe	Carroll	McLaughlin	Shelley	Ryan	Trainor	Connell	King¹	
13 Feb	H	Cobh Ramblers	2-1	12th	Grace	Tresson	Byrne¹	Crolly#	Kehoe	Carroll	McLaughlin	Shelley	Ryan	Reid	King¹	Connell	
20 Feb	A	Monaghan United	2-3	10th	Grace	Tresson	Byrne¹	Crolly	Kehoe¹	Carroll	McLaughlin	Shelley	Ryan	Reid#	King¹	Connell	Douglas
4 Mar	A	St Patrick's Ath.	3-1	10th	Kane	Tresson	Byrne	Crolly#	Kehoe	Carroll	McLaughlin•	Shelley	Ryan	Douglas	Byrne	Reynolds	Reid
11 Mar	H	Limerick	0-0	10th	Kane	Tresson	Byrne	Reid	Kehoe	Carroll	McLaughlin	Shelley	Ryan	Douglas	Byrne	Reynolds	
17 Mar	A	Dundalk	0-4	10th	Kane	Tresson	Byrne	Reid	Kehoe	Carroll	McLaughlin	Shelley	Ryan	Douglas	Byrne	Connell	
25 Mar	H	Monaghan United	1-1	12th	Kane	Tresson	Byrne	Reid•	Kehoe	Carroll	McLaughlin	Shelley	Ryan	Staunton	Byrne	Douglas	
3 Apr	A	Cobh Ramblers	0-1	12th	Kane	Tresson	Byrne	Reid	Kehoe	Carroll	McLaughlin	Shelley	Ryan	Staunton	Byrne	Douglas	Crolly

Dundalk   Premier Div.

Founded: 1922
Home: Oriel Park, Carrick Road, Dundalk, Co Louth.
        Tel. (042) 35398/35894
Capacity: 20,000; 1,600 seated
Previous Ground: Athletic Grounds (1926/27 - 1935/36)
Nickname: "Lillywhites"
Colours: White shirts, Black shorts
2nd Colours: All red
Manager: Dermot Keely; Succeeded: Tommy Connolly (Nov. 1993)
Chairman: Eamonn Hiney
Secretary: Ms Elizabeth Duffy, 183 Ard Easmuinn, Dundalk, Co. Louth.
        Tel. (042) 35750; Fax. (042) 30003

Honours:

League of Ireland Champions	:	1932/33, 1962/63, 1966/67, 1975/76,
		1978/79, 1981/82, 1987/88, 1990/91 (8)
F.A.I. Cup Winners	:	1942, 1949, 1952, 1958, 1977, 1979,
		1981, 1988 (8)
League Cup Winners	:	1977/78, 1980/81, 1986/87, 1989/90 (4)
Lague of Ireland Shield Winners	:	1966/67, 1971/72 (2)
Leinster Cup Winners	:	1951/52, 1960/61, 1970/71, 1973/74,
		1976/77, 1977/78 (6)
Dublin City Cup Winners	:	1937/38, 1942/43, 1948/49, 1967.68,
		1968/69 (5)
Top Four Winners	:	1963/64, 1966/67 (2)
Inter City Cup Winners	:	1941/42 (1)
Presidents Cup Winners	:	1930/31, 1951/52, 1963/64, 1964/65,
		1979/80, 1980/81, 1988/89, 1989/90 (8)

League Career:
Elected 1926 in place of Pioneers. Everpresent to date. Re-elected end 1951/52, 54/55, 58/59, 72/73 (4 times). Premier Division 1985/86 to date.

Players Capped (ROI): 11

First	:	Robert Egan	v	Belgium	(H) 20 Apr. 1929
Last	:	Mick Fairclough	v	Trinidad & Tobago	(A) 30 May 1982
Most	:	Willie O'Neill (11)	1935/39		

Record League Victory:
Home	:	9 - 0	v	Jacobs	06 Feb. 1932
				Shelbourne	27 Jan. 1980
Away:	:	8 - 1	v	Sligo Rovers	11 Jan. 1987

Record League Defeat:
Home	:	0 - 6	v	Drumcondra	13 Feb. 1955
Away	:	1 - 9	v	Limerick	17 Dec. 1944

European Appearances: 14

Champion's Cup:	1963/64	v	F.C. Zurich,	0 - 3, 2 - 1
	1967/68	v	Vasas Budapest,	0 - 1, 1 - 8
	1976/77	v	P.S.V. Eindhoven,	1 - 1, 0 - 6
	1979/80	v	Linfield,	1 - 1, 2 - 0
			Hibernians,	2 - 0, 0 - 1
			Glasgow Celtic,	0 - 0, 2 - 3
	1982/83	v	Liverpool,	1 - 4, 0 - 1
	1988/89	v	Red Star Belgrade,	0 - 5, 0 - 3
	1991/92	v	Kispest Honved,	0 - 2, 1 - 1
Cup Winners Cup:	1977/78	v	Hajduk Split,	1 - 0, 0 - 4
	1981/82	v	Fram Reykjavik,	4 - 0, 1 - 2
			Tottenham Hotspur,	1 - 1, 0 - 1
	1987/88	v	Ajax Amsterdam,	0 - 2, 0 - 4
Fairs Cup:	1968/69	v	D.O.S. Utrecht,	2 - 1, 1 - 1
			Glasgow Rangers,	0 - 3, 1 - 6
	1969/70	v	Liverpool,	0 - 4, 0 - 10
U.E.F.A. Cup:	1980/81	v	Oporto,	0 - 0, 0 - 1
	1989/90	v	Wettingen,	0 - 2, 0 - 3

Most League Goals:

(Match) 4: Eddie Carroll v Dolphin 4 - 1 (H) 19 Nov. 1933
Turlough O'Connor v Waterford 6 - 1 (H) 07 Dec. 1969
Seamus McDowell v Shamrock Rovers 5 - 2 (H) 14 Dec. 1975
Dessie Gorman v Sligo Rovers 8 - 1 (A) 11 Jan. 1987
(Season) 19: Liam Munroe 1959/60
(Career) 69: Joey Donnelly 1929/30 to 1931/32 & 1934/35 to 1942/43

Points in a Season:

Most	:	52	1990/91	(33 games)
		80*	1981/82	(30 games)
Least	:	11	1944/45 &	
			1946/47	(14 games)

Goals Scored in a Season:

Most	:	64	1930/31	(22 games)
Least	:	19	1972/73	(26 games)

League Appearances 1993/94:

30 Gino Lawless, Martin Lawlor, 29 Peter Hanrahan, 27 James Coll, Tom McNulty, Greg O'Dowd, 24+2 Richie Purdy, 24 Mick Doohan, 22+2 Joe Hanrahan, 19 Eddie Van Boxtel, 9+9 Matt Britton, 6+10 Trevor Donnelly, 13+2 Stephen Kelly, 13 Paul Kavanagh, 11+2 Wayne Cooney, 3+10 Tom O'Sullivan, 9+3 Keith Long, 8+3 Brian Irwin, 7+3 Alan Doherty, 4+1 Ciaran Sheehy, 3 Elden De Getrouwe, Derek Swan, Thomas Staunton, 1 Lee Robinson.
Players Used: 24

League Goalscorers 1993/94:

8 Peter Hanrahan, 4 Mick Doohan, 3 James Coll, Trevor Donnelly, Brian Irwin, Stephen Kelly, 2 Alan Doherty, Greg O'Dowd, Richie Purdy, og's. 1 Matt Britton, Elden De Getrouwe, Joe Hanrahan, Gino Lawless, Tom McNulty.
Total: 37

Dundalk 1993/94

Date	V	Opposition	Score	Pos	1	2	3	4	5	6	7	8	9	10	11	12	13
22 Aug	A	Shamrock Rovers	0-0	-	Kavanagh	Purdy	Lawlor	Doohan	Coll	Cooney	J. Hanrahan	O'Sullivan	P. Hanrahan	Lawless	O'Dowd	Irwin	
26 Aug	H	Drogheda United	0-1	9th	Kavanagh	Purdy	Lawlor	Doohan	Coll	Cooney	Irwin*	McNulty	P. Hanrahan	Lawless	O'Dowd	Donnelly	O'Sullivan
29 Aug	H	Limerick	1-0	6th	Kavanagh	Purdy*	Lawlor	Doohan	Coll	Cooney	J. Hanrahan	McNulty	P. Hanrahan	Lawless	O'Dowd	Donnelly	
5 Sep	H	Cobh Ramblers	0-2	6th	Kavanagh	Purdy*	Lawlor	Doohan	Coll	Cooney	Irwin	McNulty	P. Hanrahan*	Lawless	O'Dowd	O'Sullivan	
12 Sep	A	Derry City	4-1	5th	Kavanagh	Purdy²	Lawlor	Doohan	Coll	Cooney	J. Hanrahan¹	McNulty	P. Hanrahan¹	Lawless*	O'Dowd	O'Sullivan	Britton
19 Sep	H	Shelbourne	5-1	5th	Kavanagh	Purdy	Britton*¹	Doohan	Coll	Cooney	Doherty¹	McNulty	P. Hanrahan²	Lawless*	O'Dowd	Doherty	
26 Sep	H	St. Patrick's Ath.	0-2	5th	Kavanagh	Purdy	Lawlor	Doohan	Coll	Cooney*	J. Hanrahan	McNulty	P. Hanrahan	Lawless	O'Dowd*	Britton	
3 Oct	A	Galway United	0-0	5th	Kavanagh	Britton	Lawlor	Doohan	Coll	O'Sullivan	J. Hanrahan	McNulty	P. Hanrahan	Lawless	O'Dowd*	Doherty	O'Sullivan
10 Oct	A	Monaghan United	1-3	6th	Kavanagh	Purdy	Lawlor	Doohan	Coll	Cooney*	J. Hanrahan	McNulty	P. Hanrahan¹	Lawless	O'Dowd*	Doherty	
17 Oct	A	Cork City	1-0	6th	Kavanagh	Long	Lawlor	Doohan	Col	Doherty	J. Hanrahan	McNulty	P. Hanrahan¹	Lawless	O'Dowd*	Britton	
24 Oct	H	Bohemians	1-1	6th	Kavanagh	Long	Lawlor	Doohan	Saunton	Cooney*	Britton¹	McNulty	P. Hanrahan	Lawless	O'Dowd*	Purdy	
29 Oct	H	Shamrock Rovers	1-2	7th	Kavanagh	Purdy*	Lawlor	Coll¹	Doohan	Doherty	J. Hanrahan	McNulty¹	P. Hanrahan	Lawless	O'Dowd	Britton	
7 Nov	A	Drogheda United	3-0	6th	Kavanagh	Long	Lawlor	Coll¹	Doohan	Doherty*	J. Hanrahan	McNulty	P. Hanrahan¹	Lawless¹	O'Dowd	Britton	O'Sullivan
12 Nov	A	Limerick	0-0	7th	Van Bootel	Purdy	Lawlor	Coll	Doohan	Doherty*	J. Hanrahan	McNulty	P. Hanrahan	Lawless	O'Dowd	Cooney	
21 Nov	H	Shamrock Rovers	2-0	7th	Van Bootel	Kelly	Lawlor	Coll	Doohan	Irwin¹	Cooney*	McNulty	P. Hanrahan	Lawless	O'Dowd*	Purdy	
26 Nov	H	Derry City	2-2	5th	Van Bootel	Kelly*	Lawlor	Coll*	Purdy	Irwin#	Britton	McNulty	P. Hanrahan	Lawless	O'Dowd	Long	Donnelly¹
5 Dec	A	Shelbourne	2-1	5th	Van Bootel	Kelly	Lawlor	Long	Purdy	Irwin#	J. Hanrahan	McNulty	P. Hanrahan	Lawless	O'Dowd	Donnelly	J. Hanrahan
19 Dec	A	St. Patrick's Ath.	0-0	5th	Van Bootel	Doohan	Lawlor	Kelly	Purdy	Irwin*	McNulty	P. Hanrahan	Lawless	O'Dowd	Donnelly		
27 Dec	H	Galway United	0-0	5th	Van Bootel	Coll*	Lawlor	Kelly	Purdy	Donnelly¹	J. Hanrahan	McNulty	P. Hanrahan	Lawless	O'Dowd		
2 Jan	H	Monaghan United	0-1	8th	Van Bootel	Coll¹	Lawlor	Kelly²	Purdy	Irwin*	J. Hanrahan	Long	P. Hanrahan	Lawless	O'Dowd	O'Sullivan	Donnelly
9 Jan	H	Cork City	2-2	8th	Van Bootel	Coll	Lawlor	Kelly	Purdy	Donnelly*	J. Hanrahan	McNulty¹	P. Hanrahan¹	Lawless	O'Dowd	Britton	
14 Jan	A	Drogheda United	2-0	7th	Van Bootel	Coll¹	Lawlor	Kelly¹	Purdy	de Gezrouwe	J. Hanrahan	McNulty	P. Hanrahan	Lawless	O'Dowd	O'Sullivan	Donnelly
23 Jan	H	Cobh Ramblers	0-0	7th	Van Bootel	Coll	Lawlor	Kelly	Purdy	de Gezrouwe*¹	J. Hanrahan	McNulty	P. Hanrahan	Lawless	O'Dowd	Britton	
30 Jan	A	Monaghan United	1-1	7th	Van Bootel	Coll	Lawlor	Kelly	Purdy	de Gezrouwe	J. Hanrahan	McNulty	Swan	Lawless	O'Dowd	Britton	
13 Feb	A	St. Patrick's Ath.	0-0	7th	Van Bootel	Coll	Lawlor	Kelly	Purdy	Long	J. Hanrahan	McNulty	Swan	Lawless*	O'Dowd*	Sheedy	O'Sullivan
6 Mar	H	Monaghan United	1-1	8th	Van Bootel	Coll¹	Lawlor	Sheedy	Purdy	O'Sullivan	J. Hanrahan	McNulty	P. Hanrahan*	Donnelly*	Doohan¹	Kelly	Britton
13 Mar	A	Cobh Ramblers	1-1	8th	Van Bootel	Coll	Lawlor	Sheedy	Purdy	Britton*	J. Hanrahan	McNulty	Kelly¹	Donnelly¹	Doohan²	O'Sullivan	Irwin¹
17 Mar	A	Drogheda United	4-0	8th	Van Bootel	Coll	Lawlor	Sheedy	Purdy	Lawless*	J. Hanrahan	McNulty	P. Hanrahan¹ Kelly#	Donnelly¹	Doohan¹	Britton	Long
24 Mar	H	Limerick	2-0	8th	Van Bootel	Saunton	Lawlor	Britton	Purdy	Lawless	J. Hanrahan	P. Hanrahan¹	O'Sullivan	O'Dowd*	Doohan¹	Donnelly	Irwin
31 Mar	H	St. Patrick's Ath.	0-2	8th	Van Bootel	Coll	Lawlor	Sheedy*	Purdy	Lawless	J. Hanrahan	P. Hanrahan Robinson		Donnelly#	Doohan	Kelly	Long

Finn Harps   First Div.

Founded: 1954
Home: Finn Park, Ballybofey, Co Donegal, (074) 32635
Nickname: "Harps"
Colours: White shirts, Blue shorts
2nd Colours: All Blue
Manager: Patsy McGowan   Succeeded: Alex Harkin, caretaker (Jun. 92)
Secretary: P. Gallen, Navaney Street, Ballybofey.
           Tel. (074) 31125; (074) 31053; Fax. (074) 45582

Honours/Best Performances:
Championship	:	Runners-up 1972/73, 1975/76, 1977/78	
F.A.I. Cup Winners	:	1974	(1)
League Cup	:	Runners-up 1973/74, 1974/75	
Dublin City Cup Winners	:	1971/72	(1)
Tyler-Cup	:	Runners-up 1977/78	

League Career:
Elected with Athlone Town in 1969. Relegated end 1984/85. First Division 1985/86 to date.

European Appearances: 4
Cup Winners Cup:	1974/75	v	Bursaspor,	0 - 0, 2 - 4
U.E.F.A. Cup:	1973/74	v	Aberdeen,	1 - 3, 1 - 4
	1976/77	v	Derby County,	1 - 4, 0 - 12
	1978/79	v	Everton,	0 - 5, 0 - 5

Record League Victory:
Home	:	7 - 0	v	Athlone Town	07 Nov. 1971
			v	Drogheda United	12 Oct. 1975
Away	:	7 - 0	v	Thurles Town	01 Nov. 1981

Record League Defeat:
Home	:	1 - 7	v	Drogheda United	24 Apr. 1977
Away	:	0 - 6	v	Bohemians	12 Dec. 1976
		0 - 6	v	Waterford United	28 Nov. 1993

Most League Goals:
(Match) 6: Brendan Bradley v Sligo Rovers 6 - 2 (H) 30 Nov. 1975
(Season) 29: Brendan Bradley 1975/76
(Career) 181: Brendan Bradley 1969/70 to 1977/78 & 1982/83 to 1985/86

Points in a Season:
Most	:	42	1977/78	(30 games)
Least	:	13	1985/86	(18 games)

Goals Scored in a Season:
Most	:	62	1971/72	(26 games)
Least	:	23	1985/86	(18 games)

League Appearances 1993/94:
25+2 Seán Barrett, 22+5 Kieran Rooney, 25+1 Charlie McGeever, 24+2 Marty Gallagher, 24 Paul Hegarty, 22+2 John Gerard McGettigan, 16+9 Colm McGonnigle, 20+2 Damien Dunleavy, Martin McGinley, 16+1 Maurice Toland, 15+2 Adrian Creane, 15+1 Declan McIntyre, 11+3 Brian Lafferty, 11+1 Stephen Rushe, 10 Karl Lafferty, Ollie Reid, 9 Norman Costelloe, 4+3 Declan Sheridan, 6 Liam Sweeney, 5 John Walsh, 3+1 Dermot McCaul, 2 Declan Bonner, Dexter Sandy, Paul Trainor.
Players Used: 24

League Goalscorers 1993/94:
10 Damien Dunleavy, 6 Kieran Rooney, 4 Marty Gallagher, 3 John Gerard McGettigan, Colm McGonnigle, 2 Paul Hegarty, Charlie McGeever, Martin McGinley, Maurice Toland, 1 Ollie Reid, Stephen Rushe.
Total: 36

Patsy McGowan
Finn Harps manager points the way (EOH)

Finn Harps 1993/94

Date	V	Opposition	Score	Pos	1	2	3	4	5	6	7	8	9	10	11	12	13
19 Sep	H	Waterford United	2-0	-	Walsh	McGinley	Creane	Reid	Barrett	Bonner#	Hegarty*	McGettigan	Trainor	Rooney¹	Gallagher¹	B. Lafferty	
26 Sep	A	U.C.D.	1-4	7th	Walsh	McGinley	Creane*	Reid	Barrett	Bonner#	Hegarty	McGettigan	Trainor	Rooney¹	Gallagher	McGonnigle	B. Lafferty
3 Oct	H	Bay Wanderers	2-1	3rd	Walsh	McGinley	Creane	Reid	Sweeney	McGeever	Hegarty	McGettigan	McGonnigle¹	Rooney*	Gallagher	Barrett	
10 Oct	A	Kilkenny City	1-1	3rd	Walsh*	McGinley	Creane	Reid*	Sweeney	McGeever	Hegarty	McGettigan¹	McGonnigle	Rooney	Gallagher	McIntyre	Sheridan
17 Oct	H	Sligo Rovers	0-1	6th	Walsh*	McGinley	Creane	Barrett	Sweeney#	McGeever	Hegarty	McGettigan	McGonnigle	Rooney*	Gallagher¹	Sheridan	
24 Oct	A	St James's Gate	1-1	6th	McIntyre	McGinley¹	Reid	Barrett	Creane*	McGeever	Hegarty	McGettigan	McGonnigle	Rooney*	Gallagher¹	Creane	Dunleavy
31 Oct	H	Longford Town	1-1	5th	McIntyre	McGinley¹	Reid#	Barrett	Sweeney*	McGeever	Hegarty	Rooney	McGonnigle	Sheridan	Gallagher¹	Sheridan	Rooney
7 Nov	A	Home Farm	1-3	6th	McIntyre	McGinley¹	Creane	Barrett	Sweeney*	McGeever	Hegarty¹	McGettigan	McGonnigle	Dunleavy	Gallagher	Barrett	
14 Nov	H	Athlone Town	2-2	7th	McIntyre	McGinley	Creane	McCaul	Reid*	McGeever	Rooney	Sheridan	McGonnigle	Dunleavy	Gallagher#	Dunleavy	B. Lafferty
21 Nov	A	Athlone Town	0-1	8th	McIntyre	McGinley	Creane	Barrett	B. Lafferty	McGeever	Rooney	Sheridan	Hegarty*	Toland	Gallagher		
28 Nov	A	Waterford United	0-6	10th	McIntyre	McGinley*	McGonnigle*²	Barrett	B. Lafferty	McGeever	Rooney	K. Lafferty	Dunleavy¹	Toland	Hegarty	McGettigan	Gallagher
5 Dec	A	U.C.D.	0-0	9th	McIntyre	McGinley*²	McGonnigle	Barrett	B. Lafferty	McGeever	Rooney*	K. Lafferty	Dunleavy²	Toland	Hegarty	McGettigan	
12 Dec	A	Bay Wanderers	4-0	8th	McIntyre	McGinley	McCaul	Barrett	K. Lafferty	McGeever	Sandy	McGettigan	Dunleavy¹	Gallagher*	Hegarty	Rooney	McGonnigle
19 Dec	H	Kilkenny City	1-1	8th	McIntyre	McGinley	Toland	Barrett#	K. Lafferty	McGeever	Sandy	McGettigan	Dunleavy	Gallagher	Hegarty	McGonnigle	Rushe
26 Dec	A	Sligo Rovers	1-4	9th	McIntyre	McGinley	McCaul*	Barrett*	K. Lafferty	McGeever	B. Lafferty	McGettigan	Dunleavy	McGonnigle	Hegarty¹	Rooney	McCaul
2 Jan	H	St James's Gate	1-0	8th	McIntyre	McGinley	Toland*	Barrett	K. Lafferty	McGeever#	Gallagher¹	McGettigan	Dunleavy	McGonnigle#	Hegarty	McGeever*	Rooney
9 Jan	A	Longford Town	0-2	7th	McIntyre	McGinley	Toland¹	Barrett	B. Lafferty	Rushe	Gallagher	McGettigan	Dunleavy	Rooney	Hegarty	McGonnigle	
16 Jan	H	Home Farm	2-0	6th	McIntyre	K. Lafferty*	Toland*	Reid¹	B. Lafferty	Rushe	Gallagher	McGeever*	Dunleavy	Rooney¹	McGonnigle	Creane	
23 Jan	H	Waterford United	1-1	6th	McIntyre	McGettigan	Toland	Barrett	B. Lafferty	Rushe	Gallagher*	McGeever	Dunleavy	Rooney¹	Hegarty	McGonnigle	
30 Jan	A	U.C.D.	3-2	6th	Costelloe	McGettigan	Toland¹	Barrett	B. Lafferty	Rushe	Gallagher¹	McGeever	Dunleavy¹	Rooney¹	Hegarty		
13 Feb	H	Bay Wanderers	1-0	5th	Costelloe	McGettigan	Toland	Barrett	B. Lafferty	Rushe	Gallagher	McGeever	Dunleavy²	Rooney²	Hegarty	McGinley	McGonnigle
20 Feb	A	Kilkenny City	1-1	3rd	Costelloe	McGettigan	Toland¹	Barrett	K. Lafferty	Rushe¹	McGeever	Creane	Dunleavy	Rooney¹#	Hegarty	Toland	McGonnigle
5 Mar	H	Sligo Rovers	2-0	3rd	Costelloe	McGettigan	Toland	Barrett	McGonnigle	Rushe*	McGeever	Creane	Dunleavy*	Rooney²	Hegarty	McGinley	McGonnigle
13 Mar	A	St James's Gate	2-1	3rd	Costelloe	McGettigan¹	Toland	Barrett	McGinley	Rushe	McGeever	Creane*	Dunleavy	Rooney	Hegarty	Toland	
17 Mar	H	Longford Town	3-1	3rd	Costelloe	McGettigan¹	Gallagher	Barrett	B. Lafferty*	Rushe	McGeever	Creane	Dunleavy	Rooney	Toland	McGinley	McGonnigle
26 Mar	A	Home Farm	1-1	3rd	Costelloe	McGettigan	Gallagher	Barrett	B. Lafferty	Rushe	McGeever	Creane	Dunleavy	Rooney	Toland	Gallagher	McGonnigle
2 Apr	H	Athlone Town	1-0	p/o	Costelloe	McGettigan¹	Gallagher	Barrett	B. Lafferty	Rushe	McGeever	Creane	Dunleavy#	Rooney	Toland		
9 Apr	H	Cobh Ramblers	1-0	p/o	Costelloe	McGettigan	Hegarty	Barrett	B. Lafferty	Rushe	McGeever	Creane*	Dunleavy*	Rooney	Toland		
16 Apr	A	Cobh Ramblers	0-3	p/o	Costelloe												

30

Galway United   Premier Div.

Founded: 1977
Former Name: Galway Rovers (1977/78 to 1980/81)
Home: Terryland Park, Dyke Road, Galway. Tel. (091) 61000
Other Grounds: Crowley Park and The Sportsground (1993/94)
Nickname: "United"
Colours: Maroon & Sky blue
2nd Colours: Green Shirts, White shorts
Manager: Tony Mannion   Succeeded: Joey Malone (Jan. 1992)
Chairman: Niall O'Reilly
Secretary: Séan Hynes, 59, Seacrest, Barna Road, Galway.
             Tel. Home: (091) 591079; Office: (091) 68936; Fax. (091) 68936

Honours/Best Performances:

Championship	:	Runner-up 1984/85	
First Division Champions	:	1992/93	(1)
F.A.I. Cup Winners	:	1991	(1)
League Cup Winners	:	1985/86	(1)
First Division Shield Winners	:	1992/93	(1)

League Career:
Elected as Galway Rovers in 1977 with Thurles Town when League extended to 16 clubs. Re-elected 77/78, 81/82 (3 times). Relegated end 1991/92. Promoted end 1992/93.

European Appearances: 3

Cup Winners Cup	:	1985/86	v	Lyngby	2 - 3, 0 - 1
	:	1991/92	v	Odense	0 - 3, 0 - 4
U.E.F.A. Cup	:	1986/87	v	Groningen	1 - 3, 1 - 5

Record League Victory:

Home	:	6 - 1	v	Shelbourne	15 Dec. 1985
Away	:	7 - 2	v	Monaghan Utd.	25 Oct. 1992

Record League Defeat:

Home	:	0 - 6	v	Derry City	27 Dec. 1989
Away	:	1 - 9	v	Derry City	08 Oct. 1989

Most League Goals:
(Match) 3:

Paul Murphy	v	Waterford	3 - 0 (H)	06 Dec. 1981	
Brian Duff	v	Finn Harps	3 - 0 (H)	14 Feb. 1982	
Kevin Cassidy	v	Sligo Rovers	4 - 1 (A)	21 Nov. 1982	
Mickey McLoughlin	v	Sligo Rovers	5 - 0 (H)	25 Nov. 1984	
Tony Sherlock	v	Finn Harps	5 - 1 (H)	24 Feb. 1985	
Ricky O'Flaherty	v	Sligo Rovers	5 - 1 (H)	20 Sep. 1987	
Paul McGee	v	Limerick City	5 - 1 (A)	01 Apr. 1988	
Paul McGee	v	Athlone Town	3 - 1 (H)	22 Apr. 1990	

(Season) 20:   Paul McGee 1987/88
(Career) 74:   Paul McGee 1985/86 to 1989/90 & 1992/93

Points in a Season:
Most	:	40	1987/88	(33 games)
		50 **	1993/94	(32 games)
Least	:	13	1978/79	(30 games)

Goals Scored in a Season:
Most	:	56	1992/93	(27 games)
Least	:	13	1978/79	(30 games)

League Appearances 1993/94:
30+1 Mark Herrick, 29 Stephen Lally, 28 John Brennan, 27 Alan Gough, Noel Mernagh, 23+4 Donnie Farragher, 26 Keith Lambert, 25 Derek Rogers, 24+1 John Mannion, 24 Peter Carpenter, 18+2 Ronan Killeen, 13+6 Ollie Neary, 15+3 Gerry Mullen, 13+3 Ricky O'Flaherty, 8+1 Paul Reidy, 3+3 Kevin Cassidy, 5 Ollie Cunningham, Jimmy Nolan, 3+2 Billy Clery, 2+2 Shane Fitzgerald, 2+1 Eamonn Sherlock, 1+2 Tommy McDonald, 1+1 Donal Murray, 0+2 John Corcoran, 0+1 Eugene Halion.
Players Used: 25

League Goalscorers 1993/94:
14 John Brennan, 13 Donie Farragher, 6 Mark Herrick, Ricky O'Flaherty, 2 Noel Mernagh, 1 Peter Carpenter, Billy Clery, Ronan Killeen, Stephen Lally, Gerry Mullen, Jimmy Nolan.
Total: 47

Gerry Mullen
Galway's dynamic midfielder

Derek Rogers
At the heart of Galway's rearguard
(G.U.)

Galway United 1993/94

Date	V	Opposition	Score	Pos	1	2	3	4	5	6	7	8	9	10	11	12	13
20 Aug	A	Bohemians	0-3	-	Cunningham	Killeen	Fitzgerald*	Rogers*	O'Flaherty	Herrick	Neary	Mannion	Brennan	Memagh	Carpenter	Cassidy	Farragher
25 Aug	H*	Cork City	0-0	12th	Cunningham	Killeen	Rogers	O'Flaherty	Herrick	Neary	Farragher	Brennan[1]	Memagh	Carpenter	Sherlock	Clery[1]
29 Aug	A	Drogheda United	4-1	5th	Cunningham	Killeen	Cassidy	Reidy	O'Flaherty*	Herrick	Neary	Farragher[2]	Brennan[1]	Memagh*	Lally	Fitzgerald	Halion
4 Sep	H*	Shamrock Rovers	0-5	8th	Cunningham	Killeen*	Cassidy	Lambert	Reidy	Herrick	Neary	Sherlock*	Brennan	Clery	Lally	Corcoran	Cassidy
12 Sep	A	Cobh Ramblers	2-0	7th	Gough	Mullen	Rogers	Lambert	Reidy	Herrick[1]	Neary	Sherlock[1]	Brennan[2]	Memagh	Lally	Farragher
19 Sep	H*	Limerick	1-2	7th	Gough	Farragher	Rogers	Lambert	Herrick	Neary	Carpenter	Brennan	Memagh	Lally*	Mullen
26 Sep	A	Shelbourne	1-1	8th	Gough	Farragher[1]	Rogers	Lambert	Herrick[1]	Neary	Carpenter	Brennan	Memagh	Lally	Farragher
3 Oct	H*	Dundalk	0-0	7th	Gough	Farragher	Rogers	Reidy*	Lambert	Herrick	Neary*	Carpenter	Brennan	Memagh	Lally	Cassidy*	Mannion
10 Oct	A	St. Patrick's Ath.	3-2	5th	Gough	Farragher[1]	Rogers	Reidy	Lambert	Herrick[1]	Neary	Carpenter	Brennan[1]	Memagh	Lally	Fitzgerald
17 Oct	H*	Derry City	2-1	5th	Gough	Farragher[1]	Rogers	Lambert	Herrick	Neary*	Carpenter	Brennan	Memagh*	Lally	Mullen
24 Oct	H*	Monaghan United	1-0	5th	Gough	Farragher	Rogers	Mannion	Lambert	Herrick[1]	Neary	Carpenter	Brennan[1]	Memagh	Lally	McDonald
31 Oct	H*	Bohemians	1-3	5th	Gough	Farragher*	Rogers	Mannion*	Mullen*	Herrick	Neary	Carpenter	Brennan	Memagh	Lally	Reidy
7 Nov	H*	Cork City	1-1	5th	Gough	Farragher[1]	Lambert	Mannion	Muller*	Herrick[1]	Neary	Carpenter	Brennan	Memagh	Lally
14 Nov	A	Derry City	2-1	5th	Gough	Farragher	Lambert	Mannion*	Muller	Herrick	O'Flaherty	Carpenter	Brennan	Memagh	Lally	Neary
21 Nov	H*	Drogheda United	2-0	3rd	Gough	Farragher[1]	Lambert	Mannion	Muller	Herrick	Rogers	Carpenter	Brennan[1]	Memagh	Lally
28 Nov	A	Shamrock Rovers	1-3	4th	Gough	Farragher[1]	Lambert	Mannion*	Mullen	Herrick	Rogers	Carpenter	Brennan[2]	Memagh[2]	Lally
5 Dec	H*	Cobh Ramblers	4-0	4th	Gough	Farragher[1]	Lambert	Mannion*	Mullen	Herrick	Rogers	Carpenter	Brennan[1]	Memagh[1]*	Lally	Killeen
19 Dec	H*	Shelbourne	1-1	4th	Gough	Farragher[1]	Lambert	Mullen	Mullen	Herrick	Rogers	Carpenter	Brennan	Memagh	Lally
27 Dec	A	Dundalk	0-0	4th	Gough	Farragher	Lambert	Mullen	Mullen[1]*	Herrick	Rogers	Carpenter	Brennan[1]	Killeen	Lally
30 Dec	A	Limerick	3-0	3rd	Gough	Farragher	Lambert	Carpenter	Mullen	Herrick	Rogers	Nolan	Brennan	Memagh	Lally	Killeen	O'Flaherty
2 Jan	H*	St. Patrick's Ath.	1-2	4th	Gough	Farragher	Lambert	Carpenter	Mullen	Herrick[1]	Rogers	Brennan	Killeen	Lally[1]	Neary
9 Jan	A	Derry City	0-0	4th	Gough	Farragher	Lambert*	Carpenter	Mullen*	Herrick	Rogers	Memagh	Brennan	Killeen	Lally
16 Jan	H*	Bohemians	3-1	4th	Gough	Farragher*	Lambert*	Carpenter	Herrick	Rogers	Memagh[1]*	Brennan[1]	Killeen[1]	Lally	O'Flaherty
23 Jan	A	Shamrock Rovers	5-2	3rd	Gough	Farragher[2]	Lambert*	Carpenter	Herrick[1]	Rogers	Memagh[1]	Brennan	Killeen	Lally	Mullen
30 Jan	H*	Cork City	0-1	3rd	Gough	Mullen	Lambert	Mannion	O'Flaherty	Herrick[1]	Rogers	Memagh	Farragher	Killeen	Lally	Neary
13 Feb	A	Shelbourne	1-0	3rd	Gough	Mullen	Lambert	Mannion	O'Flaherty[1]	Nolan	Rogers	Memagh	Brennan	Killeen	Lally	Neary
6 Mar	A	Cork City	0-2	3rd	Gough	Mullen	Lambert	Brennan	Carpenter	Herrick	Rogers	Memagh	Farragher*	Killeen	Lally*	Mullen	O'Flaherty
13 Mar	H*	Shamrock Rovers	2-3	3rd	Gough	Mullen	Lambert	Brennan	Carpenter	Mannion	Rogers	Memagh	O'Flaherty[1]	Killeen[1]	Lally	Farragher	Herrick
16 Mar	A	Bohemians	1-0	3rd	Gough	Mullen	Lambert	Carpenter	Mannion	Rogers	Memagh	O'Flaherty[1]	Killeen	Lally	Fitzgerald
24 Mar	A	Derry City	1-1	3rd	Gough	Mullen	Clery	Carpenter	Mannion	Rogers	Memagh	O'Flaherty	Killeen	Lally	Mullen	Murray
27 Mar	H***	Derry City	2-1	3rd	Gough	Herrick[1]	Lambert	Carpenter*	Mannion	Rogers	Memagh	O'Flaherty[1]	Killeen	Lally	Farragher	Neary
2 Apr	H****	Shelbourne	2-5	3rd	Cunningham	Herrick	Reidy*	Clery	Neary	Mannion	Fitzgerald	Farragher[1]	O'Flaherty[1]	Killeen	Murray	Corcoran	McDonald

* Played at Sportsground
** Played at Crowley Park
*** Played at Harold's Cross, Dublin

33

Home Farm   First Div.

Founded: 1928
Previous Name: Home Farm/Drumcondra (1972/73)
Nickname: "Farm"
Home: Whitehall Stadium, 97A Swords Road, Whitehall, Dublin 9,
    Tel. (01) 8371001; Fax. (01) 8367821
Previous Ground: Tolka Park (1972/73 - 1989/90)
Colours: Blue & White Hooped shirts, Blue shorts
2nd Colours: Yellow shirts, Blue shorts
Manager: Martin Bayly   Succeeded: Theo Dunne (Apr. 1994)
Secretary: Brendan Menton, Balran House, Peacockstown, Ratoath, Dublin 15.
    Tel. (01) 8256240; Fax. (01) 6795837

Honours/Best Performances:

Championship	:	9th 1978/1979
F.A.I. Cup Winners	:	1975 (1)
League Cup	:	Semi Finalists 1981/82, 1985/86
Leinster Cup Winners	:	*1964/65 (1)
First Division Shield	:	Finalists 1990/91, 1992/93

* As a non-League club

League Career:
Joined as Home Farm/Drumcondra in 1972. Re-elected 76/77, 82/83, 83/84, 91/92 (4 times). Relegated end 1986/87. First Division 1987/88 to date.

European Appearances: 1
Cup Winners Cup: 1975/76   v   Lens   1 - 1, 0 - 6

Record League Victory:
Home : 7 - 1 v Longford Town   11 Sep. 1988
Away : 6 - 1 v Galway Rovers   17 Dec. 1978

Record League Defeat:
Home : 0 - 8 v Bohemians   05 Feb. 1978
Away : 1 - 7 v Finn Harps   27 Jan. 1974

Most League Goals:
(Match) 5:   Pat O'Connor v Longford Town 7 - 1 (H) 11 Sep. 1988
(Season) 16: Karl Gannon 1993/94
(Career) 30: Frank Devlin 1972/73 to 1975/76 & 1984/85

Points in a Season:
Most :   40*   1981/82   (30 games)
Least :   09**   1982/83   (26 games)

Goals Scored in a Season:
Most :   50   1987/88   (27 games)
Least :   15   1985/86   (22 games)

League Appearances 1993/94:
26+1 Karl Gannon, 25 Gary McCormack, 24 Martin Bayly, Stephen McGuinness, 23 James Keddy, 22+1 Aaron Lynch, 19+2 Declan Dodd, 21 Matthew Murray, 14+3 Gary Coyle, 14+2 Trevor Vaughan, 14+1 Joe Boyle, Martin Buckley, 13+1 Jason Coyle, 8+4 Wesley Robb, 7+3 Thomas Lawless, 6+2 David Foster, Liam Kelly, 6+1 Christopher Lawless, 3+4 Stephen Dixon, 2+2 Stephen Kenny, 1+2 Alan Smith, 2 Zoltan Istvan, Declan McDonnell, Cathal Warfield, 0+1 Stephen Brazil, Ger Lynch.
Players Used: 26

League Goalscorers 1993/94:
16 Karl Gannon, 4 Stephen McGuinness, 3 James Keddy, Trevor Vaughan, 2 Gary Coyle, Matthew Murray, Wesley Robb, 1 Stephen Dixon, Declan McDonnell.
Total: 34

Away from Home ... Farm!
Maurice O'Driscoll (Bohemians) and Derek Dodd (Home Farm) in action in last season's F.A.I. Cup when 'Farm' moved temporarily to Tolka Park   (The Star)

Home Farm 1993/94

Date	V	Opposition	Score	Pos	1	2	3	4	5	6	7	8	9	10	11	12	13
19 Sep	H	Sligo Rovers	0-1	-	McCormack	Foster*	McGuinness	G.Coyle	T.Lawless	A.Lynch	Keddy	Bayly	Istvan	Kelly	J.Coyle	Gannon	
26 Sep	A	Bray Wanderers	0-1	10th	McCormack	C.Lawless	McGuinness	G.Coyle	T.Lawless	A.Lynch	Keddy	Bayly	Istvan#	Kelly*	Gannon	Dixon	G.Lynch
3 Oct	H	St James's Gate	2-2	10th	McCormack	C.Lawless¹	McGuinness¹	G.Coyle	T.Lawless*	A.Lynch	Keddy	Bayly	Foster*	Kelly	Gannon#¹	Dodd	Vaughan
10 Oct	A	Athlone Town	2-2	10th	McCormack	C.Lawless	McGuinness¹	G.Coyle	T.Lawless	A.Lynch	Keddy	Bayly	Foster*	Kelly	Gannon²	Dodd	
17 Oct	A	U.C.D.	1-3	10th	McCormack	Murray	McGuinness	G.Coyle	Dodd	A.Lynch	Keddy	Dixon#¹	Foster*	Kelly	Gannon	McDonnell	Robb
24 Oct	H	Longford Town	1-0	10th	McCormack	C.Lawless*	McGuinness	G.Coyle	Dodd	A.Lynch	Keddy	Dixon	Foster	J.Coyle	Gannon¹	Kelly	Robb
31 Oct	A	Kilkenny City	1-1	9th	McCormack	Murray	McGuinness	G.Coyle	Dodd	Robb	Keddy	Bayly	Kelly#	J.Coyle	Gannon¹	T.Lawless	Brazil
7 Nov	H	Finn Harps	3-1	8th	McCormack	Murray	McGuinness	G.Coyle¹	Dodd	Robb	Keddy	Bayly	A.Lynch	J.Coyle	Gannon²	T.Lawless	
14 Nov	H	Waterford United	3-0	3rd	McCormack	Murray	McGuinness	G.Coyle	Dodd*	Robb¹	Keddy	Bayly	A.Lynch	J.Coyle	Gannon¹	T.Lawless	
21 Nov	A	Waterford United	2-4	4th	McCormack	Murray	McGuinness	G.Coyle*	T.Lawless	Robb¹	Keddy	Bayly	A.Lynch	J.Coyle	Gannon¹	C.Lawless	
28 Nov	A	Sligo Rovers	0-4	8th	McCormack	Murray	McGuinness	Dodd	T.Lawless#	Robb	C.Lawless	Bayly	A.Lynch	Foster*	Gannon	Boyle	G.Coyle
5 Dec	H	Bray Wanderers	3-2	6th	McCormack	Murray¹	McGuinness¹	Dodd	T.Lawless	Boyle	Keddy¹	Bayly	A.Lynch	G.Coyle	Gannon¹	Robb	
12 Dec	A	St James's Gate	3-2	4th	McCormack	Murray	McGuinness	Dodd	Robb*	Boyle	Keddy	Bayly	A.Lynch	G.Coyle#	Gannon²	Buckley	Vaughan
19 Dec	H	Athlone Town	1-1	4th	McCormack	Murray	McGuinness	Dodd	Buckley	Boyle	Keddy	Bayly	A.Lynch	Vaughan¹	Gannon	G.Coyle	
26 Dec	H	U.C.D.	0-0	4th	McCormack	Murray	McGuinness	Dodd*	Buckley	Boyle	Keddy	Bayly	A.Lynch	Vaughan²	Gannon*	J.Coyle	
2 Jan	A	Longford Town	2-3	4th	McCormack	Murray	J.Coyle	Dodd	Buckley	Boyle	Keddy	Bayly	A.Lynch	Vaughan²	Gannon	Foster	
9 Jan	A	Kilkenny City	1-1	5th	Warfield	Murray	J.Coyle	McGuinness¹	Buckley	Boyle	Keddy	Bayly#	A.Lynch	Vaughan	Gannon		
16 Jan	A	Finn Harps	0-2	6th	Warfield	Murray	Dodd	McGuinness	Buckley	Boyle	Keddy	Bayly	A.Lynch*	Vaughan	Gannon	Robb	Foster
23 Jan	H	Sligo Rovers	0-1	8th	McCormack	Murray*	J.Coyle	McGuinness	Buckley¹	Boyle	Keddy	Bayly	Robb*	Vaughan	Gannon	A.Lynch	Dodd
30 Jan	A	Bray Wanderers	0-0	8th	McCormack	Murray	J.Coyle	McGuinness	Buckley	Boyle	Keddy	Bayly	Robb*	Vaughan	Gannon	Dodd	
13 Feb	H	St James's Gate	3-1	7th	McCormack	Murray¹	J.Coyle	McGuinness¹	Buckley	Dodd	C.Coyle*	Bayly	A.Lynch#	Vaughan	Gannon¹	Smith	Kelly
20 Feb	A	Athlone Town	1-1	7th	McCormack	Murray	J.Coyle	Boyle	Buckley	Dodd	Keddy¹	Bayly	A.Lynch*	Vaughan	Gannon	Smith	
6 Mar	A	U.C.D.	0-0	7th	McCormack	Murray	McGuinness	Boyle	Buckley	Dodd	Smith*	Bayly	A.Lynch	Vaughan	Gannon	G.Coyle	
13 Mar	H	Longford Town	3-2	6th	McCormack	Kenny	McGuinness	McDonnell¹	Buckley	Dodd	Keddy¹	Bayly	A.Lynch	Vaughan	Gannon¹	Dixon	
17 Mar	H	Kilkenny City	0-0	6th	McCormack	Kenny	Murray	Boyle	Buckley	Dodd	Keddy	Bayly	A.Lynch	Vaughan	Gannon		
26 Mar	H	Finn Harps	1-1	6th	McCormack	G.Coyle	Murray	Boyle	Buckley	Dodd	Keddy	Bayly*	McGuinness	Vaughan	Gannon¹	Kenny	
2 Apr	H	Waterford United	1-3	6th	McCormack	G.Coyle	Murray	Boyle*	Buckley	Dodd#	Keddy	Bayly	McGuinness	Vaughan	Gannon¹	Kenny	Dixon

36

Kilkenny City   First Div.

Founded: 1966
Former Name: Emfa F.C. 1966-89
Home: Buckley Park, Tennypark, Kilkenny. Tel. (056) 51888
Nickname: "The Cats"
Colours: Amber shirts, Black shorts
2nd Colours: Claret shirts, Blue shorts
Manager: Paddy Gallagher; Succeeded: John Cleary (Jul. 1994)
Secretary: Jim Rhatigan, 7 Cedarwood Close, Loughboy, Kilkenny
         Tel. Home: (056) 22717; Office: (056) 21025; Fax. (056) 21414

Honours/Best Performances:

First Division	:	4th 1989/90
F.A.I. Cup	:	Semi-Final 1990/91
League Cup	:	Semi-Final 1989/90
First Division Shield Winners	:	1986/87 (1)

League Career:
Elected 1985 on formation of First Division. Re-elected 1985/86 to 1988/89, 1992/93 (5). First Division 1985/86 to date.

Record League Victory:

Home	: 6 - 2	v	Finn Harps	15 Oct. 1989
Away	: 5 - 2	v	Finn Harps	26 Jan. 1992

Record League Defeat:

Home	: 1 - 4	v	UCD	11 Sep. 1988
		v	Finn Harps	18 Dec. 1988
		v	Drogheda United	17 Mar. 1991
		v	Galway United	29 Nov. 1992
Away	: 1 - 7	v	U.C.D.	28 Nov. 1993

Most League Goals:

(Match) 3:	Derek O'Reilly	v UCD	3 - 1 (H) 22 Nov. 1987
	Billy Walsh	v St. James's Gate	3 - 0 (H) 16 Dec. 1990
	Derek O'Neill	v Finn Harps	5 - 2 (A) 26 Jan. 1992
(Season) 13:	Conor Best 1989/90		
(Career) 23:	John Kelly 1991/92 - 1993/94		

Points in Season:

Most	:	35	1989/90	(27 games)
Least	:	08	1985/86	(18 games)

Goals Scored in Season:

Most	:	40	1989/90	(27 games)
Least	:	17	1986/87	(18 games)

League Appearances 1993/94:
26+1 Paul McDermott, 22+3 Alan Weldrick, 24 Seanie Egan, 17+7 J.J. Reddy, 22 John Reynor, 19+3 Paul Ennis, 20+1 Jimmy Donnelly, 19+2 Charlie O'Reilly, 20 Declan Campbell, 18+1 John Kelly, 17 Dave Madden, 12+4 Owen Heery, 10+3 Jude McKenna, 10 Keith Neville, 3+7 Jason King, 9 John Cleary, 8+1 Stefan Buttner, 6 Aiden Smyth, Terry Wogan, 4+1 Willie O'Leary, 3+1 Robbie Flanagan, 2+1 Dean Cummins, 0+2 Austin Brady.
Players Used: 23

League Goalsorers 1993/94:
8 John Kelly, 6 Alan Weldrick, 5 Jimmy Donnelly, Paul Ennis, 3 J.J. Reddy, 1 Stefan Buttner, Dean Cummins, Owen Heery, Keith Neville.
Total: 31

All time League of Ireland goalscorers 1985 - 1994
23 John Kelly, 18 Ollie Walsh, 15 Conor Best, 13 Stephen Higgins, Billy Walsh, 11 Dave McCoy, 8 Jimmy Donnelly, 7 Jim Leahy, Pat Madigan, Derek O'Neill, Ian Woods, 6 Eamonn Cody, Alan Weldrick, 5 Tommy Craven, John Duffy, Paul Ennis, 4 Des Cummins, Tony Dunne, Paul McGee, Mick Madigan, Kieron Maher, Derek O'Reilly, 3 Derek Byrne, Aidan Cooney, Kevin Power, Paul Power, J.J. Reddy, John Reid, Brian Stenson, 2 Synan Braddish, Alan Curry, Paul Fahy, Greg Hayes, Colum Kavanagh, Stephen Kearney, Dave Madden, Gary Malone, Barry Murphy, Damien O'Brien, Martin Smyth, Michael Walsh, 1 Richie Bayly, John Burns, Stefan Buttner, Terry Byrne, Paul Campbell, Kevin Craven, John Croke, Tommy Cullen, Dean Cummins, Mark Girvan, Eoin Heery, Brian Irwin, Billy Lambe, Paul McDermott, Martin Morrison, Gerry Munroe, Gary Murphy, Keith Neville, Peter Nolan, Mick O'Brien, Ger O'Mahony, John Prendergast, Dave Savage, Gerry Scully: 3 Opponents
Total: 252   Games: 225   Average per game: 1.12

The 'Irish Football Programme Club'

(Programme of the year Awards)

	1981/82	Bohemians
	1982/83	Shelbourne
	1983/84	Shamrock Rovers
	1984/95	Shamrock Rovers

	Premier Division	**First Division**
1985/86	Cork City	Bray Wanderers
1986/87	Shamrock Rovers	Derry City
1987/88	Derry City	Cobh Ramblers
1988/89	Cobh Ramblers	Finn Harps
1989/90	Cork City	Cobh Ramblers
1990/91	Bohemians	Cobh Ramblers
1991/92	Bohemians	Cobh Ramblers
1992/93	Bohemians	Cobh Ramblers
1993/94	Cobh Ramblers	Sligo Rovers

"Wishes the Irish Football Handbook continued success"
For further details contact:
Shay Kett
133 Ardmore Drive, Artane, Dublin 5.

Kilkenny City 1993/94

Date	V	Opposition	Score	Pos	1	2	3	4	5	6	7	8	9	10	11	12	13
19 Sep	H	U.C.D.	3-2	-	Campbell	O'Reilly	Egan	McDermott	McKenna	McKenna	Reynor	Donnelly[1]	Kelly[*1]	Wogan	Cummins[1]	Reddy	Weldrick
26 Sep	A	Athlone Town	0-0	2nd	Campbell	O'Reilly	Egan	McDermott	McKenna	McKenna	Reynor[*]	Madden	Kelly	Wogan[*]	Cummins[*]	Reddy	Weldrick
3 Oct	A	Longford Town	1-2	4th	Campbell	O'Reilly	Egan	McDermott[#]	McKenna	McKenna	Reynor	Madden	Kelly[*1]	Wogan	Donnelly	Reddy	Weldrick
10 Oct	H	Finn Harps	1-1	5th	Campbell	O'Reilly	Egan	McDermott	Ennis	McKenna	Reynor[#]	Madden	Kelly[*1]	Wogan[*]	Donnelly	Weldrick	Reddy
17 Oct	H	Waterford United	2-2	6th	Campbell	O'Reilly	Egan	McDermott	McKenna	McKenna	Reynor	Madden	Kelly[2]	Weldrick	Donnelly	Reddy	
24 Oct	A	Sligo Rovers	1-0	3rd	Campbell	O'Reilly	Egan	McDermott	Ennis[1]	Reddy	Reynor	Madden	Kelly[*]	Weldrick	Donnelly	McKenna	
31 Oct	H	Home Farm	1-1	3rd	Wogan	O'Reilly	Egan	McDermott	Ennis[*]	Reddy[1]	Reynor	Madden	Kelly	Weldrick	Donnelly[#]	McKenna	Cummins
7 Nov	A	St. James's Gate	2-2	3rd	Campbell	O'Reilly	Egan	McDermott	Ennis	Reddy[1]	Reynor	Madden	Kelly	Weldrick	Donnelly[1]	McKenna	
14 Nov	H	Bray Wanderers	1-1	4th	Campbell	O'Reilly	Egan	McDermott	Ennis	Reddy	Reynor	Wogan	Kelly	Weldrick	Donnelly[1]	Heery	
21 Nov	A	Bray Wanderers	1-1	3rd	Campbell	O'Reilly	Egan	McDermott[*]	Ennis[*]	Reddy	Reynor	McKenna	Kelly[*1]	Weldrick	Donnelly[1]	Heery	
28 Nov	A	U.C.D.	1-7	6th	Campbell	O'Reilly	Egan	McDermott	Ennis	Cleary[*]	Reynor	Madden	Cleary	Weldrick	Donnelly	Brady	Heery
5 Dec	H	Athlone Town	1-3	7th	Campbell	O'Reilly[#]	Egan	McDermott	Ennis[1]	Cleary	Reynor	Madden	Kelly	Weldrick	Donnelly	Brady	
12 Dec	H	Longford Town	3-1	6th	Campbell	O'Reilly	Egan	McDermott	Ennis[1]	Cleary	Reynor	Madden	Reddy	Weldrick[1]	Donnelly		
19 Dec	A	Finn Harps	1-1	6th	Campbell	O'Reilly	Egan	McDermott	Ennis[1]	Cleary	Reynor	Madden	Reddy	Weldrick[2]	Donnelly		
26 Dec	A	Waterford United	0-0	6th	Campbell	O'Reilly	Egan	McDermott	Ennis[*]	Cleary	Flanagan	Madden	Reddy	Weldrick	Donnelly[*]	Heery	
2 Jan	H	Sligo Rovers	1-4	7th	Campbell	O'Reilly	Egan	McDermott	Ennis[*]	Reynor	Reynor[#]	Madden	Reddy[1]	Weldrick	Heery	Flanagan	Brady
9 Jan	A	Home Farm	1-1	7th	Campbell	Neville[1]	Neville[1]	McDermott	Ennis	Donnelly	Reynor	Madden	Reddy[1]	Weldrick	Heery[*1]	King	O'Leary
16 Jan	H	St. James's Gate	2-0	5th	Campbell	McKenna[#]	Neville	McDermott	Ennis[#]	Flanagan	Donnelly	Madden	Reddy[*]	Weldrick[1]	Heery[#]	Kelly	King
23 Jan	H	U.C.D.	1-1	5th	McKenna[#]	Neville	McDermott	O'Leary	Butner	Donnelly[1]	Kelly[*]	Reddy[*]	Weldrick[1]	Heery	King	Ennis	
28 Jan	A	Athlone Town	3-2	5th	Campbell	Egan	Neville	McDermott	Butner	Donnelly	Kelly[.]	Reddy[1]	Weldrick[1]	Heery	Ennis	King	
13 Feb	A	Longford Town	1-3	7th	Campbell	Egan	Neville	McDermott	Reynor[*]	Butner	Donnelly	Kelly	Reddy[1]	Weldrick[1]	Heery	Ennis	King
20 Feb	H	Finn Harps	1-1	6th	Smyth	Egan	Neville	McDermott	Reynor[*]	Butner[*]	Donnelly	Madden	Reddy[1]	Weldrick	Heery	Ennis	McDermott
6 Mar	A	Waterford United	0-1	7th	Smyth	Egan	O'Leary	McDermott	King[.]	Butner[*]	Donnelly	Ennis	Kelly	Weldrick	Heery	O'Reilly	King
12 Mar	A	Sligo Rovers	0-3	7th	Smyth	Egan	Heville	McDermott	Reynor	Butner[#]	Madden	Ennis	Kelly[*]	Weldrick	Heery	King	Reddy
17 Mar	H	Home Farm	0-0	7th	Smyth	Egan	Heville	McDermott	Reynor	Butner[.]	O'Reilly	O'Leary[#]	Kelly[#]	Weldrick[1]	Heery	King	Reddy
27 Mar	A	St. James's Gate	1-1	7th	Smyth	Egan	Heville	McDermott	Reynor[.]	Reddy[.]	O'Reilly	Ennis	Kelly[#]	Weldrick[1]	Heery	Butner	King
3 Apr	H	Bray Wanderers	1-1	8th	Smyth	Egan	Heville	McDermott	Reynor[*]	Butner[*]	O'Reilly	Ennis	Kelly[#1]	King	Heery	Donnelly	Reddy

39

Limerick   First Div.

Founded: 1983
Former name: Limerick City (1983-1992)
Home: Hogan Park, Rathbane North, Limerick. Tel. (061) 47874
Previous Ground: The Markets Field (1983/84)
Colours: Blue shirts, White shorts (changed in mid 1990/91 from yellow/green)
2nd Colours: White/blue
Manager: Billy Kinnane   Succeeded: Noel King
General Manager: Noel King
Chairman: Fr. Joe Young
Hon. Secretary: Noel Hanley, 16 Athlunkard Close, Shannon Banks, Corbally, Limerick
        Tel. Home: (061) 340264, Fax. (061) 330617,
        Office: (061) 417844

Honours/Best Performances:

Championship	:	3rd 1988/89
F.A.I. Cup	:	Semi-Final 1984/85
League Cup Winners	:	1992/93 (1)
First Division Winners	:	1991/92 (1)
Munster Cup Winners	:	1983/84, 1984/85, 1988/89 (3)
League of Ireland Shield Winners	:	1983/84 (1)

League Career:
Succeeded Limerick United 1983. Relegated end 1990-91. Promoted end 1991/92. Relegated end 1993/94.

Record League Victory:
Home	:	6-0	v	Drogheda United	24 Feb. 1985
Away	:	5-1	v	Galway United	03 Sep. 1988

Record League Defeat:
Home	:	1-7	v	Cork City	26 Sep. 1993
Away	:	0-7	v	Derry City	28 Apr. 1989

Most League Goals:
(Match) 3: Des Kennedy   v Sligo Rovers   4-0 (A) 28 Mar. 1984
            Tommy Gaynor   v Finn Harps   5-0 (H) 31 Mar. 1985
(Season) 21: Billy Hamilton 1988/89
(Career) 35: Tommy Gaynor 1984/85 - 1986/87

Points in Season:
Most	:	45	1988/89	(33 games)
Least	:	17	1986/87	(22 games)
		17	1990/91	(33 games)

Goals Scored in Season:

Most	:	61	1984/85	(30 games)
Least	:	21	1990/91	(33 games)

League Appearances 1993/94:
28+3 Kevin McCarthy, 30 Ray O'Halloran, 21+9 Daithi McMahon, 29 Stephen Craig, 23+6 Garret Ryan, 26+2 Johnny Walsh, 25+1 Dave Minihan, 22 Niall Keogh, 21 Michael Kerley, 17+4 Albert Finnan, 17 Brian McKenna, 16+1 Fran Hitchcock, 16 Séan Riordan, 14+1 Ray Duffy, 11+1 Joe Barriscale, 9+2 David Lawlor, 3+7 Gerry Kelly, 7 Matthew Carr, 4+2 Mick Kavanagh, 5 Julian Lyons, 3+2 Alan Shanahan, 2 John Grace, John Twomey, 1 Aidan O'Halloran.
Players Used: 24

League Goalscorers 1993/94:
8 Kevin McCarthy, 4 Daithi McMahon, 3 Garret Ryan, 2 Fran Hitchcock, 1 Albert Finnan, Gerry Kelly, Michael Kerley, Ray O'Halloran, Séan Riordan, Johnny Walsh.
Total: 23

IMPERIAL HOTEL

South Mall, Cork
Tel. 27440; Fax. 274040

Best Wishes
and
Continued Success
to the
Irish Football Handbook

Limerick 1993/94

Date	V	Opposition	Score	Pos	1	2	3	4	5	6	7	8	9	10	11	12	13
22 Aug	H	Shelbourne	0-0	-	Grace	Lyons	Finnan	Minihan*	Lawlor	Duffy	A. O'Halloran	McMahon	Kelly	Walsh	Ryan	Barriscale	McCarthy
25 Aug	A	Cobh Ramblers	0-0	7th	Grace	Lyons	Finnan	Minihan	Lawlor	Duffy	Shanahan	McMahon	Kelly	Walsh	Ryan	McCarthy	
29 Aug	H	Dundalk	0-1	10th	Barriscale	Craig	Finnan	Minihan*	Lawlor	Duffy*	R. O'Halloran	McMahon	Keeley	Walsh	McCarthy	Kelly	
5 Sep	A	St. Patrick's Ath	1-1	12th	Barriscale	Craig	Finnan	Minihan*	Lawlor	Lyons*	R. O'Halloran	McMahon[1]	Keeley[1]	Walsh	McCarthy	Kelly	Ryan
12 Sep	H	Monaghan United	2-3	12th	Barriscale	Ryan*	Finnan	Minihan	Lawlor	Lyons	R. O'Halloran	McMahon	Keeley	Walsh	McCarthy	Kelly	Shanahan
19 Sep	A	Galway United	2-1	8th	Barriscale	Craig	Finnan[1]	Minihan	Lawlor	Lyons	R. O'Halloran[1]	Shanahan	Keeley	Walsh	McCarthy		
26 Sep	H	Cork City	1-7	10th	Barriscale	Craig	Finnan	Minihan*	Lawlor*	McMahon[1]	R. O'Halloran	Shanahan	Keeley	Walsh	McCarthy		
3 Oct	A	Bohemians	0-1	12th	Barriscale	Craig	Finnan	Minihan*	Lawlor*	McMahon	R. O'Halloran	Ryan	Keogh	Walsh	McCarthy	Kelly	Shanahan
10 Oct	H	Drogheda United	1-1	12th	Barriscale	Craig	Finnan	Minihan	Carr	McMahon	R. O'Halloran	Ryan	Keogh	Walsh*	McCarthy	Kelly[1]	
17 Oct	A	Shamrock Rovers	3-7	12th	Barriscale	Craig	Finnan	Minihan	Carr	McMahon*[1]	R. O'Halloran	Hitchcock	Keogh	Walsh	McCarthy[2]	Ryan	
24 Oct	A	Derry City	0-0	12th	Barriscale	Craig*	Duffy	Minihan	Carr	McMahon	R. O'Halloran	Hitchcock	Keogh	Walsh	McCarthy[1]	Finnan	Ryan
31 Oct	H	Derry City	0-1	12th	Barriscale	Craig	Duffy	Minihan	Carr	Ryan	R. O'Halloran	Hitchcock	Keogh	Walsh*	McCarthy	McMahon	Finnan
5 Nov	A	Shelbourne	0-3	12th	Craig	Lawlor	Minihan	Carr	Ryan	R. O'Halloran	Hitchcock[1]	Keogh	Kavanagh	McMahon	Kelly		
14 Nov	H	Cobh Ramblers	1-5	12th	Twomey	Craig	Finnan	McMahon	Carr*	Ryan	R. O'Halloran	Hitchcock	Keogh	Kavanagh	McMahon	Lawlor	
21 Nov	A	Dundalk	0-0	12th	McKenna	Craig	Finnan	Minihan	Keeley	Ryan[2]	R. O'Halloran	McMahon*	Keogh	Kelly*	McCarthy	Walsh	
28 Nov	H	St. Patrick's Ath	2-1	11th	McKenna	Craig	Finnan	Kerley	Carr	Ryan	R. O'Halloran	McMahon**	Keogh	Kavanagh*	McCarthy	Kelly	Lawlor
5 Dec	A	Monaghan United	0-0	12th	McKenna	Craig	Finnan	Riordan	Kerley	Ryan	R. O'Halloran	McMahon	Keogh	Kavanagh	McCarthy	Kavanagh	
19 Dec	A	Cork City	0-3	12th	McKenna	Craig	Minihan	Riordan	Kerley	Ryan	R. O'Halloran	McMahon	Keogh*	Walsh*	McCarthy	Walsh	
27 Dec	H	Bohemians	0-0	12th	McKenna	Craig	Minihan	Riordan	Kerley	Ryan	R. O'Halloran	McMahon	Keogh	Finnan	McCarthy	Kavanagh	
30 Dec	H	Galway United	0-3	12th	McKenna	Craig	Minihan	Riordan	Kerley	Ryan[1]	R. O'Halloran	McMahon	Keogh*	Walsh	McCarthy	Walsh	
2 Jan	A	Drogheda United	2-0	11th	McKenna	Craig	Minihan	Riordan	Kerley*	Ryan	R. O'Halloran	McMahon	Keogh*	Walsh	McCarthy	Hitchcock	Finnan
9 Jan	H	Shamrock Rovers	0-2	11th	McKenna	Craig	Minihan*	Riordan	Kerley	Ryan*	R. O'Halloran	McMahon	Keogh	Walsh	McCarthy[1]	McMahon	Duffy
23 Jan	H	Drogheda United	1-0	11th	McKenna	Craig	Minihan*	Riordan	Kerley	McMahon	R. O'Halloran	Hitchcock	Keogh	Walsh*	McCarthy	Ryan	Finnan
20 Jan	A	St. Patrick's Ath	0-1	11th	McKenna	Craig*	Finnan	Riordan	Duffy	Keeley*	R. O'Halloran	Hitchcock	Ryan*	Walsh	McCarthy	McMahon	Ryan
30 Jan	A	Cobh Ramblers	0-1	11th	McKenna	Craig	Minihan	Riordan	Duffy*	Keeley	R. O'Halloran	Hitchcock	Ryan*	Walsh	McCarthy	McMahon[1]	
13 Feb	H	Monaghan United	2-1	11th	McKenna	Craig	Finnan*	Riordan	Duffy	Keeley	R. O'Halloran	Hitchcock	Ryan*	Walsh	McCarthy	Minihan*	McMahon
6 Mar	H	Cobh Ramblers	0-0	12th	McKenna	Craig	Keogh*	Riordan	Duffy	Keeley	R. O'Halloran	Hitchcock	Ryan	Walsh	McCarthy	McMahon	
12 Mar	A	Drogheda United	0-0	12th	McKenna	Craig	Keogh	Riordan	Duffy	Keeley	R. O'Halloran	Hitchcock	Ryan	Walsh	McMahon[1]	McCarthy[1]	
17 Mar	H	St. Patrick's Ath	2-2	11th	Barriscale	Craig	Keogh	Riordan	Duffy	Minihan*	R. O'Halloran	Hitchcock	Ryan*	Walsh[1]	McCarthy	McMahon	Kelly
24 Mar	A	Dundalk	0-2	11th	McKenna	Craig	Keogh	Riordan	Duffy	Minihan	R. O'Halloran	Hitchcock	Ryan*	Walsh[1]	McCarthy	McMahon	
27 Mar	H	Dundalk	2-1	11th	McKenna	Craig	Keogh*	Riordan	Duffy	Minihan*	R. O'Halloran[1]	Hitchcock[1]	Keeley	Walsh	McCarthy	McMahon	Ryan
3 Apr	A	Monaghan United	1-2	11th	McKenna	Craig	Keogh*	Riordan	Duffy	Minihan	R. O'Halloran						

42

Longford Town   First Div.

Founded: 1924
Home: Strokestown Road, Longford
Previous Grounds: Abbeycartron (1984/85 - 1992/93)
Colours: Red shirts, Black Shorts
2nd Colours: All Blue
Manager: John Cleary   Succeeded: Liam Brien (Oct. 1994)
Secretary: Mary Ginty, Aughakine, Aughnacliffe, Longford.
           Tel. (043) 84122 / 41127

Honours/Best Performances:

Championship	:	16th 1984/85
First Division	:	3rd 1985/86
F.A.I. Cup	:	Semi-Final *1937, *1955, 1988
League Cup	:	Yet to reach knock-out stages
First Division Shield	:	Final 1985/86
Leinster Cup	:	Final *1954/55

• as a non-League team.

League Career:
Elected with Cork City, 1984. Relegated end 1984/85. Re-elected 1986/87, 1990/91, 1991/92 (3). First Division 1985/86 to date.

Record League Victory:
Home	:	5 - 1 v	Derry City	12 Jan. 1986
Away	:	6 - 1 v	Finn Harps	28 Mar. 1993

Record League Defeat:
Home	:	0 - 6 v	St. Patrick's Ath.	24 Feb. 1985
Away	:	1 - 8 v	Waterford United	12 Nov. 1989

Most League Goals:
(Match) 4:   Richie Parsons v St. James's Gate 5 - 3 (H) 20 Mar. 1994
(Season) 15: Richie Parsons 1992/93
(Career) 26: Richie Parsons 1992/93 - 1993/94

Points in Season:
Most	:	29	1992/93	(27 games)
		34 **	1993/94	(27 games)
Least	:	07	1986/87	(18 games)

Goals Scored in Season:
Most	:	41	1992/93	(27 games)
Least	:	15	1989/90	(18 games)

League Appearances 1993/94:
26 James O'Callaghan, 23+3 Keith Brady, 25 Richie Parsons, 24+1 Davy Savage, 23+1 John Reid, 23 Mark Girvan, Pierce Walsh, 20+3 Derek Gough, 17+2 Dave Kealy, 13+5 Mick O'Brien, 17 George O'Hanlon, 13+1 Alan Matthews, 9+5 Eamonn Synnott, 12 Mark Devlin, 10 Aiden Smyth, 8 Stephen Kelly, 4+2 Glen Mahedy, 2+4 Joe Sullivan, 3+2 Peter Fagan, 1+1 Gary Grehan, 1 Davy Sheridan, 0+1 Tom Conway.
Players Used: 22

League Goalscorers 1993/94:
11 Richie Parsons, 5 Davy Savage, Pierce Walsh, 3 Dave Kealy, 2 Mark Devlin, Derek Gough, Stephen Kelly, Mick O'Brien, John Reid, 1 Glen Mahedy.
Total: 35

All time League of Ireland goalscorers 1985 - 1994
26 Richie Parsons, **15** Clive O'Neill, **13** Gavin Drummond, Pierce Walsh, **12** Mark Devlin, **11** Pat 'Zak' Hackett, Stephen Kelly, **7** Martin Smyth, Alan Weldrick, Dave Savage, **6** Leo Devlin, Derek Gough, Tony O'Kelly, Gerry Quigley, **5** Derek Carthy, Heysham El Khershi, Dermot Wilkins, **4** Synan Braddish, Jim Mahon, Greg O'Dowd, **3** Tom Conway, Jimmy Cullen, Gus Gillian, Dave 'Dax' Kealy, Kevin McCormack, Paul Masterson, Martin O'Sullivan, **2** Tommy Barron, Dessie Barry, Tommy Deehan, Paul Dempsey, Eamonn Donoghue, Brian Duff, Séan Egan, Tommy Hynes, John Lynch, James McGrath, J.J. Reddy, John Reid, Mick O'Brien, Donie Sweeney, Graham Quinn, **1** Noel Brady, Eddie Byrne, Joey Byrne, Kevin Cassidy, Dave Coleman, John Delamere, Declan Gallagher, Eamonn Gavin, Stephen Higgins, Dermot Lennon, Gary McCormack, Derek McCormack, Declan McGoldrick, Glenn Maheedy, Gerry Martin, Fran Moore, Johnny Morris-Burke, Joe Murphy, Derek O'Brien, Brendan Place, Wesley Robb, Mick Savage, Mick Sheridan, Terry Sheridan, Robert Stokes, Phil Wilkins, Ian Wilkinson, Tommy Wilson, Terry Wogan:
4 Opponents
Total: **257** Games: **255** Average per game: **1.01**

A Perfect 10
Luis Garcia scores the first of his two goals against Ireland (The Star)

Longford Town 1993/94

Date	V	Opposition	Score	Pos	1	2	3	4	5	6	7	8	9	10	11	12	13
19 Sep	H*	Bray Wanderers	1-0	-	Smyth	Reid	O'Callaghan	Girvan	Matthews	Walsh	Kelly[1]	O'Brien*	Gough	Parsons*	Savage	Brady	
26 Sep	A	Waterford United	2-2	3rd	Smyth	Reid	O'Callaghan	Girvan	Matthews	Walsh	Kelly	O'Brien*	Gough*	Parsons*	Savage[1]	Kelly	Brady
3 Oct	H*	Kilkenny City	2-1	3rd	Smyth	Reid*	O'Callaghan	Matthews	Matthews	Walsh	Kelly	O'Brien[1]	Gough	Parsons*	Savage[1]	Matthews	
10 Oct	A	Sligo Rovers	1-1	2nd	Smyth	Sheridan*	O'Callaghan	Girvan	Brady	Walsh	Kelly	O'Brien	Kelly	Parsons[1]	Savage		
17 Oct	H*	Athlone Town	0-0	3rd	Smyth	Matthews	O'Callaghan	Girvan	Brady	Walsh	Kelly	O'Brien	Kelly*	Parsons*	Savage	Gough	Reid
24 Oct	A	Home Farm	0-1	4th	Smyth	Reid	O'Callaghan	Girvan	Brady	Walsh[1]	Kelly[1]	Fagan*	Matthews	Parsons	Savage	O'Brien	Sullivan
31 Oct	H	Finn Harps	1-1	4th	Smyth	Reid	O'Callaghan	Girvan*	Brady	Walsh[1]	Kelly	Fagan	Matthews	Gough	Parsons[1]	Conway*	Sullivan
7 Nov	H	U.C.D.	1-2	4th	Smyth	Reid	O'Callaghan	Girvan	Brady	Walsh	Grehan	Kelly	Matthews	Gough	Parsons[1]	Grehan	
14 Nov	H	St. James's Gate	1-4	8th	Smyth	Reid	O'Callaghan	Girvan	Brady	O'Brien	Symott	Kelly*	Matthews	Gough	Parsons	Savage	
21 Nov	A	Bray Wanderers	1-0	4th	Smyth	Reid	O'Callaghan	Sullivan	Brady	Walsh*	Symott	Kelly[1]	Matthews*	Gough	Parsons	O'Brien	
28 Nov	A	Waterford United	2-1	5th	Smyth	Reid	O'Callaghan	Savage[1]	Brady	Walsh	Symott*	Kelly[1]	Matthews	Gough[1]	Parsons*	Mahedy	
5 Dec	H	Kilkenny City	1-3	5th	Smyth	Reid	O'Callaghan	Savage	Brady	Walsh[1]	Kelly	Kelly	Devlin[1]	Gough	Parsons*	Symott	Sullivan
12 Dec	H	Sligo Rovers	0-0	7th	Smyth	Reid	O'Callaghan	Savage	Brady	Walsh[1]	Kelly	Kelly	Devlin[1]	Gough*	Parsons*	Symott	
19 Dec	A	Athlone Town	1-2	7th	Smyth	Reid[1]	O'Callaghan	Savage	Brady	Walsh[1]	Girvan	Kelly	Devlin	Gough	Parsons	Symott	
26 Dec	A	Home Farm	3-2	5th	Smyth	Reid[1]	O'Callaghan	Savage[1]	Brady	Walsh[1]	Girvan	Kelly	Devlin	Gough*	Parsons	Symott	
2 Jan	H	Finn Harps	2-0	4th	Smyth	Reid[1]	O'Callaghan	Savage	Brady	Walsh[1]	Girvan	Kelly	Devlin	Gough*	Parsons*	O'Brien	
9 Jan	A	U.C.D.	2-1	4th	Smyth	Reid	O'Callaghan	Savage	Brady	Walsh	Girvan	Kealy*	Devlin.	O'Brien	Parsons	O'Brien	Symott
16 Jan	H	Bray Wanderers	1-1	4th	Smyth	Reid*	O'Callaghan	Savage	Brady	Walsh	Girvan	Kealy	Devlin[1]	Gough*	Parsons	O'Brien	Mahedy
23 Jan	A	Waterford United	0-0	4th	Smyth	Reid*	O'Callaghan	Savage	Brady	Walsh	Girvan	O'Brien	Devlin[1]	Gough#	Parsons	Symott	
30 Jan	A	Kilkenny City	3-1	3rd	Smyth	Reid*	O'Callaghan	Savage	Brady	Walsh	Girvan	O'Brien	Devlin	Gough	Parsons	Fagan	
13 Feb	H	Sligo Rovers	0-1	3rd	Smyth	Reid*	O'Callaghan	Sullivan	Symott	Matthews	Symott	Kealy*	Devlin	Gough[1]	Mahedy	Fagan	
19 Feb	H	Athlone Town	0-2	4th	Smyth	Reid*	O'Callaghan	Savage	Brady	Walsh[1]	Girvan	O'Brien	Matthews	Gough*	Parsons	Fagan	O'Brien
6 Mar	A	Home Farm	2-3	4th	Smyth	Reid*	O'Callaghan	Savage	Brady	Walsh[1]	Girvan	Symott	Kealy	Gough[1]	Parsons	O'Brien	
13 Mar	A	Finn Harps	1-3	6th	Smyth	Reid*	O'Callaghan	Savage	Brady	Walsh	Girvan	Symott	Matthews	Gough	Parsons		
17 Mar	H*	Home Farm	0-1	4th	Smyth	Reid	O'Callaghan	Girvan	Brady	Walsh	Girvan	Symott	Kealy	Fagan	Parsons[4]	Gough	
20 Mar	H	St. James's Gate	5-3	5th	Smyth	O'Hanlon	O'Callaghan	Savage	Brady	Walsh	Girvan	Symott	Devlin	Red	Parsons[1]	Gough	
27 Mar	A	U.C.D.	1-2	5th	Smyth	O'Hanlon	Mahedy*[1]	Savage	Brady	Walsh	Girvan	Symott	Devlin		Parsons	Gough	

*Played at Abbeycartron

45

Monaghan United   Premier Div.

Founded: 1979
Home: Gortakeegan, Newbliss Road, Monaghan. Tel. (047) 84450
Previous Ground: Belgium Park (1985/86 - 1987/88)
Colours: Royal Blue shirts, White shorts
2nd Colours: White shirts, Blue shorts
Manager: Bill Bagster   Succeeded: Mickey Coburn (May 1991)
Chairman: Eddie Murray
Secretary: Ian Friary, 8 Mullaghmatt, Monaghan
           Tel. Home: (047) 83001; Office: (047) 81672; Fax. (047) 83001

Honours/Best Performances:

Championship	:	7th 1993/94
First Division	:	3rd 1992/93
F.A.I. Cup	:	Quarter-Final 1991/92, 1993/94
League Cup	:	Yet to reach knock-out stages

League Career:
Elected 1985 on formation of First Division. Re-elected end 1985/86, 1989/90 & 1990/91 (3). Promoted end 1992/93.

Record League Victory:

Home	:	5 - 0	v	Longford Town	04 Oct. 1992
Away	:	4 - 1	v	Finn Harps	04 Oct. 1987
			v	Drogheda United	26 Nov. 1993

Record League Defeat:

Home	:	0 - 6	v	Waterford United	01 Oct. 1989
Away	:	0 - 5	v	Home Farm	25 Sep. 1988
			v	Home Farm	18 Feb. 1990

Most League Goals:
(Match) 3:   Peter McGee v UCD 3 - 1 (A) 15 Nov. 1987
(Season) 15: Mick Byrne 1992/93
(Career) 23: Jim Barr 1989/90, 1990/91

Points in Season:

Most	:	32	1992/93	(27 games)
		47 **	1993/94	(32 games)
Least	:	11	1986/87	(18 games)

Goals Scored in Season:

Most	:	43	1992/93	(29 games)
Least	:	19	1985/86	(18 games)

League Appearances 1993/94:
32 Brian O'Shea, 30+1 Paul Byrne, 30 Mick Byrne, 29 John Coady, Ian Woods, 28 Alan Kinsella, 26+2 Derek Murray, 22+6 Noel Melvin, 27 Ronnie Murphy, 17+9 Philip Power, 14+12 Mickey Wilson, 22+2 Paul Newe, 22 Declan Geoghegan, 11+1 Joey Malone, 6+3 Derek O'Neill, 6 Paul Fitzgerald, 1+2 Derek Smyth, 0+2 Keith Neville, Declan Smyth, 0+1 Willie O'Leary, Billy Olin.
Players Used: 21

League Goalscorers 1993/94:
11 Paul Newe, 8 Philip Power, 7 Mick Byrne, 4 Paul Byrne, 3 Noel Melvin, Derek Murray, 2 Ian Woods, 1 John Coady, Alan Kinsella, Derek O'Neill.
Total: 41

All time League of Ireland goalscorers 1985 - 1994
23 Jim Barr, 22 Mick Byrne, 19 Peter McGee, Brendan O'Callaghan, 18 Philip Power, 13 Mickey Wilson, 11 Paul Newe, 10 Mickey Coburn, 9 Derek Murray, Noel Melvin, 8 Paul Kelly, 7 Mickey Conlon, Seamus Finnegan, 6 Paul Gilliand, Bernie Savage, 4 Paul Byrne, Colm McConville, Derek O'Neill, 3 Martin Bayly, Mark Donnelly, Val Forde, Graham Quinn, Mick Wright, 2 Peter Coleman, Willie Crawley, Paul Cunningham, Danny Doran, Gavin Drummond, Alan Kinsella, Fintan Lynch, Paul McMullen, Billy Olin, Brian Quinn, Anthony O'Hare, Greg Turley, Ian Woods, 1 Austin Brady, Mick Bradley, John Coady, Ray Duffy, Dave Emerson, Paul Forde, Pat 'Zak' Hackett, Terence McCaffrey, Phil McGroggan, Paul Madden, Anthony Marron, Paul Masterson, Glenn Miller, Eamonn Lynch, John Reynor, Frank Treacy, Noel Turley, Mick McDonald: 9 Opponents.
Total: **267**   Games: **232**   Average per game: **1.15**

Keane as Mustard
Roy Keane in action against Norway   (The Star)

Monaghan United 1993/94

Date	V	Opposition	Score	Pos	1	2	3	4	5	6	7	8	9	10	11	12	13
22 Aug	A	Cork City	0-1	-	O'Shea	Kinsella	Coady	Woods	Murphy	Melvin*	P. Byrne*	Wilson	Malone	M. Byrne*	Murray	Power	
26 Aug	H	Derry City	1-1	8th	O'Shea	Kinsella	Coady	Woods	Murphy	Power[1]	P. Byrne	Wilson*	Malone	M. Byrne*	Murray	O'Neill	Neville
29 Aug	A	Bohemians	0-0	9th	O'Shea	Kinsella	Coady	Woods	Murphy	Power*	P. Byrne	Wilson	Malone*	M. Byrne	Murray	O'Neill	Smyth
5 Sep	H	Drogheda United	1-0	5th	O'Shea	Kinsella	Coady	Woods	Murphy*	Power	P. Byrne	Wilson	Malone	M. Byrne*	Murray	Melvin	
12 Sep	A	Limerick	3-2	4th	O'Shea	Kinsella	Coady	Woods	Murphy*	Malone	P. Byrne*	Melvin[1]	Power[2]	M. Byrne*	Murray	Wilson	Smyth
19 Sep	H	Shamrock Rovers	0-1	6th	O'Shea	Kinsella	Coady	Woods	Murphy	Malone	P. Byrne*	Melvin	Power	Newe	Murray	Wilson	
26 Sep	A	Cobh Ramblers	0-2	7th	O'Shea	Kinsella	Coady	Woods	Fitzgerald	Malone	Wilson*	Melvin	Smyth	M. Byrne	Murray	O'Neill	
3 Oct	H	Shelbourne	4-5	10th	O'Shea	Kinsella[1]	Coady	Woods	Fitzgerald	Malone*	O'Neill[1]	Melvin	Power[1]	M. Byrne	Murray[1]	P. Byrne[2]	Neville
10 Oct	A	Dundalk	3-1	7th	O'Shea	Kinsella	Coady	Woods	P. Byrne	Malone*	O'Neill	Melvin	Power*[1]	M. Byrne	Murray	Newe[1]	
17 Oct	H	St Patrick's Ath	1-2	9th	O'Shea	Kinsella	Coady	Woods	P. Byrne	Malone	O'Neill*	Melvin	Power	M. Byrne	Murray	O'Leary	
24 Oct	A	Galway United	0-1	9th	O'Shea	Kinsella	Coady	Woods	P. Byrne	Fitzgerald	Geoghegan	Newe*	Power[1]	M. Byrne*	Murray	Wilson	
31 Oct	H	Galway United	3-1	7th	O'Shea	Kinsella	Coady*	Woods	P. Byrne	Murphy	Geoghegan	Newe*	Power[1]	M. Byrne*[1]	Murray	Wilson	
7 Nov	H	Cork City	2-1	6th	O'Shea	Kinsella	Coady*	Woods[1]	P. Byrne	Murphy	Geoghegan	Newe*	Power*	M. Byrne[1]	Murray	Melvin	Wilson
14 Nov	A	Derry City	0-1	7th	O'Shea	Kinsella	Wilson	Woods	P. Byrne	Murphy	Geoghegan	Newe*	Melvin	M. Byrne[1]	Murray		
21 Nov	H	Bohemians	1-0	6th	O'Shea	Kinsella	Coady	Woods[1]	P. Byrne	Murphy	Geoghegan	Newe[1]	Melvin	M. Byrne[1]	Murray	Wilson	
26 Nov	A	Drogheda United	4-1	6th	O'Shea	Kinsella[1]	Coady*	Woods[1]	P. Byrne	Murphy	Geoghegan	Newe[1]	Melvin[1]	M. Byrne[1]	Murray[1]	Power	
5 Dec	H	Limerick	0-0	6th	O'Shea	Kinsella	Coady[1]	Woods	P. Byrne*	Murphy	Geoghegan	Newe	Melvin	M. Byrne*	Murray	Power	Wilson
12 Dec	A	Shamrock Rovers	1-2	6th	O'Shea	Kinsella	Coady	Woods	P. Byrne*[#1]	Murphy	Geoghegan	Newe[1]	Melvin	M. Byrne[1]	Murray*	Power	Wilson
19 Dec	H	Cobh Ramblers	2-1	7th	O'Shea	Kinsella	Coady	Woods*	P. Byrne	Murphy	Geoghegan	Newe*	Power[1]	M. Byrne[1]	Murray	Melvin	Wilson
22 Dec	A	Shelbourne	0-3	8th	O'Shea	Kinsella	Coady	Woods	P. Byrne	Murphy	Geoghegan	Newe*	Power*	M. Byrne[1]	Murray	Melvin	Wilson
2 Jan	H	Dundalk	1-0	6th	O'Shea	Kinsella	Coady	Woods	P. Byrne*	Murphy	Geoghegan	Newe	Power*	M. Byrne	Murray	Wilson	Melvin
9 Jan	A	St Patrick's Ath	0-1	7th	O'Shea	Kinsella	Coady	Woods	P. Byrne[1]	Murphy	Geoghegan	Newe	Power*	M. Byrne	Murray*	Melvin	Wilson
16 Jan	H	Cobh Ramblers	1-1	8th	O'Shea	Kinsella	Coady	O'Neill	P. Byrne[1]	Murphy	Geoghegan*	Newe[1]	Melvin	M. Byrne[1]	Murray*	Power	Wilson
23 Jan	A	St Patrick's Ath	0-0	8th	O'Shea	Kinsella	Coady	O'Neill	P. Byrne	Murphy	Geoghegan	Newe[1]	Melvin	M. Byrne	Murray		
30 Jan	H	Dundalk	1-1	8th	O'Shea	Kinsella	Coady	Woods#	P. Byrne	Murphy	Geoghegan	Newe[1]	Melvin	M. Byrne	Wilson		
13 Feb	A	Limerick	1-2	8th	O'Shea	Kinsella	Coady	Woods[1]	P. Byrne	Murphy	Geoghegan	Newe[2]	Melvin[1]	M. Byrne*	Wilson	Power	Murray
20 Feb	H	Drogheda United	3-2	7th	O'Shea	Kinsella*	Coady	Woods	P. Byrne	Murphy	Geoghegan	Newe[2]	Melvin[1]	M. Byrne*	Wilson	Power	
6 Mar	A	Dundalk	1-1	7th	O'Shea	Kinsella[2]	Coady	Woods	P. Byrne	Murphy	Geoghegan	Newe*	Melvin	M. Byrne	Wilson	Murray	
13 Mar	A	St Patrick's Ath	2-1	7th	O'Shea	Murray[2]	Coady*	Woods	P. Byrne	Murphy	Geoghegan	Newe*	Melvin	M. Byrne	Wilson	Power	
17 Mar	A	Cobh Ramblers	2-1	7th	O'Shea	O'Neill	Malone*	Power*	P. Byrne*	Murphy	Geoghegan	Newe[2]	Melvin	Fitzgerald	Wilson	Smith	Olin
25 Mar	A	Drogheda United	1-1	7th	O'Shea	Fitzgerald	Coady	Woods*	P. Byrne	Murphy	Geoghegan	Newe	Melvin	M. Byrne[1]	Wilson	Power	
3 Apr	H	Limerick	2-1	7th	O'Shea	Fitzgerald#	Murray	Woods	P. Byrne*	Murphy	Geoghegan	Power[2]	Melvin	M. Byrne	Wilson	Smith	Malone

Note Smith = Declan Smith; Smyth = Derek Smyth

St. James's Gate   First Div.

Founded: 1902
Home: Iveagh Grounds, Crumlin, Dublin 12. Tel. (01) 4556763
Previous Ground: St. James's Park (1921/22 – 1927/28)
Nickname: "The Gate"
Colours: Red shirts, Green shorts.
Manager: Pat Byrne   Succeeded: Fran Gavin (Feb. 1994)
Chairman: Peter Mulhall
Secretary: John Burke, 14 Dodder Court, Dodder Valley Park, Fir House, Dublin 24.
   Tel. Home: (01) 4597883; Office: (01) 6713355; Fax. (01) 4555062

Honours/Best Performances:

League of Ireland Champions	:	1921/22, 1939/40	(2)
F.A.I. Cup Winners	:	1922, 1938	(2)
League Cup	:	Yet to reach knock-out stages	
First Division	:	5th 1990/91, 1991/92	
League of Ireland Shield Winners	:	1935/36, 1940/41	(2)
Dublin City Cup Winners	:	1938/39	(1)
Leinster Cup Winners	:	1919/20, 1921/22, 1934/35, 1936/37, 1940/41	(5)

League Career:
Founder members 1921. Re-elected 1929/30, 1931/32, 1992/93, 1993/94 (4). Resigned end 1943/44. Elected to First Division 1990, replacing Newcastlewest.

Players Capped (R.O.I.): 8
First:	Billy Kennedy	v	Holland (A)	08 May 1932
Last:	Paddy Bradshaw & Joe O'Reilly	v	Germany (A)	23 May 1939
Most:	Joe O'Reilly (13) 1936/39			

Record League Victory:
Home	: 7 - 0	v	Shamrock Rovers	22 Apr. 1937
Away	: 8 - 0	v	Jacobs	24 Aug. 1929

Record League Defeat:
Home	: 0 - 7	v	Cork United	12 Dec. 1943
Away	: 0 - 7	v	Waterford	22 Dec. 1931
	0 - 7	v	Shamrock Rovers	27 Dec. 1943

Most League Goals:
(Match) 6: Willie Byrne v Sligo Rovers 7 - 1 (H) 30 Mar. 1938
(Season) 29: Paddy Bradshaw 1939/40
(Career) 68: Paddy Bradshaw 1939/39 to 1940/41 & 1943/44

Points In Season:
Most	:	36	1939/40	(22 games)
Least	:	03	1943/44	(14 games)

Goals Scored in a Season:
Most : 65 1937/38 (22 games)
Least : 12 1943/44 (14 games)

League Appearances 1993/94:
17+8 Paul Ussher, 24 Paul Hall, 20+4 Peter Kelly, 22+1 Colum Kavanagh, Peter Nolan, 21 Pat Trehy, 20 Eamon Balfe, 19 Mick Gorman, 18+1 Mark Farrell, 10+7 Darren Mooney, 15+1 Colm Seville, 14+1 Fran Gavin, 13 Les McAvenue, 7+6 Des Cummins, 8+2 Stephen Ralph, 6+2 Declan Reilly, 5+3 John Gallagher, 6+1 Richie Hall, 6 Robbie Flanagan, 4+2 David Gormley, 5 Tom Conway, 1+4 Alan O'Brien, 4 Joe Sullivan, 3+1 Robbie Davis, 3 Gareth Edwards, Alan Keogh, 0+3 Alessandro D'Ambrosio, 1 Keith Byrne, 0+1 Darren Roche.
Players Used: 29

League Goalscorers 1993/94:
10 Colum Kavanagh, 4 Des Cummins, 3 Mark Farrell, 2 Paul Ussher, 1 John Gallagher, Fran Gavin, Richie Hall, Colm Seville.
Total: 23

An old 'Gater'!
Joe O'Reilly, St. James's Gate's most capped player in action against Switzerland in Berne in May 1937. Ireland won by one goal to nil (D.C.)

St. James's Gate 1993/94

Date	V	Opposition	Score	Pos	1	2	3	4	5	6	7	8	9	10	11	12	13
19 Sep	H	Athlone Town	0-2		Trehy	Nolan	McAvenue	P.Hall	Baile	Gorman	Seville	Gallagher	Cummins	Keogh	Kelly	Kavanagh	Usher
26 Sep	A	Sligo Rovers	1-1	9th	Trehy	Nolan	McAvenue	P.Hall	Baile	Gorman	Usher	Gallagher#	Kavanagh[1]	Keogh	Kelly	Gavin	Farrell
3 Oct	H	Home Farm	2-2	9th	Trehy	Nolan	McAvenue	P.Hall	Baile	Gavin	Usher	Farrell	Kavanagh	Keogh	Kelly	Gallagher[1]	Cummins[1]
10 Oct	A	Waterford United	0-0	8th	Trehy	Nolan	McAvenue	P.Hall	Baile	Gavin	Usher	Farrell	Kavanagh	Gorman	Kelly	Mooney	Cummins
17 Oct	H	Bray Wanderers	0-0	8th	Trehy	Nolan	Reilly#	P.Hall	Baile	Gavin	Usher*	Farrell*	Kavanagh*	Gorman	Kelly	Gallagher	Mooney
24 Oct	A	Finn Harps	1-1	8th	Trehy	Nolan	McAvenue	P.Hall	Baile	Gavin	Usher*	Farrell[1]	Kavanagh*	Gorman	Kelly	Mooney	Cummins
31 Oct	H	U.C.D.	0-0	8th	Trehy	Nolan	Reilly	P.Hall	Baile	Gavin	Usher	Farrell	Kavanagh	Gorman	Kelly	O'Brien	Usher
7 Nov	H	Kilkenny City	2-2	9th	Trehy	Nolan	McAvenue	P.Hall	Baile	Gavin	Usher[1]	Farrell	Kavanagh[2]	Gorman	Kelly	O'Brien	Gallagher
14 Nov	A	Longford Town	4-1	5th	Trehy	Nolan	Seville*	P.Hall	Baile	Gavin	Usher[1]	Farrell	Kavanagh[3]	Gorman	Kelly*	Reilly	Gallagher
21 Nov	H	Longford Town	0-1	8th	Trehy	Ralph	Seville#	P.Hall	Baile	Gavin	Usher#	Farrell	Kavanagh#	Gorman	Kelly#	R.Hall	Roche
28 Nov	A	Athlone Town	1-3	9th	Trehy	Nolan	Mooney	P.Hall	Baile	Gavin*[1]	Usher*	Farrell	Gallagher	Gorman	Kelly	Ralph	O'Brien
5 Dec	H	Sligo Rovers	0-0	9th	Trehy	Nolan	Mooney	P.Hall	Baile	Gavin	Usher*	Farrell[2]	Kavanagh*	Gorman	Kelly	Ralph	Usher
12 Dec	H	Home Farm	2-3	10th	Trehy	Nolan	Mooney	P.Hall	Ralph	Gavin	Seville	Farrell*	Kavanagh*	Gorman	Kelly	Kelly	O'Brien
19 Dec	A	Waterford United	1-3	10th	Trehy	Nolan	McAvenue	P.Hall	Baile	Gavin	Seville*	Farrell*	Kavanagh[1]	Mooney	Kelly	Seville	O'Brien
27 Dec	H	Bray Wanderers	1-1	9th	Trehy	Nolan	McAvenue	P.Hall	R.Hall	Ralph	Seville	Farrell	Kavanagh	Mooney*	Kelly#	O'Brien	Usher
2 Jan	A	Finn Harps	0-1	10th	Trehy	Nolan	McAvenue	P.Hall	Baile	Ralph	Usher	Farrell	Kavanagh	Mooney*	Kelly#	R.Hall	Kelly
9 Jan	A	U.C.D.	0-2	10th	Trehy	Nolan	McAvenue	P.Hall	Baile	Ralph	Seville	Farrell	Kavanagh	Gavin*	R.Hall	Mooney	Kelly
16 Jan	A	Kilkenny City	0-2	10th	Trehy	Gorman#	McAvenue	P.Hall	Baile	Gavin	Seville	Farrell	Kavanagh	Mooney*	Kelly#	Ralph	D'Ambrosio
23 Jan	H	Athlone Town	0-1	10th	Trehy	Nolan	McAvenue	P.Hall	Baile	Gorman	Seville	Farrell	Kavanagh	Mooney*	Kelly#	Usher	Cummins
30 Jan	A	Sligo Rovers	1-3	10th	Trehy	Nolan	McAvenue	P.Hall	Baile	Ralph	Gorman	Farrell	Kavanagh[1]	Flanagan	Seville*	Kelly	Usher
13 Feb	A	Home Farm	1-3	10th	Trehy	Nolan	Nolan	P.Hall	Ralph	Gorman	Farrell	Usher	Kavanagh*	Flanagan	Seville*	Usher	Cummins
20 Feb	H	Waterford United	1-1	10th	Davis	Flanagan	McAvenue	P.Hall	Baile*	Ralph	Usher	Farrell	Kavanagh[1]	Reilly	Cummins*	Nolan	Mooney
6 Mar	A	Bray Wanderers	0-0	10th	Edwards#	Nolan	Flanagan	P.Hall	Reilly	Gormley	Conway*	R.Hall	Kavanagh[1]	Seville	Cummins[1]	Usher	Davis
13 Mar	H	Finn Harps	1-2	10th	Edwards	Nolan	Flanagan	P.Hall	Usher	Reilly	Conway	R.Hall	Kavanagh*	Seville	Cummins	Kelly	Gormley
17 Mar	A	U.C.D.	0-0	10th	Davis	Nolan	Mooney	Mooney	Baile	Ralph	Conway	R.Hall	Kavanagh	Seville	Cummins	D'Ambrosio	Reilly
20 Mar	H	Longford Town	3-5	10th	Edwards	Flanagan	Nolan	Sullivan	Byrne*	Reilly	Conway*	Usher	Kavanagh[1]	Flanagan*	Seville*	Nolan	Mooney
27 Mar	H	Kilkenny City	1-1	10th	Davis	Flanagan	Nolan	Sullivan	Usher	Gorman	Gormley	Cummins[1]	Kavanagh*	Seville	Kelly	D'Ambrosio	Mooney

51

St. Patrick's Athletic   Premier Div.

Founded: 1929
Home: Richmond Park, 125 Emmet Road, Inchicore, Dublin 8.
      Tel. (01) 4546211; Fax. (01) 4546211
Capacity: 6,000; 500 seated
Previous Grounds: Milltown   (1951/52 – 1953/54)
                   Chapelizod   (1954/55 – 1955/56)
                   Dalymount Park (1956/57 – 1959/60)
                   Richmond Park   (1960/61 - 1988/89)
                   Harolds Cross   (1989/90 - 1993/94)
Nickname: "The Saints"
Colours: Red shirts, White shorts
2nd Colours: Blue shirts, Blue shorts
Manager: Brian Kerr   Succeeded: Jimmy Jackson (Dec. 1986)
Asst. Manager: Liam Buckley
Chairman: Tommy Cummins
Secretary: Frank Boylan, 49 Edenmore Gardens, Raheny, Dublin 5.
          Tel. Home: (01) 8478603

Honours/Best Performances:

League of Ireland Champions	:	1951/52, 1954/55, 1955/56, 1989/90 (4)
F.A.I. Cup Winners	:	1959, 1961 (2)
League Cup	:	Final 1979/80, 1992/93
Leinster Cup Winners	:	*1947/48, 1982/83, 1986/87, 1989/90, 1990/91 (5)
League of Ireland Shield Winners	:	1959/60 (1)
Dublin City Cup Winners	:	1953/54, 1955/56, 1975/76 (3)
Presidents Cup Winners	:	1952/53, 1953/54, 1955/56, 1971/72, 1990/91 (5)

*as a non-League club

League Career:
Elected 1951 with Evergreen United (Cork Celtic). Re-elected end 1953/54, 1962/63, 1969/70 (3). Premier Division 1985/86 to date.

European Appearances: 4

Champions Cup:	1990/91	v	Dinamo Bucharest	1 - 1, 0 - 4
Cup Winners Cup:	1961/62	v	Dunfermline Athletic	0 - 4, 1 - 4
Fairs Cup:	1967/68	v	Bordeaux	1 - 3, 3 - 6
U.E.F.A. Cup	1988/89	v	Heart of Midlothian	0 - 2, 0 - 2

Players Capped (R.O.I.): 6
First: : Shay Gibbons   v West Germany (A) 04 May 1952
Last   : Noel Campbell   v Austria   (A) 10 Oct. 1971
Most   : Shay Gibbons (4) 1952/55

Record League Victory:
Home : 8 - 0 v Limerick 10 Dec. 1967
Away : 6 - 0 v Transport 04 Apr. 1959
          v Longford Town 24 Feb. 1985

Record League Defeat:
Home : 2 - 8 v Cork Celtic 21 Jan. 1962
Away : 0 - 7 v Bohemians 04 Apr. 1974

Most League Goals:
(Match) 5: Shay Gibbons v Cork Athletic 6-2 (H) 22 Feb. 1953
(Season) 28: Shay Gibbons 1954/55
(Career) 108: Shay Gibbons 1951/52 to 1956/57

Points In Season:
Most : 52   1989/90   (33 games)
        56* 1981/82   (30 games)
Least : 13   1962/63   (18 games)

Goals Scored in Season:
Most : 62   1954/55   (22 games)
Least : 22   1986/87   (22 games)

League Appearances 1993/94:
32 John McDonnell, 31 Tony O'Dowd, 30+1 Derek Dunne, 30 Dave Campbell, 28+1 John Byrne, 27 Ian Hill, 22+4 Paul Campbell, 25 Mark O'Neill, 17+8 Jason Byrne, 19+3 John Tracey, 17+1 Mark Ennis, 5+10 Kieran O'Brien, 14 Eddie Gormley, 10+2 Christy McElligott, 9 Pascal Keane, 8 Martin Nugent, 5+3 Ray Carolan, 7 Mark Browne, 6+1 P.J. O'Connell, 4+2 James Reilly, 2+4 Lee King, 3+2 David McEnroe, 0+4 Brian Morrisroe, 1+1 Gareth Byrne, 0+2 Liam Buckley, 0+1 Thomas Fallon.
Players Used: 26

League Goalscorers 1993/94:
7 Jason Byrne, 6 Mark Ennis, 4 Dave Campbell, Derek Dunne, 2 Pascal Keane, John McDonnell, Martin Nugent, P.J. O'Connell, 1 Lee King, David McEnroe, Mark O'Neill.
Total: 32

Jason Byrne
Top scorer for St. Pat's in 1993-94 (St.P.A.)

Brian Kerr
The National League's longest serving manager (St.P.A.)

St. Patrick's Athletic 1992/93

Date	V	Opposition	Score	Pos	1	2	3	4	5	6	7	8	9	10	11	12	13
28 Aug	A	Dundalk	0-0	-	O'Dowd	Hill	Byrne	Reid	Kelch	Carolan	Tracey*	Dunne	P Campbell	Ryan	Newe	Osam	
6 Sep	H	Shamrock Rovers	1-0	3rd	O'Dowd	Hill	Byrne	Reid	Kelch	Carolan	Osam[1]	Tracey	P Campbell	Ryan	Newe[1]	Browne	
13 Sep	A	Cork City	1-2	6th	O'Dowd	Hill	Byrne	Reid	Kelch	Carolan[1]	Osam*	Tracey	P Campbell	Ryan	Newe[1]	Dunne	McElligott
20 Sep	H	Bohemians	1-1	7th	O'Dowd	Hill	Byrne	Reid	Kelch	Carolan*	Dunne	Tracey	P Campbell#	Ryan	Newe#	O'Brien	Browne
27 Sep	A	Waterford United	2-0	5th	O'Dowd	Hill	Byrne	Reid	Kelch	O'Brien	Dunne	Tracey	Robb	Ryan	Newe[1]	Browne[1]	McElligott
4 Oct	H	Sligo Rovers	2-0	3rd	O'Dowd	Hill	Byrne	D Campbell	Kelch	Carolan	Dunne	Browne[1]	Robb	Ryan	Newe[1]		
11 Oct	H	Derry City	1-1	3rd	O'Dowd	Hill	Byrne	McElligott	Tracey	Carolan	Dunne[1]	Browne	P Campbell	Ryan	Newe	Dolan	
18 Oct	A	Drogheda United	1-1	4th	O'Dowd	Hill	Byrne	D Campbell	Tracey	Carolan	Dunne*	Browne	P Campbell	Ryan	Newe[1]		
24 Oct	A	Shelbourne	1-1	5th	O'Dowd	Hill	Kelch	D Campbell	Byrne	Tracey	Dunne	Browne*	P Campbell*	Dolan[1]	Newe#	Ryan	Robb
25 Oct	H	Bray Wanderers	1-1	6th	O'Dowd	Hill	Carolan	D Campbell	Byrne	Tracey	Dunne	Browne	Robb	Ryan[1]	Newe#	Dolan	Fallon
1 Nov	A	Limerick	0-0	5th	O'Dowd	Hill	Kelch	D Campbell	Byrne	Tracey	Dunne	Browne	Dolan	Ryan	Newe#	Carolan	
8 Nov	A	Limerick City	0-2	6th	O'Dowd	Hill	Carolan	D Campbell	Fitzgerald	Tracey	Dunne	Browne*	Dolan	Osam	Newe.	P Campbell	Ryan
15 Nov	H	Dundalk	0-0	6th	O'Dowd	Hill	Kelch	D Campbell	Fitzgerald	Tracey	Dunne	Browne	Dolan	Osam	Newe.	Ryan	
22 Nov	A	Shamrock Rovers	1-1	6th	O'Dowd	Hill	Kelch	D Campbell	Fitzgerald	Tracey	Dunne	Browne	Dolan	Osam	P Campbell[1]	P Campbell[1]	
29 Nov	H	Cork City	2-1	6th	O'Dowd	Hill	Kelch[1]	D Campbell	McDonnell	Tracey	Dunne	Browne	Dolan	Osam	P Campbell	Ryan	
4 Dec	A	Bohemians	0-0	6th	O'Dowd	Hill	Kelch	D Campbell	McDonnell	Tracey	Dunne	Buckley	Dolan	Osam*	P Campbell		
13 Dec	H	Waterford United	2-1	5th	O'Dowd	Hill	Kelch	D Campbell	McDonnell	Fallon	Dunne	Ryan[2]	Dolan	Osam*	P Campbell	Tracey	Browne
20 Dec	A	Sligo Rovers	0-1	6th	O'Dowd	Hill	Kelch	D Campbell	McDonnell	Fallon	Dunne	P Campbell	Dolan	Osam*	Newe	Carolan	
27 Dec	A	Derry City	0-1	7th	O'Dowd	Hill	Kelch	McElligott	McDonnell	Fallon	Dunne[1]	P Campbell	Dolan[1]	Tracey	Ryan*	Browne	
3 Jan	H	Drogheda United	2-2	6th	O'Dowd	Hill	Kelch*	McElligott	McDonnell	Tracey	Carolan	P Campbell	Dolan[1]	Ryan[1]	Newe	Browne	Dunne
10 Jan	A	Bray Wanderers	1-1	6th	O'Dowd	Hill	Kelch	McElligott	McDonnell	Tracey	Carolan	P Campbell	Dolan	Ryan[1]	Dunne	Carolan	
17 Jan	H	Shelbourne	0-0	6th	O'Dowd	Hill	Kelch*	McElligott	McDonnell	Tracey*	Fallon*	P Campbell	Dolan	Ryan	Dunne	P Campbell[1]	Newe
24 Jan	A	Sligo Rovers	1-3	7th	O'Dowd	Hill	Kelch*	McElligott	McDonnell	Tracey.	O'Connell	Carolan	Dolan	Ryan	Dunne	Carolan	
31 Jan	H	Bray Wanderers	0-0	7th	O'Dowd	Hill	Carolan	McElligott	McDonnell	P Campbell	O'Connell	Browne	Dolan	Ryan	Dunne	Newe	
7 Feb	A	Waterford United	1-1	7th	O'Dowd	Hill	Carolan	McElligott	McDonnell	Fallon*	O'Connell	Browne	Dolan	Ryan	O'Brien	P Campbell[1]	Fitzgerald
21 Feb	A	Drogheda United	0-2	7th	O'Dowd	Hill	Carolan*	McElligott	McDonnell	Dunne#	P Campbell	Browne	Dolan	Ryan	O'Brien	McNeill	O'Connell
28 Feb	H	Waterford United	2-1	7th	O'Dowd	Hill	Kelch	McElligott	McDonnell	Tracey	O'Brien	Osam[1]	Browne	P Campbell*[1]	Ryan[1]	Dunne	
14 Mar	H	Waterford United	4-0	7th	O'Dowd	Hill	Kelch*	McElligott[1]	McDonnell	Tracey*	O'Brien	D Campbell	Browne	Dolan[1]	Ryan[1]	Newe	Fallon[1]
21 Mar	A	Bray Wanderers	0-0	7th	O'Dowd	Hill	Kelch*	McElligott	McDonnell	Tracey	O'Brien	D Campbell	Browne	Dolan	Ryan#	Newe	Fitzgerald
4 Apr	A	Shamrock Rovers	0-1	7th	O'Dowd	Hill	D Campbell	McElligott	McDonnell	Tracey	O'Brien	Osam	Browne	Dolan	Ryan	P Campbell	Newe
7 Apr	H	Sligo Rovers	0-1	7th	O'Dowd	Hill	D Campbell	McElligott	McDonnell	Kelch	O'Brien	Osam	Browne#	P Campbell	Ryan	Newe	
11 Apr	H	Drogheda United	0-1	7th	O'Dowd	Hill	Kelch	McElligott*	McDonnell	Fitzgerald	O'Brien	Fallon	Browne	P Campbell#	Ryan	Reid	Carolan

54

Shamrock Rovers   Premier Div.

Founded: 1901
Home: Royal Dublin Society (RDS), Ballsbridge, Dublin 4.
Previous Grounds: Glenmalure Park   (1922/23 - 1986/87)
                   Tolka Park   (1987/88)
                   Dalymount Park   (1988/89 - 1989/90)
Nickname: "The Hoops"
Colours: Green & White Hooped shirts, Green shorts
2nd Colours: All purple
Manager: Ray Treacy   Succeeded: Noel King (Jan 1992)
Asst. Manager: Tony Macken
Chairman: John McNamara
Secretary: Brian Murphy, c/o 11/12 York Road, Ringsend Dublin 4.
          Tel. Home: (01) 2840926; Office: (01) 6685433; Fax. (01) 6606950; Mobile (088) 551620

Honours:

League Champions	:	1922/23, 1924/25, 1926/27, 1931/32, 1937/38, 1938/39, 1953/54, 1956/57, 1958/59, 1963/64, 1983/84, 1984/85, 1985/86, 1986/87, 1993/94 (15)
F.A.I. Cup Winners	:	1925, 1929, 1930, 1931, 1932, 1933, 1936, 1940, 1944, 1945, 1948, 1955, 1956, 1962, 1964, 1965, 1966, 1967, 1968, 1969, 1978, 1985, 1986, 1987. (24)
League Cup Winners	:	1976/77 (1)
Shield Winners	:	1924/25, 1926/27, 1931/32, 1932/33, 1934/35, 1937/38, 1941/42, 1949/50, 1951/52, 1954/55, 1955/56, 1956/57, 1957/58, 1962/63, 1963/64, 1964/65, 1965/66, 1967/68. (18)
Dublin City Cup Winners	:	1944/45, 1947/48, 1952/53, 1954/55, 1956/57, 1957/58, 1959/60, 1963/64, 1966/67, 1983/84. (10)
Leinster Cup Winners	:	1922/23, 1926/27, 1928/29, 1929/30, 1932/33, 1937/38, 1952/53, 1954/55, 1955/56 1956/57, 1957/58, 1963/64, 1968/69, 1981/82, 1984/85 (15)
Inter-City Cup Winners	:	1945/46, 1946/47, 1948/49 (3)
Blaxnit Cup Winners	:	1967/68 (1)
Tyler Cup Winners	:	1977/78 (1)
Top 4 Cup Winners	:	1955/56, 1957/58, 1965/66 (3)
Presidents Cup Winners	:	1933/34, 1940/41, 1942/43, 1943/44, 1944/45, 1945/46, 1948/49, 1954/55, 1956/57, 1957/58, 1959/60, 1962/63, 1968/69, 1969/70, 1970/71, 1972/73, 1984/85, 1985/86, 1986/87, 1987/88. (20)

League Career:
Elected 1922 as league extended from 8 to 12 clubs. Re-elected end 1975/76. Premier Division 1985/86 to date.

European Appearances: 16

Champions Cup:		1957/58	v	Manchester United	0 - 6, 2 - 3
		1959/60	v	Nice	1 - 1, 2 - 3
		1964/65	v	Rapid Vienna	0 - 2, 0 - 3
		1984/85	v	Linfield	1 - 1, 0 - 0
		1985/86	v	Honved	1 - 3, 0 - 2
		1986/87	v	Celtic	0 - 1. 0 - 2
		1987/88	v	Omonia Nicosia	0 - 1, 0 - 0
Cup Winners Cup:		1962/63	v	Botev Plovdiv	0 - 4, 0 - 1
		1966/67	v	Spora Luxembourg	4 - 1, 4 - 1
				Bayern Munich	1 - 1, 2 - 3
		1967/68	v	Cardiff City	1 - 1, 0 - 2
		1968/69	v	Randers Freja	1 - 2, 0 - 1
		1969/70	v	Schalke 04	2 - 1, 0 - 3
		1978/79	v	Apoel Nicosia,	2 - 0, 1 - 0
				Banik Ostrava	1 - 3, 0 - 3
Fairs Cup:		1963/64	v	Valencia	0 - 1, 2 - 2
		1965/66	v	Real Zaragoza	1 - 1, 1 - 2
U.E.F.A. Cup:		1982/83	v	Fram Reykjavik,	4 - 0, 3 - 0
				Univ. Craiova	0 - 2, 0 - 3

Players Capped (R.O.I.): 62

First:	Dinny Doyle, John Fagan			
	John Joe Flood, Bob Fullam,	v	Italy	(A) 21 Mar. 1926
Last:	Pat Byrne	v	Czechoslovakia	(N) 27 May 1986
Most:	Frank O'Neill (20) 1961/71			

Record League Victory:
Home	: 11 - 0	v	Bray Unknowns	28 Oct. 1928
Away	: 8 - 0	v	Jacobs	31 Jan. 1932

Record League Defeat:
Home	: 1 - 6	v	Sligo Rovers	27 Dec. 1936
Away	: 0 - 7	v	St. James's Gate	22 Apr .1937

Most League Goals:
(Match) 6: Paul Scully v Bray Unknowns 9-3 (H) 10 Nov. 1935
(Season) 27: Bob Fullam 1922/23
(Career) 109: Paddy Ambrose 1949/50 to 1959/60

Points in Season:
Most	:	49	1984/85	(30 games)
		66 **	1993/94	(32 games)
		76*	1981/82	(30 games)
Least	:	14	1945/46	(14 games)
			1947/48	(14 games)

Goals Scored in Season:
Most   :   77   1922/23   (22 games)
Least   :   20   1944/45   (14 games)

League Appearances 1993/94:
32 Gino Brazil, Alan O'Neill, 31 John Toal, 30+1 Stephen Geoghegan, 30 Willie Burke, 28+2 Eoin Mullen, 29 Peter Eccles, 28 Alan Byrne, 25+2 Derek McGrath, 25 Terry Eviston, 18 Paul Osam, 12+2 John Nolan, 6+5 John Bacon, 4+4 Paul Cullen, 2+6 Derek Treacy, 5+2 Paul Cashin, 3+3 Alan Dodd, 3+1 Terry Berry, 0+4 Chris Giles, 2+1 Gareth Kelly, Derek Swan, 2 Pat O'Toole, 1 Christian Bowes, Ed Greene, John Power, 0+1 Mark McCormack, Padraig Redmond.
Players Used: 27

League Goalscorers 1993/94:
23 Stephen Geoghegan, 10 John Toal, 7 Derek McGrath, 6 Terry Eviston, 4 Peter Eccles, 3 Eoin Mullen, 1 John Bacon, Terry Berry, Gino Brazil, Willie Burke, Alan Byrne, Paul Cashin, Paul Cullen, Alan Dodd, Paul Osam.
Total: 62

Hoopla!
Champions Shamrock Rovers pop the champagne cork   (The Star)

Shamrock Rovers 1993/94

Date	V	Opposition	Score	Pos	1	2	3	4	5	6	7	8	9	10	11	12	13
22 Aug	H	Dundalk	0-0	-	O'Neill	Burke	Nolan	Brazil	Eccles	Toal	Osam	McGrath	Eviston*	Swan	Byrne	Geoghegan	
25 Aug	A	Shelbourne	0-1	10th	O'Neill	Burke	Nolan	Brazil	Eccles	Toal	Osam	McGrath	Eviston	Swan	Byrne		
4 Sep	A	Galway United	5-0	6th	O'Neill	Burke[1]	Nolan*	Brazil	Eccles[1]	Toal[3]	Osam	McGrath	Eviston*	Geoghegan[#]	Byrne	Cashin[1]	Mullen
12 Sep	H	Cork City	3-0	5th	O'Neill	Burke[1]	Nolan*	Brazil	Eccles	Toal	Osam	McGrath	Eviston*	Geoghegan[2]	Byrne	Mullen	
15 Sep	A	St Patrick's Ath.	2-0	2nd	O'Neill	Burke	Mullen	Brazil	Eccles	Toal	Osam	McGrath	Eviston*	Geoghegan[2]	Byrne	Bacon	
19 Sep	H	Monaghan United	1-0	1st	O'Neill	Burke	Mullen	Brazil[1]	Berry[1]	Toal	Osam	McGrath	Eviston	Geoghegan	Byrne		
26 Sep	H	Bohemians	2-1	1st	O'Neill	Burke	Mullen	Brazil	Eccles	Toal	Osam	McGrath	Eviston	Geoghegan	Byrne		
30 Sep	A	Drogheda United	1-2	2nd	O'Neill	Burke	Mullen	Brazil	Eccles	Toal	Osam[1]	McGrath*	Eviston	Geoghegan	Cashin	Treacy	
10 Oct	A	Derry City	0-0	2nd	O'Neill	Kelly	Mullen	Brazil	Eccles	Toal	Osam	McGrath[3]	Eviston	Geoghegan	Byrne[1]	Swan	
17 Oct	H	Limerick	7-3	1st	O'Neill	Kelly	Mullen	Brazil	Eccles	Toal*	Osam	McGrath	Eviston[#2]	Geoghegan[2]	Byrne*	Giles	Cullen
24 Oct	A	Cobh Ramblers	3-1	1st	O'Neill	Burke	Mullen	Brazil	Eccles	Toal	Osam	McGrath	Eviston*[1]	Geoghegan[3]	Byrne	Cullen[#]	Giles
31 Oct	H	Cobh Ramblers	3-0	1st	O'Neill	Burke	Mullen	Brazil	Eccles	Toal[#]	Osam	McGrath	Eviston[1]	Geoghegan[1]	Byrne	Cullen	Giles
7 Nov	A	Dundalk	2-1	1st	O'Neill	Burke	Mullen	Brazil	Eccles	Toal	Osam	Cullen*[1]	Eviston[1]	Geoghegan[1]	Byrne	Treacy	
14 Nov	H	Shelbourne	2-0	1st	O'Neill	Burke	Mullen	Brazil	Eccles	Toal	Osam	Cullen	Eviston[1]	Geoghegan	Byrne	Treacy	
21 Nov	H	St Patrick's Ath.	1-0	1st	O'Neill	Burke	Mullen	Brazil	Eccles[1]	Toal	Osam	McGrath	Eviston	Geoghegan	Byrne		
28 Nov	H	Galway United	3-1	1st	O'Neill	Burke	Mullen	Brazil	Eccles	Toal[1]	Osam	McGrath	Eviston	Geoghegan[1]	Byrne	Treacy	Nolan
5 Dec	A	Cork City	2-2	1st	O'Neill	Burke	Mullen	Brazil	Eccles	Toal	Osam*	McGrath[#]	Eviston[1]	Geoghegan[1]	Byrne	Nolan	Treacy
12 Dec	H	Monaghan United	2-1	1st	O'Neill	Burke	Mullen	Brazil	Eccles	Toal	Osam*	McGrath	Eviston	Geoghegan	Byrne	Treacy	
17 Dec	A	Bohemians	0-2	1st	O'Neill	Burke	Mullen	Brazil	Eccles	Toal	Nolan[1]	McGrath[1]	Eviston	Geoghegan	Byrne	Bacon	
27 Dec	H	Drogheda United	2-0	1st	O'Neill	Burke	Mullen	Brazil	Eccles	Toal	Cashin	McGrath[1]	Eviston	Geoghegan	Byrne	Bacon	
2 Jan	H	Derry City	0-1	1st	O'Neill	Burke	Mullen	Brazil	Eccles[1]	Toal	Cashin	Treacy	Eviston[1]	Geoghegan[1]	Byrne	McGrath	Bacon
9 Jan	A	Limerick	2-0	1st	O'Neill	Burke	Mullen	Brazil	Eccles	Toal	Cashin*	Treacy	Eviston	Geoghegan	Byrne	Kelly[#]	Bacon
16 Jan	A	Derry City	0-1	1st	O'Neill*	Burke	Mullen	Brazil[#]	Eccles	Toal	O'Toole	McGrath[1]	Eviston	Geoghegan	Byrne	Redmond	Cullen
23 Jan	H	Galway United	2-5	1st	O'Neill[1]	Burke	Mullen	Brazil	Eccles	Toal	O'Toole	Cullen	Eviston*	Geoghegan[1]	Bowes	Cashin	
30 Jan	H	Bohemians	1-2	1st	O'Neill	Burke	Mullen	Brazil	Eccles	Toal	Nolan[#]	Cullen[#]	Power*	Geoghegan	Byrne	McGrath	Berry
13 Feb	A	Cork City	1-2	2nd	O'Neill	Burke	Mullen	Brazil	Eccles	Toal[1]	Nolan	McGrath[1]	Bacon	Geoghegan	Byrne	Dodd	
6 Mar	A	Bohemians	2-1	2nd	O'Neill	Burke	Mullen[1]	Brazil	Eccles*	Toal[1]	Nolan	McGrath[1]	Bacon[#]	Geoghegan[1]	Dodd		
13 Mar	A	Galway United	3-2	1st	O'Neill	Burke	Mullen[1]	Brazil	Berry	Dodd[1]	Nolan	McGrath[1]	Bacon[1]	Geoghegan	Byrne	Dodd	Greene
17 Mar	A	Derry City	3-0	1st	O'Neill	Burke	Mullen[1]	Brazil	Berry[1]	Toal[1]	Nolan	McGrath*	Bacon	Geoghegan	Byrne		
25 Mar	A	Shelbourne	3-0	1st	O'Neill	Burke	Mullen	Brazil	Berry	Toal[1]	Nolan	McGrath[1]	Bacon[1]	Geoghegan[1]	Byrne[#]	Dodd	
30 Mar	H	Shelbourne	2-1	1st	O'Neill	Burke	Mullen	Brazil	Eccles[1]	Toal	Nolan*	Dodd	Bacon	Geoghegan[1]	Greene[#]	McCormack	Giles
3 Apr	H	Cork City	2-0	1st	O'Neill	Burke	Mullen	Brazil	Eccles[1]	Toal	Nolan*	Dodd	Bacon	Geoghegan[1]	Greene[#]	McCormack	Giles

Shelbourne   Premier Div.

Founded: 1895
Home: Tolka Park, Richmond Road, Drumcondra, Dublin 3.
   Tel. (01) 8373091 / 8368781
Capacity: 10,000; all seated
Previous
Grounds: Shelbourne Park (1921/22 - 1948/49)
   Milltown   (1949/50 - 1950/51)
   Dalymount Park   (1951/52 - 1953/54, 1974/75)
   Irishtown   (1955/56)
   Harold's Cross   (1975/76 - 1976/77, 1982/83 - 1988/89)
   Tolka Park   (1954/55, 1956/57 - 1973/74, 1977/78 - 1981/82, 1989/90 to date)
Nickname: "Shels"/"The Reds"
Colours: Red shirts, Red shorts
2nd Colours: Sky Blue shirts, White shorts
Manager: Eamonn Gregg   Succeeded: Eoin Hand (Jan. 1994)
President: Brian Lenihan
Chairman: Finbarr Flood
Secretary: Ollie Byrne, c/o Tolka Park. Tel. (01) 8375536/8375754; Fax. (01) 8375588

Honours/Best Performances:

League of Ireland Champions	:	1925/26, 1928/29, 1930/31, 1943/44,	
		1946/47, 1952/53, 1961/62, 1991/92	(8)
F.A.I. Cup Winners	:	1939, 1960, 1963, 1993	(4)
League Cup	:	Finalists 1993/94	
First Division	:	Runners-up 1986/87	
League of Ireland Shield Winners	:	1921/22, 1922/23, 1925/26, 1929/30	
		1943/44, 1944/45, 1948/49, 1970/71	(8)
Dublin City Cup Winners	:	1941/42, 1946/47, 1962/63, 1964/65	(4)
Leinster Cup Winners	:	1899/1900, 1900/01, 1903/04, 1905/06,	
		1907/08, 1908/09, 1912/13, 1913/14,	
		1916/17, 1918/19, 1923/24, 1930/31,	
		1945/46, 1948/49, 1962/63, 1967/68,	
		1971/72, 1993/94	(18)
Top 4 Cup Winners	:	1961/62	(1)
Presidents Cup Winners	:	1939/40, 1960/61, 1993/94	(3)
North South Cup	:	Final 1961/63	
I.F.A. Cup Winners	:	1906, 1911, 1920	(3)

League Career:
Founder members 1921. Resigned end 1933/34. Re-admitted 1936 in place of Reds United. Re-elected end 1940/41, 1945/46, 1966/67, 1973/74, 1974/75, 1979/80, 1980/81 (7). Relegated end 1985/86. Promoted end 1986/87. Premier Division 1987/88 to date.

59

European Appearances: 6

Champions Cup:	1962/63	v	Sporting Lisbon	0 - 2, 1 - 5	
	1992/93	v	Tavria Simferopol	0 - 0, 1 - 2	
Cup Winners Cup:	1963/64	v	Barcelona	0 - 2, 1 - 3	
	1993/94	v	Karpaty Lvov	3 - 1, 0 - 1	
		v	Panathinaikos	1 - 2, 0 - 3	
Fairs Cup:	1964/65	v	Belenenses	0 - 0, 1 - 1, 2 - 1	
		v	Athletico Madrid	0 - 1, 0 - 1	
U.E.F.A. Cup:	1971/72	v	Vasas	1 - 1, 0 - 1	

Players Capped (ROI): 23

First : Mick Foley, Fran Watters v Italy (A) 21 Mar. 1926
Last : Mick Gannon, Paddy Roche v Austria (A) 10 Oct. 1971
Most : Joe Haverty (7) 1965/66

Players Capped (NI): 5

First : Val Harris v England (H) 17 Feb. 1906
Last : Eddie Brookes v Scotland (A) 13 Mar. 1920
Most : Val Harris (6) 1906/08

Record League Victory:

Home : 9 - 0 v Bray Unknowns 04 Sep. 1926
Away : 9 - 0 v Pioneers 16 Dec. 1922

Record League Defeat:

Home : 1 - 7 v Shamrock Rovers 26 Jan. 1969
Away : 0 - 9 v Dundalk 27 Jan. 1980

Most League Goals:

(Match) 6: John Ledwidge v Jacobs 9 - 1 (H) 10 Oct .1929
Alexander Hair v Jacobs 7 - 0 (H) 06 Sep. 1930
(Season) 29: Alexander Hair 1930/31
(Career) 126: Eric Barber 1958/59 to 1965/66 & 1971/72 to 1974/75

Points in Season:

Most : 49 1991/92 (33 games)
Least : 08 1945/46 (14 games)

Goals Scored in Season:

Most : 72 1922/23 (22 games)
Least : 15 1985/86 (22 games)

League Appearances 1993/94:

32 Jody Byrne, 30 Brian Mooney, Mick Neville, Anto Whelan, 28+2 Greg Costello, 25 Mark Rutherford, 22+2 Ken O'Doherty, 15+8 Stephen Cooney, 20+1 Paul Doolin, 20 Brian Flood, 19 Vinny Arkins, 18+1 Tommy Dunne, 15+2 Barry O'Connor, 15 Kevin Brady, 4+11 Tony Izzi, 13+1 Aaron Callaghan, 5+4 Bobby Browne, 3+2 Karl Wilson, 2+2 Darren Kelly, Seán Riordan, 2 Padraig Dully, 1 Pat Byrne, Dave Smith, 0+1 Anto Brennan.
Players Used: 24

League Goalscorers 1993/94:

8 Barry O'Connor, 7 Vinny Arkins, 6 Stephen Cooney, Brian Mooney, 3 Tony Izzi, Ken O'Doherty, 2 Mark Rutherford, Anto Whelan, 1 Bobby Browne, Jody Byrne, Aaron Callaghan, Paul Doolin, Séan Riordan.
Total: 42

Mark two ...
Two of the National League's finest, Mark Rutherford (Shelbourne) and Mark Herrick (Galway United), tussle for possession (The Star)

Shelbourne 1993/94

Date	V	Opposition	Score	Pos	1	2	3	4	5	6	7	8	9	10	11	12	13
22 Aug	A	Limerick	0-0	-	J. Byrne	Brady	Dunne	Neville	Whelan	Doolin	Mooney[#]	Costello	Izzi[•]	O'Doherty	Rutherford	Browne	Wilson
25 Aug	H	Shamrock Rovers	1-1	4th	J. Byrne	Flood	Brady	Neville[•]	Whelan[1]	Doolin[1]	Mooney	Costello	O'Doherty	Wilson	Rutherford[1]	Browne	
29 Aug	A	Cobh Ramblers	2-0	3rd	J. Byrne	Flood	Brady	Neville	Whelan[•]	Doolin[1]	Mooney	Costello	O'Doherty	Wilson[#]	Rutherford[1]	Browne	Izzi
5 Sep	H	Derry City	2-0	2nd	J. Byrne	Flood	Brady	Neville	Whelan	Doolin	Mooney[1]	Costello	Dully	Izzi[•]	Rutherford[1]	Cooney[1]	
10 Sep	H	St Patrick's Ath.	1-0	1st	J. Byrne	Flood	Brady	Neville	Riordan	Doolin	Mooney	Costello	O'Doherty[1]	Cooney[#]	Rutherford	Browne[1]	Izzi
19 Sep	A	Dundalk	1-5	4th	J. Byrne	Costello	Wilson[•]	Riordan	Whelan[1]	Doolin	Mooney	P. Byrne	O'Doherty	Browne	Rutherford[#]	O'Doherty	Cooney[1]
26 Sep	H	Galway United	1-1	3rd	J. Byrne	Flood	Brady	Neville[•]	Whelan[1]	Doolin	Mooney	Costello	Dully	Cooney[•]	Rutherford[1]	Wilson	Riordan[1]
3 Oct	A	Monaghan United	5-4	3rd	J. Byrne[1]	Flood	Brady	Neville[#]	Whelan	Doolin	Browne	O'Doherty	Izzi[2]	Cooney[1]	Rutherford	Izzi	Riordan
8 Oct	H	Cork City	0-1	4th	J. Byrne	Flood	Brady	Neville	Whelan	Doolin	Mooney	Costello	O'Doherty	Dunne[•]	Rutherford	Izzi	
15 Oct	A	Bohemians	0-1	4th	J. Byrne	Flood	Dunne	Brady	Whelan	Doolin	Browne[•]	Costello	Cooney	Mooney	Rutherford	Izzi	
24 Oct	H	Drogheda United	1-0	4th	J. Byrne	Flood	Brady	Neville	Whelan	Browne[•]	Mooney	Costello	Atkins	O'Doherty	Rutherford	Cooney	Costello
29 Oct	A	Drogheda United	2-2	4th	J. Byrne	Flood	Dunne	Neville	Whelan	Cooney[1]	Mooney[1]	O'Doherty	Atkins[1]	Izzi[•1]	Rutherford[1]	Costello	
5 Nov	H	Limerick	3-0	4th	J. Byrne	Flood	Dunne	Neville	Whelan	Doolin	Mooney[•]	Cooney[1]	Atkins[1]	O'Doherty[•1]	Rutherford	Izzi	Costello
14 Nov	A	Shamrock Rovers	0-2	4th	J. Byrne	Flood	Brady	Neville	Whelan	Doolin[1]	Mooney	Dunne[•]	Atkins[1]	Cooney	Rutherford	O'Connor	
19 Nov	H	Cobh Ramblers	1-0	3rd	J. Byrne	Costello	Dunne	Neville	Whelan	Doolin[1]	Browne	O'Doherty[•]	Atkins[1]	O'Connor	Rutherford	Cooney	
28 Nov	A	Derry City	4-1	3rd	J. Byrne	Costello	Dunne	Neville	Whelan	Cooney[1]	Mooney	O'Doherty[1]	Atkins[2]	O'Connor	Rutherford		
5 Dec	A	St Patrick's Ath.	2-2	3rd	J. Byrne	Costello	Dunne	Neville	Whelan	Cooney[2]	Mooney[•]	O'Doherty[1]	Atkins	O'Connor	Rutherford	Callaghan	Izzi
10 Dec	H	Dundalk	1-2	3rd	J. Byrne	Callaghan	Dunne	Neville	Whelan	O'Doherty[#]	Mooney[1]	Costello	Atkins[1]	O'Connor	Rutherford[•]	Izzi	Doolin
19 Dec	A	Galway United	1-1	3rd	J. Byrne	Callaghan	Dunne	Neville	Whelan	Doolin	Mooney	Costello	Atkins[1]	O'Connor	Rutherford[•]	Cooney[1]	
22 Dec	H	Monaghan United	3-0	3rd	J. Byrne	Callaghan[1]	Dunne	Neville	Whelan	Doolin	Mooney[•]	Costello	Atkins[•]	O'Connor	Rutherford	Cooney[1]	
7 Jan	H	Bohemians	2-1	3rd	J. Byrne	Callaghan	Brady	Neville	Whelan	Doolin	Mooney[1]	Costello	O'Doherty	Cooney[1]	Rutherford		
16 Jan	H	Cork City	1-1	3rd	J. Byrne	Callaghan	Brady[•]	Neville	Whelan	Doolin	Mooney	Costello	O'Doherty[•]	Cooney[•]	Rutherford	O'Connor	
21 Jan	A	Bohemians	0-2	4th	J. Byrne	Callaghan	Brady	Neville	Whelan	Doolin	Mooney	Costello	Atkins	O'Connor[1]	Rutherford	Cooney	Dunne
28 Jan	H	Derry City	1-1	4th	J. Byrne	Callaghan	Brady	Neville	Whelan	Doolin	Mooney	Costello	Atkins	O'Connor[1]	Rutherford	Cooney	
13 Feb	A	Galway United	0-1	4th	J. Byrne	Flood	Dunne	Neville	Whelan	Doolin	Mooney	Costello[•]	Atkins	O'Connor	Rutherford	O'Doherty	Izzi
5 Mar	A	Derry City	0-0	4th	J. Byrne	Callaghan	Dunne	Neville	Whelan	O'Doherty	Mooney	Costello	Atkins	Cooney	Flood		
11 Mar	H	Bohemians	0-2	6th	J. Byrne	Flood	Callaghan	Neville	Whelan	O'Doherty	Mooney[1]	Costello	Atkins	O'Connor	Cooney[•]	Brennan	
17 Mar	A	Cork City	1-1	6th	J. Byrne	Flood	Callaghan	Neville	Whelan	O'Doherty	Mooney[1]	Costello	Atkins	O'Connor	Cooney[1]		
20 Mar	A	Cork City	1-3	6th	J. Byrne	Callaghan	Dunne	Neville	Whelan	Flood	Mooney	Costello	Atkins	O'Connor	Cooney[1]	Kelly	
25 Mar	H	Shamrock Rovers	0-3	6th	J. Byrne	Smith	Dunne	Neville	Whelan[•]	Flood	Mooney[1]	Costello[•]	Atkins	O'Connor	Cooney[1]	Izzi	Kelly
30 Mar	A	Shamrock Rovers	1-2	6th	J. Byrne	Callaghan	Dunne	Neville	Whelan	Flood	Mooney[1]	Costello	Atkins[1]	O'Connor	Kelly	Izzi	
2 Apr	A	Galway United	5-2	5th	J. Byrne	Callaghan	Dunne	Neville	O'Doherty	Flood	Mooney[1]	Costello	Atkins[1]	O'Connor[3]	Kelly		

Sligo Rovers   Premier Div.

Founded: 1928
Home: The Showgrounds, Sligo. Tel. (071) 71212; Fax. (071) 71331
Correspondence: P.O. Box 275, Sligo.
Nickname: "Rovers"/"The Bit of Red"
Colours: Red shirts, Red shorts
Chairman: Kevin Dykes
Manager: Lawrie Sanchez   Succeeded: Willie McStay (Sep. 1994)
Asst. Manager: Chris Rutherford
Secretary: Kevin Colreavy, 39 Martin Savage Terrace, Sligo
    Tel. Home: (071) 42204; Office: (071) 42141; Fax. (071) 41119

Honours/Best Performances:

League of Ireland Champions	:	1936/37, 1976/77	(2)
F.A.I. Cup Winners	:	1983, 1994	(2)
League Cup	:	Final 1975/76, 1976/77	
First Division Champions	:	1993/94	(1)
First Division Shield Winners	:	1993/94	(1)
League of Ireland Shield	:	Runners-up 1939/40	
Dublin City Cup Winners	:	1936/37	(1)
Blaxnit Cup	:	Runners-up 1969/70	

League Career:

Elected 1934 with Waterford. Resigned end 1939/40. Re-admitted 1948 with Transport. Excluded end 1961/62 with Transport. Re-admitted 1963 with Drogheda. Re-elected end 1957/58, 1960/61, 1967/68, 1971/72, 1973/74, 1974/75, 1983/84, 1988/89 (8). Relegated end 1984/85. Promoted end 1985/86. Relegated end 1987/88. Promoted end 1989/90. Relegated end 1992/93. Promoted end 1993/94.

European Appearances: 2

Champions Cup:	1977/78	v	Red Star Belgrade	0 - 3, 0 - 3
Cup Winners Cup	1983/84	v	Valkeakosken Haka	0 - 1, 0 - 3

Players Capped (R.O.I.): 1

Paddy Monahan (2) v Switzerland (A) 05 May 1935
              v Germany   (A) 08 May 1935

Record League Victory:

Home	:	9 - 0	v	Dolphin	20 Dec. 1936
Away	:	6 - 1	v	Shamrock Rovers	27 Dec. 1936

Record League Defeat:

Home	:	2 - 9	v	Cork Celtic	04 Dec. 1960
Away	:	0 - 9	v	Waterford	25 Feb. 1968

Most League Goals:
(Match) 5: W.R."Dixie"" Dean v Waterford 7-1 (H) 19 Mar. 1939
(Season) 19: Harry Litherland 1936/37
(Career) 85: Johnny Armstrong 1951/52 to 1963/64

Points in Season:
Most	:	39	1976/77	(26 games)
		50**	1993/94	(27 games)
	:	62*	1981/82	(30 games)
Least	:	05	1961/62	(22 games)

Goals Scored in Season:
Most	:	68	1936/37	(22 games)
Least	:	16	1992/93	(32 games)

League Appearances 1993/94:
27 Mark McLean, 26 Declan Boyle, Johnny Kenny, 24 Gavin Dykes, 22+2 Eddie Annand, 23 Willie McStay, 21+2 Gerry Carr, 20+2 Martin McDonnell, 21 Will Hastie, 17+2 David Reid, 12+6 Ian Lynch, 14+3 Padraig Moran, 14+1 Gerry Kelly, 5+7 Pierce Devanney, 11 Ger Houlahan, 8 Ricardo Gabbiadini, 4 Robert Spence, 2 Calum Campbell, 0+2 Trevor Scanlan, 0+1 John Lynch, David McDermott, Aidan Rooney.
Players Used: 22

League Goalscorers 1993/94:
10 Eddie Annand, 8 Johnny Kenny, 7 Ger Houlahan, 4 Padraig Moran, 3 Will Hastie, 2 Pierce Devanney, Ricardo Gabbiadini, 1 Declan Boyle, Gerry Carr, Gavin Dykes, Gerry Kelly, David Reid, og.
Total: 42

That winning feeling ...
Goalscorer Gerry Carr celebrates Sligo's F.A.I. Cup win over Derry City (The Star)

Sligo Rovers 1993/94

Date	V	Opposition	Score	Pos	1	2	3	4	5	6	7	8	9	10	11	12	13
19 Sep	A	Home Farm	1-0		McLean	McSlay	LLynch	Boyle	Dykes[1]	Reid	Kenny	Hastie	Moran	Annand	Houlahan	Devanney[1]	
26 Sep	H	St. James's Gate	1-1	4th	McLean	McSlay	LLynch	Kelly	Dykes	Reid	Kenny	Hastie	Moran[1]	Annand	Houlahan[.]	Devanney	
3 Oct	A	Waterford United	1-2	5th	McLean	Boyle	LLynch	Kelly[*]	Dykes	Reid	Kenny	Hastie	Moran	Annand	Devanney[#1]	Carr	
10 Oct	A	Longford Town	1-1	6th	McLean	Carr	LLynch	Boy,e	Dykes	Reid	Kenny	Hastie	Moran[1]	Annand	Devanney[*]	McDonnell	
17 Oct	A	Finn Harps	1-0	4th	McLean	McSlay	McDonnell	Boyle	Dykes	Reid	Kenny	Hastie	Moran[*]	Annand	Carr	Devanney[1]	
24 Oct	H	Kilkenny City	0-1	5th	McLean	McSlay	McDonnell	Boyle	Dykes	Reid[*]	Kenny	Hastie[*]	Moran	Annand[1]	Carr	Annand	
31 Oct	A	Athlone Town	1-2	7th	McLean	McSlay	McDonnell	Boyle	Dykes	Reid[*]	Kenny	Hastie	Moran[1]	Devanney	Carr	Devanney	
7 Nov	H	Bray Wanderers	1-1	5th	McLean	McSlay	McDonnell	Boyle	Dykes	Devanney	Kenny	Hastie[*]	Moran[1]	Annand[1]	Carr	LLynch	
14 Nov	A	U.C.D.	1-1	6th	McLean	McSlay[.]	McDonnell	Boyle	Dykes	LLynch	Kenny	Hastie	Moran	Annand	Carr[1]	Devanney	
21 Nov	H	U.C.D.	1-1	7th	McLean	McSlay[*]	McDonnell	Boyle	Dykes	Devanney	Kenny	Moran	Annand[*1]	Annand	Carr	Red	
26 Nov	H	Home Farm	4-0	4th	McLean	McSlay	McDonnell[*]	Boyle	Dykes	Reid[1]	Kenny[1]	Moran	Annand[1]	Carr	LLynch		
5 Dec	A	St. James's Gate	0-0	5th	McLean	McSlay	McDonnell	Boyle	Dykes	Hastie[#]	Kenny	Houlahan[1]	Moran[*1]	Annand[2]	Carr	Devanney	Kelly
11 Dec	A	Waterford United	4-1	3rd	McLean	McSlay	LLynch	Boyle	Dykes	Hastie	Kenny	Houlahan	Moran	Annand[1]	Carr	McDonnell	
19 Dec	H	Longford Town	0-0	3rd	McLean	McSlay	LLynch	Boyle	Dykes	Hastie	Kenny	Houlahan[2]	Red[*]	Annand[1]	Carr	Devanney	Sanlon
26 Dec	A	Finn Harps	4-1	2nd	McLean	McSlay	McDonnell	Eoyle	Kelly	Hastie[1#2]	Kenny[2]	LLynch	Moran[#]	Annand[1]	Carr	Sanlon	Carr
2 Jan	A	Kilkenny City	4-1	2nd	McLean	McSlay[*]	McDonnell	Boyle	Dykes	Hastie	Kenny[2]	Houlahan	Red	Annand	Kelly[*1]	Moran	
8 Jan	H	Athlone Town	2-2	3rd	McLean	Reid	McDonnell	Eoyle	Dykes	Reid[*]	Kenny	Houlahan[#3]	Carr	Campbell	Kelly	J.Lynch	Rooney
16 Jan	A	Bray Wanderers	3-0	2nd	McLean	McSlay	McDonnell	Boyle	Dykes	Reid[*]	Kenny	LLynch	Annand[1]	Kelly	Moran		
23 Jan	H	Home Farm	1-0	2nd	McLean	McSlay	McDonnell	Boyle	Dykes	Hastie[*]	Kenny[2]	Campbell	Annand[1]	Kelly	LLynch		
29 Jan	H	St. James's Gate	3-1	2nd	Carr	McDonnell	Boyle	Dykes	Hastie	Kenny[2]	Spence[#]	Gabbiadini	Annand[1]	Kelly			
13 Feb	A	Waterford United	1-0	1st	McLean	McSlay	McDonnell	Boyle	Dykes	Hastie	Kelly[.]	Spence[#]	Gabbiadini	Annand[1]	Carr		
19 Feb	H	Longford Town	1-0	1st	McLean	McSlay	McDonnell	Boyle	Dykes	Hastie	Kenny	Kelly	Gabbiadini	Annand[1]	Carr	Red	LLynch
5 Mar	H	Finn Harps	0-2	2nd	McLean	McSlay	McDonnell	Boyle	Red[#]	Hastie	Kenny[2]	Kelly	Gabbiadini	Annand	Carr	LLynch	
12 Mar	H	Kilkenny City	3-0	1st	McLean	McSlay	McDonnell	Boyle[1]	Dykes	Hastie	Kenny[2]	Kelly	Gabbiadini	Spence[*]	Carr	McDermott	LLynch
16 Mar	A	Athlone Town	2-0	1st	McLean	McSlay	McDonnell[*]	Boyle	Red	Hastie	Kenny	Kelly	Gabbiadini	Houlahan	Carr	Annand	
26 Mar	H	Bray Wanderers	1-0	1st	McLean	McSlay	LLynch[*]	Boyle	Dykes	Red	Kenny	Kelly	Gabbiadini[1]	Annand[*]	Carr	Annand[1]	
2 Apr	A	U.C.D.	0-1	1st	McLean	McSlay	McDonnell[*]	Boyle	Dykes	Red[*]	Kenny	Kelly[#]	Gabbiadini	Annand	Carr	Moran	LLynch

Note: LLynch = Ian Lynch; J. Lynch = John Lynch

65

University College Dublin   First Div.

Founded: 1895
Home: Belfield Park, Stillorgan, Dublin 4.
Nickname: "The Students"
Colours: Navy blue shirts and shorts, sky blue trim
2nd Colours: St. Patrick's blue & white striped shirts, sky blue shorts
Manager: Theo Dunne   Succeeded: Tony O'Neill (Jul. 1994)
President: Michael McNulty
Chairman: Gerry Horkan
General Manager: Dr. Tony O'Neill
Secretary: Brendan Dillon, 184 Stillorgan Road, Donnybrook, Dublin 4.
           Tel. Home: (01) 2601155; Office: (01) 2960666; Fax. (01) 2960982

Honours/Best Performances:

Championship	:	4th 1984/85	
F.A.I. Cup Winners	:	1984	(1)
League Cup	:	Yet to reach quarter-finals.	
Leinster Cup Winners	:	1980/81	(1)
First Division	:	Runners-up 1988/89	
League of Ireland Shield	:	Runners-up 1983/84	

League Career:
Elected 1979 in place of Cork Celtic. Re-elected end 1979/80, 1982/83 (2). Relegated end 1985/86. Promoted end 1988/89. Relegated end 1989/90. First Division 1990/91 to date.

European Appearances: 1
Cup Winners Cup: 1984/85   v   Everton   0 - 0, 0 - 1

Record League Victory:
Home   :   7 - 1   v   Kilkenny City   28 Nov. 1993
Away: 5 - 1   v   St. James's Gate   02 Dec. 1990

Record League Defeat:
Home   :   0 - 7   v   Limerick United   23 Dec. 1979
Away   :   1 - 7   v   Shamrock Rovers   13 Apr. 1980

Most League Goals
(Match)   4:   David Cassidy v Shelbourne 5-1 (H) 18 Nov. 1979
(Season) 13:   Darren O'Brien 1993/94
(Career) 46:   Darren O'Brien 1986/87 - 1993/94

Points in Season:
Most	:	38	1984/85	(30 games)
		40 **	1993/94	(27 games)
Least	:	08	1985/86	(22 games)

Goals Scored in Season:
Most	:	41	1984/85	(30 games)
Least	:	19	1985/86	(22 games)

League Appearances 1993/94:
27 Seamus Kelly, Packie Lynch, Michael O'Byrne, Terry Palmer, Jonathan Treacy, 26 Conor Timmons, 25+1 Darren O'Brien, 22 Jason Colwell, 21 Ciaran Kavanagh, 19+1 Robert Griffin, 16 Declan Fitzgerald, 15+1 Robert Keogh, 12+2 Paul Burton, 2+6 Andy Myler, 2+4 John Gibbons, 0+2 Stafford Quaid, 1 Tony McDonnell, Barra Sheridan, 0+1 Fergal Coleman.
Players Used: 19

League Goalscorers 1993/94:
13 Darren O'Brien, 6 Michael O'Byrne, 4 Jason Colwell, Robert Griffin, Ciaran Kavanagh, 1 Declan Fitzgerald, John Gibbons, Robert Keogh, Packie Lynch, Andy Myler, Terry Palmer
Total: 37

All time League of Ireland goalscorers 1979 - 1994
46 Darren O'Brien, 27 Paul Cullen, 25 Martin Moran, 22 Robert Griffin, Ken O'Doherty, 21 David Cassidy, 20 Mark McKenna, 17 Dave Tilson, 13 Peter Hanrahan, 11 Joe Hanrahan, Michael Kavanagh, 10 Shane Leonard, Brendan Murphy, 9 Jason Colwell, Ciaran Kavanagh, David Norman, Aidan Reynolds, 8 John Cullen, Gary O'Sullivan, 7 Robbie Lawlor, Martin O'Sullivan, 6 Ralston Dunlop, Robbie Gaffney, Patrick Lynch, Michael O'Byrne, 5 Brent Barling, Eugene Davis, Keith Duignam, Paul Hughes, Zoltan Istvan, Donal Murphy, Ultan McCabe, Connor Timmons, 4 Ian Murray, 3 Colm Begley, Paul Caffrey, Ciáran Duffy, Michael Giles, Kevin Henry, Tony McCarthy, Paul McGovern, Sammy Saundh, 2 Peter Burke, Tom Burke, Paul Burton, Dave Cowhie, Fintan Drury, Pádraig Gallagher, Séan Nolan, Larry O'Gara, Paul Roche, Jonathan Treacy, Pierce Walsh, 1 Pat Cowhie, Kieron Deeney, Richard Earle, Declan Fitzgerald, John Gibbons, Paul Glennon, Paul Hale, Stephen Holt, Timothy Hyland, Dermot Keely, Robert Keogh, Janos Lenart, Simon Lysaght, Pat McKeown, Andy Myler, Terry Palmer, Peter Prendergast, Gerry Scully, Nick Skelly, George Strachan, Brian Swords, Bela Tettamanti, Zolt Torok.
8 Opponents:
Total: **436**   Games: **407**   Average per game: **1.07**

A pressing matter!
Charlton faces the media   (EOH)

68 U.C.D. 1993/94

Date	V	Opposition	Score	Pos	1	2	3	4	5	6	7	8	9	10	11	12	13
19 Sep	A	Kilkenny City	2-3	-	Kelly	Lynch	Treacy	Palmer	Timmons	O'Byrne	Kavanagh[1]	O'Brien[1]	Griffin[1]	Colwell	Fitzgerald		
26 Sep	H	Finn Harps	4-1	5th	Kelly	Lynch	Treacy	Palmer	Timmons	O'Byrne[1]	Kavanagh[1]	O'Brien[2]	Griffin[#]	Colwell	Fitzgerald[*]	Quaid	Gibbons
3 Oct	H	Athlone Town	0-1	7th	Kelly	Lynch	Treacy	Palmer	Timmons	O'Byrne	Kavanagh	O'Brien	Griffin	Colwell	Fitzgerald[#]	Burton	Gibbons
10 Oct	A	Bray Wanderers	2-0	4th	Kelly	Lynch	Treacy	Palmer	Timmons	O'Byrne[1]	Kavanagh	O'Brien[2]	Griffin	Colwell	Fitzgerald		
17 Oct	H	Home Farm	3-1	1st	Kelly	Lynch	Treacy	Palmer	Timmons	O'Byrne[1]	Kavanagh[1]	O'Brien[2]	Griffin	Colwell	Fitzgerald		
24 Oct	A	Waterford United	1-1	1st	Kelly	Lynch	Treacy	Palmer	Timmons	O'Byrne	Burton	O'Brien	Griffin	Colwell[1]	Fitzgerald	Burton	
31 Oct	A	St James's Gate	0-0	2nd	Kelly	Lynch	Treacy	Palmer	Timmons	O'Byrne	Burton	O'Brien	Griffin[*]	Colwell	Fitzgerald		
7 Nov	A	Longford Town	2-1	1st	Kelly	Lynch	Treacy	Palmer	Timmons	O'Byrne	Burton	O'Brien[2]	Sheridan[*]	Colwell	Fitzgerald	Quaid	
14 Nov	H	Sligo Rovers	1-1	1st	Kelly	Lynch	Treacy	Palmer[1]	Timmons	O'Byrne	Burton	O'Brien[1]	Keogh[1]	Colwell	Fitzgerald	Gibbons	
21 Nov	A	Kilkenny City	1-1	2nd	Kelly	Lynch	Treacy	Palmer	Timmons	O'Byrne[2]	Burton	O'Brien[2]	Keogh[1]	Colwell[1]	Fitzgerald[1]		
28 Nov	H	Finn Harps	7-1	2nd	Kelly	Lynch	Treacy	Palmer	Timmons	O'Byrne	Burton	O'Brien	Keogh	Colwell	Fitzgerald		
5 Dec	A	Athlone Town	0-0	2nd	Kelly	Lynch	Treacy	Palmer	Timmons	O'Byrne	Burton[#]	O'Brien[1]	Kavanagh	Colwell	Fitzgerald	Gibbons	Coleman
12 Dec	H	Bray Wanderers	0-2	2nd	Kelly	Lynch	Treacy	Palmer	Timmons	O'Byrne	Keogh	O'Brien[1]	Kavanagh	Colwell	Fitzgerald[1]	Griffin	
19 Dec	A	Home Farm	1-2	3rd	Kelly	Lynch	Treacy	Palmer	Timmons	O'Byrne	Keogh	O'Brien	Kavanagh	Colwell	Griffin		
26 Dec	A	Waterford United	1-0	3rd	Kelly	Lynch[1]	Treacy	Palmer	Timmons	O'Byrne	Keogh	O'Brien	Kavanagh	Colwell	Griffin[1]		
2 Jan	H	St James's Gate	2-0	2nd	Kelly	Lynch[1]	Treacy	Palmer	Timmons	O'Byrne	Keogh	O'Brien	Kavanagh	Colwell	Griffin[*1]	Myler	
9 Jan	H	Longford Town	1-2	3rd	Kelly	Lynch	Treacy	Palmer	Timmons	O'Byrne	Keogh	O'Brien	Kavanagh	Colwell[1]	Griffin[*]	Myler	
16 Jan	A	Kilkenny City	1-1	3rd	Kelly	Lynch	Treacy	Palmer	Timmons	O'Byrne	Keogh	O'Brien	Kavanagh	Colwell	Griffin[*]		
23 Jan	H	Finn Harps	2-3	3rd	Kelly	Lynch	Treacy	Palmer	Timmons	O'Byrne	Keogh	O'Brien	Kavanagh[1]	Colwell[1]	Griffin[*]	Myler	
30 Jan	H	Athlone Town	0-0	4th	Kelly	Lynch	Treacy	Palmer	Timmons	O'Byrne[*#]	Burton	O'Brien[*]	Kavanagh	Colwell[*]	Griffin	Myler	Myler
13 Feb	H	Home Farm	0-0	4th	Kelly	Lynch	Treacy	Palmer	Timmons	O'Byrne[1]	Burton	O'Brien	Kavanagh	Colwell	Griffin[1]	Keogh	
6 Mar	A	Waterford United	3-0	4th	Kelly	Lynch	Treacy	Palmer	Timmons	O'Byrne	Keogh	Gibbons[1]	Kavanagh	Fitzgerald[*]	Griffin[1]		
17 Mar	A	St James's Gate	0-0	4th	Kelly	Lynch	Treacy	Palmer	Timmons	O'Byrne	Keogh	Gibbons[#]	Kavanagh[1]	Fitzgerald[*]	Griffin	O'Brien	Myler
27 Mar	A	Longford Town	2-1	4th	Kelly	Lynch	Treacy	Palmer	McDonnell	O'Byrne	Keogh	O'Brien	Kavanagh[1]	Burton	Myler[1]		
31 Mar	A	Bray Wanderers	0-1	4th	Kelly	Lynch	Treacy	Palmer	Timmons	O'Byrne	Keogh	O'Brien	Kavanagh	Burton	Myler		
2 Apr	H	Sligo Rovers	1-0	4th	Kelly	Lynch	Treacy	Palmer	Timmons	O'Byrne	Keogh	O'Brien[1]	Kavanagh	Burton	Griffin		

Waterford United   First Div.

Founded: 1982
Ground: **Waterford Regional Sports Centre, Cork Road, Waterford.**
Previous Ground: Kilcohan Park (1982/83 - 1992/93)
Nickname: "The Blues"
Colours: **Blue & white striped shirts, white shorts**
2nd Colours: All White with Blue trim
Manager: **Johnny Matthews**   Succeeded: Brendan Ormsby (Jul. 1994)
Asst. Manager: Dave Kirby
Reserve Team Manager: Shamie Coad
Physio: Peter Corcoran
Chairman: Bertie Rogers
Secretary: Willie Moran, 49 Roselawn, Tramore, Co. Waterford.
    Tel. Home: (051) 381749; Office: (051) 381036; Fax. (051) 90334

Honours/Best Performances:

Championship	:	4th 1986/87	
F.A.I. Cup	:	Final 1986	
League Cup winners	:	1984/85	(1)
First Division winners	:	1989/90	(1)
First Division Shield	:	Finalists 1993/94	
Munster Cup winners	:	1985/86, 1986/87	(2)

League Career:
Elected 1982, replacing Waterford F.C. Relegated end 1988/89. Promoted end 1989/90. Relegated end 1990/91 Promoted end 1991/92. Relegated end 1992/93.

European Appearances: 1
Cup Winners Cup: 1986/87   v   Bordeaux   1 - 2, 0 - 4

Record League Victory:
Home : 8 - 1 v   Longford Town   12 Nov. 1989
Away : 7 - 1 v   Sligo Rovers   13 Sep. 1987

Record League Defeat:
Home : 0 - 5 v   Bohemians   07 Nov. 1982
                v   St. Patrick's Athletic 09 Sep. 1990
Away : 0 - 6 v   Bohemians   30 Aug. 1992
                v   Shelbourne   26 Dec. 1992

Most League Goals:
(Match) 3: Pat Morley   v Finn Harps   4-1 (A) 25 Nov. 1984
             Martin Reid   v Athlone Town   3-2 (H) 29 Dec. 1985
             Michael Bennett   v Sligo Rovers   7-1 (A) 13 Sep. 1987
             Kevin Kelly   v Cobh Ramblers   3-1 (A) 29 Mar. 1992
             Paul Stokes   v Home Farm   4-2 (H) 21 Nov. 1994
             Darren Lonergan   v Finn Harps   6-0 (H) 28 Nov. 1994
(Season) 16: Pascal Keane 1992/93
(Career) 49: Michael Bennett 1982/83 - 1987/88

Points in Season:
Most   :   37   1989/90   (27 games)
Least   :   17   1990/91   (33 games)

Goals Scored in Season:
Most   :   58   1989/90   (27 games)
Least   :   21   1988/89   (33 games)

League Appearances 1993/94:
26 Alan Reynolds, 23 Brendan Ormsby, 22 Peter Crowley, 20+1 Darren Lonergan, 19+2 Clem Fanning, 14+7 Jimmy Barden, 16+3 Brian Arrigan, 17 Alan Barry, 13+4 Christy O'Halloran, 15 Brian Barry, 13 Dominique Wouters, 11+2 Paul Stokes, 10+3 Pascal Keane, 9+4 John Lacey, 10+1 Mark Browne, Stephen Hall, 8 Gary Kelly, 3+4 Michael Butler, 4+2 Brian Farrell, 3+3 Paul Devereaux, 4+1 Alan Kelly, Derek O'Connor, 4 Colm Fanning, Robert Markovac, 3 Billy Askew, Paul Flynn, Andrew Kersham, Umberto Oliva, 2+1 Keith Greene, 0+2 Richie Hale, 1 Gerry Norris, 0+1 Derek Galbert.
Players Used: 32

League Goalscorers 1993/94:
7 Paul Stokes, 4 Darren Lonergan, 3 Brian Arrigan, Mark Browne, Christy O'Halloran, 2 Clem Fanning, Brendan Ormsby, og's, 1 Jimmy Barden, Alan Barry, Keith Greene, Pascal Keane, John Lacey, Alan Reynolds.
Total: 32

All time League of Ireland goalscorers 1982 - 1994
48 Michael Bennett, 43 Martin Reid, 35 Paschal Keane, 24 Vinny McCarthy, 19 Pat Morley, 18 Kevin Kelly, 14 Paul Cashin, 13 Terry Kearns, Derek O'Connor, 10 Derek Grace, 9 Jimmy Browne, 8 Kevin Power, Mick Madigan, 7 Eamonn Cody, Jimmy Donnelly, Chris Jones, Paddy Joyce, Paul Stokes, 6 Brian Arrigan, Pat Arrigan, Frank Hayes, Darran Lonergan, 5 Alan Barry, Brian Barry, Mark Browne, Richie Hale, Johnny Matthews, 4 Paschal Cashin, Timmy Dixon, 3 Jim Brown, John Burns, Greg Hayes, Mick Jones, Tony Macken, Pat Madigan, Christy O'Halloran, Ken O'Neill, 2 Matthew Carr, Clem Fanning, Tommy Fitzgerald, Kieran McCabe, Kevin O'Halloran, Tony O'Kelly, Brendan Ormsby, Kieran O'Toole, John 'Tramore' Power, 1 Jimmy Barden, Noel Bollard, Ciao Brazil, Duncan Burns, Paul Cleary, Paul Deveraux, Keith Greene, Andy King, Paul Kirkham, John Lacey, Paul McGee, Jim McMenamim, George Mellerick, Ger O'Mahony, Derek O'Neill, Rick O'Neill, Phillip O'Regan, Alan Reynolds, Paul Ryan, Brendan Storan, Terence Walsh. 11 Opponents
Total: **428**   Games: **342**   Average per game: **1.25**

Waterford United 1993/94

Date	V	Opposition	Score	Pos	1	2	3	4	5	6	7	8	9	10	11	12	13
19 Sep	A	Finn Harps	0-2	.	Flynn	Cl. Fanning	Lonergan	Reynolds	A. Barry	Artigan	Crowley#	Farrell	Norris	Hall*	Hale	A. Kelly
26 Sep	H	Longford Town	2-2	8th	G. Kelly	B. Barry	Lonergan	Reynolds	A. Barry	Ormsby	Artigan'	Crowley#	Farrell	O'Halloran'	Hall*	Cl. Fanning
3 Oct	H	Sligo Rovers	2-1	6th	G. Kelly	B. Barry#	Lonergan	Reynolds#	A. Barry	Ormsby	Artigan	Crowley	Farrell	O'Halloran'	Barden	Devereaux
10 Oct	A	St. James's Gate	0-0	7th	G. Kelly	B. Barry	Lonergan	Reynolds	A. Barry	Ormsby	Artigan	Crowley	Farrell	O'Halloran'	Oliva	Barden
17 Oct	A	Kilkenny City	2-2	7th	G. Kelly	B. Barry	Lonergan	Reynolds	A. Barry	Ormsby	Crowley'	Devereaux	Keane	O'Halloran'	Oliva*	Lacey
24 Oct	H	U.C.D.	1-1	7th	G. Kelly	Lacey*	Lonergan	Reynolds	A. Barry	Ormsby	Crowley#	Reynolds	Browne'	O'Halloran'	Keane	Farrell
31 Oct	A	Bray Wanderers	1-1	6th	G. Kelly	Lacey*	Lonergan	Reynolds	A. Barry	Ormsby	Crowley	Reynolds	Browne	O'Halloran'	Stokes'	Devereaux
7 Nov	H	Athlone Town	1-1	7th	G. Kelly	B. Barry*	Cl. Fanning	Reynolds	A. Barry	Ormsby	Crowley	Co. Fanning#	Barden	O'Halloran	Stokes'	
14 Nov	H	Home Farm	0-3	9th	B. Barry#	Hall	Cl. Fanning	Reynolds#1	A. Barry	Lonergan	Crowley	Reynolds*	Browne'	O'Halloran	Stokes'	Artigan
21 Nov	A	Home Farm	4-2	6th	Wouters	Hall	Cl. Fanning	Reynolds	A. Barry	Lonergan	Crowley	Reynolds*	Barden*	O'Halloran	Stokes'	Butler
28 Nov	H	Finn Harps	6-0	3rd	Wouters	Ormsby	Cl. Fanning	Reynolds	A. Barry#1	Artigan#1	Crowley	Barden*	Barden*	O'Halloran	Stokes2	Lacey'
5 Dec	A	Longford Town	1-2	4th	Wouters	Ormsby	Cl. Fanning	Reynolds	A. Barry'	Artigan	Crowley	Barden'	Barden*	O'Halloran	Stokes*	Hale
11 Dec	A	Sligo Rovers	1-4	7th	Wouters	Ormsby'	Cl. Fanning	Reynolds	A. Barry	Artigan	Lonergan	Hall*	Barden	Keane	Lacey	Stokes
19 Dec	H	St. James's Gate	3-1	5th	Wouters	Ormsby	B. Barry	Reynolds	A. Barry	Artigan	Lonergan	O'Halloran'	Browne#1	Keane*	Stokes'	Hall*
26 Dec	H	Kilkenny City	0-0	5th	Wouters	Ormsby	B. Barry*	Reynolds	A. Barry	Artigan	Lonergan	O'Halloran'	Browne	Keane	Lacey'	Barden
2 Jan	A	U.C.D.	0-1	6th	Wouters	Ormsby'	Butler	Reynolds	A. Barry	Butler	Co. Fanning	Barden'	Stokes	Lacey'	Cl. Fanning	
5 Jan	A	Athlone Town	2-2	6th	Wouters	Ormsby1	Hall	Reynolds	Crowley	Browne	Lonergan	Barden1	Stokes	Keane	Cl. Fanning1	Keane
23 Jan	A	Finn Harps	1-1	7th	Wouters	Ormsby	Hall	Reynolds	Crowley	Artigan	Co. Fanning#	Barden	Stokes	Keane	Cl. Fanning	Lonergan
30 Jan	H	Longford Town	0-0	7th	Ormsby	Lonergan	Askew	Reynolds	Crowley	Markovac	Co. Fanning	Barden'	Keane	Cl. Fanning	Butler	Barden
13 Feb	H	Sligo Rovers	0-1	8th	Ormsby	Lonergar	Askew	Reynolds*	Crowley	Markovac	Reynolds'	Barden	Stokes	Keane'	Cl. Fanning	Browne
20 Feb	A	St. James's Gate	1-1	8th	Ormsby	Lonergan	Hall	Reynolds	Crowley	Markovac	Reynolds'	Barden	Keane'	Reynolds'	Cl. Fanning	O'Connor
6 Mar	A	Kilkenny City	1-0	8th	Ormsby	Lonergan1	O'Connor*	Reynolds	Crowley	Hall	Keane	Barden	Browne'	O'Halloran1	Galbert	Artigan
13 Mar	H	U.C.D.	0-3	8th	Flynn	Ormsby	O'Connor	Reynolds	Crowley	Keane	Artigan'	Barden	Browne	Devereaux	Devereaux	Lacey
17 Mar	A	Bray Wanderers	0-0	8th	Flynn	Cl. Fanning	A. Kelly	Reynolds	Crowley	B. Barry	Artigan	Reynolds	Barden	O'Halloran	O'Halloran	Farrell
20 Mar	H	Bray Wanderers	0-0	8th	Flynn	Cl. Fanning	A. Kelly	O'Connor'	Crowley	B. Barry	Artigan*	Reynolds	Barden	O'Halloran	Greene	Butler
27 Mar	H	Athlone Town	0-1	8th	Kersham	Cl. Fanning	A. Kelly	O'Connor	Crowley	B. Barry	Markovac*	Reynolds#	Greene	Lacey'	O'Halloran	Artigan
2 Apr	A	Home Farm	3-1	7th	Kersham	Cl. Fanning'	A. Kelly	Ormsby	Crowley	B. Barry	Barden	Reynolds#	Reynolds	Lacey	Barden	Butler

Note: Cl.Fanning = Clem Fanning; Co.Fanning = Colm Fanning

The Lilywhites ...
Dundalk F.C. line up for the new season (R.N.)

ARE YOU PICKING UP *SPORT* ON

729MW / 89FM ?

RTE RADIO CORK

* WEEKEND SPORT EACH SATURDAY & SUNDAY FROM 2-5PM
* REGULAR SPORTS BULLETINS, PROFILES, INTERVIEWS & PREVIEWS
* ALSO, LIVE COVERAGE OF LOCAL & NATIONAL SPORTING EVENTS

HOME AND AWAY - YOU'RE A WINNER WITH

RTE RADIO CORK

"Where They Played"
(A summary of League of Ireland grounds)
1921-22 to 1993-94

Abbeycartron, Longford	Longford Town	1984/85 to 1992/93	(9)
Anglesea Road, Dublin	Dublin United	1922/23	(1)
	Shelbourne United	1922/23	(1)
Athletic Grounds, Dundalk	Dundalk	1926/27 to 1935/36	(10)
Ballinlough, Cork	Fordsons	1924/25 to 1928/29	(5)
Ballygowan Park/Demesne, Newcastlewest Co. Limerick	Newcastle United/ Newcastlewest	1985/86 to 1989/90	(5)
Beech Hill, Dublin	Dublin United	1921/22	(1)
Belfield, Dublin	U.C.D.	1979/80 to Date	(15)
Belgium Park, Monaghan	Monaghan United	1985/86 to 1987/88	(3)
Bellevue Lodge, Dublin	Olympia	1921/22	(1)
Bishopstown, Cork	Cork City	1992/93 to Date	(2)
Brandywell, Derry	Derry City	1985/86 to Date	(9)
Buckley Park, Kilkenny	Emfa/Kilkenny City	1985/86 to Date	(9)
Carlisle Grounds, Bray	Bray Unknowns	1929/30 to 1942/43	(14)
	Transport	1948/49 to 1950/51	(3)
	Bray Wanderers	1985/86 to Date	(9)
Chalgrove Terrace, Dublin	Brooklyn	1923/24 to 1924/25	(2)
Chapelizod, Dublin	St. Patrick's Athletic	1954/55 to 1955/56	(2)
Claremont Road, Dublin	Y.M.C.A.	1921/22	(1)
Crowley Park, Galway	Galway United (J)	1993/94	(1)
Dalymount Park, Dublin	Bohemians	1921/22 to Date	(73)
	Shelbourne	1951/52 to 1953/54 & 1974/75	(4)
	St. Patrick's Athletic	1956/57 to 1959/60	(4)
	Shamrock Rovers	1988/89 to 1989/90	(2)
Dolphin Park, Dublin	Dolphin (A)	1930/31 to 1931/32 & 1934/35 to 1936/37	(5)
Finn Park, Ballybofey	Finn Harps	1969/70 to Date	(25)
Flower Lodge, Cork	Cork Hibernians	1962/63 to 1975/76	(14)
	Cork Celtic (B)	1969/70 to 1970/71 & 1978/79	(3)
	Albert Rvs./C. Alberts /Cork United	1976/77 to 1979/80	(4)
	Cork City	1984/85 to 1985/86	(2)
Gortakeegan, Monaghan	Monaghan United	1988/89 to Date	(5)
Green Lanes, Dublin	Brideville (C)	1939/40	(1)
Greyhound Park, Cork	Cork Bohemians (D)	1932/33 to 1933/34	(2)
Greyhound Stadium, Thurles	Thurles Town	1977/78 to 1981/82	(5)

Harolds Cross, Dublin	Brideville	(G)	1929/30	
		(C)	1930/31 to 1931/32 & 1935/36 to 1942/43	(11)
	Dolphin		1932/33 to 1933/34	(2)
	Transport		1951/52 to 1961/62	(11)
	Shelbourne		1975/76 to 1976/77 & 1982/83 to 1988/89	(9)
	St. Patrick's Athletic	(H)	1989/90 to 1993/94	(5)
Irishtown, Dublin	Shelbourne		1955/56	(1)
Iveagh Grounds, Dublin	St. James's Gate		1928/29 to 1943/44 & 1990/91 to Date	(20)
Kilcohan Park, Waterford	Waterford		1930/31 to 1931.32 1934/35 to 1940/41 1945/46 to 1981/82	(46)
	Waterford United		1982/83 to 1992/93	(11)
Lourdes Stadium, Drogheda	Drogheda/Drogheda Utd		1963/64 to 1978/79	(16)
Mardyke, Cork	Fordsons		1929/30	(1)
	Cork/Cork City	(E)	1930/31 to 1939/40	(10)
	Cork United	(E)	1939/40 to 1947/48	(9)
	Cork Athletic		1948/49 to 1956/57	(9)
	Evergreen Utd/ Cork Celtic	(F)	1953/54 to 1958/59 & 1961/62	(7)
	Cork Hibernians		1957/58 to 1961/62	(5)
Markets Field, Limerick	Limerick/Limerick Utd		1937/38 to 1982/83	(46)
	Limerick City		1983/84	(1)
Milltown, Dublin	Shamrock Rovers		1922/23 to 1986/87	(65)
	Shelbourne Utd.		1923/24	(1)
	Reds Utd.		1935/36	(1)
	Shelbourne		1949/50 to 1950/51	(2)
	St. Patrick's Athletic		1951/52 to 1953/54	(3)
Oriel Park, Dundalk	Dundalk		1936/37 to Date	(58)
R.D.S., Dublin	Shamrock Rovers		1990/91 to Date	(4)
Ranelagh Grounds, Athlone	Athlone Town		1926/27 to 1927/28	(2)
Rathbane, Limerick	Limerick City/Limerick		1984/85 to Date	(10)
Rathmines, Park, Dublin	Rathmines Athletic		1922/23	(1)
Regional Sports Centre, Waterford	Waterford United		1993/94	(1)
Richmond, Hill, Dublin	Frankfort		1921/22	(1)
Richmond Park, Dublin	Brideville	(G)	1925/26 to 1929/30	(5)
	St. Patrick's Athletic	(H)	1960/61 to 1988/89 & 1993/94	(30)
Rutland Avenue, Dublin	Jacobs		1921/22 to 1931/32	(11)
St. Colmans Park, Cobh	Cobh Ramblers		1985/86 to Date	(9)

St. James Park, Dublin	St. James's Gate		1921/22 to 1927/28	(7)
St. Mels Park, Athlone	Athlone Town		1969/70 to Date	(25)
Shelbourne Park, Dublin	Shelbourne		1921/22 to 1933/34 & 1936/37 to 1948/49	(26)
Showgrounds, Sligo	Sligo Rovers		1934/35 to 1939/40 1948/49 to 1961/62 & 1963/64 to Date	(51)
Sportsground, Athlone	Athlone Town		1922/23 to 1925/26	(4)
Sportsground, Galway	Galway United	(J)	1993/94	(1)
Strand Road, Dublin	Pioneers		1922/23	(1)
Strokestown Road, Longford	Longford Town		1993/94	(1)
Terryland Park, Galway	Galway Rovers/ Galway United		1977/78 to 1992/93	(16)
The Thatch, Dublin	Midland Athletic		1922/23 to 1923/24	(2)
	Pioneers		1923/24 to 1925/26	(3)
Tolka Park, Dublin	Drumcondra		1928/29 to 1971/72	(44)
	Dolphin	(A)	1935/36 to 1936/37	(2)
	Shelbourne		1954/55 1956/57 to 1973/74 1977/78 to 1981/82 1989/90 to Date	(29)
	Home Farm		1972/73 to 1989/90	(18)
	Shamrock Rovers		1987/88	(1)
Turners Cross, Cork	Cork Bohemians	(D)	1933/34	(1)
	Evergreen Utd/ Cork Celtic	(B) (F)	1951/52 to 1968/69 & 1970/71 to 1977/78	(26)
	Cork United		1980/81 to 1981/82	(2)
	Cork City		1986/87 to 1991/92	(6)
United Park, Drogheda	Drogheda United		1979/80 to Date	(15)
Whitehall, Dublin	Home Farm		1990/91 to Date	(4)
Woodbrook, Dublin	Bray Unknowns		1924/25 to 1928/29	(5)

NOTES:

A In Season 1935/36 Dolphin played at both Dolphin Park and Tolka Park.
B In Season 1970/71 Cork Celtic played at both Flower Lodge and Turners Cross.
C In Season 1939/40 Brideville played at both Green Lanes and Harold's Cross.
D In Season 1933/34 Cork Bohemians played at both Greyhound Park and Turner's Cross.
E Cork United took over Cork City's remaining fixtures in February 1940.
F In Seasons 1953/54 , 1954/55, 1956/57 & 1957/58 Evergreen United played at both Mardyke and Turners Cross.
G In Season 1929/30 Brideville played at both Richmond Park and Harold's Cross.
H In season 1993/94 St. Patrick's Athletic played at both Harolds Cross and Richmond Park
J In season 1993/94 Galway United played at both Crowley Park and Sportsground.
* Many different grounds have been used for League of Ireland games over the years, some only once in a season for e.g. Harolds Cross for Galway United v Shelbourne 2 Apr 1994. This section lists only those grounds used by a club for a substantial part of any one season.

"COMINGS AND GOINGS"

In 1921 the very first 'Football League of the Irish Free State' began with eight Dublin based teams ... **Bohemians, Dublin United, Frankfort, Jacobs, Olympia, St. James's Gate, Shelbourne** and **Y.M.C.A.** In the intervening 73 years there have been many changes in personnel and quite a few name changes too. Below is a list of those happenings.

Year	In	Out
1922	Athlone Town, Midland Athletic, Pioneers, Rathmines Athletic, Shamrock Rovers, Shelbourne United	Frankfort, Y.M.C.A.
1923	Brooklyn	Dublin United, Olympia, Rathmines Athletic
1924	Bray Unknowns, Fordsons	Midland Athletic, Shelbourne United
1925	Brideville	Brooklyn
1926	Dundalk	Pioneers
1928	Drumcondra	Athlone Town
1930	Dolphin, Waterford, Cork	
1932	Cork Bohemians	Brideville, Jacobs, Waterford.
1934	Sligo Rovers, Waterford	Cork Bohemians, Shelbourne
1935	Brideville, Reds United	
1936	Shelbourne	Reds United
1937	Limerick	Dolphin
1938	Cork City	
1940	Cork United (1940)	Cork City (1938), Sligo Rovers,
1941		Waterford
1943		Bray Unknowns, Brideville
1944	Brideville	St. James's Gate
1945	Waterford	Brideville
1948	Cork Athletic, Sligo Rovers, Transport	Cork United (1940)
1951	Evergreen United, St. Patrick's Athletic	
1957	Cork Hibernians	Cork Athletic
1959	Cork Celtic *(Evergreen United)*	
1962		Sligo Rovers, Transport
1963	Drogheda, Sligo Rovers	
1969	Athlone Town, Finn Harps	
1972	Home Farm / Drumcondra	
1973	Home Farm *(H.F./Drumcondra)*	
1975	Drogheda United *(Drogheda)*	
1976	Albert Rovers	Cork Hibernians
1977	Galway Rovers, Thurles Town, Cork Albert, Cork Alberts *(Albert Rovers)*	
1979	U.C.D., Cork United (1979), *(Cork Alberts)* Limerick United *(Limerick)*	Cork Celtic

Year	In	Out
1981	Galway United *(Galway Rovers)*	
1982	Waterford United	Cork United (1979), Thurles Town, Waterford
1983	Limerick City	Limerick United
1984	Cork City, Longford Town	
1985	Bray Wanderers, Cobh Ramblers, Derry City, Emfa, Monaghan United, Newcastle United	
1986	Newcastlewest *(Newcastle United)*	
1989	Kilkenny City *(Emfa)*	
1990	St. James's Gate	Newcastlewest
1992	Limerick (1992) *(Limerick City)*	

Notes:
(1) Teams underlined indicate a change of name   (2) Teams *in italics* indicate the original name.

Happy Wanderers!
Bray Wanderers, one of the National League's most recent additions   (M.D.)

The International Review
incorporating Ireland at the World Cup Finals

Ireland, following a hugely successful 1992/93 campaign culminating in successive away victories in Albania, Latvia and Lithuania, began the new season within striking distance of a place in the World Cup finals in America. With just three games remaining for Charlton's men in this most exhausting of qualifying groups, realistically only three countries were left in contention for those two precious places in the U.S.A. Along with the Irish the other big players were Spain, improving all the time under new manager Clemente, and Denmark, still a huge threat, but as yet struggling to rediscover that European Championship winning form of two years previously. A point clear at the top and with home games to Lithuania and Spain yet to come, the odds did seem to favour Ireland, but not surprisingly perhaps, qualification was to prove a hard road in the end, a final nerve wracking shoot out in the boiling cauldron of Windsor Park, Belfast very nearly putting paid to the American dream.

Getting There
The opening game for Ireland came early, on September 8th, when Lithuania paid their first ever visit to Dublin. Despite their well deserved reputation for being the most potent of the so called 'weaker nations' in Group 3, Ireland's last game, in Vilnius earlier in the summer had yielded a comfortable victory. Expectations were high that this game too would prove a none too taxing task in advance of the visit of Spain to Lansdowne Road some five weeks later.
The Irish line-up showed just one change from that which took to the field in Lithuania, veteran Kevin Moran replacing Paul McGrath at the heart of the defence. Once again despite the rather modest quality of the opposition Lansdowne Road was packed to capacity.
Ireland began as if victory would ensure a qualification spot, forcing their opponents back with an early tidal wave of green shirted endeavour. Within four minutes of the start, this Irish 'blitzkrieg' was rewarded with the opening score, Steve Staunton's powerful cross being hammered to the net by the inrushing John Aldridge. It was a magnificent start, and Ireland continued the onslaught throughout a totally one-sided opening phase. The only real surprise was that it took until the 25th minute for a second goal to materialise. Having seen Kevin Moran's header from his corner kick cleared off the line, Denis Irwin whipped over the clearance for Alan Kernaghan, rising highest, to power a header past goalkeeper Stauce, his first ever strike for Ireland.
In the run-up to half time, numerous other chances went a begging for the home side as the Lithuanians continued to act in the supporting role.
What a contrast in the second period however, with the visitors, perhaps sensing Ireland's increasing frustration at failing to capitalise on a hatful of good scoring opportunities, began to put their own attacking game together, exposing some gaping holes in the centre of the Irish rearguard. Kernaghan in particular looked vulnerable, especially with the ball on the group, and a half of acute

disappointment for the home support saw the visitors waste the two best openings, Kirilovas and Sturmby the guilty parties.

With a little more luck on their side, it could have been so very different for Lithuania, but at least the main objective, a brace of points for Ireland, was realised. Charlton however fumed, publically criticising his players. *"That was our worst performance in a very long time. We won't get away with that type of thing against Spain next month."* How accurate those words would prove to be. Having comfortably defeated Albania in Tirana a fortnight prior to coming to Dublin, the Spaniards trailed Ireland by a mere two points whilst enjoying the advantage of a significantly better goal difference. A brace of points in this one would definitely see the Irish through, a single point would leave them in a very advantageous position indeed. As things turned out however, a superb Spanish performance, full of guile, craft, skill and muscle too, left the home side floundering in the wake of a devastating show of incisive counter attacking football. *"Spaniards in the works, Republics American dream turns to nightmare"* ran the Irish Independent headline. And a nightmare it was, as a fifteen minute period in the opening half saw Spain score three times without reply to numb the home support. It had been quite some time since anything even remotely like this had been witnessed at Lansdowne Road, and it wasn't a pleasant feeling. Afterwards, in the inevitable post match dissection, much was made of Ireland's tactical naivety, particularly the choice of a very conservative five-man midfield formation and Niall Quinn's impossible isolation up front. But little praise was reserved for Clemente, whose homework had been thorough and whose side, previously labelled as soft by Spanish standards, had played with great commitment.

The opening moments of the game gave little indication of the disasters about to befall the Irish who looked confident going forward. After just eight minutes, however, Ferrer quickly threw to centre forward Salinas who laid a lovely ball back for Caminero, and he fairly rifled a shot past Bonner. The roof caved in four minutes later, a long ball from Camaraso finding Salinas who exploited Kernaghan's immobility on the ground to squeeze the ball in from a narrow angle. With Moran forced to depart the scene through injury Ireland's bewilderment was plain for all to see. His replacement John Sheridan had an unfortunate introduction, inadvertently knocking an innocuous looking long ball into the path of Salinas, who again finished in style. Ireland were simply blown away by the Spanish hunger for success, the half time whistle could not come quickly enough.

Understandably the second half saw the visitors sitting back on a lead which they could hardly have imagined would be theirs before the game began. As a result Ireland's game recovered somewhat and fifteen minutes from the end a poor clearance fell to Sheridan who volleyed home to raise the spirits a little. We were not to know it then but that one moment would later prove crucial to Ireland's chances of a second successive World Cup finals appearance. With this defeat to Spain, the initiative in Group 3 had been lost in advance of the final game in Belfast, exactly the scenario that Republic supporters had hoped might be avoided. It was now imperative to get a result from this game though even a draw might not necessarily ensure qualification.

Northern Ireland, still smarting from their nil-three defeat in Dublin in March, needed no further incentive than to halt the Republic's march to the United States. In the highly charged and hostile atmosphere, sometimes bordering on the hysterical, which was Windsor Park on the night of November 17th every ounce of Charlton's side indomitable spirit was called on to survive and without, officially, a single supporter from south of the border to cheer them on. With Spain hosting Denmark on the same night in Seville, and the Republic and the Spanish now level on points one behind the Danes, it was always likely to prove a nailbiting climax. In the end having fallen behind to a goal worthy of winning any game, the Republic's salvation came from an unlikely source, substitute Alan McLoughlin, for so long confined to the fringes of the Irish set-up.

As might have been expected, it did not turn out to be a game for the purist. A dreadful first half almost totally devoid of constructive football, ground to an almost inevitable scoreless interval with the visitors having perhaps the better of the meagre chances which came. The second half was a great deal better with Ray Houghton and Roy Keane coming close early on. Then, just as news filtered through that Spain had taken the lead in Seville, Northern Ireland struck. Ian Dowie, just on as a substitute, laid the ball off for Jimmy Quinn, and the Reading man smashed a 20 yards volley past Bonner. It was a tremendous strike from the prolific Quinn and with it Southern hearts sank and the doubts began to creep in. Would the glory be snatched away at the very last hurdle after all? Enter McLoughlin, whose precious goal three minutes later in the 76th minute assured the Portsmouth mid-fielder a special place in Irish hearts and minds forever.

The goal came as a result of Gerry Taggart's poor clearance from a Denis Irwin cross, the ball falling nicely for McLoughlin to volley left footed just inside Tommy Wright's post.

What followed was probably the most excruciating fourteen minutes plus injury time ever experienced by Republic supporters as the other match in Seville seemed almost more important than the one we were all watching. However Spain, despite being reduced to ten men and ironically the team which had humbled the Irish a mere five weeks earlier, now crucially denied Denmark a place in the finals grimly, hanging on to a lead given them by Hierro. In fact, with identical points totals and goal differences records, it was on goals scored that the Republic booked their place, a situation which would have seemed most unlikely when Group 3 began some seventeen months earlier. Charlton summed up everybody's feelings *"The credit is due to the lads who have worked like crazy in the previous qualifiers. Fair play to the North they made it hard for us out there."*

Getting Prepared

Having had ample time to ponder the permutations of the World Cup Finals draw in Las Vegas, which paired them with Italy, Mexico and Norway, Ireland remerged from their winter hibernation to begin a five match build-up to America with a home game on March 23rd against fellow qualifiers Russia, geographically the largest and potentially the strongest of the former Soviet republics. With injury, and in the visitors case internal wrangling, rendering both sides very much understrength, Charlton availed of the opportunity to introduce some as yet untried potential, whilst at the same time affording fringe performers such as Carey, McLoughlin, O'Brien and McGoldrick a rare first team outing. The introduction of debutants Phil Babb, Jason McAteer and Gary Kelly lent an even more unfamiliar look to the Irish side though all three, particularly Kelly, who was a popular 'man of the match' choice, made impressive starts. Subsequently all three would play a big part in Ireland's challenge in the United States.

On a miserably wet and windy day at Lansdowne Road, Ireland, despite such an inexperienced line-up, played the first forty five minutes with great cohesion and drive. Tranmere's Liam O'Brien was most unfortunate to see a well struck free kick rebound out from the crossbar while McAteer was denied a debut strike by some excellent goalkeeping by Chelsea's Dimitri Kharine. Russia for their part had a goal from Borodiouk disallowed for handball against Salenko, who would score five goals against Cameroon in the finals themselves.

This however, was an isolated attack by the visitors and it was Ireland who dominated proceedings without finding that vital breakthrough. In a second half best forgotten, the game eventually petered out to a scoreless draw, a result which increasingly appeared to be the height of the visitors ambition.

As April 20th, the date of Ireland's next assignment, against Holland in the compact Gemeentelijk Sportspark, Tilburg, drew near, Jack Charlton grew increasingly more agitated about his worsening injury crisis. Unusually for him, the man himself publicly admitted to being very worried about the prospect of taking on the Dutch without the services of people like McGrath, Quinn, Aldridge, Irwin, Keane and Townsend. As it turned out he need not have worried, indeed after the game his grin was as broad as the river Tyne, as Ireland's 'babes' fashioned an excellent one-nil win. Even the restricting of Koeman, Jonk and Bergkamp to forty five minutes play by prior agreement with their respective clubs offered little excuse for a Dutch side out fought and out thought by a fiercely determined Irish eleven.

Ireland dominated the first half, reducing the home side to just one clear cut chance, a Rijkaard header which was comfortably held by Bonner. With the tight pitch seeming to be to the visitors advantage particularly in curbing the width on offer to wingers Overmars and Roy, Sheridan, Coyne and McGoldrick all came close to opening the scoring. However it was in defence that Ireland really shone, Moran and Babb flawless in the centre, Kelly and Phelan raiding up the flanks. Ten minutes into the second period the Irish scored the game's only goal. Ronnie Whelan in a rare outing, played a neat ball into the path of Sheridan, and his clinical cross made the finish easy for Tommy Coyne. Although there was one heart-stopping moment right at the death, Ronald De Boers header glancing off the crossbar, Ireland played with supreme composure throughout, to gain a memorable victory, their first against the Dutch in fourteen years. After the excitement of Tilburg the next game, a first ever encounter with Bolivia, in Dublin on May 24th, was always likely to prove something of an anti-climax. Whilst for Pat Bonner there was the satisfaction of equalling Liam Brady's record of 72 Irish caps, and for the fans a late winning goal to celebrate, overall there was little to distinguish this particular international fixture.

Certainly the Bolivians, warming up for their first World Cup finals appearance since 1950, did play a pleasing brand of eye catching one-touch football, but up front glaringly lacked punch, a failing which would also burden them in the U.S.A. With a cluttered five-man midfield, leaving Tommy Coyne as the sole front runner, Ireland's attacking capabilities were limited too, much to the frustration of another big home crowd.

Reduced to a handful of half chances, the best two of which fell to an out of sorts Coyne, Ireland had to wait eighty six minutes for the vital breakthrough, Terry Phelan's piledriver being deflected into the path of John Sheridan who finished in style from twenty two yards. On an evening of anguish for the home support, the winning score did at least bring with it a measure of relief, though the overall performance was well below par.

Just days after the Bolivian game, the Irish returned to the scene of what many consider to be their best ever performance under Jack Charlton, the Niedersachsenstadion in Hannover where on June 15th, 1988, a powerful Soviet Union side, later to contest the final, were run ragged for over an hour in a European Championship finals match. Now for this most prestigious of friendlies, away to Germany, on a ground where the World Cup holders were unbeaten in more than forty years, Ireland once again rose to great heights in recording a terrific two-nil win. Indeed such was Ireland's superiority at times in this game you almost felt you needed to pinch yourself to be certain it really was true!

Once again Charlton's decision to give youth its fling paid rich dividends. With goalkeeper Alan Kelly, whose inclusion temporarily delayed Bonner's record breaking appearance, playing the proverbial 'blinder,' as did McAteer, Babb and Gary Kelly, a half time substitute for Irwin, the capacity 50,000 home crowd were stunned into silence long before the final whistle.

After Germany had enjoyed slightly the better of the opening exchanges, Klinsmann coming closest to breaking the deadlock, Ireland shocked their hosts after 31 minutes. The goal stemmed from McAteer's excellent run and cross, which deflected slightly off the head of Strunz straight to Cascarino and the Chelsea man, struggling in the reserves, headed his twelfth goal for Ireland. The home sides response was immediate with newcomer Basler striking the base of an upright and Strunz whalloping a twenty yarder off the crossbar. However the Irish goal survived to the interval despite coming under increasing pressure.

The second and clinching goal came after 69 minutes when Gary Kelly, cutting in from the right wing, struck a left foot shot which took a slight deflection off the backpedalling Berthold to completely decieve goalkeeper Illgner. After that there was only going to be one winner as an increasingly agitated home crowd vented their frustration on Berti Vogts and his side. Now only the Czech Republic in Dublin a week later lay ahead of Ireland's journey to Orlando to prepare for the finals. Typically, despite such a magnificent performance Charlton preached caution *"I just hope people do not read too much into this result, and put us under even more pressure before we get to America."*

Although Whit Sunday was a truly miserable day for a game of football, with high winds and driving rain, the capacity Lansdowne crowd set to give their heroes a rousing send off against the Czech's were determined not to let the conditions dampen their spirits. A very special welcome was reserved for Pat Bonner on the occasion of his record breaking 73rd cap although almost unnoticed 'big Cas' notched up his half century. Unfortunately for all concerned the celebrations were not rewarded with either a win or indeed a good performance as for the second time in six months Ireland were well beaten on a ground where for so long they had looked invincible. Of course on the very eve of their journey to the U.S.A. the home side's commitment was bound to be somewhat diluted, and a skilful Czech team took full advantage to register a prestigious win.

The visitors took the lead in the 25th minute, Terry Phelan blatantly tripping Kuka in the box and the same player coolly dispatching the resultant spot kick. The goal finally sparked Ireland into action and after a couple of near misses skipper Andy Townsend equalised with the help of a deflection on the stroke of half time.

On the resumption it was once again the Czech's who looked the more intent on gaining victory and after ten minutes their industry bore fruit. It was an unfortunate goal from Packie Bonner's point of view as having made a superb save from Frydek at point blank range Kuka knocked in the rebound. Six minutes from the end the impressive Suchoparek, playing as sweeper, exploited a large hole in Ireland's defence to squeeze the ball inside Bonner's right hand post. Such a comprehensive defeat coming within a week of the superb performance in Hannover meant the post match mood was a strange mixture of disappointment tempered with anticipation at the prospect of once again being a part of the world's greatest sporting event. In a season in which the pendulum of fortune had swung high and low so many times all was now focused on Giants Stadium, New Jersey and the opening encounter with the mighty Italians on June 18th.

The Main Event

The arrival of Ireland in Orlando coincided with some rather freakish weather conditions as monsoon type rains put a damper on the team's preparations, though not their high morale. Whilst expressing himself happy with the build up to USA '94, Charlton did admit to being worried about the extremes of heat and humidity which the players would face, especially in their second opening phase game against Mexico in Orlando where a noon day kick-off would further exacerbate matters.

The other great fear was the huge media attention focusing in on the Irish party, particularly as neither England nor any of the other teams from these islands had reached the final stages. Fortunately good work by all concerned meant another trouble free tournament for Ireland in this regard. In fact media coverage was on a colossal scale and R.T.E. in particular were hugely comprehensive. While the introduction of new panelists and a regular studio discussion spot were only partly successful, the contribution of Niall Quinn, sadly missing a second consecutive World Cup finals with crucial ligament problems was a definite plus. No doubt we will see the big Manchester City man behind the microphone again in the future.

Once more Irish supporters were asked to pay out large sums of money in order to see their heroes play, and whilst inevitably some were unfortunate enough to encounter problems most thoroughly enjoyed their American experience. Indeed for many Irish the pre-tournament worries were not financial ones but centered around whether or not given the F.A.I.'s paltry tickets allocation, they would in fact get to see the games at all. In the event, almost all did, and once again as we have come to expect and to celebrate, the conduct of the travelling fans was superb, once more leaving a very positive impression behind.

Overall, despite much scepticism about the lack of knowledge and lack of interest in the World Cup, the American public turned up in their hundreds of thousands to help sell out many of the games and swell the average attendance over the fifty two games to a record 68,604. And while there were moments of conflict, most notably those involving Charlton and Aldridge with Orlando officialdom during the game with Mexico, nevertheless the U.S. organisation was excellent. Indeed the smooth running of things helped enormously in realising the high expectations beforehand that this might be an especially good tournament. The introduction by FIFA, amongst other innovations, of three points for a group phase win, a change in the offside law and a stretcher for all injuries to speed up the game, proved to be big successes.

The most exciting finals since Mexico in 1970, saw that most important of ingredients, goals, in greater abundance than for some time, while the emergence of so called 'smaller nations' like Bulgaria, Romania and Sweden as major players added a new refreshing dimension. Unfortunately the single most disappointing factor was a very poor final between Brazil and Italy, two names synonymous with good football, but both of whom failed miserably at the Pasadena Rose Bowl to do justice to an excellent tournament. With the selling of the game of soccer to the American public high on the agenda another poor final following on from the scandalous display by Argentina against West Germany in the climax to Italia 90, was regrettable. As for Ireland, it certainly was to prove an eventful second finals appearance, with perhaps slightly more low's than high's than we might have expected as the team made final preparations to meet the Italians in New York.

After all the many hours of talking, preparing, anticipating, the day of reckoning, 18th June, and the opening game with the three times world champions finally arrived. In the searing heat of one of America's most famous sporting arenas, the Giants Stadium, New Jersey, where in a near capacity crowd of 74,826, Irish supporters were expected to be hugely outnumbered by Italians, all the images were those of a vociferous, heaving, triumphant sea of green, white and orange.

After all the pre-tournament fuss about the lack of tickets available to the Irish, how could so many have made it to the game? we wondered, how indeed! A triumph for perseverence it would seem and a deep, deep pocket! Those Italians who stayed in the bars of 'Little Italy' and elsewhere, comfortable in the knowledge that their team would triumph, were to be sorely disappointed. What in fact transpired was an electrifying opening to Ireland's World Cup challenge. In what ranks as perhaps the best ever result by an Irish eleven anywhere, arguably on a par with Stuttgart, Hannover, Genoa, even Goodison Park, a star studded Italian outfit, with high hopes themselves were reduced to a poor second best. Having exited from Italia 90 at the hands of the same opponents, Schillachi et al., and having lost every one of our previous seven meetings with Italy this victory in New York was a very special one. Once again as had been seen in Tilburg and Hannover in the weeks leading up to USA '94, given the right set of circumstances, Ireland's commitment to the cause bordered almost on the fanatical.

As for Ray Houghton, who had featured in just one of the warm-up games and whose place in the team looked under serious threat from the swashbuckling McAteer, once again as he did six years earlier in Stuttgart, the Aston Villa man emerged as the hero of the hour.

With the exception of the ever improving Babb replacing an injured Kevin Moran, Charlton's line up for this crucial game held few surprises. The new single front runner system so successful against Holland was again used, giving Tommy Coyne the nod over John Alridge. John Sheridan as expected secured a starting place on the strength of some impressive performances earlier in the season. Italy for their part were a side full of household names from Baresi to Baggio and on paper it was difficult to imagine a tougher test for Ireland. On the day however it was those wearing green shirts who won all the individual battles.

Ireland were on top from early on, Paul McGrath setting the tone just two minutes in with a superb tackle which denied Signori a goalscoring opportunity. In the sweltering heat which reached 93°F, Ireland's work rate, particularly at midfield where Keane reigned supreme in front of the back four, was quite phenomenal. After just eleven minutes play, the start every man, woman and child in Ireland had secretly wished for, and prayed for, materialised. Denis Irwin began the move, whipping over a cross for Coyne whose downward header was taken on the chest by Houghton running diagonally across the penalty area some twenty yards out. At first it looked as though the Aston Villa linkman might be forced wide, but suddenly having brushed past Baresi, he looked up and planted a sublime volley over the head of Pagliuca and under the crossbar. As he cartwheeled away in triumph, surely an image that will remain in the mind for many years to come, an entire nation erupted in celebration. Not surprisingly the goal stung the Italians into action, but despite their neat passing game and measured build up, there was little bit up front, and the Irish defence with Babb and McGrath outstanding gave nothing away. The interval arrived without Bonner having a save of note to make. Having replaced Tassotti with Inter's Berti, Italy began the second half with renewed purpose. After ten minutes Ireland survived their biggest scare when Dino Baggio fell heavily in the 'area' under challenge from Babb. Despite the animated protestations of the Italians, however, Dutch referee Van Der Ende signalled a corner kick. By the mid-point of the half when a tiring Houghton had been replaced by the livewire McAteer, the pendulum had once again swung in Ireland's favour. John Sheridan squandered a great chance to increase the lead when set up by a brilliant Keane run, but the Sheffield Wednesday man struck the crossbar when it seemed he must score. Despite that miss however, the Irish team held their nerve right up to the fourth minute of injury time, the final whistle confirming a marvellous victory, and one of the real shocks of USA '94. A smiling, cigar smoking Charlton summed the mood up nicely. *"That was an inspired start to the competition and a wonderful win. Mexico, next Friday, will of course be another big test."*

Having somewhat unluckily lost their opening game to Norway, Mexico were under tremendous pressure to achieve a result against the Irish in Orlando, where the choice of a noon kick-off was always going to prove a huge burden for Charlton's men to surmount. This was especially true as the Mexicans themselves were very much at home in these extreme conditions.

With an unchanged starting line-up Ireland began well despite pitch level temperatures touching a staggering 103°F. Both Coyne, from Phelan's cross, and Andy Townsend, fluffing a diving header set up by Staunton, had good opportunities to register an early score. Mexico however were proving to be a much more potent outfit than the Italians had been. Their neat, accurate passing game, using the width of the pitch to good effect, gradually began to drain the Irish reserves of stamina, players like Staunton, Irwin and Sheridan suffering greatly in the heat. Having played their hearts out in the opening period disaster struck for the Irish at a psychologically devastating time, two minutes from the break. The goal was created with a flowing three man move involving Ambrizzi and Hermosillo, with the ball being eventually laid back into the path of Luis Garcia, and the Athletico Madrid midfielder swept a glorious 25 yarder low into the corner of Pat Bonner's net.

Twelve minutes into the second half Ireland's best chance to equalise again fell to the boot of John Sheridan, but unfortunately his attempted lob was weak and easily held by Campos in the Mexican goal. Within minutes the central American side pounced, once again through Luis Garcia to put the game beyond the Irish. Much of the blame for the goal lay with Irwin, who was turned inside out by Garcia Aspe, and his neat lay off was clinically dispatched by Luis Garcia, Bonner having no chance.

To their credit Ireland battled on bravely as Mexico understandably sat back on their two goal lead. The introduction of McAteer and Aldridge for Houghton and Coyne was vital and it was these two who combined for an Irish score in the 84th minute, 'Aldo' powering home a header from the Bolton youngster's teasing cross. The goal gave Charlton's man a much needed boost, but despite a fighting finish, Ireland had to settle for defeat. The last notable incident was Townsend's marvellous drive superbly saved at full stretch by Campos.

With Italy having scraped through against Norway, courtesy of a single Dino Baggio strike the 'Group of Death' which Group E had been dubbed was proving to be just that with all teams now equal on points. The one crucial difference however was that Mexico and Ireland having scored an extra goal held the most slender of advantages.

Having already fallen foul of the authorities more than once with his fortright comments during this World Cup, Jack Charlton's outburst at the delay in allowing John Aldridge on as a substitute against Mexico earned him a fine and a one match touchline ban for the next assignment, against Norway back in New York. Meanwhile on the pitch, bookings for both Irwin and Phelan in Orlando, their second offences, meant both received a one match ban, thus Ireland were forced to plan for this game without their regular full backs. As expected Gary

Kelly and Steve Staunton provided the cover whilst Jason McAteer was given his first start to a game in USA '94, and 'Aldo's' short but telling contribution against the Mexicans relegated Tommy Coyne to the substitute's bench.

With the cushion of holding second place in Group E, Charlton's number one objective was of course to avoid defeat and in this the team proved successful although not before we all suffered a nailbiting ninety minutes. The game began well for the Irish with Egil Olsen's team looking anything but an outfit which urgently required a positive result. It was to Ireland's credit that they took the game to their tough uncompromising and tactically sterile opponents throughout the opening half. The pity was that they could not convert their obvious superiority into a lead goal which would have opened the game up. Despite good opportunities falling to Sheridan and Townsend neither were taken and the game remained scoreless to half-time.

Norway of course were boxing clever waiting for news of goals in the other Group E game between Italy and Mexico in Washington D.C. With that game also scoreless at the interval the Norwegians came out for the second half with a completely different attitude, knowing that a brace of scoreless draws would spell disaster for their hopes of reaching the last sixteen. The problem for them however was that Ireland were still clearly the better side and despite their best efforts Bonner was rarely troubled. Ireland's biggest fright came in the 74th minute when Goran Sorloth's looping effort bounced back of the crossbar and away to safety, a lucky escape. In the end however it was Charlton's men who once again finished the stronger, Roy Keane shooting just over following an electrifying seventy yard run. And so referee Torres of Colombia finally brought and end to the nailbiting action and 'Big Jack' could celebrate once again as he had done in Italia '90, masterminding a safe passage through a group fraught with danger. As his side completed a lap of honour around the huge Giants Stadium, the party at home and in the USA began. Surely a scoreless draw can never before have sparked such joyful celebrations!

With the other Group E game also ending in a draw, one goal each, it was Mexico who deservedly took the honours in the extremely tight affair. Despite having an identical record to the Italians, Ireland claimed the runners-up spot by virtue of having beaten Arrigo Sacchi's men in New York, whilst Norway equal with everybody else on four points, more than some of the sides who advanced, finished bottom of Group E and were on their way home.

With second place secured, Ireland now awaited the outcome of Group F, the winners of which they would meet in Orlando on Independence Day, July 4th. Although Belgium had looked the most likely to top the group, indeed Charlton took in their final game against Saudi Arabia, a surprise defeat meant that Belgiums near neighbours Holland actually topped Group F and so would meet the Republic in the eighth finals.

Whilst Ireland were not happy with having to return to the scorching heat of Orlando, at least following their excellent win in Tilburg less than three months earlier, confidence was high that the Dutch could be overcome again. The winners would certainly face a very enticing quarter final against either Brazil or U.S.A. in Dallas. This would in fact be the third occasion on which the Irish would meet Holland in three major tournament finals following defeat at Euro

'88 in Germany and that famous draw in Palermo during Italia '90. Despite missing the huge talents of Gullit and Van Basten nevertheless manager Dick Advocaat still had a wealth of talent from which to choose including the likes of Roy, Bergkamp, Jonk, Koeman and Rijkaard.

Ireland for their part made a couple of line-up changes from the clash with Norway, Coyne replacing Aldridge and Phelan returning at the expense of Jason McAteer. Unfortunately it was not to prove a happy reintroduction for the dimunitive Manchester City man as his error after only 10 minutes gift wrapped the Dutch a vital breakthrough goal. In truth however the goal was coming almost from the kick-off, as a fluid Dutch midfield and attack carved up a ponderous Irish rearguard with pace and inventiveness. There seemed to be little danger as Phelan rose just inside his own half to head a long ball presumably towards the safety of the touchline. Inexplicably however he headed it back in the general direction of Bonner, and the alert Overmars was in like a flash to sprint to the line and cross for the inrushing Bergkamp to finish in style. It was an unfortunate goal from an Irish viewpoint, but to be fair Dick Advocaat's side were well worth their lead. Holland's tremendous pace, particularly on the flanks, coupled with the accuracy of their passing, continued to keep Ireland much too busy at the back to make any real impression in attack. With oceans of time and space, Koeman and Co. looked world class, which was especially frustrating given their total eclipse in Tilburg. Ironically it was just as Charlton's men seemed to be gaining a foothold in the game in the moments coming up to the half time whistle, that disaster struck a second time, Jonk's speculative long range effort fumbled over his own goal line by Bonner.

It was a desperately disappointing moment for the big Donegal-man who had looked to have the shot covered, and undoubtedly it was the crucial moment of the game, as a one-nil interval deficit would have seemed almost a success given that Ireland were so outclassed in the opening 45 minutes.

Desperately chasing the game in the second period, the Irish not surprisingly had a great deal more of the play especially following McAteer's introduction for a very tired looking Steve Staunton. Two good chances, both of which fell to Houghton, were spurned however, and even the introduction of big Tony Cascarino, who up to this had had his world cup finals ruined by injury, failed to make much of an impression.

Ireland did have the ball in the Dutch net in the final minute, McGrath turning in McAteer's cross, however the goal was quite rightly disallowed for foot up against the Aston Villa defender. It simply wasn't meant to be Ireland's day, the unfortunate errors by Phelan and Bonner only symptoms of a well below par performance. Understandably there was a great feeling of regret that the journey had come to an end, but certainly any attempts to apportion the blame for Ireland's exit from USA '94 to certain individuals, as was attempted by some journalists who should have known better, was both hugely unfair and totally inaccurate. Ireland could have no complaints about the result in Orlando, now twice in quick succession the graveyard of our hopes. We simply lost to a better prepared team who unfortunately for us, played their best football of the tournament on the day.

It was a pity too that in the aftermath of the final defeat, a row should break out about the appearance of Charlton and the team at a civic reception in Dublin. A little more consideration towards players who, unaware of the event, had made family plans at the end of almost twelve consecutive months of non-stop football, would not have gone amiss. To their credit they did return to Dublin and appropriately the final words in a season full of highlights, especially those at Windsor Park, Tilburg, Hannover and Giants Stadium should be Charlton's. *"We gave it all we had,"* he said, *"but at the end of the day it just wasn't enough. But let there be no recriminations in defeat - this team has represented Ireland well in America."*

Chasin' Jason ...
Lars Bohinen of Norway in McAteer's wake   (The Star)

IRELAND AT THE WORLD CUP FINALS 1994

18 Jun. at Giants Stadium, Meadowlands, New Jersey
Rep. of Ireland (1) 1 *(Houghton 12)*
Italy 0
Rep.of I.: Bonner (Celtic 74), Irwin (Man. Utd. 27), McGrath (Aston Villa 66), Babb (Coventry C. 6), Phelan (Man. City 23), Houghton (Aston Villa 59), Keane (Man. Utd. 23), Townsend (Aston Villa 46), Sheridan (Sheffield Wed. 21), Coyne (Motherwell 15), Staunton (Aston Villa 48).
Subs: McAteer (Bolton W. 6) for Houghton 67 mins. Aldridge (Tranmere Rov. 58) for Coyne 89 mins.
Italy: Pagliuca, Tassotti (Berti h-time), Baresi, Costacurta, Maldini, Donadoni, D. Baggio, Albertini, Evani, R. Baggio, Signori (Massaro 70).
Referee: van der Ende (Holland)   Att: 74,326
Bookings: Ireland - Phelan, Irwin, Coyne: Italy - none.

28 Jun. at Giants Stadium, Meadowlands, New Jersey
Rep. of Ireland 0
Norway 0
Rep.of I.: Bonner (Celtic 76), G. Kelly (Leeds Utd. 6), McGrath (Aston Villa 68), Babb (Coventry C. 8), Staunton (Aston Villa 50), McAteer (Bolton W. 8), Keane (Man. Utd. 25), Townsend (Aston Villa 48), Sheridan (Sheffield Wed. 23), Houghton (Aston Villa 61), Aldridge (Tranmere Rov. 60).
Subs: D. Kelly (Wolverhampton W. 17) for Aldridge 64 mins. Whelan (Liverpool 50) for Townsend 74 mins.
Norway: Thorstvedt, Berg, Bratseth, Johnsen, Bjornebye, Flo, Leonhardsen (Bohinen 67), Rekdal, Mykland, Halle (Jakobsen 34), Sorloth.
Referee: J. Torres (Colombia)   Att: 76,322
Bookings: Ireland - Keane, Houghton, G. Kelly
Norway - Johnsen, Sorloth.

24 Jun. at Florida Citrus Bowl, Orlando
Rep. of Ireland (0) 1 *(Aldridge 83)*
Mexico (1) 2 *(Luis Garcia 43, 67)*
Rep.of I.: Bonner (Celtic 75), Irwin (Man. Utd. 28), McGrath (Aston Villa 67), Babb (Coventry C. 7), Phelan (Man. City 24), Houghton (Aston Villa 60), Keane (Man. Utd. 24), Townsend (Aston Villa 47), Sheridan (Sheffield Wed. 22), Coyne (Motherwell 16), Staunton (Aston Villa 49).
Subs: McAteer (Bolton W. 7) for Staunton 66 mins. Aldridge (Tranmere Rov. 59) for Coyne 66 mins.
Mexico: Campos, Suarez, Perales, Ambrizzi, Bernal, Hermosillo (Salvador 80), Garcia Aspe, Del Olmo, Rodriguez (Gutierrez 80), Luis-Garcia, Alvez
Referee: K. Roethlisberger (Switzerland) Att: 61,219
Bookings: Ireland - Irwin, Phelan:
Mexico - Campos, Del Olmo

4 July at Florida Citrus Bowl, Orlando
Rep. of Ireland 0
Holland (2) 2 *(Bergkamp 10, Jonk 41)*
Rep.of I.: Bonner (Celtic 77), G. Kelly (Leeds Utd. 7), McGrath (Aston Villa 69), Babb (Coventry C. 9), Phelan (Man. City 25), Houghton (Aston Villa 62), Keane (Man. Utd. 26), Townsend (Aston Villa 49), Sheridan (Sheffield Wed. 24), Coyne (Motherwell 17), Staunton (Aston Villa 51).
Subs: McAteer (Bolton W. 9) for Staunton 63 mins. Cascarino (Chelsea 51) for Coyne 74 mins.
Holland: de Goey, F. de Boer, Koeman, Rijkaard, Valckx, Witschge (Numan 80), Jonk, Winter, Overmars, Van Vossen (Roy 70), Bergkamp.
Referee: P. Mikkelsen (Denmark)   Att: 61,355
Bookings: Holland - Koeman: Ireland - none.

Ireland line-up vs Mexico (EOH)

USA '94 Results Round-Up

Group A

18 Jun. at The Silverdome, Pontiac, Detroit   Att: 74,325
U.S.A.   (1) 1 (Wynalda 44)
Switzerland   (1) 1 (Bregy 39)

18 Jun. at The Rose Bowl, Pasadena   Att: 91,865
Colombia   (1) 1 (Valencia 42)
Romania   (2) 3 (Raducioiu 15, 88, Hagi 34)

22 Jun. at The Silverdome, Pontiac, Detroit   Att: 61,428
Romania   (1) 1 (Hagi 35)
Switzerland   (1) 4 (Sutter 16, Chapuisat 52, Knup 65, Bregy 72)

22 Jun. at The Rose Bowl, Pasadena   Att: 93,194
U.S.A.   (1) 2 (Escobar (og) 34, Stewart 52)
Colombia   (0) 1 (Valencia 90)

26 Jun. at Stanford Stadium, Palo Alto, San Francisco   Att:83,769
Colombia   (1) 2 (Gaviria 44, Lozano 90)
Switzerland   0

26 Jun. at The Rose Bowl, Pasadena   Att: 93,869
U.S.A.   0
Romania   (1) 1 (Petrescu 17)

	P.	W.	D.	L.	F.	A.	GD	Pts.
Romania	3	2	-	1	5	5	(0)	6
Switzerland	3	1	1	1	5	4	(+1)	4
USA	3	1	1	1	3	3	(0)	4
Colombia	3	1	-	2	4	5	(-1)	3

Group B

19 Jun. at The Rose Bowl, Pasadena   Att: 83,959
Cameroon   (1) 2 (Embe 31, Omam-Biyik 47)
Sweden   (1) 2 (Ljung 8, Dahlin 75)

20 Jun. at Stanford Stadium, Palo Alto, San Francisco   Att:81,061
Brazil   (1) 2 (Romario 26, Rai 53 (pen))
Russia   0

24 Jun. at Stanford Stadium, Palo Alto, San Francisco   Att:83,401
Brazil   (1) 3 (Romario 39, Santos 65, Bebeto 73)
Cameroon   0

24 Jun. at The Silverdome, Pontiac, Detroit   Att: 71,528
Russia   (1) 1 (Salenko 4 (pen))
Sweden   (1) 3 (Brolin 39 (pen), Dahlin 60, 82)

28 Jun. at Stanford Stadium, Palo Alto, San Francisco   Att:74,914
Cameroon   (0) 1 (Milla 47)
Russia   (3) 6 (Salenko 15, 41, 45 (pen), 73, 75, Radchenko 82)

28 Jun. at The Silverdome, Pontiac, Detroit   Att: 77,217
Brazil   (0) 1 (Romario 47)
Sweden   (1) 1 (K.Andersson 23)

	P.	W.	D.	L.	F.	A.	GD	Pts.
Brazil	3	2	1	-	6	1	(+5)	7
Sweden	3	1	2	-	6	4	(+2)	5
Russia	3	1	-	2	7	6	(+1)	3
Cameroon	3	-	1	2	3	11	(-8)	1

Group C

17 Jun. at Soldier Field, Chicago   Att: 63,117
Bolivia   0
Germany   (0) 1 (Klinsmann 60)

17 Jun. at The Cotton Bowl, Dallas   Att: 56,247
South Korea   (0) 2 (Myung Bo 84, Jung Won 90)
Spain   (0) 2 (Salinas 50, Goikoetxea 55)

21 Jun. at Soldier Field, Chicago   Att: 63,113
Germany   (0) 1 (Klinsmann 47)
Spain   (1) 1 (Goikoetxea 14)

23 Jun. at Foxboro Stadium, Boston   Att: 53,456
Bolivia   0
South Korea   0

27 Jun. at Soldier Field, Chicago   Att: 63,089
Bolivia   (0) 1 (Sanchez 67)
Spain   (1) 3 (Guardiola 19 (pen), Caminero 66, 71)

27 Jun. at The Cotton Bowl, Dallas   Att: 63,998
Germany   (3) 3 (Klinsman 12, 36, Riedle 20)
South Korea   (0) 2 (Sun Hong 52, Myung Bo 62)

	P.	W.	D.	L.	F.	A.	GD	Pts.
Germany	3	2	1	-	5	3	(+2)	7
Spain	3	1	2	-	6	4	(+2)	5
South Korea	3	-	2	1	4	5	(-1)	2
Bolivia	3	-	1	2	1	4	(-3)	1

Group D

21 Jun. at Foxboro Stadium, Boston — Att: 53,486
Argentina (2) **4** *(Batistuta 2, 44, 90, Maradona 60)*
Greece **0**

21 Jun. at The Cotton Bowl, Dallas — Att: 44,932
Bulgaria **0**
Nigeria (2) **3** *(Yekini 21, Amokachi 43, Ammuniki 54)*

25 Jun. at Foxboro Stadium, Boston — Att: 54,453
Argentina (2) **2** *(Caniggia 21, 28)*
Nigeria (1) **1** *(Siasia 8)*

26 Jun. at Soldier Field, Chicago — Att: 63,160
Bulgaria (1) **4** *(Stoichkov 5, 56 (pens), Letchkov 66, Borimorov 90)*
Greece **0**

30 Jun. at The Cotton Bowl, Dallas — Att: 63,998
Argentina **0**
Bulgaria (0) **2** *(Stoichkov 61, Sirakov 90)*

30 Jun. at Foxboro Stadium, Boston — Att: 53,001
Greece **0**
Nigeria (1) **2** *(George 45, Amokachi 90)*

	P.	W.	D.	L.	F.	A.	GD	Pts.
Nigeria	3	2	-	1	6	2	(+4)	6
Bulgaria	3	2	-	1	6	3	(+3)	6
Argentina	3	2	-	1	6	3	(+3)	6
Greece	3	-	-	3	0	10	(-10)	0

Group E

18 Jun. at The Giants Stadium, New Jersey — Att: 74,826
Italy **0**
Rep. of Ireland (1) **1** *(Houghton 11)*

19 Jun. at RFK Stadium, Washington — Att: 52,359
Mexico **0**
Norway (0) **1** *(Rekdal 85)*

23 Jun. at The Giants Stadium, New Jersey — Att: 74,624
Italy (0) **1** *(D. Baggio 69)*
Norway **0**

24 Jun. at The Citrus Bowl, Orlando — Att: 61,219
Mexico (1) **2** *(Garcia 44, 66)*
Rep. of Ireland (0) **1** *(Aldridge 84)*

28 Jun. at RFK Stadium, Washington — Att: 53,186
Italy (0) **1** *(Massaro 48)*
Mexico (0) **1** *(Bernal 58)*

28 Jun. at The Giants Stadium, New Jersey — Att: 76,322
Norway **0**
Rep. of Ireland **0**

	P.	W.	D.	L.	F.	A.	GD	Pts.
Mexico	3	1	1	1	3	3	(0)	4
Rep. of Ireland	3	1	1	1	2	2	(0)	4
Italy	3	1	1	1	2	2	(0)	4
Norway	3	1	1	1	1	1	(0)	4

Group F

19 Jun. at The Citrus Bowl, Orlando — Att: 60,790
Belgium (1) **1** *(Degryse 11)*
Morocco **0**

20 Jun. at RFK Stadium, Washington — Att: 52,535
Holland (0) **2** *(Jonk 50, Taument 86)*
Saudi Arabia (1) **1** *(Amin 19)*

25 Jun. at The Citrus Bowl, Orlando — Att: 62,387
Belgium (0) **1** *(Albert 65)*
Holland **0**

25 Jun. at The Giants Stadium, New Jersey — Att: 72,404
Morocco (1) **1** *(Chaouch 26)*
Saudi Arabia (2) **2** *(Al Jaber 7 (pen), Amin 45)*

29 Jun. at RFK Stadium, Washington — Att: 52,959
Belgium **0**
Saudi Arabia (1) **1** *(Owairan 5)*

29 Jun. at The Citrus Bowl, Orlando — Att: 60,578
Holland (1) **2** *(Bergkamp 43, Roy 78)*
Morocco (0) **1** *(Nader 47)*

	P.	W.	D.	L.	F.	A.	GD	Pts.
Holland	3	2	-	1	4	3	(+1)	6
Saudi Arabia	3	2	-	1	4	3	(+1)	6
Belgium	3	2	-	1	2	1	(+1)	6
Morocco	3	-	-	3	2	5	(-3)	0

Second Round

2 Jul. at Soldier Field, Chicago — Att: 60,246
Belgium (1) **2** *(Grun 7, Albert 90)*
Germany (3) **3** *(Voeller 5, 39, Klinsmann 10)*

2 Jul. at RFK Stadium, Washington — Att: 53,121
Spain (1) **3** *(Hierro 15, Luis Enrique 74, Beguiristain 87 (pen))*
Switzerland **0**

3 Jul. at The Cotton Bowl, Dallas — Att: 60,277
Saudi Arabia (0) **1** *(Al Ghesheyan 85)*
Sweden (1) **3** *(Dahlin 6, K.Andersson 51, 88)*

3 Jul. at The Rose Bowl, Pasadena　　　　　　Att: 90,469
Argentina　　(1) **2**　*(Batistuta 16 (pen), Balbo 75)*
Romania　　(2) **3**　*(Dumitrescu 11, 18, Hagi 56)*

4 Jul. at The Citrus Bowl, Orlando　　　　　　Att: 61,355
Holland　　(2) **2**　*(Bergkamp 11, Jonk 41)*
Rep. of Ireland　　**0**

4 Jul. at Stanford Stadium, Palo Alto,
　　　　San Francisco　　　　　　　　　　　Att: 84,147
Brazil　　(0) **1**　*(Bebeto 74)*
USA　　**0**

5 Jul. at Foxboro Stadium, Boston　　　　　　Att: 54,367
Italy　　(0) **2**　*(R.Baggio 89, 102 (pen))*
Nigeria　　(1) **1**　*(Ammuniki 26)*　　AET

5 Jul. at The Giants Stadium, New Jersey　　Att: 71,030
Bulgaria　　(1) **1**　*(Stoichkov 7)*
Mexico　　(1) **1**　*(Garcia Aspe 18 (pen))* AET
　　(Bulgaria won 3-1 on penalties)

Quarter-Finals

9 Jul. at Foxboro Stadium, Boston　　　　　　Att: 54,605
Italy　　(1) **2**　*(D.Baggio 26, R.Baggio 88)*
Spain　　(0) **1**　*(Caminero 59)*

9 Jul. at The Cotton Bowl, Dallas　　　　　　Att: 63,998
Brazil　　(0) **3**　*(Romario 52, Bebeto 62,*
　　　　　　　　　　　　　　Branco 81)
Holland　　(0) **2**　*(Bergkamp 64, Winter 76)*

10 Jul. at The Giants Stadium, New Jersey　　Att: 72,416
Bulgaria　　(0) **2**　*(Stoichkov 76, Letchkov 79)*
Germany　　(0) **1**　*(Matthaeus 49 (pen))*

10 Jul. at Stanford Stadium, Palo Alto,
　　　　San Francisco　　　　　　　　　　　Att: 81,715
Romania　　(0) **2**　*(Raducioiu 89, 101)*
Sweden　　(0) **2**　*(Brolin 79, K.Andersson 115)*
　　(Sweden won 5-4 on penalties)　　AET

Semi-Finals

13 Jul. at The Giants Stadium, New Jersey　　Att: 77,094
Bulgaria　　(1) **1**　*(Stoichkov 44 (pen))*
Italy　　(2) **2**　*(R.Baggio 21, 26)*

13 Jul. at The Rose Bowl, Pasadena　　　　　Att: 84,569
Brazil　　(0) **1**　*(Romario 79)*
Sweden　　**0**

3rd/4th Place Play-Off

16 Jul. at The Rose Bowl, Pasadena　　　　　Att: 83,716
Bulgaria　　**0**
Sweden　　(4) **4**　*(Brolin 8, Mild 30, Larsson 37,*
　　　　　　　　　　　　K.Andersson 39)

FINAL

17 Jul. at The Rose Bowl, Pasadena　　　　　Att: 94,194
Brazil　　**0**
Italy　　**0**
(Brazil won 3-2 on penalties)　AET　(Romario, Branco, Dunga/Albertini, Evani)

Brazil:　Taffarel, Jorginho, Aldair, Marcio Santos, Branco, Mauro Silva, Dunga, Mazinho, Zinho, Bebeto, Romario
　　　　　Subs: Cafu for Jorginho (21 mins.)
　　　　　　　　Viola for Mazinho (106 mins.)

Italy:　Pagliuca, Mussi, Baresi, Maldini, Benarrivo, Berti, Albertini, D.Baggio, Donadoni, R.Baggio, Massaro
　　　　　Subs: Apolloni for Mussi (34 mins)
　　　　　　　　Evani for D. Baggio (94 mins.)
　　　　　　　　　　　　　　　　　　　　　　　Ref: S. Puhl (Hungary)

Top Scorers

6　　Oleg Salenko (Russia), Hristo Stoichkov (Bulgaria)
5　　Kennet Andersson (Sweden), Roberto Baggio (Italy), Jurgen Klinsmann (Germany), Romario (Brazil)
4　　Gabriel Batistuta (Argentina), Martin Dahlin (Sweden), Florin Raducioiu (Romania)
3　　Bebeto (Brazil), Dennis Bergkamp (Holland), Tomas Brolin (Sweden), Caminero (Spain), Gheorghe Hagi (Romania)

Top: The Italian Job Ray Houghton's golden strike against Italy (The Star)
Bottom: B Class Babb bearing down on Bergkamp (The Star)

Senior Internationals 1993-94

World Cup Qualifying Games

8 Sep. at Landsdowne Road
Rep. of Ireland (2) **2** *(Aldridge 4, Kernaghan 25)*
Lithuania 0
Rep.of I.: Bonner (Celtic 67), Irwin (Man.Utd. 22), Moran (Blackburn Rov. 68), Kernaghan (Man. City 7), Phelan (Man. City 16), Keane (Man. Utd. 17), Houghton (Aston Villa 54), Townsend (Aston Villa 40), Quinn (Man. City 41), Aldridge (Tranmere Rov. 55), Staunton (Aston Villa 42)
Subs: Whelan (Liverpool 45) for Townsend 69 mins. Cascarino (Chelsea 44) for Quinn 75 mins.
Lithuania: Stauce, Ziukas, Baltusnikas, Kalvaitis, Tereskinas, Aspavicius, Baranauskas, Skarbauus (Stalyas 84), Sturmby, Kirilovia (Maciulevicius 69), Slekys.
Referee: R. Pederson (Norway)   Att. 33,000

13 Oct. at Landsdowne Road
Rep. of Ireland (0) **1** *(Sheridan 78)*
Spain (3) **3** *(Caminero 8, Salinas 12, 26)*
Rep.of I.: Bonner (Celtic 68), Irwin (Man.Utd. 23), Moran (Blackburn Rov. 69), Kernaghan (Man. City 8), Phelan (Man. City 17), Keane (Man. Utd.18), McGrath (Aston Villa 62), Whelan (Liverpool 46), Houghton (Aston Villa 55), Quinn (Man. City 42), Staunton (Aston Villa 43)
Subs: Sheridan (Sheffield Wed. 16) for Moran 22 mins. Cascarino (Chelsea 45) for Staunton h.time.
Spain: Zubizarreta, Ferrer, Voro, Nadal, Giner, Hierro, Goikoexea, Camarasa, Salinas (Guardiola 67), Caminero (Bakero 30), Luis-Enrique
Referee: F. Baldas (Italy)   Att: 34,000

17 Nov. at Windsor Park, Belfast
Northern Ireland (0) **1** *(Quinn 73)*
Rep. of Ireland (0) **1** *(McLoughlin 76)*
N. Ireland: Wright, Fleming, Worthington, Taggert, McDonald, Donaghy, Wilson (Black 78), Magilton, Quinn, Gray (Dowie 72), Hughes.
Rep.of I.: Bonner (Celtic 69), Irwin (Man.Utd. 24), McGrath (Aston Villas 63), Kernaghan (Man. City 9), Phelan (Man. City 18), Keane (Man. Utd. 19), Townsend (Aston Villa 41), Houghton (Aston Villa 56), Quinn (Man. City 43), Aldridge (Tranmere Rov. 56), McGoldrick (Arsenal 9)
Subs: McLoughlin (Portsmouth 15) for Houghton 70 mins. Cascarino (Chelsea 46) for Aldridge 81 mins.
Referee: A. Caker (Turkey)   Att. 10,500

Other Group 3 Results 1993/94

Aug. 25th **Denmark** (2) **4** *(Olsen, B.Laudrup, Pingle, Vilfort)*
Lithuania 0

Sep. 8th **Albania** 0
Denmark (1) **1** *(Pingle)*

Northern Ireland (1) **2** *(Quinn, Gray)*
Latvia 0

Sep. 22nd **Albania** (1) **1** *(Kushta)*
Spain (3) **5** *(Salinas 3, Munoz, Caminero)*

Oct. 13th **Denmark** (0) **1** *(B.Laudrup)*
Northern Ireland 0

Nov. 17th **Spain** (0) **1** *(Hierro)*
Denmark 0

	P.	W.	D.	L.	F.	A.	Pts.
Spain	12	8	3	1	27	4	19
*Rep. of Ireland	12	7	4	1	19	6	18 (+13)
Denmark	12	7	4	1	15	2	18 (+13)
N.Ireland	12	5	3	4	14	13	13
Lithuania	12	2	3	7	8	21	7
Latvia	12	0	5	7	4	21	5
Albania	12	1	2	9	6	26	4

*Republic of Ireland qualified having scored more goals than Denmark although having an identical points and goal difference total.

U-21 Internationals 1993/94

12 Oct. at United Park, Drogheda
Rep. of Ireland 0
Spain (1) **2** *(Guerrero 38, Oscar 63)*
Spain: Valencia, Velasco, Ramon, Samti, Lasa, Acosta (Carreras 80), Oscar, Imaz, Garcia San Juan, Guerrero (Galvez 65), Alfonso
Referee: Mr. C. Fallstrom (Sweden)   Att: 5,000

Friendly Games

24 Mar. at Landsdowne Road
Rep. of Ireland 0
Russia 0
Rep.of I.: Bonner (Celtic 70), G. Kelly (Leeds United 1), Carey (Leicester C. 3), Babb (Coventry C. 1), McGoldrick (Arsenal 10), McAteer (Bolton W. 1), Whelan (Liverpool 47), O'Brien (Tranmere Rov. 11), McLoughlin (Portsmouth 16), Cascarino (Chelsea 47), D. Kelly (Wolverhampton W. 16). Subs: A. Kelly (Shefield Utd. 2) for Bonner h.time. Coyne (Motherwell 10) for D. Kelly 65 mins.
Russia: Kharine, Khlestov, Gorloukovitch, Kakhimov, Koutown, Tetradze, Komeev (Tchertshev 60), Popov, Salenko, Borodiouk, Radchenko (Kossocapov 86)
Referee: C. Fallstrom (Sweden)   Att. 34,550

20 Apr. at Gemeentelijk Sportpark, Tilburg
Holland 0
Rep. of Ireland (0) 1   *(Coyne 55)*
Holland: de Goey, Valckx, Koeman (de Wolf h-time), F.de Boer, Davids, Jonk (Winter h.time), Overmars, Rijkaard, R. de Boer, Bergkamp (Taument h-time), Roy.
Rep.of I.: Bonner (Celtic 71), G. Kelly (Leeds United 2), Moran (Blackburn Rov. 70), Babb (Coventry C. 2), Phelan (Man. City 19), McGoldrick (Arsenal 11), Sheridan (Sheffield Wed. 17), Townsend (Aston Villa 42), Whelan (Liverpool 48), Coyne (Motherwell 11), Staunton (Aston Villa 44). Subs: McAteer (Bolton W. 2) for McGoldrick 70 mins. Coyle (Bolton W. 1) for Coyne 83 mins. (McLoughlin (Portsmouth 17) for Phelan 83 mins.
Referee: H. Strampe (Germany)   Att. app. 14,000

24 May at Landsdowne Road
Rep. of Ireland (0) 1   *(Sheridan 86)*
Bolivia 0
Rep.of I.: Bonner (Celtic 72), Irwin (Man. Utd. 25), Babb (Coventry C. 3), Moran (Blackburn Rov. 71), Phelan (Man. City 20), Sheridan (Sheffield Wed. 18), Houghton (Aston Villa 57), Townsend (Aston Villa 43), Keane (Man. Utd. 20), Coyne (Motherwell 12), Staunton (Aston Villa 45). Subs: G. Kelly (Leeds United 3) for Irwin h-time. Kernaghan (Man. City 10) for Moran h-time. McAteer (Bolton W. 3) for Houghton 59 mins. Cascarino (Chelsea 48) for Coyne 82 mins.
Bolivia: Trucco, Soruco, (J.M. Pena 50), Sandy, Angel, Quinteros, Ramos, Pinedo (Borja 50), Melgar, A. Pena (Castillo 68), Baldivesto, Cristaldo.
Referee: A. Howells (Wales)   Att: 32,500

29 May at Niedersachen Stadium Hannover
Germany 0
Rep. of Ireland (1) 2   *(Cascarino 31, G. Kelly 69)*
Germany: Illgner, Strunz, Kohler, Matthaus, Buchwald (Berthold 35), Moller, Sammer, Wagner, Basler, Riedle (Voller 67), Klinsmann.
Rep.of I.: A. Kelly (Sheffield Utd. 3), Irwin (Man. Utd. 26), Babb (Coventry C. 4), McGrath (Aston Villa 64), Phelan (Man. City 21), Sheridan (Sheffield Wed. 19), Keane (Man. Utd. 21), Townsend (Aston Villa 44), McAteer (Bolton W. 4), Cascarino (Chelsea 49), Staunton (Aston Villa 46). Subs: G. Kelly (Leeds Utd. 4) for Irwin h-time. Whelan (Liverpool 49) for Sheridan h-time. Coyne (Motherwell 13) for Cascarino 70 mins. Houghton (Aston Villa 58) for McAteer 87 mins.
Referee: J. Aranda-Encinar (Spain)   Att: 50,000

5 Jun. at Landsdowne Road
Rep. of Ireland (1) 1   *(Townsend 43)*
Czech Republic (1) 3   *(Kuka 25 (p), 55, Suchoparek 84)*
Rep.of I.: Bonner (Celtic 73), G. Kelly (Leeds United 5), McGrath (Aston Villa 65), Kernaghan (Man. City 11), Phelan (Man. City 22), McGoldrick (Arsenal 12), Townsend (Aston Villa 45), Sheridan (Sheffield Wed. 20), Aldridge (Tranmere Rov. 57), Cascarino (Chelsea 50), Staunton (Aston Villa 47). Subs: Keane (Man. Utd. 22) for McGoldrick 55 mins. McAteer (Bolton W. 5) for Aldridge 55 mins. Coyne (Motherwell 14) for Cascarino 66 mins. Babb (Coventry C. 5) for McGrath 79 mins.
Czech R.: Kouba, Repka, Suchoparek, Kotulek, Kubik, Smejkal, Nemec (Nedved 88), Novotny, Kuka, Poborsky, Frydkek (Samec 90).
Referee: Sundell (Sweden)   Att: 43,465

Tommy Coyne celebrates in Tilburg
(The Star)

Representative Matches

23 Jul. at Tolka Park
B.G. National League (1) **2** *(Tilson 43, Fenlon 78)*
Leeds United (0) **2** *(Shutt 64, Speed 76)*
National L.: Henderson (Bohemians), Neville (Shelbourne), Coll (Dundalk), Gauld (Derry City), Dunne (Dundalk), Byrne (Shamrock Rovers), McNulty (Dundalk), Carlyle (Derry City), Dully (Shelbourne), Fenlon (Bohemians), Tilson (Bohemians).
Subs: Barry (Cork City) for Dunne (27 mins)
Whelan (Bohemians) for Coll (54 mins)
Swan (Shamrock Rovers) for Dully (86 mins)
Leeds Utd.: Beeney, Kelly, Dorigo, Batty, Wetherall, Newsome, Strachan, Rod Wallace, Tobin (Shutt 60), McAllister, Speed.
Referee: O. Cooney (Dublin)   Att. 7,000 approx.

10 Aug. at Tolka Park
B.G. National League   **0**
Blackburn Rovers (0) **1** *(Newell 74)*
National L.: Henderson (Bohemians), Purdy (Dundalk), Coll (Dundalk), Neville (Shelbourne), Dunne (Dundalk), Byrne (Shamrock Rovers), McNulty (Dundalk), Doolin (Shelbourne), Morley (Cork City), Fenlon (Bohemians), Tilson (Bohemians).
Subs: O'Connor (Bohemians) for Byrne (60 mins.)
McGrath (Shamrock R.) for McNulty (60 m.)
Swan (Shamrock Rovers) for Morley (75 mins)
McDonnell (St Patrick's A.) for Dunne (86 m.)
Blackburn Rovers: Mimms, Berg, Dobson, Anderson, Marker (Morrison 52), Moran (May 52), Ripley, Atkins (Makel 67), Gallagher, Newell, Wilcox.
Referee: B. Shorte (Kildare)   Att. n/a

17 Aug. at Tolka Park
B.G. National League (0) **1** *(O'Connor 72)*
RCS (Czechoslovakia) (1) **4** *(Hapal 6, Postulka 53, Latal 57, Kuka 89)*
National L.: Henderson (Bohemians), Purdy (Dundalk), Curran (Derry City), Gauld (Derry City), Lawlor (Dundalk), McNulty (Dundalk), Carlyle (Derry City), Byrne (Shamrock Rovers), Swan (Shamrock Rovers), Fenlon (Bohemians), Tilson (Bohemians)
Subs: McGrath (Shamrock R.) for Tilson (59 m.)
O'Connor (Drogheda Utd.) for Swan (72 mins)
O'Driscoll (Bohemians) for Byrne (80 mins)
R.C.S.: Kouba (Stupala HT), Latal, Suchoparek, Krabec (Smicer HT), Novotny (Kinder HT), Hapal, Kubik (Repka HT), Berger (Molnar HT), Kuka, Postulka, Moravcik.
Referee: D. McArdle (Dundalk)   Att. 800 approx.

19 Oct. at Landsdowne Road
(Official switching on of new floodlights)
B.G. National League (1) **1** *(Morley 13)*
Liverpool (0) **2** *(Hutchinson 81, Coll (og) 89)*
National L.: Henderson (Bohemians), McNulty (Dundalk), Best (Bohemians), Coll (Dundalk), Brady (Shelbourne), Mooney (Shelbourne), Byrne (Shamrock Rovers), Doolin (Shelbourne), O'Connor (Drogheda United), Fenlon (Bohemians), Morley (Cork City).
Subs: O'Neill (Shamrock R.) for Henderson (HT)
Eviston (Shamrock R.) for Morley (65 mins.)
Liverpool: Grobbelaar, Matteo, Bjornebye, Nicol, Piechnik, Ruddock, Fowler (Hutchinson 72), Stewart, Rush (Patterson 55), Redknapp, Walters.
Referee: J. Seery (Northern Irl.)   Att. 28,000 approx.

Tony Gale Testimonial

8 May at Upton Park
West Ham United XI (0) **4** *(Dicks, Stuart 2, Mitchell)*
Rep. of Ireland XI (1) **2** *(Townsend 39, Dunne 60)*
R.O.I. XI: Bonner (Kelly H.T.), Kenna, Phelan, Townsend (Dunne 55), Moran (Scully H.T.), Fitzgerald, Byrne, Houghton, Stapleton, Rush, Staunton.
Att. 8,000 approx.

Kevin Moran Testimonial

11 May at Landsdowne Road
Republic of Ireland XI (0) **5** *(Sheridan 46, D. Kelly 69, 88, Moran 77 (pen.) Houghton 85)*
National Lottery XI (0) **1** *(Shearer 73)*
R.O.I. XI: Bonner (A. Kelly H.T.), McGoldrick, Moran, Kernaghan, Phelan, Staunton, Townsend (Babb H.T.), Sheridan, Houghton, Aldridge (Coyne H.T.), D. Kelly.
N.Lottery XI: Flowers (Blackburn Rov.), Jones (Liverpool), Nicol (Liverpool), Hendry (Blackburn Rov.), Le Saux (Blackburn Rov.), Sherwood (Blackburn Rov.), Strachan (Leeds United), McAllister (Leeds United), Barnes (Liverpool), Cole (Newcastle Utd.), Shearer (Blackburn Rov.)
Subs: Berg (Blackburn Rov.) for Le Saux (H.T.)
Rush (Liverpool) for Strachan (61 mins)
May (Blackburn Rov.) for Nicol (61 mins)
A. O'Neill (Shamrock R.) for Flowers (77 m.)
Referee: P. Kelly (Cork)   Att. 42,630

European Championship 1994-96 Group 6

1994

Apr. 20th	Northern Ireland	(3)	4	*(Quinn 2, Dowie, Lomas)*
	Liechtenstein	(0)	1	*(Hasler)*
Sep. 7th	Latvia		0	
	Rep. of Ireland	(2)	3	*(Aldridge 2 (1 pen.) Sheridan)*
	Liechtenstein		0	
	Austria	(3)	4	*(Polster 3, Aigner)*
	Northern Ireland	(0)	1	*(Quinn (pen))*
	Portugal	(1)	2	*(Costa, Oliviera)*
Oct. 9th	Latvia	(0)	1	*(Monjaks)*
	Portugal	(1)	3	*(Pinto: 2, Figo)*
Oct. 12th	Austria	(1)	1	*(Polster)*
	Northern Ireland	(2)	2	*(Gillespie, Gray)*
	Rep. of Ireland	(3)	4	*(Coyne: 2, Quinn 2)*
	Liechtenstein		0	

Nov. 13th	Portugal v Austria
Nov. 15th	Liechtenstein v Latvia
Nov. 16th	Northern Ireland v **Rep. of Ireland**
Dec. 18th	Portugal v Liechtenstein

1995

Mar. 29th	**Rep. of Ireland** v Northern Ireland
	Austria v Latvia
Apr. 26th	**Rep. of Ireland** v Portugal
	Latvia v Northern Ireland
	Austria v Liechtenstein
Jun. 3rd	Liechenstein v **Rep. of Ireland**
	Portugal v Latvia
Jun. 7th	Northern Ireland v Latvia
Jun. 11th	**Rep. of Ireland** v Austria
Aug. 15th	Liechtenstein v Portugal
Aug. 16th	Latvia v Austria
Sep. 3rd	Portugal v Northern Ireland
Sep. 6th	Austria v **Rep. of Ireland**
	Latvia v Liechtenstein
Oct. 11th	Austria v Portugal
	Liechtenstein v Northern Ireland
	Rep. of Ireland v Latvia
Nov. 15th	Northern Ireland v Austria
	Portugal v **Rep. of Ireland**

Black n' Blue
New York's finest keep a watchful eye at the Giant's Stadium (EOH)

Ladies Soccer 1993-94 Honours List
(Summer Season 1993)

	Winners	Runners-up	
LFAI Senior Cup	*Benfica*	College Corinthians	3-0
LFAI Presidents Cup	*Cork Rangers*	Lifford	2-1
Leinster Senior League	*Elm Rovers*	Brighton Celtic	
Leinster Senior Cup	*Brighton Celtic*	Verona	2-1
Munster Senior League	*Cork Rangers*	Benfica	
Munster Senior Cup	*Benfica*	Cork Rangers	1-0
Civil Service League	*Castle Rovers*	O'Connell Chics	
Civil Service Senior Cup	*Castle Rovers*	Drumcondra	3-0
Open Cup	*Castle Rovers*	Ballymun	2-0
Bracken Senior Cup	*Leinster 'A'*	Munster	2-0

FAI Senior Player of the Year   Susan Ronan (Welsox)

Friendly Internationals

24 Oct. '93 at Ray McSharry Park, Sligo
    Republic of Ireland   2 *(Towler, Leahy)*
    Northern Ireland   0
Rep. of Ireland: Susan Hayden, Nicki O'Neill, Imelda O'Hanlon, Caroline Nagle, Yvonne Lyons, Bernie O'Reilly, Liz Towler, Sue Ronan, Therese Leahy, Siobhán Furlong, Christine Dias.
    Subs used: Jackie McCarthy, Mary Shire, Jackie Braddish, Evelyn Carnegie

5 Jun. '94 at Pembroke
    Wales   0
    Republic of Ireland   2 *(Furlong (pen), Gallagher)*
Rep. of Ireland: S. Hayden, N. O'Neill, Y. Lyons, C. Nagle, Ronnie Nagle, T. Leahy, S. Ronan, Olivia O'Toole, L. Towler, S. Furlong (capt.), Marie Gallagher.
    Subs used: B. O'Reilly and Katie Liston

"Republic of Ireland - the First

Game No.	Date	Opponents	V	City	Stadium	Comp	H.T.	F.T.	Referee	1	2	3
1	210326	Italy	A	Turin	Montovelodromo	F	(0-3)	0-3	Ruoff (Swi)	Cannon	F.Brady	J.McCarthy
2	230427	Italy 'B'	H	Dublin	Landsdowne R.	F	(1-0)	1-2	Langenus (Bel)	Collins	F.Brady	Kirkland
3	120228	Belgium	A	Liege	Standard Liege	F	(0-2)	4-2	Kingscott (Eng)	Cannon	Robinson	J.McCarthy
4	200429	Belgium	H	Dublin	Dalymount Pk.	F	(1-0)	4-0	Westwood (Eng)	Farquharson	Maguire	Burke
5	110530	Belgium	A	Brussels	Astrid Parc	F	(1-1)	3-1	Melcon (Eng)	Farquharson	Lacey	J.McCarthy
6	260431	Spain	A	Barcelona	Montjoich	F	(1-1)	1-1	Romanhino (Por)	Farquharson	Lennox	Reid
7	131231	Spain	H	Dublin	Dalymount Pk.	F	(0-3)	0-5	Langenus (Bel)	Farquharson	Lennox	L.Doyle
8	080532	Holland	A	Amsterdam	De-Meer	F	(1-0)	2-0		M.McCarthy	J.Daly	P.Byrne
9	250234	Belgium	H	Dublin	Dalymount Pk.	WC	(1-2)	4-4	Crew (Eng)	J.Foley	Lynch	T.Burke
10	080434	Holland	A	Amsterdam	De-Meer	WC	(1-1)	2-5		J.Foley	Chatton	P.Byrne
11	151234	Hungary	H	Dublin	Dalymount Pk.	F	(1-2)	2-4	Langenus (Bel)	J.Foley	O'Kane	P.Bermingham[1]
12	050535	Switzerland	A	Basle	Ranv-Hov	F	(0-0)	0-1	Berenele (Aus)	J.Foley	O'Kane	L.Dunne
13	080535	Germany	A	Dortmund	Kampfbahn R.E.	F	(1-1)	1-3	A.Krist (Czech)	J.Foley	O'Kane	L.Dunne[1]
14	081235	Holland	H	Dublin	Dalymount Pk.	F	(3-2)	3-5	Bauwens (Ger)	Harrington	W.O'Neill	McGuire
15	170336	Switzerland	H	Dublin	Dalymount Pk.	F	(1-0)	1-0	Langenus (Bel)	Harrington	W.O'Neill	Gorman
16	030536	Hungary	A	Budapest	Hungaria Uti	F	(2-1)	3-3	Bruell (Czech)	Harrington	W.O'Neill	Gorman
17	090536	Luxembourg	A	Luxembourg	Stade Municipale	F	(1-0)	5-1	Bauwens (Ger)	Harrington	W.O'Neill	Gorman
18	171036	Germany	H	Dublin	Dalymount Pk.	F	(2-2)	5-2	Webb (Sco)	J.Foley	W.O'Neill	Gorman
19	061236	Hungary	H	Dublin	Dalymount Pk.	F	(1-2)	2-3	Nattrass (Eng)	J.Foley	W.O'Neill	Gorman
20	170537	Switzerland	A	Berne	Wankdorf	F	(1-0)	1-0	Lewington (Eng)	Breen	W.O'Neill	Feenan
21	230537	France	A	Paris	Colombes	F	(0-0)	2-0	A.Krist (Czech)	Breen	W.O'Neill	Feenan
22	101037	Norway	A	Oslo	Ullevaal	WC	(1-1)	2-3	Bauwens (Ger)	McKenzie	Williams	Hoy
23	071137	Norway	H	Dublin	Dalymount Pk.	WC	(1-2)	3-3	Gibbs (Eng)	McKenzie	W.O'Neill	Gorman
24	180538	Czechoslovakia	A	Prague	AC Sparta	F	(1-1)	2-2	Barlassina (Ita)	McKenzie	Gaskins	Gorman
25	220538	Poland	A	Warsaw	Military	F	(0-3)	0-6	Majorsky (Hun)	McKenzie*	Gaskins	Gorman
26	180938	Switzerland	H	Dublin	Dalymount Pk.	F	(3-0)	4-0	Mortimer (Eng)	McKenzie	Hoy	Gorman
27	131138	Poland	H	Dublin	Dalymount Pk.	F	(2-1)	3-2	Bauwens (Ger)	McKenzie	Hoy	Gorman
28	190339	Hungary	H	Cork	Mardyke	F	(1-1)	2-2		McKenzie	Hoy	Gorman
29	180539	Hungary	A	Budapest	MTK	F	(0-1)	2-2		McKenzie	Hoy	W.O'Neill
30	230539	Germany	A	Bremen	Weser	F	(0-1)	1-1	Remke (Den)	McKenzie	Hoy	W.O'Neill
31	160646	Portugal	A	Lisbon	Of Light	F	(0-3)	1-3		Courtney*	McMillan	Aherne
32	230646	Spain	A	Madrid	Metropolitano	F	(1-0)	1-0	Wartburg (Swi)	C.Martin	McMillan	Aherne
33	300946	England	H	Dublin	Dalymount Pk.	F	(0-0)	0-1	Webb (Sco)	Breen	Gorman	W.E.Hayes
34	020347	Spain	H	Dublin	Dalymount Pk.	F	(2-1)	3-2	Barrick (Eng)	Breen	J.McGowan	P.D.Farrell
35	040547	Portugal	H	Dublin	Dalymount Pk.	F	(0-2)	0-2	Pearse (Eng)	Breen	Gorman	W.E.Hayes
36	230548	Portugal	A	Lisbon	Of Light	F	(0-2)	0-2		G.Moulson	K.Clarke	C.Martin
37	300548	Spain	A	Barcelona	Montjuich	F	(1-1)	1-2	Szel (Fra)	G.Moulson	K.Clarke	C.Martin
38	051248	Switzerland	H	Dublin	Dalymount Pk.	F	(0-0)	0-1	Reader (Eng)	G.Moulson	Keane	C.Martin
39	240449	Belgium	H	Dublin	Dalymount Pk.	F	(0-0)	0-2	Sdez (Fra)	W.J.Hayes	O'Byrne	C.Martin
40	220549	Portugal	H	Dublin	Dalymount Pk.	F	(1-0)	1-0	Le Foll (Fra)	Godwin	Koane	C.Martin
41	020649	Sweden	A	Stockholm	Resunda	WC	(1-2)	1-3	Baert (Bel)	Godwin	Keane	C.Martin
42	120649	Spain	A	Dublin	Dalymount Pk.	F	(1-3)	1-4	Ellis (Eng)	Godwin	Keane	C.Martin
43	080949	Finland	H	Dublin	Dalymount Pk.	WC	(2-0)	3-0	Evans (Eng)	Godwin	Aherne	C.Martin[2]
44	210949	England	A	Liverpool	Goodison Pk.	F	(1-0)	2-0	Mowat (Sco)	Godwin	Aherne	C.Martin[1]
45	091049	Finland	A	Helsinki	Olympic	WC	(0-0)	1-1	Bronkhorst (Hol)	Godwin	Aherne	C.Martin
46	131149	Sweden	H	Dublin	Dalymount Pk.	WC	(0-2)	1-3	Ling (Eng)	Godwin	Aherne	C.Martin
47	100550	Belgium	A	Brussels	Century	F	(0-3)	1-5	Bronkhorst (Hol)	Aherne	Aherne	C.Martin
48	261150	Norway	H	Dublin	Dalymount Pk.	F	(1-2)	2-2	Pearce (Eng)	Godwin	Aherne	S.Fallon
49	130551	Argentina	H	Dublin	Dalymount Pk.	F	(0-0)	0-1	Leafe (Eng)	Kiernan	Aherne	C.Martin
50	300551	Norway	A	Oslo	Ullevaal	F	(1-1)	3-2	Jorgensen (Den)	Kiernan	Aherne	Clinton
51	171051	W.Germany	H	Dublin	Dalymount Pk.	F	(2-0)	3-2	Ling (Eng)	Kiernan	Aherne	S.Fallon
52	040552	W.Germany	A	Cologne	Mungesdorfer	F	(0-1)	0-3	Ellis (Eng)	Kiernan	Aherne	S.Fallon
53	070552	Austria	A	Vienna	Praeter Pk.	F	(0-4)	0-6	Reinhardt (W.Ger)	Kiernan	Aherne	S.Fallon
54	010652	Spain	A	Madrid	Chamartin	F	(0-4)	0-6	Leafe (Eng)	J.O'Neill	Aherne	S.Fallon
55	161152	France	H	Dublin	Dalymount Pk.	F	(1-0)	1-1	Alsteen (Bel)	J.O'Neill	Aherne	S.Fallon[1]
56	250353	Austria	H	Dublin	Dalymount Pk.	F	(0-0)	4-0	Ellis (Eng)	J.O'Neill	JR.Lawler	O'Farrell[1]
57	041053	France	A	Dublin	Dalymount Pk.	WC	(0-2)	3-5	Franken (Bel)	J.O'Neill	Aherne	O'Farrell[1]
58	281053	Luxembourg	H	Dublin	Dalymount Pk.	WC	(1-0)	4-0	Bond (Eng)	J.O'Neill	JR.Lawler	Gannon
59	251153	France	A	Paris	Parc de Princes	WC	(0-0)	0-1	Van Noffel (Bel)	J.O'Neill	JR.Lawler	Gannon
60	070354	Luxembourg	A	Luxembourg	Stade Municipale	WC	(0-0)	1-0	Ausum (Hol)	Scannell	Traynor	M.Galagher

150 games 1926 - 1975"

Game No.	4	5	6	7	8	9	10	11	12	13
1	M.Foley	D.Doyle	J.Connolly	Flood	Grace	Watters	B.Fullam	J.Fagan		
2	Glen	O'Brien	Muldoon	Lacey	Duggan	Martin	B.Fullam[1]	Kendrick		
3	J.Kinsella	Sullivan[1]	Barry	Lacey[1]	J.Byrne	White[2]	Dowdall	Golding		
4	Glen	O'Brien	Barry	J.Bermingham	Flood[3]	D.Byrne[1]	Dowdall	Egan		
5	Glen	O'Brien	McLoughlin	Duggan	Flood[1]	J.Dunne[2]	Horlacher	Golding		
6	P.Byrne	Robinson	Chatton	S.Byrne	Flood	Dowdall	Moore[1]	Kavanagh		
7	Glen	McLoughlin	Chatton	Gallagher	Flood	D.Byrne	Horlacher	Kavanagh		
8	O'Reilly[1]	O'Brien	O.Kinsella	Kennedy	Stevenson	Moore[1]	Horlacher	J.Kelly		
9	Gaskins	O'Reilly	Kendrick	Kennedy	D.Byrne	Moore[4]	O'Keeffe	J.Kelly		
10	Gaskins	O'Reilly	Kendrick	Kennedy	Squires[1]	Moore[1]	W.Jordan*	Meehan	Horlacher[40]	
11	Gaskins	Lennon	Horlacher	Griffiths	J.Donnelly[1]	Moore	Rigby	W.Fallon		
12	Gaskins	Lennon	Hutchinson	J.Daly	Ellis	J.Donnelly	Rigby	Monahan		
13	Gaskins	Lennon	Hutchinson	Moore	Ellis	J.Donnelly	Rigby	Monahan		
14	Glen	Andrews	O'Reilly	Moore	Ellis[1]	J.Donnelly	Horlacher[2]	Kendrick		
15	Glen	C.Turner	O'Reilly	J.Dunne[1]	Ellis	J.Donnelly	Horlacher	J.Kelly		
16	Glen	C.Moulsen	O'Reilly	J.Dunne[2]	Duggan	J.Donnelly	Madden[1]	W.Fallon		
17	Glen	C.Moulsen	O'Reilly	J.Dunne[2]	Duggan	J.Donnelly[1]	Ellis	J.Kelly[2]		
18	C.Turner	H.Connolly	O'Reilly	Moore	Geoghegan[1]	J.Donnelly[2]	Ellis	Davis[2]		
19	C.Turner	C.Moulsen	O'Reilly	Moore	W.Fallon[1]	J.Donnelly	Ellis	Davis[1]		
20	C.Turner	C.Moulsen	O'Reilly	Brown	D.Jordan	J.Dunne[1]	P.Farrell	W.Fallon		
21	C.Turner	C.Moulsen	O'Reilly	Brown[1]	D.Jordan[1]	J.Dunne	P.Farrell	W.Fallon		
22	C.Turner	O.Kinsella	O'Reilly	J. Donnelly	T.Donnelly	J.Dunne[1]	W.Jordan	Geoghegan[1]		
23	C.Turner	Arrigan	O'Reilly	K.O'Flanagan	Duggan[1]	J.Dunne[1]	Carey	Foy		
24	C.Turner	O'Mahoney	O'Reilly	K.O'Flanagan	Davis[1]	J.Dunne[1]	Carey	O'Keeffe		
25	C.Turner	O'Mahoney	O'Reilly	K.O'Flanagan	Davis	J.Dunne	Carey	O'Keeffe	Harrington[69]	
26	Lunn	O'Mahoney	O'Reilly	T.Donnelly[1]	Bradshaw[2]	J.Dunne[1]	Carey	W.Fallon		
27	Lunn	O'Mahoney	O'Reilly	K.O'Flanagan	Bradshaw	J.Dunne[1]	Carey[1]	W.Fallon[1]		
28	C.Turner	Weir	O'Reilly	K.O'Flanagan	Bradshaw[1]	J.Dunne	Carey[1]	Foy		
29	O'Mahoney	Weir	O'Reilly	K.O'Flanagan[2]	Bradshaw	J.Dunne	Carey	W.Fallon		
30	O'Mahoney	Weir	O'Reilly	K.O'Flanagan	Bradshaw[1]	J.Dunne	Carey	W.Fallon		
31	Carey	Vernon	PD.Farrell	JK.O'Reilly[1]	Sloan	D.Walsh	McAlinden	Eglington	C.Martin[30]	
32	Carey	Vernon	PD.Farrell	JK.O'Reilly	Sloan[1]	D.Walsh	McAlinden	Eglington		
33	Carey	C.Martin	W.Walsh	K.O'Flanagan	Coad	M.O'Flanagan	Stevenson	Eglington		
34	Carey	C.Martin	W.Walsh	Coad[1]	D.Walsh[2]	Stevenson	Eglington			
35	Carey	PD.Farrell	W.Walsh	K.O'Flanagan	Coad	D.Walsh	Stevenson	Eglington		
36	Carey	PD.Farrell	W.Walsh	Henderson	Coad	D.Walsh	Stevenson	Eglington		
37	Carey	PD.Farrell	W.Walsh	Henderson	Coad	D.Walsh	Stevenson	Moroney[1]		
38	Carey	PD.Farrell	Gannon	O'Driscoll	Coad	D.Walsh	Stevenson	Eglinton		
39	Carey	Gannon	W.Walsh	O'Driscoll	Coad	JK.Lawlor	Carroll	Malone		
40	Carey	Gannon	Moroney	Corr	Coad[1]	D.Walsh*	D.McGowan	Eglinton	PD.Farrell[35]	
41	Carey	Gannon	Moroney	O'Driscoll	Coad	D.Walsh[1]	D.McGowan	Eglinton		
42	Carey	Gannon	Moroney	Corr	PD.Farrell	D.Walsh	D.McGowan	Hartnett		
43	Carey	Gannon	Moroney	Gavin[1]	Fitzsimons	Carroll*	Desmond	TM.O'Connor	P.Daly[20]	
44	Carey	W.Walsh	Moroney	Corr	PD.Farrell[1]	D.Walsh	Desmond	TM.O'Connor		
45	Carey	Coffey	Moroney	Gavin	PD.Farrell[1]	D.Walsh	Desmond	TM.O'Connor		
46	Carey	W.Walsh	Ryan	Corr	PD.Farrell	D.Walsh	Desmond	TM.O'Connor		
47	Moroney	W.Walsh	Ryan	Murray	Fitzsimons	Duffy[1]	M. Clarke	Colfer		
48	Moroney	Gannon	Ryan	C.Giles	JK.Lawlor	D.Walsh[1]	Carey[1]	Eglinton		
49	PD.Farrell	Ringstead	Ryan	Higgins	JK.Lawlor	D.Walsh	Carey	Eglington		
50	PD.Farrell[1]	Ringstead[1]	Ryan	Moroney	Cunneen*	D.Walsh	Carey	Colfer	Coad[1 42]	Posipal o.g.
51	PD.Farrell	Ringstead	Ryan	Moroney	Fitzsimons[1]	Glynn[1]	F.Burke	Eglington		
52	PD.Farrell	Ringstead	Ryan	Gannon	Fitzsimons	Gibbons	C.Martin	Eglington		
53	PD.Farrell	Ringstead	Ryan	Gannon	Fitzsimons	O'Farrell	C.Martin	Eglington		
54	PD.Farrell	Ringstead	Ryan	Coad	Fitzsimons	D.Walsh	C.Martin	Eglington		
55	PD.Farrell	S.Dunne	Ryan	Cusack	Fitzsimons	Gavin	Carey	Eglington		
56	PD.Farrell	S.Dunne	Ryan	Ringstead[2]	Fitzsimons	D.Walsh	Carey	Eglington[1]		
57	PD.Farrell	S.Dunne	Ryan[1]	C.Martin	Fitzsimons	D.Walsh[1]	Moroney	Eglington		
58	Cantwell	S.Dunne	Ryan[1]	Munroe	Fitzsimons[2]	Gibbons	Cummins	Eglington[1]		
59	Clinton	C.Martin	Ryan	PD.Farrell	Fitzsimons	D.Walsh	Ringstead	Eglington		
60	Clinton	C.Martin	Saward	Gavin	N.Kelly	F.Kearns	Cummins[1]	Hartnett		

101

Game No.	Date	Opponents	V	City	Stadium	Comp	H.T.	F.T.	Referee	1	2	3
61	081154	Norway	H	Dublin	Dalymount Pk.	F	(0-1)	2-1	Clough (Eng)	J.O'Neill	JR.Lawler	Donovan
62	010555	Holland	H	Dublin	Dalymount Pk.	F	(0-0)	1-0	Luty (Eng)	J.O'Neill	JR.Lawler	Donovan
63	250555	Norway	A	Oslo	Bislett	F	(1-1)	3-1	Meissner (W.Ger)	J.O'Neill	JR.Lawler	Donovan
64	280555	W.Germany	A	Hamburg	Volkspark	F	(0-1)	1-2	Vandermeer (Hol)	J.O'Neill	JR.Lawler	Donovan
65	191055	Yugoslavia	H	Dublin	Dalymount Pk.	F	(1-3)	1-4	Murdock (Eng)	J.O'Neill	JR.Lawler	Murphy
66	271155	Spain	H	Dublin	Dalymount Pk.	F	(1-2)	2-2	Ellis (Eng)	J.O'Neill	S.Dunne	Cantwell
67	100556	Holland	A	Rotterdam	Feynoord	F	(0-0)	4-1	Penning (W.Ger)	Godwin	S.Dunne	Cantwell
68	031056	Denmark	H	Dublin	Dalymount Pk.	WC	(2-0)	2-1	Bond (Eng)	J.O'Neill	S.Dunne	Cantwell
69	251156	W.Germany	H	Dublin	Dalymount Pk.	F	(0-0)	3-0	Murdock (Eng)	A.Kelly	S.Dunne	Cantwell[1]
70	080557	England	A	London	Wembley	WC	(0-4)	1-5	Phillips (Sco)	A.Kelly	Donovan	Cantwell
71	190557	England	H	Dublin	Dalymount Pk.	WC	(1-0)	1-1	Phillips (Sco)	Godwin	S.Dunne	Cantwell
72	021057	Denmark	A	Copenhagen	Idraetspark	WC	(0-0)	2-0	Schulz (E.Ger)	Godwin	S.Dunne	Cantwell
73	110558	Poland	A	Katowice	Slaski	F	(1-1)	2-2	Romain (Aus)	Godwin	S.Dunne	Cantwell
74	140558	Austria	A	Vienna	Praeter Pk.	F	(0-1)	1-3	Wyssling (Swi)	J.O'Neill	S.Dunne	Cantwell
75	051058	Poland	H	Dublin	Dalymount Pk.	F	(2-2)	2-2	Clough (Eng)	J.O'Neill*	S.Dunne	Cantwell[2]
76	050459	Czechoslovakia	H	Dublin	Dalymount Pk.	EC	(2-0)	2-0	Van Nuffel (Bel)	J.O'Neill	McNally	Cantwell[1]
77	100559	Czechoslovakia	A	Bratislava	Thelnepole	EC	(0-1)	0-4	Barberan (Fra)	J.O'Neill	Whittaker	Cantwell
78	011159	Sweden	H	Dublin	Dalymount Pk.	F	(2-2)	3-2	Holland (Eng)	Dwyer	Carolan	Cantwell
79	300360	Chile	H	Dublin	Dalymount Pk.	F	(1-0)	2-0	Aston (Eng)	Dwyer	Carolan	Cantwell[1]
80	110560	W.Germany	A	Dusseldorf	Rhinestadion	F	(1-0)	1-0	Ellis (Eng)	Dwyer	S.Dunne	McGrath
81	180560	Sweden	A	Malmö	Malmö	F	(0-3)	1-4	Bronkhurst (Hol)	Dwyer#	S.Dunne	McGrath
82	280960	Wales	H	Dublin	Dalymount Pk.	F	(1-1)	2-3	Best (USA)	Dwyer	P.Kelly	McGrath
83	061160	Norway	H	Dublin	Dalymount Pk.	F	(2-1)	3-1	Bowman (Sco)	Dwyer	P.Kelly	Cantwell
84	030561	Scotland	A	Glasgow	Hampden Pk.	WC	(0-2)	1-4	Guique (Fra)	Dwyer	McNally	Cantwell
85	070561	Scotland	H	Dublin	Dalymount Pk.	WC	(0-2)	0-3	Grandin (Bel)	Dwyer	P.Kelly	Cantwell
86	081061	Czechoslovakia	H	Dublin	Dalymount. Pk.	WC	(1-1)	1-3	Holland (Eng)	Dwyer	P.Kelly	Cantwell
87	291061	Czechoslovakia	A	Prague	Strahove	F	(0-4)	1-7	Lundell (Swe)	Dwyer	P.Kelly	Cantwell
88	080462	Austria	H	Dublin	Dalymount Pk.	F	(0-1)	2-3	Gulde (Swi)	A.Kelly*	A.Dunne	Cantwell[1]
89	120862	Iceland	H	Dublin	Dalymount Pk.	EC	(2-1)	4-2	Smith (Wal)	A.Kelly	A.Dunne	Cantwell[2]
90	020962	Iceland	A	Reykjavik	Laugardalsvöllur	EC	(0-1)	1-1	Nielsen (Nor)	A.Kelly	McNally	Cantwell
91	090663	Scotland	H	Dublin	Dalymount Pk.	F	(1-0)	1-0	Howley (Eng)	A.Kelly	A.Dunne	Cantwell[1]
92	250963	Austria	A	Vienna	Praeter Pk.	EC	(0-0)	0-0	Gere (Hun)	A.Kelly	Browne	R.Brady
93	131063	Austria	H	Dublin	Dalymount Pk.	EC	(1-1)	3-2	Poulsen (Den)	A.Kelly	A.Dunne	R.Brady
94	110364	Spain	A	Seville	Sanchez Pizjuan	EC	(1-4)	1-5	Van Nuffel (Bel)	A.Kelly	T.Foley	R.Brady
95	080464	Spain	H	Dublin	Dalymount Pk.	EC	(0-1)	0-2	Versyp (Bel)	A.Kelly	A.Dunne	R.Brady
96	100564	Poland	A	Crakow	Vistula	F	(1-1)	1-3	Kainer (Aus)	A.Kelly*	A.Dunne	R.Brady
97	130564	Norway	A	Oslo	Ullevaal	F	(2-0)	4-1	Malka (W.Ger)	Dwyer	A.Dunne	R.Brady
98	240564	England	H	Dublin	Dalymount Pk.	F	(1-2)	1-3	Davidson (Sco)	Dwyer	A.Dunne	Cantwell
99	251064	Poland	H	Dublin	Dalymount Pk.	F	(1-2)	3-2	Clements (Eng)	Dwyer	A.Dunne	Cantwell
100	240365	Belgium	H	Dublin	Dalymount Pk.	F	(0-1)	0-2	Bogaerts (Hol)	A.Kelly	Meagan	F.Brennan
101	050565	Spain	H	Dublin	Dalymount Pk.	WC	(0-0)	1-0	Callaghan (Wal)	P.Dunne	A.Dunne	S.Brennan
102	271065	Spain	A	Seville	Sanchez Pizjuan	WC	(1-2)	1-4	Freitas (Por)	P.Dunne	A.Dunne	Meagan
103	101165	Spain	N	Paris	Colombes	WC	(0-0)	0-1	Schwinte (Fra)	P.Dunne	A.Dunne	Meagan
104	040566	W.Germany	H	Dublin	Dalymount Pk.	F	(0-2)	0-4	Mullen (Sco)	P.Dunne	Strahan	Hurley
105	220566	Austria	A	Vienna	Praeter Pk.	F	(0-0)	0-1	Gere (Hun)	A.Kelly	A.Dunne	Hurley
106	250566	Belgium	A	Liege	Standard Liege	F	(1-2)	3-2	Schwinte (Fra)	A.Kelly	A.Dunne	Hurley
107	231066	Spain	H	Dublin	Dalymount Pk.	EC	(0-0)	0-0	Carlsson (Swe)	A.Kelly	A.Dunne	Conway
108	161166	Turkey	H	Dublin	Dalymount Pk.	EC	(0-0)	2-1	Sorensen (Den)	P.Dunne	A.Dunne	Conway
109	071266	Spain	A	Valencia	Mestalla	EC	(0-2)	0-2	Roomer (Hol)	A.Kelly	A.Dunne	Conway
110	220267	Turkey	A	Ankara	May 19th	EC	(0-1)	1-2	Roumenchev (Bul)	A.Kelly	Kinnear	Finucane
111	210567	Czechoslovakia	H	Dublin	Dalymount Pk.	EC	(0-1)	0-2	Schaut (Bel)	A.Kelly	T.Foley	Finucane
112	221167	Czechoslovakia	A	Prague	Slavia	EC	(0-0)	2-1	Vetter (E.Ger)	A.Kelly	Kinnear	Conway
113	150568	Poland	H	Dublin	Dalymount Pk.	F	(0-2)	2-2	Jennings (Eng)	A.Kelly	Kinnear	T.Carroll
114	301068	Poland	A	Katowice	Slaski	F	(0-0)	0-1		A.Kelly*	A.Dunne	T.Carroll
115	101168	Austria	H	Dublin	Dalymount Pk.	F	(0-1)	2-2	Davidson (Sco)	A.Kelly	Kinnear	T.Carroll
116	041268	Denmark	H	Dublin	Dalymount Pk.	WC	(1-1)	1-1	Syme (Sco)	A.Kelly	A.Dunne	T.Carroll
117	040569	Czechoslovakia	H	Dublin	Dalymount Pk.	WC	(1-0)	1-2	Ribeiro (Por)	A.Kelly	Mulligan	S.Brennan
118	270569	Denmark	A	Copenhagen	Idraetspark	WC	(0-1)	0-2	Arkhipov (USSR)	A.Kelly	Mulligan	S.Brennan
119	080669	Hungary	H	Dublin	Dalymount Pk.	WC	(0-1)	1-2	Loraux (Bel)	A.Kelly	Mulligan	S.Brennan
120	210969	Scotland	H	Dublin	Dalymount Pk.	F	(1-1)	1-1	Burtenshaw (Eng)	A.Kelly	Mulligan	S.Brennan
121	071069	Czechoslovakia	A	Prague	Sparta	F	(0-3)	0-3	Lo-Bello (Ita)	Fitzpatrick	Mulligan	S.Brennan
122	151069	Denmark	H	Dublin	Dalymount Pk.	WC	(1-0)	1-1	Patterson (Sco)	A.Kelly	Mulligan	S.Brennan

Game No.	4	5	6	7	8	9	10	11	12	13
61	Gannon	C.Martin[1]	Ryan[1]	PD.Farrell	F.Fagan	Ambrose	Cummins	Eglington		
62	O'Farrell	C.Martin	Gavin	PD.Farrell	Fitzsimons	Ambrose	J.Fitzgerald[1]	Eglington		
63	O'Farrell	C.Martin	Gannon	Ringstead	Fitzsimons	S.Fallon	Cummins[2]	Glynn		
64	Gavin	C.Martin	Gannon	PD.Farrell	Fitzsimons	S.Fallon[1]	Cummins	Eglington		
65	O'Farrell	C.Martin	PD.Farrell	Ringstead	Fitzsimons[1]	Gibbons	Cummins	Tuohy		
66	Ryan	C.Martin	PD.Farrell	Ringstead[1]	Fitzsimons[1]	Gibbons	Cummins	Eglington		
67	O'Farrell	C.Martin	T.Dunne	Ringstead[1]	Fitzsimons[2]	J.Fitzgerald	L.Whelan	Haverty[1]		
68	Mackey	Nolan	T.Dunne	Gavin[1]	Fitzsimons	Curtis[1]	L.Whelan	Haverty		
69	Mackey	Nolan	T.Dunne	McCann[1]	Fitzsimons	Curtis	Peyton	Haverty[1]		
70	Mackey	PD.Farrell	Saward	Ringstead	Fitzsimons	Curtis[1]	L.Whelan	Haverty		
71	Hurley	Nolan	Saward	Ringstead[1]	Fitzsimons	Curtis	L.Whelan	Haverty		
72	Hurley	O'Farrell	Saward	Ringstead	Fitzsimons	Curtis[1]	Cummins[1]	Haverty		
73	Hurley	Nolan	Saward	Ringstead	Fitzsimons	Curtis[1]	Cummins[1]	Haverty		
74	Hurley	McGrath	Saward	Ringstead	Fitzsimons	Curtis[1]	Cummins	Haverty		
75	S.Keogh	McGrath	Saward	Ringstead	Curtis	Cummins	Haverty	Taylor		
76	Hurley	McGrath	Saward	Ringstead	Hamilton	C.Doyle	Cummins	Tuohy[1]		
77	Hurley	McGrath	O'Farrell	Ringstead	Hamilton	Fitzsimons	Cummins	Tuohy		
78	Hurley	McGrath	Saward	J.Giles[1]	F.Fagan	Curtis[2]	Cummins	Haverty		
79	Hurley	Nolan	Saward	J.Giles	F.Fagan	Curtis[1]	Cummins	Haverty		
80	Hurley	Nolan	Saward	Fogarty	F.Fagan[1]	Curtis	Cummins	Peyton		
81	Hurley	Nolan	Saward	Fogarty	F.Fagan[1]	Curtis	Cummins	Cantwell*	Peyton 43	Swan h.t.
82	Hurley	JS.O'Neill	Saward	J.Giles	F.Fagan[2]	P.Fitzgerald	Peyton	Haverty		
83	Hurley	Fullam	Saward	J.Giles	F.Fagan[1]	P.Fitzgerald[2]	Curtis	Haverty		
84	Hurley	McEvoy	Saward	J.Giles	Fogarty	Cummins	Curtis	Haverty[1]		
85	Hurley	McEvoy	Meagan	J.Giles	F.Fagan	Cummins	P.Fitzgerald	Haverty		
86	Hurley	McGrath	Nolan	J.Giles[1]	Fogarty	F.O'Neill	P.Fitzgerald	Haverty		
87	Hurley	McGrath	Nolan	J.Giles	Fogarty[1]	F.O'Neill	P.Fitzgerald	Haverty		
88	Hurley	Traynor	Meagan	J.Giles	Saward	Curtis	Hale	Tuohy[1]	Lowry 34	
89	Hurley	Traynor	Meagan	J.Giles	Saward	Fogarty[1]	Hale	Tuohy[1]		
90	Hurley	Traynor	Nolan	Curtis	Saward	Fogarty	Peyton*	Tuohy[1]		
91	Hurley	Traynor	McGrath	J.Giles	McEvoy	P.Turner	Peyton*	Haverty	Fogarty h.t.	
92	Hurley	Traynor	McGrath	J.Giles	R.Whelan	Fogarty	Curtis	Tuohy		
93	Hurley	Traynor	McGrath	J.Giles	McEvoy	Fogarty	Cantwell[2]	Haverty		Koller o.g.
94	Hurley	Traynor	Meagan	J.Giles	McEvoy	Fogarty	Hale	Haverty		
95	Hurley	Browne	Fullam	J.Giles	McEvoy	Cantwell	Hale	P.Turner		
96	Hurley	T.Foley	Fullam	J.Giles	McEvoy	Strahan	Ambrose	Haverty	Dwyer 50	
97	Hurley[2]	T.Foley	Fullam	J.Giles[1]	McEvoy[1]	Strahan	Ambrose	Haverty		
98	Bailham	Browne	McGrath	J.Giles	McEvoy	Strahan[1]	Ambrose	Haverty*	R.Whelan 5	
99	T.Foley	F.O'Neill	McGrath	Hennessey	McEvoy[2]	Strahan	Mooney[1]	Haverty		
100	T.Foley	F.O'Neill	McGrath	Hennessey	McEvoy	Conmy	Mooney	Tuohy		Iribar o.g.
101	Hurley	F.O'Neill	McGrath	Hennessey	McEvoy	J.Giles	Cantwell	Haverty		
102	T.Foley	F.O'Neill	McGrath	Barber	McEvoy[1]	J.Giles	Cantwell	Haverty		
103	T.Foley	F.O'Neill	S.Brennan	Dunphy	McEvoy	J.Giles	Cantwell	Haverty		
104	T.Foley*	F.O'Neill	McGrath	Dunphy	Hennessey	Treacy	Gilbert	Haverty	J.Keogh 10	
105	S.Brennan	F.O'Neill	McGrath	Meagan	Fullam	J.Giles	Cantwell	Haverty		
106	S.Brennan	Barber	McGrath	Meagan	Fullam[1]	J.Giles	Cantwell[2]	Haverty		
107	S.Brennan	F.O'Neill	McEvoy	Meagan	Treacy	J.Giles	Cantwell	O'Connell		
108	S.Brennan	F.O'Neill[1]	McEvoy[1]	Meagan	Hurley	J.Giles	Dunphy	Haverty		
109	S.Brennan	F.O'Neill	Dempsey	Meagan	Hurley	Hale	Dunphy	Haverty		
110	McGrath	F.O'Neill	Cantwell[1]	Meagan	Hurley	J.Giles	Dunphy	Gallagher		
111	Dempsey	Conmy	McEvoy	Meagan	Hurley	Treacy	Dunphy	Gallagher		
112	Dempsey	Conmy	Rogers	Meagan	Hurley	Treacy[1]	Dunphy	TR.O'Connor[1]		
113	Dempsey[1]	Conmy	Rogers*	Meagan	Hurley	Treacy	Dunphy	Fullam	Hale[1] 71	
114	Dempsey	F.O'Neill	Rogers	Hale	Hurley	Treacy	Dunphy	Fullam	Smyth 61	
115	Dempsey	F.O'Neill	Rogers[1]	Hale[1]	Hennessey*	J.Giles	Dunphy	Fullam	Conway 54	mins. due to fog
116	Dempsey	F.O'Neill	Rogers	Hale	Hurley	J.Giles[1]	Dunphy	Fullam	Abandoned 51	
117	Dempsey	F.O'Neill	Rogers[1]	Finucane	Hurley	J.Giles	Leech*	Treacy	Hand 40	
118	Dempsey	Newman*	Rogers	Finucane	Dunphy	Givens	Leech	Treacy	F.O'Neill 55	
119	A.Dunne	Conway	Rogers	Finucane	Dunphy	Givens[1]	Leech	Hurley*	F.O'Neill h.t.	
120	Meagan	Conway	Rogers	Finucane	Hale	Givens[1]	J.Giles	Treacy		
121	Kinnear	Conway	T.Carroll	Finucane	Hale	Givens*	Conroy	Conmy	Fullam h.t.	
122	Kinnear	Conway	Rogers	T.Byrne	Dunphy	Givens[1]	Conroy	Treacy		

103

Game No.	Date	Opponents	V	City	Stadium	Comp	H.T.	F.T.	Referee	1	2	3
123	051169	Hungary	A	Budapest	Nep	WC	(0-1)	0-4	Jakse (Yug)	A.Kelly	Mulligan	S.Brennan
124	060570	Poland	A	Poznan	Warta	F	(0-2)	1-2		A.Kelly	Mulligan	Hand
125	090570	W.Germany	A	Berlin	Olympic	F	(0-1)	1-2	Boström (Swe)	A.Kelly	Mulligan[1]	Hand
126	230970	Poland	H	Dublin	Dalymount Pk.	F	(0-2)	0-2	Lyden (Eng)	A.Kelly*	Mulligan	Hand
127	141070	Sweden	H	Dublin	Dalymount Pk.	EC	(1-0)	1-1	Halles (Fra)	A.Kelly	Mulligan	T.Carroll*[1]
128	281070	Sweden	A	Stockholm	Fotbollstadion	EC	(0-0)	0-1	Kazakov (USSR)	A.Kelly	Dunning	Finucane
129	081270	Italy	A	Florence	Comunale	EC	(0-2)	0-3	Schaut (Bel)	A.Kelly	Dunning	Finucane
130	100571	Italy	H	Dublin	Landsdowne Rd.	EC	(1-1)	1-2	Schulenburg (E.Ger)	A.Kelly	Kinnear	Mulligan
131	300571	Austria	H	Dublin	Dalymount Pk.	EC	(0-3)	1-4	Hoberg (Nor)	A.Kelly	JC.Dunne	Hand
132	101071	Austria	A	Linz	Linzer	EC	(0-3)	0-6	Goppel (Swi)	Roche	Gannon	Herrick
133	110672	Iran	N	Recife	Santa Cruz	F	(0-1)	2-1	Angonese (Ita)	A.Kelly	Kinnear	Dempsey
134	180672	Ecuador	N	Natal	New Lake	F	(1-1)	3-2	Kitabjan (Fra)	A.Kelly	Kinnear	Dempsey
135	210672	Chile	N	Recife	Isle of Retiro	F	(0-0)	1-2	Arpi (Bra)	A.Kelly	Kinnear	Dempsey
136	250672	Portugal	N	Recife	Isle of Retiro	F	(1-2)	1-2	Coerezza (Arg)	A.Kelly	Kinnear	T.Carroll
137	181072	U.S.S.R.	H	Dublin	Landsdowne Rd.	WC	(0-0)	1-2	Hoberg (Nor)	A.Kelly	Kinnear	T.Carroll
138	151172	France	H	Dublin	Dalymount Pk.	WC	(1-0)	2-1	Rasmussen (Den)	A.Kelly	Kinnear	Holmes
139	130573	U.S.S.R.	A	Moscow	Lenin	WC	(0-0)	0-1	Dalberg (Swe)	A.Kelly	T.Carroll	Holmes
140	160573	Poland	A	Wroclaw	Olympic	F	(0-1)	0-2	Kunz (E.Ger)	A.Kelly	T.Carroll	Holmes
141	190573	France	A	Paris	Parc de Princes	WC	(0-0)	1-1	Rainea (Rom)	A.Kelly	T.Carroll*	Holmes
142	060673	Norway	A	Oslo	Ullevaal	F	(1-0)	1-1	Hirvinemi (Fin)	A.Kelly	T.Carroll	Holmes
143	210173	Poland	H	Dublin	Dalymount Pk.	F	(1-0)	1-0	Matthewson (Eng)	Thomas*	Kinnear	Holmes
144	050574	Brazil	A	Rio de Janeiro	Maracana	F	(0-0)	1-2	Velasquez (Col)	Thomas	Kinnear	Holmes*
145	080574	Uruguay	A	Montevideo	Centenario	F	(0-2)	0-2	Barreto (Urg)	M.Kearns	Kinnear	A.Dunne
146	120574	Chile	A	Santiago	Nacional	F	(1-0)	2-1		M.Kearns	Kinnear	A.Dunne
147	301074	U.S.S.R.	H	Dublin	Dalymount Pk.	EC	(2-0)	3-0	Axelryd (Swe)	Roche	Kinnear	Holmes
148	201174	Turkey	A	Izmir	Stade D'Ataturk	EC	(0-0)	1-1	Srodecki (Pol)	Roche	Kinnear	A.Dunne
149	110375	W.Germany 'B'	H	Dublin	Dalymount Pk.	F	(0-0)	1-0	Homewood (Eng)	Roche	Kinnear	A.Dunne
150	100575	Switzerland	H	Dublin	Landsdowne Rd.	EC	(2-0)	2-1	Schiller (Aus)	Roche	Kinnear	A.Dunne

Notes: (A) * Ireland used a third substitute in games 143 (Hale 85 for +) and 149 (Dennehy 83 for +)
(B) Team Captain underlined.

Swiss Timing - 1937!
Ireland line-up prior to the game with Switzerland in Berne in May 1937.
Ireland won courtesy of a goal from Jimmy Dunne, third from left front row(D.C.)

Game No.	4	5	6	7	8	9	10	11	12	13
123	Kinnear	Conway	Rogers	A.Dunne	Dunphy	Givens	Conroy*	Dempsey	Treacy 40	
124	Kinnear	Conway	T.Carroll*	T.Byrne	Dunphy	Givens1	Conroy#	J.Giles	S.Brennan h.t.	Treacy h.t.
125	S.Brennan	Conway*	T.Carroll	T.Byrne	Dempsey	Givens#	Conroy	J.Giles	Dunphy 58	Treacy 87
126	S.Brennan	Treacy	Dunphy	T.Byrne	Dempsey	M.Lawlor	Conroy	Heighway#	M.Kearns 76	Hale 85
127	A.Dunne	Givens#	Dunphy	T.Byrne	Dempsey	M.Lawlor	Conroy	Heighway	Kinner 70	Treacy 83
128	S.Brennan	Treacy	Dunphy	T.Byrne	Dempsey	M.Lawlor	Conroy	Heighway		
129	S.Brennan	Treacy	Dunphy*	T.Byrne	Dempsey	Givens	Conroy	Rogers	M.Lawlor 43	
130	A.Dunne	J.Giles	Dunphy*	T.Byrne	Conway 1	Givens#	Heighway	Rogers*	Finucane h.t	
131	A.Dunne	Treacy	Dunphy*	T.Byrne	Conway	Givens#	Heighway	Rogers1	Campbell h.t.	Holmes 74
132	McConville	Finucane	Mulligan	Kearin*	F.O'Neill	Leech	M.Martin#	T.R.O'Connor	Richardson 62	Hale 69
133	T.Carroll	Campbell	Mulligan	M.Martin	Givens 1	Leech*1	Treacy	Rogers	T.R.O'Connor 78	
134	T.Carroll	Campbell	Mulligan	M.Martin1	Givens	Leech#	Treacy*	Rogers1	T.R.O'Connor 1 h.t.	Dennehy
135	T.Carroll*	Campbell	Mulligan	M.Martin	T.R.O'Connor	Dennehy	Treacy	Rogers1	Herrick	
136	Mulligan	Dempsey	Campbell	M.Martin	Rogers	Givens	Treacy*	Leech1	O'Connor	
137	McConville	Hand	Campbell	M.Martin	Rogers*	Conroy1	Treacy	Heighway	Leech 62	
138	McConville	Hand	Mulligan	T.Byrne*	J.Giles	Conroy#1	Treacy1	Givens	Campbell 75	T.R.O'Connor 89
139	McConville	Hand	Mulligan	M.Martin	J.Giles*	Conroy#	Treacy	Givens	T.Byrne h.t.	Dennehy h.t.
140	McConville	Hand	Mulligan	M.Martin	M.Lawlor*	Dennehy#	Treacy	Givens	G.Daly h.t.	T.R.O'Connor 67
141	McConville	Hand	Mulligan	M.Martin1	T.Byrne	Dennehy	Treacy	Givens	Herrick 25	
142	Conroy	G.Daly	Mulligan	M.Martin	T.Byrne*	Dennehy1	Treacy*	Givens	Richardson 10	E.Fagan 80
143	Conroy+	Hand	Mulligan	M.Martin	T.Byrne	Mancini	Treacy	Givens#	Dennehy 10 1	M.Kearns h.t.
144	Conroy	Hand	Mulligan	M.Martin	J.Giles	Mancini1	Treacy#	Givens	A.Dunne h.t.	G.Daly h.t.
145	Conroy	Hand	Mulligan	M.Martin	J.Giles	Mancini	Conway	Givens*	G.Daly 73	
146	Conroy	Hand1	Mulligan	M.Martin	J.Giles	Mancini	Conway1	Givens		
147	L.Brady	Heighway	Mulligan	M.Martin	J.Giles	Mancini	Treacy	Givens3		
148	L.Brady	Heighway	Mulligan	M.Martin	J.Giles	Hand	Conroy*	Givens1	Dennehy 86	
149	L.Brady	Heighway	Campbell#	M.Martin	G.Daly+	Hand	Treacy*	Givens	Conroy h.t.	Conway 1 65 *
150	L.Brady	Conroy	Mulligan	M.Martin1	J.Giles	Hand	Treacy1	Givens		

Put it there Boy!
Ireland's captain Charlie Turner shakes hands with Swiss skipper Minelli prior to the game in Berne. The referee is Lewington of England. (D.C.)

Republic of Ireland International Players 1926 - 1975

Aherne, Thomas 'Bud' (Belfast Celtic) 1946, Luton Town 1949-53 **(16)**
Ambrose, Paddy (Shamrock Rovers) 1954-1964 **(5)**
Andrews, Paddy (Bohemians) 1935 **(1)**
Arrigan, Tom (Waterford) 1937 **(1)**
Bailham, Eddie (Shamrock Rovers) 1964 **(1)**
Barber, Eric (Shelbourne) 1965-1966 **(2)**
Barry, Paddy (Fordsons) 1928-1929 **(2)**
Bermingham, Jimmy (Bohemians) 1929 **(1)**
Bermingham, Paddy (St. James's Gate) 1934 **(1)**
Bradshaw, Paddy (St. James's Gate) 1938-1939 **(5)**
Brady, Frank (Fordsons) 1926-1927 **(2)**
Brady, Liam (Arsenal) 1974-1980[2], Juventus 1980[3]-1982[3], Sampdoria 1982[4]-1984[2], Inter Milan 1984[3]-1986[1], Ascoli 1986[2]-1987, West Ham United 1989-1990 **(72)**
Brady, Ray (Queens Park Rangers) 1963-1964 **(6)**
Breen, Tommy (Manchester United) 1937, (Shamrock Rovers) 1946-1947 **(5)**
Brennan, Fran (Drumcondra) 1965 **(1)**
Brennan, Shay (Manchester United) 1965-1970[4], (Waterford) 1970[5], **(19)**
Brown, Johnny (Coventry City) 1937 **(2)**
Browne, Willie (Bohemians) 1963-1964 **(3)**
Burke, Florrie (Cork Athletic) 1951 **(1)**
Burke, John (Shamrock Rovers) 1929 **(1)**
Burke, Tom (Cork) 1934 **(1)**
Byrne, David 'Babby' (Shelbourne) 1929, (Shamrock Rovers) 1931, (Coleraine) 1934 **(3)**
Byrne, Jack 'Squib' (Bray Unknowns) 1928 **(1)**
Byrne, Paddy (Dolphin) 1931, (Shelbourne) 1932, (Drumcondra) 1934 **(3)**
Byrne, Seán (Bohemians) 1931 **(1)**
Byrne, Tony (Southampton) 1969-1973 **(14)**
Campbell, Noel (St. Patrick's Athletic) 1971, (Fortuna Cologne) 1972-77 **(11)**
Cannon, Harry (Bohemians) 1926-1928 **(2)**
Cantwell, Noel (West Ham United) 1953-1960, (Manchester United) 1961-1967 **(36)**
Carey, Johnny (Manchester United) 1937-1952 **(29)**
Carolan, Joe (Manchester United) 1959-1960 **(2)**
Carroll, Brendan (Shelbourne) 1949 **(2)**
Carroll, Tommy (Ipswich Town) 1968-1970, (Birmingham City) 1972-1973 **(17)**
Chatton, Harry (Shelbourne) 1931[1], (Dumbarton 1931[2], (Cork) 1934 **(3)**
Clarke, Kevin (Drumcondra) 1948 **(2)**
Clarke, Mattie (Shamrock Rovers) 1950 **(1)**
Clinton, Tommy (Everton) 1951-1954 **(3)**
Coad, Paddy (Shamrock Rovers) 1946-1952 **(11)**
Coffey, Jimmy (Drumcondra) 1949 **(1)**
Colfer, Martin (Shelbourne) 1950-1951 **(2)**
Collins, Frank (Jacobs) 1927 **(1)**
Conmy, Ollie (Peterborough United) 1965-1969 **(5)**
Connolly, Hugh (Cork) 1936 **(1)**
Connolly, James (Fordsons) 1926 **(1)**
Conroy, Terry (Stoke City) 1969-1976 **(26)**
Conway, Jimmy (Fulham) 1966-1976, (Manchester City) 1977 **(20)**

Corr, Peter (Everton) 1949 **(4)**
Courtney, Edward 'Ned' (Cork United) 1946 **(1)**
Cummins, George (Luton Town) 1953-1961 **(19)**
Cunneen, Tim (Limerick) 1951 **(1)**
Curtis, Dermot (Shelbourne) 1956, (Bristol City) 1957-1958[2], (Ipswich Town) 1958[3]-1962, (Exeter City) 1963 **(17)**
Cusack, Seán (Limerick) 1952 **(1)**
Daly, Gerry (Manchester United) 1973-1975, (Derby County) 1976-1980[4], (Coventry City) 1980[5]-1984[1], (Birmingham City) 1984[2]-1985, Shrewsbury Town 1986 **(48)**
Daly, Jimmy (Shamrock Rovers) 1932-1935 **(2)**
Daly, Pat (Shamrock Rovers) 1949 **(1)**
Davis, Tom (Oldham Athletic) 1936, (Tranmere Rovers) 1938 **(4)**
Dempsey, John (Fulham) 1966-1968, (Chelsea) 1969-1972 **(19)**
Dennehy, Miah (Cork Hibernians) 1972, (Nottingham Forest) 1973-1975, (Walsall) 1976 **(10)**
Desmond, Peter (Middlesborough) 1949 **(4)**
Donnelly, Joey (Dundalk) 1934-1937 **(10)**
Donnelly, Tom (Drumcondra) 1937, (Shamrock Rovers) 1938 **(2)**
Donovan, Don (Everton) 1954-1957 **(5)**
Dowdall, Charlie (Fordsons) 1928, (Barnsley) 1929, (Cork) 1931 **(3)**
Doyle, Christy (Shelbourne) 1959 **(1)**
Doyle, Denis (Shamrock Rovers) 1926 **(1)**
Doyle, Larry (Dolphin) 1931 **(1)**
Duffy, Bobby (Shamrock Rovers) 1950 **(1)**
Duggan, Harry (Leeds United) 1927-1936, (Newport County) 1937 **(5)**
Dunne, Jimmy (Sheffield United) 1930, (Arsenal) 1936, (Southampton) 1937[2], (Shamrock Rovers) 1937[3]-1939 **(15)**
Dunne, Jimmy C. (Fulham) 1971 **(1)**
Dunne, Leo (Manchester City) 1935 **(2)**
Dunne, Pat (Manchester United) 1965-1966 **(5)**
Dunne, Seamus (Luton Town) 1952-1960 **(15)**
Dunne, Tommy (St. Patrick's Athletic) 1956 **(3)**
Dunne, Tony 'A' (Manchester United) 1962-1971, (Bolton Wanderers) 1974-1975 **(33)**
Dunning, Paddy (Shelbourne) 1970 **(2)**
Dunphy, Eamonn (York City) 1965, (Millwall) 1966-1971 **(23)**
Dwyer, Noel (West Ham United) 1959-1960[3], (Swansea Town) 1960[4]-1964 **(14)**
Egan, Robert (Dundalk) 1929 **(1)**
Eglington, Tommy (Shamrock Rovers) 1946[2], (Everton) 1946[3]-1955 **(24)**
Ellis, Plevna 'Plev' (Bohemians) 1935-1936 **(7)**
Fagan, Eamonn (Shamrock Rovers) 1973 **(1)**
Fagan, Fionan (Manchester City) 1954-1959, (Derby County) 1960-1961 **(8)**
Fagan Jack 'Kruger' (Shamrock Rovers) 1926 **(1)**
Fallon, Seán (Celtic) 1950-1955 **(8)**
Fallon, Willie (Notts County) 1934-1938, (Sheffield Wednesday) 1939 **(9)**

Farquharson, Tom (Cardiff City) 1929-1931 **(4)**
Farrell, Paddy (Hibernian) 1937 **(2)**
Farrell, Peter 'D' (Shamrock Rovers) 1946, (Everton) 1947-1957 **(28)**
Feenan, Johnny (Sunderland) 1937 **(1)**
Finucane, Al (Limerick) 1967-1971 **(11)**
Fitzgerald, Jack (Waterford) 1955-1956 **(2)**
Fitzgerald, Peter (Leeds United) 1960-1961*[1]*, (Chester City) 1961*[2]* **(5)**
Fitzpatrick Kevin (Limerick) 1969 **(1)**
Fitzsimons Arthur (Middlesborough) 1949-1958, (Lincoln City) 1959 **(26)**
Flood, John Joe (Shamrock Rovers) 1926-1931 **(5)**
Fogarty, Ambrose 'Amby' (Sunderland) 1960-1963, (Hartlepool United) 1964 **(11)**
Foley, Jim 'Fox' (Cork) 1934*[1]*, (Celtic) 1934*[2]*-1936 **(7)**
Foley, Mick 'Boxer' (Shelbourne) 1926 **(1)**
Foley, Theo (Northampton Town) 1964-1967 **(9)**
Foy, Tommy (Shamrock Rovers) 1937-1939 **(2)**
Fullam, Bob (Shamrock Rovers) 1926-1927 **(2)**
Fullam, Johnny (Preston N.E.) 1960, (Shamrock Rovers) 1964-1969 **(11)**
Gallagher, Charlie (Celtic) 1967 **(2)**
Gallagher, Matt (Hibernian) 1954 **(1)**
Gallagher, Patsy (Falkirk) 1931 **(1)**
Gannon, Eddie (Notts County) 1948, Sheffield Wednesday) 1944-1953, (Shelbourne) 1954-1955 **(14)**
Gannon, Mick (Shelbourne) 1971 **(1)**
Gaskins, Paddy (Shamrock Rovers) 1934-1935, (St. James's Gate) 1938 **(7)**
Gavin, Johnny (Norwich City) 1949-1954, (Tottenham) 1955, (Norwich City) 1956 **(7)**
Geoghegan, Matt (St. James's Gate) 1936-1937 **(2)**
Gibbons, Shay (St. Patrick's Athletic) 1952-1955 **(4)**
Gilbert, Bobby (Shamrock Rovers) 1966 **(1)**
Giles, Christy (Doncaster Rovers) 1950 **(1)**
Giles, Johnny (Manchester United) 1959-1963*[1]*, (Leeds United) 1963*[2]*-1975*[3]*, (West Bromwich Albion) 1975*[4]*-1977*[3]*, (Shamrock Rovers) 1977*[4]*-1979 **(59)**
Givens, Don (Manchester United) 1969-1970*[1]*, (Luton Town) 1970*[2]*-1972*[3]*, (Queens Park Rangers) 1972*[4]*-1978*[2]*, (Birmingham City) 1978*[3]*-1981*[1]*, (Neuchatel Xamax) 1981*[2]* **(56)**
Glen, William 'Sacky' (Shamrock Rovers) 1927-1936 **(8)**
Glynn, Dessie (Drumcondra) 1951-1955 **(2)**
Godwin, Tommy (Shamrock Rovers) 1949*[5]*, (Leicester City) 1949*[6]*-1957*[1]*, (Bournemouth) 1957*[2]*-1958 **(13)**
Golding, Joseph (Shamrock Rovers) 1928-30 **(2)**
Gorman, Bill (Bury) 1936-1938, (Brentford) 1939-1947 **(13)**
Grace, Joe (Drumcondra) 1926 **(1)**
Griffiths, R. (Walsall) 1934 **(1)**
Hale, Alfie (Aston Villa) 1962*[1]*, (Doncaster Rovers) 1962*[2]*-1964, (Waterford) 1966-1971 **(13)**
Hamilton, Tommy (Shamrock Rovers) 1959 **(2)**
Hand, Eoin (Portsmouth) 1969-1975 **(20)**
Harrington, Bill (Cork) 1935-1938 **(5)**
Hartnett, Jim (Middlesborough) 1949-1954 **(2)**

Haverty, Joe (Arsenal) 1956-1961*[2]*, (Blackburn Rovers) 1961*[3]*-1963*[1]*, (Millwall) 1963*[2]*-1964*[4]*, (Celtic) 1964*[5]*, (Bristol Rovers) 1965*[1]*, (Shelbourne) 1965*[2]*-1966 **(32)**
Hayes, Billy (WE) (Huddersfield Town) 1946-1947 **(2)**
Hayes, Willie (WJ) (Limerick) 1949 **(1)**
Heighway, Steve (Liverpool) 1970-1981*[2]*, (Minnesota Kicks) 1981*[3]* **(34)**
Henderson, Benny (Drumcondra) 1948 **(2)**
Hennessy, Jackie (Shelbourne) 1964-1966, (St. Patrick's Athletic) 1968 **(5)**
Herrick, John (Cork Hibernians) 1971-1972, (Shamrock Rovers) 1973 **(3)**
Higgins, Jim (Birmingham City) 1951 **(1)**
Holmes, Jimmy (Coventry City) 1971-1976, (Tottenham Hotspur) 1977-1979, (Vancouver Whitecaps) 1981 **(30)**
Horlacher, Fred (Bohemians) 1930-1936 **(7)**
Hoy, Mick (Dundalk) 1937-1939 **(6)**
Hurley, Charlie (Millwall) 1957*[1]*, (Sunderland) 1957*[2]*-1969*[1]*, (Bolton Wanderers) 1969*[2]* **(40)**
Hutchinson, Freddie (Drumcondra) 1935 **(2)**
Jordan, Billy 'W' (Bohemians) 1934-1937 **(2)**
Jordan, Davy (Wolverhampton Wanderers) 1937 **(2)**
Kavanagh, Peter (Celtic) 1931 **(2)**
Keane, Tom (Swansea) 1948-1949 **(4)**
Kearin, Mick (Shamrock Rovers) 1971 **(1)**
Kearns, Fred (West Ham United) 1954 **(1)**
Kearns, Mick (Oxford United) 1970, (Walsall) 1973-1978, (Wolverhampton Wanderers) 1979 **(18)**
Kelly, Alan (Drumcondra) 1956-1957, (Preston, N.E.) 1962-1973 **(47)**
Kelly, Jimmy (Derry City) 1932-1936 **(4)**
Kelly, Noel (Nottingham Forest) 1954 **(1)**
Kelly, Phil (Wolverhampton Wanderers) 1960-1961 **(5)**
Kendrick, Joe (Everton) 1927, (Dolphin) 1934-1935 **(4)**
Kennedy, Billy (St. James's Gate) 1932-1934 **(3)**
Keogh, John (Shamrock Rovers) 1966 **(1)**
Keogh, Shay (Shamrock Rovers) 1958 **(1)**
Kiernan, Fred (Shamrock Rovers) 1951*[2]*, (Southampton) 1951*[3]*-1952 **(5)**
Kinnear, Joe (Tottenham) 1967-1975*[4]*, (Brighton H.A.) 1975*[5]* **(26)**
Kinsella, Joe (Shelbourne) 1928 **(1)**
Kinsella, Owen (Shamrock Rovers) 1932-1937 **(2)**
Kirkland, Alec (Shamrock Rovers) 1927 **(1)**
Lacey, Billy (Shelbourne) 1927-1930 **(3)**
Lawler, Joseph 'Robin' (Fulham) 1953-1955 **(8)**
Lawlor, John 'Kit' (Drumcondra) 1949, (Doncaster Rovers) 1950-1951 **(3)**
Lawlor, Mick (Shamrock Rovers) 1970-1973 **(5)**
Leech, Mick (Shamrock Rovers) 1969-1972 **(8)**
Lennon, Charlie (St. James's Gate) 1934-1935 **(3)**
Lennox, George (Dolphin) 1931 **(2)**
Lowry, Dinny (St. Patrick's Athletic) 1962 **(1)**
Lunn, Dick (Dundalk) 1938 **(2)**
Lynch, Jeremiah (Cork Bohemians) 1934 **(1)**
McAlinden, Jimmy (Portsmouth) 1946 **(2)**
McCann, Jimmy 'Maxie' (Shamrock Rovers) 1956 **(1)**
McCarthy, Jack (Bohemians) 1926-1930 **(3)**
McCarthy, Mick (Shamrock Rovers) 1932 **(1)**

107

McConville, Tommy (Dundalk) 1971, (Waterford) 1972-1973 **(6)**
McEvoy, Andy (Blackburn Rovers) 1961-1967 **(17)**
McGowan, Daniel (West Ham United) 1949 **(3)**
McGowan, John (Cork United) 1947 **(1)**
McGrath, Mick (Blackburn Rovers) 1958-1965, (Bradford Park Avenue) 1966-1967 **(22)**
McGuire, Bill (Bohemians) 1935 **(1)**
McKenzie, George (Southend United) 1937-1939 **(9)**
McLoughlin, F. (Fordsons) 1930, (Cork) 1931 **(2)**
McMillan, Billy (Belfast Celtic) 1946 **(2)**
McNally, Brendan (Luton Town) 1959-1962 **(3)**
Mackey, Gerry (Shamrock Rovers) 1956-1957 **(3)**
Madden, Owen (Cork) 1936 **(1)**
Maguire, Jim (Shamrock Rovers) 1929 **(1)**
Malone, Gerry (Shelbourne) 1949 **(1)**
Mancini, Terry (Queens Park Rangers) 1973-1974*[3]*, (Arsenal) 1974*[4]* **(5)**
Martin, C. (Borroustouness) 1927 **(1)**
Martin, Con (Glentoran) 1946, (Leeds United) 1947-1948*[2]*, (Aston Villa) 1948*[3]*-1956 **(30)**
Martin, Mick (Bohemians) 1971-1972, (Manchester United) 1973-1975*[4]*, (West Bromwich Albion) 1975*[5]*-1977, (Newcastle United) 1979-1983 **(52)**
Meagan, Mick (Everton) 1961-1964, (Huddersfield Town) 1965-1968, (Drogheda) 1969 **(17)**
Meehan, Paddy (Drumcondra) 1934 **(1)**
Monahan, Paddy (Sligo Rovers) 1935 **(2)**
Mooney, Jackie (Shamrock Rovers) 1964-1965 **(2)**
Moore, Paddy (Shamrock Rovers) 1931-1932, (Aberdeen) 1934-1935*[1]*, (Shamrock Rovers) 1935*[2]*-1936 **(9)**
Moroney, Tommy (West Ham United) 1948-1951, (Evergreen United) 1953 **(12)**
Moulson, Con (Lincoln City) 1936*[2]*, (Notts County) 1936*[3]*-1937 **(5)**
Moulson, George (Lincoln City) 1948 **(3)**
Muldoon, Tommy (Aston Villa) 1927 **(1)**
Mulligan, Paddy (Shamrock Rovers) 1969*[6]*, (Chelsea) 1969*[7]*-1972*[4]*, (Crystal Palace) 1972*[5]*-1975*[3]*, (West Bromwich Albion) 1975*[4]*-1979*[3]*, (Shamrock Rovers) 1979*[4]* **(50)**
Munroe, Liam (Shamrock Rovers) 1953 **(1)**
Murphy, Albie (Clyde) 1955 **(1)**
Murray, Terry (Dundalk) 1950 **(1)**
Newman, Billy (Shelbourne) 1969 **(1)**
Nolan, Ronnie (Shamrock Rovers) 1956-1962 **(10)**
O'Brien, Mick (Derby County) 1927, (Walsall) 1929, (Norwich City) 1930, (Watford) 1932 **(4)**
O'Byrne, Lar (Shamrock Rovers) 1949 **(1)**
O'Connell, Tony (Dundalk) 1966, (Bohemians) 1970 **(2)**
O'Connor, Tommy (TY) (Shamrock Rovers) 1949 **(4)**
O'Connor, Turlough (TH) (Fulham) 1967, (Dundalk) 1971-1972*[4]*, (Bohemians) 1972*[5]*-1973 **(8)**
O'Driscoll, John (Swansea) 1948-1949 **(3)**
O'Farrell, Frank (West Ham United) 1952-1956, (Preston N.E.) 1957-1959 **(9)**
O'Flanagan, Kevin (Bohemians) 1937-1939, (Arsenal) 1946-1947 **(10)**
O'Flanagan, Michael (Bohemians) 1946 **(1)**
O'Kane, Paddy (Bohemians) 1934-1935 **(3)**

O'Keeffe, Tim (Cork) 1934, (Waterford) 1938 **(3)**
O'Mahoney, Matt (Bristol Rovers) 1938-1939 **(6)**
O'Neill, Frank (Shamrock Rovers) 1961-1971 **(20)**
O'Neill, Jimmy (Everton) 1952-1959 **(17)**
O'Neill, John 'Sonny' (Preston N.E.) 1960 **(1)**
O'Neill, William (Dundalk) 1935-1939 **(11)**
O'Reilly, Jack (JK) (Cork United) 1946 **(2)**
O'Reilly, Joe (Brideville) 1932, (Aberdeen) 1934, (Brideville) 1935-1936*[3]*, (St. James's Gate) 1936*[4]*-1939 **(20)**
Peyton, Noel (Shamrock Rovers) 1956, (Leeds United) 1960-1962 **(6)**
Reid, Charlie (Brideville) 1931 **(1)**
Richardson, Damien (Shamrock Rovers) 1971, (Gillingham) 1973-1979 **(3)**
Rigby, Alf (St. James's Gate) 1934-1935 **(3)**
Ringstead, Alf (Sheffield United) 1951-1959 **(20)**
Robinson, Jeremiah (Bohemians) 1928, (Dolphin) 1931 **(2)**
Roche, Paddy (Shelbourne) 1971, (Manchester United) 1974-1975 **(8)**
Rogers, Eamonn (Blackburn Rovers) 1967-1971, (Charlton Athletic) 1972 **(19)**
Ryan, Reg (West Bromwich Albion) 1949-1953, (Derby County) 1954-1955 **(16)**
Saward, Pat (Millwall) 1954, (Aston Villa) 1957-1960, (Huddersfield Town) 1961-1962 **(18)**
Scannell, Ted (Southend United) 1954 **(1)**
Sloan, Josiah 'Paddy' (Arsenal) 1946 **(2)**
Smyth, Mick (Shamrock Rovers) 1968 **(1)**
Squires, Johnny (Shelbourne) 1934 **(1)**
Stevenson, Alex (Dolphin) 1932, (Everton) 1946-1948 **(7)**
Strahan, Freddie (Shelbourne) 1964-1966 **(5)**
Sullivan, Jack (Fordsons) 1928 **(1)**
Swan, Maurice (Drumcondra) 1960 **(1)**
Taylor, Tommy (Waterford) 1958 **(1)**
Thomas, Peter (Waterford) 1973-1974 **(2)**
Traynor, Tommy (Southampton) 1954-1964 **(8)**
Treacy, Ray (West Bromwich Albion) 1966-1967*[1]*, (Charlton Athletic) 1967*[2]*-1971, (Swindon Town) 1972-1973, (Preston N.E.) 1974-1976, (West Bromwich Albion) 1977, (Shamrock Rovers) 1978-1979 **(42)**
Tuohy, Liam 'Rasher' (Shamrock Rovers) 1955-1959, (Newcastle United) 1962, (Shamrock Rovers) 1963-1965 **(8)**
Turner, Charlie (Southend) 1936-1937, (West Ham United) 1938-1939 **(10)**
Turner, Paddy (Celtic) 1963-1964 **(2)**
Vernon, Jackie (Belfast Celtic) 1946 **(2)**
Walsh, Davy (West Bromwich Albion) 1946-1950, (Aston Villa) 1952-1953 **(20)**
Walsh, Willie (Manchester City) 1946-1950 **(9)**
Watters, Fran (Shelbourne) 1926 **(1)**
Weir, E. 'Ned' (Clyde) 1939 **(3)**
Whelan, Liam (Manchester United) 1956-1957 **(4)**
Whelan, Ronnie (Snr.) (St. Patrick's Athletic) 1963-1964 **(2)**
White, Jimmy (Bohemians) 1928 **(1)**
Williams, Joe (Shamrock Rovers) 1937 **(1)**
Whittaker, Richard 'Dick' (Chelsea) 1959 **(1)**

B International Results & Line-Ups

21 Oct. '57 *at Dalymount Pk*
Rep. of Ireland (1) 1 (Neville)
Romania (1) 1 (Semenescu)
Dwyer (Wolves), Whittaker (Chelsea), McNally (Luton), Gavin (Doncaster), Keogh (Shamrock R.), McGrath (Blackburn), Fagan (Man City) Peyton (Shamrock R.), Neville (West Ham), Meagan (Everton), Tuohy (Shamrock R.)

11 Aug. '58 *at Reykjavik*
Iceland (0) 2 (Bjoergvinsson, Fhordarsen)
Rep. of Ireland (1) 3 (Doyle, Nolan, McCann)
Taylor (Waterford), Mackey (Shamrock R.), O'Brien (Shelbourne), Nolan (Shamrock R.), Keogh (Shamrock R.), Rowe (Drumcondra), McCann (Shamrock R.), Doyle (Shelbourne), Ambrose (Shamrock R.), O'Rourke (St. Patricks A.), Tuohy (Shamrock R.)

11 Oct. '58 *at Tolka Park*
Rep. of Ireland (0) 1 (Doyle)
South Africa 0
Taylor (Waterford), Fullam (Drumcondra), O'Brien (Shelbourne), Nolan (Shamrock R.), Browne (UCD), Rowe (Drumcondra), McCann (Shamrock R.), Doyle (Shelbourne), Ambrose (Shamrock R.), O'Rourke (St. Patricks A.), Tuohy (Shamrock R.)
Sub: Dunne (St. Patricks A.) for Browne

11 Sep. '60 *at Dalymount Park*
Rep. of Ireland (1) 2 (Hennessy 2)
Iceland (1) 1 (Beck)
Darcy (Shamrock R.), Fullam (Drumcondra), O'Brien (Shelbourne), Nolan (Shamrock R.), Farrell (Shamrock R.), Dunne (St. Patricks A.), O'Donovan (Cork Celtic), Hamilton (Shamrock R.), Fitzgerald (Waterford), Hennessy (Shelbourne), Conroy (Shelbourne)

27 Mar. '90 *at Turners Cross*
Rep. of Ireland (2) 4 (McLoughlin, D. Kelly (pen), Quinn 2)
England (1) 1 (Atkinson)
G. Kelly (Bury), Irwin (Oldham), Brazil (Man Utd.), Scully (Arsenal), Beglin (Leeds U.), McLoughlin (Swindon), Mooney (Preston), Milligan (Oldham), M. Kelly (Portsmouth), Quinn (Man City), D. Kelly (Leicester)
Subs: Phelan (Wimbledon) for Irwin; De Mange (Hull C.) for McLoughlin; Waddock (Millwall) for Milligan; Coyle (Airdrie) for D. Kelly

12 Feb. '92 *at Tolka Park*
Rep. of Ireland (1) 2 (Fenlon, D. Kelly)
Denmark 0
Peyton (Everton), Cunningham (Millwall), Scully (Southend), Fitzgerald (Wimbledon), McDonald (Tottenham), McGoldrick (Crystal P.), McLoughlin (Southampton), Fenlon (Bohemians), Russell (Portadown), Coyle (Airdrie), D Kelly (Newcastle)
Subs: M. Kelly (Portsmouth) for D. Kelly; Arkins (St. Johnstone) for Coyle; Power (Norwich C) for Fenlon.

Republic of Ireland B Appearances

Ambrose, Paddy (Shamrock R.) 58-59 v Ice, S.A.
Arkins, Vinny (St. Johnstone) 91-92 v Den (sub)
Beglin, Jim (Leeds U.) 89-90 v Eng
Brazil, Derek (Manchester U.) 89-90 v Eng
Browne, Willie (UCD) 58-59 v S.A.
Conroy, Ollie (Shelbourne) 60-61 v Ice
Coyle, Owen (Airdrie) 89-90 v Eng (sub), 91-92 v Den
Cunningham, Ken (Millwall) 91-92 v Den
Darcy, Eamonn (Shamrock R.) 60-61 v Ice
De Mange, Ken (Hull City) 89-90 v Eng (sub)
Doyle, Christy (Shelbourne) 58-59 v Ice (*), S.A. (*)
Dunne, Tommy (St. Pats) 58-59 v S.A. (sub), 60-61 v Ice
Dwyer, Noel (Wolves) 57-58 v Rom
Fagan, Fionan (Manchester C.) 57-58 v Rom
Farrell, Tommy (Shamrock R.) 60-61 v Ice
Fenlon, Pat (Bohemians) 91-92 v Den (*)
Fitzgerald, Jack (Waterford) 60-61 v Ice
Fitzgerald, Scott (Wimbledon) 91-92 v Den
Fullam, Christy (Drumcondra) 58-59 v S.A., 60-61 v Ice
Gavin, Paddy (Doncaster R.) 57-58 v Rom
Hamilton, Tommy (Shamrock R.) 60-61 v Ice
Hennessy, Jackie (Shelbourne) 60-61 v Ice (**)
Irwin, Denis (Oldham A.) 89-90 v Eng
Kelly, David (Leicester C.) 89-90 v Eng (*p) (Newcastle U.) 91-92 v Den (*)
Kelly, Gary (Bury) 89-90 v Eng
Kelly, Mark (Portsmouth) 89-90 v Eng, 91-92 v Den (sub)
Keogh, Shay (Shamrock R.) 57-58 v Rom, 58-59 v Ice
McCann, Jim (Shamrock R.) 58-59 v Ice (*), S.A.
McDonald, Dave (Tottenham) 91-92 v Den
McGoldrick, Eddie (Crystal P.) 91-92 v Den
McGrath, Mick (Blackburn) 57-58 v Rom
Mackey, Gerry (Shamrock R.) 58-59 v Ice
McLoughlin, Alan (Swindon) 89-90 v Eng (*), (Southampton) 91-92 v Den
McNally, Brendan (Luton) 57-58 v Rom
Meagan, Mick (Everton) 57-58 v Rom
Milligan, Mike (Oldham A.) 89-90 v Eng
Mooney, Brian (Preston) 89-90 v Eng
Neville, Billy (West Ham) 57-58 v Rom (*)
Nolan, Ronnie (Sham R.) 58-59 v Ice (*), S.A., 60-61v Ice
O'Brien, Brendan (Shelbourne) 58-59 v Ice, S.A., 60-61 v Ice
O'Donovan, Paul (Cork Celtic) 60-61 v Ice
O'Rourke, Paddy (St. Patricks A.) 58-59 v Ice, S.A.
Peyton, Gerry (Everton) 91-92 v Den
Peyton, Noel (Shamrock R.) 57-58 v Rom
Phelan, Terry (Wimbledon) 89-90 v Eng (sub)
Power, Lee (Norwich C.) 91-92 v Den (sub)
Quinn, Niall (Manchester C.) 89-90 v Eng (**)
Rowe, Tommy (Drumcondra) 58-59 v Ice, S.A.
Russell, Martin (Portadown) 91-92 v Den
Scully, Pat (Arsenal) 89-90 v Eng, (Southend) 91-92 v Den
Taylor, Tommy (Waterford) 58-59 v Ice, S.A.
Tuohy, Liam (Sham R.) 57-58 v Rom, 58-59 v Ice, S.A.
Waddock, Gary (Millwall) 89-90 v Eng (sub)
Whittaker, Richard (Chelsea) 57-58 v Rom

U-23 International Results & Line-Ups

5 Jun. '66   *at Dalymount Park*
Rep. of Ireland   0
France   0
Dunne (Manchester U.), Carroll (Cambridge C.), Mulligan (Shamrock R.), Finucane (Limerick), Pugh (Sligo R.), Treacy (West Brom), McGrath (Drumcondra), Dunphy (Millwall), McEwan (Manchester U.), Morrissey (Coventry C.) Rogers (Blackburn).

14 Nov. '72   *at Lorient*
France   0
Rep. of Ireland   0
Roche (Shelbourne), Doran (Bohemians), Martin (Bohemians), Sheehan (Cork Hibs), O'Brien (Shelbourne), Minnock (Athlone T.), Doherty (Finn Harps), Lawlor (Shamrock R.), Shortt (Waterford), Dennehy (Cork Hibs), Sheehy (Preston).
Sub: Fagan (Shamrock R.) for Doherty.

20 May '73   *at Dalymount Park*
Rep. of Ireland   0
France   0
Roche (Shelbourne), Gregg (Bohemians), Dunning (Shelbourne), Sheehan (Cork Hibs), O'Brien (Manchester U.), Fagan (Shamrock R.) Macken (Waterford), Minnock (Athlone T.), Shortt (Waterford), Allen (Cork Hibs), Fairclough (Huddersfield T.).
Subs: Sheehy (Preston) for Allen.

11 Apr. '89   *at Dalymount Park*
Rep. of Ireland   (2) 3   (McCarthy, Irwin, Sheridan (p))
Northern Ireland   0
G. Kelly (Newcastle), Irwin (Oldham), Fleming (St. Patricks A.), McCarthy (Celtic), Brazil (Manchester U.), Sheridan (Leeds U.), Milligan (Oldham). O'Brien (Newcastle), Coyle (Clydebank), Mooney (Preston), M. Kelly (Portsmouth).
Subs: Swan (Bohemians) for McCarthy; De Mange (Hull C.) for O'Brien; McGee (Wimbledon) for M. Kelly.

15 May '90   *at Portadown*
Northern Ireland   (2) 2   (McBride, Devine)
Rep. of Ireland   (0) 3   (Quinn, D. Kelly 2, 1 pen)
A. Kelly (Preston), Fleming (St. Patricks A.), Scully (Arsenal), Brazil (Manchester U.), Phelan (Wimbledon), Mooney (Preston), Waddock (Millwall), Sheridan (Sheffield W.), M. Kelly (Portsmouth), D. Kelly (Leicester), Quinn (Manchester C.).
Sub: Russell (Middlesbrough) for M. Kelly.

Republic of Ireland U-23 Appearances

Allen Denis (Cork Hibs) 72-73 v Fra
Brazil, Derek (Manchester U.) 88-89 v N.I., 89-90 v N.I.
Carroll, Tommy (Cambridge C.) 65-66 v Fra
Coyle, Owen (Clydebank) 88-89 v N.I.
De Mange, Ken (Hull City) 88-89 v N.I. (Sub)
Dennehy, Miah (Cork Hibs) 72-73 v Fra
Doherty, Gerry (Finn Harps) 72-73 v Fra
Doran, John, (Bohemians) 72-73 v Fra
Dunne, Pat (Manchester U.) 65-66 v Fra
Dunning, Paddy (Shelbourne) 72-73 v Fra
Dunphy, Eamonn (Millwall) 65-66 v Fra
Fagan, Eamonn (Shamrock R.) 72-73 v Fra (sub), Fra
Fairclough, Mick (Huddersfield T.) 72-73 v Fra
Finucane, Al (Limerick) 65-66 v Fra
Fleming, Curtis (St. Pats A.) 88-89 v N.I., 89-90 v N.I.
Gregg, Eamonn (Bohemians) 72-73 v Fra
Irwin, Dennis (Oldham A) 88-89 v N.I.(*)
Kelly, Alan (Preston) 89-90 v N.I.
Kelly, David (Leicester C.) 89-90 v N.I.(**p)
Kelly, Gary (Newcastle U.) 88-89 v N.I.
Kelly, Mark (Portsmouth) 88-89 v N.I., 89-90 v N.I.
Lawlor, Mick (Shamrock R.) 72-73 v Fra
McCarthy, Mick (Celtic) 88-89 v N.I. (*)
McEwan, Frank (Manchester U.) 65-66 v Fra
McGee, Paul (Wimbledon) 88-89 v N.I. (sub)
McGrath, Joe (Drumcondra) 65-66 v Fra
Macken, Tony (Waterford) 72-73 v Fra
Martin, Mick (Bohemians) 72-73 v Fra
Milligan, Mike (Oldham A.) 88-89 v N.I.
Minnock, John (Athlone T.) 72-73 v Fra (2)
Mooney, Brian (Preston) 88-89 v N.I., 89-90 v N.I.
Morrissey, Pat (Coventry C.) 65-66 v Fra
Mulligan, Paddy (Shamrock R.) 65-66 v Fra
O'Brien, Liam (Newcastle U.) 88-89 v N.I.
O'Brien, Ray (Shelbourne) 72-73 v Fra, (Man U.) v Fra
Phelan, Terry (Wimbledon) 89-90 v N.I.
Pugh, David (Sligo R.) 65-66 v Fra
Quinn, Niall (Manchester C.) 89-90 v N.I. (*)
Roche, Paddy (Shelbourne) 72-73 v Fra (2)
Rogers, Eamonn (Blackburn R.) 65-66 v Fra
Russell, Martin (Middlesbrough) 89-90 v N.I. (sub)
Scully, Pat (Arsenal) 89-90 v N.I.
Sheehan, Martin (Cork Hibs) 72-73 v Fra (2)
Sheehy, Sean (Preston) 72-73 v Fra, Fra (sub)
Sheridan, John (Leeds U.) 88-89 v N.I. (*p), (Sheffield W.) 89-90 v N.I.
Shortt, Paddy (Waterford) 72-73 v Fra (2)
Swan, Derek (Bohemians) 88-89 v N.I. (sub)
Treacy, Ray (West Brom) 65-66 v Fra
Waddock, Gary (Millwall) 89-90 v N.I.

110

U-21 International Results & Line-ups

(FR) 8 Mar. '78 *at Dalymount Park*
Rep. of Ireland (1) 1 (Murray)
Northern Ireland (1) 1 (Blackledge)
O'Neill (Shamrock R.), Nolan (Limerick), Anderson (West Brom), Daly (Wolves), Devine (Arsenal), Braddish (Dundalk), Madigan (Waterford), Grimes (Manchester U.) Murray (Everton), McGee (QPR), Lane (Cork Alberts).

(TT) 15 May '78 *At Toulon*
Poland (1) 1 (Nocko)
Rep. of Ireland 0
Finucane (Limerick), Wade (Ilford), Anderson (West Brom), Malone (Bohemians), Daly (Wolves), Meagan (Shamrock R.), Braddish (Liverpool), Sheedy (Hereford), L. Murray (Shamrock R.), M Murray (Everton), Foley (Oxford).
Sub: Walker (Gillingham) for Sheedy.

(TT) 17 May '78 *at Toulon*
Mexico (1) 1 (Malone OG)
Rep. of Ireland (1) 1 (M. Murray)
Finucane (Limerick), Wade (Ilford), Anderson (West Brom.), Malone (Bohemians), Daly (Wolves), Meagan (Shamrock R.),Braddish (Liverpool), Sheedy (Hereford) L Murray (Shamrock R.), M Murray (Everton), Foley (Oxford)
Sub: Coyle (Blackpool) for L Murray

(TT) 19 May '78 *at Toulon*
France (2) 2 (Francois, Zaromba)
Rep. of Ireland 0
Finucane (Limerick), Wade (Ilford), Anderson (West Brom), Malone (Bohemians), Daly (Wolves), Meagan (Shamrock R.), Braddish (Liverpool), Sheedy (Hereford), Coyle (Blackpool), M MUrray (Everton), Foley (Oxford).
Sub: L. Murray (Shamrock R) for Coyle

(TT) 20 May '78 *at La Seyne*
Iran 0
Rep. of Ireland 0 (Iran won on pens)
Henderson (Shamrock R.), Wade (Ilford), Anderson (West Brom), Malone (Bohemians), Nolan (Limerick), Meagan (Shamrock R.), Braddish (Liverpool), Sheedy (Hereford), L Murray (Shamrock R.), M Murray (Everton), Foley (Oxford)
Subs: Walker (Gillingham) for M Murray; Coyle (Blackpool) for Meagan.

(TT) 18 Jun. '79 *at Toulon*
USSR (0) 1 (Suslaparov)
Rep. of Ireland 0
O'Neill (Shamrock R.), Carroll (Liverpool), Lawlor (Dundalk), O'Leary (Shamrock R.), Anderson (West Brom.), Bayly (Shamrock R.), Hayes (Southampton), Meagan (Shamrock R.), O'Doherty (Fulham), Grimes (Manchester U.), O'Callaghan (Millwall)
Subs: Murray (Everton) for Bayly; Coyle (Blackpool) for O'Callaghan.

(TT) 20 Jun. '79 *at Draguignan*
Argentina (3) 4 (Alvez (pen), Diaz, Fortunato 2)
Rep. of Ireland (1) 1 (Grimes (pen))
Bonner (Celtic), O'Doherty (Fulham), Anderson (West Brom), O'Leary (Shamrock R.), Lawlor (Dundalk), Grimes (Manchester U.), Bayly (Shamrock R.), Meagan (Shamrock R.), O'Callaghan (Millwall), Hayes (Southampton), Foley (Oxford)
Subs: Lawless (Bohemians for Bayly; Murray (Everton) for Foley.

(TT) 22 Jun. '79 *at Toulon*
Hungary (0) 3 (Gymesi, Pekker, Toma)
Rep. of Ireland 0
Bonner (Celtic), Anderson (West Brom.), O'Leary (Shamrock R.), Lawlor (Dundalk), O'Doherty (Fulham), Grimes (Manchester U.), Bayly (Shamrock R.), Meagan (Shamrock R), O'Callaghan (Millwall), Hayes (Southampton), Foley (Oxford)
Sub: Carroll (Liverpool) for O'Doherty.

(TT) 23 Jun. '79 *at La Seyne*
Yugoslavia (1) 2 (Lawlor OG, Smajic)
Rep. of Ireland (0) 1 (Murray)
Bonner (Celtic), Carroll (LIverpool), Anderson (West Brom), Lawlor (Dundalk), O'Leary (Shamrock R.), Grimes (Manchester U.), Bayly (Shamrock R.), Meagan (Shamrock R.), O'Callaghan (Millwall), Hayes (Southampton), Foley (Oxford)
Subs: Lawless (Bohemians) for Bayly; Murray (Everton) for Foley.

(Fr) 12 Sep. '79 *at Tolka Park*
Rep of Ireland (0) 1 (Grimes (pen))
Poland (1) 1 (Fajt)
Henderson (Shamrock R.) Devine (Arsenal), Grimes (Manchester U.), O'Leary (Shamrock R.), Anderson (Preston), Waddock (QPR), Gaffney (Shamrock R.), Chandler (Blackpool), Hayes (Southampton), Kinsella (Millwall), O'Callaghan (Millwall)
Sub: Lawlor (Dundalk) for Waddock

(FR) 25 Feb. '81 *at Anfield*
England (1) 1 (Shaw)
Rep of Ireland 0
Bonner (Celtic), A. Whelan (Manchester U.), McDonagh (Bohemians), Anderson (Preston), Hughton (Orient), Atkinson (Wolves), R. Whelan (Liverpool), Sheedy (Liverpool), O'Connor (Athlone T.), Donovan (Aston V.), McGee (Preston).
Subs: Kinsella (Millwall) for Sheedy; Buckley (Shamrock R.) for O'Connor.

(TT) 5 Jun. '83 *at Toulon*
France (0) 1 (Anziani)
Rep. of Ireland 1 (Howlett)
Peyton (Fulham), O'Regan (Brighton), Pender (Wolves), Coyle (Limerick U.), Beglin (Liverpool), O'Driscoll (Fulham), O'Brien (Bohemians), Howlett (Brighton), Wilson (Fulham), O'Keefe (Wigan A), Kennedy (Middlesbrough).
Sub: Gorman (Arsenal) for O'Brien.

(TT) 7 Jun. '83 *at Hyeres*
Argentina (1) 1 (Gasperini)
Rep. of Ireland 0
O'Hanlon (Middlesbrough), O'Regan (Brighton), Pender (Wolves), McDonagh (Shamrock R.), Beglin (Liverpool), O'Driscoll (Fulham), Wilson (Fulham), Gorman (Arsenal), Howlett (Brighton), O'Keefe (Wigan A..), Kernan (Wolves).
Subs: Kennedy (Middlesbrough) for Wilson; O'Brien (Bohemians) for Kernan.

(TT) 9 Jun. '83 *at Toulon*
USSR (1) 1 (Mikhailichenko)
Rep. of Ireland 0
Peyton (Fulham), O'Regan (Brighton), Pender (Wolves), McDonagh (Shamrock R.), Beglin (Liverpool), Gorman (Arsenal), O'Driscoll (Fulham), Kennedy (Middlesbrough), Howlett (Brighton), O'Brien (Bohemians), O'Keefe (Wigan A.).
Subs: Kelly (Preston) for O'Driscoll; Kernan (Wolves) for Howlett.

(TT) 11 Jun. '83 *at Six-Fours*
China (0) 1 (Song)
Rep. of Ireland (2) 5 (O'Keefe 4, Gorman)
O'Hanlon (Middlesbough), O'Regan (Brighton), Coyle (Limerick U.), Pender (Wolves), Beglin (Liverpool), McCabe (Shelbourne), Gorman (Arsenal), Howlett (Brighton), Kelly (Preston), O'Brien (Bohemians), O'Keefe (Wigan A.).
Subs: McDonagh (Shamrock R.) for O'Regan; Kernan (Wolves) for Kelly.

(FR) 25 Mar. '85 *at Portsmouth*
England (2) 3 (Waiters, Fairclough, Wilkinson)
Rep. of Ireland (0) 2 (Kennedy 2 pens)
O'Neill (Bohemians), Coyle (Limerick C.), O'Regan (Brighton), O'Doherty (Crystal P.), Pender (Wolves), Kennedy (Portsmouth), Collins (Southampton), De Mange (Liverpool), Mooney (Liverpool), Sheridan (Leeds U.), Ryan (Brighton)
Subs: Kelly (Newcastle) for O'Neill; Donnellan (Chelsea) for Sheridan; O'Connor (Bristol R.) for Mooney; Hanrahan (UCD) for Ryan.

(EC) 9 Sep. '86 *at Lokeren*
Belgium 0
Rep. of Ireland 0
Kelly (Newcastle), Irwin (Oldham), Dolan (Walsall), Collins (Portsmouth), Bollard (Waterford U.), Callaghan (Stoke), De Mange (Liverpool), Daly (Shrewsbury), Quinn (Arsenal), Swan (Bohemians), Russell (Manchester U.)

(EC) 14 Oct. '86 *at Oriel Park*
Rep. of Ireland (0) 1 (De Mange)
Scotland (0) 2 (Shannon, Gallacher)
Kelly (Newcastle), Irwin (Oldham), Brazil (Manchester U.), Collins (Portsmouth), Dolan (Walsall), Callaghan (Stoke), Milligan (Oldham), De Mange (Liverpool), Quinn (Arsenal), Mooney (Liverpool), Russell (Manchester U.)

(EC) 17 Feb. '87 *at Edinburgh*
Scotland (2) 4 (Fleck 3, Ferguson)
Rep. of Ireland (1) 1 (Coyle)
Kelly (Newcastle), Irwin (Oldham), Phelan (Swansea), O'Shea (Tottenham), Brazil (Manchester U.), Sheridan (Leeds U.), De Mange (Liverpool), Russell (Manchester U.), Mooney (Liverpool), Dolan (West Ham), Coyle (Dumbarton)
Sub: Collins (Portsmouth) for Russell

(EC) 28 Apr. '87 *at Turners Cross*
Rep. of Ireland (0) 1 (P. Dolan)
Belgium (0) 1 (Christiaens) **(see notes)**
Kelly (Newcastle), O'Shea (Tottenham), P. Dolan(Walsall), Brazil (Manchester U.), Staunton (Liverpool), De Mange (Liverpool), Russell (Leicester C), Mooney (Liverpool), E. Dolan (West Ham), Collins (Portsmouth), Coyle (Dumbarton).
Subs: Swan (Bohemians) for Coyle; Bayly (Sligo R.) for P. Dolan.

(TT) 5 Jun. '89 *at Toulon*
Senegal 0
Rep. of Ireland 2 (Dolan, McGee)
G. Kelly (Newcastle), Fleming (St. Patricks A.), Brazil (Manchester U), Scully (Arsenal), Daish (Cambridge), Kenna (Southampton), Poutch (Luton), Fenlon (St. Patricks A.), Dolan (West Ham), D. Kelly (West Ham), McGee (Wimbledon).
Subs: Gormley (Tottenham) for Fenlon; Fitzgerald (Tottenham) for Poutch.

(TT) 7 Jun. '89 *at Toulon*
Bulgaria (1) 2 (Trendafilov, Mitharski)
Rep. of Ireland 0
Gough (Portsmouth), Fleming (St. Patricks A.), Staunton (Liverpool), Scully (Arsenal), Daish (Cambridge), Gormley (Tottenham), Brazil (Manchester U.) McGee (Wimbledon), Quinn (Arsenal), Kelly (West Ham), Tighe (Luton).
Subs: Poutch (Luton) for Gormley; Dolan (West Ham) for Tighe

(TT) 9 Jun. '89 *at Toulon*
England 0
Rep. of Ireland 0
Kelly (Newcastle), Fleming (St. Patricks A.), Scully (Arsenal), Daish (Cambridge), Kenna (Southampton), Poutch (Luton), Brazil (Manchester U.), Staunton (Liverpool), McGee (Wimbledon), Dolan (West Ham), Quinn (Arsenal).

(TT) 10 Jun. '89 *at Toulon*
France "B" 0
Rep. of Ireland (0) 1 (D. Kelly)
G. Kelly (Newcastle), Fleming (St. Patricks A.), Scully (Arsenal), Daish (Cambridge), Kenna (Southampton), Poutch (Luton), Staunton (Liverpool), Brazil (Manchester U.), Tighe (Luton), Quinn (Arsenal), Fitzgerald (Tottenham).
Subs: McGee (Wimbledon) for Tighe; D. Kelly (West Ham) for Fitzgerald; Gormley (Tottenham) for Staunton.

(FR)   24 Apr. '90 *at Oriel Park*
Rep. of Ireland   (0) 1   (Cousins)
Malta   (1) 1   (Licari)
Gough (Portsmouth), Poutch (Luton), Scully (Arsenal), McCarthy (UCD), O'Donoghue (Cork City), Byrne (F.C. Boom), Collins (Liverpool), Kelly (Portsmouth), Arkins (Shamrock R.), Ampadu (Arsenal), Power (Norwich).
Subs: Roche (Celtic) for Kelly; O'Dowd (Shelbourne) for Gough; Cousins (Dundalk) for Power; King (Bohemians) for Ampadu.

(FR)   30 May. '90 *at Valetta*
Malta   (1) 1   (Sultana)
Rep. of Ireland   (1) 1   (Cousins)
Gough (Portsmouth), Fleming (St. Patricks A.), Kenna (Southampton), Daish (Cambridge), Fenlon (St. Patricks A.), McGrath (Brighton), Scully (Arsenal), Poutch (Luton), Power (Norwich), Cousins (Dundalk), Ampadu (Arsenal).
Subs: Arkins (Shamrock R.) for Power; O'Dowd (Leeds U.) for Gough; McCarthy (Brighton) for Scully; King (Bohemians) for Daish.

(EC)   16 Oct. '90 *at Dalymount Park*
Rep. of Ireland   (1) 3   (Cousins 2, 1 pen, Arkins)
Turkey   (1) 2   (Tas 2)
O'Dowd (Leeds U.), O'Donoghue (Cork City), Cunningham (Millwall), McCarthy (Derry C.), Scully (Arsenal), Keane (Nottm. Forest), Ampadu (Arsenal), Brady (Dundalk), Arkins (Shamrock R.), Cousins (Liverpool), Kelly (Portsmouth).
Subs: Poutch (Shamrock R.) for Ampadu; Power (Norwich) for Kelly.

(EC)   13 Nov. '90 *at Turners Cross*
Rep of Ireland   0
England   (1) 3   (Shearer 2, Olney)
O'Dowd (Leeds U.), Cunningham (Millwall), O'Donoghue (Cork City), Scully (Arsenal), McCarthy (Brighton), Poutch (Shamrock R.), Keane (Nottm. Forest), Roche (Celtic), Power (Norwich), Cousins (Liverpool), Kelly (Portsmouth).
Subs: Arkins (Shamrock R.) for Roche; Brady (Sunderland) for Kelly.

(EC)   26 Mar. '91 *at Brentford*
England   (1) 3   (Wallace, Shearer, Cundy)
Rep. of Ireland   0
Gough (Portsmouth), Cunningham (Millwall), Kenna (Southampton), Scully (Arsenal), Fitzgerald (Wimbledon), McGrath (Brighton), Keane (Nottm. Forest), Collins (Liverpool), Power (Norwich), Arkins (Shamrock R.), O'Donoghue (Cambridge).
Subs: McCarthy (Brighton) for O'Donoghue; Roche (Partick T.) for Collins.

(EC)   30 Apr. '91 *at Oriel Park*
Rep. of Ireland   (0) 1   (Fitzgerald)
Poland   (1) 2   (Mielcarski, Waldoch)
Gough (Portsmouth), McDonald (Tottenham), Fitzgerald (Wimbledon), P McCarthy (Brighton), Kenna (Southampton), McGrath (Brighton), Keane (Nottm. Forest), Cousins (Liverpool), Power (Norwich), Brady (Sunderland), O'Donoghue (Cambridge).
Subs: Arkins (Shamrock R.) for Brady; T. McCarthy (Derry C.) for P. McCarthy.

(EC)   15 Oct. '91 *at Bydgoszcz*
Poland   (0) 2   (Juskowiak 2)
Rep. of Ireland   0
McKenna (UCD), McDonald (Tottenham), Fitzgerald (Wimbledon), McCarthy (Shelbourne), Kenna (Southampton), Rush (West Ham), Collins (Liverpool), O'Donoghue (Cambridge), Dunne (St. Johnstone), Arkins (Shamrock R.), Cousins (Liverpool).
Subs: Cunningham (Millwall) for O'Donoghue; Toal (Manchester U.) for Dunne.

(EC)   12 Nov. '91 *at Istanbul*
Turkey   (1) 2   (Cafer, Hakan)
Rep. of Ireland   (0) 1   (O'Connor)
McKenna (UCD), McDonald (Tottenham), Fitzgerald (Wimbledon), McCarthy (Shelbourne), Kenna (Southampton), Toal (Manchester U.), Collins (Liverpool), O'Donoghue (Cambridge), Dunne (St. Johnstone), O'Connor (Shamrock R.), Power (Norwich).
Subs: Rush (West Ham) for Dunne; Arkins (Shamrock R.) for Power.

(FR)   24 Mar. '92 *at Tolka Park*
Rep. of Ireland   (1) 1   (Struder OG)
Switzerland   (0) 1   (Hohener)
Connolly (Bohemians), Collins (Liverpool), Carey (Manchester U.), McCarthy (Brighton), Curtis (Leeds U.), J. Dunne (Gillingham), Toal (Manchester U.), Bacon (Arsenal), L. Dunne (St. Johnstone), Ampadu (West Brom), Power (Norwich).
Subs: Fenlon (Bohemians) for Ampadu; Dempsey (Gillingham) for L. Dunne; O'Connor (Shamrock R.) for Power; Byrne (Bangor) for Curtis.

(EC)   25 May '92 *at Tolka Park*
Rep. of Ireland   (1) 3   (Kinsella, Curtis, Power)
Albania   (1) 1   (Baholli)
Connolly (Bohemians), Napier (Cork City), Gillard (Luton), McGrath (Shamrock R.), McCarthy (Brighton), Curtis (Leeds U.), Kinsella (Colchester), Toal (Manchester U.), Gallen (Watford), Power (Norwich), Dempsey (Gillingham).
Subs: Brady (Sunderland) for Dempsey; Collins (Liverpool) for Toal.

(EC)   13 Oct '92 *at Copenhagen*
Denmark   (3) 3   (Christensen, Moller 2)
Rep. of Ireland   (1) 2   (Dempsey, McGrath)
Colgan (Chelsea), Byrne (Bangor), Dunne (Dundalk), Breen (Gillingham), Greene (Luton T.), Kinsella (Colchester), Rush (West Ham), McGrath (Shamrock Rovers), Power (Norwich), Bacon (Arsenal), Dempsey (Gillingham).
Subs: J. Gallen (Watford) for Bacon: Kavanagh (Middlesbrough) for Rush.

(EC)   17 Nov '92 *at Jerez*
Spain   (2) 2   (Kiko, Alphonso)
Rep. of Ireland   (0) 1   (McCarthy)
McKenna (U.C.D.), Broughan (Bohemians), Dunne (Dundalk), Greene (Luton), McCarthy (Brighton), Kinsella (Colchester), McGrath (Shamrock Rovers), Kavanagh (Middlesbrough), Brady (Doncaster), J. Gallen (Watford), Rush (West Ham).
Subs: Kelly (Leeds United) for Rush: Dempsey (Gillingham) for Kinsella.

113

(EC)   9 Mar '93 *at Dalymount Park*
Rep. of Ireland   0
Germany   (0) 1   (Wuck)
Colgan (Chelsea), S. Gallen (Q.P.R.), Greene (Luton T.), Carr (Coventry), Dunne (Dundalk), Kinsella (Colchester), McGrath (Shamrock Rovers), Kavanagh (Middlesbrough), Sheridan (Coventry), J. Gallen (Watford), Kelly (Leeds United)

(EC)   23 Mar '93 *at Baunatal*
Germany   (3) 8   (Lottner, Herrlich (2), Wuck, Nerlinger, Munch, Haber, Worns)
Rep. of Ireland   0
Colgan (Chelsea), Kavanagh (Middlesbrough), S. Gallen (Q.P.R.), Greene (Luton), Kinsella (Colchester), Hardy (Wrexham), Toal (Manchester U.), McGrath (Shamrock Rovers), Sheridan (Coventry), Kelly (Leeds Utd.), J. Gallen (Watford).
Subs: McKenna (U.C.D.) for Colgan; O'Rourke (Cobh Ramblers) for S. Gallen.

(EC)   27 Apr '93 *at Tolka Park*
Rep. of Ireland   0
Denmark   (1) 2   (Ekelund, Wael)
Colgan (Chelsea), Kinsella (Colchester), Dunne (Dundalk), McCarthy (Brighton), Greene (Luton), Kavanagh (Middlesbrough), McGrath (Shamrock Rovers), Sheridan (Coventry), Power (Norwich), Turner (Tottenham), O'Connor (Drogheda Utd.)
Subs: J. Gallen (Watford) for Power; Bacon (Arsenal) for McGrath.

(EC)   26 May '93 *at Tirana*
Albania   (0) 1   (Quendo)
Rep. of Ireland   (0) 1   (Power)
Colgan (Chelsea), Purdy (Dundalk), McCarthy (Brighton), S. Gallen (Q.P.R.), Hardy (Wrexham), Bacon (Arsenal), Kinsella (Colchester), Sheridan (Coventry), Dempsey (Gillingham), Power (Norwich), Kelly (Leeds United)
Subs: Dunne (Dundalk) for Purdy; O'Connor (Drogheda United) for Power.

(EC)
Rep. of Ireland   0
Spain   (1) 2   (Guerrero, Oscar)
Colgan (Chelsea), Kelly (Leeds United), McCarthy (Brighton), Greene (Luton), Kinsella (Colchester), Hardy (Wrexham), Buckley (Cork City), Boland (Coventry), J.Gallen (Shrewsbury), O'Connor (Drogheda United), Turner (Tottenham)
Subs: Sheridan (Coventry for Boland; Power (Norwich) for Gallen

Notes

The result of the Republic of Ireland v Belgium U-21 match played on 28th April 1987 was subsequently changed to read 3-0 in Ireland's favour as Belgium had fielded ineligible players.

Symbols used in the International Section
EC = European Championship
Fr = Friendly
TT = Toulon Tournament
WC = World Cup

Under-21 Fixtures - Euro '96

06 Sep. 1994	Latvia	v	*Republic of Ireland*
15 Nov. 1994	England	v	*Republic of Ireland*
28 Mar. 1995	*Republic of Ireland*	v	England
25 Apr. 1995	*Republic of Ireland*	v	Portugal
10 Jun. 1995	*Republic of Ireland*	v	Austria
05 Sep. 1995	Austria	v	*Republic of Ireland*
10 Oct. 1995	*Republic of Ireland*	v	Latvia
14 Nov. 1995	Portugal	v	*Republic of Ireland*

Note: England replace Northern Ireland in group 6 of Under-21 Competition and Liechtenstein do not take part.

Moran's Moment
Kevin and family salute the crowd at his testimonial at Lansdowne Road (The Star)

Cork City Supporters Club   Est. 1989.
Are you a Cork City Supporter?

If the answer is yes, then shouldn't you consider joining the official Cork City Supporters Club.

With regular weekly meetings at our base in the **Telecom Club, McCurtain St., Cork,** CCSC organises a wide range of activities, including away trips, social events, player of the month awards and much more besides. Membership of the CCSC is open to all ages so why not come along and join us on Tuesday nights at the Telecom Club where we regularly take in the big game on t.v.

For further information contact any of the following committee members.
Ger Byrne (Chairman) 300212, **Denis Slyne** (Secretary) 270317

Best Wishes to Gerry & Dave - once again the CCSC is delighted to support the Irish Football Handbook.

Republic of Ireland U-21 Appearances

Ampadu, Kwame (Arsenal) 89-90 v Mal (2), 90-91 v Tur, (West Brom) 91-92 v Swz **4**
Anderson, John (West Brom) 77-78 v N.I., Mex, Pol, Fra, Iran, 78-79 v USSR, Arg, Hun, Yug, (Preston) 79-80 v Pol, 80-81 v Eng **11**
Arkins, Vinny (Shamrock R.) 89-90 v Mal, Mal (sub), 90-91 v Tur (*), Eng (sub), Eng, Pol (sub), 91-92 v Pol, Tur (sub) **8**
Atkinson, Hugh (Wolves) 80-81 v Eng **1**
Bacon, John (Arsenal) 91-92 v Swz, 92-93 v Den, Den (sub), Alb **4**
Bayly, Martin (Sligo R.) 86-87 v Bel (sub) **1**
Bayly, Richie (Sham R.) 78-79 v USSR, Arg, Hun, Yug **4**
Beglin, Jim (Liverpool) 82-83 v Fra, Arg, USSR, Chn **4**
Boland, Willie (Coventry City) 93-94 v Spn **1**
Bollard, Noel (Waterford U.) 86-87 v Bel **1**
Bonner, Packie (Celtic) 78-79 v Arg, Hun, Yug, 80-81 v Eng **4**
Braddish, Synan (Dundalk) 77-78 v N.I., (Liverpool) v Pol, Mex, Fra, Iran **5**
Brady, Kieron (Doncaster Rvs.) 90-91 v England (sub), Pol, 91-92 v Alb (sub), 92-93 v Spn **4**
Brady, Paul (Dundalk) 90-91 v Tur **1**
Brazil, Derek (Manchester U.) 86-87 v Sco (2), Bel, 88-89 v Sen, Bul, Eng, Fra (B) **7**
Breen, Gary (Gillingham) 92-93 v Den **1**
Broughan, Donal (Bohemians) 92-93 v Spn **1**
Buckley, Anthony (Cork City) 93-94 v Spn **1**
Buckley, Liam (Shamrock R.) 80-81 v Eng (Sub) **1**
Byrne, Paul (Bangor) 92-93 v Den **1**
Byrne, Tommy (F.C. Boom (Bel)) 89-90 v Mal, 91-92 v Swz (sub) **2**
Callaghan, Aaron (Stoke C.) 86-87 v Bel, Sco **2**
Carey, Brian (Manchester U.) 91-92 v Swz **1**
Carr, Gerard (Coventry City) 92-93 v Ger **1**
Carroll, Derek (L'pool) 78-79 v USSR, Hun (sub), Yug **3**
Chandler, Jeff (Blackpool) 79-80 v Pol **1**
Colgan, Nicky (Chelsea) 92-93 Den (2), Ger (2), Alb, 93-94 v Spn **6**
Collins, David (Liverpool) 89-90 v Mal, 90-91 v Eng, 91–92 v Pol, Tur, Swz, Alb (sub) **6**
Collins, Eamon (Southampton) 84-85 v Eng, (Portsmouth) 86-87 v Bel (2), Sco (sub), Sco **5**
Connolly, John (Bohemians) 91-92 v Swz, Alb **2**
Cousins, Tony (Dundalk) 89-90 v Mal (*sub), Mal (*sub), 90-91 v Tur (**p), Eng, Pol, 91-92 v Pol **6**
Coyle, Owen (Dumbarton) 86-87 v Sco (*), Bel **2**
Coyle, Pat (Blackpool) 77-78 v Mex (sub), Fra, Iran, (sub), 78-79 v USSR (sub) **4**
Coyle, Peter (Limerick U.) 82-83 v Fra, Chn, (Limerick C.) 84-85 v Eng **3**
Cunningham, Ken (Millwall) 90-91 Tur, Eng (2), 91-92 v Pol (sub) **4**
Curtis, Len (Leeds U.) 91-92 v Swz, Alb (*) **2**
Daish, Liam (Cambridge U.) 88-89 v Sen, Bul, Eng, Fra (B), 89-90 v Mal **5**
Daly, Gerry (Shrewsbury T.) 86-87 v Bel **1**
Daly, Maurice (Wolves) 77-78 v N.I., Pol, Mex, Fra **4**
De Mange, Ken (Liverpool) 84-85 v Eng, 86-87 v Bel (2), Sco (*), Sco **5**

Dempsey, Mark (Gillingham) 91-92 v Swz (sub), Alb, 92-93 v Den (*), Spn (sub), Alb **5**
Devine, John (Arsenal) 77-78 v N.I., 79-80 v Pol **2**
Dolan, Eamonn (West Ham) 86-87 v Sco, Bel, 88-89 v Sen (*), Bul (sub), Eng **5**
Dolan, Pat (Walsall) 86-87 v Bel, Bel (*), Sco **3**
Donnellan, Leo (Chelsea) 84-85 v Eng (sub) **1**
Donovan, Terry (Aston V.) 80-81 v Eng **1**
Dunne, Joey (Gillingham) 91-92 v Swz **1**
Dunne, Liam (St.. Johnstone) 91-92 v Pol, Tur, Swz **3**
Dunne, Tommy (Dundalk) 92-93 Den (2), Spn, Ger, Alb (sub) **5**
Fenlon, Pat (St. Patricks A.) 88-89 v Sen, 89-90 v Mal, (Bohemians) 91-92 v Swz (sub) **3**
Finucane, Tony (Limerick) 77-78 v Pol, Mex, Fra **3**
Fitzgerald, Scott (Wimbledon) 90-91 v Eng, Pol (*), 91-92 v Pol, Tur **4**
Fitzgerald, Tommy (Spurs) 88-89 v Sen (sub), Fra (B) **2**
Fleming, Curtis (St. Patricks A.) 88-89 v Sen, Bul, Eng, Fra (B), 89-90 v Mal **5**
Foley, Peter (Oxford U.) 77-78 v Pol, Mex, Fra, Iran, 78-79 v Arg, Hun Yug **7**
Gaffney, Robbie (Shamrock R.) 79-80 v Pol **1**
Gallen, Joe (Watford) 91-92 v Alb, 92-93 v Den (sub) (2), Spn, Ger (2) (Shrewsbury) 93-94 v Spn **7**
Gallen, Stephen (QPR) 92-93 v Ger (2), Alb **3**
Gillard, Ken (Luton T.) 91-92 v Alb **1**
Gorman, Paul (Arsenal) 82-83 v Fra (sub), Arg, USSR, Chn (*) **4**
Gormley, Eddie (Tottenham) 88-89 v Sen (sub), Bul, Fra (B), (sub) **3**
Gough, Alan (Portsmouth) 88-89 v Bul, 89-90 v Mal (2), 90-91 v Eng, Pol **5**
Greene, David (Luton Town) 92-93 v Den (2), Spn, Ger (2) 93-94 v Spn **6**
Grimes, Ashley (Manchester U.) 77-78 v N.I., 78-79 v USSR, Arg (*p), Hun, Yug, 79-80 v Pol (*p) **6**
Hanrahan, Joe (UCD) 84-85 v Eng (sub) **1**
Hardy, Phil (Wrexham) 92-93 v Ger, Alb 93-94 v Spn **3**
Hayes, Austin (Southampton) 78-79 v USSR, Arg, Hun, Yug, 79-80 v Pol **5**
Henderson, Dave (Shamrock R.) 77-78 v Iran, 79-80 v Pol **2**
Howlett, Gary (Brighton) 82-83 v Fra (*), Arg, USSR, Chn **4**
Hughton, Henry (Orient) 80-81 v Eng **1**
Irwin, Denis (Oldham A.) 86-87 v Bel, Sco (2) **3**
Kavanagh, Graham (Middlesbrough) 92-93 v Den (sub), Spn, Ger (2), Den **5**
Keane, Roy (Nottm. F) 90-91 v Tur, Eng (2), Pol **4**
Kelly, David (West Ham) 88-89 v Sen, Bul, Fra (B) (*sub) **3**
Kelly, Gary (Newcastle Utd.) 84-85 v Eng (sub), 86-87 v Bel (2), Sco (2), 88-89 v Sen, Eng, Fra (B) **8**
Kelly, Gary (Leeds Utd.) 92-93 v Spn (sub), Ger (2), Alb 93-94 v Spn **5**
Kelly, John (Preston) 82-83 v USSR (sub) Chn **2**
Kelly, Mark (Portsm'th) 89-90 v Mal, 90-91 v Tur, Eng **3**
Kenna, Jeff (Southampton) 88-89 v Sen, Eng, Fra (B), 89-90 v Mal, 90-91 v Eng, Pol, 91-92 v Pol, Tur **8**
Kennedy, Mick (Middlesbrough) 82-83 v Fra, Arg (sub), USSR, (Portsmouth) 84-85 v Eng (**pp) **4**

116

Kernan, Tony (Wolves) 82-83 v Arg, USSR (sub), Chn (sub) **3**
King, Lee (Bohemians) 89-90 v Mal (sub), v Mal (sub) **2**
Kinsella, Mark (Colchester U.) 91-92 v Alb (*), 92-93 v Den (2), Spn, Ger (2), Alb 93-94 v Spn **8**
Kinsella, Tony (M'wall) 79-80 v Pol, 80-81 v Eng (sub) **2**
Lane, Redmond (Cork Alberts) 77-78 v N.I. **1**
Lawless, Gino (Bohs) 78-79 v Arg (sub), Yug (sub) **2**
Lawlor, Martin (Dundalk) 78-79 v USSR, Arg, Hun, Yug, 79-80 v Pol (sub) **5**
McCabe, Kieran (Shelbourne) 82-83 v Chn **1**
McCarthy, Paul (Brighton) 89-90 v Mal (Sub, 90-91 v Eng, Eng (sub), Pol, 91-92 v Swz, Alb, 92-93 v Spn (*), Den, Alb 93-94 Spn **10**
McCarthy, Tony (UCD)89-90 v Mal, (Derry C.) 90-91 v Tur, Pol (sub), (Shelbourne) 91-92 v Pol, Tur **5**
McDonagh, Jacko (Bohemians) 80-81 v Eng, (Shamrock R.) 82-83 v Arg, USSR, Chn (sub) **4**
McDonald, Dave (Tottenham) 90-91 v Pol, 91-92 v Pol, Tur **3**
McGee, Paul (QPR) 77-78 v N.I., (PNE) 80-81 v Eng **2**
McGee, Paul (Wimbledon) 88-89 v Sen (*), Bul, Eng, Fra (B) (sub) **4**
McGrath, Derek (Brighton) 89-90 v Mal, 90-91 v Eng, Pol, (Shamrock R.) 91-92 v Alb, 92-93 v Den (*), Spn, Ger (2), Den **9**
McKenna, Brian (UCD) 91-92 v Pol, Tur, 92-93 v Spn, Ger (sub) **4**
Madigan, Mick (Waterford) 77-78 v N.I. **1**
Malone, Joey (Bohemians) 77-78 v Pol, Mex, Fra, Iran **4**
Meagan, Mark (Shamrock R.) 77-78 v Pol, Mex, Fra, Iran, 78-79 v USSR, Arg, Hun, Yug **8**
Milligan, Mike (Oldham A) 86-87 v Sco **1**
Mooney, Brian (Liverpool) 84-85 v Eng, 86-87 v Sco (2), Bel **4**
Murray, Larry (Shamrock R.) 77-78 v Pol, Mex, Fra (sub), Iran **4**
Murray, Martin (Everton) 77-78 v N.I. (*), Pol, Mex (*), Fra, Iran, 78-79 v USSR (sub), Arg (sub), Yug (*sub) **8**
Napier, Stephen (Cork City) 91-92 v Alb **1**
Nolan, Pat (Limerick) 77-78 v N.I., Iran **2**
O'Brien, David (Bohemians) 82-83 v Fra, Arg (sub), USSR, Chn **4**
O'Callaghan, Kevin (Millwall) 78-79 v USSR, Arg, Hun, Yug, 79-80 v Pol **5**
O'Connor, Barry (Drogheda U.) 91-92 v Tur (*), Swz (sub), 92-93 v Alb (sub) 93-94 Spn **4**
O'Connor, Mark (Bristol R.) 84-85 v Eng (sub) **1**
O'Connor, Michael (Athlone T.) 80-81 v Eng **1**
O'Doherty, Declan (Fulham) 78-79 v USSR, Arg, Hun **3**
O'Doherty, Ken (Crystal P.) 84-85 v Eng **1**
O'Donoghue, Fergus (Cork City) 89-90 v Mal, 90-91 v Tur, Eng, (Camb Utd.) v Eng, Pol, 91-92 v Pol, Tur **7**
O'Dowd, Tony (Shelbourne) 89-90 v Mal (sub), (Leeds U.) v Mal (sub), 90-91 v Tur, Eng **4**
O'Driscoll, Sean (Fulham) 82-83 v Fra, Arg, USSR **3**
O'Hanlon, Kelham (Middlesbrough) 82-83 v Arg, Chn **2**
O'Keefe, Eamonn (Wigan A) 82-83 v Fra, Arg, USSR, Chn (****) **4**
O'Leary, Pierce (Shamrock R.) 78-79 v USSR, Arg, Hun, Yug, 79-80 v Pol **5**
O'Neill, Alan (Sham R.) 77-78 v N.I., 78-79 v USSR **2**
O'Neill, Dermot (Bohemians) 84-85 v Eng **1**
O'Regan, Kieran (Brighton) 82-83 v Fra, Arg, USSR, Chn, 84-85 v Eng **5**

O'Rourke, Kenny (Cobh Ramblers) 92-93 v Ger (sub) **1**
O'Shea, Tim (Tottenham) 86-87 v Sco, Bel **2**
Pender, John (Wolves) 82-83 v Fra, Arg, USSR, Chn, 84-85 v Eng **5**
Peyton, Gerry (Fulham) 82-83 v Fra, USSR **2**
Phelan, Terry (Swansea) 86-87 v Sco **1**
Poutch, Neil (Luton T.) 88-89 v Sen, Bul (sub), Eng, Fra (B), 89-90 v Mal (2), (Shamrock R.) 90-91 v Tur (sub), Eng **8**
Power, Lee (Norwich C.) 89-90 v Mal (2), 90-91 v Tur (sub), Eng (2), Pol, 91-92 v Tur, Swz, Alb (*), 92-93 v Den (2), Alb (*) 93-94 v Spn (sub), **13**
Purdy, Richie (Dundalk) 92-93 v Alb **1**
Quinn, Niall (Arsenal) 86-87 v Bel, Sco, 88-89 v Bul, Eng, Fra (B) **5**
Roche, Declan (Celtic) 89-90 v Mal, 90-91 v Eng, (Partick T.) v Eng (sub) **3**
Rush, Matthew (West Ham) 91-92 v Pol, Tur (sub), 92-93 v Den, Spn **4**
Russell, Martin (Manchester U.) 86-87 v Bel, Sco (2), (Leicester C.) v Bel **4**
Ryan, Gerry (Brighton) 84-85 v Eng **1**
Scully, Pat (Arsenal) 88-89 v Sen, Bul, Eng, Fra (B), 89-90 v Mal (2), 90-91 v Tur, Eng (2) **9**
Sheedy, Kevin (Hereford U.) 77-78 v Pol, Mex, Fra, Iran, (Liverpool) 80-81 v Eng **5**
Sheridan, John (Leeds U.) 84-85 v Eng, 86-87 v Sco **2**
Sheridan, Tony (Coventry City) 92-93 v Ger (2), Den, Alb 93-94 Spn (sub), **5**
Staunton, Steve (Liverpool) 86-87 v Bel, 88-89 v Bul, Eng, Fra (B) **4**
Swan, Derek (Bohemians) 86-87 v Bel, Bel (sub) **2**
Tighe, Aaron (Luton T.) 88-89 v Bul, Fra (B) **2**
Toal, Kieran (Manchester U.) 91-92 v Pol (sub), Tur, Swz, Alb, 92-93 v Ger **5**
Turner, Andy (Tottenham) 92-93 v Den 93-94 v Spn **2**
Waddock, Gary (QPR) 79-80 v Pol **1**
Wade, Roger (Ilford) 77-78 v Pol, Mex, Fra, Iran **4**
Walker, Pat (Gillingham) 77-78 v Pol (sub), Iran, (sub) **2**
Whelan, Anto (Manchester U.) 80-81 v Eng **1**
Whelan, Ronnie (Liverpool) 80-81 v Eng **1**
Wilson, Robert (Fulham) 82-83 v Fra, Arg **2**

Note: (*) = Goals Scored

Mick Milligan
Capped at U21 level vs Scotland in 1986 (DC)

117

Body Czech!
Alan Mahon (Ireland) and Roman Graca (R.C.S.) in action during the UEFA U16 Championship Finals
(The Star)

My Ball!
John Burns (Republic of Ireland) and Stephen Clemence (England) race for possession during their U16 clash at Tolka Park   (The Star)

UEFA U-16 Championship Finals

Group A

26 Apr. at Oriel Park, Dundalk
Albania (0) 0
Austria (1) 1 *(Plassnegger 21)*
Albania: Shehi, Zeqiri (Tarja 57), Pinari, Ibrahimi, Domi, Dibra, Hoxha (Ruko 68), Maliqi, Koka, Qosja, Merkoci.
Austria: Fuka, Hiden, Krogler, Schandl, Saler, Kuljic (Graf 78), Klein, Plassnegger, Ramic, Rauscher, Weiss.
Referee: O'Hanlon (Rep. Ireland)   Att. 200 approx.

26 Apr. at United Park, Drogheda
Belarus (0) 1 *(Ryndiuk 65)*
Spain (0) 0
Belarus.: Gayev, Lukashevic, Vavilov, Kirilenko, Baranov, Kapelian, Likhtarovich, Tabola, Novitski, Ryndiuk, Osipenko
Spain: Teruel, Canego, Cabezas Garcia, Navarro, Perez, Goya (Pizarro 53), Zapata, Lizardi, Cabello Garcia, De La Mata, Raso (Bootello 65).
Referee: Albrecht (Germany)   Att. n/a

28 Apr. at Oriel Park, Dundalk
Austria (1) 1 *(Klein 39)*
Spain (1) 1 *(Canego 29)*
Austria: Fuka, Hiden, Schandl, Saler, Kuljic, Klein, Plassnegger, Praprotnig, Ramic (Resner 74), Rauscher (Graf 61), Weiss.
Spain: Teruel, Canego, Navarro, Perez, Goya, Dominguez, Zapata (Bootello 64), Lizardi, Cabello Garcia, De La Mata, Salvador.
Referee: Mendes Pratas (Portugal)   Att. n/a

28 Apr. at United Park, Drogheda
Albania (0) 1 *(Merkoci 51)*
Belarus (0) 1 *(Gavrilovich 42)*
Albania: Shehi, Pinari, Ibrahimi, Domi, Dibra, Hoxha (Ruko 72), Maliqi (Sinani 76), Koka, Qosja, Merkoci, Tarja.
Belarus: Gayev, Lukashevic, Vavilov, Kirilenko, Baranov, Kapelian, Likhtarovich, Tabola (Ignatik 60), Novitski (Gavrilovich 40), Ryndiuk, Osipenko.
Referee: Cakman (Turkey)   Att. 600 approx.

30 Apr. at Oriel Park, Dundalk
Albania (0) 0
Spain (3) 4 *(Cabello Garcia 19, 31, Lizardi 29, 52)*
Albania: Shehi, Pinari, Ibrahimi, Domi, Dibra (Ruko 68), Hoxha (Sinani 52), Maliqi, Koka, Qosja, Merkoci, Tarja.
Spain: Teruel (Martinez 58), Canego, Cabezas Garcia, Navarro, Perez, Goya, Dominguez, Lizardi, Cabello Garcia, De La Mata (Salvador 64), Pizarro.
Referee: Fisker (Denmark)   Att. 150 approx.

30 Apr. at United Park, Drogheda
Austria (0) 1 *(Plassnegger 47)*
Belarus (0) 1 *(Ryndiuk 79)*
Austria: Fuka, Hiden, Schandl, Saler, Kuljic, Klein, Plassnegger (Resner 78), Praprotnig, Ramic (Graf 57), Rauscher, Weiss.
Belarus: Gayev, Lukashevic, Vavilov, Kirilenko, Baranov, Kapelian, Likhtarovich, Tabola, Osipenko, Gavrilovich (Ignatik 68), Balin (Ryndiuk 79).
Referee: Hrinak (RCS)   Att.1,000 approx.

Belarus won 5-4 on penalty kicks to decide group winners

Group B

26 Apr. at Frank Cooke Park, Dublin
England (1) 1 *(Cassidy 15)*
Portugal (0) 0
England: Wright, Millett, Hilton, Broomes, Wallwork, Shore, Richardson, Clemence, Carragher (Heskey 66), Ducros (Quashie 73), Cassidy.
Portugal: Dos Santos, Ramos, Soares (A) (Vargas 65), Pacheco, Pereira, Meira (Fernandes 40), Monteiro, Basto, Soares (Z), Lima, Patacas.
Referee: Levnikov (Russia)   Att: 300 approx.

26 Apr. at Tolka Park, Dublin
RCS (1) 1 *(Nemeth 21)*
Rep. of Ireland (0) 0
RCS: Mucha, Graca, Chribik (Adam 55), Toth, Minarovic, Czinege, Kamancza, Hasprun, Bagocky (Cukan 71), Nemeth, Laclavik.
Rep.of I.: O'Connor (Crumlin Utd.), Worrell (Home Farm), Murphy (Belvedere), Hawkins (Newcastle, Galway), Darcy (Stella Maris), O'Hanlon (Stella Maris) [Kirby (Johnville) 56], Cummins (Crumlin Utd.) [Cassin (Belvedere) 74], Burns (Belvedere), Mannix (Stella Maris), Mahon (Crumlin Utd.), Frawley (Belvedere).
Referee: Ancion (Belgium)   Att. 2,300 approx.

28 Apr. at Tolka Park, Dublin
England (0) 1 *(Clemence 78)*
Rep. of Ireland (1) 1 *(Frawley 26)*
England: Wright, Millett, Hilton, Broomes, Wallwork, Quashie (Shore 46), Richardson, Clemence, Ducros (Heath 72), Cassidy, Heskey.
Rep.of I.: O'Connor, Worrell, Murphy, Hawkins, Darcy, Kirby, Cummins [Webb (Stella Maris) 49], Burns, Mannix, Mahon (Cassin 40), Frawley.
Referee: Meier (Switzerland)   Att.7,000 approx.

28 Apr. at Whitehall, Dublin
Portugal (2) **2** *(Soares (Z) 20, 24)*
RCS **0**
Portugal: Dos Santos, Ramos (Meira 78), Pacheco, Pereira, Monteiro, Basto, Soares (Z), Patacas, Vargas (Lima 65), Rodrigues, Fernandes.
RCS: Mucha, Graca, Chribik (Cukan 51), Toth, Minarovich, Czinege, Kamancza, Hasprun (Lojdl 58), Bagocky, Nemeth, Lacklavik.
Referee: Shmolik (Belarus) Att. n/a

28 Apr. at Plassey Bowl, Limerick
Denmark (0) **3** *(Thorup 43, Olsen 77, Hansen 78)*
Russia (1) **2** *(Bout 39, 64)*
Denmark: Johansen, Gronkjaer, Heiselberg, Iversen, Nielsen (Hansen 55), Lauritsen, Olsen, Lektonen (Lund-Burmeister 68), Poulsen, Thorup, Vigh.
Russia: Tchitchkine, Meerovitch, Aksenov, Sedunov, Zaikine, Kobenko, Fichman, Bout, Afonin, Povorov, Topounov (Zaranko 19).
Referee: Gallagher (England) Att: n/a

30 Apr. at Dalymount Park, Dublin
England (2) **2** *(Cassidy 2, Richardson 28)*
RCS (0) **1** *(Bagocky 42)*
England: Millett, Wright, Hilton, Broomes, Richardson, Clemence, Carragher, Cassidy, Heath (Quashie 68), Shore, Crooks (Heskey 57).
RCS: Mucha, Graca (Adam 51), Toth, Minarovich, Czinege, Kamancza, Bagocky, Nemeth, Laclavik, Chribik (Hasprun 41), Cukan.
Referee: Schuttengruber (Austria) Att: 100 approx.

28 Apr. at Cooke Park, Tipperary
Germany (3) **5** *(Frohlich 9, Nehrbauer 34, Thurre (og) 40, Reich 45), Saur 62)*
Switzerland (1) **1** *(Sansonnens 21)*
Germany: Enke, Levy, Bauer, Disteldorf, Scherbe, Wiblishauser, Saur, Reich (Villa 68), Nehrbauer, Frohlich (Kallus 65), Koch.
Swi: Roth (Bernet 28), Eich, Jenny, Lampreu (Bieli 42), Sansonnens, Kehrli, Pizzinat, Riedwyl, Ziegler, Renfer, Thurre.
Referee: Melnichuk (Ukraine) Att. 2,000 approx.

30 Apr. at Tolka Park, Dublin
Portugal (1) **3** *(Soares (Z) 34, 61, Ramos 54)*
Rep.of I. **0**
Portugal: Dos Santos, Ramos (Vargas 74), Pacheco (Lima 66), Pereira, Monteiro, Basto, Soares (Z), Caneira, Patacas, Rodrigues, Fernandes.
Rep.of I.: O'Connor, Worrell, Murphy, Hawkins, Darcy, Cummins (Cassin 52), Burns [Baker (Manchester Utd.) 61], Mannix, Mahon, Frawley, Kirby
Referee: Albrecht (Germany) Att: 4,100 approx.

30 Apr. at Bishopstown, Cork
Denmark (3) **3** *(Thorup 7, 15, Hansen 11)*
Germany (2) **4** *(Levy 25, Reich 40, Parlatan 52, Saur 69)*
Denmark: Johansen, Gronkjaer (Lund-Burmeister 67), Hansen, Heiselberg, Iversen, Lauritsen, Lektonen, Olsen, Poulsen (Nielsen 54), Thorup, Vigh.
Germany: Enke, Levy, Bauer (Koch 66), Disteldorf (Kallus 66), Scherbe, Wiblishauser, Parlatan, Saur, Reich, Nehrbauer, Frohlich.
Referee: Gallagher (England) Att. 400 approx.

Group C

26 Apr. at Turner's Cross, Cork
Denmark (4) **4** *(Gronkjaer 9, 30, Hansen 12, Laursen 21)*
Switzerland (0) **3** *(Ziegler 56, 70, Thurre 66)*
Denmark: Johansen, Gronkjaer, Hansen, Iversen (Jorgensen 62), Jensen, Lauritsen, Laursen (Poulsen 41), Lektonen, Olsen, Thorup, Vigh.
Swi.: Roth, Eich, Jenny (Renfer 62), Julmy, Sansonnens, Vanetta, Kehrli, Pizzinat, Ziegler, Bieli (Tschopp 67), Thurre.
Referee: Orrason (Iceland) Att. 200 approx.

30 Apr. at Turner's Cross, Cork
Russia (1) **5** *(Bout 14, 49, 77, Afonin 41, Lampreu (og) 67)*
Switzerland (0) **1** *(Tschopp 55)*
Russia: Vorobiev (D), Meerovitch, Aksenov, Sedunov, Zaikine, Kobenko (Vorobiev (I), 32), Fichman, Bout, Afonin, Povorov, Zaranko (Mazitov 67).
Swi.: Bernet, Tschopp, Eich (Lampreu 64), Jenny, Julmy, Sansonnens, Vanetta, Kehrli, Ziegler (Riedwyl 52), Bieli, Thurre.
Referee: Orrason (Iceland) Att: 200 approx.

26 Apr. at St. Colman's Park, Cobh
Germany **0**
Russia (0) **2** *(Bout 46, Afonin 79)*
Germany: Enke, Levy, Bauer (Koch 72), Disteldorf (Kallus 72), Scherbe, Wiblishauser, Parlatan, Saur, Reich, Nehrbauer, Frohlich.
Russia: Tchitchkine, Meerovitch, Aksenov, Sedunov, Zaikine, Kobenko, Fichman, Bout, Afonin, Povorov, Zaranko.
Referee: Brito Arceo (Spain) Att: 570

Group D

26 Apr. at Belfield Park, Dublin
Belgium (0) **1** *(Van De Paar 74)*
Ukraine (2) **2** *(Iachtchouk 6, Fedorouk 9)*
Belgium: Desmet, Dhooge, Foets, Hoefkens, Rouffignon, Schockaert (Roussel 51), Thys, Turco, Van De Paar, Verdonck, Vermoesen (Durka 25).
Ukraine: Perkhoun, Koltchine (Kouptsov 78), Fedorouk, Nazarov, Michkov, Gopkalo (Belokon 73), Zoubov, Slioussar, Zgoura, Omelianovitch, Iachtchouk
Referee: Hrinak (RCS) Att: n/a

26 Apr. at Iveagh Grounds, Dublin
Iceland (1) 1 *(Gudjohnsen 20)*
Turkey (0) 2 *(Meric 43, 55)*
Iceland: Magnusson (G), Agustsson, Haraldsson, Ingimarsson, Vidarsson, Pjetursson (Magnusson (J) 75), Asgeirsson, Johannesson (Gudmundsson (S) 69), Gislason, Sveinsson.
Turkey: Tuncay, Caliskan, Tan, Seletli, Ozke, Duranoglu, Habiboglu (Yaman 79), Tekke, Bayhan, Meric, Saglam (Aydin 68).
Referee: Schuttengruber (Austria)   Att: 60

28 Apr. at Iveagh Grounds, Dublin
Belgium (0) 2 *(Roussel 48, Verdonck 65)*
Iceland (0) 1 *(Ingimarsson 77)*
Belgium: Desmet, Hoefkens, Janne, Pardo, Rouffignon, Roussel, Durka, Thys (Vermoesen 41), Turco, Van De Paar, Verdonck (Schockaert 74).
Iceland: Magnusson (G), Agustsson, Haraldsson, Ingimarsson, Vidarsson, Asgeirsson, Johannesson (Gudmundsson (J) 54), Gudjohnsen, Gislason, Sveinsson, Magnusson (J) (Pjetursson 63).
Referee: Pregja (Albania)   Att: 100 approx.

28 Apr. at RDS, Dublin
Turkey (1) 1 *(Bayhan 11)*
Ukraine (1) 1 *(Zoubov 20)*
Turkey: Tuncay, Caliskan, Tan, Seletli, Ozke, Duranoglu (Aydin 80), Habiboglu, Tekke, Bayhan, Meric (Yaman 71), Saglam.
Ukraine: Ostapenko, Koltchine, Fedorouk, Nazarov, Michkov, Gopkalo, Zoubov, Slioussar, Zgoura, Omelianovich (Belokon 78), Iachtchouk (Golovko 70).
Referee: Fisker (Denmark)   Att: n/a

30 Apr. at RDS, Dublin
Belgium   0
Turkey (2) 4 *(Habiboglu 1, 63, Bayhan 6, Tekke 57)*
Belgium: Desmet, Hoefkens, Janne (Schockaert 52), Pardo (Thys 40), Rouffignon, Roussel, Durka, Turco, Van De Paar, Verdonck, Vermoesen.
Turkey: Tuncay, Caliskan, Tan (Onur 73), Seletli, Ozke, Duranoglu (Gok 64), Habiboglu, Tekke, Bayhan, Meric, Saglam.
Referee: Shmolik (Belarus)   Att: 350 approx.

30 Apr. at Belfield Park, Dublin
Iceland (1) 1 *(Gislason 17)*
Ukraine (0) 2 *(Iachtchouk 56, Slioussar 68)*
Iceland: Magnusson (G), Agustsson, Haraldsson (Valgeirsson 74), Ingimarsson, Vidarsson, Pjetursson, Gudjohnsen, Gislason, Sveinsson, Magnusson (J) (Asgeirsson 29), Gudmundsson (J).
Ukraine: Ostapenko, Koltchine, Fedorouk, Nazarov, Michkov, Gopkalo (Klimenko 46), Zoubov, Slioussar, Zgoura, Omelianovich, Iachtchouk (Golovko 78).
Referee: O'Hanlon (Rep. of Ireland)   Att: 30

Group A	P.	W.	D.	L.	F.	A.	Pts.
Belarus	3	1	2	-	3	2	5
Austria	3	1	2	-	3	2	5
Spain	3	1	1	1	5	2	4
Albania	3	-	1	2	1	6	1

Group B	P.	W.	D.	L.	F.	A.	Pts.
England	3	2	1	-	4	2	7
Portugal	3	2	-	1	5	1	6
RCS	3	1	-	2	2	4	3
Rep. of Ireland	3	-	1	2	1	5	1

Group C	P.	W.	D.	L.	F.	A.	Pts.
Russia	3	2	-	1	9	4	6
Denmark	3	2	-	1	10	9	6
Germany	3	2	-	1	9	6	6
Switzerland	3	-	-	3	5	14	-

Group D	P.	W.	D.	L.	F.	A.	Pts.
Turkey	3	2	1	-	7	2	7
Ukraine	3	2	1	-	5	3	7
Belgium	3	1	-	2	3	7	3
Iceland	3	-	-	3	3	6	-

Quarter-Finals

3 May at Dalymount Park, Dublin
Belarus (1) 1 *(Osipenko 21)*
Denmark (2) 3 *(Olsen 31, Thorup 39, Gronkjaer 50)*
Belarus: Gayev, Lukashevich, Vavilov, Kirilenko, Baranov, Kapelian, Likhtarovich, Ryndiuk, Osipenko, Gavrilovich, Narushevich (Tabola 66).
Denmark: Johansen, Gronkjaer, Hansen, Heiselberg, Iversen, Lauritsen, Lektonen (Jensen 28), Olsen (Nielsen 59), Poulsen, Thorup, Vigh.
Referee: Ancion (Belgium)   Att: 100 approx.

3 May at R.D.S., Dublin
England (1) 2 *(Carragher 4, Ducros 57)*
Ukraine (0) 2 *(Fedorouk 47, Omelianovitch 80)*
A.E.T.
England: Wright, Millett, Hilton, Broomes, Wallwork, Richardson, Clemence, Carragher (Quashie 86), Ducros (Heskey 74), Cassidy, Shore
Ukraine: Ostapenko, Koltchine, Fedorouk, Nazarov, Michkov, Klimenko, Zoubov (Gopkalo 76), Slioussar, Zgoura, Omelianovitch, Belokon (Golovko 74).
Referee: Mendes Pratas (Portugal)   Att: n/a
Ukraine won 7-6 on penalty kicks

121

3 May at Tolka Park, Dublin
Austria (0) **2** *(Plassnegger 60, Pomper 71)*
Russia 0
Austria: Fuka, Hiden, Schandl, Kiesenebner (Pomper 59), Kuljic, Klein, Plassnegger (Graf 76), Praprotnig, Ramic, Rausher, Weiss.
Russia: Tchitchkine, Meerovitch, Aksenov, Sedunov, Zaikine, Kobenko, Fichman, Bout, Afonin, Povorov, Zaranko (Vorobiev (I) 56).
Referee: Brito Arceo (Spain) Att: n/a

3 May at Oriel Park, Dundalk
Portugal 0
Turkey 0 A.E.T.
Portugal: Dos Santos, Ramos (Pereira Vargas 84), Pacheco, Pereira, Monteiro, Basto, Soares (Z), Caneira, Patacas, Rodrigues (Lima 68), Fernandes.
Turkey: Tuncay, Caliskan, Tan, Seletli, Ozke, Duranoglu (Aydin 67), Habiboglu, Tekke, Bayhan, Meric (Yaman 88), Saglam.
Referee: Meier (Switzerland) Att: 380
Turkey won 5-3 on penalty kicks

SEMI-FINALS

5 May at Tolka Park, Dublin
Austria 0
Turkey (1) **1** *(Saglam 14)*
Austria: Fuka, Hiden, Krogler (Resner 57), Pomper, Schandl, Kuljic, Plassnegger, Praprotnig, Ramic (Graf 34), Rauscher, Weiss.
Turkey: Tuncay, Cariskan, Tan, Seletli, Ozke, Duranoglu, Habiboglu (Aydin 77), Tekke, Bayhan, Meric, Saglam (Yaman 80).
Referee: Gallagher (England) Att: 700 approx.

5 May at Dalymount Park, Dublin
Denmark (1) **2** *(Lektonen 37, Thorup 80)*
Ukraine (0) **2** *(Belokon 42, Gopkalo 61)* A.E.T.
Denmark: Johansen, Gronkjaer, Hansen, Heiselberg, Iversen, Lauritsen, Laursen (Poulsen 52), Lektonen (Nielsen 62), Olsen, Thorup, Vigh.
Ukraine: Ostapenko, Koltchine, Fedorouk, Nazarov, Michkov, Klimenko (Gopkalo 40), Zoubov Slioussar, Zgoura, Omelianovitch, Belokon (Golovko 73).
Referee: O'Hanlon (Rep. of Ireland) Att: 300 approx.
Denmark won 5-3 on penalty kicks

3RD/4TH PLAY-OFF

8 May at R.D.S., Dublin
Austria 0
Ukraine (1) **2** *(Iachtchouk 34, Zgoura 78)*
Austria: Fuka, Hiden, Pomper, Schandl, Praprotnig, Graf, Klein, Rauscher, Kuljic, Plassnegger, Resner (Krogler 69).
Ukraine: Ostapenko, Koltchine, Fedorouk, Nazarov, Michkov, Gopkalo, Kouptsov, Zoubov, Slioussar, Zgoura, Iachtchouk.
Referee: Levnikov (Russia) Att: n/a

FINAL

8 May at R.D.S., Dublin
Denmark 0
Turkey (0) **1** *(Meric 51)*
Denmark: Johansen, Lauritsen, Iversen, Vigh, Olsen, Heiselberg, Lektonen (Nielsen 26), Poulsen (Jensen 64), Thorup, Gronkjaer, Hansen.
Turkey: Tuncay, Caliskan, Seletli, Ozke, Habiboglu, Onur, Aydin, Meric, Saglam, Tekke, Bayhan.
Referee: Albrecht (Germany) Att: 2,000 approx.

Top Scorers:
Vladimir Bout (Russia) 6
Kenny Thorup (Denmark) 5
Zeferino Soares (Portugal) 4

Highest Scoring Teams:
Denmark 15
Ukraine 11

Games Played: 32 **Goals Scored:** 93 **Goal Average:** 2.91

Note: in the Group C Final Table (page 121) it should be observed that Denmark qualified ahead of Germany despite having an inferior goal difference. According to UEFA Rules for the tournament (Article 6, Rule 11), Russia also becomes involved in the equation as terms finishing *"equal on points after having played all the matches in their group, the following criteria shall be used to determine the ranking in the order given:*
1. Higher number of points obtained in the matches between the teams concerned.
2. Goal difference in the matches between the teams concerned."

Republic of Ireland Players *(Club by Club)*

The following is a list of clubs which have supplied players to Free State/Republic of Ireland teams in all Senior International matches up to and including the World Cup clash with Holland on July 4th, 1994. The number in brackets after each clubs name is the total of players supplied by that club. In the case of League of Ireland clubs details, of the last player to be capped are included. It should be noted that in the case of players being 'on loan' when capped it is the club to which the player is contracted and not to which he is 'loaned' that is included.

(A) League of Ireland: (Present Members): 8

Bohemians	(20)	Barry Murphy	v	Uruguay	(h)	1-1	23 Apr 86
Drogheda U	(3)	Jerome Clarke & Cathal Muckian	v	Poland	(a)	0-3	12 Apr 78
Dundalk	(11)	Mick Fairclough	v	Trinidad & Tobago	(a)	1-2	30 May 82
St. James's Gate	(8)	Paddy Bradshaw & Joe O'Reilly	v	Germany	(a)	1-1	23 May 39
St. Patricks Ath.	(6)	Noel Campbell	v	Austria	(h)	1-4	30 May 71
Shamrock R.	(62)	Pat Byrne	v	Czechoslovakia	(n)	1-0	27 May 86
Shelbourne	(23)	Mick Gannon & Paddy Roche	v	Austria	(a)	0-6	30 May 71
Sligo Rovers	(1)	Paddy Monahan	v	Germany	(a)	1-3	8 May 35

(B) League of Ireland: (Past Members): 14

Bray Unknowns	(1)	Jack Byrne	v	Belgium	(a)	4-2	12 Feb 28
Brideville	(2)	Joe O'Reilly	v	Luxembourg	(a)	5-1	9 May 36
Cork	(9)	Hugh Connolly	v	Germany	(h)	5-2	17 Oct 36
Cork Athletic	(1)	Florrie Burke	v	W. Germany	(h)	3-2	17 Oct 51
Cork Bohemians	(1)	Miah Lynch	v	Belgium	(h)	4-4	26 Feb 34
Cork Hibernians	(2)	Miah Dennehy	v	Chile	(n)	1-2	25 Jun 72
Cork United	(3)	Johnny McGowan	v	Spain	(h)	3-2	2 Mar 47
Dolphin	(5)	Joe Kendrick	v	Holland	(h)	3-5	8 Dec 35
Drumcondra	(13)	Fran Brennan	v	Belgium	(h)	0-2	24 Mar 65
Evergreen U	(1)	Tommy Moroney	v	France	(h)	3-5	4 Oct 53
Fordsons	(6)	Frank McLoughlin	v	Belgium	(a)	3-1	11 May 30
Jacobs	(1)	Frank Collins	v	Italy 'B'	(h)	1-2	23 Apr 27
Limerick/Lim U	(6)	Johnny Walsh	v	Trinidad & Tobago	(a)	1-2	30 May 82
Waterford	(8)	Peter Thomas	v	Brazil	(a)	1-2	5 May 74

(C) Irish League: (Present Members): 2
Coleraine (1), *Glentoran* (1)

(D) Irish League: (Past Members): 2
Belfast Celtic (3), *Derry City* (1)

(E) Football League: (Present Members): 72

Arsenal (12), *Aston Villa* (11), *Barnsley* (1), *Birmingham City* (6), *Blackburn Rovers* (6), *Blackpool* (1), *Bolton Wanderers* (5), *AFC Bournemouth* (2), *Brentford* (1), *Brighton & H.A.* (8), *Bristol City* (1), *Bristol Rovers* (2), *Bury* (1), *Cambridge United* (1), *Cardiff City* (2), *Charlton Athletic* (2), *Chelsea* (5), *Chester City* (1), *Coventry City* (5), *Crystal Palace* (3), *Derby County* (8), *Doncaster Rovers* (3), *Everton* (15), *Exeter City* (1), *Fulham* (7), *Gillingham* (2), *Grimsby Town* (1), *Hartlepool United* (1), *Huddersfield Town* (3), *Hull City* (1), *Ipswich Town* (3), *Leeds United* (8), *Leicester City* (3), *Leyton Orient* (1), *Lincoln City* (3), *Liverpool* (9), *Luton Town* (7), *Manchester City* (8), *Manchester United* (21), *Middlesbrough* (6), *Millwall* (8), *Newcastle United* (6), *Notts County* (5), *Northampton Town* (1), *Norwich City* (4), *Nottingham Forest* (3), *Notts County* (5) *Oldham Athletic* (2), *Oxford United* (4), *Peterborough United* (1), *Portsmouth* (6), *Port Vale* (1), *Preston North End* (8), *Queens Park Rgs.* (8), *Rotherham United* (1), *Sheffield United* (3), *Sheffield Wednesday* (4), *Shrewsbury Town* (1), *Southampton* (6), *Stoke City* (2), *Sunderland* (5), *Swansea City* (3), *Swindon Town* (3), *Southend United* (3), *Tottenham Hotspur* (5) *Tranmere Rovers* (4), *Walsall* (5), *Watford* (1), *West Bromwich Albion* (7), *West Ham United* (10), *Wimbledon* (1), *Wolverhampton Wanderers* (5),*York City* (1)

(F) Football League: (Past Members): 2
Bradford Park Avenue (1), *Newport County* (1)

(G) Scottish League: (Present Members): 7
Aberdeen (2), *Celtic* (9), *Clyde* (2), *Dumbarton* (1), *Falkirk* (1), *Hibernian* (2), *Motherwell* (1)

(H) Scottish League: (Past Members): 1
Borroustounness (1)

(I) Europe: 14

Belgium	:	*Waregem* (1)
France	:	*LeHavre* (2); *Olympic Lyon* (1)
Germany	:	*Fortuna Cologne* (1)
Holland	:	*Ajax Amsterdam* (1)
Italy	:	*Ascoli* (1), *Inter Milan* (1), *Juventus* (1), *Sampdoria* (1)
Portugal	:	*Porto* (1)
Spain	:	*Real Sociedad* (1), *Santander* (1), *Sporting Gijon* (1)
Switzerland	:	*Neuchatal Xamax* (1)

(J) North America: 4

Canada	:	*Vancouver Whitecaps* (1)
USA	:	*Minnesota Kicks* (1), *Philadelphia Fury* (1), *Wichita Wings* (1)

Mickey Walsh (F.C. Porto)
Unique in being the only player capped for the 'Republic' whilst playing in Portugal (DC)

The 'Copa Independencia do Brazil'

International FLASHBACK

With Brazilians celebrating the 150th anniversary of their country's independence from Portuguese rule, and with no major footballing event such as a World Cup finals or South American Championships scheduled, the summer of 1972 saw the C.B.F. (Brazilian Football Association) honour the occasion by organising their own 'Copa Independencia,' the biggest international tournament of its kind ever in the history of the game. Frequently, though inaccurately referred to as the 'Mini World Cup' such was the size of this huge undertaking that for close on a month eighteen different countries and two intercontinental selections from across the globe played no fewer than forty four games in twelve different cities, a logistical feat comparable with the hosting of the World Cup finals themselves.

Despite the magnitude of the task however, such has always been the enormous feeling and almost religious fervour reserved for the game of football in South America's biggest country, that this event was of great importance there, not just in a sporting context, but politically as well. Certainly the huge amounts of money invested in the pre-tournament upgrading of facilities, many at venues remote in a footballing sense which had never before played host to international football, bore testament to the importance placed in its hosting not alone by the country's soccer community but by the Brazilian government itself. The fact that Brazil were World Cup holders having won the Jules Rimet trophy outright for a record third time in the Aztec Stadium, Mexico City, just two years previously afforded even greater prestige to this unique and exciting occasion.

Among those invited to the 'Copa' were all ten South American CONMEBOL members, whilst the proximity of the final stages of the European Championships in Belgium meant that some of Europe's top teams, including West Germany, Spain and Belgium did not travel, although the Soviet Union, beaten finalists in Brussels that year did make it across the Atlantic Ocean for phase two of the competition. The non availability of some top European sides probably explains the rather unexpected invitation extended to the Republic of Ireland, an offer which delighted team manager Liam Tuohy and one which the F.A.I. quickly accepted.

In all seven European sides including Portugal, Scotland and France were present, whilst the remaining berths went to Iran, holders of the Asian International Cup and representative selections from Africa and CONCACAF (Central America). Given that the number of teams involved was a rounded twenty, the format adopted was rather bizzare. Five countries, Brazil, Czechoslovakia, Scotland, Soviet Union and Uruguay were given a bye to the second phase, effectively the Quarter Finals, where the eventual winners of the two, four team mini leagues, would provide the tournament finalists at the

125

Maracana Stadium, Rio de Janeiro on July 9th. Before that however the remaining fifteen invitees would play-off in three groups of five, the winners only of each round-robin series advancing to join the others in the second phase.

Ireland for their part were drawn in Group B which also included Portugal, who were clear favourites, Chile, and two sides, Iran and Ecuador, never previously encountered on the international stage. Group B games would take place in the sprawling metropolis of Recife at the 'Santa Cruz' and 'Isle of Retiro' stadiums and in the nearby city of Natal, at the newly constructed and rather strangely titled 'New Lake Stadium.' Group A which included both the African and Central American selections, had as joint favourites Argentina and France, whilst Group C saw Yugoslavia fly the lone European flag amongst four South Americans, including Peru, quarter finalists in Mexico two years earlier.

Along with the football, there was also a financial dimension to the competition with each nation guaranteed expenses of Stg.£6,000 per preliminary group match, a not inconsiderable sum in 1972. Thus Ireland could expect a minimum £24,000 for their first four games and should they qualify for the quarter final stage this match fee would rise to £10,000. Overall the winners of the 'Copa Independencia' would receive a further £20,000, the runners-up £12,000 and so on.

As for Ireland's pre-tournament preparations, not surprisingly the weeks leading up to the team's departure on June 7th saw Liam Tuohy's original eighteen man squad hit by a number of late withdrawals. Particularly disappointing were the unavoidable defections of captain Johnny Giles, who had a groin strain which had troubled him for much of Leeds United's season, and Jimmy Holmes whose club Coventry City insisted on the full back accompanying them on a tour of Japan. With Liverpool's Steve Heighway and Fulham's Jimmy Conway also unable to travel, Tuohy called up three home based players Mick Martin (Bohemians), Al Finucane (Limerick), Turlough O'Connor (Dundalk), along with Mick Fairclough of Huddersfield Town as replacements. This brought the total League of Ireland representation to eight with Miah Dennehy of Cork Hibernians the only uncapped player in the travelling party.

One notable omission and one which drew much media comment was that of Alfie Hale of Waterford who along with Cork Hibernian's Tony Marsden had finished the domestic season as top goalscorers with a haul of twenty two strikes apiece. The exclusion of Hale, an experienced campaigner in the green of Ireland, did not go down at all well with certain sections of the Irish sporting media. However Tuohy was keen to give youth its chance and so at thirty three the ex-Aston Villa and Doncaster Rovers man remained at home.

In truth it would have been difficult to chastise Tuohy for attempting to introduce something new to the team or indeed envy him the monumental task of reviving Ireland's flagging fortunes. For on the eve of this journey to Brazil the Republic's standing really was at an all time low. Bereft of a victory in twenty consecutive matches, an unprecedented and dismal sequence stretching back nearly five years, Tuohy was badly in need of a little magic with which to turn things around and halt the slide which had seen the country's soccer team become an also ran. Not since November 1967 and an unlikely European Championship victory in Czechoslovakia, where Turlough O'Connor and Ray Treacy had been the goalscoring heroes, had Ireland tasted the sweetness of victory. A depressing run of sixteen defeats and just four draws had culminated in a soul destroying 0-6 loss to Austria the previous autumn in what had in fact been Liam Tuohy's first ever game in charge.

That outing, also a European Championship qualifier, in Linz, had seen virtually a League of Ireland selection (captain Paddy Mulligan of Chelsea the only exception) steamrolled by their experienced opponents, bringing an embarrassing climax to what had once again proved to be a fruitless qualifying campaign. Now six months later and without an outing since, Tuohy had certainly had a great deal of time to consider the possibilities. Not surprisingly having also had time to reflect, Ireland's supporters were looking forward with renewed hope to the autumn when a World Cup qualifying series with the Soviet Union and France was due to begin. Firstly however they were hoping that the 'Copa Independencia' might prove to be something of a watershed in their team's fortunes.

In the absence of John Giles, it was Paddy Mulligan who assumed captaincy of the squad and at Dublin Airport ahead of a gruelling seventeen hour journey to Recife, including a stop off at Lisbon to collect the Portuguese party, the Chelsea man had this to say: *"Despite the loss of players such as Giles, Heighway, and Conway, nevertheless morale is high and although qualification for phase two is perhaps a little unrealistic, then at least with a little luck we can end that long wait for an International victory."*

At the same time Liam Tuohy declared, *"Frankly I know virtually nothing of the Iranian and Ecuadorian sides, but we have a full dossier on both Portugal and Chile and what I have learnt is not very encouraging from our point of view. However, this tournament will provide invaluable experience ahead of our World Cup preliminary games with France and Russia."*

In retrospect, whilst pragmatic perhaps, the views expressed were hardly the most positive by a manager and his team captain on the eve of participation in a major international tournament.

The 'Copa Independencia' kicked off on Sunday June 11 1972 with a brace of games in each of the three preliminary groups, including Ireland's opener against Iran in the 'Santa Cruz' stadium Recife where oppressive heat and humidity was to prove a huge burden for the players. Despite Tuohy's claim that virtually nothing was known about the Iranian side, nevertheless all Irish expectations were for a comfortable start to the tournament, one which would yield a relatively easy victory.

The Asians however were to prove rather more formidable opponents than was expected and Ireland's error of judgment in this regard almost cost them dearly. In fact this was a far better side than was widely recognised and in the ten years from 1968 and their first 'Asian Intercontinental Cup' success, Iran would twice retain their title winning in Thailand in 1972 and at home in Iran in 1976. The country would also make its mark on the broader world stage with participation in the 1978 World Cup Finals in Argentina, acquitting themselves well in the process with a draw against Scotland in a tough group which also included Peru and beaten finalists Holland. However radical changes to the country's political structures following the return from exile in 1979 of the Ayatollah Ruhollah Khomeni lead to the suppression of many of the personal and sporting freedoms enjoyed under the Shah Pahlavi and signalled an end to the most successful period in Iran's footballing history. In Recife, Ireland would get a taste of the form which made the Iranians Asia's most powerful footballing nation for over a decade.

Prior to the action of the Santa Cruz stadium getting under way the pre-match ceremonies provided a chaotic if humourous opening to proceedings. The cause of the problem was a breakdown some distance from the ground of a bus which was carrying the local police band entrusted with the playing of the national anthems. This resulted in the band members having to continue their journey on foot whereupon arriving at the stadium it was discovered that the music which had been brought for Amhrán na bhFiann was in fact that for 'God save the Queen'! At this point with the kick off delayed for over an hour, it was wisely decided to dispense completely with the musical formalities and the action began.

Unfortunately for Ireland it began in whirlwind fashion for the Iranians and after just ten minutes play disaster struck. With Alan Kelly caught badly out of position, striker Hessenali curled a lovely shot from just inside the 'area' into the corner of the Preston man's net. Forced for long periods on the defensive, the Irish lads had few answers in a one sided opening period, although Kelly went a long way towards atoning for his earlier error by making a string of fine saves, keeping the scoreline to a single goal at the interval.

The turning point in the game came just fifteen minutes after the resumption and what a controversial moment it proved to be. Following a delightful run through a static Irish rearguard, midfielder Parvis slammed the ball past Kelly only for Italian referee Aurelo Angonese to disallow the score claiming Parvis had obstructed an Irish defender en route to goal. It was a decision which incensed not just the Iranians but the watching crowd who were no doubt anticipating an upset.

Whilst the Asians surrounded the referee in vehement protest at his decision, Ireland lent even greater fuel to the fires by immediately breaking upfield to equalise. It was goalscorer Mick Leech who began the move himself, playing a neat one-two with Noel Campbell which left the Shamrock Rovers man clear to coolly beat goalkeeper Nasser and claim his first goal for his country in his fifth appearance.

Incredibly, within four minutes, Ireland had taken the lead and the whole aspect of the game had swung so dramatically that a by now demoralised opposition barely raised a threat from there to the final whistle. The winning goal was the direct result of a mistake by right back Ibraim who up to that point had done an excellent man marking job on Don Givens, but who now crucially gifted the Luton Town striker the opportunity to strike. After that the Irish were comfortable, and although they had ridden their luck somewhat in the first hour's play, a precious opening victory was secured and a depressing five year long hiatus was ended.

Immediately following the game, Iranian officials lodged a strong complaint with the organisers about the refereeing of Angonese claiming not only had Parvis's goal been perfectly legitimate but both of Ireland's efforts had been offside! A local newspaper 'O Globo' also found sympathy with the losers and a story appeared credited to the Brazilian Press Agency which left a sour taste in the mouths of the Irish party. Under the heading *"Ireland train on whiskey"* the report claimed that *"the Irish sleep late, get up late and can frequently be seen with a glass of whiskey in their hands."* There was also some pretty silly stuff about all night parties involving the players and American nurses based near to the teams' hotel.

Naturally, a furious Tuohy swiftly denied any such antics were taking place citing the fact that the team trained hard each morning at eight o'clock and whilst obviously enjoying a relaxing beer, whiskey was not allowed. Thankfully following the manager's comments there were no further reports along these lines. However in a telephoned interview with the 'Irish Times' Tuohy spoke of the upset caused by the report and of the sunburn and breathing difficulties being experienced by the squad which had now moved on to Natal in preparation for the game against Ecuador. The last word on the 'whiskey' incident lay with F.A.I. chairman Sam Prole who responding to a question at Dublin airport on the teams return said *"I have nothing but praise for all eighteen players in the party. They behaved impeccably both on and off the field and were a credit to their association and their country."*

Despite the fact that this was Ecuador's eighty seventh international fixture, their overall playing record was comfortably the worst of any side on the South American continent. Since their first outing in 1938 against neighbours Bolivia they had only ever managed a paltry seven victories, five of which had come against another neighbour, Colombia. During that time they had consistently failed to make even the slightest impression on the South American Championship and invariably finished bottom of each of their World Cup qualifying groups. On the eve of this match, only their second ever against European opposition Ecuador had not won in ten outings including a 0-3 reverse to Portugal in their opening 'Cora Independencia' fixture. Two years previously, England, en route to the 1970 World Cup finals in Mexico, had won a friendly encounter two-nil in Quito in the same week in which their captain Bobby Moore was falsely accused of involvement in the infamous bracelet stealing incident in the Colombian capital, Bogota. With such a poor record, not surprisingly Ireland were favourites to secure a maximum points return from this one despite the difficult conditions, even more oppressive than those in Recife a week earlier.

In complete contrast to their opening encounter, Ireland began this game in the 'New Lake' Stadium at great pace and just twelve minutes had elapsed when a 'cannonball' free kick by Eamonn Rogers from just outside the penalty area had them ahead. It was a dream start and although the Irish continued to dominate unfortunately they were hampered by some very poor defending. This proved costly in the thirty sixth minute when midfielder Coronel went on a solo run which totally wrongfooted the Irish rearguard and he confidently beat Kelly with a strong shot.

Again in the second half Ireland began strongly and after sixteen minutes Don Givens put Mick Martin clear, and the Bohemians man restored the lead. At this point things were looking good but shortly after the goal Givens was controversially sent off by referee Kitabjan of France, allegedly for rough play. It was a decision which greatly upset the Irish and Ecuador capitalised on their unease, to equalise through a rather scrappy goal from another midfielder Lasso, with only six minutes remaining. To their credit, what might have seemed a satisfactory division of the spoils given the circumstances was transferred into a brave win with just moments left by a jaded Irish side. The goal stemmed from a long kick out by Kelly, which fell nicely for substitute Turlough O'Connor and he beat Ecuador's number one, Maldonado with ease. Initially there was some confusion as to the winning goalscorer, as some Irish newspapers credited the other substitute Miah Dennehy, who was making his debut in a green shirt with the golden strike. Things were soon sorted out however and though the Corkman would indeed go on to score for his country, it would not happen on this particular trip.

With victory in their opening two games, there was now a great deal more confidence in the Irish camp, who whilst acknowledging the difficulty of the task ahead against a talented Chilean side, nevertheless felt a win was now *"well within our compass."* Taking the results to date in Group B, a victory against the South Americans would leave an exciting showdown with Portugal, in the final first phase encounter, to determine group honours. Following clear cut victories over Ecuador, Iran and Chile, the Portuguese now lead the Group with a 100% record. Both Ireland and Chile had accumulated four points with the Irish having played a game less, and Iran and Ecuador already out of contention.

For this third match Ireland moved to Reife's second stadium the 'Isle of Retiro' and what would be only their second ever meeting with Chile. The first had been at Dalymount Park some twelve years earlier when a brace of goals from Noel Cantwell had sent the home crowd away in happy mood. Unfortunately on this occasion the Irish fans were to be disappointed.

In an even, competitive, if scoreless opening period, Ireland's best opportunity fell to Mick Martin who was brilliantly thwarted at the base of his upright by goalkeeper Neff. The opening period of the second half saw the Chilians up the tempo considerably and Ireland again suffering the disadvantage of the difficult conditions of heat and humidity were forced more and more on the defensive. Half way through they cracked, when Fouilloux sent Cazelly through and the center forward rifled a shot past Kelly. Within eight minutes it was two nil to Chile and again the same doubt act was involved, this time Fouilloux knocking in a Cazelly cross. Seconds after the restart and the roof caved in on Ireland. Turlough O'Connor, who up to then was having a barnstorming game for the Irish was dismissed by referee Arpi of Brazil. It was a silly incident with O'Connor trying to charge goalkeeper Neff who stepped aside whereupon the Irishman crashed into fullback Azocar. In frustration O'Connor tore off his jersey and flung it into the jeering and obviously appreciative crowd.

Despite such a catalogue of adversity Ireland continued to battle bravely and were rewarded after seventy nine minutes when Eamonn Rogers headed a fine goal from a Mick Martin cross. This naturally gave Tuohy's men renewed hope but try as they might they could not find a precious equaliser, indeed it was the Chileans who had the better of the late exchanges. Thus it was a very disappointed Irish party which returned to base to prepare for their last game against the Portuguese.

Following their defeat to Chile, Ireland now required a clear five goal winning margin against Portugal to advance at the expense of the Iberians, a most unlikely scenario. This fact obviously influenced the team selection of opposing manager Josef Agusto who rested a number of key players, though not the great Eusebio who had proved to be in excellent scoring form to date and who was keenly chasing Coluna's record of 60 appearances for Portugal.

In spite of Ireland's punishing schedule, their line up for this match, again at the 'Isle of Retiro' Stadium showed just two changes from their last outing, Leech and Givens replacing O'Connor and Dennehy as the frontline partnership. However, mental and physical fatigue was to effect some of the Irish players in the latter stages of the game, reports citing some players as being *'close to exhaustion'* on another day of oppressive heat and humidity. Joe Kinnear, manager of Wimbledon and a panelist on R.T.E.'s U.S.A.'94 coverage has made reference to never having suffered conditions as difficult in his long career as those he experienced in his four games at full back on this Irish team in Brazil.

The game itself began with Ireland having slightly the better of the exchanges in the opening quarter. A quiet game was suddenly brought to life after that with three goals almost in as many minutes. The first of these came in the thirty fifth minute when Peres beat Kelly with a rising shot from twenty yards. Within two minutes of that, a rare mistake by Mulligan let in Nene, and he made no mistake. So for the second successive game Ireland were two goals adrift, but almost immediately got in on the act themselves with a super strike from Mich Leech. Taking a short pass from Ray Treacy, Leech cleverly played the ball around his marker before whalloping it clinically past goalkeeper Jose Enrique.

This revived the Irish spirit a great deal and from there to the interval and beyond it was a case of an Irish eleven growing ever more tired striving manfully to conjure up an equaliser against technically superior opponents who also enjoyed the bulk of the play. Indeed such was Ireland's dogged conviction that the Brazilian crowd grew increasingly vocal in their support of the men in green as the game wore on. Of course it has to be born in mind that in this celebration of Brazilian independence, Ireland's opponents were of course the Portuguese! Despite a brave effort however, one marked by some superb defensive play, the Irish lads just could not find a way through this Portuguese team who thus finished top of Group B with a maximum points haul of eight from their four matches, and went forward to the second phase.

Ireland with two wins, two defeats and seven goals scored had pleased manager Tuohy with both their commitment and the manner of their performances. Particularly pleasing was the choice of both Mulligan and Leech in the Brazilian Sports Writers best xi chosen from Group B. And so it was a very upbeat party which returned to Dublin Airport on June 27th where Liam Tuohy had this to say: *"I was tremendously impressed by the performance of all the players. They gave me everything they had and I honestly believe that were it not for the conditions out there, and some slices of very bad luck, we would have qualified for the Quarter finals. You would have to have been out there to realise just what the handicaps were, the humidity, the language barrier and of course the referees, all combined to make the job of winning that much harder. Frankly the entire trip exceeded by expectations."*

So then a slightly, though understandably, biased view from the manager, but perhaps the 'Copa Independencia' did prove something of a watershed for the Irish after all. Although failing once again to qualify from their subsequent World Cup qualifying group nevertheless the performance level, with three from a possible four points plundered from the French was considerably improved. Indeed it has continued from then on to improve right up to the present day through a succession of managers who have followed on from Liam Tuohy. It may well be that the cold statistical facts of wins over opposition such as Ecuador and Iran would hardly qualify to set the world alight but nevertheless it was a start, at a time when we desperately needed to start somewhere.

Whilst Portugal were comfortably securing their berth in the next phase, the other two preliminary groups were also of course in full swing. In Group A, Argentina and France confirmed their status as joint favourites by reaching the final game, against each other, both with a 100% record. However, as the South Americans enjoyed a considerably better goal difference, a scoreless draw in this game, the only goalless encounter in the entire thirty game opening phase, was enough to see Argentina through to join Portugal, Soviet Union and the reigning South American champions Uruguay.

Meanwhile in Group C where Peru proved to be a huge disappointment, it was Yugoslavia who blazed a trail, ensuring early qualification ahead of the surprise packets in this group Paraguay, and scoring fifteen goals in four outings, including ten against a hapless Venezuela. Centre forward Bajevic who notched five in that game subsequently finished as the tournament's top striker with thirteen goals. Thus the Yugoslavs joined Brazil, Scotland and Czechoslovakia in an eagerly awaited second Quarter final grouping.

The honour of opening phase two fell to hosts Brazil and Czechoslovakia who played out a scoreless draw in front of 120,000 spectators in the Maracana Stadium on June 28th. For a Brazilian side which included such stars of the Mexico World Cup as Rivelino, Gerson, Jairzinho, and Tostao it was hardly an ideal start, although Viktor in the Czechoslovak's goal was quite outstanding, and the homesters enjoyed little luck.

Four days later in Sao Paolo however, their luck changed and Yugoslavia, perhaps Brazil's biggest threat to a place in the final were unceremoniously dismissed on a scoreline of three goals to nil. This result meant that victory over Scotland in their last group match would see the hosts comfortably through. The Scots, already with draws against Czechoslovakia (0-0) and Yugoslavia (2-2) (where Lou Macari was twice on the scoresheet) under their belts, could of course have made the final themselves if they had won. Despite a brave effort in Rio however, Tommy Docherty's men lost to a single goal scored by Jairzinho and with the home side going through, Yugoslavia pipped Scotland for the third/fourth place play-off spot.

In the second Quarter final grouping the crucial game came as early as the opening fixture when Portugal were emphatic three-one winners over fellow qualifiers Argentina. Despite dropping a point to Uruguay in their second game, a single goal victory in their last group outing against the Soviet Union was enough to see Portugal through to the final everybody in Brazil wanted as a climax to the 'Copa Independencia.' Argentina meanwhile whose only points dropped were those against the Portuguese qualified to meet Yugoslavia in that third/fourth place play-off.

In that play-off match in Rio Yugoslavia once again found their scoring touch beating the Argentinians by four goals to two and so finished the tournament with a whopping twenty three goals in eight matches.

That same day July 9th saw the Maracana Stadium once again packed to its 120,000 capacity for the 'Copa Independencia' final between Brazil and Portugal. The home side included six players who had played in the 1970 World Cup Final against Italy whilst the Portuguese boasted perhaps their greatest ever forward line of Eusebio, Jordao, Dinis and Peres. Sadly however the prolific Nene, Portugal's all-time leading goalscorer was injured for this game.

Unfortunately as is so often seen in major tournament deciders the importance of the occasion seemed to affect the performance of the players and a rather dour encounter was settled by a single goal from Jairzinho whose feat of scoring in every one of Brazil's games in Mexico in 1970 had earned him a particular place in the hearts of Brazilian fans. And so the 'Copa Independencia,' this hugely ambitious undertaking, came to a close with ironically the result every Brazilian wished for, victory in the 'Maracana' against the colonial power which for centuries had ruled their country.

Republic of Ireland in the 'Copa Independencia do Brazil'

(i) **11th June 1972 at Santa Cruz Stadium, Recife**
Referee: A. Angonese (Italy)   Att. 10,500
Republic of Ireland   (0)   **2**   *(Leech 61, Givens 64)*
Iran   (1)   **1**   *(Hessenali 10)*

Kelly (Preston North End), Kinnear (Tottenham Hotspur), Dempsey (Chelsea), Mulligan (C) (Chelsea), Carroll (Birmingham City), Campbell (Fortuna Cologne), Martin (Bohemians), Rogers (Charlton Athletic), Treacy (Swindon Town), Leech (Shamrock Rovers), Givens (Luton Town),
Sub: O'Connor (Dundalk) for Leech 78 mins.

(ii) **18th June 1972 at New Lake Stadium, Natal**
Referee: Kitabjan (France)
Republic of Ireland   (1)   **3**   *(Rogers 12, Martin 61, O'Connor 88)*
Ecuador   (1)   **2**   *(Coronel 36, Lasso 78)*

Kelly, Kinnear, Dempsey, Mulligan (C), Carroll, Campbell, Martin, Rogers, Treacy, Leech, Givens
Subs: O'Connor for Treacy h.t., Dennehy (Cork Hibernians) for Leech.

(iii) **21st June 1972 at Isle of Retiro Stadium, Recife**
Referee: Arpi (Brazil)
Republic of Ireland   (0)   **1**   *(Rogers 79)*
Chile   (0)   **2**   *(Cazelly 60, Fouilloux 68)*

Kelly, Kinnear, Dempsey, Mulligan (C), Carroll, Campbell, Martin, Rogers, Treacy, Leech, Givens
Subs: Herrick (Cork Hibernians) for Carroll 82 mins.

(iv) **25th June 1972 at Isle of Retiro Stadium, Recife**
Referee: Coerezza (Argentina)   Att. 13,000
Republic of Ireland   (1)   **1**   *(Leech 38)*
Portugal   (2)   **2**   *(Peres 35, Nene 37)*

Kelly, Kinnear, Dempsey, Mulligan (C), Carroll, Campbell, Martin, Rogers, Treacy, Leech, Givens
Sub: O'Connor for Treacy

Players not used: Peter Thomas (Waterford), Al Finucane (Limerick), Tommy McConville (Dundalk) and Mick Fairclough (Huddersfield Town)

'Copa Independencia do Brazil' June / July 1972

Participants: African XI, Argentina, Bolivia, Brazil, Chile, Colombia, Concacaf XI, Czechoslovakia, Ecuador, France, Iran, Paraguay, Peru, Portugal, Republic of Ireland, Scotland, Soviet Union, Uruguay, Venezuela, Yugoslavia.

FIRST ROUND

Group A: (Aracaju, Macejo, Salvador)

Argentina	CONCACAF XI	7-0	Colombia	CONCACAF XI	4-3
Argentina	Colombia	4-1	Colombia	France	2-3
Argentina	France	0-0	CONCACAF XI	African XI	0-0
Argentina	African XI	2-0	CONCACAF XI	France	0-5
Colombia	African XI	0-3	France	African XI	2-0

Final Placings: *Argentina 7* (+12), France 7 (+8), African XI 3, Colombia 2, Concacaf XI 1

Group B: (Natal, Recife)

Chile	Ecuador	2-1	Ecuador	Portugal	0-3
Chile	Iran	2-1	Ecuador	Rep. Ireland	2-3
Chile	Portugal	1-4	Iran	Portugal	0-3
Chile	Rep. Ireland	2-1	Iran	Rep. Ireland	1-2
Ecuador	Iran	1-1	Portugal	Rep. Ireland	2-1

Final Placings: *Portugal 8*, Chile 6, Rep. of Ireland 4, Ecuador 1, Iran 1

Group C: (Campo Grande, Curitiba, Manaus)

Bolivia	Paraguay	1-6	Paraguay	Venezuela	4-1
Bolivia	Peru	0-3	Paraguay	Yugoslavia	1-2
Bolivia	Venezuela	2-2	Peru	Venezuela	1-0
Bolivia	Yugoslavia	1-1	Peru	Yugoslavia	1-2
Paraguay	Peru	1-0	Venezuela	Yugoslavia	1-10

Final Placings: *Yugoslavia 7*, Paraguay 6, Peru 4, Bolivia 2, Venezuela 1

Byes: Brazil, Czechoslovakia, Scotland, Soviet Union, Uruguay

SECOND ROUND

Group A: (Belo Horizonte, Porto Alegre, Rio de Janeiro, Sao Paulo)

Brazil	Czechoslovakia	0-0	Czechoslovakia	Scotland	0-0
Brazil	Scotland	1-0	Czechoslovakia	Yugoslavia	1-2
Brazil	Yugoslavia	3-0	Scotland	Yugoslavia	2-2

Final Placings: *Brazil 5*, Yugoslavia 3, Scotland 2, Czechoslovakia 2

Group B: (Belo Horizonte, Porto Alegre, Rio de Janeiro, Sao Paulo)

Argentina	Portugal	1-3	Portugal	Soviet Union	1-0
Argentina	Soviet Union	1-0	Portugal	Uruguay	1-1
Argentina	Uruguay	1-0	Soviet Union	Uruguay	1-0

Final Placings: *Portugal 5*, Argentina 4, Soviet Union 2, Uruguay 1

THIRD PLACE PLAY-OFF

9th July in Rio de Janeiro

        Argentina   2
        Yugoslavia 4

FINAL

9th July at Maracana Stadium, Rio de Janeiro   Att: 120,000

        Brazil   1   (Jairzinho)
        Portugal 0

Brazil: Leao, Ze Maria, Brito, Vantuir, Marco Antonio (Rodrigues-Neto), Clodoaldo, Gerson, Jairzinho, Leivinha (Dazio-Dada), Tostao, Rivelino.

Portugal: Marques, Correia, Humberton, Coelho, Timula (Alisto), Toni, Jamie-Garcia, Peres, Jordao (Jorge), Eusebio, Dinis

Mc Gold *Trick*!
Eddie celebrates qualification at Windsor Park   (The Star)

European Review
Mixed Fortunes for National League Clubs

Champions' Cup CORK CONQUER CWMBRAN BUT TOPPLE TO TURKS

Having clinched their first ever league title the previous May, Cork City found themselves facing a short hop across the Irish Sea to take on Cwmbran Town, inaugural winners of the Konica Welsh League and thus the principality's Champions' Cup debutants, in the preliminary round. The proximity of the away leg enticed upwards of 500 Leeside fans to take the Swansea ferry, ensuring new boss Damien Richardson's side solid vocal backing.
Gone from the ranks were two wily campaigners, Paul Bannon and Gerry McCabe, and their accumulated experience was sorely missed by City in a hesitant and nervous opening period. The Corkmen were in the unusual position for a National League side of going into an away game as favourites but paid a heavy price for their cautious approach. There were barely five minutes gone when Dave Barry unnecessarily and clumsily challenged Francis Ford as the Welshman actually carried the ball out of the box and the Icelandic referee immediately awarded a penalty. Full-back Simon King rifled the spot-kick past compatriot Phil Harrington and Cwmbran were in an unexpected lead.
City had good possession but no finish to several sweeping moves before being rocked to the core by a Cwmbran double strike inside sixty seconds midway through the half. Mickey Dicks and Wayne Goodridge combined neatly to send a ball into the danger area and Ford, unchallenged, headed to the net. The local celebrations were still ringing around the ground when Ford struck again, exploiting Cork's uncharacteristic defensive timidness to race through and slot past the stranded Harrington. With on-loan centre-back Paul Hague of Gillingham looking distinctly uncomfortable, the Welsh side threatened every time they gained possession though, quite ironically, City easily had the bulk of the play but spurned a stream of decent chances.
Not long after the third goal hit the rigging, midfield maestro Dave Barry pulled up injured and it seemed the fates had conspired against the Leesiders. It had been a curious first half: despite a very high percentage possession, a few elementary errors had been punished in full and elimination, even at this early stage, seemed more probable than possible.
A huge effort was required to salvage something from the match and, in fairness, City tightened up and patiently took control. After 63 minutes John Caulfield, on for Johnny Glynn just moments earlier, pulled a goal back. Harringtons long kick was knocked on by Tommy Gaynor, Morley played it into Caulfield's path and City were back in the hunt. A quarter of an hour later Caulfield turned provider, hammering a low drive across the face of the home goal which Morley missed but Anthony Buckley, who had replaced Barry, steered past Patrick O'Hagan. It was all to play for now as Cork strove to amend their disastrous opening but still the chances were squandered right to the end with Hague heading against the bar and Declan Hyde's late, late effort cleared off the line. It had been a tremendous second half recovery but Cork had set themselves too big a task with

137

their early defensive ineptitude.

Due to ongoing work at their Bishopstown stadium, the return was played at Turner's Cross which itself was under reconstruction and without perimeter fencing. Beneath a blazing sun and depleted by Barry's absence, City still created several scoring opportunities but couldn't get their act together in front of goal. Cwmbran played a neat and tidy brand of football, more effective than the locals' frenetic efforts and surprisingly increased their aggregate lead after just eight minutes. Phil McNeil drilled a dead ball from just outside the box which ricocheted upwards off Nicky Copeman's head. It seemed an easy catch for Harrington but, under pressure from Ford, he fumbled it and Ford back-heeled for the inrushing McNeil to ram to the net.

Now facing a two-goal deficit, City continued to huff and puff but a catalogue of missed chances was all they had to show for their exertions. Cwmbran almost killed the tie stone dead after 52 minutes when Harrington parried McNeil's shot and Ford, with the goal gaping, hit the rebound towards the keeper who instinctively deflected the ball to safety from a prone position.

It was fitness as much as anything else which turned the game in City's favour as Cwmbran slowly wilted under the heat and the relentless pressure. Following a corner, a session of head tennis ended when Caulfield nodded across the goal and the alert Morley bundled the ball over the line.

Fifteen minutes to go and the homesters went into overdrive. The winning score, and the one which finally decided the tie, arrived with five minutes remaining. Daly lofted in a deep free which was only partially cleared. Gaynor returned it into the crowded goalmouth where Glynn thundered in to head home from six yards amid scenes of wild jubilation.

For the first round proper City travelled to Istanbul to take on Galatasaray, Turkey's most famous side and one gradually building up a solid European pedigree. Cork, without goal hero Glynn, performed out of their skins against the talented and speedy locals. Twice in the opening ten minutes the impressive Buckley drew saves from Hayrettin and midway through the first half Gaynor had a well-crafted score ruled out for a marginal offside. With just over half an hour gone the Turks broke through when Kubilay Turkilmaz exchanged passes with Gotz Falko, one of two Germans bolstering the Gala side, to pierce the Irish defence and plant the ball beyond Harrington. Before half-time Gaynor had a fleeting chance to equalise, his volley dropping just the wrong side of the post with Hayrettin stranded.

Gala came roaring forward on the turnover and increased their lead after 52 minutes when Arif blasted home Kubilay's low cross after Hakan had failed to connect. The flares and firecrackers exploded all around the beautiful Ali Sami Yen stadium and within minutes Swiss international Kubilay, the games undoubted star, was only denied by the crossbar. City drew deep within themselves to stem the tide and, in a rare breakaway, plundered a priceless away goal after 63 minutes. Hyde, playing a blinder, outpaced the giant Reinhard Stumpf and his deep cross was met by Dave Barry whose shot deflected to the net off Falko. Thereafter, the Corkmen were very disciplined and strong in defence and kept their goal intact for a very creditable result in an intimidating arena.

Bishopstown had its European debut for the return and the event was added to by a large and colourful party of Gala fans, many of whom had travelled from Britain. City played five across the middle with Gaynor, surprisingly, and not Morley as the lone frontman. The game was on a knife-edge throughout though Cork had the better possession and chances. The best fell to Hyde whose stinging volley was deflected over by Falko and, in the second half, to Buckley who dragged the ball wide of Hayrettin but hit the side netting. Stumpf marshalled the Turkish backline superbly, limiting City's emerging superiority to just a few clearcut opportunities, while at the other end Harrington was in the right place to hold Kubilay's header from Galatasaray's only threatening move. Just when it seemed the home side might break the deadlock as the Turks defended desperately, an unforced error by Barry was seized upon by Tugay whose pass sliced open the stretched City rearguard for Kubilay to slip the ball low past Harrington with just fourteen minutes to go.

City continued to press to the end and were denied the consolation of a deserved equaliser when Glynn blasted high in injury time when it looked easier to score.

Cork City have the unique distinction among all the continents clubs of being the only one ever to engage Welsh opposition in the Champions' Cup as well as the unwanted label of the last Irish club to participate in the competition.

Cup Winners' Cup EASTERN PROMISE FOR SHELS BEFORE GREEK TRAGEDY

After undertaking a long haul to the Crimea the previous season when clashing with Tavria Simferopol, Shelbourne could be forgiven for thinking that the football gods had not smiled too kindly on them when faced with another trip to the Ukraine for an encounter with Karpaty from the ancient city of Lvov. The away leg also came very early in the domestic season as the Tolka Park outfit had the further misfortune to end up in the preliminary round.

Karpaty had qualified when losing the Ukranian Cup final to double winners Dynamo Kiev and Shels, having come very close to squeezing out Tavria on away goals were confident of giving a good account of themselves. In humid conditions Karpaty began the game at a hectic pace yet offered little threat up front against a Shels side packed with experience and well in control defensively. It was a game of fleeting chances, with Jody Byrne dealing capably with the few long range efforts that penetrated his protective shield though Mokrizki caused a moment of worry with a screaming free-kick inches off target after 34 minutes.

Shelbourne's containing game exposed Karpaty as moderate opponents who lacked the guile and tactical awareness normally encountered at this level. Still, nothing should take from a very fine display from the Dubliners, marred only by the concession of a late goal at a time when more ambition might even have yielded a famous victory. A brief lapse in concentration as Pat Byrne attempted to substitute Bobby Browne for Vinny Arkins allowed Evtushok to steal in and snatch an undeserved winner.

Two weeks later at Tolka it was a very different story as the Reds came out of their defensive shell to claim not only their finest European result but also an inspirational performance. In a re-shuffled line out Brian Flood came in for Tommy Dunne and Padraig Dully replaced Arkins. Following some early pressure from the Ukranians, Shelbourne levelled the aggregate after just eight minutes when a loose ball broke to Greg Costello, hero of the Cup Final, and he thumped it home with the aid of a deflection. Ken O'Doherty was a constant aerial threat and should have made the scoresheet, receiving great supply from the raiding Mooney and Flood. The home side had a let-off after half an hour when Plotko miskicked from the edge of the six yard box while Mick Neville thundered a free-kick off the crossbar from over thirty yards as the interval loomed.

If Neville was denied a spectacular score, Brian Mooney made amends after 66 minutes, crashing another long range effort past Strontzizki to give the Dubliners a deserved overall lead. The goal lifted Shels to even greater efforts with the scent of glory now clearly in the air and victory became tangible ten minutes later when sbustitute Tony Izzi collected a long clearance from Jody Byrne and feinted past two defenders before slotting home from twelve yards. Mark Rutherford, who had given an exhibition in the second period, might have had a fourth but his header came back off the woodwork. Karpaty's frustration came to the boil when Pokladok was red carded for chopping the elusive Rutherford. Just as Shels seemed to be coasting it, the game took a dramatic turn when Byrne parried Mokrizki's shot and Masur tucked away the rebound. In a hectic closing period Shels held out to record a well merited and stylish triumph.

Shelbourne's reward was a very difficult trip to Athens to take on Panathinaikos, while not the most successful Greek side domestically, certainly the one to have made the greatest impact at European level. In front of 30,000 passionate supporters, Panathinaikos grabbed an early lead in the 11th minute when Yorgos Donis shot home past a beleagured Irish defence minus the services of skipper Mick Neville. Shels hit back and Stephen Cooney crashed a shot off the crossbar four minutes later for the Dubliners' best scoring chance of the night. The Reds absorbed constant pressure but wilted again after 37 minutes. A free kick by Kostas Frantzeskos was tipped onto the bar by Jody Byrne and Dimitris Saravakos, following up, made sure of the rebound.

After the interval, Ken O'Doherty was pulled back to central defensive duties in an effort to bolster the barricades but once again Shels conceded an early goal when Kristov Warzycha, a Polish international, brought the tally to three after 48 minutes. It was a long way to the final whistle after that but the Reds gradually plugged the gaps and with the Greeks content with their lot the storm had died well before the end.

Neville returned for the home leg, though carrying an injury and on an evening of teeming rain Shelbourne searched desperately for an early goal to reduce the aggregate deficit. O'Doherty was narrowly off target from Floods cross and Mooney headed over when well placed. The Reds forced seven corners without reply in the opening half yet it was the Greeks who opened the scoring through Georgiadis after 24 minutes when he finished Spiros Maragos' floater past the helpless Byrne. Paul Doolin was close to an equaliser following another corner when his swivel volley drew the best from Polish national keeper Jozef Wandzyk, the tall netminder tipping the ball to safety at full stretch. Shels had had the best of the first half yet had fallen further behind.

In the 57th minute Saravakos increased the visitors' lead following a dubious free-kick award and thereafter Panathinaikos, with the tie now safe, displayed their full repertoire of swift and skilful passes. Shelbourne battled gamely to the end and finally had some reward for their labours when Mooney beautifully curled a free beyond Wandzyk following a foul on the tireless O'Doherty four minutes from time.

Euroshels
Ken O'Doherty goes close against Karpaty Lvov (The Star)

UEFA Cup BOHS BLASTED BY BORDEAUX

Bohemians, following the heartbreak of seeing the 1992-93 championship slip through their fingers, settled for the consolation of a UEFA Cup spot, entering the competition for the eighth time, a National League record. Unlike fellow Euro qualifiers Cork City and Shelbourne, the Dalymount men were directly through to the first round and had an extra month on their countrymen to prepare for the fray. And preparation would be needed for the Gypsies had been drawn to face one of the great names in French football, FC Girondins de Bordeaux, a club which had reached Champions' Cup and Cup Winners' Cup semi-final stages in the past. Although fallen from such dizzy heights in recent times after serious financial difficulties resulted in enforced relegation, Bordeaux were back in the big time nationally and eager to re-establish a reputation on the continent. It was an onerous task for Bohs but the Phibsboro side had always performed honourably on this stage, particularly at home.

Bohemians' best hopes were to achieve a Dalymount victory and on a soaking surface that target was not beyond them. Certainly the conditions made for an open game and so it proved with the fans seeing a really entertaining encounter and Bohs giving it their gutsy best. Les Girondins were the first to threaten when Laurent Croci swung in a corner and Christophe Dugarry headed past Dave

Henderson but Mick Moody was well positioned to clear off the line. In the 16th minute Dave Tilson, on the attack, misplaced a pass which was intercepted by Bixente Lizarazu and his long delivery looked to be heading straight for Henderson when Robbie Best knocked it out of his path to the grateful Dugarry who swept the ball to the net from a narrow angle despite the best efforts of Pat Kelch.

This unfortunate goal spurred an immediate response from the Irish side and a period of pressure almost produced an equaliser after 24 minutes when Tommy Fitzgerald evaded the offside trap only to be dispossessed by Bordeaux keeper, Gaetan Huard. Dugarry was again menacing after 32 minutes but Tony O'Connor cut out the danger and Henderson was called into action five minutes later, diving full length to keep out Croci's fierce long-range free.

A mix-up between Huard and Jean-luc Dogon presented a chance for Tony Cousins but his clever lob bounced back off the bar. Dugarry caused more problems as half-time approached, outjumping Henderson from a corner but this time Pat Fenlon cleared from between the posts.

French international Philippe Vercruysse was guilty of poor finishing five minutes after the break when he blasted high with only Henderson to beat. With Bordeaux gradually slowing the pace of the game, the Gypsies began to find more space but the closest they came was Fenlon's well flighted free-kick which once again struck the woodwork. Huard saved from Fitzgerald but the visitors finished strongest and Henderson needed to be at his best to keep out the ubiquitous Dugarry and Jean-François Daniel. Although denied a share of the spoils Bohemians could take heart from a brave and professional performance.

Any chance that Bohs might sneak a breakaway goal at the Lescure Stadium was quickly quashed as the Dubliners struggled to get out of their own half such was the onslaught they faced from an uptempo Bordeaux, keen to give their fans an impressive show. With Brazilian Marcio Santos, just months away from a World Cup winners medal, recalled to central defence with Didier Senac, the prospect of lone striker Cousins hitting gold always looked forlorn.

Bordeaux were up several gears from the first encounter, moving the ball precisely and with great speed but guilty of squandermania, most notably from the boot of young Zinedine Zidane. The inevitable opening goal came after 22 minutes when Zidane finally atoned for his earlier lapses, knocking in Stephane Paille's low centre. One minute later Vercruysse, in splendid isolation, headed number two and Bohs knew they were in for a rough night. Les Girondins stretched the Gypsies' defence with full-backs Donal Broughan and Pat Kelch having a torrid time, yet Bohs gallantly battened the hatches to half time.

The worst, however, was far from over as time and again the white wave swept forward and Bohemians had their backs to the wall until the final whistle. Henderson was positively brilliant in goal, stemming the tide almost single handedly on occasion as his defence was torn to shreds. Paille, Youssouf Fofana and Vercruysse completed the rout as a bedraggled Bohemians left the pitch following their biggest Euro hammering since a Champions' Cup tie in Dresden in 1978. The gulf in class had been obvious from the kick-off and Bohemians had toiled hard to hold the French to five.

Not such Turkish Delight
Cork City's Fergus O'Donoghue clears from Galatasaray's Swiss international, Kubilay (EOH)

National League Clubs in Europe 1993-94

Champions Cup

Preliminary Round / 1st leg
18 Aug. at Cwmbran Stadium; Referee: G. Orraison (Iceland)
Cwmbran Town (3) 3 *(King (p) 5, Ford, 26,27)*
Cork City (0) 2 *(Caulfield 63, Buckley 76)*
Cwmbran T: O'Hagan, Burrows, Blackie, Dicks (McNeill 80), King, Copeman, Parselle (Payne 75), Goodridge, Ford, Wharton, Powell.
Cork C: Harrington, Daly, Hague, O'Donoghue, Napier, Roche, Barry (Buckley 30), Hyde, Glynn (Caulfield 58), Morley, Gaynor.
Att: 3,000

Preliminary Round / 2nd leg
1 Sep. at Turner's Cross; Referee: J. Reyjwort (Holland)
Cork City (0) 2 *(Morley 75, Glynn 85)*
Cwmbran Town (1) 1 *(McNeill 8)*
Cork C: Harrington, Daly, Hague, O'Donoghue, Napier, Buckley, Roche (Glynn 56), Hyde (Murphy 76), Caulfield, Morley, Gaynor.
Cwmbran T: O'Hagan, Burrows, Blackie, Dicks (Vaughan 86), King, Copeman, Goodridge, McNeill, Payne, Ford, Wharton (Smith 76)
Att: approx. 4,000
(Aggregate 4-4, Cork City win on away goals)

First Round / 1st leg
15 Sep. at Ali Sami Yen Stadium, Istanbul; Referee: J. Garcia (Spain)
Galatasaray (1) 2 *(Kubilay 31, Arif 52)*
Cork City (0) 1 *(Barry 63)*
Galatasaray: Hayrettin, Stumpf, Bulent, Yusuf, Falko, Tugay, Arif (Mustafa 78), Hakan, Suat, Kubilay, Hamza.
Cork C: Harrington, Cotter, Daly, O'Donoghue, Napier, Buckley, Barry (Roche 81), Hyde, Murphy, Morley (Caulfield 89), Gaynor.
Att: approx. 30,000

First Round / 2nd leg
29 Sep. at Bishopstown; Referee: D. Pauchard (France)
Cork City 0
Galatasaray (0) 1 *(Kubilay 76)*
Cork C: Harrington, Cotter (Glynn 80), Daly, O'Donoghue, Napier, Buckley, Barry (Roche 83), Hyde, Murphy, Morley, Gaynor.
Galatasary: Hayrettin, Stumpf, Bulent, Yusuf, Falko, Tugay, Ergdal (Arif 65), Hamza, Hakan, Suat, Kubilay (Mert 88).
Att: approx. 7,000
(Aggregate 1-3)

Cup Winners Cup

Preliminary Round / 1st leg
18 Aug. at Ukraine Stadium Lvov
Karpaty Lvov (0) 1 *(Evtushok 82)*
Shelbourne 0
K. Lvov: Stronzizki, Mokrizki, Evtushok, Romanishin, Plotko, Stelmakh (Riznik 67), Chizevcki, Rafalshyk (Shylytizki h.t.), Petrik, Karolosh, Poklodok.
Shels: Byrne, Neville, Whelan, Brady, Dunne, Mooney, Doolin, Costello, Rutherford, Arkins (Browne 82), O'Doherty.
Att: 25,000

Preliminary Round / 2nd leg
1 Sep. at Tolka Park; Referee: P. Leduc (France)
Shelbourne (1) 3 *(Costello 9, Mooney 65, Izzi 76)*
Karpaty Lvov (0) 1 *(Masur 89)*
Shels: Byrne, Flood, Brady, Neville, Whelan, Doolin, Mooney, Costello, Dully (Izzi 54), O'Doherty, Rutherford.
K. Lvov: Stronzizki, Evtushok, Tchijevsky, Masur, Mokrizki, Petrik, Poklodok, Karolosh (Shoulatitsky 78), Riznik, Plokto, Stelmakh (Rafalshyk 45).
Att: 6,500

First Round / 1st leg
15 Sep. at Olympic Stadium, Athens
Referee: B. Heinemann (Germany)
Panathinaikos (2) 3 *(Donis 11, 37, Warzycha 48)*
Shelbourne 0
Pana: Wandzyk, Mavridis, Kalitzakis, Apostolakis, Donis, Fratzeskos, Christodoulou (Markov 63), Eskorgladif, Maragos (Giotsas 63), Warzycha, Saravakos.
Shels: Byrne, Flood, Whelan, Brady, Wilson (Browne 52), Mooney, Costello, Rutherford, Cooney, O'Doherty.
Att: 30,000

First Round / 2nd leg
29 Sep. at Tolka Park: Referee: B. Markowalczyk (Poland)
Shelbourne (0) 1 *(Mooney 86)*
Panathinaikos (1) 2 *(Deerbiakis 24, Saravakos 57)*
Shels: Byrne, Flood, Neville, Whelan, Brady, Mooney, Doolin, Costello, Rutherford (Browne 67), O'Doherty, Dully (Cooney 60).
Pana: Wandzyk, Mavridis, Kalitzakis, Apostolakis, Donis (Giotsas 61), Nibuas, Deerbiakis (Fratbeskos 61), Saravakos, Warzycha, Maragos, Antonios.
Att: 2,000

U.E.F.A. Cup

First Round / 1st leg
14 Sep. at Dalymount Park; Referee S. Rvangelos (Greece)
        Bohemians 0
        Bordeaux (1) 1 *(Dugarry 16)*
Bohs: Henderson, O'Connor, Best, O'Driscoll, Kelch, Dunne, Moody, Fitzgerald (King 89), Cousins (Geoghegan 66), Fenlon, Tilson.
Bordeaux: Huard, Croci, Lizarazu, Senac, Dogon, Lucas, Zidane (Witschge 70), Guerit, Daniel, Vercruysse, Dugarry (Fofana 74).
Att: 6,000

First Round / 2nd leg
28 Sep. at Lescure Stadium, Bordeaux;
        Referee: M. Rothlisberger (Switzerland)
        Bordeaux (2) 5 *(Zidane 22, Vercruysse 25, 72, Paille 60, Fofana 67)*
        Bohemians 0
Bordeaux: Huard, Croci, Lizarazu, Senac, Santos, Dib (Daniel 63), Zidane, Guerit, Paille (Grenet 63), Vercruysse, Fofana.
Bohs: Henderson, Broughan (Crawford 76), Best, O'Driscoll, Kelch, Dunne, Moody, O'Connor, Cousins (Fitzgerald 72), Fenlon, Tilson.
Att: 18,000
(Aggregate 6-0)

Allez Les Bohs, Allez!
Maurice O'Driscoll bursts through the Bordeaux midfield (The Star)

LEAGUE OF IRELAND clubs in the CHAMPIONS CUP

Season	Rd	Club	Opponent	Country	Result
1957/58	Pr.	**Shamrock Rovers**	Manchester United	(Eng)	(h) 0-6
					(a) 2-3 McCann, Hamilton
1958/59	Pr.	**Drumcondra**	Athletico Madrid	(Spa)	(h) 1-5 Fullam (pen)
					(a) 0-8
1959/60	Pr.	**Shamrock Rovers**	Nice	(Fra)	(h) 1-1 Hennessy
					(a) 2-3 Hamilton, Tuohy
1960/61	Pr.	**Limerick**	Young Boys Berne	(Swz.)	(h) 0-5
					(a) 2-4 Lynam, O'Reilly
1961/62	Pr.	**Drumcondra**	Nurenberg	(W.Ger.)	(h) 1-4 Fullam
					(a) 0-5
1962/63	Pr.	**Shelbourne**	Sporting Lisbon	(Por)	(h) 0-2
					(a) 1-5 Hennessy
1963/64	Pr.	**Dundalk**	Zurich	(Swz)	(h) 0-3
					(a) 2-1 Cross, Hasty
1964/65	Pr.	**Shamrock Rovers**	Rapid Vienna	(Aus)	(h) 0-2
					(a) 0-3
1965/66	Pr.	**Drumcondra**	Vorwaerts Berlin	(E.Ger)	(h) 1-0 Morrissey
					(a) 0-3
1966/67	Pr.	**Waterford**	Vorwaerts Berlin	(E.Ger)	(h) 1-6 Lynch
					(a) 0-6
1967/68	1.	**Dundalk**	Vasas Budapest	(Hun)	(h) 0-1
					(a) 1-8 Hale
1968/69	1	**Waterford**	Manchester United	(Eng)	(h) 1-3 Matthews
					(a) 1-7 Casey
1969/70	1	**Waterford**	Galatasary	(Tur)	(h) 2-3 Morley, Buck
					(a) 0-2
1970/71	1	**Waterford**	Glentoran	(N.Irl)	(h) 1-0 Casey
					(a) 3-1 Casey, O'Neill, McGeough
	2	**Waterford**	Glasgow Celtic	(Sco)	(h) 0-7
					(a) 2-3 Og Matthews
1971/72	1	**Cork Hibernians**	Borussia Moenchengladbach	(W.Ger)	(h) 0-5
					(a) 1-2 Dennehy
1972/73	1	**Waterford**	Omonia Nicosia	(Cyp)	(h) 2-1 Hale: 2
					(a) 0-2
1973/74	1	**Waterford**	Ujpest Dozsa	(Hun)	(h) 2-3 O'Neill, Kirby
					(a) 0-3
1974/75	1	**Cork Celtic**	Omonia Nicosia	(Cyp)	Walk Over
			Ararat Erevan	(USSR)	(h) 1-2 Tambling
					(a) 0-5
1975/76	1	**Bohemians**	Glasgow Rangers	(Sco)	(h) 1-1 T. O'Connor
					(a) 1-4 T. Flanagan
1976/77	1	**Dundalk**	PSV Eindhoven	(Hol)	(h) 1-1 McDowell
					(a) 0-6
1977/78	1	**Sligo Rovers**	Red Star Belgrade	(Yug)	(h) 0-3
					(a) 0-3
1978/79	1	**Bohemians**	Omonia Nicosia	*(Cyp)	(h) 1-0 Joyce
					(a) 1-2 P. O'Connor
	2	**Bohemians**	Dynamo Dresden **	(E.Ger.)	(h) 0-0
					(a) 0-6

146

Season	Rd	Club	Opponent	Country	Result	Scorers
1979/80	Pr.	**Dundalk**	Linfield	(N.Irl)	(h) 1-1	Devine
				***	(a) 2-0	Mucklan: 2
	1	**Dundalk**	Hibernians	(Mal)	(h) 2-0	Carlyle, Devine
					(a) 0-1	
	2	**Dundalk**	Glasgow Celtic	(Sco)	(h) 0-0	
					(a) 2-3	Mick Lawlor, Mucklan
1980/81	1	**Limerick**	Real Madrid	(Spal)	(h) 1-2	Kennedy
					(a) 1-5	Kennedy
1981/82	1	**Athlone Town**	KB Copenhagen	(Den)	(h) 2-2	Davis: 2
					(a) 1-1	M. O'Connor
		(Agg. 3-3, KB won on away goals)				
1982/83	1	**Dundalk**	Liverpool	(Eng)	(h) 1-4	Flanagan
					(a) 0-1	
1983/84	1	**Athlone Town**	Standard Liege	(Bel)	(h) 2-3	R. Collins, Salmon
					(a) 2-8	Hitchcock, Salmon
1984/85	1	**Shamrock Rovers**	Linfield	(N.Irl)	(h) 1-1	Eccles
		(Agg. 1-1, Linfield won on away goals)			(a) 0-0	
1985/86	1	**Shamrock Rovers**	Honved	(Hun)	(h) 1-3	Coady
					(a) 0-2	
1986/87	1	**Shamrock Rovers**	Glasgow Celtic	(Sco)	(h) 0-1	
					(a) 0-2	
1987/88	1	**Shamrock Rovers**	Omonia Nicosia	(Cyp)	(h) 0-1	
					(a) 0-0	
1988/89	1	**Dundalk**	Red Star Belgrade	(Yug)	(h) 0-5	
					(a) 0-3	
1989/90	1	**Derry City**	Benfica	(Por)	(h) 1-2	Carlyle
					(a) 0-4	
1990/91	1	**St. Patrick's Athletic**	Dinamo Bucharest	(Rom)	(h) 1-1	Fenlon
					(a) 0-4	
1991/92	1	**Dundalk**	Kispest Honved	(Hun)	(h) 0-2	
					(a) 1-1	McEvoy
1992/93	P	**Shelbourne**	Tavria Simferopol	(Ukr)	(h) 0-0	
					(a) 1-2	Dully
1993-94	P	**Cork City**	Cwmbran Town	(Wal)	(h) 2-1	Morley, Glynn
					(a) 2-3	Caulfield, Buckley
		(Agg. 4-4, Cork City won on away goals)				
	1	**Cork City**	Galatasaray	(Tur)	(h) 0-1	
					(a) 1-2	Barry

Note: * Played at Flower Lodge; ** Played at Oriel Park; *** Played in Haarlem (Holland)

Summary of Appearances in the CHAMPIONS CUP
7 Shamrock Rovers, Dundalk; 6 Waterford; 3 Drumcondra; 2 Athlone Town, Bohemians, Limerick, Shelbourne; 1 Cork Celtic, Cork City, Cork Hibernians, Derry City, St. Patrick's Athletic, Sligo Rovers.

LEAGUE OF IRELAND clubs in the CUP WINNERS CUP

1961/62	Pr.	**St. Patrick's Athletic**	Dunfermline Ath	(Sco)	(h) 0-4	
					(a) 1-4	O'Rourke
1962/63	1	**Shamrock Rovers**	bye			
	2	**Shamrock Rovers**	Botev Plovdiv	(Bul)	(h) 0-4	
					(a) 0-1	
1963/64	1	**Shelbourne**	Barcelona	(Spa)	(h) 0-2	
					(a) 1-3	Bonham (pen)
1964/65	1	**Cork Celtic**	Slavia Sofia	(Bul)	(h) 0-2	
					(a) 1-1	Leahy
1965/66	1	**Limerick**	CSKA Sofia	(Bul)	(h) 1-2	O'Connor
					(a) 0-2	
1966/67	1	**Shamrock Rovers**	Spora Luxembourg	(Lux)	(h) 4-1	O'Neill (pen), Dixon, Fullam, Kearin
					(a) 4-1	O'Neill, Fullam, Dixon 2
	2	**Shamrock Rovers**	Bayern Munich	(W.Ger)	(h) 1-1	Dixon
					(a) 2-3	Gilbert, Tuohy
1967/68	1	**Shamrock Rovers**	Cardiff City	(Wal)	(h) 1-1	Gilbert
					(a) 0-2	
1968/69	1	**Shamrock Rovers**	Randers Freja	(Den)	(h) 1-2	Fullam
					(a) 0-1	
1969/70	1	**Shamrock Rovers**	Shalke 04	(W.Ger)	(h) 2-1	Barber: 2
					(a) 0-3	
1970/71	Pr.	**Bohemians**	Gottwaldov	(Czh)	(h) 1-2	Swan (Pen)
					(a) 2-2	O'Connell, Dunne
1971/72	1	**Limerick**	Torino	(Ity)	(h) 0-1	
					(a) 0-4	
1972/73	1	**Cork Hibernians**	Pezoporikos	(Cyp)	(h) 4-1	Lawson: 2, Wallace, Dennehy
					*(a) 2-1	Lawson (pen), Sheehan
		(*Both games played at Flower Lodge)				
	2	**Cork Hibernians**	Shalke 04	(W.Ger)	(h) 0-0	
					(a) 0-3	
1973/74	1	**Cork Hibernians**	Banik Ostrava	(Czh)	(h) 1-2	Humphries
					(a) 0-1	
1974/75	1	**Finn Harps**	Bursapor	(Tur)	(h) 0-0	
					(a) 2-4	Ferry, Bradley
1975/76	1	**Home Farm**	Lens	(Fra)	(h) 1-1	Brophy
					(a) 0-6	
1976/77	1	**Bohemians**	Esbjerg	(Den)	(h) 2-1	OG Ryan
					(a) 1-0	Mitten
	2	**Bohemians**	Slask Wroclaw	(Pol)	(h) 0-1	
					(a) 0-3	
1977/78	1	**Dundalk**	Hajduk Split	(Yug)	(h) 1-0	T. Flanagan
					(a) 0-4	
1978/79	1	**Shamrock Rovers**	Apoel Nicosia	(Cyp)	(h) 2-0	Giles, Lynex
					(a) 1-0	Lynex
	2	**Shamrock Rovers**	Banik Ostrava	(Czh)	(h) 1-3	Giles
					(a) 0-3	
1979/80	1	**Waterford**	Gothenburg	(Swe)	(h) 1-1	Keane
					(a) 0-1	

Season	Rd	Club	Opponent	Country	Result	Scorers
1980/81	1	**Waterford**	Hibernians	(Mal)	(h) 4-0	Finucane, Fitzpatrick, Kirk: 2
					(a) 0-1	
	2	**Waterford**	Dynamo Tbilisi	(USSR)	(h) 0-1	
					(a) 0-4	
1981/82	1	**Dundalk**	Fram Reykjavik	(Icl)	(h) 4-0	L. Flanagan (pen), Fairclough, Duff, Martin Lawlor
					(a) 1-2	Fairclough
	2	**Dundalk**	Tottenham Hotspur	(Eng)	(h) 1-1	Fairclough
					(a) 0-1	
1982/83	1	**Limerick United**	AZ.67	(Hol)	(h) 1-1	Nolan
					(a) 0-1	
1983/84	1	**Sligo Rovers**	Haka Valkeakosen	(Fin)	(h) 0-1	
					(a) 0-3	
1984/85	1	**U.C.D.**	Everton	(Eng)	(h) 0-0	
					(a) 0-1	
1985/86	1	**Galway United**	Lyngby	(Den)	(h) 2-3	Bonner, Murphy
					(a) 0-1	
1986/87	1	**Waterford United**	Bordeaux	(Fra)	(h) 1-2	Synnott
					(a) 0-4	
1987/88	1	**Dundalk**	Ajax Amsterdam	(Hol)	(h) 0-2	
					(a) 0-4	
1988/89	1	**Derry City**	Cardiff City	(Wal)	(h) 0-0	
					(a) 0-4	
1989/90	1	**Cork City**	Torpedo Moscow	(USSR)	(h) 0-1	
					(a) 0-5	
1990/91	Pr.	**Bray Wanderers**	Trabzonspor	(Tur)	(h) 1-1	Nugent
					(a) 0-2	
1991/92	Pr.	**Galway United**	Odense	(Den)	(h) 0-3	
					(a) 0-4	
1992/93	1	**Bohemians**	Steaua Bucharest	(Rom)	(h) 0-0	
					(a) 0-4	
1993-94	P	**Shelbourne**	Karpaty Lvov	(Ukr)	(h) 3-1	Costello, Mooney, Izzi
					(a) 0-1	
	1	**Shelbourne**	Panathinaikos	(Gre)	(h) 1-2	Mooney
					(a) 0-3	

Summary of Appearances in the CUP WINNERS CUP

6 Shamrock Rovers; 3 Bohemians, Dundalk, Limerick/Limerick United; 2 Cork Hibernians, Galway United, Shelbourne, Waterford; 1 Bray Wanderers, Cork Celtic, Cork City, Derry City, Finn Harps, Home Farm, St. Patrick's Athletic, Sligo Rovers, U.C.D, Waterford United.

LEAGUE OF IRELAND club in the FAIRS/UEFA CUP

FAIRS CUP:

1962/63	1	**Drumcondra**	Odense BK09	(Den)	(h) 4-1	Morrissey, McCann, Dixon: 2
					(a) 2-4	Morrissey, Rice
	2	**Drumcondra**	Bayern Munich	(W.Ger)	(h) 1-0	Dixon
					(a) 0-6	
1963/64	1	**Shamrock Rovers**	Valencia	(Spa)	(h) 0-1	
					(a) 2-2	O'Neill, Mooney
1964/65	1	**Shelbourne**	Belenenses	(Por)	(h) 0-0	
					(a) 1-1	Barber
				(play off)	(h) 2-1	Hannigan, Conroy
	2	**Shelbourne**	Athletico Madrid	(Spa)	(h) 0-1	
					(a) 0-1	
1965/66	1	**Shamrock Rovers**	bye			
	2	**Shamrock Rovers**	Real Zaragosa	(Spa)	(h) 1-1	Tuohy
					(a) 1-2	Fullam
1966/67	1	**Drumcondra**	Eintract Frankfort	(W.Ger)	(h) 0-0	
					(a) 1-6	Whelan
1967/68	1	**St. Patrick's Athletic**	Bordeaux	(Fra)	(h) 1-3	Hennessey
					(a) 3-6	Ryan, Campbell: 2
1968/69	1	**Dundalk**	DOS Utrecht	(Hol)	(h) 2-1	Stokes, Morrissey
					(a) 1-1	Stokes
	2	**Dundalk**	Glasgow Rangers	(Sco)	(h) 0-3	
					(a) 1-6	Murray (pen)
1969/70	1	**Dundalk**	Liverpool	(Eng)	(h) 0-10	
					(a) 0-4	
1970/71	1	**Cork Hibernians**	Valencia	(Spa)	(h) 0-3	
					(a) 1-3	Wiggington

UEFA CUP:

1971/72	1	**Shelbourne**	Vasas Budapest	(Hun)	(h) 1-1	Murray
					(a) 0-1	
1972/73	1	**Bohemians**	IFC Cologne	(W.Ger)	(h) 0-3	
					(a) 1-2	Daly
1973/74	1	**Finn Harps**	Aberdeen	(Sco)	(h) 1-3	Harkin
					(a) 1-4	Harkin
1974/75	1	**Bohemians**	SV Hamburg	(W.Ger)	(h) 0-1	
					(a) 0-3	
1975/76	1	**Athlone Town**	Valerengen	(Nor)	(h) 3-1	Davis: 2, Martin
					(a) 1-1	Martin
	2	**Athlone Town**	A.C. Milan	(Ity)	(h) 0-0	
					(a) 0-3	
1976/77	1	**Finn Harps**	Derby County	(Eng)	(h) 1-4	OG
					(a) 0-12	
1977/78	1	**Bohemians**	Newcastle United	(Eng)	(h) 0-0	
					(a) 0-4	
1978/79	1	**Finn Harps**	Everton	(Eng)	(h) 0-5	
					(a) 0-5	
1979/80	1	**Bohemians**	Sporting Lisbon	(Por)	(h) 0-0	
					(a) 0-2	

Season	Rd	Club	Opponent	Country	Result	Scorers
1980/81	1	**Dundalk**	Oporto	(Por)	(h) 0-0	
					(a) 0-1	
1981/82	1	**Limerick United**	Southampton	(Eng)	(h) 0-3	
					(a) 1-1	Morris
1982/83	1	**Shamrock Rovers**	Fram Reykjavik	(Icl)	(h) 4-0	O'Carroll, Buckley, Beglin, Gaynor
					(a) 3-0	Gaynor, Campbell, R. Murphy
	2	**Shamrock Rovers**	Uni Craiova	(Rum)	(h) 0-2	
					(a) 0-3	
1983/84	1	**Drogheda United**	Tottenham Hotspur	(Eng)	(h) 0-6	
					(a) 0-8	
1984/85	1	**Bohemians**	Glasgow Rangers	(Sco)	(h) 3-2	O'Brien: 2, Lawless
					(a) 0-2	
1985/86	1	**Bohemians**	Dundee United	(Sco)	(h) 2-5	Lawless, O'Brien
					(a) 2-2	Jameson, O'Brien
1986/87	1	**Galway United**	Groningen	(Hol)	(h) 1-3	P. Murphy
					(a) 1-5	McGee (Pen)
1987/88	1	**Bohemians**	Aberdeen	(Sco)	(h) 0-0	
					(a) 0-1	
1988/89	1	**St. Patrick's Athletic**	Heart of Midlothian	(Sco)	(h) 0-2	
					(a) 0-2	
1989/90	1	**Dundalk**	Wettingen	(Swz)	(h) 0-2	
					(a) 0-3	
1990/91	1	**Derry City**	Vitesse Arnhem	(Hol)	(h) 0-1	
					(a) 0-0	
1991/92	1	**Cork City**	Bayern Munich	(Ger)	(h) 1-1	Barry
					(a) 0-2	
1992/93	1	**Derry City**	Vitesse Arnhem	(Hol)	(h) 1-2	Mooney
					(a) 0-3	
1993-94	1	**Bohemians**	Bordeaux	(Fra)	(h) 0-1	
					(a) 0-5	

Summary of Appearances in the UEFA/FAIRS CUP

8 Bohemians; 4 Dundalk; 3 Finn Harps, Shamrock Rovers; 2 Derry City, Drumcondra, St. Patricks Athletic, Shelbourne; 1 Cork City, Cork Hibernians, Drogheda United, Galway United, Limerick United, Athlone Town.

Summary of LEAGUE OF IRELAND club appearances in all EURO. competitions:
not including season 1994/95

16 Shamrock Rovers; 14 Dundalk; 13 Bohemians; 8 Waterford; 6, Limerick/Limerick United; Shelbourne; 5 Drumcondra 4 Cork Hibernians, Derry City, Finn Harps, St. Patrick's Athletic; 3 Athlone Town, Cork City, Galway United; 2 Cork Celtic, Sligo Rovers; 1 Bray Wanderers, Drogheda United, Home Farm, U.C.D., Waterford United.

EUROPEAN CLUB COMPETITIONS 1994-95

Champions Cup: Preliminary Round

AEK Athens (Gce)	v Glasgow Rangers (Sco)	2-0 1-0
Avenir Beggen (Lux)	v Galatasaray (Tur)	1-5 0-4
Legia Warsaw (Pol)	v Hajduk Split (Cro)	0-1 0-4
Maccabi Haifa (Isr)	v Casino Salzburg (Aus)	1-2 1-3
Paris St. Germain (Fra)	v Vac Samsung (Hun)	3-0 2-1
Silkeborg (Den)	v Dynamo Kiev (UKR)	0-0 1-3
Sparta Prague (Czh)	v IFK Goteburg (Swe)	1-0 0-2
Steaua Bucharest (Rom)	v Servette Geneva (Swi)	4-1 1-1

Champions League

Group **A** - Barcelona, Galatasaray, IFK Goteburg, Manchester Utd.
Group **B** - Bayern Munich, Dynamo Kiev, Paris St.G., Spartak Moscow
Group **C** - Anderlecht, Benfica, Hajduk Spit, Steaua Bucharest
Group **D** - A.C. Milan, AEK Athens, Ajax, Salzburg

Sep. 14th

Barcelona	2,	Manchester U.	4,	Paris St.G.	2,	Dynamo Kiev 3
Galatasaray	1,	Goteburg	2,	Bayern M.	0,	Spartak Moscow 2
Anderlecht	0,	Hajduk Split	0,	Salzburg	0,	Ajax 2
Steaua Buch.	0,	Benfica	0,	AEK Athens	0,	A.C.Milan 0

Sep. 28th

Galatasaray	0,	Goteburg	2,	Bayern M.	1,	Spartak M. 1
Manchester U.	0,	Barcelona	1,	Dynamo Kiev	0,	Paris St.G. 2
Steaua Buch.	0,	Benfica	3,	AEK Athens	1,	A.C. Milan 3
Hajduk Split	1,	Anderlecht	1,	Ajax	2,	Salzburg 0

Winners and Runners-up in each group to advance to the quarter finals.

Cup Winners Cup - Preliminary Round

Bangor (N.Ire)	v Tatran Presov (Slv)	0-1 0-4
Barry Town (Wal)	v Zhalgiris Vilnius (Lit)	0-1 0-6
Bodo Glimt (Nor)	v Olimpija Riga (Lat)	6-0 0-0
Fandok Bobruisk (Bela)	v Tirana * (Alb)	4-1 0-3
Ferencvaros (Hun)	v FGI Diddeleng (Lux)	6-1 6-1
Floriana (Mal)	v **Sligo Rovers** (Irl)	2-2 0-1
IBK Kebflavik (Ice)	v Maccabi Tel-Aviv (Isr)	1-2 1-4
Norma Tallinn (Est)	v Marbor Branik (Slvn)	1-4 0-10
F.C. Pirin (Bul)	v Schaan (Liec)	3-0 1-0
Sandoyar Itrott (F.Is)	v H.J.K. Helsinki (Fin)	0-5 0-2
Tiligui Tiraspol (Mol)	v Omonia Nicosia (Cyp)	0-1 1-3
Viktoria Zizkov (Czh)	v IFK Norrkoping (Swe)	1-0 3-3

First Round

Besiktas (Tur)	v H.J.K. Helsinki	2-0 1-1
Bodo Glimt	v Sampdoria	3-2 0-2
Brondby (Den)	v Tirana	3-0 1-0
Chelsea (Eng)	v Viktoria Zizkov	4-2 0-0
Croatia Zagreb (Cro)	v Auxerre (Fra)	3-1 0-3
CSKA Moskow (Rus)	v Ferencvaros **	2-1 1-2
Dundee United (Sco)	v Tatran Presov	3-2 1-3
Grasshoppers (Swi)	v Chernomorets Odessa (Ukr)	3-0 0-1

Maribor Branik	v Austria Vienna (Aus)	1-1 0-3
Omonia Nicosia	v Arsenal (Eng)	1-3 0-3
F.C. Pirin	v Panathinaikos (Gce)	0-2 1-6
F.C. Porto (Por)	v LKS Lodz (Pol)	2-0 1-0
Real Zaragoza (Spa)	v Gloria Bistrita (Rom)	4-0 1-2
Sligo Rovers	v Club Brugge (Bel)	1-2 1-3
Werder Bremen (Ger)	v Maccabi Tel-Aviv	2-0 0-0
Zhalgiris Vilnius	v Feyenoord Rotterdam (Hol)	1-1 1-2

Second Round

Arsenal	v Brondby	2-2 2-1
Austria Vienna	v Chelsea *	1-1 0-0
Besiktas	v Auxerre	2-2 0-2
Club Brugge	v Panathinaikos	1-0 0-0
Feyenoord Rotterdam	v Werder Bremen	1-0 4-3
F.C. Porto	v Ferencvaros	6-0 0-2
Sampdoria	v Grasshoppers	3-0 2-3
Tatran Presov	v Real Zaragoza	0-4 1-2

U.E.F.A. Cup - Preliminary Round

Aarau (Swi)	v F.C. Mura (Slo)	1-0 2-0
Ararat Erevan (Arm)	v C.S.K.A. Sofia (Bul)	0-0 0-3
Anjalankoski (Fin)	v Inter Bratislava (Slv)	0-1 3-0
Anorthosis Famagusta (Cyp)	v F.C. Shumen (Bul)	2-0 2-1
Aris Thessaloniki (Gce)	v Hapoel Beer Sheva (Isr)	3-1 2-1
Bangor City (Wal)	v Akranes (Ice)	1-2 0-2
F.C. Copenhagen (Den)	v F.C. Jazz (Fin)	0-1 4-0
Dinamo Minsk (Bela)	v Hibernians (Mal)	3-1 3-4
Dinamo Tbilisi (Geo)	v Univ. Craiova (Rom)	2-0 2-1
Fenerbache (Tur)	v Touran (Kaz)	5-0 2-0
Gornik Zabrze (Pol)	v **Shamrock Rovers** (Ire)	7-0 1-0
Gotu Itrottarfelag (F.Is)	v Trelleborgs (Swe)	0-1 2-3
Hafnarfjordur (Ice)	v Linfield (N.Ire)	1-0 1-3
Inter Cardiff (Wal)	v G.K.S. Katowice (Pol)	0-2 0-6
Kispest Honved (Hun)	v Zimbru Chisinau (Mol)	4-1 1-0
Lillestrom (Nor)	v Shakhter Donetsk (Ukr)	4-1 0-2
Motherwell (Sco)	v Havnar Boltgelag (F.Is)	3-0 4-1
Odense Bk (Den)	v Flora Tallinn (Est)	3-0 3-0
Sct Olimpija (Slo)	v Levski Sofia (Bul)	3-2 2-1
Portadown (N.Ire)	v Slovan Bratislava (Slv)	0-2 0-3
F.C. Romar (Lit)	v A.I.K. Stockholm (Swe)	0-2 0-2
Rosenborg Bk. (Nor)	v CS Grevenmacher (Lux)	6-0 2-1
Skonto Riga * (Lat)	v Aberdeen (Sco)	0-0 1-1
Slavia Prague (Czh)	v **Cork City** (Irl)	2-0 4-0
Teuta (Alb)	v Apollon (Cyp)	1-4 2-4
Valletta (Mal)	v Rapid Bucharest (Rom)	1-5 1-1
F.C. Vardar (Mac)	v Bekescsabai (Hun)	1-1 0-1

First Round

Aarau	v Martimo (Por)	0-0 0-1
Admira Wacker (Aus)	v Gornik Zabrze	5-2 1-1
A.I.K. Solna	v Slavia Prague	0-0 2-2
Anorthosis Famagusta	v Athletico Bilbao (Spa)	2-0 0-3

Apollon	v F.C. Sion (Swi)	1-3 3-2
Antwerp (Bel)	v Newcastle United (Eng)	0-5 2-5
Bayer Leverkusen (Ger)	v P.S.V. Eindhoven (Hol)	5-4 0-0
Blackburn Rovers (Eng)	v Trelleborgs	0-1 2-2
Boavista (Por)	v Mypa (Fin)	2-1 1-1
Bordeaux (Fra)	v Lillestrom	3-1 2-0
Borussia Dortmund (Ger)	v Motherwell	1-0 2-0
Cannes (Fra)	v Fenerbache	4-0 5-0
C.S.K.A. Sofia	v Juventus (Ita)	3-2 0-5
Dinamo Minsk	v Lazio (Ita)	0-0 1-4
Dinamo Tiblisi	v Innsbruck (Aus)	1-0 1-5
Eintracht Frankfurt (Ger)	v Sct Olimpija	2-0 1-1
Inter Milan (Ita)	v Aston Villa ** (Eng)	1-0 0-1
Kaiserslautern (Ger)	v Akranes	4-1 4-0
G.K.S. Katowice	v Aris Salonika (Gce)	1-0 1-1
Linfield	v Odense Bk	1-1 0-5
Napoli (Ita)	v Skonto Riga	2-0 1-0
Olympiakos Piraeus (Gce)	v Marseille (Fra)	1-2 0-3
Real Madrid * (Spa)	v Sporting Lisbon (Por)	1-0 1-2
Rotor Volgograd (Rus)	v Nantes (Fra)	3-2 0-3
Rosenborg	v Deportivo La Coruna (Spa)	1-0 1-4
Rapid Bucharest	v Charleroi (Bl)	2-0 1-2
Seraing (Bel)	v Dinamo Moskow ** (Rus)	3-4 1-0
Slovan Bratislava	v F.C. Copenhagen	1-0 1-1
Tek'ikKamychine (Rus)	v Bekescsabai	6-1 0-1
Trabzonspor (Tur)	v Dinamo Bucharest (Rom)	2-1 3-3
F.C. Twente (Hol)	v Kispest Honved	1-4 3-1
Vitesse Arnhem (Hol)	v Parma (Ita)	1-0 0-2

Second Round

Admira Wacker	v Cannes	1-1 4-2
Boavista	v Napoli	1-1 1-2
Dinamo Moskow	v Real Madrid	2-2 0-4
Innsbruck	v Deportivo La Coruna	2-0 0-4
Juventus	v Martimo	2-0 1-0
Kaiserlautern	v Odense Bk.*	1-1 0-0
Katowice	v Bordeaux	1-0 1-1
Kispest Honved	v Bayer Leverkusen	0-2 0-5
Lazio	v Trelleborgs	1-0 0-0
Newcastle United	v Athletico Bilbao *	3-2 0-1
Rapid Bucharest	v Eintracht Frankfurt	2-1 0-5
Sion*	v Marseille	2-0 1-3
Slovan Bratislava	v Borussia Dortmund	2-1 0-3
Trabzonspor *	v Aston Villa	1-0 1-2
Tek'ikKamychine	v Nantes	1-2 0-2

* Won on away goals
** Won on penalties

Champions clash in Cwmbran
Fergus O'Donoghue (Cork City) tackles Francis Ford (Cwmbran Town) (The Star)

153

Athlone Town's European Debut
v Valerengens IF & AC Milan
UEFA Cup 1975/76

Euro Flashback

Founded in 1887 and claiming to be the Republic's oldest club, Athlone Town has had, in League of Ireland terms, a curious history. In 1922 they became the first provincial side to enter league ranks, rubbing shoulders with eleven clubs from the capital. Despite an early major success when capturing the FAI Cup - or the Free State Cup as it was then known - in 1924, the midlanders' flirtation with league football lasted a mere five seasons, the club resigning in 1928 having finished bottom and walloped at home in the first round of the Cup by non-league Drumcondra. There followed four decades of relative obscurity before a gradual resurgence led to a famous Intermediate Cup run in 1968 which saw the 'Town going all the way to the final against the renowned Home Farm. Although ultimate glory was denied Athlone, after a replay, football fever had returned once more to St. Mel's Park and when the league was extended in 1969-70 they successfully applied for membership. In the company of Finn Harps they re-entered the league fold, back once again among the big boys.

Whether it was a grim determination to do better second time around or just pure exuberance, Athlone claimed their first trophy within three months of their return by trouncing Shelbourne 4-0 in the Leinster Senior Cup decider. One season later, the same teams faced up in the Shield final at a time when this old competition carried with it a passport to the European Inter Cities Fairs Cup. Not long out of the backwaters, Athlone Town suddenly found themselves on the threshold of Europe with barely more than a season of senior experience behind them. Shelbourne, however, avenging the earlier humiliation, frustrated what would have been a truly meteoric rise with a single goal victory though Athlone had stubbornly held out for a second replay. Defeated but defiant, Athlone's appetite had been whetted and they longed for another opportunity to reach the continents lush green swards.

After their initial enthusiasm had burned out the club had a period of consolidation, team-building and managerial change. Amby Fogarty was appointed in November '74 and his first game, a 4-0 home victory against Limerick, seemed an omen for better things ahead. The tough little Dubliner soon had the side on track as the season slowly came to the boil. Bohemians may have been unassailable in their rush to a first championship in nearly forty years but there was a tremendous scramble for the vital, Euro-clinching, runners-up position between Finn Harps, Cork Hibernians, Dundalk and Athlone. In the end the outcome hinged on the last game at St. Mel's when Hibs, who had been Euro contestants for the previous four seasons, were the visitors. Although two points in arrears, a victory by any margin would have seen the Leesiders through on goal average. A tense encounter was decided in favour of the homesters when John Minnocks free-kick rattled Joe Grady's net and there was no way back for Hibs after John Lawson failed with a second half penalty. Six seasons after returning from the wilderness Athlone Town had reached Europe's promised land and eagerly awaited a glamour tie to set Shannonside abuzz.

In a competition littered with the games glitterati – Ajax, Porto, Cologne, Liverpool, Red Star Belgrade, Hamburg, Sporting Lisbon, Roma, Lazio, Barcelona and Honved were all there – Athlone's supporters were left with somewhat mixed emotions when their favourites were paired with little-known Valerengens from Oslo, an amateur outfit whose best result had been achieved on Irish soil nine years earlier when Linfield were held to a 1-1 draw at Windsor Park.

Before the home leg, Fogarty revealed his bold approach. *"Our task today is to destroy and construct – to hit the Norwegians hard at the start and then build on their troubles."* His team duly obliged and grabbed the lead as early as the third minute when Valerengens' keeper, Areld Blomfeldt, blocked out Minnock's powerful free-kick and Paul Martin raced in to knock home the loose ball. It was the perfect start and Athlone played with purpose and confidence but were suddenly caught by a swift counter which ended with Kell Eriksen splitting the home defence for Tarva Olsen to hit the target from twelve yards. With just twelve minutes elapsed and an away goal already conceded, Athlone did not relent from their policy of all-out attack and they persisted with their onslaught for the remainder of the half. Time and again the Norwegians were ripped apart but a combination of good goalkeeping, bad luck and poor finishing ensured that the interval arrived with the scores still level. The pressure continued to mount in the second period but the lead goal proved elusive. Noel Larkin, pushed up to centre forward, had a goal ruled out and the woodwork intervened on a couple of occasions as Valerengens were pinned back in a desperate rearguard action. Then, in the 66th minute, came the inevitable breakthrough when Minnock flung over a teasing cross and Eugene Davis ghosted in to steer the ball to the net from six yards. Valerengens were a ragged outfit by the time Davis pounced again with five minutes remaining, seizing on a poor back-pass from Haslie and rounding Blomfeldt to ignite the celebrations on the terraces.

Athlone's dominance lead Peter Byrne of the Irish Times to write: *"The spectacle of an Irish team in full spate in European competition is rare enough to warrant the acclaim of all but the sternest critic and for ninety minutes yesterday we watched Athlone utterly outclass the Norwegians everywhere except on the scoreline."*

For the return leg Fogarty gave prior notice of his intention to include Joe Healy, who had replaced Paul Martin in the first game, from the start. Media speculation was rife that Martin would be omitted despite scoring a hat-trick against Finn Harps in a Dublin City Cup tie the previous weekend. Healy, had seen his home club Derry City oust Norwegian opposition before when the Candystripes, with Dougie Wood a key figure, knocked Lyn Oslo out of the Champions' Cup a decade earlier. Wood, an abrasive defender and former player-manager at St. Mel's, was back for his second stint at the club after a short spell at Shamrock Rovers.

Valerengens came into the game without skipper Trod Hoedvedt, suspended by coach Tore Skaug for a breach of club discipline. Hoedvedt, something of a maverick, had a tenuous Athlone connection having once been a team-mate of Joe Haverty who trained Town's Dublin-based players, when both lined out with Boston Shamrock. The Oslo side had other problems, too, and more pressing ones. With their domestic season only weeks from its conclusion, Valerengens were rushing headlong towards relegation. UEFA added to their troubles by deeming that their home ground, the Bislett Stadium, which enjoyed world ranking in Athletics, was unsuitable because of inadequate perimeter fencing and the match was switched to the national Ullevaal Stadium.

If there was disruption in the home camp, Fogarty was once again in positive mood before the kick-off: "*A team must play to its strengths and our strength is going forward. Frankly, I don't think we are capable of closing it up and playing for keeps.*" Contrary to reports, Paul Martin retained his place, with Healy coming in as sweeper and Wood, surprisingly, being left on the bench.

After the expected early pressure from the home side passed without serious threat, the Irish took control and were rewarded in the twentieth minute when Martin, collecting on halfway from Minnock, turned quickly and out-sprinted the central defensive cover on a thirty yard dash before side-stepping Haslie and lobbing Blomfeldt for a superb individual score. For the remainder of the half the homesters were tormented by the accuracy and pace of Athlone's attacks, particularly on the flanks, but poor finishing which seemed to carry over from the first meeting meant there was only a goal in it at the changeover.

"*Abandoning the concept of depth in defence when playing away from home, they took the game to the Norwegians with uninhibited fervour and if the marksmanship never quite attained the exalted level of the build-up, it all made for a rollicking robust struggle which needed only atmosphere on the terraces to give it enduring grandeur,*" was how the Irish Times viewed Fogarty's mens' display, observing on the use of a sweeper that "*the strategy worked like a dream, for Healy, providing extra pace behind Andy Stephenson, was quite magnificent.*"

The pattern remained the same after the re-start until Valerengens struck a stunning, unexpected, equaliser in the 54th minute when Eriksen sent a scorching left-foot drive past Mick O'Brien, quite against the run of play. It was like an echo from the St. Mel's match. Mel Moffat, writing in the Irish Press, described the midlanders' response. "*Athlone's reaction to this (goal) almost ended in the complete demoralisation of Valerengen. They charged forward with a blitz of attacking moves that were only denied the goal tag by some slack finishing and goal-line clearances.*" Scoring hero Martin was perhaps the most culpable, missing the proverbial sitter from six yards when set up by Carl Humphries. Amazingly, the Norwegians almost won the match when Wood, a late substitute for Martin, upended Harry Karlsen inside the box. From the resultant spot-kick, Hyving hit the post but O'Brien saved brilliantly when Arek Foss was first to the rebound.

Moffat summed up Athlone's performance as *"The most arrogant display I have ever seen by an Irish team in a foreign country,"* adding that *"only bad finishing by Athlone prevented an avalanche of goals."* This view was shared by Fogarty: *"As the game panned out we could have had as many as five goals, but the important thing tonight was to qualify."* The Irish Times reported *"on a night when all eleven players were heroes in varying degrees, the top accolade should go to Carl Humphries. Positively brilliant on the ball, Humphries taunted and teased the Norwegians with his uncanny close control and eventually threw Valerengen into total disarray."*

Humphries' career, in all probability, could have been over just a year earlier at the age of 23 when, disillusioned by Dave Bacuzzi's strict training regime at Cork Hibernians, he drifted out of Flower Lodge and the League of Ireland. Fogarty, however, who had had the gifted player under his wing when boss of Cork Celtic, stepped in to sign him for Athlone and rescued Humphries from inter-firm football. His managers faith had been repaid in full on this soaking wet night in Oslo.

The squad returned home to blazing bonfires and a civic reception and hoped their efforts would be rewarded with more exciting opposition in the next round. *"If we could draw Liverpool, it would be absolutely superb,"* Fogarty stated, confidently adding, *"we might not win the tie overall, but of this I am convinced – we would not be beaten in the home game."* When the pairings were made, the manager was moved to say, *"God drew this one for us."* Liverpool would not be travelling to St. Mel's but no less a luminary than AC Milan were on the way.

The Milanese aristocrats had accumulated nine Italian *scudettos*, two European Champions' Cups, two European Cup Winners' Cup and had attained the pinnacle of club football when clinching the World Club Championship against Argentinian side Estudiantes de la Plata in 1969, just as Athlone Town sought league membership. While Athlone were knocking out Valerengens, Milan had removed Everton from the competition.

The immediate problem posed by Milan's visit was the suitability of St. Mel's to host the match. Fogarty believed the game should be played in Dublin with the increased revenue then being used to upgrade their own facilities. The club directors thought otherwise and with a lot of voluntary help and UEFA's approval Milan would indeed run out at the compact little stadium on the banks of the Shannon with its seating accommodation for 200 and a stretched capacity of 9-10,000.

As the big day approached media interest was specifically focused on Milan's initial reaction to Athlone's humble circumstances. The Italians' regimental coach, Nero Rocco, not a man to mince words, declared, *"As far as my players and I were concerned, the big worry before we arrived here was the state of the playing surface. Now that we have seen it I am satisfied. I am not particularly worried about the closeness of the crowd to the playing area for once the game starts we will be concentrating exclusively on what happens on the pitch. Athlone's players may only be part-time professionals, but I shall be happy enough to go home with a scoreless draw. We shall be playing for a result and thinking about the important things when Athlone come out to Milan."*

Fogarty, epitomising the sides attitude to the Euro encounters, exuded confidence. *"I cannot imagine the Italians settling for defeat today and yet I am convinced that we are in with a reasonable chance of winning. I think we can hand them a few surprises."* Recent good form was a further morale booster as Athlone had travelled to Milltown and beaten Shamrock Rovers 2-1 and overturned Cork Hibs by the same score at home with Minnock and Martin, who was in a rich scoring vein, on the mark in both games. Once again, Wood was recalled to a more conventional defensive formation with Healy returning to substitute duties as 9,000 crammed St. Mel's to the rafters to see the mighty and the minnows. For much of the game, the uneducated observer would have had difficulty distinguishing David from Goliath as Athlone roared out of the starting blocks in a fashion which rocked their illustrious opponents. Frequently the home sides rhythm was interrupted by the ever increasing malicious play of the Italians. It was not a game for the squeamish with Bill George commenting in the Cork Examiner that *"Milan were destructive in their tactics and destructive in inclination. They were guilty of what was probably the most negative performance seen from one of Europe's top-flight sides in Ireland and compounded the cynicism of their approach with an element of physical play that bordered on the violent at times."*

Athlone showed skill, passion and a necessary hardness in their game to overcome the blatant provocation but weak refereeing saw only Scala and Gorin cautioned though any one of several Italians could have been dismissed as, indeed, could John Duffy, the Athlone captain, following a wild tackle on Vincenzi.

But it was not all cynical and negative. Daly and Humphries continually probed the Milan defensive wall for cracks while Duffy, probably the home sides best player on the day, was a constant menace with his penetrating overlaps from full back. The home defence was solid and it was midway through the opening period before Calloni, from thirty yards, produced the visitors' first serious attempt on O'Brien's goal. The game was being carried by Athlone when on the half hour Davis released a ball which Terry Daly picked up at full throttle and crashed through the Milanese shield only to be felled by Scala. The Danish referee pointed to the spot and the entire midlands held it's breath as a strange hush descended on the stadium when Minnock prepared for the kick. Enrico Albertosi, who had guarded the *Azzuri's* net in the Mexico World Cup Final stood between John Minnock and a place in Irish football folklore. Whether burdened by the sudden weight of history or haunted by a couple of recent penalty failures, Minnock barely stepped back before stubbing a feeble effort straight at the Milan custodian. The ensuing groans were momentary for despite this huge disappointment, players and supporters were soon re-focused on the target of achieving a famous result. Duffy came close as the half ended, shooting instinctively but weakly from just six yards out.

The Italians seemed more composed after the break, perhaps realising Athlone would not come so close again, with Albertosi in particular very assured in his handling. Davis and the AC skipper, Romeo Benetti, appeared intent on exchanging shirts before the final whistle in an ongoing tussle as the Dubliner's influence grew. But the second period, by and large, was an anti-climax. Milan had set their stall beforehand and, once let off the hook, were content to escape with a scoreless draw. The game ended with Cyril Barnicle replacing Larkin in a final effort to unhinge a locked defence but the chances, although few, had come and gone and were not availed of. As Declan Lynch would later recall in Hot Press Magazine, *"The final score read a stupendous 0-0 victory for Athlone Town."* It was, unquestionably, a superb display and, despite the missed penalty, a magnificent, improbable result. Milan's negativity is best highlighted by their being the first team to fail to score at the venue in almost eleven months.

If at times events on the pitch had resembled a battle zone, then the aftermath produced a bitter war of words with both managers angrily accusing the opposition of questionable behaviour. Fogarty believed *"three or four of the Milan players should have been sent-off,"* while Rocco, speaking of the return leg, retorted that he doubted Athlone would *"finish with even five players if they use the same violence as in the first game,"* defining the Irish sides performance as *"brutal aggression."* Both managers agreed that referee Sorenson had badly handled affairs with Fogarty saying, *"Had he asserted himself early on, I think we would have been spared a lot of the nastiness which followed."* Athlone's Golden Day may have left a sour taste but there was no disputing that all of the plaudits had been earned by the gallant homesters.

If domestic results before the home leg had gone well for Athlone, the same could not be said of their run-up to the return. A goal from Davis had salvaged a point at Sligo but the Sunday before flying to Italy the team had lost in Drogheda where Healy had sustained an ankle injury which cast a doubt over his participation in the San Siro. A repeat of his Oslo heroics seemed slim and Fogarty was forced to retain Wood in an unchanged eleven. The gulf in facilities and status was hugely evident on arrival in Italy. Where Athlone's squad trained in four different towns – at home under Fogarty's watchful eye, in Dublin under Haverty, the Derry contingent in the Maiden City under Eunan Blake, a former Athlone manager, and Humphries on Leeside with Cork Celtic – their opponents enjoyed state of the art amenities at their specially designed sumptuous training camp at Milanello. The San Siro itself was a cathedral of the world game, an awe-inspiring monument to Milan's power and affluence.

Rocco made two changes from the first leg as Milan, lying third in Serie A, sought to overrun the Irish upstarts with a goal feast for their fanatical *tifosi*. Anquilletti was replaced by Sabadini at right back but the sensational news came with the recall of the revered veteran Gianni Rivera, an idol of the whole country, so adored, in fact, that he had been appointed club president.

As the teams lined up for what was Milan's 99th European game, Rivera, who had not played for six months, was accorded due worship by the 42,500 awaiting the slaughter of the sacrificial lambs. True to their manager's philosophy, however, brave Athlone had not come merely to defend and as early as the sixth minute Davis scuffed a half chance and four minutes later Minnock drew the best from Albertosi with a cracking twenty yarder. Milan were not in cynical defensive mode and gradually moved up the gears to slowly take control though Athlone thwarted every threat with O'Brien superb between the posts and Kevin Smith the pick of a resolute defence. On the flanks Daly was subdued but Humphries positively revelled in this theatre of dreams with Benetti, outfoxed once too often, finally booked for a callous off the ball foul on the quicksilver winger. It was a moment out of context with the rest of the game as pre-match fears of a kicking sequel never materialised and the game blossomed from the off. It took a huge, draining effort from the blue-and-black shirted Irishmen, so reminescent of Milan's great rivals Internazionale, to hold the tie scoreless to the interval much to the annoyance of the impatient home support who hurled fruit and a chorus of derision from the towering stands. Rivera, a pale shadow of his former greatness, had hardly seen the ball as Athlone chased and harried every pass. It was all a little too frenetic for the ageing Gianni.

The badly needed break offered a chance to replenish the reserve tanks and to patch up any fraying edges but Fogarty knew that now, three quarters of the way through the tie, his men were still trading on a par with genuine giants of the game. Milan again upped the tempo with Benetti a player transformed from the first leg and Vincenzi a constant danger but still wave after wave of Italian assaults were held at bay as time steadily ebbed away. Amazingly, following such impressive discipline, the tie turned on an unforced error nineteen minutes into the second period. O'Brien, faultless up to then, miscued a kick-out which placed the immaculate Smith under unexpected pressure and he was dispossessed by the lurking Gorin who returned a deep cross into the area to which Bigon got the faintest flick allowing the menacing Vincenzi an easy stab to the net from just four yards. The roar which greeted this surprise gift was more one of relief than celebration and with Athlone tiring rapidly and still twenty-five minutes to go, Milan were suddenly out for blood. Healy was immediately thrown into action for the ineffective Daly but Milan struck again within five minutes. This time Benetti thundered a thirty yard free through a porous defensive wall and O'Brien was once again picking the ball from the net as the party began on the tiered decks. Padraic Nicholson replaced Davis in a further damage limitation exercise but one final drama remained. With ten minutes left, Rivera finally made a telling contribution, his incisive pass releasing substitute Calloni who was brought down by Wood's reckless challenge. Benetti claimed his second from the spot. At 3-0, the result was a travesty for Athlones warriors who were denied any consolation when Albertosi brought off a fine save from Nicholson in the dying moments. It had been heroic but, gallingly, all the scores came directly from the self-destruct button.

The part-timers had performed way beyond their station and earned the begrudging admiration of the Italians. Humphries was accorded an unique honour, an opposition player applauded from the pitch at fiercely partisan San Siro and achieving favourable comparison with George Best among sections of the Italian media.

"For 63 minutes," wrote the Irish Times, *"Athlone refused to die. Chasing, runing, often presumptuous enough to put their foot on the ball and invite the lunging tackle, the Irishmen slowly, incredibly turned the carnival atmosphere into one of acute tension. Jubilation hardened to frustration as Milan probed in vain for the gaps which aching legs were beginning to leave."* Derek Potter of the Daily Express, said *"La Scala remembers Irish tenor John McCormack alongside Gigli in it's roll of honour. San Siro should not easily forget the courage, skill and calm of Athlone's League of Ireland part-timers in the UEFA Cup."*

Athlone had performed with honour and dignity, with passion and pride, with skill and self-belief. With just a little luck in the first leg they might have caused a sensation but they had fearlessly grabbed the lions tail and shaken it hard. They had proven their manager's belief that Irish players had skill to match the best and that only professional fitness and the ability to convert chances to goals were the key differences at European level football. They had shown that League of Ireland clubs had a right to participate in UEFA competitions and with the correct attitude Irish teams need fear nobody. Athlone Town had kept AC Milan scoreless for over two and a half hours of hard competitive combat during which time they were never out of their depth. It was an achievement for all associated with the club and a lesson for their fellows. They had climbed from the anonymity of the Leinster Junior League to base camp at San Siro's everest in just a few short years. It was the stuff of comic book fiction. It was also the stuff of football fact.

1st Round/1st Leg 18 Sep. '75 at St. Mel's Park
    Athlone Town (1) **3** *(Martin 3, Davis 66, 85)*
    Valerengens (1) **1** *(Olsen 12)*
Athlone: O'Brien, Duffy, Smith, Wood, Stephenson, Larkin, Minnock, Humphries, Martin (Healy 54), Davis, Daly.
Valerengens: Blomfeldt, Hansen (Skojli 48), Brekke, Haslie, Jorgensen, Edner, Eriksen, Hoedvedt, Olavson (Foss 33), Karlsen, Olsen
    Referee: B. Hoppenbrouwer (Hol.)
    Att: 4,000 approx.

1st Round/2nd Leg 1 Oct. '75 at Ullevaal Stadium, Oslo
    Valerengens (0) **1** *(Eriksen 54)*
    Athlone Town (1) **1** *(Martin 20)*
Valerengens: Blomfeldt, Hansen, Brekke, Haslie, Jorgensen, Edner, Eriksen, Foss, Olavson (Hyving 76), Karlsen, Olsen
Athlone: O'Brien, Duffy, Smith, Healy, Stephenson, Larkin, Minnock, Humphries, Martin (Wood 81), Davis, Daly.
    Referee: H. Johansson (Sweden)
    Att: 800 approx.
(Athlone Town won 4-2 on aggregate)

2nd Round/1st Leg 22 Oct. '75 at St. Mel's Park
    Athlone Town 0
    AC Milan 0
Athlone: O'Brien, Duffy, Smith, Wood, Stephenson, Larkin, (Barnicle 86), Minnock, Humphries, Martin (Healy 60), Davis, Daly.
Milan: Albertosi, Anquilletti, Maldera, Bet, Turone, Scala, Gorin, Benetti, Calloni (Sabadini 45), Bigon, Vincenzi
    Referee: U. Sorenson (Denmark)
    Att: 9,000 approx.

2nd Round/2nd Leg 5 Nov. '75 at San Siro Stadium, Milan
    AC Milan (0) **3** *(Vincenzi 64, Benetti 70, 80 (pen))*
    Athlone Town 0
Milan: Albertosi, Sabadini (Anquilletti 75), Maldera, Turone, Bet, Scala, Gorin, Benetti, Bigon, Rivera, Vincenzi (Calloni 75)
Athlone: O'Brien, Duffy, Smith, Wood, Stephenson, Minnock, Larkin, Humphries, Martin, Davis (Nicholson 75), Daly (Healy 65).
    Referee: P. Gheti (Romania)
    Att: 42,500 approx.
(Milan won 3-0 on aggregate)

The Championship Review
A Rovers Return

After all the trauma of recent times, the loss of their spiritual home at Glenmalure Park, and the fall from the great heights of glory days in the 1980's when four consecutive League of Ireland titles were won, this season saw the rehabilitation of Shamrock Rovers completed. Having inherited little more than a name just a few short years ago, with neither a ground nor a team to grace it, this first title in seven years stands as a magnificent tribute to the commitment and foresight of all at this famous club, particularly Chairman John McNamara and his fellow directors. Their decision to entrust the on-field task of recapturing past glories to Ray Treacy, and their determination to allow the ex-Republic of Ireland man ample time in which to succeed, despite the huge pressures resulting from last season's poor form, has been fully vindicated with this fifteenth Championship success. And it was a thoroughly deserved win, their seven poins final margin over Cork City, with whom they had fought a tremendous season long battle, clearly illustrating that. Indeed for all but a couple of weeks of the 1993-94 season it was these two rivals who filled the top two positions in the National League. Once again Cork demonstrated their consistency having now finished first, second (twice) and third in the past four seasons. But on this occasion the 'Hoops,' finding just the right blend of youth and experience, particularly with new signings Alan O'Neill, Terry Eviston, Eoin Mullen and Alan Byrne on board, were simply too good for Damien Richardson's charges.

Elsewhere towards the top end of the table it was an excellent season for Tony Mannion's youngsters at Galway who finished a very creditable third, whilst the other surprise packets were newly promoted Monaghan United who greatly impressed in their first ever season of Premier Division football. As for 'Rovers' great Dublin rivals Shelbourne and Bohemians there was little for either to enthuse over, finishing fifth and sixth respectively, while Dundalk had their poorest campaign for many years.

Meanwhile at the opposite end of the spectrum, Limerick failed to maintain their progress from the previous campaign, and their on-going financial difficulties were not helped by a season spent exclusively in the company of Cobh Ramblers and Drogheda United, fighting off the threat of relegation to the First Division. Unfortunately for both the 'Shannonsiders' and Drogheda, it was ultimately to prove a losing battle.

Shamrock Rovers began the season indifferently, taking just one point from a possible six on offer. Having thrashed Galway United 5-0 at the Sportsgrounds, however, they were on their way. Making maximum use of the extra point on offer for a victory this season, thirteen wins in their next sixteen outings, meant that by mid-December, the Dubliners were fully eight points clear of nearest rivals Cork City who themselves had a five point cushion over Shelbourne and Galway. With the prolific goalscoring of another of Treacy's shrewd acquisitions, Steve Geoghegan, who had already notched up a hugely impressive sixteen Championship strikes, the 'Hoops' were looking unstoppable, even at this early stage.

At the bottom of the Premier, a five-nil thrashing at the hands of Cork City in United Park, their seventh defeat in nine games, left Drogheda just a single point ahead of bottom side Limerick who boasted just two wins all season and who had already conceded seven to both of the top sides.

Despite their apparent invincibility approaching the turn of the year, a controversial defeat at great rivals Bohemians on December 17th seemed to badly bruise 'Rovers' confidence, and slowly but surely over the next eight weeks the chasing pack led by Cork City closed in. By mid-February, at the end of a dismal sequence of four consecutive defeats, the last of which came at Bishopstown, the once comfortable lead had been surrendered to Cork who were now ahead on goal difference and had a game in hand. It looked as though the pendulum was swinging south, although with an impressive Galway now just five points adrift of the joint leaders, we were set for an exciting climax to the Championship race.

Meanwhile at the opposite end of things, the weeks had seen little change with Cobh, Drogheda and Limerick in descending order, still filling the crucial three bottom places, with just a single point separating them, but all three were well adrift of next best placed St. Patrick's Athletic. Probably the single most significant day in the entire league season occurred on March 13th when the fortunes of the two main protagonists could not have been more different. For while the 'Hoops' battled magnificently to turn a two goal deficit in Galway into a vital three points, Cork meanwhile had twice squandered the lead in Derry to eventually lose 2-3 in controversial circumstances. The effect of these results were not just to restore 'Rovers' lead but also their confidence. Indeed they would subsequently win each one of their four remaining games to squeeze out the Corkmen's challenge. Having comfortably disposed of both Derry City and Shelbourne, Shamrock Rovers arrived at their penultimate assignment, a re-arranged fixture, again against Shelbourne, this time at the R.D.S. knowing that victory would secure the League title. Anything less would mean their final game against Cork City the following Sunday would constitute a Championship shoot-out.

The very large crowd which turned up at the R.D.S. on March 30th got a good soaking as the downpour which preceeded the game almost led to referee Michael Tomney postponing it. However despite the driving rain he decided to go ahead, and within seven minutes of the start 'Rovers' fans were very glad he had done so, as John Bacon scored the opener after good work by Geoghegan. By the 35th minute they had scored again and looked to be coasting to victory. The goal came when Geoghegan was impeded inside the penalty area by Neville and John Toal made no mistake from the spot kick. On the stroke of half-time a superb drive by Mooney brought 'Shels' back into the frame but, despite their best efforts, some excellent defending, particularly by Berry kept the 'Reds' at bay. As the final whistle blew the 'Hoops' fans breathed a huge sigh of relief. The celebrations could now start in earnest. The ongoing battle to avoid relegation and secure a play-off spot went right down to the wire for all the three protagonists, with amazingly just a single point separating them on the final day of League action. Spice was added with the meeting of Cobh and Drogheda at St. Colman's Park while Limerick travelled to Gortakeegan to take on Billy Bagster's Monaghan United. Unfortunately for the 'Shannonsiders,' despite a brave performance and a consolation score from Fran Hitchcock they were always second best on the day, losing by two goals to one, and so dropped to the lower division for the second time.

Meanwhile a tense affair at St. Colman's was finally settled with only ten minutes remaining, Alan Kane's error in dropping a corner kick punished by an alert Alan O'Neill.

So then, it was Cobh who eventually made it to the play-off where they would in fact meet Finn Harps over two legs, whilst Drogheda relegated for a third time in nine years, joined Limerick in the lower division.

And whilst Cork celebrated joining Shamrock Rovers in the UEFA Cup, Monaghan and Galway likewise did so for their fine campaigns and Cobh for having survived the dreaded drop, it was of course the 'Hoops' fans who really had most to celebrate. It took a 'Rovers' old boy, Cork's manager Damien Richardson, to sum things up nicely. *"Rovers were worthy champions,"* he said, *"we pushed them hard but they deservedly got there in the end, both sides are a credit to the League."*

Splashdown!
John Toal wades past Shelbourne's Darren Kelly as Rovers clinch the title (The Star)

Team Multi-Channel
For all the best in Local Sport,
'Weekend Sport'
every Monday and Friday night on
The Cork Local Channel
6.30pm, 8.00pm, 9.30pm & 11.00pm

First and Last ... almost!
Action from Bray v Sligo at the Carlisle Grounds.
Sligo finished as Champions, Bray were re-elected. (The Star)

165

First Division Championship Review
A speedy return for Sligo

Having failed to halt Sligo Rovers slide out of Premier Division football, following his appointment the previous season, manager Willie McStay and his side certainly made up for that disappointment with a truly remarkable campaign this time round. Not only did Sligo capture their first ever Shield title, and more prestigiously, a glorious second F.A.I. cup success, but they also bounced right back in the League, to clinch the First Division title, and so regain their place amongst the country's elite. In fact this was Sligo's third occasion on which to gain promotion from the lower division, in just eight seasons, though their first as champions.

What made their success all the more remarkable was the fact that their early season form was so mediocre as to give no clue of the triumphs ahead. Indeed the divisional runners-up Athlone Town had for much of the campaign looked virtually unstoppable after opening with a superb run of nineteen consecutive games unbeaten. However, that total had included no fewer than ten draws, and so when the 'Westerners' finally got into the groove, given that a win now yielded three points, they stormed to the top of the table with surprising speed. At the finish both sides filled the two automatic promotion places with relative ease, whilst below them a very interesting battle for the play-off spot developed, with U.C.D. and Finn Harps eventually taking the fight right to the final day of league action.

At the opposite end of the table St. James's Gate, despite appointing the experienced Pat Byrne to the managerial chair in mid-season, failed to avoid the disappointment of propping up the others by a considerable margin, for a second consecutive year. Above them, avoidance of the second re-election spot eventually came down to a straight fight between Kilkenny City and Bray Wanderers. Unfortunately for the 'Seasiders,' having fallen from the heights of FAI Cup and European glory just a few short years ago, it was they who suffered the ignominy of having to re-apply for membership. Elsewhere Longford Town, despite a brief showing in the play-off frame during February, Waterford United and Home Farm all experienced very mediocre seasons.

Having supplemented their local crop of promising youngsters with the experience of Paul Brady, Tommy Keane and Barry Murphy amongst others, it was Athlone Town who blazed an early trail, Michael O'Connor's side enjoying a seven point advantage over a solid if unspectacular U.C.D., with a third of the season completed in early December. Sligo at this point, having had floodlights installed at the 'Showgrounds' in late November, a move which was to capture the imagination of the town's soccer going public, were a further two points adrift. However, they were just beginning to get into their stride, and of their eight home games under lights, seven would end in victory, the other being a 2-2 draw with fellow leaders Athlone. Meanwhile at the bottom of the table things were already taking on a familiar look with St. James's Gate in last position, a point adrift of Bray.

On February 13th following a one-nil home win over Waterford United, their fourth in succession, Sligo finally overtook the 'Midlanders' at the top of the table, to lead on goal difference, with now just six series of matches remaining. Behind the leading two, the battle for third place continued apace between Harps, U.C.D. and now Longford, although defeats to both of the top two sides in the next fortnight ensured that the hopes of the Abbeycartron side were short lived. By now St. James's Gate had fallen six points behind Bray who were themselves struggling to keep in touch with the mid table sides.

The First Division's 'match of the season' took place on March 16th when Athlone played host to Willie McStay's team, for a game which was likely to prove the Championship decider, even if both sides still had two games left to play. In the event it was the visitors who were in command throughout, goals from Gabbiadini and Boyle confirming their superiority, whilst a week later at the 'Showgrounds' Eddie Annand's single strike against struggling Bray was sufficient to give the 'Westerners' the title. The following day at the Regional Sports Centre in Waterford, Donal Golden's goal for Athlone confirmed their promotion to the Premier Division also.

In the ongoing battle for third spot U.C.D., two points in arrears and with a game in hand against Bray, needed to win both remaining games to be sure of overtaking Finn Harps. However, a surprise win for the 'Seasiders' at the Carlyle Grounds on March 31st shocked the 'Students,' and with both clubs successful on the final day, U.C.D. against champions Sligo, and Harps' against Athlone, it was the Donegal outfit who earned the right to challenge Cobh Ramblers for a place in the Premier Division.

At the bottom Bray's surprise win against U.C.D. gave them a slight chance in their final game at Kilkenny, of relegating the 'Cats' to a re-election place. However, a one-all draw at Buckley Park, did not prove sufficient for the Co. Wicklow side to succeed.

The first play-off game took place at Finn Park on April 9th, with the bulk of a large 2,500 attendance hoping to see 'Harps' take a first step towards ending nine years of exile in the lower division. A tough uncompromising affair was settled ten minutes from the break when a superbly struck 25 yarder from midfielder John Gerard McGettigan flew past Henderson in the Cobh goal. Given the chances for the home side in the game, however, a single goal return, was for them a disappointing one. The second game at St. Colman's Park a week later was nicely set up.

The breakthrough goal in the game at Cobh came after twenty five minutes play, and crucially it came to the homesters as Kevin Kelly's accurate corner kick was powerfully headed home at the near post by Seán Francis. Within ten minutes a bad error from Harps' keeper Norman Costelloe was punished by the veteran Paul Bannon and with this goal the Donegalmen visibly wilted. In the 73rd minute the old warhorse Bannon once again stole it at the near post to head in another Kelly corner, and so Cobh avoided the drop to the First Division whilst Harps after a brave effort must wait at least another year. However the congratulations must in the main go to Athlone and in particular Sligo Rovers who bounced back in style in 1993-94.

Premier Division Table 1993/94
(after first series 22 matches - 9 Jan. 1994)

	HOME P	W	D	L	F	A	AWAY P	W	D	L	F	A	TOTAL P	W	D	L	F	A	Pts.
Shamrock Rovers	11	9	1	1	25	7	11	6	2	3	18	9	22	15	3	4	43	16	48
*Cork City	10	5	3	2	14	7	11	6	2	3	26	16	21	11	5	5	40	23	38
*Shelbourne	11	8	1	2	16	5	10	2	5	3	16	19	21	10	6	5	32	24	36
Galway United	11	4	4	3	13	12	11	5	3	3	17	14	22	9	7	6	30	26	34
Bohemians	11	7	2	2	15	5	11	1	5	5	8	12	22	8	7	7	23	17	31
Derry City	11	4	4	3	11	10	11	4	3	4	10	11	22	8	7	7	21	21	31
Monaghan United	11	6	2	3	16	12	11	3	1	7	11	15	22	9	3	10	27	27	30
Dundalk	11	1	5	5	12	16	11	6	3	2	13	4	22	7	8	7	25	20	29
St. Patrick's Athletic	11	2	6	3	14	14	11	4	3	4	10	10	22	6	9	7	24	24	27
Cobh Ramblers	11	2	3	6	8	15	11	3	1	7	12	19	22	5	4	13	20	34	22
Limerick	11	1	3	7	7	24	11	2	5	4	8	16	22	3	8	11	15	40	17
Drogheda United	11	1	2	8	8	30	11	3	3	5	8	14	22	4	5	13	16	44	17

* Cork City v Shelbourne was not played until March 20th, 1994

Group A - Final Table

	HOME P	W	D	L	F	A	AWAY P	W	D	L	F	A	TOTAL P	W	D	L	F	A	Pts.
Shamrock Rovers	16	12	1	3	35	15	16	9	2	5	27	15	32	21	3	8	62	30	66
Cork City	16	10	4	2	29	13	16	7	4	5	31	23	32	17	8	7	60	36	59
Galway United	16	6	4	6	22	23	16	8	4	4	25	19	32	14	8	10	47	42	56
Derry City	16	7	6	3	20	13	16	5	4	7	17	22	32	12	10	10	37	35	46
Shelbourne	16	8	3	5	18	13	16	3	7	6	24	29	32	11	10	11	42	42	43
Bohemians	16	8	3	5	20	12	16	3	5	8	14	23	32	11	8	13	34	35	41

Group B - Final Table

	HOME P	W	D	L	F	A	AWAY P	W	D	L	F	A	TOTAL P	W	D	L	F	A	Pts.
Monaghan United	16	8	5	3	23	17	16	5	3	8	18	21	32	13	8	11	41	38	47
Dundalk	16	3	7	6	19	19	16	7	6	3	18	8	32	10	13	9	37	27	43
St. Patrick's Athletic	16	3	7	6	17	24	16	6	5	5	15	14	32	9	12	11	32	38	39
Cobh Ramblers	16	4	4	8	12	19	16	4	4	8	19	22	32	8	8	16	31	41	32
Limerick	16	4	5	7	14	28	16	2	6	8	9	22	32	6	11	15	23	50	29
Drogheda United	16	3	4	9	13	34	16	4	3	9	13	24	32	7	7	18	26	58	28

First Division 1993/94

	|HOME|					|AWAY|					|TOTAL|					
	P	W	D	L	F	A	P	W	D	L	F	A	P	W	D	L	F	A	Pts
Sligo Rovers	13	7	5	1	26	10	14	7	3	4	16	10	27	14	8	5	42	20	50
Athlone Town	13	5	6	2	18	14	14	6	7	1	16	8	27	11	13	3	34	22	46
Finn Harps	14	8	5	1	19	8	13	3	4	6	16	27	27	11	9	7	35	35	42
U.C.D.	14	5	5	4	21	12	13	5	5	3	16	11	27	10	10	7	37	23	40
Longford Town	14	7	3	4	22	19	13	2	4	7	13	20	27	9	7	11	35	39	34
Home Farm	14	6	5	3	22	16	13	1	6	6	12	23	27	7	11	9	34	39	32
Waterford United	13	4	6	3	19	13	14	2	7	5	13	20	27	6	13	8	32	33	31
Kilkenny City	14	3	8	3	18	19	13	2	7	4	13	23	27	5	15	7	31	42	30
Bray Wanderers	13	3	7	3	6	12	14	1	8	5	11	15	27	4	15	8	17	27	27
St. James's Gate	13	0	7	6	9	17	14	1	6	7	14	24	27	1	13	13	23	41	16

Promotion / Relegation Play-Off

First Leg Apr. 9th at Finn Park
Finn Harps (1) 1 *(McGettigan 35)*

Cobh Ramblers 0

Cobh won 3-1 on aggregate.

Second Leg Apr. 16 at St. Colman's Park
Cobh Ramblers (2) 3 *(Francis 24, Bannon 36, 73)*

Finn Harps 0

Mick Neville can't Mark Ennis
Shelbourne's experienced defender has trouble with the Saints' striker (The Star)

Premier Division Results 1993/94

	1	2	3	4	5	6	7	8	9	10	11	12
1. Bohemians	✕	2-0	3-4 1-1	2-0 1-3	0-1	1-0	3-0 0-1	1-0	0-0	0-0	2-0 1-2	1-0 2-0
2. Cobh Ramblers	0-0	✕	2-1	1-3	1-2 1-0	0-2 1-1	0-2	0-0 1-0	2-0 1-2	0-1 0-1	1-3	1-1
3. Cork City	2-0 3-1	2-0	✕	1-0 4-2	1-1	0-1	1-2 2-0	3-0	1-0	1-1	2-2 2-1	3-1 1-1
4. Derry City	3-0 4-0	2-0	0-1 3-2	✕	1-1	1-4	0-0 1-1	0-0	1-0	2-0	0-0 1-0	1-4 0-0
5. Drogheda U.	0-4 2-1	1-3	0-5	0-1	✕	0-3 0-2	1-4	0-2 0-0	1-4 1-1	1-1 2-0	2-1	2-2
6. Dundalk	1-1	0-2 0-0	2-2	2-2	0-1 4-0	✕	0-0	0-0 2-0	1-3 1-1	0-2 0-2	1-2	5-1
7. Galway U.	1-1 3-1	4-0	0-0 0-1	2-1 2-1	2-0	0-0	✕	1-2	1-0	1-2	0-5 2-3	1-1 2-5
8. Limerick	0-0	1-5 0-0	1-7	0-1	1-1 1-0	0-1 2-1	0-3	✕	2-3 2-1	2-1 2-2	0-2	0-0
9. Monaghan U.	1-0	2-1 1-1	2-1	1-1	1-0 3-2	1-0 1-1	3-1	0-0 2-1	✕	1-2 0-0	0-1	4-5
10. St.Patrick's Ath.	0-0	1-1 0-5	3-4	0-0	4-1 1-3	0-0 0-0	2-3	1-1 1-0	1-0 1-2	✕	0-2	2-2
11. Shamrock R.	2-1 1-2	3-1	3-0 2-0	0-1 3-0	2-0	0-0	3-1 2-5	7-3	2-1	1-0	✕	2-0 2-1
12. Shelbourne	2-1 0-2	1-0	0-1 1-1	2-0 1-1	1-0	1-2	1-1 0-1	3-0	3-0	1-0	1-0 0-3	✕

First Division Results 1993/94

	1	2	3	4	5	6	7	8	9	10
1. Athlone Town	✕	1-1 0-0	1-0	2-2 1-1	0-0 2-3	2-1	3-1	2-1 0-2	2-0	2-2
2. Bray Wanderers	0-0	✕	0-4	1-0 0-0	1-1	2-1	0-0 0-0	0-3	0-2 1-0	1-1 0-0
3. Finn Harps	2-2 1-0	2-1 1-0	✕	2-0	1-1	1-1 3-1	1-0	0-1 2-0	0-0	2-0 1-1
4. Home Farm	1-1	3-2	3-1 1-1	✕	1-1	1-0 3-2	2-2 3-1	0-1 0-1	0-0	3-0 1-3
5. Kilkenny City	1-3	1-1 1-1	1-1 1-1	1-1 0-0	✕	3-1	2-0	1-4	3-2 1-1	2-2 0-1
6. Longford Town	0-0 0-2	1-0 1-1	2-0	3-2	2-1 3-1	✕	1-4 5-3	0-0	1-2 1-2	2-1
7. St. James's Gate	0-2 0-1	1-1	1-1 1-2	2-3	2-2 1-1	0-1	✕	0-0	0-2	0-0 1-1
8. Sligo Rovers	2-2	1-1 1-0	4-1	4-0	0-1 3-0	1-1 1-0	1-1 3-1	✕	1-1	4-1
9. U.C.D.	0-1 0-0	1-2	4-1 2-3	3-1 0-0	7-1	1-2	0-0 0-0	1-1 1-0	✕	1-0
10. Waterford U.	1-1 0-1	0-0	6-0	4-2	0-0	2-2 0-0	3-1	2-1 0-1	1-1 0-3	✕

MOST GOALS SCORED IN A SEASON
(League of Ireland 1921 - 1994)

Goals scored	Season	Team	No. of Games	Ave. per Game	Final Position	Top Scorer
77	1922/23	Shamrock Rovers	22	3.50	1st	(27 *Bob Fullam*)
76	1937/38	Waterford	22	3.45	2nd	(21 *Tim O'Keeffe*)
74	1977/78	Bohemians	30	2.46	1st	(24 *Turlough O'Connor*)
73	1935/36	Bohemians	22	3.29	1st	(16 *Benny Gaughran*)
72	1922/23	Shelbourne	22	3.27	2nd	(26 *Ralph Ardiff*)
72	1922/23	Bohemians	22	3.27	3rd	(14 *Christy Robinson*)
71	1961/62	Cork Celtic	23*	3.09	2nd	(18 *Donal Leahy*)
70	1931/32	Shamrock Rovers	22	3.18	1st	(18 *Paddy Moore*)
70	1971/72	Cork Hibernians	26	2.69	2nd	(22 *Tony Marsden*)

(First Division 1985 - 1993)

60	1989/90	Waterford United	29**	2.06	1st	(13 *Pascal Keane*)

* Including League Play-Off game.   ** Including two Play-Off games.

Highest Goal Average per game in a Season

In the 1944/45 season **Cork United** remained unbeaten over their 14 Championship games, scoring a whopping 59 goals on the way to a fourth league success in five seasons. This magnificent total, which included a personal haul of twenty-six goals for Séan McCarthy represents a goal average per game of (4.21), the highest ever in League of Ireland history.

Cork Hibernians 1971-72
Top scorer Tony Marsden third from right, back row   (EB)

STATISTICS 1993/94

Premier Division

Games Played	:	192
Home Wins	:	76
Total Goals	:	472
Most Frequent Scoreline:	1-0 (36 times)	

Away wins : 63 Draws : 53
Av. per game : 2.46 1992/93 Av. : 2.06

Biggest Wins
7 - 1	Cork City	v Limerick (A)	26 Sep.
7 - 3	Shamrock Rov.	v Limerick (H)	17 Oct.
5 - 0	Cobh Ramblers	v St. Pat's Ath. (A)	26 Mar.
	Cork City	v Drogheda Utd. (A)	12 Dec.
	Shamrock Rov.	v Galway Utd. (A)	4 Sep.

Highest Agg.Score
7 - 3	Shamrock Rov. v Limerick	17 Oct.
4 - 5	Monaghan Utd. v Shelbourne	3 Oct.

Most Goals in a Match (3)
Liam Coyle (Derry City)	v Bohemians (H)	3-0	12 Dec.
Stephen Geoghegan (Shamrock Rovers)	v Cobh Ramblers (H)	3-0	31 Oct.
Derek McGrath (Shamrock Rovers)	v Limerick (H)	7-3	17 Oct.
Barry O'Connor (Shelbourne)	v Galway United (A)	5-2	2 Apr.
John Toal (Shamrock Rovers)	v Galway United (A)	5-0	4 Sep.

Top Scorers:
23	Stephen Geoghegan	(Shamrock Rovers)
15	Pat Morley	(Cork City)
14	John Brennan	(Galway United)
12	Donnie Farragher	(Galway United)
11	Tommy Gaynor	(Cork City)
	Paul Newe	(Monaghan United)
10	John Toal	(Shamrock Rovers)

Stephen Geoghegan
Top Premier marksman (The Star)

John "Jumbo" Brennan
Topped the Galway goalcharts (GU)

First Division

Games Played	:	135
Home Wins	:	48
Away wins	:	30
Draws	:	57
Total Goals	:	320
Av. per game	:	2.37
1992/93 Av.	:	2.53

Most Frequent Scoreline: 1-1 (28 times)

Biggest Wins : 7-1 U.C.D. v Kilkenny City (H) 28 Nov.
6-0 Waterford Utd. v Finn Harps (H) 28 Nov.

Highest Agg.Score : 7-1 U.C.D. v Kilkenny City (H) 28 Nov.
5-3 Longford T. v St. James's Gate (H) 20 Mar.

Most Goals in a Match:
(4) Richie Parsons (Longford T.) v St. James's Gate (H) 5-3 20 Mar.
(3) Colum Kavanagh (St. James's Gate) v Longford Town (A) 4-1 14 Nov.
(3) Ger Houlahan (Sligo Rovers) v Bray Wanderers (A) 3-0 16 Jan.
(3) Darren Lonergan (Waterford Utd.) v Finn Harps (H) 6-0 28 Nov.
(3) Paul Stokes (Waterford Utd.) v Home Farm (H) 4-2 21 Nov.

Top Scorers:
16 Karl Gannon (Home Farm)
13 Darren O'Brien (U.C.D.)
11 Richie Parsons (Longford Town)
10 Eddie Annand (Sligo Rovers)
10 Damien Dunleavy (Finn Harps)
10 Colum Kavanagh (St. James's Gate)

3 League Wins:
Athlone Town v St. James's Gate (H) 3-1, (A) 2-0, 1-0
Finn Harps v Bray Wanderers (H) 2-1, 1-0, (A) 4-0
Sligo Rovers v Home Farm (H) 4-0, (A) 1-0, 1-0

3 League Draws:
Athlone Town v Bray Wanderers (H) 1-1, 0-0, (A) 0-0
Athlone Town v Home Farm (H) 2-2, 1-1, (A) 1-1
Bray Wanderers v St. James's Gate (H) 0-0, 0-0, (A) 1-1
Bray Wanderers v Waterford United (H) 1-1, 0-0, (A) 0-0
Kilkenny City v Bray Wanderers (H) 1-1, 1-1, (A) 1-1
Kilkenny City v Home Farm (H) 1-1, 1-1, (A) 1-1
Kilkenny City v Finn Harps (H) 1-1, 0-0, (A) 1-1

Karl Gannon
First Division top gun and club record
(The Star)

Colum Kavanagh
Among the goals despite the 'Gates struggles (PM)

League of Ireland Championship 1921/22 to 1993/94

Season	Winners	P	W	D	L	F	A	Pts	Runners-Up	Pts.
1921-22	St. James's Gate	14	11	1	2	31	8	23	Bohemians	21
1922-23	Shamrock Rovers	22	18	3	1	77	19	39	Shelbourne	34
1923-24	Bohemians	18	16	0	2	56	20	32	Shelbourne	28
1924-25	Shamrock Rovers	18	13	5	0	67	12	31	Bohemians	28
1925-26	Shelbourne	18	14	3	1	65	23	31	Shamrock Rovers	29
1926-27	Shamrock Rovers	18	14	4	0	60	20	32	Shelbourne	29
1927-28	Bohemians	18	15	1	2	53	20	31	Shelbourne	28
1928-29	Shelbourne	18	16	1	1	49	12	33	Bohemians	32
1929-30	Bohemians	18	14	2	2	51	18	30	Shelbourne	29
1930-31	Shelbourne	22	13	5	4	52	22	31	Dundalk	28
1931-32	Shamrock Rovers	22	13	6	3	70	34	32	Cork	29
1932-33	Dundalk	18	13	3	2	44	21	29	Shamrock Rovers	24
1933-34	Bohemians	18	11	5	2	38	23	27	Cork	26
1934-35	Dolphin	18	12	4	2	48	21	28	St. James's Gate	27
1935-36	Bohemians	22	17	2	3	73	27	36	Dolphin	33
1936-37	Sligo Rovers	22	16	2	4	68	30	34	Dundalk	24
1937-38	Shamrock Rovers	22	14	4	4	71	47	32	Waterford	31
1938-39	Shamrock Rovers	22	16	4	2	60	32	36	Sligo Rovers	27
1939-40	St. James's Gate	22	17	2	3	63	27	36	Shamrock Rovers	30
1940-41	Cork United	20	13	4	3	50	23	30	Waterford	30 (1)
1941-42	Cork United	18	13	4	1	54	20	30	Shamrock Rovers	28
1942-43	Cork United	18	12	3	3	42	14	27	Dundalk	26
1943-44	Shelbourne	14	9	3	2	46	20	21	Limerick	20
1944-45	Cork United	14	11	0	3	59	24	22	Limerick	17
1945-46	Cork United	14	9	3	2	46	20	21	Drumcondra	19
1946-47	Shelbourne	14	8	3	3	34	24	19	Drumcondra	18
1947-48	Drumcondra	14	7	4	3	29	22	18	Dundalk	17
1948-49	Drumcondra	18	12	5	1	34	23	29	Shelbourne	23
1949-50	Cork Athletic	18	10	5	3	43	26	25	Drumcondra	25
1950-51	Cork Athletic	18	12	2	4	46	22	26	Sligo Rovers	25
1951-52	St. Patrick's Ath.	22	16	2	4	59	34	34	Shelbourne	31
1952-53	Shelbourne	22	12	6	4	46	24	30	Drumcondra	29
1953-54	Shamrock Rovers	22	11	8	3	44	20	30	Evergreen United	28
1954-55	St. Patrick's Ath.	22	17	2	3	62	31	36	Waterford	33
1955-56	St. Patrick's Ath.	22	16	2	4	61	34	34	Shamrock Rovers	31
1956-57	Shamrock Rovers	22	15	6	1	68	24	36	Drumcondra	31
1957-58	Drumcondra	22	15	3	4	51	23	33	Shamrock Rovers	31
1958-59	Shamrock Rovers	22	15	4	3	58	29	34	Evergreen United	29
1959-60	Limerick	22	15	0	7	46	26	30	Cork Celtic	28
1960-61	Drumcondra	22	16	1	5	59	21	33	St. Patrick's Ath.	32
1961-62	Shelbourne	22	15	5	2	55	23	35	Cork Celtic	35 (2)
1962-63	Dundalk	18	9	6	3	39	23	24	Waterford	23
1963-64	Shamrock Rovers	22	14	7	1	68	27	35	Dundalk	30
1964-65	Drumcondra	22	14	4	4	35	22	32	Shamrock Rovers	31
1965-66	Waterford	22	16	4	2	53	26	36	Shamrock Rovers.	34
1966-67	Dundalk	22	15	4	3	54	19	34	Bohemians	27
1967-68	Waterford	22	16	2	4	59	18	34	Dundalk	30
1968-69	Waterford	22	16	4	2	68	30	36	Shamrock Rovers	31
1969-70	Waterford	26	16	6	4	55	33	38	Shamrock Rovers	36

174

1970-71	Cork Hibernians	26	12 11 3	38 17	35	Shamrock Rovers	35	(3)
1971-72	Waterford	26	21 2 3	66 35	44	Cork Hibernians	40	
1972-73	Waterford	26	20 2 4	67 21	42	Finn Harps	41	
1973-74	Cork Celtic	26	18 6 2	50 25	42	Bohemians	38	
1974-75	Bohemians	26	18 6 2	36 12	42	Athlone Town	33	
1975-76	Dundalk	26	15 10 1	54 26	40	Finn Harps	36	
1976-77	Sligo Rovers	26	18 3 5	48 20	39	Bohemians	38	
1977-78	Bohemians	30	17 10 3	74 25	44	Finn Harps	42	
1978-79	Dundalk	30	19 7 4	57 25	45	Bohemians	43	
1979-80	Limerick United	30	20 7 3	67 24	47	Dundalk	46	
1980-81	Athlone Town	30	23 5 2	67 22	51	Dundalk	45	
1981-82	Dundalk	30	20 6 4	61 24	80	Shamrock Rovers	76	(4)
1982-83	Athlone Town	26	20 5 1	61 24	65	Drogheda United	49	(5)
1983-84	Shamrock Rovers	26	19 4 3	64 15	42	Bohemians	36	
1984-85	Shamrock Rovers	30	22 5 3	63 21	49	Bohemians	43	

Premier Division

1985-86	Shamrock Rovers	22	15 3 4	44 17	33	Galway United	31	
1986-87	Shamrock Rovers	22	18 3 1	51 16	39	Dundalk	30	
1987-88	Dundalk	33	19 8 6	54 32	46	St. Patrick's Ath.	45	
1988-89	Derry City	33	24 5 4	70 21	53	Dundalk	51	
1989-90	St. Patrick's Ath.	33	22 8 3	51 22	52	Derry City	49	
1990-91	Dundalk	33	22 8 3	51 17	52	Cork City	50	
1991-92	Shelbourne	33	21 7 5	57 29	49	Derry City	44	
1992-93	Cork City	38	19 10 9	53 38	48	Bohemians	46	(7)
1993-94	Shamrock Rovers	32	21 3 8	62 30	66	Cork City	59	(5)

First Division

1985-86	Bray Wanderers	18	11 6 1	30 10	28	Sligo Rovers	27	
1986-87	Derry City	18	16 1 1	45 14	33	Shelbourne	27	
1987-88	Athlone Town	27	19 1 7	42 22	39	Cobh Ramblers	38	
1988-89	Drogheda United	27	16 7 4	38 22	39	U.C.D.	34	
1989-90	Waterford United	27	16 5 6	58 28	37	Sligo Rovers	37	(6)
1990-91	Drogheda United	27	15 11 1	38 14	41	Bray Wanderers	38	
1991-92	Limerick City	27	14 10 3	47 27	38	Waterford United	33	
1992-93	Galway United	27	16 6 5	56 27	38	Cobh Ramblers	32	
1993-94	Sligo Rovers	27	14 8 5	42 20	50	Athlone Town	46	(5)

Summary of LOI / Premier Division Winners

15 Shamrock Rovers; 8 Dundalk; 7 Bohemians; 6 Waterford; 5 Cork United, Drumcondra; 4 St. Patrick's Athletic; 2 Athone Town, Cork Athletic, Limerick/Limerick United, St. James's Gate, Sligo Rovers; 1 Cork Celtic, Cork City, Cork Hibernians, Derry City, Dolphin

Summary of First Division Winners

2 Drogheda United
1 Athlone Town, Bray Wanderers, Derry City, Galway United, Limerick City, Sligo Rovers, Waterford United

** Notes **

(1) Cork United awarded the Title: Waterford players in dispute over payment for the play off.
(2) Shelbourne won play-off (1-0)   (3) Cork Hibernians won play-off (3-1)
(4) 4 Pts Away win, 3 Pts Home win, 2 Pts Away Draw, 1 Pt. Home Draw.
(5) 3 Pts Win, 1 Pt Draw.   (6) Waterford Utd. won play-off (2-1) on agg.
(7) After two play-off series

Football League of Ireland Hotshots

	Top Scorer	Club	Goals	
1921-22	Jack Kelly	(St. James's Gate)	11	
22-23	Bob Fullam	(Shamrock Rovers)	27	Club Record
23-24	Dave Roberts	(Bohemians)	20	
24-25	Billy Farrell	(Shamrock Rovers)	25	
25-26	Billy Farrell	(Shamrock Rovers)	24	
26-27	David Byrne	(Shamrock Rovers)	17	
	John McMillan	(Shelbourne)	17	
27-28	Charlie Heinemann	(Fordsons)	24	Club Record
28-29	Eddie Carroll	(Dundalk)	17	
29-30	Johnny Ledwidge	(Shelbourne)	16	
30-31	Alexander Hair	(Shelbourne)	29	Club Record
31-32	Pearson Ferguson	(Cork)	21	
	Jack Forster	(Waterford)	21	
32-33	George Ebbs	(St. James's Gate)	20	
33-34	Alf Rigby	(St. James's Gate)	13	
34-35	Alf Rigby	(St. James's Gate)	17	
35-36	Jimmy Turnbull	(Cork)	37	All-Time Record
36-37	Bob Slater	(Shelbourne 19, Waterford 1)	20	
37-38	Willie Byrne	(St. James's Gate)	25	
38-39	Paddy Bradshaw	(St. James's Gate)	22	
39-40	Paddy Bradshaw	(St. James's Gate)	29	Club Record
40-41	Mick O'Flanagan	(Bohemians)	19	
41-42	Tommy Byrne	(Limerick)	20	Club Record
42-43	Séan McCarthy	(Cork United)	16	
43-44	Séan McCarthy	(Cork United)	16	
44-45	Séan McCarthy	(Cork United)	26	Club Record
45-46	Paddy O'Leary	(Cork United)	15	
46-47	Paddy Coad	(Shamrock Rovers)	11	
	Alf Hanson	(Shelbourne)	11	
47-48	Séan McCarthy	(Cork United)	13	
48-49	Bernard Lester	(Transport)	12	
	Eugene Noonan	(Waterford)	12	
	Paddy O'Leary	(Cork Athletic)	12	
49-50	Dave McCulloch	(Waterford)	19	
50-51	Dessie Glynn	(Drumcondra)	20	
51-52	Shay Gibbons	(St. Patricks Athletic)	26	
52-53	Shay Gibbons	(St. Patricks Athletic)	22	
53-54	Danny Jordan	(Bohemians)	14	
54-55	Jimmy Gauld	(Waterford)	30	Club Record
55-56	Shay Gibbons	(St. Patricks Athletic)	21	
56-57	Tommy Hamilton	(Shamrock Rovers)	15	
	Donal Leahy	(Evergreen United)	15	
57-58	Donal Leahy	(Evergreen United)	16	
58-59	Donal Leahy	(Evergreen United)	22	
59-60	Austin Noonan	(Cork Celtic)	27	Club Record
60-61	Dan McCaffrey	(Drumcondra)	29	Club Record
61-62	Eddie Bailham	(Shamrock Rovers)	21	
62-63	Mick Lynch	(Waterford)	12	
63-64	Eddie Bailham	(Shamrock Rovers)	18	
	Jimmy Hasty	(Dundalk)	18	
	Johnny Kingston	(Cork Hibernians)	18	
64-65	Jackie Mooney	(Shamrock Rovers)	16	
65-66	Mick Lynch	(Waterford)	17	

66-67	Johnny Brooks	(Sligo Rovers)	15	
	Danny Hale	(Dundalk)	15	
67-68	Carl Davenport	(Cork Celtic)	15	
	Ben Hannigan	(Dundalk)	15	
68-69	Mick Leech	(Shamrock Rovers)	19	
69-70	Brendan Bradley	(Finn Harps)	18	
70-71	Brendan Bradley	(Finn Harps)	20	
71-72	Alfie Hale	(Waterford)	22	
	Tony Marsden	(Cork Hibernians)	22	Club Record
72-73	Alfie Hale	(Waterford)	20	
	Terry Harkin	(Finn Harps)	20	
73-74	Terry Flanagan	(Bohemians)	18	
	Turlough O'Connor	(Bohemians)	18	
74-75	Brendan Bradley	(Finn Harps)	21	
75-76	Brendan Bradley	(Finn Harps)	29	Club Record
76-77	Syd Wallace	(Waterford)	16	
77-78	Turlough O'Connor	(Bohemians)	24	Club Record
78-79	John Delamere	(Shelbourne 15, Sligo R 2)	17	
79-80	Alan Campbell	(Shamrock Rovers)	22	
80-81	Eugene Davis	(Athlone Town)	23	Club Record
81-82	Michael O'Connor	(Athlone Town)	22	
82-83	Noel Larkin	(Athlone Town)	18	
83-84	Alan Campbell	(Shamrock Rovers)	24	
84-85	Tommy Gaynor	(Limerick City)	17	
	Michael O'Connor	(Athlone Town)	17	

Premier Division

85-86	Tommy Gaynor	(Limerick City)	15	
86-87	Mick Byrne	(Shamrock Rovers)	12	
87-88	Jonathan Speak	(Derry City)	24	Club & Premier Division Record.
88-89	Billy Hamilton	(Limerick City)	21	Club Record
89-90	Mark Ennis	(St. Patricks Athletic)	19	
90-91	Peter Hanrahan	(Dundalk)	18	
91-92	John Caulfield	(Cork City)	16	
92-93	Pat Morley	(Cork City)	20	Club Record
93-94	Stephen Geoghegan	(Shamrock Rovers)	23	

First Division

85-86	Con McLaughlin	(Finn Harps)	11	
	Harry McLoughlin	(Sligo Rovers)	11	
86-87	Alex Krstic	(Derry City)	18	
87-88	Con McLaughlin	(Finn Harps)	20	1st. Div. Record
88-89	Pat O'Connor	(Home Farm)	14	
89-90	John Ryan	(Bray Wanderers)	16	Club Record
90-91	Jim Barr	(Monaghan United)	12	
	Con McLaughlin	(Finn Harps)	12	
91-92	Con McLaughlin	(Finn Harps)	12	
	Barry Ryan	(Limerick City)	12	
92-93	Mick Byrne	(Monaghan United)	15	Club Record
	Richie Parsons	(Longford Town)	15	Club Record
93-94	Karl Gannon	(Home Farm)	16	Club Record

The Records

Career	235	Brendan Bradley (Harps/Athlone/Sligo/Derry) 1969-86
Season	37	Jimmy Turnbull (Cork FC) 1935-36
Match	7	Jimmy Munro (Cork FC) v St. James's Gate 7-3 (A) 2 Feb 31

"The 100 Club"
(All time top scorers in League of Ireland football)

Season 1993/94 saw the inclusion of two more names to this illustrious list - those of *Mick Byrne* and *Pat Morley*. In addition *Michael O'Connor* continued to add to his tally.

235	Brendan Bradley	(Finn Harps, Athlone Town, Sligo Rovers, Derry City)
178	Turlough O'Connor	(Bohemians, Dundalk)
162	Donal Leahy	(Evergreen United/Cork Celtic, Limerick)
156	Johnny Matthews	(Waterford, Limerick United)
153	Alfie Hale	(Waterford, Cork Celtic, St. Patrick's Athletic, Limerick, Thurles Town)
143	Paul McGee	(Sligo Rovers, Shamrock Rovers, Waterford, Dundalk, Galway United, Athlone Town, Finn Harps)
141	Eric Barber	(Shelbourne, Shamrock Rovers)
135	Sean McCarthy	(Cork United, Evergreen United)
132	Mick Leech	(Shamrock Rovers, Waterford, Drogheda United)
130	Eugene Davis	(Shamrock Rovers, Athlone Town, St. Patrick's Athletic, Bohemians, U.C.D., Bray Wanderers)
	Jack Fitzgerald	(Waterford, Cork Hibernians)
129	Austin Noonan	(Evergreen Utd/Cork Celtic, Cork Hibernians)
126	Paddy Coad	(Waterford, Shamrock Rovers)
120	Shay Gibbons	(St. Patrick's Athletic, Cork Hibernians, Dundalk)
118	Paddy O'Leary	(Limerick, Cork United, Cork Athletic)
117	Des Kennedy	(Limerick/Limerick United, Galway Rovers, Limerick City, Newcastlewest)
115	David "Babby" Byrne	(Shamrock Rovers, Shelbourne, Brideville)
	Michael O'Connor	(Athlone Town, Shamrock Rovers, Dundalk)
111	Des Glynn	(Drumcondra, Shelbourne)
110	Pat Morley	(Waterford United, Limerick City, Cork City)
109	Paddy Ambrose	(Shamrock Rovers)
	Con McLaughlin	(Finn Harps)
	Ronnie Whelan	(St. Patrick's Athletic, Drogheda)
106	Garry Hulmes	(Sligo Rovers, Limerick United)
105	Tim O'Keeffe	(Cork, Waterford, Cork United)
103	Mick Byrne	(Bohemians, Shelbourne, Shamrock Rovers, Sligo Rovers, Monaghan United)

Note: Several Players in the "100 Club" have also lined out with other League of Ireland sides. The clubs listed here are those with which the players actually scored.

Current Top Scorers in League of Ireland Football
(as at end season 1993-94)

This feature details those players who have scored 50 or more goals in the L.O.I. championship and who made at least one appearance during last season. In both this and an accompanying section on 'All time top scorers' every effort has been made to ensure the accuracy of the information included, however it should be noted that differences of opinion especially concerning the controversial subject of 'own goals' occasionally arise.

Amongst the players listed at the end of the 1992-93 season who did not play League of Ireland football this season were Damien Byrne, Denis Clarke, Dessie Gorman, Vinny McCarthy, Con McLaughlin, Paul McGee and Larry Wyse. New names to the list this time round are *Pat Fenlon* and *Tommy Gaynor*.

Total	Players	Clubs	Debut Scoring Season
115	Michael O'Connor	(Athlone Town, Shamrock Rovers, Dundalk)	1979-80
110	Pat Morley	(Waterford United, Limerick City, Cork City)	1984-85
103	Mick Byrne	(Bohemians, Shelbourne, Shamrock Rovers, Sligo Rovers, Monaghan United)	1979-80
96	Terry Eviston	(Home Farm, Bohemians, Athlone Town, Dundalk, Shamrock Rovers)	1975-76
84	Paul Newe	(Shelbourne, Drogheda United, Dundalk, Cobh Ramblers, Monaghan United)	1982-83
78	Mark Ennis	(Shelbourne, St. Patrick's Athletic, Derry City)	1986-87
75	Liam Buckley	(Shelbourne, Shamrock Rovers)	1978-79
71	John Caulfield	(Cork City)	1986-87
	Paul Doolin	(Bohemians, Shamrock Rovers, Derry City, Shelbourne)	1981-82
64	Derek Swan	(Bohemians, Shamrock Rovers)	1986-87
	Tommy Gaynor	(Limerick United, Shamrock Rovers, Dundalk, Limerick City, Cork City)	1981-82
63	Pádraig Dully	(Athlone Town, Shelbourne)	1985-86
60	Peter Hanrahan	(U.C.D., Limerick City, Dundalk)	1986-87
53	Pat Fenlon	(St. Patrick's Athletic, Bohemians)	1987-88
52	Johnny Walsh	(Limerick/Limerick United, Limerick City)	1976-77

Mark Ennis
One of the National League's ace goalpoachers (St.P.A.)

FAI Cup Joy for Sligo Rovers
Derry denied in North West Derby Final

It was, in many ways, a strange cup year. The competition produced a couple of epics, the Dundalk-Galway replay cliffhanger and most notably the Bohemians-Shamrock Rovers first round mini series; the holders, Shelbourne, were dumped out in their opening defence and league champions Cork City were humbled at Sligo one round later. The minnows, for a second successive season, failed to capture a league scalp. But the '94 FAI Cup may perhaps be best remembered for other reasons such as the toll the weather took with a string of postponed games, several of which caused acrimony due to late announcements. The appalling conditions claimed both semi-finals as victims and the re-fixtures prompted Limerick to threaten to pull out just one step from the decider. Most embarrassing, however, was the ultimate change in venue and date for the Final itself which the FAI insisted would take place at Tolka Park on April 24th. The game, eventually, was at Lansdowne Road three weeks later.

The biggest on-field upset came in the very first game when Limerick, all season long in the relegation zone, beat Shelbourne with a goal from teenager Garrett Ryan. Two attractive all-premier division ties served up tremendous first round fare. Dundalk returned from Galway with a scoreless drawn, the replay was abandoned at half-time but when the sides met again a week later Dundalk overturned a two-goal deficit before Galway's Donnie Farragher, in the dying moments, took the tie to extra-time where Mick Doohan finally settled the issue in favour of the Lilywhites. At Dalymount, Tony Cousins and Stephen Geoghegan exchanged goals and the RDS re-match was heading for a scoreless stalemate when Tommy Byrne popped up to give the Gypsies the lead with just four minutes to go only for Geoghegan to rescue the Hoops in the last seconds. In extra-time Tony O'Connor once again powered Bohs in front but Willie Burke levelled to set up a third instalment. The old Dublin rivals had produced drama, skill and controversy over the three games which were finally decided by a single strike from Cousins which denied Rovers, who were steaming along in the league, any hopes of a possible double run.

Derry City, although displaying indifferent form, were once again among the cup favourites and came from behind to beat a stubborn challenge from Drogheda United while Cobh Ramblers travelled to Waterford and stole a 1-0 victory thanks to a superb display from keeper Stephen Henderson.

In all-First Division clashes Monaghan pipped Longford courtesy of John Coady's goal but replays were required for Finn Harps and Home Farm to oust U.C.D. and Athlone Town.

Sligo, showing scant evidence of what would follow in the weeks ahead needed a freak Declan Boyle effort to stay afloat against non-league Glenmore Celtic and scraped through in the replay at Dalymount. Bray also had a sticky time before out-gunning Leinster Senior League Champions elect Cherry Orchard, a replay and extra-time on the menu before Alan Smith's brace won the day. At Buckley Park the competitions only hat-trick, from John Kelly, helped despatch debutants Casement Celtic while St. James's Gate, with an early salvo were too strong for College Corinthians, a game in which Mark Farrell registered the fastest goal of the tournament.

St. Patrick's Athletic and Cork City had comfortable victories against Garda and Elm Rovers but two sides at least would carry the non-league banner forward, Fermoy, who accounted for much-vaunted Bluebell United, and Glebe North who saw off Whitehall Rangers, both tussles needing replays.

After coming out tops in two classics Dundalk and Bohemians were paired for the third year running at the second round stage with the Dubliners avenging the previous seasons defeat on the strength of goals from Jim Crawford and, once again, Cousins. The shock of the round was reserved for Sligo Rovers who buried Cork City with a quick-fire second half double burst from skipper Gavin Dykes and Ricardo Gabbiadini. St. Pat's, easing into their stride, handed the 'Gate a five-goal hammering while Cobh took care of Kilkenny by the odd goal in three and Derry also brushed aside lower division opposition in Bray Wanderers despite conceding a lead goal. Donal O'Brien struck twice for the Candystripes.

Monaghan United reached the quarter-finals for only the second time when Mick Byrnes effort against Finn Harps proved decisive at Gortakeegan, the original match having finished scoreless. The remaining non-leaguers bit the dust when Mike Kerley's early goal was enough for Limerick to dispose of plucky Fermoy and Glebe North fell to Home Farm.

Derry were favoured with a home tie for the third round in succession and triumphed over luckless St. Patrick's with Garry Heaney's solitary goal on the stroke of half-time. Monaghan were quietly confident of making record progress when paired with lowly Limerick, particularly when Paul Newe cancelled out Johnny Walsh's goal but, within a minute, the battling Shannonsiders had claimed a badly needed tonic when Dave Minihan hit the winner. Once again Sligo humbled premier opponents at the Showgrounds but Cobh Ramblers made a fight of it before submitting to Ger Houlahan's second-half goal. Home Farm, facing a Dublin derby with Bohemians switched to Tolka and almost caused a sensation when Karl Gannon shot the amateurs in front but a late Howie King reply saved the Phibsboro blushes. In the rounds only replay Bohs proved much too strong, crossing the line by 4-1.

The semi-final draw placed the two favourites, Bohemians and Derry, together leaving the longer odds Limerick and Sligo with plenty to play for. There was huge controversy when both games were washed out and the re-fixtures set for midweek. Limerick, facing a trip to Sligo quite literally on a shoestring following an abysmal season and a serious arson attack at Rathbane, claimed they could neither afford to get their players off work nor afford to play such a vital game without them. They threatened to pull out unless the game was re-scheduled for the weekend, which was a free date. Finally, under protest, the Limerick club relented and mustered its depleted forces. Playing with pride and passion, and aware that their home ground was now unsuitable for any possible replay, Limerick battled for a victory which was denied them when Scotsman Eddie Annand struck the games only goal midway through the second period.

The other game did not have such an off the field preamble and Derry City, at last drawn out of the Brandywell, were superb in knocking out Bohemians, Donal O'Brien, just before half-time, securing the precious result to the huge disappointment of the homesters, cup winners only two years before.

The outcome was a novel North West derby final, a situation which forced Merrion Square to switch from Tolka Park's limited capacity to Lansdowne, though work at the Ballsbridge venue meant an unanticipated three week delay, an extension to a season which had already seen both championship programmes completed. An unnecessary hiatus, perhaps, but the FAI were left with little option.

It was an amazing situation for both finalists. Derry had seen the much heralded Roy Coyle vacate the managers chair and former Foyleside favourite Tony O'Doherty stepped in as caretaker boss. It took some time but O'Doherty hauled the club off the floor and while they were never contenders in the league race he had guided his hometown club to an unexpected League Cup triumph. He now stood on the verge of a cup double, from the ashes to the doorstep of Europe.

If the talk in the Maiden City was of doubles, down Showgrounds way the buzz was about the possibility of an unprecedented treble. Willie McStay had been asked to stem the threat of relegation and had failed. Now, in his first full season, he had coaxed and cajoled his rejuvenated squad to the First Division title and the First Division Shield and all of a sudden the FAI Cup, that famous old pot, was within reach. The change of fortune spoke volumes for McStay's powers of motivation.

Carr heads for Home
Gerry Carr gets the vital touch and Sligo get the Cup (The Star)

Final Day arrived with the elements still faithfully unkind as they had been almost throughout the competition, restricting the attendance but not dampening the enthusiasm of either side or their supporters. It was typical derby action from the start with every ball keenly contested but the better chances falling to the Premier outfit. O'Brien glanced a header onto the post and Kevin McKeever lifted the rebound over the crossbar. Sligo replied with a weaving Gabbiadini run which saw his shot blocked before Peter Hutton released Liam Coyle, the skilful striker hitting the target but called back for offside. After 21 minutes O'Brien cracked a shot to the side netting and four minutes later Gabbiadini's chip carried too far after another mazy dribble. Half-time arrived with Sligo's confidence growing but Derry ruing some missed opportunities.

Joe Lawless, a cup winner with Bohemians in '92, had an early Derry chance on the changeover but McLean easily saved after appeals for offside had been turned down. Within minutes Paul Curran miskicked at the other end and Johnny Kenny sent over a fine cross but Gabbiadini headed wide. It was end to end now with a McKeever drive from 25 yards clearing the bar and the evidence growing that a single goal would decide the issue.

That goal arrived on 72 minutes when Eddie Annand's corner skimmed off Gerry Carr's head and ended up in the far corner of Dermot O'Neill's net. It was a score reminiscent of Lawrie Sanchez's famous winner for Wimbledon against Liverpool in the '88 FA Cup final and proved just as decisive. A frustrated Coyle was booked a minute later and Sligo threatened again but O'Neill rushed outside his penalty area to thwart Annand. Derry, the popular fancies, strove gallantly in search of an equaliser and with seven minutes to go it seemed their moment had come. McKeever suddenly found himself clean through on goal and shot from ten yards but Mark McLean saved brilliantly and this was the final inspiration needed to carry his team mates to the last whistle. Sligo's defence was excellently marshalled by young Declan Boyle, a player of strength, pace and enormous potential, and a worthy recipient of the Man of the Match award. The teamwork and covering by McStay's crew was the foundation on which this famous result was achieved and the blue riband was destined for Yeats' country for the first time since 1983 when, by a cruel coincidence, Dermot O'Neill, then of Bohemians, was also the oppositions netminder.

Harp Lager FAI Cup 1993-94

First Round

Feb. 4th	**Shelbourne**	0	
	Limerick	(0) 1	*(Ryan 66')*
Feb. 5th	**Finn Harps**	(1) 1	*(Dunleavy 29)*
	U.C.D.	(1) 1	*(Griffin 19)*
	St. Patricks Athletic	(2) 3	*(Dunne 7, O'Neill 39 Treacy 65)*
	Garda	0	
	Sligo Rovers	(0) 1	*(Boyle 52)*
	Glenmore Celtic	(1) 1	*(Hannigan 41)*
Feb. 6th	**Athlone Town**	0	
	Home Farm	0	
	▽ **Bluebell United**	0	
	Fermoy	0	
	Bohemians	(1) 1	*(Cousins 33)*
	Shamrock Rovers	(1) 1	*(Geoghegan 42)*
	Bray Wanderers	(1) 1	*(Farrell 7)*
	Cherry Orchard	(1) 1	*(Glynn (p) 45)*
●	**Cork City**	(2) 4	*(Glynn 36,60, Morley 44, Caulfield 65)*
	Elm Rovers	(0) 1	*(Curry 89)*
	Derry City	(0) 2	*(Vaudequin 50, O'Brien 61)*
	Drogheda United	(1) 1	*(Ryan 26)*
	Galway United	0	
	Dundalk	0	
	Kilkenny City	(1) 4	*(Kelly 25, 51, 72, Donnelly 79)*
	Casement Celtic	(0) 2	*(Luxford 46, 57)*
	Monaghan United	(0) 1	*(Coady 60)*
	Longford Town	0	
	St. James's Gate	(3) 3	*(Farrell 1, 29, McAvenue 5)*
	College Corinthians	(0) 1	*(Abbott 52)*
Feb. 10th	**Waterford United**	0	
	Cobh Ramblers	(0) 1	*(Francis 58)*
Feb. 13th	**Whitehall Rangers**	0	
▶	Glebe North	0	

First Round Replays

Feb. 9th	☆ **Cherry Orchard**	(1) 1	*(Glynn 80)*
	Bray Wanderers	(1) 2	*(Smith 10, 112)* AET
	Shamrock Rovers	(0) 2	*(Geoghegan 90, Burke 115)*
	Bohemians	(0) 2	*(Byrne 86, O'Connor 103)* AET
Feb. 10th	**Dundalk**	0	
	Galway United	0	*(abandoned at h.t.)*
	✗ **Glenmore Celtic**	(0) 1	*(Flynn 49)*
	Sligo Rovers	(1) 2	*(Annand (p) 14, Carr 82)*
	Home Farm	(0) 2	*(Keddy 67, Vaughan 84)*
	Athlone Town	(1) 1	*(O'Connell 37)*
	U.C.D.	(0) 1	*(O'Brien 65)*
	Finn Harps	(2) 3	*(Lafferty 22, Gallagher 32, Dunleavy 64)*
Feb. 13th	**Fermoy**	(0) 2	*(McMahon 49, Myers 75)*
△	Bluebell United	0	
Feb. 17th	**Dundalk**	(0) 4	*(Coll 57, J.Hanrahan 67, Donnelly 85, Doohan 111)*
	Galway United	(2) 3	*(Brennan 10, Nolan 15, Farragher 88)* AET
Feb. 20th	**Glebe North**	(0) 1	*(Durran 75)*
⊕	Whitehall Rangers	0	

First Round Second Replay

Feb. 16th	**Bohemians**	(0) 1	*(Cousins 49)*
	Shamrock Rovers	0	

Second Round

Feb. 25th	**St. James's Gate**	0	
	St. Patrick's Athletic	(2) 5	*(D.Campbell 17, 86(p), Ennis 35, Jn.Byrne 76, Gormley 88)*
Feb. 26th	**Finn Harps**	0	
	Monaghan United	0	
	Sligo Rovers	(0) 2	*(Dykes 52, Gabbiadini 56)*
	Cork City	0	

Feb. 27th	**Cobh Ramblers**	(1) 2	*(Cragoe 28, K.Kelly 75)*
	Kilkenny City	(0) 1	*(Buttner 55)*
	Derry City	(2) 3	*(O'Brien 44, 45, Coyle 56)*
	Bray Wanderers	(1) 1	*(Gormley 26)*
	△ Fermoy	0	
	Limerick	(1) 1	*(Kerley 11)*
Mar. 3rd	Dundalk	0	
	Bohemians	(1) 2	*(Crawford 45, Cousins 67)*
Mar. 9th	Glebe North	0	
	✪ **Home Farm**	(1) 2	*(Vaughan 28, Bayly (p) 77)*

SECOND ROUND REPLAY

| Mar. 10th | **Monaghan United** | (1) 1 | *(M.Byrne 13)* |
| | Finn Harps | 0 | |

QUARTER-FINALS

Mar. 19th	**Sligo Rovers**	(0) 1	*(Houlahan 71)*
	Cobh Ramblers	0	
Mar. 20th	**Derry City**	(1) 1	*(Heaney 45)*
	St. Patrick's Athletic	0	
	☐ **Home Farm**	(0) 1	*(Gannon 65)*
	Bohemians	(0) 1	*(King 85)*
	Limerick	(0) 2	*(Walsh 52, Minihan 67)*
	Monaghan United	(0) 1	*(Newe 66)*

QUARTER-FINAL REPLAY

| Mar. 24th | **Bohemians** | (2) 4 | *(King 14, Broughan (p) 32, Cousins 54, 60)* |
| | Home Farm | (1) 1 | *(Vaughan 26)* |

SEMI-FINALS

Apr. 13th	Bohemians	0	
	Derry City	(1) 1	*(O'Brien 44)*
	Sligo Rovers	(0) 1	*(Annand 67)*
	Limerick	0	

FINAL

May 15th at Lansdowne Road
Sligo Rovers (0) 1 *(Carr 72)*
Derry City 0

Sligo Rovers: McLean, McStay, Boyle, Dykes, McDonnell, Moran, Hastie, Carr, Kenny, Gabbiadini, Annand
Derry City: O'Neill, Vaudequin, Curran, Gauld, McLaughlin, Hutton, McKeever, O'Brien, Kinnaird, Lawless, Coyle (Heaney 85)

Referee: D. McArdle (Dundalk)   Att: 13,800

△ at Carraig Park   ▽ at Red Cow
✗ at Dalymount Park   ☆ at Richmond Park
✪ at Market Green   ☐ at Tolka Park
▶   ●

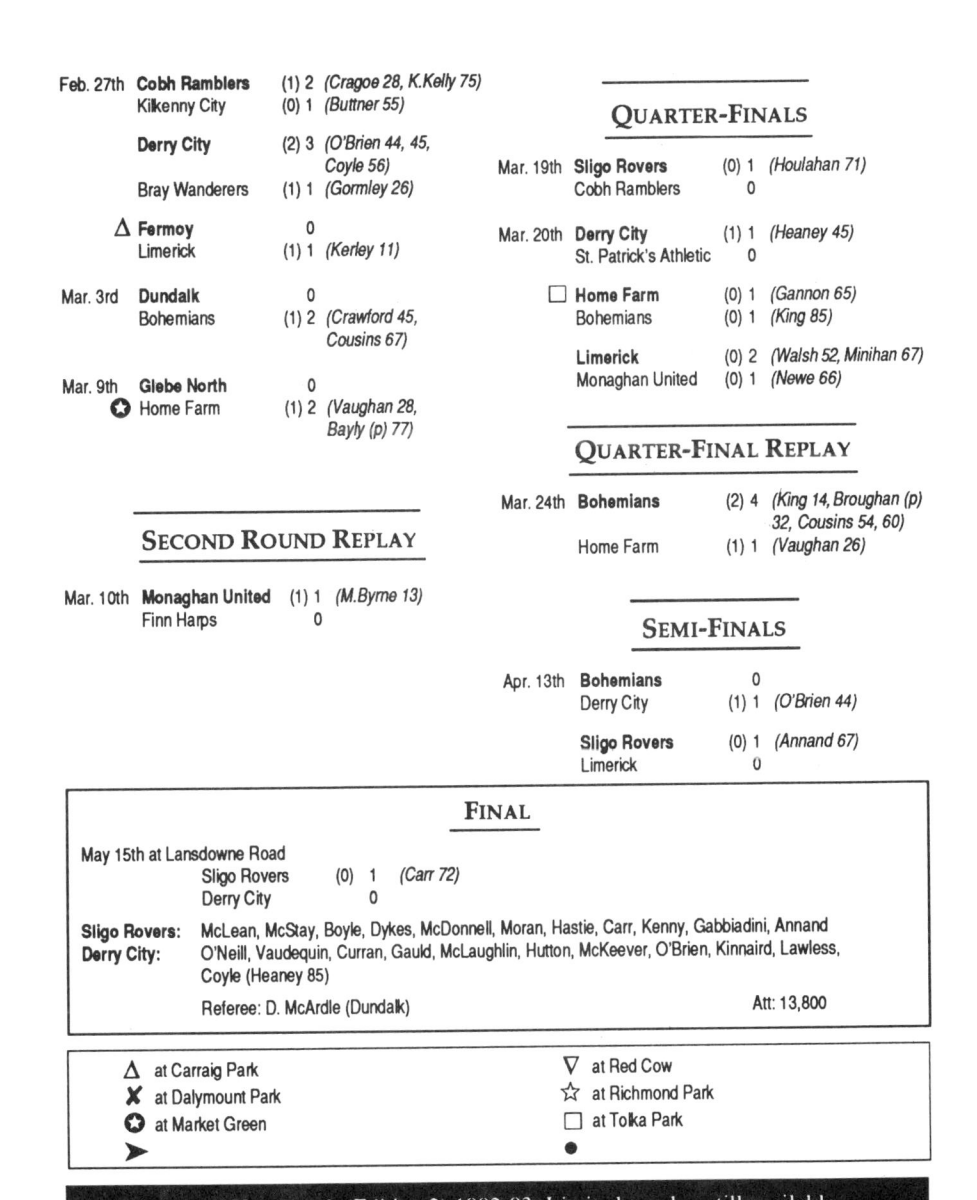

Irish Football Handbook (Edition 2) 1992-93: Limited number still available.
Unique features include:
Summary of L.O.I. opposition in Europe; Shamrock Rovers v Bayern Munich 1966; Jimmy Turnbull - Double Record Holder; The First League Cup Final; Original Munster Football Association 1901-1914; Defunct Competitions.
From
Red Card Publications
P.O. Box 10, Eglinton Street, Cork, R.O.I.
£4.99 post free (R.O.I./U.K.) + £2 postage (Europe) + £4 postage (worldwide)

F.A.I. Cup Final Results

	Winners	Runners-Up	Score	
1922	St. James's Gate	Shamrock Rovers	1-1	1-0
1923	Alton United	Shelbourne		1-0
1924	Athlone Town	Fordsons		1-0
1925	Shamrock Rovers	Shelbourne		2-1
1926	Fordsons	Shamrock Rovers		3-2
1927	Drumcondra	Brideville	1-1	1-0 (a)
1928	Bohemians	Drumcondra		2-1
1929	Shamrock Rovers	Bohemians	0-0	3-0 (a)
1930	Shamrock Rovers	Brideville		1-0
1931	Shamrock Rovers	Dundalk	1-1	1-0
1932	Shamrock Rovers	Dolphin		1-0
1933	Shamrock Rovers	Dolphin	3-3	3-0
1934	Cork	St. James's Gate		2-1
1935	Bohemians	Dundalk		4-3
1936	Shamrock Rovers	Cork		2-1
1937	Waterford	St. James's Gate		2-1
1938	St. James's Gate	Dundalk		2-1
1939	Shelbourne	Sligo Rovers	1-1	1-0
1940	Shamrock Rovers	Sligo Rovers		3-0
1941	Cork United	Waterford	2-2	3-1
1942	Dundalk	Cork United		3-1
1943	Drumcondra	Cork United		2-1
1944	Shamrock Rovers	Shelbourne		3-2
1945	Shamrock Rovers	Bohemians		1-0
1946	Drumcondra	Shamrock Rovers		2-1
1947	Cork United	Bohemians	2-2	2-0
1948	Shamrock Roverss	Drumcondra		2-1
1949	Dundalk	Shelbourne		3-0
1950	Transport	Cork Athletic	2-2 2-2	3-1
1951	Cork Athletic	Shelbourne		1-0
1952	Dundalk	Cork Athletic	1-1	3-0
1953	Cork Athletic	Evergreen United	2-2	2-1
1954	Drumcondra	St. Patrick's Athletic		1-0
1955	Shamrock Rovers	Drumcondra		1-0
1956	Shamrock Rovers	Cork Athletic		3-2
1957	Drumcondra	Shamrock Rovers		2-0
1958	Dundalk	Shamrock Rovers		1-0
1959	St. Patrick's Athletic	Waterford	2-2	2-1
1960	Shelbourne	Cork Hibernians		2-0
1961	St. Patrick's Athletic	Drumcondra		2-1
1962	Shamrock Rovers	Shelbourne		4-1
1963	Shelbourne	Cork Hibernians		2-0

	Winners	Runners-Up	Score	
1964	**Shamrock Rovers**	Cork Celtic	1-1	2-1
1965	**Shamrock Rovers**	Limerick	1-1	1-0
1966	**Shamrock Rovers**	Limerick		2-0
1967	**Shamrock Rovers**	St. Patrick's Athletic		3-2
1968	**Shamrock Rovers**	Waterford		3-0
1969	**Shamrock Rovers**	Cork Celtic	1-1	4-1
1970	**Bohemians**	Sligo Rovers	0-0 0-0	2-1
1971	**Limerick**	Drogheda	0-0	3-0
1972	**Cork Hibernians**	Waterford		3-0
1973	**Cork Hibernians**	Shelbourne	0-0	1-0 (b)
1974	**Finn Harps**	St. Patricks Athletic		3-1
1975	**Home Farm**	Shelbourne		1-0
1976	**Bohemians**	Drogheda United		1-0
1977	**Dundalk**	Limerick		2-0
1978	**Shamrock Rovers**	Sligo Rovers		1-0
1979	**Dundalk**	Waterford		2-0
1980	**Waterford**	St. Patrick's Athletic		1-0
1981	**Dundalk**	Sligo Rovers		2-0
1982	**Limerick United**	Bohemians		1-0
1983	**Sligo Rovers**	Bohemians		2-1
1984	**U.C.D.**	Shamrock Rovers	0-0	2-1 (c)
1985	**Shamrock Rovers**	Galway United		1-0
1986	**Shamrock Rovers**	Waterford United		2-0
1987	**Shamrock Rovers**	Dundalk		3-0
1988	**Dundalk**	Derry City		1-0
1989	**Derry City**	Cork City	0-0	1-0
1990	**Bray Wanderers**	St. Francis		3-0 (d)
1991	**Galway United**	Shamrock Rovers		1-0 (d)
1992	**Bohemians**	Cork City		1-0 (d)
1993	**Shelbourne**	Dundalk		1-0 (d)
1994	**Sligo Rovers**	Derry City		1-0 (d)

Notes

All matches played at Dalymount Park except:

(a) played at Shelbourne Park   (b) played at Flower Lodge
(c) played at Tolka Park   (d) played at Landsdowne Road

Summary of Winners

24 Shamrock Rovers, 8 Dundalk, 5 Bohemians, Drumcondra, 4 Shelbourne, 2 Cork Athletic, Cork Hibernians, Cork United, Limerick/Limerick United, St. Patricks Athletic, St. James's Gate, Sligo Rovers, Waterford, 1 Alton United, Athlone Town, Bray Wanderers, Cork, Derry City, Finn Harps, Fordsons, Galway United, Home Farm, Transport, U.C.D.

Non-League Clubs in the F.A.I. Cup
1922 – 94

Aer Lingus (Dublin)

52	1	Shamrock Rovers	H	0-3
82	1	*Workmans Club*	A	1-0
		Burnett		
	2	Bye		
	3	Limerick United	A	0-4

AIB (Dublin)

78	1	Waterford	H	0-1
80	1	Athlone Town	H	1-4
		O'Reilly		
89	1	Limerick City	H	0-2

Albert Rovers (Cork)

50	1	*Longford Town*	H	2-2
		O'Connell, Allen		
	R	*Longford Town*	A	0-0
	R	*Longford Town*	N	2-1
		Allen 2		
	2	Sligo Rovers	A	0-2
54	1	Bohemians	A	1-1
		Cremin		
	R	Bohemians	H	1-2
		Hackett		
55	1	Evergreen United	A	2-2
		Dwan, Cremin		
	R	Evergreen United	H	1-2
		O'Connell (J.)		
56	1	Waterford	A	0-3
59	1	Dundalk	A	3-3
		Collins (T.) 2, Hickey		
	R	Dundalk	H	0-0
	R	Dundalk	N	0-4
61	1	*Tycor Athletic*	A	0-2

Cup Fact Alton United have the unique distinction of never having lost a Cup match. Being the first non-leaguers to win the trophy in 1923, they never returned to defend it. They are also the only club from outside the Republic to lift the Cup.

Alton United (Belfast)

23	1	Midland Athletic	H	5-0
		Ward 3, Duffy, Brennan (pen)		
	2	Shelbourne United	A	1-1
		Duffy		
	R	Shelbourne United	H	2-0
		Ward, McSherry		
	SF	*Fordsons*	N	4-2
		Ward 3, Brennan (pen)		
	F	Shelbourne	N	1-0
		McSherry		

AOH (Cork)

50	1	Dundalk	H	2-1
		Madden, O'Sullivan (G)		
	2	*St. Patrick's Athletic*	H	0-1
51	1	Limerick	A	1-2
		O'Sullivan (G)		
52	1	Evergreen United	H	2-1
		Murphy (J) 2		
	2	Dundalk	H	0-4
53	1	*Longford Town*	H	2-2
		Dunlea, Murphy		
	R	*Longford Town*	A	0-3
57	1	Sligo Rovers	H	0-1

Ashtown Villa (Dublin)

91	1	Dundalk	A	1-0
		Murphy		
	2	Derry City	A	2-1
		Hannigan, Murphy		
	QF	Kilkenny City	A	0-1
92	1	Bray Wanderers	A	1-2
		Dillon		
93	1	*Glenmore Celtic*	A	4-4
		Donnelly, Kelly 2, Lynch (pen)		
	R	*Glenmore Celtic*	H	0-1

Explanatory notes for this section are at end of Summary Table.

Athlone Town

22	1	YMCA	A	4-3
		Js. Sweeney 2, Ghent, Jn. Sweeney (pen)		
	2	Bohemians	A	1-7
		Js. Sweeney		
68	1	Shelbourne	H	0-2

Avondale United (Cork)

78	1	Galway Rovers	H	0-2
85	1	Galway United	H	0-4
88	1	*Tramore Athletic*	H	0-2

B & I (Dublin)

35	1	Cork	A	0-0
	R	Cork	A	0-3
36	1	Dundalk	A	1-7
		Kavanagh		

Ballina Town

90	1	Shelbourne	H	0-4

Ballyfermot United (Dublin)

81	1	Cork United	H	2-5
		Cleary, Farrell (pen)		
84	1	*Bank Rovers*	H	0-1
86	1	Longford Town	H	1-2
		Howell		
88	1	Longford Town	H	1-1
		Foley		
	R	Longford Town	A	0-1
90	1	Bohemians	H	0-1

Bank Rovers (Dundalk)

84	1	*Ballyfermot United*	A	1-0
		og		
	2	Waterford United	H	0-5
85	1	Cork City	A	0-2
87	1	Bohemians	H	1-2
		Cunningham		
93	1	*Tramore Athletic*	A	0-0
	R	*Tramore Athletic*	H	0-3

Barrackton United (Cork)

26	1	Jacobs	A	1-5
		McVeigh (pen)		

Belgrove (Dublin)

65	1	Transport	H	2-1
		Sullivan, Reardon		
	2	Cork Celtic	A	1-1
		O'Riordan		
	R	Cork Celtic	H	0-1
75	1	Limerick	A	0-2

Bendigo (Dublin)

28	1	Bray Wanderers	A	1-6
		Cummins		

Bluebell United (Dublin)

71	1	St. Patrick's Athletic	A	0-2
82	1	Limerick United	H	0-1
83	1	Athlone Town	A	0-2
86	1	*Crofton Celtic*	A	0-0
	R	*Crofton Celtic*	H	0-1
88	1	St. Mary's (Cork)	H	3-2
		Marshall, Cassidy, Brown		
	2	St. Patrick's Athletic	H	0-3
90	1	U.C.D.	H	2-2
		Cullen (T.), O'Brien		
	R	U.C.D.	A	1-4
		Swift		
92	1	Bohemians	A	1-2
		O'Brien		
93	1	Sligo Rovers	A	0-1
94	1	*Fermoy*	H	0-0
	R	*Fermoy*	A	0-2

Botanic (Dublin)

54	1	Cork Athletic	A	1-4
		Murphy		

Boyne Rovers (Drogheda)

90	1	Sligo Rovers	A	1-1
		McGroggan		
	R	Sligo Rovers	H	0-1

189

Bray Unknowns

23	1	Bohemians	A	0-9
24	1	Brooklyn	A	2-1
		o.g., Carroll		
	2	Bohemians	A	0-1

Bray Wanderers

56	1	*Longford Town*	H	2-0
		Duggan, Giles		
	2	*Workmans Club*	A	0-0
	R	*Workmans Club*	H	0-1
58	1	Shelbourne	H	1-2
		Seerey		
59	1	*Chapelizod*	H	1-2
		Bennett		
60	1	Sligo Rovers	A	2-4
		Bennett (2 pens)		
77	1	Bye		
	2	Shelbourne	A	0-2

Brendanville (Dublin)

89	1	Dundalk	A	1-3
		Marshall		

Brideville (Dublin)

33	1	*Sligo Rovers*	A	1-3
		Thomas (pen)		
34	1	*Queens Park*	A	2-2
		Quinlan, o.g.		
	R	*Queens Park*	H	0-2

Bridewell (Cork)

67	1	Drogheda	A	1-1
		O'Connor		
	R	Drogheda	H	0-3

Buncrana Hearts

89	1	Athlone Town	A	1-2
		Smith		

Butchers (Cork)

35	1	*Distillery*	A	1-1
		Staunton		
	R	*Distillery*	H	0-0
	R	*Distillery*	A	0-3

Cahir Park

30	1	*Glasnevin*	A	1-2
		Ryan		

Carndonagh

91	1	Limerick City	H	0-0
	R	Limerick City	A	0-3

Casement Celtic (Cork)

94	1	Kilkenny City	A	2-4
		Luxford 2		

Castleview (Cork)

93	1	U.C.D.	A	0-2

Chapelizod (Dublin)

58	1	Shamrock Rovers	A	1-4
		O'Connor		
59	1	*Bray Wanderers*	A	2-1
		Bailey 2 (1 pen)		
	2	St. Patrick's Athletic	H	1-4
		Sherry		

Cherry Orchard (Dublin)

94	1	Bray Wanderers	A	1-1
		Glynn (pen)		
	R	Bray Wanderers	H	1-2
		Glynn		

C.I.E. (Dublin)

74	1	Dundalk	A	1-5
		Corcoran		

C.I.E. Mosney

83	1	Finn Harps	A	0-0
	R	Finn Harps	H	0-0
	R	Finn Harps	A	0-2

C.I.E. Transport (Dublin)

76	P	Sligo Rovers	A	0-3
80	1	St. Patrick's Athletic	H	2-2
		Smith, Cassidy		
	R	St. Patrick's Athletic	A	2-3
		Cassidy, O'Brien		

Clifton (Cork)

24	1	Shelbourne United	H	0-2

Cup Fact Dundalk are the league club to have had their colours lowered most often, five times in all. Distillery (1940), AOH (1950), Workman's Club (1956), Cobh Ramblers (1983) and Ashtown Villa (1991) have all seen off the Lilywhites. Next in line are Bohemians and Home Farm with three losses apiece. Bohs were caught by Shamrock Rovers in the first ever running of the Cup in 1922 and by Drumcondra in 1927 but did not slip up again for 63 years until St. Francis surprisingly came out tops in the 1990 semi-final. Home Farm are the only league side to fall in successive years, in 1991 and 1992, to Portlaoise and Fanad United.

Cup Fact Cobh Ramblers (23 games) and Jacobs (24) share the highest number of qualifications to the FAI Cup proper with fifteen apiece, though Longford, from two qualifications less, have played the most games, 25.

Cobh Ramblers

27	1	Brideville	A	1-2
		Kelleher		
28	1	Bohemians	A	0-7
32	1	Bohemians	A	0-8
38	1	*Distillery*	A	1-2
		Wall		
39	1	*Cork Bohemians*	H	1-2
		Quaine		
40	1	Sligo Rovers	A	2-3
		Quaine 2		
48	1	*St. Patrick's Athletic*	H	1-4
		Forde		
54	1	Drumcondra	A	0-6
58	1	Sligo Rovers	A	1-2
		og.		
59	1	Drumcondra	H	0-1
63	1	*Transport*	A	0-5
75	1	Drogheda	A	1-0
		Meade		
	2	St. Patrick's Athletic	H	1-3
		Ward		
80	1	Home Farm	H	0-0
	R	Home Farm	A	0-2
81	1	Galway Rovers	H	3-1
		O'Leary, McDaid		
		F. O'Neill		
	2	Finn Harps	H	1-4
		P. O'Neill		
83	1	Dundalk	H	2-1
		McDaid, O'Halloran		
	2	Bye		
	3	Finn Harps	H	1-0
		F. O'Neill		
	SF	Sligo Rovers	H	1-1
		O'Halloran (pen)		
	R	Sligo Rovers	A	2-2
		Crowley, O'Flynn		
	R	Sligo Rovers	H	0-0
	R	Sligo Rovers	A	2-3
		F. O'Neill 2		

Cobh Wanderers

90	1	Limerick City	H	0-2

Colepark United (Dublin)

87	1	Swilly Rovers	A	0-1

College Corinthians (Cork)

90	1	Newcastlewest	H	1-3
		O'Leary		
92	1	Shelbourne	A	0-2
93	1	Shamrock Rovers	A	0-3
94	1	St. James's Gate	A	1-3
		Abbott		

Cork Bohemians

25	1	Athlone Town	A	3-5
		O'Driscoll, O'Leary 2		
28	1	Fordsons	H	2-4
		Noonan, Buckley		
29	1	*Waterford Celtic*	A	1-1
		Lynch (pen)		
	R	*Waterford Celtic*	H	4-1
		Buckley, O'Sullivan 2, Geaney		
	2	Drumcondra	A	1-3
		Kane		
30	1	Dundalk	H	1-2
		Delea		
31	1	Drumcondra	H	3-2
		Delea, Hayes 2		
	2	Dundalk	A	1-3
		Delea		
32	1	Drumcondra	A	1-3
		Foley (pen)		
38	1	Drumcondra	A	1-2
		Curtin		
39	1	*Cobh Ramblers*	A	2-1
		Byrne, Fitzgerald		
	2	Bohemians	A	1-3
		Byrne		
41	1	Shamrock Rovers	A	3-8
		Whitnell, Curtin, Byrne		
42	1	Cork United	H	2-5
		Carroll, Whitnell		

Cork City

28	1	St. James's Gate	A	0-4

Crofton Celtic (Cork)

79	1	Drogheda United	H	0-2
84	1	Galway United	A	0-4
86	1	*Bluebell United*	H	0-0
	R	*Bluebell United*	A	1-0
		Neville		
	2	Cobh Ramblers	H	0-0
	R	Cobh Ramblers	A	0-1
87	1	Sligo Rovers	A	2-4
		Neville, McCarthy		

Crosshaven

86	1	Newcastle United	H	0-3

Culdaff United

88	1	Home Farm	A	0-5
89	1	Shamrock Rovers	H	0-3

CYM (Dublin)

72	1	Cork Celtic	H	0-1
75	1	Bye		
	2	Waterford	H	1-0
		Garvan		
	3	St. Patrick's Athletic	A	0-1

Dale United (Bray)

93	1	Cork City	A	0-7

Dalkey United (Dublin)

66	1	*Transport*	H	3-1
		Byrne, McDonnell, Kane		
	2	Waterford	H	0-2
73	1	Home Farm/ Drumcondra	A	2-1
		Byrne, Wildes		
	2	Bye		
	3	Shelbourne	A	0-0
	R	Shelbourne	H	0-1
76	P	Limerick	A	1-0
		Devlin		
	1	Athlone Town	H	0-0
	R	Athlone Town	A	1-4
		Heffernan		
78	1	Finn Harps	H	0-1

Distillery (Dublin)

35	1	*Butchers*	H	1-1
		Recusin		
	R	*Butchers*	A	0-0
	R	*Butchers*	H	3-0
		Dorney, Redmond, Molloy		
	2	Dundalk	H	1-2
		Ward		
38	1	*Cobh Ramblers*	H	2-1
		Hogan, Martini		
	2	Drumcondra	A	4-0
		Molloy, Campbell, Lambert 2		
	SF	St. James's Gate	N	2-2
		Martini, Doyle		
	R	St. James's Gate	N	2-3
		Byrne, Lambert		
39	1	Brideville	A	5-1
		Brazil 3, Doyle (pen), Maxwell		
	2	Sligo Rovers	A	1-3
		Scully		
40	1	Dundalk	A	2-1
		Scully, Reid		
	2	St. James's Gate	A	0-2
41	1	Limerick	A	0-1
42	1	Dundalk	A	1-2
		Cullen		
43	1	Drumcondra	A	1-1
		Molloy		
	2L	Drumcondra	H	1-4
		Ward (Agg. 2-5)		

Dolphin (Dublin)

29	1	Jacobs	A	1-1
		Kenny		
	R	Jacobs	H	2-3
		Burch, Hand (pen)		
30	1	*Mullingar Celtic*	H	5-1
		Hand 2 (1 pen), Swan 3		
	2	Brideville	A	1-1
		Hand		
	R	Brideville	N	2-2
		Hand 2		
	R	Brideville	N	1-5
		Swan		

Drumcondra (Dublin)

25	1	Bye		
	2	Athlone Town	A	0-2
27	1	Jacobs	A	3-0
		McCarney 2, Murray		
	2	Bye		
	SF	Bohemians	N	3-1
		Swan, Coyle, Murray		
	F	Brideville	N	1-1
		McCarney		
	R	Brideville	N	1-0
		Murray		
28	1	Athlone Town	A	9-3
		McCarney 4, Swan 3, Keogh, Doyle		
	2	Bray Unknowns	A	2-2
		Murray 2		
	R	Bray Unknowns	H	4-1
		McCarney 3, Doyle		
	SF	Fordsons	A	3-0
		McCarney, Doyle 2		
	F	Bohemians	A	1-2
		Keogh		

Edenmore (Dublin)

91	1	Sligo Rovers	H	1-2
		Craven		
92	1	Cork City	A	0-3

Edenville (Dublin)

31	1	*St. Vincents*	A	3-1
		Bell 2, Lewis		
	2	Bohemians	A	1-5
		Bell		
32	1	Jacobs	H	2-1
		Mundow (pen), Kane		
	2	Shamrock Rovers	A	2-4
		Mundow (pen), Kane		

Elm Rovers (Dublin)

91	1	Monaghan United	A	2-1
		Hilliard, Farrell		
	2	Limerick City	A	0-1
94	1	Cork City	A	1-4
		Curry		

Evergreen United (Cork)

37	1	*Longford Town*	A	1-2
		Fitzgerald		
41	1	Cork United	H	0-2
51	1	Shamrock Rovers	H	1-3
		O'Connell		

Everton (Cork)

86	1	Cobh Ramblers	A	0-1

Fanad United

87	1	Galway United	A	1-1
		og.		
	R	Galway United	H	0-3
88	1	Bohemians	A	0-1
92	1	Home Farm	A	2-0
		Grier 2		
	2	St. James's Gate	A	1-1
		Harkin		
	R	St. James's Gate	H	1-1
		McGeever		
	R	St. James's Gate	H	2-3
		Harkin, McIlwaine		

Fearons Athletic (Dublin)

37	1	Bray Unknowns	H	4-1
		Leonard, Byrne 2, Reid		
	2	Cork	A	0-0
	R	Cork	A	1-0
		Hogan		
	SF	St. James's Gate	N	0-4

Fermoy

29	1	*Richmond United*	H	0-1
92	1	Galway United	A	1-3
		Lawlor		
94	1	*Bluebell United*	A	0-0
	R	*Bluebell United*	H	2-0
		McMahon, Myers		
	2	Limerick	H	0-1

Fordson (Cork)

23	1	Rathmines Athletic	H	W/O
	2	Dublin United	A	3-2
		O'Sullivan 3		
	SF	*Alton United*	N	2-4
		Buckle 2		
24	1	Bye		
	2	Jacobs	A	2-0
		Collins 2		
	SF	St. James's Gate	H	4-0
		Collins 3, Pinkney		
	F	Athlone Town	N	0-1

Freebooters (Cork)

49	1	Shelbourne	H	0-3

Garda (Dublin)

86	1	Derry City	A	0-5
89	1	Shelbourne	H	1-1
		Hennebry		
	R	Shelbourne	A	1-2
		Flynn (pen)		
94	1	St. Patrick's Athletic	A	0-3

Glasheen (Cork)

64	1	Drogheda	A	0-1
65	1	Shamrock Rovers	H	0-1

Glasnevin (Dublin)

30	1	*Cahir Park*	H	2-1
		Drumgoole 2		
	2	Dundalk	A	0-5

Glebe North

94	1	*Whitehall Rangers*	A	0-0
	R	*Whitehall Rangers*	H	1-0
		Durran		
	2	Home Farm	H	0-2

Glenmore Celtic (Dublin)

92	1	Moyle Park College	H	0-0
	R	Moyle Park College	A	0-1
93	1	Ashtown Villa	H	4-4
		O'Brien, Masterson, Dooney, Kelly (pen)		
	R	Ashtown Villa	A	1-0
		Byrne		
	2	Tramore Athletic	A	3-1
		Flynn (pen), Byrne Brien		
	QF	Shelbourne	A	0-6
94	1	Sligo Rovers	A	1-1
		Hannigan		
	R	Sligo Rovers	H	1-2
		Flynn		

Grangegorman (Dublin)

55	1	St. Patrick's Athletic	A	0-4

Grattan United (Cork)

40	1	Bray Unknowns	A	2-5
		Ring 2 (1 pen)		

GSR (Cork)

36	1	Reds United	H	1-4
		Buckle		

Hammond Lane (Dublin)

81	1	Dundalk	A	0-1
85	1	Waterford United	A	0-4

Cup Fact Only five of the current 22 league clubs have never lost against the small fry. These are Cork City (4 games), Limerick (City) (8), St. Patrick's Athletic (15) and U.C.D. (5). The Saints' unbeaten record now stretches back 40 years, from their initial pairing with Jacobs in 1954.

Home Farm (Dublin)

63	1	Limerick	A	1-3
		Dixon		
66	1	Waterford	A	0-4
67	1	Drumcondra	H	1-0
		og.		
	2	Shamrock Rovers	A	1-2
		Daly		
68	1	St. Brendan's	A	3-1
		Duffy, 2 og's		
	2	Drumcondra	H	1-2
		Daly		
70	1	Rialto	A	0-0
	R	Rialto	H	1-2
		Daly		

Hospitals' Trust (Dublin)

36	1	Sligo Rovers	A	2-5
		Molloy 2 (1 pen)		

Cup Fact On no less than three occasions non-league sides have knocked out the Cup holders. In 1949 St. Patrick's Athletic became the first to record this feat, sensationally ousting Shamrock Rovers by 2-1 in a replay at Milltown. One year later AOH embarrassed Dundalk on the same score line at the Mardyke while Midleton from east Cork completed the hat-trick in 1991, dumping Bray Wanderers 2-0 at Knockgriffin Park.

Cup Fact In over seven decades of competition, Cobh Ramblers can claim to be the only minnows to have humbled reigning League of Ireland Champions. At St. Colman's Park in 1983 they caught Dundalk napping by 2-1 at the outset of their own famous charge to the semi-final. Thus, 33 years after being shocked by AOH, the Co. Louth side suffered the unique ignominy of falling to non-league opponents as both Cup holders and League champions.

Jacobs (Dublin)

33	1	Shelbourne	A	0-5
34	1	Dolphin	H	0-5
41	1	Drumcondra	A	1-2
		Martini		
43	1	Brideville	A	1-2
		Hollingsworth		
	2L	Brideville	H	3-3
		Hollingsworth 2, Kirwan (agg. 4-5)		
50	1	Shamrock Rovers	H	0-1
51	1	Dundalk	H	1-2
		Malone		
52	1	Drumcondra	A	0-0
	R	Drumcondra	H	1-2
		Duffy (pen)		
53	1	Transport	H	3-1
		McEvoy, Ward, Keegan		
	2	Evergreen United	A	1-1
		Duffy		
	R	Evergreen United	H	0-1
54	1	St. Patrick's Athletic	H	1-1
		Hutchinson (pen)		
	R	St. Patrick's Athletic	A	0-1
55	1	*Longford Town*	H	0-1
60	1	Transport	A	1-3
		Dixon		
61	1	Transport	A	1-0
		Sinclair		
	2	Cork Hibernians	H	0-0
	R	Cork Hibernians	A	1-2
		Murphy (pen)		
63	1	Shelbourne	H	1-3
		Kane		
64	1	Waterford	H	2-1
		Waters 2		
	2	Bohemians	H	2-3
		Brennan, og.		
69	1	*Ringmahon Rangers*	H	0-0
	R	*Ringmahon Rangers*	A	1-3
		Keogh		

Lindon (Dublin)

26	1	Pioneers	H	4-2
		Hoey 3, Flanagan		
	2	Jacobs	H	1-1
		Carey		
	R	Jacobs	A	2-4
		Hoey (pen), Flanagan		

Longford Town

37	1	*Evergreen United*	H	2-1
		McManus, Clarke (P.)		
	2	Drumcondra	H	2-1
		Clarke (W.), Clarke (P.)		
	SF	Waterford	N	1-4
		Clarke (P.)		
40	1	Waterford	A	1-3
		Griffin		
41	1	Shelbourne	H	0-5
50	1	*Albert Rovers*	A	2-2
		Clarke, McDaid		
	R	*Albert Rovers*	H	0-0
	R	*Albert Rovers*	N	1-2
		Leavy		
51	1	Bohemians	A	1-3
		McNamara		
53	1	*AOH*	A	2-2
		Gilbert 2		
	R	*AOH*	H	3-0
		Gilbert 3		
	2	Limerick	A	1-1
		Gilbert		
	R	Limerick	H	1-1
		Gilbert		
	R	Limerick	N	0-0
	R	Limerick	N	1-2
		Collins		
55	1	*Jacobs*	A	1-0
		Ward		
	2	Transport	A	3-2
		Gilbert 2, Ward		
	SF	Shamrock Rovers	N	0-3
56	1	*Bray Wanderers*	A	0-2
57	1	Drumcondra	H	1-5
		Archbold		
60	1	Limerick	A	0-6
62	1	*Pike Rovers*	A	1-2
		Dodrill		
69	1	Sligo Rovers	H	2-0
		Hogan, Bermingham		
	2	Shelbourne	H	0-2
72	1	Dundalk	H	0-3

Mallow United

91	1	Athlone Town	H	0-1

Mervue United (Galway)

85	1	U.C.D.	H	1-2
		Collins		
87	1	Longford Town	H	1-0
		Collins		
	2	Rockmount	H	2-2
		Farragher, Fallon		
	R	Rockmount	A	0-1
88	1	Monaghan United	H	1-2
		McDonnell		

Midleton

89	1	Parkvilla	A	1-1
		O'Keeffe		
	R	Parkvilla	H	0-0
	R	Parkvilla	A	2-3
		O'Keeffe, Daly		
91	1	Bray Wanderers	H	2-0
		Quinn, O'Connor		
	2.	St. James's Gate	H	0-1

Moyle Park College (Dublin)

90	1	Galway United	A	0-3
92	1	Glenmore Celtic	A	0-0
	R	Glenmore Celtic	H	1-0
		Burns		
	2	Limerick City	H	1-2
		Condron		

Mullingar Celtic

30	1	Dolphin	A	1-5
		Henry		

Ormeau (Dublin)

32	1	Shamrock Rovers	A	3-9
		Morton, Snowe, Hughes		

Parkvilla (Navan)

75	1	Shamrock Rovers	H	0-0
	R	Shamrock Rovers	A	1-5
		Kennedy		
86	1	TEK United	A	0-1
89	1	Midleton	H	1-1
		Conway (pen)		
	R	Midleton	A	0-0
	R	Midleton	H	3-2
		O'Neill, McCabe		
		Conway		
	2	Home Farm	H	0-2
91	1	Drogheda United	A	1-4
		Rodgers (pen)		

Pegasus (Dublin)

77	1	Home Farm	H	2-2
		Dolan 2		
	R	Home Farm	A	2-1
		Travers, Henry		
	2	Dundalk	A	1-2
		McGrath		
88	1	Newcastlewest	H	1-2
		Skelly		
92	1	Limerick City	H	0-1

Pike Rovers (Limerick)

52	1	Waterford	A	1-2
		Meaney		
60	1	Cork Hibernians	A	3-4
		Tuite, Lipper, Cunneen		
62	1	Longford Town	H	2-1
		Hackett, Costelloe		
	2	Shelbourne	H	1-2
		Casey		

Portlaoise

91	1	Home Farm	H	3-1
		Comerford, Conroy,		
		Burke		
	2	Kilkenny City	H	2-3
		McCormack, Griffey		

Queen's Park (Dublin)

34	1	*Brideville*	H	2-2
		Walsh, Bermingham (F.)		
	R	*Brideville*	A	2-0
		MacDonnell, Bermingham (E.)		
	2	Dolphin	H	1-1
		MacDonnell		
	R	Dolphin	A	0-1
37	1	Cork	A	2-3
		Ryan, Bermingham (J.)		

Railway Union (Dublin)

87	1	St. Patrick's Athletic	H	0-3

Reds United (Dublin)

35	1	Bohemians	H	3-3
		Doyle, Lappin 2		
	R	Bohemians	A	3-4
		Lappin, Flood, Finnegan		

Rialto (Dublin)

70	1	*Home Farm*	H	0-0
	R	*Home Farm*	A	2-1
		Campbell, Farrell		
	2	Bye		
	3	Sligo Rovers	A	0-4
72	1	Waterford	A	1-11
		Dempsey		
73	1	Cork Hibernians	A	1-3
		Norton		

Richmond Rovers (Dublin)

29	1	Dundalk	A	0-2

Richmond United (Dublin)

29	1	*Fermoy*	A	1-0
		Fagan		
	2	Shamrock Rovers	A	0-4

Ringmahon Rangers (Cork)

62	1	Drumcondra	A	0-3
69	1	*Jacobs*	A	0-0
	R	*Jacobs*	H	3-1
		Coleman, Gosnell 2		
	2	Shamrock Rovers	A	0-4
70	1	Waterford	H	0-7
76	1	Bohemians	A	0-1
83	1	Shamrock Rovers	A	0-2

Rockmount (Cork)

86	1	Limerick City	A	0-4
87	1	Monaghan United	A	3-1
		Hinchin, Lawless, O'Sullivan		
	2	*Mervue United*	A	2-2
		og., Philpott (pen)		
	R	*Mervue United*	H	1-0
		Philpott (pen)		
	QF	Dundalk	H	0-2
89	1	U.C.D.	A	0-2
90	1	Bray Wanderers	A	0-3

Rossville (Dublin)

31	1	Waterford	A	3-5
		Byrne, McCormack 2		
33	1	Cork	A	1-6
		Quirke		

St. Brendan's (Dublin)

68	1	Home Farm	H	1-3
		og.		
76	1	Sligo Rovers	H	1-3
		Kennedy		

Cup Fact The first league sides to tumble were Olympia (1-3 v Shamrock Rovers) and YMCA (3-4 v Athlone Town) both of whom were embarrassed on 14 Jan 1922. The most recent upsets were caused by Fanad United (2-0 at Home Farm) and Wayside Celtic (1-0 at Waterford United), both wins coming on 16 Feb 1992.

St. Francis (Dublin)

90	1	Kilkenny City	A	1-0
		Kerr		
	2	Cobh Ramblers	A	2-2
		Kerr, Toner		
	R	Cobh Ramblers	H	3-0
		Coleman, Toner, Byrne		
	QF	Newcastlewest	A	3-0
		Connolly, Hilliard, og.		
	SF	Bohemians	N	1-0
		Murphy		
	F	Bray Wanderers	N	0-3

St. James's Gate (Dublin)

48	1	Cork United	A	1-5
		Colfer		
50	1	Sligo Rovers	A	0-3
51	1	Sligo Rovers	A	1-4
		Menzies		
78	1	Home Farm	H	1-5
		Dunne		
89	1	Cobh Ramblers	A	0-3

St. Joseph's Boys (Dublin)

88	1	Derry City	A	0-6
91	1	Waterford United	A	1-2
		Knight		

St. Mary's (Athlone)

84	1	Shamrock Rovers	H	0-3

St. Mary's (Cork)

88	1	Bluebell United	A	2-3
		Long (pen), O'Brien		

St. Patrick's Athletic (Dublin)

48	1	Cobh Ramblers	A	4-1
		Cassidy 2, McDonald, McCormack		
	2	Bye		
	SF	Shamrock Rovers	N	2-8
		Shields, McCormack		
49	1	Shamrock Rovers	A	1-1
		Cassidy		
	R	Shamrock Rovers	H	2-1
		Gregg, Rogers		
	2	Shelbourne	H	0-1
50	1	Shelbourne	H	3-1
		Cassidy, og., Collins		
	2	AOH	A	1-0
		Donnelly		
	SF	Cork Athletic	N	1-1
		Comerford		
	R	Cork Athletic	N	2-2
		Cassidy 2		
	R	Cork Athletic	A	2-4
		Maher 2		
51	1	Drumcondra	H	1-2
		Cassidy		

St. Vincent's (Cork)

31	1	Edenville	H	1-3
		Herrick		

Shamrock Rovers (Dublin)

22	1	Olympia	A	3-1
		Flood, Cowzer 2		
	2	Dublin United	H	5-1
		Fullam 2, Cowzer 2, Flood		
	SF	Bohemians	A	1-0
		Flood		
	F	St. James's Gate	N	1-1
		Campbell		
	R	St. James's Gate	N	0-1

199

Sligo Celtic

23	1	Dublin United	A	3-3
		Tiernan 2, Dykes		
	R	Dublin United	H	0-0
	R	Dublin United	A	1-3
		og.		

Sligo Rovers

33	1	*Brideville*	H	3-1
		Westby, Callaghan, Fallon		
	2	Shelbourne	A	2-5
		Monaghan, Donnelly		
34	1	Dundalk	A	0-4

Strandville (Dublin)

28	1	Jacobs	A	1-2
		McGrane		

Swilly Rovers

73	1	Cork Celtic	H	2-2
		Og., Cassidy		
	R	Cork Celtic	A	0-6
79	1	*Tramore Athletic*	A	1-0
		O'Keeffe		
	2	Galway Rovers	A	0-1
87	1	*Colepark United*	H	1-0
		O'Neill		
	2	Dundalk	A	0-3

Cup Fact There have been two epics involving clubs from outside the League of Ireland which have gone down in Cup folklore. In the 1953 second round, Longford took Limerick to a third replay before finally surrendering by the odd goal in three after extra-time in the fourth game following 1-1, 1-1 and 0-0 draws. In the 1983 semi-final Cobh Ramblers also brought Sligo Rovers, the eventual Cup winners, to a fourth meeting losing 2-3 (after leading 2-0), the sides having earlier drawn 1-1, 2-2 and 0-0.

TEK United (Dublin)

64	1	Shelbourne	H	3-7
		Giles 2, Johnston		
65	1	Shelbourne	H	1-3
		Brock		
70	1	Limerick	A	0-5
71	1	Finn Harps	A	1-5
		Fogarty (pen)		
72	1	Drogheda	A	0-3
74	1	Bye		
	2	St. Patrick's Athletic	H	0-2
77	1	Bye		
	2	Waterford	A	3-3
		Bell (pen), Heffernan, Monaghan		
	R	Waterford	H	1-2
		Monaghan		
86	1	*Parkvilla*	H	1-0
		McGuirk		
	2	Dundalk	A	0-4
89	1	Longford Town	H	2-3
		Carroll (pen), O'Neill		

Temple United (Cork)

90	1	Athlone Town	A	0-3
93	1	Derry City	A	0-3

Terenure Athletic (Dublin)

38	1	Shamrock Rovers	A	0-0
	R	Shamrock Rovers	A	1-2
		Staunton		

Cup Fact Current league clubs most often drawn against non-leaguers: Bohemians (25 times), Dundalk (25), Shelbourne (24), Sligo Rovers (23), Shamrock Rovers (22). Most matches, including replays, is Sligo's 30, a sequence which has seen the "Bit o' Red" surprised just once — by Longford Town in 1969.

Tramore Athletic (Cork)

66	1	Shelbourne	H	1-4
		Fitzgerald		
67	1	Dundalk	A	1-6
		Goggin (pen)		
68	1	St. Patrick's Athletic	H	0-3
79	1	*Swilly Rovers*	H	0-1
80	1	Sligo Rovers	A	0-0
	R	Sligo Rovers	H	0-2
81	1	Drogheda United	H	0-3
82	1	Galway United	A	1-2
		O'Regan		
87	1	Home Farm	A	1-1
		Jackson		
	R	Home Farm	H	0-5
88	1	*Avondale United*	A	2-0
		Hayes (J.), Hayes (P.)		
	2	Home Farm	H	1-2
		O'Sullivan		
93	1	*Bank Rovers*	H	0-0
	R	*Bank Rovers*	A	3-0
		Morgan, O'Connor, Hoare		
	2	*Glenmore Celtic*	H	1-3
		Leahy		

Transport (Dublin)

48	1	Waterford	A	1-3
		Lester		
63	1	*Cobh Ramblers*	H	5-0
		Bailey 2, Dixon, Byrne 2		
	2	Limerick	A	2-2
		Bennett, McDonagh		
	R	Limerick	H	1-2
		Bennett		
64	1	Bohemians	A	2-2
		Byrne, Bennett (pen)		
	R	Bohemians	H	2-3
		Bennett, Burke		
65	1	*Belgrove*	A	1-2
		Burke (pen)		
66	1	*Dalkey United*	A	1-3
		Byrne		
69	1	Shelbourne	A	0-0
	R	Shelbourne	H	2-3
		Cowzer, Boyce		
71	1	Drogheda	H	0-3
74	1	Bye		
	2	Limerick	A	1-0
		Leavy		
	3	Athlone Town	A	1-2
		Conroy		

Tramore Rookies

33	1	Drumcondra	H	0-8
34	1	Bohemians	A	0-9
35	1	Drumcondra	A	0-3
36	1	Brideville	H	1-5
		Flaherty		

Tullamore

67	1	Bohemians	A	0-3
71	1	Sligo Rovers	A	1-3
		Geraghty (pen)		
87	1	Shamrock Rovers	A	0-6

Cup Fact Eight clubs have won the FAI Cup and it's non-league equivalent, the Intermediate Cup. Drumcondra, in fact, won both in the same year, 1927. Bray Wanderers, Home Farm, St. James's Gate, St. Patrick's Athletic, Sligo Rovers, Transport and UCD are the others to notch up victories in both competitions. The "Gate" and Transport did things backwards, so to speak, winning the FAI Cup first and subsequently the Intermediate Cup. Cobh Ramblers and Longford Town are the only current league members capable of joining this exclusive group.

Tycor Athletic (Waterford)

58	1	St. Patrick's Athletic	A	1-2
		McEvoy		
61	1	*Albert Rovers*	H	2-0
		Woods, Quinn		
	2	Drumcondra	H	0-2

Cup Fact A total of five non-league outfits have made it to Cup Final Day. Shamrock Rovers (1922), Alton United (1923, winners), Fordsons (1924), Drumcondra (1927, winners and 1928) were all early finalists while only St. Francis (1990) have made such a significant impact in modern times. Like Rovers and Alton, St. Francis reached the final at the first attempt.

201

University College Dublin

35	1	Waterford	A	2-4
		Hooper, Doherty		
39	1	Bray Unknowns	H	1-1
		Crean		
	R	Bray Unknowns	A	0-1
53	1	Sligo Rovers	A	3-3
		Doris, Cassidy, Lenehen (pen)		
	R	Sligo Rovers	H	2-3
		Lenehen, Cassidy		
57	1	Cork Athletic	A	2-4
		og., Plunkett		

Valeview (Dublin)

86	1	Monaghan United	H	0-2

Waterford

33	1	Bohemians	H	0-4
34	1	Bray Unknowns	H	0-3

Waterford Celtic

29	1	Cork Bohemians	H	1-1
		Haygood		
	R	Cork Bohemians	A	1-4
		Arrigan		
30	1	Brideville	A	0-1

Wayside Celtic (Dublin)

91	1	St. James's Gate	H	0-2
92	1	Waterford United	A	1-0
		Mooney		
	2	Monaghan United	H	2-2
		Duignan (pen), Keating		
	R	Monaghan United	A	0-1
93	1	Cobh Ramblers	H	0-0
	R	Cobh Ramblers	A	1-3
		Mooney		

Wembley (Cork)

73	1	Waterford	A	1-3
		Long (pen)		
74	1	Sligo Rovers	A	1-2
		Long (pen)		
77	1	Bohemians	H	0-6
70	1	Cork Alberts	A	0-3

West Ham (Belfast)

22	1	Shelbourne	H	0-0
	R	Shelbourne	A	1-2
		Kerr		

Whitehall Rangers (Dublin)

94	1	Glebe North	H	0-0
	R	Glebe North	A	0-1

Workmans Club (Dublin)

56	1	Dundalk	H	3-1
		Millar, Mooney, Hill		
	2	Bray Wanderers	H	0-0
	R	Bray Wanderers	A	1-0
		Hill		
	SF	Shamrock Rovers	N	1-2
		May		
57	1	Transport	H	1-0
		Duggan		
	2	Drumcondra	H	0-1
61	1	Drumcondra	A	1-2
		O'Leary		
62	1	Shelbourne	H	0-2
82	1	Aer Lingus	H	0-1

Cup Fact The biggest win enjoyed by non-leaguers was Drumcondra's resounding 9-3 victory at Athlone in 1928. This total included 4 strikes from Owen McCarney and a hat-trick from George Swan. McCarney recorded 8 goals from 4 games before drawing a blank in the decider against Bohemians which Drums lost though they did have the honour of being the only non-League of Ireland side to reach successive finals.

Non-League Clubs in The F.A.I. Cup
Summary Table

	P	W	D	L	F	A
Aer Lingus	3	1	-	2	1	7
AIB	3	-	-	3	1	7
Albert Rovers	13	1	6	6	12	24
Alton United	5	4	1	-	13	3
Cup Winners 1923						
AOH	8	2	1	5	7	15
Ashtown Villa	6	2	1	3	8	9
Athlone Town	3	1	-	2	5	12
Avondale United	3	-	-	3	-	8
B & I	3	-	1	2	1	10
Ballina Town	1	-	-	1	-	4
Ballyfermot United	6	-	1	5	4	11
Bank Rovers	6	1	1	4	2	12
Barrackton United	1	-	-	1	1	5
Belgrove	4	1	1	2	3	5
Bendigo	1	-	-	1	1	6
Bluebell United	13	1	3	9	7	22
Botanic	1	-	-	1	1	4
Boyne Rovers	2	-	1	1	1	2
Bray Unknowns	3	1	-	2	2	11
Bray Wanderers	7	1	1	5	6	11
Brendanville	1	-	-	1	1	3
Brideville	3	-	1	2	3	7
Bridewell	2	-	1	1	1	4
Buncrana Hearts	1	-	-	1	1	2
Butchers	3	-	2	1	1	4
Cahir Park	1	-	-	1	1	2
Carndonagh	2	-	1	1	-	3
Casement Celtic	1	-	-	1	2	4
Castleview	1	-	-	1	-	2
Chapelizod	3	1	-	2	4	9
Cherry Orchard	2	-	1	1	2	3
CIE	1	-	-	1	1	5
CIE Mosney	3	-	2	1	-	2
CIE Transport	3	-	1	2	4	8
Clifton	1	-	-	1	-	2
Cobh Ramblers	23	4	4	15	21	59
Semi-Finalists 1983						

	P	W	D	L	F	A
Cobh Wanderers	1	-	-	1	-	2
Colepark United	1	-	-	1	-	1
College Corinthians	4	-	-	4	2	11
Cork Bohemians	14	3	1	10	26	43
Cork City	1	-	-	1	-	4
Crofton Celtic	7	1	2	4	3	11
Crosshaven	1	-	-	1	-	3
Culdaff United	2	-	-	2	-	8
CYM	3	1	-	2	1	2
Dale United	1	-	-	1	-	7
Dalkey United	9	3	2	4	7	10
Distillery	16	5	4	7	26	24
Semi-Finalists 1938						
Dolphin	6	1	3	2	12	13
Drumcondra	10	6	2	2	27	12
Cup Winners 1927; Finalists 1928						
Edenmore	2	-	-	2	1	5
Edenville	4	2	-	2	8	11
Elm Rovers	3	1	-	2	3	6
Evergreen United	3	-	-	3	2	7
Everton	1	-	-	1	-	1
Fanad United	7	1	3	3	7	10
Fearon's Athletic	4	2	1	1	5	5
Semi-Finalists 1937						
Fermoy	5	1	1	3	3	5
Fordson	6	4	-	2	11	7
Finalists 1924						
Freebooters	1	-	-	1	-	3
Garda	4	-	1	3	2	11
Glasheen	2	-	-	2	-	2
Glasnevin	2	1	-	1	2	6
Glebe North	3	1	1	1	1	2
Glenmore Celtic	8	2	3	3	10	15
Grangegorman	1	-	-	1	-	4
Grattan United	1	-	-	1	2	5
GSR	1	-	-	1	1	4
Hammond Lane	2	-	-	2	-	5
Home Farm	8	2	1	5	8	14

203

	P	W	D	L	F	A
Hospitals Trust	1	-	-	1	2	5
Jacobs	24	3	6	15	21	43
Lindon	3	1	1	1	7	7
Longford Town *Semi-Finalists 1937, 1955*	25	6	6	13	26	52
Mallow United	1	-	-	1	-	1
Mervue United	5	1	1	3	5	7
Midleton	5	1	2	2	5	5
Moyle Park College	4	1	1	2	2	5
Mullingar Celtic	1	-	-	1	1	5
Ormeau	1	-	-	1	3	9
Parkvilla	8	1	3	4	6	15
Pegasus	5	1	1	3	6	8
Pike Rovers	4	1	-	3	7	9
Portlaoise	2	1	-	1	5	4
Queens Park	5	1	2	2	7	7
Railway Union	1	-	-	1	-	3
Reds United	2	-	1	1	6	7
Rialto	5	1	1	3	4	19
Richmond Rovers	1	-	-	1	-	2
Richmond United	2	1	-	1	1	4
Ringmahon Rangers	7	1	1	5	3	18
Rockmount	7	2	1	4	6	14
Rossville	2	-	-	2	4	11
St. Brendan's	2	-	-	2	2	6
St. Francis *Finalists 1990*	6	4	1	1	10	5
St. James's Gate	5	-	-	5	3	20
St. Joseph's Boys	2	-	-	2	1	8

	P	W	D	L	F	A
St. Mary's (Athlone)	1	-	-	1	-	3
St. Mary's (Cork)	1	-	-	1	2	3
St. Patrick's Athletic *Semi-Finalists 1948, 1950*	11	4	3	4	19	22
St. Vincent's	1	-	-	1	1	3
Shamrock Rovers *Finalists 1922*	5	3	1	1	10	4
Sligo Celtic	3	-	2	1	4	6
Sligo Rovers	3	1	-	2	5	10
Strandville	1	-	-	1	1	2
Swilly Rovers	6	2	1	3	4	12
TEK United	11	1	1	9	12	37
Temple United	2	-	-	2	-	6
Terenure Athletic	2	-	1	1	1	2
Tramore Athletic	15	2	3	10	11	32
Tramore Rookies	4	-	-	4	1	25
Transport	13	2	3	8	19	25
Tullamore	3	-	-	3	1	12
Tycor Athletic	3	1	-	2	3	4
University College Dublin	6	-	2	4	10	16
Valeview	1	-	-	1	-	2
Waterford	2	-	-	2	-	7
Waterford Celtic	3	-	1	2	2	6
Wayside Celtic	6	1	2	3	4	8
Wembley	4	-	-	4	2	14
West Ham	2	-	1	1	1	2
Whitehall Rangers	2	-	1	1	-	1
Workmans Club *Semi-Finalists 1956*	9	3	1	5	7	9

Notes: Year is given in left-hand column. Figures in second column (1, 2, 3) are round numbers. Also in this column P = preliminary round; R = replay; QF = quarter-final; SF = semi-final; F = final; 2L = second leg.

Teams in italics are fellow non-leaguers. For presentation purposes the round of entry for League of Ireland clubs has been classed the first round, though in reality this has often officially varied anywhere from first to fifth round. Occasionally, a brief preliminary round, including one or two league sides, was necessary to balance subsequent rounds. In certain years a short supplementary round involving as few as four teams was introduced after a full first round for the same purpose. Any team not having to play in this supplementary round is, again for balanced presentation, considered to have received a bye. Venues have been generalised. Where a non-league side availed of local facilities other than it's own, or used a neighbouring League of Ireland ground, the club is deemed to have played at "home." Where a non-league club has been drawn at home but conceded that advantage (e.g. Garda v Derry City, 1986 and Glenmore Celtic v Shelbourne in 1993) to the opposition, the venue is deemed as "away."

THE LEAGUE CUP
'Derry back on Song'

Having missed out on a place in the final last season, for the first time in five years, this League Cup campaign witnessed a return by Derry City to their recent domination of the competition, as they captured their fourth title in just six years. Following a particularly difficult opening to their championship season, one beset by turmoil both on and off the pitch and one which saw the 'Candystripes' fortunate to scrape into the top six group for the league's second phase, this League Cup success came as a welcome boost particularly for beleagured manager Tony O'Doherty. Indeed it marked the first ever trophy win as manager for the popular Derry supremo, whose playing career had included so many highlights.

For the first time in many years, the format for this League Cup competition was changed from the familiar group system to a more slimline straight knockout one, with non-leaguers Mervue United of Galway and Buncrana Hearts from Donegal invited to participate. Unfortunately neither fared particularly well in the first round as Mervue playing at the Galway Showgrounds lost heavily to holders Limerick for whom Gerry Kelly scored the competition's only hat-trick whilst Hearts were out-classed by newly promoted Monaghan United at Gortakeegan. Elsewhere the regionalised draw threw up a number of interesting local derbies with Sligo Rovers the only First Division outfit to claim a premier scalp, that of Galway United at their own Showgrounds. The first round's closest battle however was fought out at nearby Finn Park where the eventual winners Derry City needed a penalty shoot-out to see off the plucky challenge of homester's Finn Harps.

With four first round winners, Cork City, St. Patrick's Athletic, Shelbourne and Waterford, all receiving a bye to the quarter finals, a curtailed second round saw Limerick relinquish their title at Sligo by a single goal whilst Monaghan United exited by a similar scoreline at Derry. There were good away wins for Bray at Shamrock Rovers and Drogheda at Athlone Town. All four quarter finals took place on October Bank Holiday Monday where the most emphatic performance was that of Sligo who thrashed Drogheda at United Park. Elsewhere Derry, St. Pat's and Shelbourne all enjoyed hard earned one-nil home wins over Waterford United, Cork City and Bray Wanderers respectively. However an appeal against St. Pat's victory, on the basis that one of their players, Mark Ennis, was cuptied, was upheld and the game replayed only for the Premier Division side to once again emerge victorious.

The first semi-final on December 21st produced a smashing game between Derry and Sligo, the side which had knocked the Foylesiders out, at the Brandywell, the previous season. This time at the Showgrounds, a second half strike from Peter Hutton was enough to reverse that result and secure Derry a berth in the final.

The second semi on December 29th, an all Dublin clash between Shelbourne and

St. Pat's, both semi-finalists the previous season proved to be an equally exciting affair. Two goals to the good at the interval following strikes from John Byrne and Dave Campbell, the Inchicore side looked set for the final, but a second half hat-trick in just eighteen minutes from Greg Costello shattered 'St. Pat's' and saw Shelbourne through to their first ever League Cup decider.

By February 22nd and the final first leg at the Brandywell, Shelbourne were not enjoying the best of times. Dumped out of the F.A.I. Cup by Limerick and experiencing a poor time in the League, their fortunes would not improve much in this game. They felt aggrieved as early as the 2nd minute, when following a long free kick by Derry full back Pascal Vaudequin, the offside appeals of the out-rushing 'Reds' defenders were ignored by both referee and linesman, leaving Kevin McKeever ample time to pick his spot and beat goalkeeper Jody Byrne. Two minutes into the second period and a miserable night for the visitors was complete when Peter Hutton clinically finished off a superb Liam Coyle through ball.

On a freezing cold night, before a small attendance, the second leg on 8th March at Tolka Park produced a very lively game of football. Despite Shelbourne enjoying the greater degree of possession in the opening period, Derry looked assured throughout and effectively secured the title when Coyle scored with a clever piece of opportunism minutes before the break. Within a minute of the restart, the 'Reds' had equalised through their semi-final hero Costello, and this score signalled an all out effort from the home side to try and retrieve the game. Derry however held on comfortably enough for a share of the spoils on the night and yet another League Cup success.

Spanish Sheri
Emerging to play a vital role for Ireland, John Sheridan evades Spain's Andoni Goekoetxea (The Star)

Bord Gais League Cup 1993-94

First Round

Aug. 14th
Bohemians	0		
Shelbourne	(1) 1	*(Whelan 45)*	

Cobh Ramblers	(1) 2	*(K. Kelly 35, Martin (p) 56)*
Cork City	(1) 4	*(Caulfield 43, 52, Gaynor 46, Roche 70)*

Mervue United	(0) 1	*(McSweeney (p) 85)*
Limerick	(2) 5	*(McMahon 35, Walsh 40, Kelly 60, 67, 76)*

(Played at Galway Sportsground)

Aug. 15th
Dundalk	0	
Drogheda United	(1) 1	*(O'Connor 15)*

Finn Harps	0	
Derry City	0	*(Derry City won 5-3 on penalties)*

Kilkenny City	(1) 1	*(McKenna 23)*
Waterford United	(1) 2	*(Farrell 31, Crowley 105) AET*

Longford Town	(0) 1	*(Parsons 77)*
Athlone Town	(1) 2	*(Keane 37, Golden 58)*

Monaghan United	(2) 4	*(Byrne 19, 58, Wilson 37, 69)*
Buncranna Hearts	0	

St. James's Gate	0	
Shamrock Rovers	(0) 3	*(Treacy 48, Eviston 74, Geoghegan 78)*

St. Patrick's Ath.	(0) 1	*(O'Brien 87)*
Home Farm	0	

Sligo Rovers	(0) 2	*(Annand 47, Kenny 62)*
Galway United	(0) 1	*(O'Flaherty (p) 90)*

U.C.D.	(1) 1	*(O'Brien 37)*
Bray Wanderers	(1) 3	*(Douglas 30, 119, Nugent 110) AET*

Second Round

Aug. 19th
Athlone Town	(1) 1	*(Golden 6)*
Drogheda United	(2) 2	*(Ryan 16, Crolly 17)*

Shamrock Rovers	(1) 1	*(Swan 15)*
Bray Wanderers	(0) 3	*(Nugent 62, Coyle 65, Best 69)*

Sligo Rovers	(0) 1	*(Dykes 85)*
Limerick	0	

Sep. 9th
Derry City	(1) 1	*(Coyle 7)*
Monaghan United	0	

Quarter Finals

Oct. 25th
Derry City	(0) 1	*(McLaughlin 76)*
Waterford United	0	

Drogheda United	(2) 2	*(Crolly 19, 21)*
Sligo Rovers	(3) 5	*(Annand 20, 31, Carr 44, Reid 65, Kenny 75)*

* St. Patrick's Ath.	(1) 1	*(Dunne 26)*
Bray Wanderers	0	

Shelbourne	(1) 1	*(Whelan 44)*
Cork City	0	

Quarter Final-Re-Fixture

Nov. 23rd
St. Patrick's Ath.	(0) 1	*(Buckley 74)*
Bray Wanderers	0	

Semi-Finals

Dec. 21st
Derry City	(1) 2	*(Vaudequin 5, Hutton 70)*
Sligo Rovers	(1) 1	*(Kenny 13)*

Dec. 29th
Shelbourne	(0) 3	*(Costello 47(p), 49, 65)*
St. Patrick's Ath.	(2) 2	*(John Byrne 17, D. Campbell 21)*

* Game re-played as St. Patrick's used cup-tied player, Mark Ennis

---

FINAL

1st Leg at Brandywell 22nd Feb.   Referee: J. Stacey (Athlone)   Att: 3,000

Derry City	(1) 2	*(McKeever 2, Hutton 49)*
Shelbourne	0	

Derry City: O'Neill, Vaudequin, McLoughlin, Curran, Hutton, Gauld, McKeever, Sayers (Lawless 69), Coyle, O'Brien, Kinnaird
Shels: Byrne, Flood, Neville, Whelan, Dunne, O'Doherty, Mooney, Costello, Arkins, Callaghan, Rutherford (Cooney 81)

2nd Leg at Tolka Park 8th Mar.   Referee: M. Caulfield (Dublin)   Agg: 1-3

Shelbourne	(0) 1	*(Costello 46)*
Derry City	(1) 1	*(Coyle 39)*

Shels: Byrne, Flood, Dunne, Neville, Whelan, Brennan (Izzi 70), Mooney, Costello, Arkins, O'Doherty, Cooney
Derry City: O'Neill, Vaudequin, McLoughlin, Hutton, Curran, Gauld, McKeever, Lawless, Coyle (Sayers 41), O'Brien, Kinnaird

207

Previous League Cup Finals

1973/74   Waterford (2) 2   *(Buck, Matthews (pen)*
         Finn Harps (0) 1   *(Ferry)*
25 Oct 73   at Tolka Park; Referee: D.V. Byrne (Dublin)
W/ford: Bryan, Brennan, Sleator, McConville, Finucane, Macken, Buck, Hale, Kirby, O'Neill, Matthews.
Finn Harps: Murray, McDowell, Hutton, McGrory, Sheridan, McDermott, Smith, Ferry, Bradley, Harkin, Nicholl.

1974/75   Bohemians (1) 1   *(Mitten)*
         Finn Harps (0) 1   *(Fullam (OG))*
1 Jan '75   at Oriel Park; Referee: E. Farrell (Dublin)
Bohemians: Smyth, Doran, Gregg, Kelly, Burke, Fullam, Byrne, P. O'Connor, T. O'Connor, Flanagan (Sheehy), Mitten.
Finn Harps: Murray, McGranaghan, Hutton, O'Doherty, Sheridan, McDowell, McGee, McLoughlin (McGrory), Bradley, Ferry, Smith.

Replay   Bohemians (0) 2   *(Mitten, Fullam)* A.E.T.
         Finn Harps (0) 1   *(Smith)*
9 Jan '75   at Tolka Park; Referee: E. Farrell (Dublin)
Bohemians: Smyth, Doran, Gregg, Kelly, Burke, Fullam, Byrne, P. O'Connor, Ingoldsby, Sheehy (McCormack), Mitten.
Finn Harps: Murray, McGranaghan, Hutton, McDowell, Sheridan, McGrory, McGee, McLoughlin (Forbes), Carlyle, Smith, Ferry.

1975/76   Limerick (2) 4   *(Duggan 2, Kennedy, Meaney (pen))*
(1st Leg)   Sligo Rovers 0
16 Oct '75   at Markets Field; Referee P. Mulhall (Dublin)
Limerick: Fitzpatrick, M. O'Mahony, Lymer, Nolan, Fitzgerald, J. O'Mahony, Quinlivan, Ryan, Duggan, Kennedy, Meaney.
Sligo Rvs: Patterson, Robertson, Fox, Fagan, Rutherford, Pugh, Boyle, McGee, Leonard, Frickleton, Scannell (Sinclair).

(2nd leg):   Sligo Rvs. (1) 1   *(Leonard)*
         Limerick 0
5 Nov. 75   at the Showgrounds; Referee: P. Mulhall (Dublin)
Sligo Rvs.:   Patterson, Robertson, Fox, Sinclair, Rutherford, Pugh, McGee, Fagan, Leonard, Frickleton, Boyle (Kent).
Limerick: Fitzpatrick, M. O'Mahony, Lymer, Nolan, Fitzgerald, J. O'Mahony (Grey), Ryan, Duggan, Kennedy, Meaney.
(Limerick won 4-1 on Aggregate)

1976/77   Shamrock Rvs (0) 1   *(Leech)*
         Sligo Rovers 0
6 Oct '76   at Dalymount Park; Referee: J. Carpenter (Dublin)
Shamrock R: O'Neill, Doran, McNevin, Wyse, Synnott, Fullam, Leech, Conway, Meagan, (Magee), Lyons, Gaffney.
Sligo Rvs: Patterson, McManus, Fox, Sinclair (Stenson), Rutherford, Betts, Fagan, Fielding, McGee, Leonard (Bailey), Hulmes.

1977/78   Dundalk (1) 2   *(Flanagan, Dainty)*
(1st Leg)   Cork Alb. (0) 2   *(Finnegan, C. McCarthy)*
6 Apr. 78   at Oriel Park; Referee: P. Daly (Dublin)
Dundalk: Blackmore, McConville, O'Brien, Dunning, Carroll, Braddish, Ingoldsby, King, Flanagan, Lawlor, Dainty.
Cork Alb: Ludzik, Tobin (J. McCarthy), Brohan (Waters), O'Mahony, Daly, Finnegan, Nodwell, Lawson, C. McCarthy, Murphy, Lane.

(2nd Leg)   Cork Alb (1) 2   *(Finnegan, Nodwell)*
         Dundalk (2) 2   *(Lawlor, Flanagan)*
12 Apr. 78   at Flower Lodge; Referee: J. Carpenter (Dublin)
Cork Alb: Ludzik, J. McCarthy, Notley, O'Mahony, Brohan, Finnegan, Lawson (Punch), Nodwell, Murphy, C. McCarthy, Lane.
Dundalk: Blackmore, O'Brien, Dunning, Carroll, McConville, Nixon, King, Ingoldsby, Dainty, Flanagan, Lawlor.
(Aggregate 4-4, Dundalk won 4-3 on penalties)

1978/79   Bohemians (1) 2   *(O'Connor 2 (1 pen))*
         Shamrock R 0
22 Mar 79   at Dalymount Park; Referee: P. Daly (Dublin)
Bohemians: Smyth, Gregg, Burke, McCormack, Brady, Bailey (Byrne), Kelly, Lawless, Joyce (O'Riordan), O'Connor, Eviston.
Shamrock R: O'Neill, Gannon, Fullam, Burke, O'Leary, Bayly, Gaffney, Meagan, Murray, Murphy, Byrne.

1979/80   Athlone T. (3) 4   *(Salmon, Whelan 3 (2 pens))*
         St. Pats Ath (0) 2   *(Jameson, Browning)*
28 Nov, 79   at Richmond Park; Referee: P. Daly (Dublin)
Athlone T: Smyth, Fenuik, Fullam, Whelan, Smith, O'Connor, Wyse, Clarke, Salmon, Devlin, Davis.
St. Pats Ath: O'Brien, Kearney, Murphy (O'Donnell), Doyle, Daly, Malone, Munelly, Browning, Carthy, Jameson, Kirwan.

1980/81   Galway Rovers 0
(1st Leg)   Dundalk 0
1 Jan 81   at Terryland Park; Referee: K. O'Sullivan (Cork)
Galway Rvs: Lally, Daly, Collins, Herrick, Sheehan, Nolan, Quinlivan, McDonnell, Humphries, Cassidy (Fay), McLoughlin.
Dundalk: Blackmore, McKenna, Lawlor, McConville, Dunning, Braddish, Flanagan, Byrne, Clarke, Crawley (Archbold), Fairclough (Duff).

(2nd Leg)   Dundalk 0   A.E.T.
         Galway Rovers 0
8 Jan '81   at Oriel Park; Referee: P. Mulhall (Dublin)
Dundalk: Blackmore, McConville, Keely, Dunning, Lawlor, Clarke, Flanagan, McKenna, Byrne (Crawley), Fairclough, Archbold (Braddish).
Galway Rvs: Lally, Daly, Herrrick, Sheehan, Collins, Nolan, Cassidy (Quinlivan), McDonnell, Humphries, McLoughlin, Fay (Mannion).
(Aggregate 0-0; Dundalk won 3-2 on pens)

1981/82   **Athlone T.** (0) 1   *(Fitzpatrick)*
          Shamrock R   0
1 Jan '82   *at Tolka Park; Referee: J. Carpenter (Dublin)*
Athlone T: Smyth, Larkin, Carroll, McCue, Conway, Salmon, Wyse, Clarke, O'Connor, Devlin, Fitzpatrick.
Shamrock R: O'Neill, Murphy, Eccles, Synnott, Beglin Gaffney, Burns, Barratt, Campbell, Buckley, Maher.

1982/83   **Athlone T** (0) 2   *(McCue, Larkin (pen))*
          Dundalk (1) 1   *(Ralph)*
30 Dec. '82   *at Tolka Park; Referee: P. Daly (Dublin)*
Athlone T: Grace, Fenuik, O'Connor (p), McCue, Conway, Carroll, Wyse, Meagan, O'Connor (M), Larkin, Murray.
Dundalk: Byrne (J), Lawlor (R), McConville, Dunning, Lawlor (M), Byrne (S), King, Flanagan, Kelly, Ralph, Cunningham (McLaughlin).

1983/84   **Drogheda U** (1) 3   *(Dillon 2, Martin)*
          Athlone T (0)1   *(Collins)*
5 Jan '84   *at Tolka Park; Referee: J. Carpenter (Dublin)*
Drogheda U: Flynn, Byrne (Murphy), Bradley, Flanagan, Macken, Martin, Murray, Quinlan, Parker, Dillon, Gallacher.
Athlone T: Grace, Fenuik, P. O'Connor, Larkin, Carroll, Byrne, Wyse, Meagan, M. O'Connor, Collins, Hitchcock.

1984/85:   **Waterford U** (0) 2   *(Morley, Bennett)*
          Finn Harps (1) 1   *(Arkwright)*
18 Mar 85   *at Kilcohan Park; Referee: P.J. Walsh (Limerick)*
Waterford U: Flavin, Power, O'Regan, Burns, Hayes, Walsh, Madigan, Dixon, McCarthy (O'Neill), Bennett, Morley.
Finn Harps: McIntyre, P. McNutt, Boyle, McDermott, McGeever, Arkwright, McGroarty, Kelly, McLaughlin (Ferry), S. McNutt, Harkin.

1985/86   **Galway U** (1) 2   *(Bonner, McGee)*
          Dundalk   0
15 Jan '86   *at Tolka Park; Referee: M. Caulfield (Dublin)*
Galway U: Blackmore, Gardner, Cassidy, Bonner, Nolan, Deacy (Mernagh), Mannion, McDonnell, Steedman, McGonigle, McGee.
Dundalk: O'Neill, Connell, McConville, McCue, Shelley, Carroll (L. Murray), M. Murray, Kehoe, Malone, Gorman, McNulty.

1986/87   **Dundalk** (1) 1   *(Murray (pen))*
          Shamrock R   0
1 Jan 87   *at Dalymount Park; Referee: P. Kelly (Cork)*
Dundalk: O'Neill, Carroll, McCue, Malone, Lawlor, Wyse, Murray, Devereaux, Matthews (Callan), Gorman, McNulty.
Shamrock R: J. Byrne, Kenny, Keely, Larkin, Nolan, Doolin, P. Byrne, Neville, Glynn, Murphy, M. Byrne.

1987/88   **Cork City** (0) 1   *(Myers)*
          Shamrock R   0
21 Oct. '87   *at Turners Cross; Referee: J. Purcell (Dublin)*
Cork City: Kelly, Neiland, Healy, Murphy, Long, Bowdren, Barry, O'Keeffe, Freyne, Myers, Caulfield.
Shamrock R: J. Byrne, Kenny, Eccles, Neville, Brady, Steedman (Flynn), Doolin, Toal, McCarthy, M. Byrne, Carlyle.

1988/89   **Derry City** (3) 4   *(Doolin 2, Speak, Larkin)*
          Dundalk   0
13 Oct '88   *at Oriel Park; Referee: J. Purcell (Dublin)*
Derry City: Dalton, Keay, Brady, Neville, Curran, Doolin, Carlyle (Gauld), Larkin, Speak, Coady, Healy (Cunningham)
Dundalk: O'Neill, Mackey, Lawlor, Murray, Cleary, Malone, Wyse, Kehoe, Eviston, Gorman. Cousins.

1989/90   **Dundalk** (1) 1   *(Newe)* A.E.T.
          Derry City (1) 1   *(Healy)*
9 Nov. 89   *at Oriel Park; Referee: J. Spillane (Cork)*
Dundalk: O'Neill, Lawless, Coll, Malone (Cleary), Lawlor, McNulty, Wyse, Shelley, Cousins, Murray, Newe.
Derry City: Dalton, Vaudequin, Curran, Neville, Brady, Carlyle, Doolin, Healy, Coady, Krstic, Speak.
(Dundalk won 4-1 on penalties)

1990/91   **Derry City** (1) 2   *(Hanrahan, Healy)*
          Limerick C   0
27 Feb. '91   *at Brandywell; Referee O. Cooney (Dublin)*
Derry City: Dalton, Vaudequin, Brady (McCann), Curran, McCarthy (Gorman), Healy, Carlyle, Hegarty, Speak, Gauld, Hanrahan.
Limerick C: Grace, J. Lyons, Kerley (D. Lyons), O'Halloran, Power, Shanahan, Hogan, Hartnett (Finnan), Fitzgerald, Walsh, Ryan.

1991/92   **Bohemians**   0
          Derry City (0) 1   *(Speak)*
27 Feb. '92   *at Dalymount Park Referee G. McGrath (Wicklow)*
Bohemians: Grace, M. Byrne, Whelan, Best, P. Byrne, King (Murray 106), A. Byrne, Fenlon, McDermott (Douglas 90), Tilson, Lawless.
Derry City: O'Neill, Mooney, Curran, Gauld, Coady, Kearney, Hutton, Mannion, Hanrahan, Speak, O'Brien (Carlyle 62).

1992/93   **St. Pat's Ath.**   0
          Limerick (1) 2   *(H.King, Mumby)*
30 Dec. '92   *at Harold's Cross Referee: M. Tomney (Dublin)*
St.Pat's Ath: O'Dowd, Hill, McDonnell, D. Campbell (Ryan), Kelch, Tracey, Osam, Dolan, P.Campbell, Fallon (Newe), Dunne
Limerick: Grace, Kerley (Finnan), Minihan, O'Halloran, Duffy, Craig, De Mange, Walsh, Ryan (McMahon), Mumby, H.King.

209

NON-LEAGUE CLUBS IN LEAGUE CUP
1976/77 - 1993/94

Bluebell United   (Dublin)

88	G	St. Patrick's Athletic	H	2-1
		Mackey (pen), Reddy		
	G	Bray Wanderers	A	1-3
		Reddy		
	G	U.C.D.	A	0-1

Buncrana Hearts

94	1	Monaghan United	A	0-4

Castlebar Celtic

93	G	Longford Town	A	0-5
	G	Galway United	A	1-1
		Ruane (pen)		
	G	Limerick City	H	0-2

Cobh Ramblers

77	G	Waterford	H	2-1
		F.O'Neill, Mellerick		
	G	Cork Celtic	A	2-2
		Flynn, Ward		
	G	*Kilkenny*	A	1-0
		F.O'Neill		
	SF	Shamrock Rovers	H	0-3
83	G	Waterford United	A	2-0
		O'Halloran, Crowley		
	G	Galway United	A	1-1
		F.O'Neill		
	G	Limerick United	H	1-3
		McCarthy		
84	G	Waterford United	H	2-1
		Wilshaw, McDaid		
	G	Galway United	H	0-2

Connaught Senior League

88	G	Newcastlewest	A	0-0
	G	Limerick City	A	1-7
		Mullen		
	G	Galway United	H	1-3
		Mullen		
89	G	Newcastlewest	A	1-3
		Halion		
	G	Galway United	A	1-1
		Halion		
	G	Limerick City	H	3-4
		McEllin 2, Halion		
90	G	Newcastlewest	A	0-0
	G	Galway United	A	2-4
		Halion 2		
	G	Limerick City	A	0-2
91	G	Longford Town	A	1-2
		Brennan		
	G	Limerick City	H	1-3
		Halion		
	G	Galway United	A	0-5

Culdaff United

90	G	Finn Harps	A	1-1
		Moran		
	G	Derry City	A	1-6
		Ming		
	G	Sligo Rovers	H	0-2

Note: Year given represents second part of season, i.e. 88 = 1987-88. G = group match; 1 = first round. Both Connaught Senior League and Kilkenny are regional selections and not club sides. It should be particularly noted that the latter was not Kilkenny City in non-league guise. There has only been one all-non-league encounter in the competition, that of Cobh Ramblers v Kilkenny in 1976-77. Non-league participation is by invitation.

Fanad United

88	G	Sligo Rovers	H	3-0
		Kelly, Harkin, Ferry		
	G	Derry City	A	3-2
		Kelly 2, Ferry		
	G	Finn Harps	H	1-0
		McElwaine		
	QF	Galway United	H	1-0
		Kelly		
	SF	Shamrock Rovers	H	1-4
		McGonigle		
89	G	Sligo Rovers	A	2-2
		Toland, Kelly		
	G	Derry City	H	1-1
		Ferry		
	G	Finn Harps	A	2-2
		McLoughlin, McFadden		
91	G	Finn Harps	H	1-1
		Grier		
	G	Sligo Rovers	H	1-0
		Grier		
	G	Derry City	A	0-8
92	G	Derry City	H	0-1
	G	Finn Harps	A	1-1
		McElwaine (pen)		
	G	Sligo Rovers	H	0-4
93	G	Derry City	A	3-4
		McGonigle 2, Ferry		
	G	Finn Harps	A	1-0
		McGonigle		
	G	Sligo Rovers	A	0-5

Galway Rovers

77	G	Athlone Town	H	0-0
	G	Finn Harps	A	1-1
		Nolan		
	G	Sligo Rovers	H	0-1

Kilkenny

77	G	Cork Celtic	H	3-2
		Murphy, Lannon, Semple		
	G	Waterford	A	3-5
		Lannon (3)		
	G	Cobh Ramblers	H	0-1

Longford Town

83	G	Athlone Town	A	0-1
	G	Sligo Rovers	H	1-2
		Gardiner		
	G	Finn Harps	A	0-1
84	G	Athlone Town	H	0-3
	G	Finn Harps	H	1-2
		Murray		
	G	Sligo Rovers	A	2-2
		El Khershi, Murray		

Mervue United   (Galway)

94	1	Limerick	H	1-5
		McSweeney (pen)		

Salthill Devon   (Galway)

92	G	Galway United	H	0-4
	G	Longford Town	H	1-2
		Long (pen)		
	G	Limerick City	A	2-2
		Treacy, O'Shea		

	P	W	D	L	F	A	Progress
Bluebell United	3	1	-	2	3	5	Never beyond group.
Buncrana Hearts	1	-	-	1	-	4	First round.
Castlebar Celtic	3	-	1	2	1	8	Never beyond group.
Cobh Ramblers	9	4	2	3	11	13	Semi-final 1976-1977.
Connaught Senior League	12	-	3	9	11	34	Never beyond group.
Culdaff United	3	-	1	2	2	9	Never beyond group.
Fanad United	17	6	5	6	21	35	Semi-Final 1987-1988.
Galway Rovers	3	-	2	1	1	2	Never beyond group.
Kilkenny	3	1	-	2	6	8	Never beyond group.
Longford Town	6	-	1	5	4	11	Never beyond group.
Mervue United	1	-	-	1	1	5	First round.
Salthill Devon	3	-	1	2	3	8	Never beyond group.

First Division Shield
A First for Sligo Rovers

In a truly memorable year, one which yielded an unprecedented three trophies, Sligo Rovers' first major honour for more than eleven years came with their mid-season victory over Waterford United in the Shield final. As with last season's winners Galway United, once again the Shield honours were captured by the First Division champions, whilst like the 'Tribesmen' also, Sligo were successful at the first time of asking in a Shield decider.

As for Waterford, this was the 'Blues' second defeat in three years in a Shield final, having lost to U.C.D., also over two legs, in 1991. It was another disappointing chapter in a very mediocre season for Brendan Ormbsy's side. This year's Northern Section saw the United's of Galway and Monaghan, both promoted at the end of the 92/93 season, replaced by Sligo and St. James's Gate, the latter having moved over from the Southern Section where Bray Wanderers and Waterford replaced promoted Cobh Ramblers and of course the 'Gate.' In line with changes introduced to this season's Championship, the Shield also saw three points awarded for a win whilst a two-legged final was re-introduced.

In the Northern Section Sligo began steadily with a home win over St. James's Gate followed by a share of the spoils at Finn Park and another success at Longford Town. This left the 'Westerners' final game against Athlone Town, who had themselves opened up with straight wins over Longford and the 'Gate,' as crucial to determining group honours. In the event Sligo were comfortable two-nil winners over Michael O'Connor's side and so qualified for their first Shield final whilst Athlone's visit to Finn Park was of academic interest only.

The Southern Section proved to be a tight affair with just two points separating four sides at the finish. Waterford began impressively with wins at Kilkenny and Bray, while Home Farm's amateurs followed up an opening day win at Bray with draws at both U.C.D. and Kilkenny. Thus the meeting of the two at Whitehall, Farm's last assignment, was a vital one. Unfortunately for the home side, however, a scoreless draw was not enough to see them overtake the 'Suirsiders,' whilst a similar scoreline at Belfield where U.C.D. entertained Bray denied the 'Students' the chance to enter the fray themselves. Despite having a home game against U.C.D. yet to play, Waterford were already through to the decider.

The first leg of the final, in Waterford on December 28th, brought little Christmas cheer to the home side who found themselves two goals in arrears, ironically the goals which would ultimately win this Shield competition, within twenty minutes of the kick-off. The first came after just eleven minutes when a mistimed tackle by Peter Crowley let in the First Division's player of the year, Johnny Kenny, who scored with ease. Eight minutes later poor marking from Padraig Moran's corner kick allowed Gerry Carr a free header and the hero of

Sligo's FAI Cup final win over Derry City made no mistake. Waterford for their part tried hard to recover from such a disastrous start and restored some hope with a scrambled effort from Jimmy Barden on the stroke of half time. In a tame second period however, the visitors comfortably held their advantage.

The return leg a week later under the 'Showgrounds' new floodlights drew a sizeable crowd who witnessed a tense, closely fought game with Waterford having perhaps slightly the better of things. Despite this, scoring chances were at a premium, and although finishing strongly, with no fewer than six corners won in the final few minutes, Waterford could not produce the crucial breakthrough, much to the relief of a by now subdued home support. Thus with this Shield victory, Sligo returned to trophy winning form after a long barren spell and set the scene for probably the most memorable season in the club's long history.

Reasons to be cheerful, part three
Player-manager Willie McStay led Sligo to a memorable treble (The Star)

Bord Gais First Division Shield 1993-94

NORTHERN SECTION

Aug. 22nd	**Longford Town**	(2)	2	*(Parsons 22, Sullivan 26)*
	Finn Harps		0	
	Sligo Rovers	(1)	3	*(Houlahan 32, Devanney 80, 84)*
	St. James's Gate	(1)	1	*(McAvenue 43)*
Aug. 25th	**Athlone Town**	(1)	1	*(Dowling 44)*
	Longford Town		0	
	Finn Harps	(1)	1	*(Lafferty 40)*
	Sligo Rovers	(1)	1	*(Moran 2)*
Aug. 29th	St. James's Gate		0	
	Athlone Town	(1)	2	*(Dowling 15, Keane 49)*
	Longford Town		0	
	Sligo Rovers	(1)	1	*(Annand 25)*
Sep. 5th	Finn Harps	(0)	1	*(Hegarty 84)*
	St. James's Gate	(0)	1	*(Kelly 47)*
	Sligo Rovers	(1)	2	*(Annand 29, Reid 79)*
	Athlone Town		0	
Sep. 12th	Athlone Town	(0)	2	*(Keane 72, Golden 77)*
	Finn Harps	(2)	2	*(Gallagher 10, Trainor 37)*
	St. James's Gate		0	
	Longford Town	(1)	1	*(Fagan 6)*

	P.	W.	D.	L.	F.	A.	Pts.
Sligo Rovers	4	3	1	0	7	2	10
Athlone Town	4	2	1	1	5	4	7
Longford Town	4	2	0	2	3	2	6
Finn Harps	4	0	3	1	4	6	3
St. James's Gate	4	0	1	3	2	7	1

SOUTHERN SECTION

Aug. 22nd	**Home Farm**	(1)	1	*(Keddy 16)*
	Bray Wanderers		0	
	Kilkenny City	(1)	4	*(McKenna 45, 76, Wogan 49, 87)*
	U.C.D.	(1)	2	*(Griffin 10, Colwell (p) 52)*
Aug 26th	Kilkenny City		0	
	Waterford United	(1)	1	*(Farrell 10)*
	U.C.D.		0	
	Home Farm		0	
Aug. 29th	Bray Wanderers		0	
	Waterford United	(1)	1	*(Farrell 18)*
	Kilkenny City	(0)	1	*(Wogan 85)*
	Home Farm	(0)	1	*(Istvan 58)*
Sep. 5th	Home Farm		0	
	Waterford United		0	
	U.C.D.		0	
	Bray Wanderers		0	
Sep. 12th	Waterford United	(0)	1	*(Farrell 80)*
	U.C.D.	(2)	3	*(Treacy 4, O'Byrne 38, O'Brien 90)*
	Bray Wanderers		0	
	Kilkenny City		0	

	P.	W.	D.	L.	F.	A.	Pts.
Waterford United	4	2	1	1	3	3	7
Home Farm	4	1	3	0	2	1	6
Kilkenny City	4	1	2	1	5	4	5
U.C.D.	4	1	2	1	5	5	5
Bray Wanderers	4	0	2	2	0	2	2

FINAL

Dec. 28th 1st Leg at the Waterford Regional Sports Centre
    Waterford United (1) 1 *(Barden 45)*
    Sligo Rovers (2) 2 *(Kenny 11, Carr 20)*
Waterford U.: Wouters, Lonergan, B. Barry, Kelly, A. Barry, Crowley, Arrigan (Keane 68), Halloran, Lacey, Stokes, Barden.
Sligo Rovers: McLean, McStay, McDonnell, Carr (Devanney h.t), Dykes, Kenny, Hastie, Kelly, Houlahan, Annand, Moran (Scanlan h.t.).
Referee: Mr. J. Barry (Limerick)

Jan. 5th 2nd Leg at the Showgrounds
    Sligo Rovers 0
    Waterford United 0 *(Agg 2-1)*
Sligo Rovers: McLean, McStay, McDonnell, Boyle, Dykes, Kenny, Hastie, Kelly, Houlahan, Annand, Reid (Carr 58).
Waterford U.: Wouters, Lonergan, B. Barry, Reynolds, A. Barry Ormsby, Butler, Clem Fanning, Crowley, Barden, Colm Fanning.
Referee: Mr. J. Stacey (Athlone) Att. app.2,500

Previous First Division Shield Finals

1985/86 (1st leg) 13 Apr. 1986	Derry City (1) 3 *(Gauld (p) 9, Da Gama 68, Smyth og 89)* Longford T. (1) 1 *(Masterson 29)* at Brandywell; Referee: *W. Wallace (Donegal)*	(2nd leg) 20 Apr. 1986	Longford T. 0 Derry City (2) 3 *(Da-Gama 22, 44, 90 (p))* at Showgrounds: Referee: *O. Cooney (Dublin)*

Derry City: Quigley, McGuinness (McDermott HT),Quigg, Da Silva, McDowell, King, O'Neill, Da Gama, Bradley, Gauld, Mahon.
Longford: Kelly, Salmon, Smyth, Chubb, Pidgeon, Hackett (O'Sullivan 75), Walsh, Martin, Higgins, Masterson, Craven.

Longford T.: Kelly, Hackett, Smyth, Chubb, Pidgeon, Craven, Walsh, Martin, Higgins, Masterson (Salmon 63), O'Sullivan
Derry City: Quigley, McDermott, Quigg, Da Silva, McDowell, King (O'Doherty 80), O'Neill, Da Gama, Bradley (McCreadie 73), Gauld, Mahon.

1986/87 Emfa (2) 4 *(P. Madigan 7, Geoghegan 44, McGee, 54, 59)*
Finn Harps (1) 2 *(Greer 38, McKeever)*
19 Apr. 1987 at Oriel Park

Emfa: Cheevers, Hayes, Breen, M. Madigan, O'Mahony, P. Madigan, Craven, Higgins, Coady (Ryan), Geoghegan (Morgan 73), McGee.
Finn Harps: McCrystal, McDermott, Slevin, Walsh, L. Bonner, Cunningham, Greer, McLaughlin, McDaid (Martin 70), Arkwright (McMullen 70), McKeever.

1990/91 (1st leg) 18 Mar. 1991	Home Farm 0 Drogheda U. 0 at Whitehall: Referee: *P.J. Coyne (Kildare)*	(2nd leg) 1 Apr. 1991	Drogheda U.(0) 1 *(D. Geoghegan 88)* Home Farm 0 at United Park: Referee: *P. Leamy (Dublin)*

Home Farm: Smyth, Buckley, Morrissey, McKane, Mullen, Kieran, Milne, Redmond, Duff, Dunne, Bowes
Drogheda: Horgan, Brerton, Flanagan (O'Reilly 50), Girvan, D. Geoghegan, Carton, Toal, Donnelly, Scully, R. Kelly, Doyle.

Drogheda: Horgan, D. Geoghegan, Girvan, O'Reilly, Flanagan, Toal, D. Kelly (Scully 70), Donnelly, O'Callaghan, R. Kelly, Cunningham
Home Farm: Smyth, Buckley, Morrissey, Mullen, McKane, Bollard, Dunne, Redmond, Duff, Milne (Campbell HT), Murray.

1991/92 (1st leg) 23 Oct. 1991	U.C.D. (1) 1 *(Duffy 10)* Waterford U. 0 at Belfield; Referee: *T. Traynor (Dublin)*	(2nd leg) 28 Oct. 1991	Waterford U.(1) 1 *(J. Browne 38)* U.C.D. (1) 1 *(O'Brien 16)* at Kilcohan Park; Referee: *A. Gunning (Cork)*

U.C.D.: McKenna, Kavanagh, Lynch, Timmons, Treacy, McCabe (Colwell 79), Istvan, O'Sullivan, O'Brien, Duffy, Cullen
Waterford: Quinlivan, K. Kelly, A. Barry, Carr, Brazil (A. Kelly 44), Maher, (M. Browne HT), Devereaux, Cashin, Walsh, J. Browne, O'Connor

Waterford: Quinlivan, K. Kelly, A. Barry, Carr, A. Kelly, Walsh, Kielty (B. Barry HT), Cashin, M. Browne (Hale HT), J. Browne, O'Connor.
U.C.D.: McKenna, Kavanagh, Lynch, Timmons, Treacy, Colwell (Hyland 84), O'Sullivan, Istvan, O'Brien, Duffy (McCabe 84), Cullen.

1992/93 Galway U. (1) 3 *(McGee 15, 88; McCormack og. 67)*
Home Farm 0
10 Dec. '92 at Dalymount Park   Referee: *J. Stacey (Athlone)*

Galway U.: Cunningham, Kenny, Cassidy, Rogers, Nolan, Lally, Mullen, Mannion, McGee, Mernagh (Halion 83), Carpenter.
Home Farm: McCormack, Buckley, O'Reilly, Murray, McGuinness, Mullen, Gannon, A.Lynch (Dodd 75), Keddy (Costigan 75), King, Donnelly.

THE LEINSTER SENIOR CUP
Shelbourne end a barren spell

It's hard to believe that this season's Leinster Senior Cup win, was a first for Shelbourne in twenty two years. Indeed it was also their first appearance in a provincial decider, since that last success back in January 1972, when Bohemians were defeated by three goals to one at Dalymount Park. Having waited so long for a seventeenth title, the pity was that their clash with Dundalk at Tolka Park on March 21st was all too forgetable. A bad tempered affair which included four sendings off and precious little good football, was just the latest in a line of disappointing Leinster finals. At least we were spared the disgraceful terrace antics which had marred the previous final between Bohemians and Shamrock Rovers.

Having included no fewer than nineteen non-League sides in the first round last year, this season just three Ashtown Villa, St. Francis and Whitehall Rangers made it to the same stage. Appropriately enough, it was in fact Shelbourne who began proceedings by hosting Kilkenny City on August 4th, where they gave little clue as to their later triumph, scraping home courtesy of Greg Costello's goal in extra time. The non-Leaguers fared badly, those great cup battlers St. Francis suffering the competition's worst defeat, nil-six at Home Farm, whilst Ashtown Villa and Whitehall also lost out to St. James's Gate and U.C.D. respectively. Elsewhere Dundalk and Longford Town enjoyed good local derby wins at Drogheda and Athlone, holders Bohemians were very impressive in overcoming St. Patrick's Athletic, while Bray secured the shock of the round, knocking out Shamrock Rovers.

The quarter finals included three Premier/First Division clashes, with Bohemians, Dundalk and Shelbourne all making the most of home advantage to defeat St. James's Gate, Bray Wanderers and Home Farm. The fourth tie at Belfield ensured First Division representation in the semi's with U.C.D. hosting Longford Town. The visitors won a close encounter, with a single first half effort from Richie Parsons sufficient for success.

For their first Leinster semi-final since 1960, Longford travelled to Oriel Park where despite a fine performance, Alan Doherty's lone strike secured Dundalk, their first provincial final appearance in ten years. The second semi between Shelbourne and holders Bohemians at Dalymount Park was undoubtedly the pick of the crop in this season's competition. Having swapped second half goals through Doolin and Broughan, an absorbing tie went to extra time and eventually to a penalty shoot-out. Not for the first time it was goalkeeper Jody Byrne who was the 'Reds' hero, saving three spot kicks, while Anto Whelan's final strike stripped the holders of their title and ensured 'Shels' an overdue Leinster final appearance.

Unfortunately for the paltry attendance (approx. 300), which left the comfort of their armchairs on March 21st and made their way to Tolka Park, their efforts were not rewarded with much of a spectacle. Indeed by far the busiest man on the pitch was not any of the players, but referee Dave Allen who presided over a tetchy, free ridden ninety minutes. After a very poor first half, Dundalk skipper James Coll and Shelbourne's Ken O'Doherty were dismissed minutes into the second period after a punch-up in the 'Lillywhites' goalmouth. The winning goal after 73 minutes was one of the few bright spots as Antonio Izzi, who ten minutes earlier had replaced Brennan, volleyed home Vinny Arkins cross in style. The goal however did little to improve the quality of play, and just before the end referee Allen again flashed a brace of red cards, this time in the direction of Shelbourne's Greg Costello and Dundalk's Tom O'Sullivan who had swapped punches, after a bad tackle by the 'Shels' player. The final whistle moments later, brought relief, and whilst Shelbourne celebrated the end of a long barren run in the Leinster Senior Cup, it was a pity that their triumph had not been marked by a better spectacle, than this most disappointing of finals.

Izzi good or what?
Tony Izzi hit the Final winner
(CL)

Long Ball?
Brian Mooney (Shelbourne) takes on Keith Long (Dundalk) (The Star)

217

Leinster Senior Cup 1993/94

First Round

Aug. 4th	Shelbourne	(0) 1	(Costello (p))
	Kilkenny City	0	AET
Aug. 6th	Drogheda United	(0) 1	(Crolly)
	Dundalk	(2) 2	(Donnelly, O'Sullivan)
Aug. 8th	Bray Wanderers	(1) 1	(Douglas)
	Shamrock Rovers	(1) 1	(Osam)

(Bray Wanderers won 3-2 on pens after extra time)

Sep. 3rd	Home Farm	(3) 6	(G.Coyle 3, Kelly 2, C. Lawless)
	St. Francis	0	
Sep. 9th	Ashtown Villa	(0) 1	(Lynch)
	St. James's Gate	(1) 2	(Kelly, Gorman)
	Athlone Town	(0) 2	(Golden, Kiernan)
	Longford Town	(1) 3	(Green, Reid, Kelly (p))
Oct. 6th	Bohemians	(2) 3	(O'Connor 2, O'Driscoll)
	St. Patrick's Athletic	0	
Oct. 20th	U.C.D.	(2) 3	(O'Byrne 2, O'Brien)
	Whitehall Rangers	(0) 1	(McDonagh)

Quarter Finals

Nov. 2nd	Bohemians	(0) 2	(Fenlon, Cousins)
	St. James's Gate	(1) 1	(Farrell)
Nov. 9th	Shelbourne	(1) 2	(Rutherford, Arkins)
	Home Farm	0	
Nov. 11th	U.C.D.	0	
	Longford Town	(1) 1	(Parsons)
Nov. 14th	Dundalk	(3) 3	(Doherty, Britton, O'Sullivan)
	Bray Wanderers	(1) 1	(Brien)

Semi Finals

Jan. 19th	Dundalk	1	(Doherty)
	Longford Town	0	
Jan. 24th	Bohemians	(0) 1	(Broughan)
	Shelbourne	(0) 1	(Doolin)

(Shelbourne won 4-3 on pens after extra time)

FINAL

21st Mar. 1994 at Tolka Park   Referee: Mr. D. Allen (Dublin)   Att: approx. 300

| Shelbourne | (0) 1 | (Izzi 73) |
| Dundalk | 0 | |

Shelbourne: Byrne, Flood, Neville, Whelan, Smith, Brennan (Izzi 63), Costello, Kelly, Mooney, O'Doherty, Arkins

Dundalk: Kavanagh, Long, Coll, Staunton, Lawless, O'Dowd, P.Hanrahan, Britton, Doherty (O'Leary 75), Donnelly (O'Sullivan 64), Irwin.

LEINSTER SENIOR CUP FINALS:

Season	Winners	Runners-Up	Score
1892/93	Leinster Nomads	Dublin University	2-1
1893/94	Bohemians	Dublin University	2-2, 3-0
1894/95	Bohemians	Dublin University	1-1, 3-1
1895/96	Bohemians	Athlone Town	3-1
1896/97	Bohemians	Dundalk	3-2
1897/98	Bohemians	Shelbourne	3-1
1898/99	Bohemians	Richmond Rovers	2-1
99/1900	Shelbourne	Freebooters	1-0
1900/01	Shelbourne	Bohemians	2-1
1901/02	Bohemians	Tritonville	1-0
1902/03 *	Bohemians		
1903/04	Shelbourne	Bohemians	3-2
1904/05	Bohemians	Shelbourne	1-0
1905/06	Shelbourne	Royal Irish Rifles	3-1
1906/07	Bohemians	Reginald	0-0, 4-0
1907/08	Shelbourne	Royal Berkshires	3-1
1908/09	Shelbourne	Lancashire Fusiliers	3-1
1909/10	Bohemians	Inniskilling Fusiliers	3-0
1910/11	Bohemians	Shelbourne	1-0
1911/12	Bohemians	Manchester Regiment	3-0
1912/13	Shelbourne	Bohemians	4-0
1913/14	Shelbourne	St. James's Gate	0-0, 0-0, 2-0
1914/15	Bohemians	Clarence	6-0
1915/16	Bohemians	Shelbourne	0-0, 3-2
1916/17	Shelbourne	St. James's Gate	2-0
1917/18	Olympia	Shelbourne	1-0
1918/19	Shelbourne	St. James's Gate	3-0
1919/20	St. James's Gate	Bohemians	0-0, 1-1, 2-1
1920/21	Dublin United	St. James's Gate	1-0
1921/22	St. James's Gate	Jacobs	1-0
1922/23	Shamrock Rovers	Bohemians	3-1
1923/24	Shelbourne	Brideville	2-1
1924/25 **	Brideville	Glasnevin	1-0
1925/26	Bohemians	Shelbourne	2-2, 2-1
1926/27	Shamrock Rovers	Bohemians	2-2, 2-1
1927/28	Bohemians	Shelbourne	0-0, 3-1
1928/29	Shamrock Rovers	Dundalk	0-0, 1-0
1929/30	Shamrock Rovers	Shelbourne	2-1
1930/31	Shelbourne	Dolphin	1-0
1931/32	Dolphin	Shelbourne	3-0
1932/33	Shamrock Rovers	Dolphin	2-1
1933/34	Drumcondra	Shamrock Rovers	3-2
1934/35	St. James's Gate	Dundalk	2-1
1935/36	Drumcondra	Dundalk	2-0
1936/37	St. James's Gate	Dundalk	1-0
1937/38	Shamrock Rovers	Brideville	2-0
1938/39	Drumcondra	Dundalk	2-1
1939/40	Bohemians	Shamrock Rovers	2-0
1940/41	St. James's Gate	Bohemians	4-2
1941/42	Distillery	Bray Unknowns	4-1
1942/43	Drumcondra	St. James's Gate	4-2
1943/44	Drumcondra	Shamrock Rovers	3-2

1944/45		Drumcondra	Shelbourne	2-1
1945/46		Shelbourne	Shamrock Rovers	4-0
1946/47		Bohemians	Grangegorman	11-0
1947/48		St. Patrick's Athletic	Transport	3-2
1948/49		Shelbourne	Shamrock Rovers	5-2
1949/50		Drumcondra	Shelbourne	4-1
1950/51		Dundalk	St. Patrick's Athletic	2-1
1951/52		Transport	Shelbourne	3-0
1952/53		Shamrock Rovers	Bohemians	1-1, 2-0
1953/54		Drumcondra	St. Patrick's Athletic	3-1
1954/55		Shamrock Rovers	Longford Town	2-1
1955/56		Shamrock Rovers	St. Patrick's Athletic	3-1
1956/57		Shamrock Rovers	Drumcondra	2-0
1957/58		Shamrock Rovers	Drumcondra	1-1, 1-0
1958/59		Drumcondra	Dundalk	5-2
1959/60		Drumcondra	Transport	1-0
1960/61		Dundalk	Drumcondra	1-0
1961/62		Drumcondra	Dundalk	1-0
1962/63		Shelbourne	Shamrock Rovers	2-1
1963/64		Shamrock Rovers	St. Patrick's Athletic	3-0
1964/65		Home Farm	Dundalk	2-1
1965/66		Bohemians	Shelbourne	3-2
1966/67		Bohemians	Dundalk	1-0
1967/68		Shelbourne	Drumcondra	4-0
1968/69		Shamrock Rovers	Bohemians	3-0
1969/70		Athlone Town	Shelbourne	4-0
1970/71		Dundalk	Shamrock Rovers	5-2
1971/72		Shelbourne	Bohemians	3-1
1972/73		Bohemians	Shamrock Rovers	3-1
1973/74		Dundalk	Bohemians	0-0, 1-0
1974/75		Bohemians	Shamrock Rovers	1-1, 1-0
1975/76		Bohemians	Athlone Town	4-3
1976/77	***	Dundalk	Bohemians	1-0
1977/78		Dundalk	Bohemians	1-0
1978/79		Bohemians	Shamrock Rovers	2-1
1979/80		Bohemians	Athlone Town	2-0
1980/81		U.C.D.	St. Patrick's Athletic	2-1
1981/82		Shamrock Rovers	Dundalk	2-1
1982/83		St. Patrick's Athletic	Drogheda United	3-2
1983/84		Bohemians	U.C.D.	1-0
1984/85		Shamrock Rovers	U.C.D.	2-1
1985/86		Bohemians	Drogheda United	1-0
1986/87		St. Patrick's Athletic	Bohemians	1-0
1987/88		Athlone Town	St. Patrick's Athletic	1-0
1988/89		Bohemians	Bray Wanderers	1-1, 1-0
1989/90		St. Patrick's Athletic	Bray Wanderers	2-0
1990/91		St. Patrick's Athletic	Bohemians	1-1, 1-0
1991/92		Athlone Town	St. Francis	0-0, 4-2
1992/93		Bohemians	Shamrock Rovers	1-0
1993/94		Shelbourne	Dundalk	1-0

* Shelbourne withdrew in protest at the appointed referee ** Due to a dispute League clubs did not take part *** Competition confined to these two clubs

SUMMARY OF WINNERS

30 Bohemians, 18 Shelbourne, 15 Shamrock Rovers, 11 Drumcondra, 6 Dundalk,
5 St. Patricks Athletic, St. James's Gate, 3 Athlone Town, 1 Brideville, Distillery, Dolphin,
Dublin United, Home Farm, Leinster Nomads, Olympia, Transport, U.C.D.

Munster Senior Cup 1993-94
Five in a row for Cork City

The 85th running of the Munster Senior Cup was another fragmented affair which dragged on from September right through to May, fully five weeks after the League of Ireland Championship was completed. Having completely dominated this competition in recent times Cork City were chasing their fifth title in a row, and their seventh consecutive appearance in a Munster Cup decider. Once again this year three rounds were completed before the province's League of Ireland sides joined the fray, though unfortunately Limerick again declined to take part. The first round saw seventeen games played with Blarney United and Mayfield United both awarded walkovers whilst Everton received a bye. Greenmount Rangers, with a 6-0 drubbing of fellow Corkonians Dunbar Celtic, and Avenue United from Ennis, who hit five without reply against Greenwood, provided the highlights of the round. Surprisingly, the previous season's finalists Fermoy lost out at the first hurdle on this occasion.

Despite the fact that all matches were decided on the day, if necessary either through extra-time or penalties, the second round took six weeks to complete. The big game was the meeting of the then top two placed sides in the Premier Division of the Munster Senior League, Everton and Avondale United, with the former, as they did in the race for MSL honours, coming out on top.

The tightest encounter in round 3 was that between Mayfield United and Crofton Celtic with the latter winning on penalties after an exciting 3-3 draw. Elsewhere Cork sides Tramore Athletic, Everton and St. Mary's joined the aforementioned Avenue United in the quarter finals.

The most clear cut quarter final win came at St. Colman's Park, Cobh, where in the first ever game under floodlights at the venue, the homesters scored five without reply against Crofton. Holders Cork City, also had a comfortable home win, against Avenue United, whilst performance of the round came at Waterford where the 'Blues' went down 0-2 to visitors Tramore Athletic. In the only all non-league clash, Everton needed penalties to see off the challenge of St. Mary's.

In a disappointing first semi-final at Bishopstown, late goals from Morley and Gaynor saw Cork City overcome Tramore, while later that evening in Cobh, a lone strike from Alan O'Neill was sufficient to see 'Ramblers' through to their first Munster Cup decider since 1987 at the expense of Everton, in what was another poor encounter.

The Final itself, a week later on May 8th at Turners Cross, was thankfully a great deal more exciting than either of the semi's, the local derby aspect adding an extra dimension. Cork City opened the scoring on the quarter hour, Pat Morley whipping a volley past Michael Devine in the Cobh goal. It was Morley's fourth successive final to notch a goal, giving the ace striker a unique Munster Cup record. Within nine minutes, however, Cobh were on level terms through Alan O'Neill, and ten minutes after that Brian Healy, making his first team debut, put them ahead. 'Ramblers' held this lead to the interval but within two minutes of the restart some good approach work from Anthony Buckley was finished to the net by Billy Woods. And so the scoreline remained at 2-2 even throughout extra-time, mainly due to the excellence of goalkeepers Harrington and in particular Devine. So for a third time the Munster Cup Final was decided on a penalty shoot-out where the holders triumphed 4-2 to retain their stranglehold on this particular competition.

In the family ...
Father and son, Jackie and Pat Morley, who have both scored in Munster Senior Cup Finals (EOH)

Munster Senior Cup 1993/94

First Round

Sep. 12th **Avenue United** (Clare) (3) **5** *(Hehir 3, Ryan, Mannion)*
Greenwood 0

Avondale United (0) 1 *(O'Connell)*
Nenagh (0) 1 *(Quinlivan)* AET
(Avondale won 4-3 on pens)

Ballincollig (0) **2** *(Brady, Horgan)*
Douglas Hall (0) 1 *(Cotter)*

Blarney United Walkover / Askeaton withdrew
Askeaton

Casement Celtic (1) **4** *(Caulfield, Swan 2, Nagle)*
Waterford Bohs. (2) 3 *(Twomey, McCormack, Madigan)* AET
(Score after 90 mins. 3-3)

College Corinth. 0
St. Mary's 0 AET
(St. Mary's won 4-2 on pens.)

Fairview Rangers (1) **1** *(Constadine)*
Midleton 0

Fermoy (1) 2 *(Van Wijnen 2)*
Tramore Athletic (2) 2 *(Forde 2)*
(Tramore Athletic won 5-4 on pens.)

Greenmount R. (2) **6** *(Goulding 3, Scannell, O'Leary, Fitzgerald)*
Dunbar Celtic 0

Mayfield United Walkover / Johnville withdrew
Johnville

Newcastlewest 1
Mallow United 3

Ringmahon R. (1) 1 *(O'Mahony)*
Springfield (1) **2** *(McDonagh (p), Burns)*

Rockmount (2) **3** *(Ahern 2, Cronin)*
Crosshaven (0) 1 *(Kelleher)*

St. John Bosco (1) 2 *(McSweeney, Boylan)*
Carrigaline Utd. (1) **4** *(Cahill 2, Keating 2)*

Temple United 0
Crofton Celtic (1) **1** *(O'Neill)*

Wembley (2) **3** *(Long, Manning, Curtin)*
Glasheen (1) 2 *(Healy (p), Cronin)*

Wilton United (1) 1 *(Butler)*
Cobh Wanderers (1) **2** *(Lane, O'Neill)*

Sep. 19th **St. Michaels** (Tipp) **1** *(Grace)*
Tralee Dynamoes 0

Oct. 3rd **Castleview** (1) 2 *(Magnier, O'Brien)*
U.C.C. (3) **4** *(Monaghan, Sweeney, Cronin, Graigner)*

Bye: Everton

Second Round

Oct. 17th **Mallow United** 0
U.C.C. (1) **4** *(O'Keeffe, Bird, Dennehy, Carroll)*

Rockmount (1) **2** *(Long, O'Mahony)*
Wembley (1) 1 *(Courtney)*

St. Mary's (0) **4** *(Hyde, T.Long 2, G.Long)*
Ballincollig (0) 2 *(Prendeville, og.)* AET
(Score after 90 mins. 1-1)

Springfield 0
Tramore Athletic (1) **1** *(Hegarty)*

Oct. 24th **Everton** (1) **2** *(Nagle, Browne)*
Avondale Utd. (0) 1 *(O'Leary)*

Mayfield United **2**
Blarney United 0

Nov. 7th **Greenmount R.** (1) 2 *(Goulding, Kiely)*
Avenue United (0) **3** *(Gilligan, Corry, Miniter)*

Nov. 8th **Crofton Celtic** (0) **2** *(O'Neill, Connolly)*
St. Michaels (1) 1 *(Ryan)*

Fairview Rangers 2
Casement Celtic 2
(Casement Celtic won on pens. AET)

Nov. 21st **Cobh Wanderers** (1) **2** *(Coughlan, Shanahan (p))*
Carrigaline Utd. (1) 1 *(O'Neill (p))*

Third Round

Dec. 12th **Avenue United** (1) **1** *(Gilligan)*
U.C.C. 0

St. Mary's (1) **4** *(T.Long 2, Hyde, Commyns)*
Rockmount (1) 1 *(Dennehy)*

Dec. 27th **Fairview Rangers** 0
Everton (1) **2** *(O'Regan, Nagle)*

Jan. 16th **Carrigaline United** 0
Tramore Athletic (1) **3** *(Forde, Hegarty, Morgan)*

Jan. 30th **Mayfield United** 3
Crofton Celtic 3
(Crofton Celtic won 5-3 on pens. AET)

Quarter Finals

Mar. 15th **Cobh Ramblers** (2) **5** *(K.Kelly 3, Kenneally 2)*
Crofton Celtic 0

Apr. 10th **Everton** **2** *(M.O'Regan, T.O'Regan)*
St. Mary's **2** *(Long, Hyde)*
(Everton won 5-4 on pens. AET)

Waterford United 0
Tramore Athletic (2) **2** *(Forde 2)*

Apr. 17th **Cork City** (2) **4** *(Buckley, Morley (p), Woods 2)*
Avenue United (1) **1**

Semi-Finals

Mar. 1st **Cork City** (0) **2** *(Morley, Gaynor)*
Tramore Athletic 0

Cobh Ramblers (0) **1** *(O'Neill)*
Everton 0

FINAL

May 8th at Turner's Cross Referee: Mr. A. O'Regan (Cork)
Cork City (1) **2** *(Morley 15, Woods 47)*
Cobh Ramblers (2) **2** *(O'Neill 24, Healy 34)* AET
(Cork City won 4-2 on penalties)

Cork City: Harrington, Daly, O'Donoghue, Ashton, Napier, Buckley, Barry, Murphy, McCarthy (Warren extra-time), Woods, Morley.

Cobh Ramblers: Devine, P.Kelly, Lynch, Bannon, Long, Kenneally (O'Flaherty 17), K.O'Rourke, J.O'Rourke, K.Kelly, Healy, O'Neill (Greene 70).

Irish Football Handbook (Edition 3) 1993-94: Limited number still available.
Unique features include:
Ireland's Euro tour 1939; Bohemians v Glasgow Rangers 1984; Cork Athletic v Evergreen United; 1953 F.A.I. Cup Final (Raich Carter); Unbeaten Sequences.
From:
Red Card Publications
P.O. Box 10, Eglinton Street, Cork, R.O.I.
£5.99 post free (R.O.I./U.K.) + £2 postage (Europe) + £4 postage (worldwide)

MUNSTER SENIOR CUP FINALS

1901-02	6th Prov. Battalion (Fermoy) Royal Engineers	2 1		T
1902-03	Royal Engineers (Camden) CIYMA	5 3		T
1903-04	Cork Celtic Leinster Regiment	3 1		T
1904-05	Manchester Reg. Haulbowline	5 1		T
1905-06	3rd Dragoon Guards Durham Lt. Infantry	4 1		T
1906-07	Sherwood Foresters Durham Lt. Infantry			?
1907-08	Royal Field Artillery Royal Welsh Fusiliers	2 1 (AET)		T
1908-09	Royal Welsh Fusiliers South Lancs. Regt.	2 1		T
1909-10	Royal Welsh Fusiliers Highland Lt. Infantry	1 0		T
1910-11	Rifle Brigade (Tipp.) Highland Lt. Infantry	2 0		V
1911-12	North Staffs Regt. East Surrey Regt.	3 2		V
1912-13	Kings O Yorks Lt. Inf. North Staffs Regt.	1 0		B
1913-14	Rifle Brigade (Cork) Royal Field Artillery	1 5 1 1		V, V
1922-23	Fordsons FC Shandon	4 1	(O'Sullivan, Buckley, Collins 2) (J. Ryan (pen))	V
1923-24	Fordson FC Barrackton United	3 0	(Ward, Collins 2)	V
1924-25	Cobh Ramblers Cork City	4 2	(Brookes, Webb, Davidson, Woodward) (Falvey, Bishop (pen))	V
1925-26	Fordson FC Cork Bohemians	2 1	(O'Driscoll, Kelly) (J. Stanton)	V
1926-27	Cork Bohemians Cahir Park	2 1	(O'Sullivan 2) (Crowley)	V
1927-28	Cork Bohemians Barrackton United	2 2	(Keane, Noonan) (Herlihy, 2 pens)	M
Replay	Cork Bohemians Barrackton United	1 0	(Noonan)	M

1928-29	Fordson FC Fermoy	3 0	*(Buckle, Hannon 2)*	M
1929-30	Fordson "B" Cork Bohemians	1 0	*(McCarthy)*	M
1930-31	Cork Bohemians Cork "B"	3 1	*(Buckley, Fletcher, Cunneen)* *(Hannon)*	GT
1931-32	Cork Bohemians Barrackton United	2 2	*(O'Sullivan, Cunneen)* *(Hickey (pen), Collins)*	GT
Replay	Cork Bohemians Barrackton United	2 0	*(Cunneen, Buckley)*	M
1932-33	Cork Bohemians Waterford	3 0	*(Cunneen 2, O'Neill)*	GT
1933-34	Cork Southern Rovers	4 0	*(Coleman 2, O'Keeffe 2)*	T
1934-35	Waterford Cobh Ramblers	2 1	*(Ryan, Walsh)* *(Farrelly)*	T
1935-36	Southern Rovers Grattan United	2 1	*(Murray, Allen)* *(Murphy)*	T
1936-37	Cork Cobh Ramblers	3 1	*(Monaghan, Ryng, O'Connell)* *(Burke (pen)*	M
1937-38	Limerick Cork	2 2	*(Kelly, Aherne)* *(O'Donoghue, Thompson)*	M
Replay	Limerick Cork	2 0	*(Noonan, Davis)*	MF
1938-39	Cork City Limerick	0 0		M
Replay	Cork City Limerick	4 0	*(Turnbull 3, O'Neill)*	M
1939-40	Cork United Limerick		*(Final not played)*	
1940-41	Cork United Evergreen	2 0	*(O'Neill, McCarthy)*	M
1941-42	St. Kevins Dunlop FC	3 0	*(Keane, Murphy (pen), Corbett)*	T
1942-43	Cork Bohemians Richmond Celtic	2 0	*(Philpott 2)*	T
1943-44	Cobh Ramblers Coastal Defence	3 3	*(Keating, Quaine, O'Mahony)* *(McCarthy, O'Keeffe, Ross)*	M
Replay	Cobh Ramblers Coastal Defence	2 1	*(Hannigan, O'Reilly)* *(Ross)*	M
1944-45	Cork United "B" Blackrock	1 1	*(Cotter)* *(Cremin)*	M
Replay	Cork United "B" Blackrock	4 1	*(Desmond, O'Connell 2, Broderick)* *(Cremin)*	T

1945-46	Waterford	1	*(Curtin)*		M
	Cork United	1	*(McCarthy)*	*final not replayed*	
1946-47	Cork United	2	*(O'Leary 2)*		M
	Waterford	1	*(Cronin)*		
1947-48	Cork United	1	*(D. Noonan)*		M
	Waterford	1	*(Curtin)*	*final not replayed*	
1948-49	Limerick	1	*(Carroll)*		M
	Waterford	1	*(Curtin (pen))*		
Replay	Limerick	2	*(Flynn, Cusack)*		M
	Waterford	1	*(McMullen)*		
1949-50	Albert Rovers	2	*(Allen, Singleton)*		T
	Cork Athletic	1	*(O'Reilly (pen))*		
1950-51	Cork Athletic	4	*(O'Leary, Lennox 2, Hennessy)*		M
	Limerick	0			
1951-52	Evergreen United	2	*(McCarthy 2)*		M
	Waterford	2	*(Keating, Barry)*		
Replay	Evergreen United	5	*(McCarthy 4, T. Fitzgerald (OG))*		M
	Waterford	1	*(D. Fitzgerald)*		
1952-53	Cork Athletic	1	*(Cotter (pen))*		M
	Limerick	1	*(Cronin)*		
Replay	Cork Athletic	5	*(O'Leary 3, Broderick, Carter)*		M
	Limerick	2	*(Cusack, Hayes)*		
1953-54	Limerick	5	*(Cronin, Gilbert 2, Callopy (pen), Lynam)*		M
	Albert Rovers	1	*(Collins)*		
1954-55	Cork Athletic	4	*(J. Moloney, Collins, Wallace, W. Moloney)*		M
	Waterford	1	*(O'Grady)*		
1955-56	Waterford	3	*(McIlvenny, J. Fitzgerald 2)*		M
	Cork Athletic	0			
1956-57	Waterford	5	*(D. Fitzgerald, A. Hale 2, Martin (pen), McFarlane)*		M
	Evergreen United	1	*(Madden)*		
1957-58	Evergreen United		*Final not played*		
	Limerick				
1958-59	Limerick	3	*(Dillon, Lynam 2, (1 pen))*		M
	Evergreen United	1	*(Moloney)*		
1959-60	Cork Celtic	3	*(Leahy 2, McCarthy)*		M
	Waterford	1	*(Casey)*		
1960-61	Cork Hibernians	3	*(Galvin, Morley, Allen)*		M
	Waterford	2	*(J. Fitzgerald, McGrath)*		
1961-62	Cork Celtic	3	*(Lynam 2, Leahy)*		M
	Limerick	0			
1962-63	Limerick	1	*(F. McNamara)*		FL
	Cork Hibernians	1	*(Jordan)*		
Replay	Limerick	1	*(O'Connor)*		MF
	Cork Hibernians	0			

Season	Teams	Score	Scorers	
1963-64	Cork Celtic	2	*(Noonan, Leahy)*	FL
	Limerick	1	*(Fenton)*	
1964-65	Cork Hibernians	3	*(Wallace, Gosnell, Fitzgerald)*	T
	Cork Celtic	1	*(O'Donovan)*	
1965-66	Waterford	4	*(Casey, Matthews 2, Coad)*	K
	Cobh Ramblers	1	*(Devlin)*	
1966-67	Waterford	2	*(Matthews, Hale)*	FL
	Cork Hibernians	2	*(Noonan 2)*	
Replay	Waterford	2	*(Hale 2, (1 pen)*	K
	Cork Hibernians	1	*(Noonan)*	
1967-68	Cork Hibernians	3	*(Noonan, McSweeney, Wallace)*	MF
	Limerick	1	*(McGrath)*	
1968-69	Cork Hibernians	4	*(Davenport, Wallace, Wigginton, Dennehy)*	K
	Waterford	1	*(Hale)*	
1969-70	Cork Hibernians	2	*(Wigginton, Henderson (pen))*	FL
	Waterford	2	*(Hale, Buck)*	
Replay	Cork Hibernians	3	*(Eddie, Davenport 2)*	K
	Waterford	2	*(Matthews 2, 1 pen)*	
1970-71	Cork Hibernians	4	*(Dennehy 2, Dreaper, Marsden (pen))*	FL
	Limerick	1	*(McEvoy)*	
1971-72	Cork Celtic	3	*(J. McCarthy 2, Ryan)*	T
	Waterford	1	*(Keane)*	
1972-73	Cork Hibernians	4	*(Wigginton, Coyne 3)*	FL
	Limerick	2	*(Doyle, Kennedy)*	
1973-74	Cork Celtic	6	*(Madden, Notley 2, Ludzik (pen), Shortt, Hannigan)*	T
	Limerick	1	*(Hogan)*	
1974-75	Cork Hibernians	3	*(Brohan, Lawson, Davenport OG)*	T
	Cork Celtic	0		
1975-76	Waterford	2	*(Leech 2)*	FL
	Cork Hibernians	1	*(Trainer)*	
1976-77	Limerick	3	*(Kennedy, O'Mahony, Fitzgerald)*	P
	Cork Celtic	2	*(Shortt, Barry)*	
1977-78	Cork Alberts	2	*(Finnegan, Notley)*	M
	Limerick	1	*(McDonnell)*	
1978-79	Cobh Ramblers		final not played	
	Limerick			
1979-80	Cork United	2	*(Allen, Madden)*	FL
	Crosshaven	0		
1980-81	Waterford	2	*(Madigan, Bennett)*	K
	Tramore Athletic	1	*(Bruton)*	
1981-82	Cork United	0		FL
	Waterford	0		
Replay	Cork United	0		K
	Waterford	0	(5-4pens)	

1982-83	Cobh Ramblers	5	(O'Halloran, Wilshaw, F. O'Neill, Crowley (pen), McCarthy)	T
	Clonmel Town	1	(Ryan)	
1983-84	Limerick City	1	(Kennedy)	S
	Cobh Ramblers	0		
1984-85	Limerick City	1	(Hulmes (pen))	R
	Cobh Ramblers	1	(Mellerick)	
Replay	Limerick City	2	(McDaid, Morris)	S
	Cobh Ramblers	2	(O'Halloran, Piggott) (3-1 pens)	
1985-86	Waterford United	4	(Jones, Bennett 2 (1 pen), Dixon)	T
	Wembley	0		
1986-87	Waterford United	2	(Grace (pen), Cashin)	K
	Limerick City	1	(Morley)	
1987-88	Cork City	1	(Barry)	T
	Cobh Ramblers	0		
1988-89	Limerick City	1	(Walsh (pen))	R
	Cork City	0		
1989-90	Cork City	3	(Barry, Kenneally, Nagle)	T
	Tramore Athletic	0		
1990-91	Cork City	3	(Morley, Caulfield, Gallagher)	T
	Limerick City	0		
1991-92	Cork City	6	(Caulfield 3, Morley, McCabe, Bannon)	T
	Everton	1	(Browne)	
1992-93	Cork City	3	(Morley 2, Barry)	T
	Fermoy	1	(Lawlor)	
1993-94	Cork City	2	(Morley, Woods)	T
	Cobh Ramblers	2	(O'Neill, Healy) (4-2 pens)	

Key to Venues

B = Ballintemple FL = Flower Lodge GT = Greyhound Track
K = Kilcohan Park M = Mardyke MF = The Markets Field
P = Priory Park R = Rathbane S = St. Colman's Park
T = Turner's Cross V = Victoria Cross

1. 1906-07 Final possibly never played.
2. Cork Celtic, the first civilian team to win the Cup, had no connection with Cork Celtic 1959-79.
3. Competition suspended on outbreak of World War I.
4. New Munster Football Association formed, 1922.

* Awarded to Waterford   ** Awarded to Cobh Ramblers

Summary of Winners 1922-23 / 1993-94

8. Cork Hibernians, Waterford, 6. Cork Bohemians, Cork Celtic / Evergreen United, Cork City (1984), Limerick, 4. Albert Rovers / Cork United, Cobh Ramblers, Fordson F.C., 3. Cork Athletic, Cork United (1940), Limerick City, 2. Cork F.C., Waterford United 1. Cork City (1938), Cork United "B", Fordson "B" St. Kevins, Southern Rovers.

THE PRESIDENTS CUP

1993/94 Final
11th Aug. 1993 at Tolka Park, Referee: J. McDermott (Dublin)
Shelbourne (1) **3** *(Arkins 17, Mooney 87, 110)*
Bohemians (0) **2** *(L.King 65, Devlin 72) A.E.T.*

Shelbourne: Byrne, Riordan, Dunne, Neville, Whelan (Izzi 97), Doolin, Mooney, Costello, Arkins, Wilson (Flood 74), Rutherford.

Bohemians: Henderson, Broughan, Geoghegan, Best, Moody, Dunne, Devlin (Neville 100), O'Connor, King L., Fenlon, King H.

Season	Winners	Runners-up	Score	Venue
1929-30	Shamrock Rovers	Shelbourne	1-1*	S
1930-31	Dundalk	Shamrock Rovers	1-1, 7-3	S, D
1931-32	*This competition was not completed*			
1932-33	Shamrock Rovers	Dundalk	2-0	D
1933-34 to 1938-39 *no competition*				
1939-40	Shelbourne	Shamrock Rovers	2-1	S
1940-41	Shamrock Rovers	St. James's Gate	2-1	S
1941-42	Shamrock Rovers	Drumcondra	3-3, 4-4, 5-3	T, D, M
1942-43	No Competition			
1943-44	Shamrock Rovers	Dundalk	3-2	M
1944-45	Shamrock Rovers	Drumcondra	2-0	M
1945-46	Shamrock Rovers	Shelbourne	3-2	M
1946-47	Drumcondra	Shamrock Rovers	2-2, 1-0	D, D
1947-48	Drumcondra	Shelbourne	2-2*	
1948-49	Shamrock Rovers	Drumcondra	3-2	M
1949-50	Drumcondra	Dundalk	2-1	T
1950-51	Drumcondra	Transport	2-0	T
1951-52	Dundalk	Drumcondra	2-1	T
1952-53	St. Patrick's Ath.	Dundalk	1-1, 5-0	T, D
1953-54	St. Patricks Ath.	Shelbourne	2-2, 3-1	T, T
1954-55	Shamrock Rovers	Drumcondra	2-1	T
1955-56	St. Patricks Ath.	Shamrock Rovers	3-1	T
1956-57	Shamrock Rovers	St. Patrick's Ath.	1-0	D
1957-58	Shamrock Rovers	Drumcondra	3-3, 1-0	D, D
1958-59	Drumcondra	Dundalk	4-3	D
1959-60	Shamrock Rovers	St. Patrick's Ath.	1-1, 2-0	D, T
1960-61	Shelbourne	Shamrock Rovers	1-1, 1-1, 3-1	D, T, T
1961-62	Drumcondra	St. Patrick's Ath.	3-0	D
1962-63	Shamrock Rovers	Shelbourne	1-0	D
1963-64	Dundalk	Shelbourne	4-3	D

Season	Winners	Runners-up	Score	Venue
1964-65	Dundalk	Shamrock Rovers	1-1, 4-2	D, D
1965-66	Bohemians	Shamrock Rovers	1-1, 3-2	D, D
1966-67	Drumcondra	Shamrock Rovers	1-0	T
1967-68	Bohemians	Drumcondra	0-0, 3-2	D, T
1968-69	Shamrock Rovers	Dundalk	3-2	T
1969-70	Shamrock Rovers	St. Patrick's Ath	4-3	T
1970-71	Shamrock Rovers	Drogheda	3-3, 3-1	D, T
1971-72	St. Patricks Ath.	Bohemians	0-2, 2-1	D, T
1972-73	Shamrock Rovers	Dundalk	3-1	D
1973-74	Waterford	Cork Hibernians	2-0	F
1974-75	Bohemians	St. Patrick's Ath.	4-1	T
1975-76	Bohemians	Home Farm	4-0	D
1976-77	Bohemians	Dundalk	1-1, 1-0	D, O
1977-78	Bohemians	Dundalk	2-1	O
1978-79	Bohemians	Shamrock Rovers	3-1	M
1979-80	Dundalk	Bohemians	2-1	O
1980-81	Dundalk	St. Patrick's Ath.	1-1, 3-0	
1981-82	Dundalk	Athlone T.	2-1, 2-2 (4-3)	O, SM
1982-83	Bohemians	Dundalk	1-0, 2-3 (3-3)	D, O
	(Bohemians won on away goals)			
1983-84	Athlone Town	Bohemians	2-1, 1-3 (5-1)	SM, D
1984-85	Shamrock Rovers	U.C.D.	3-2	T
1985-86	Shamrock Rovers	Bohemians	1-0	M
1986-87	Shamrock Rovers	Dundalk	3-2	O
1987-88	Shamrock Rovers	Dundalk	0-0	O
	(Shamrock Rovers won 3-1 on penalties)			
1988-89	Dundalk	St. Patrick's Ath.	3-2	T
1989-90	Dundalk	Bray Wanderers	3-1	C
1990-91	St. Patrick's Ath	Bray Wanderers	2-2	C
	(St. Patrick's Ath. won 5-4 on penalties)			
1992-93	Bohemians	Shelbourne	0-0	T
	(Bohemians won 4-2 on penalties)			
1993-94	Shelbourne	Bohemians	3-2 AET	T

Note:
The 1991-92 Presidents Cup Final due to be contested by Dundalk and Shamrock Rovers was not played as the clubs failed to agree on a suitable date.

Summary of Winners 1929-30/1993-94
20 Shamrock Rovers, 9 Bohemians, Dundalk, 6 Drumcondra,
5 St. Patrick's Athletic, 3 Shelbourne, 1 Athlone Town, Waterford.

*1929/30 Final not replayed
1981/82, 1982/83, 1983/84 finals two-legged.

Key to Venues
C = Carlisle Grounds, D = Dalymount Park, F = Flower Lodge, M = Milltown,
O = Oriel Pk., S = Shelbourne Park, SM = St. Mels Park, T = Tolka Park.

EBS Leinster Senior Leagues 1993/94

Senior Division

	P	W	D	L	Pts.
Cherry Orchard	30	18	10	2	46
Glenmore Celtic	30	19	7	4	45
Ashtown Villa	30	18	8	4	44
Wayside Celtic	30	18	8	4	44
Glebe North	30	13	7	10	33
St. Francis	30	11	8	11	30
CYM	30	10	8	12	28
Belgrove FC	30	9	9	12	27
Bluebell United	30	8	11	11	27
Ballyfermot United	30	10	6	14	26
Newbridge Town	30	9	8	13	26
Lusk United	30	6	12	12	24
Pegasus	30	9	4	17	22
St. Joseph Boys	30	7	6	17	20
Moyle Park C.	30	5	9	16	19
Elm Rovers	30	5	9	16	19

Division 1A

	P	W	D	L	Pts.
Whitehall Rangers	30	22	5	3	49
Aer Lingus	30	20	7	3	47
Wicklow Rovers	30	16	7	7	39
Trinity SL	30	13	9	8	35
CIE Ranch	30	14	6	10	34
AFC Belgrove	30	13	8	9	34
Malahide United	30	14	5	11	33
Drumcondra	30	12	6	12	30
Larkview Boys	30	13	3	14	29
Cross Celtic	30	10	7	13	27
College of Tech.	30	9	9	12	27
St. Mary's (Athlone)	30	8	9	13	25
Drogheda Celtic	30	9	6	15	24
Bank of Ireland	30	8	5	17	21
Dalkey United	30	6	4	20	16
Swords Celtic	30	1	8	21	10

Division 1

	P	W	D	L	Pts.
Railway Union	30	20	5	5	45
Garda	29	16	7	6	39
Parkvilla	30	14	9	7	37
Dunleary Celtic	30	13	10	7	36
Manortown United	30	13	9	8	35
Workmans Club	30	10	13	7	33
Dale United	30	10	12	8	32
Tullamore	29	10	11	8	31
TEK United	30	11	7	12	29
Bank Rovers	30	7	13	10	27
Brendanville	30	10	6	14	26
Crumlin United	30	8	8	14	24
Vale View Sh.	30	9	5	16	23
Celbridge Town	30	6	10	14	22
Boyne Rovers	30	6	10	14	22
AIB	30	5	7	18	17

* Note Garda v Tullamore was not played

Division 1B

	P	W	D	L	Pts.
Arklow Town	28	20	6	2	46
Landsdowne Rang.	28	21	4	3	46
Dublin Bus	28	17	3	8	37
Ballybrack Boys	28	13	7	8	33
Mount Tallant	28	10	9	9	29
Leixlip United	28	12	4	12	28
Portlaoise	28	11	5	12	27
St. Joseph's (Glas.)	28	11	5	12	27
Iveagh Celtic	28	10	7	11	27
Meath Rangers	28	9	7	12	25
Mullingar Town	28	8	7	13	23
Quay Celtic	28	10	2	16	22
Rathgar S.C.	28	7	5	16	19
Loughshinney Utd.	28	6	7	15	19
St. Mochta's	28	4	4	20	12

Play Off

Arklow Town 1 Lansdowne Rangers 1 AET
(Finnegan) (Young)
Arklow won 3-2 on penalties

Leinster Senior Leagues Winners (since 1970-71)

1970-71	TEK United	1982-83	Bluebell United
1971-72	St. Brendan's	1983-84	St. Mary's, Athlone
1972-73	Rialto	1984-85	St. Mary's, Athlone
1973-74	CYM Terenure	1985-86	Bluebell United
1974-75	TEK United	1986-87	Bluebell United
1975-76	Pegasus	1987-88	St. James's Gate
1976-77	Belgrove	1988-89	St. James's Gate
1977-78	TEK United	1989-90	St. Francis
1978-79	Pegasus	1990-91	Pegasus
1979-80	Workman's Club	1991-92	Bluebell United
1980-81	Pegasus	1992-93	St. Francis
1981-82	Hammond Lane	1993-94	Cherry Orchard

Munster Senior Leagues 1993/94

Senior Premier Division

	P	W	D	L	F	A	Pts.
Everton	22	17	3	2	46	14	54
Avondale Utd.	22	14	5	3	43	24	47
St.Mary's	22	10	7	5	29	22	37
Casement C.	22	9	4	9	34	33	31
Cobh R.	22	7	8	7	40	37	29
Tramore Ath.	22	8	5	9	36	34	29
College Cor.	22	8	4	10	30	39	28
Glasheen	22	7	5	10	24	24	26
Fermoy	22	7	4	11	32	35	25
Rockmount	22	6	7	9	30	33	25
Cork City	22	4	10	8	33	47	22
Carrigaline U.	22	1	6	15	30	65	9

Senior First Division

	P	W	D	L	F	A	Pts.
UCC	24	17	3	4	66	23	54
Mallow Utd.	24	14	3	7	48	35	45
Cobh W.	24	12	6	6	45	31	42
Crofton C.	24	12	5	7	50	34	41
Midleton	24	11	4	9	36	35	37
Douglas Hall	24	8	6	10	40	43	30
Wembley	24	8	3	13	33	53	27
Ringmahon R	24	8	2	14	37	51	26
Crosshaven	24	1	3	20	14	65	6

F.A.I./Harp Lager Intermediate Cup '93/94

Third Round

14 Nov.

Belgrove F.C.	1	(A.Daly)
Portlaoise	1	(G.Conway)
Bluebell United	3	(J.Cullen, E.Stokes, S.Coffey)
Iveagh Celtic	0	
Carndonagh	1	(A.McGuinness)
Ballincollig	1	(M.O'Mahony)
Carrigaline United	3	(M.Collins, M.Coughlin, M.Dennehy)
St. Joseph's Boys	3	(M. McDonald; 2, K. O'Brien)
CYM	2	(J.Duffin, S. Cannon)
Everton	1	(T. O'Regan)
Fermoy	1	(D. O'Connor)
Glasheen	0	
Glenmore Celtic	2	(K.Brien, L.Wyse)
Avondale United	1	(K. O'Riordan)
Gweedore Celtic	0	
Casement Celtic	2	(P.Mulcahy, D.Luxford)
Lansdowne Rangers	1	(P. Gordon)
Castleview	1	(N. Curtin (p))
Malahide United	0	
College Corinthians	1	(E.Barrett)
Meath Rangers	0	
Temple United	5	(K.McCarthy; 2, S. Walsh, A. Elliott, G. Cooney)
St. Mochta's	1	(A. McClure)
Moyle Park	3	(D.Looney, D. Kelly, C.Stynes)
Whitehall Rangers	3	(P.Kavanagh; 2, P.Dowling)
Mallow United	0	

21 Nov.

Cherry Orchard	1	(S. Hatch)
Ballyfermot United	0	
Elm Rovers	2	(P.Heary, G.Gaynor)
Lusk United	1	(P.Linden)
Garda	7	(D.Kavanagh; 2, J.McCarthy, D.Reilly, D.McGrath, G.Miller, D. Mulhall)
Castlebar Town	1	(K. Ryan)
Glebe North	3	(S.McGarry, M.McNamee, G.Richards)
Workman's Club	1	(M. Finn)
St. Mary's (Cork)	0	
Ashtown Villa	0	

Note: Details of Bonaghee United v Quay Celtic and Fanad United v Mervue United unavailable.

Third Round Replays

21 Nov.

Portlaoise	1	(M. O'Loughlin)	
Belgrove F.C.	1	(J. O'Flaherty)	AET

(Belgrove F.C. won 5-4 on penalties)

Ballincollig	0	
Carndonagh	2	(J. Farran, N. Doherty)

28 Nov.

Ashtown Villa	2	(J. O'Reilly, S. Kearney)
St. Mary's (Cork)	1	(J. Hyde (p))
St. Joseph's Boys	2	(G. Lewins, P. Mitchell)
Carrigaline United	3	(M. Collins 2; C. Cahill)

5 Dec.

Castleview	5	(T. Barrett 2, I. O'Brien, D. Duggan, N. Curtin)
Lansdowne Rangers	2	(G. Kennedy, P. Goggins)

Fourth Round

5 Dec.

Carndonagh	0	
Elm Rovers	3	
Carrigaline United	0	
Bluebell United	0	
Casement Celtic	2	(S. Caulfield, D. Luxford)
Fanad United	2	(O. Harkin, E. McGinley)
Cherry Orchard	2	(S. Hatch, C. Notaro)
Temple United	0	
Fermoy	3	(R. O'Connor, K. Myers, W. Van Wignen (p))
Ashtown Villa	2	(K. Craven, S. Donnelly)
Glebe North	1	(D. Quinlan)
C.Y.M.	1	(J. Duffin (p))
Glenmore Celtic	1	(P. Keogh)
Moyle Park	1	(J. Kernan (p))
Whitehall Rangers	2	(P. Dowling 2)
Belgrove F.C.	1	(J. Doyle)

12 Dec.

Castleview	0	
Garda	2	(J. McCarthy, D. Mulhall)

2 Jan.

College Corinthians	2	(D. Geelan 2)
Bonaghee United	1	(D. McLoughlin)

Fourth Round Replays

12 Dec.

Bluebell United	2	(E. Stokes, W. Devereaux)
Carrigaline United	1	(T. Coughlan)

Fanad United	1	(E. McGinley)
Casement Celtic	2	(P. Bowdren, D. Luxford)

19 Dec.
C.Y.M.	4	(J. Duffin 2; M. McCabe, A. Lonergan)
Glebe North	5	(G. Richards 2; M. McNamee (p), D. Quinlan, C. Dunne)
Moyle Park	2	(J. Kernan, K. Byrne)
Glenmore Celtic	6	(B. Byrne 2; G. Irwin 2; P. Keogh, C. Flynn (p))

Fifth Round

23 Jan.
Fermoy	1	(R. O'Connor)
Glenmore Celtic	3	(G. Irwin, P. Keogh, E. Hannigan)
Cherry Orchard	3	(J. Hatch 2; G. Murphy)
Garda	2	(G. Murphy 2)

Quarter Finals

30 Jan.
Casement Celtic	2	(P. O'Keeffe, P. Bowdren)
Whitehall Rangers	6	(D. McDonagh 3; B. Toner, P. Dowling, B. Connolly)
College Corinthians	0	
Bluebell United	1	(J. Cassidy)
Glebe North	4	(S. McGarry 3; D. Quinlan)
Elm Rovers	3	(S. Curry 2; J. Clohessey)
Glenmore Celtic	0	
Cherry Orchard	1	(C. Notaro)

Semi Finals

6 Mar.
Bluebell United	3	(P. Finegan 2; A. Behan)
Glebe North	0	
Cherry Orchard	0	
Whitehall Rangers	0	

Semi Final Replay

13 Mar.
Whitehall Rangers	1	(B. Toner)
Cherry Orchard	2	(G. Murphy, C. Notaro)

FINAL

30 Mar at Richmond Park   Referee: N. Garry (Dublin)
Cherry Orchard	2	(Notaro, Hatch)
Bluebell United	1	(Devereaux)

(abandoned, due to weather, 63 mins.)

FINAL REPLAY

6 Apr. at Richmond Park   Referee: N. Garry (Dublin)
Bluebell United	(1) 1	(Behan)
Cherry Orchard	0	

Bluebell United: Séan Coffey, Doolin, Stokes, T. Cullen, Reilly, Saunders, Devlin, Stephen Coffey, Devereaux, Behan (J. Cullen 79), Clarke

Cherry Orchard: Barnwell, Coughlan, Kennedy, Murphy, Curley, Glynn (Byrne 73), Dunne, McDermott, Hatch, O'Riordan, (Carrick 78), Notaro

Orange Order
Aron Winter and Wim Jonk celebrate the No. 8's decisive goal against Ireland
(The Star)

INTERMEDIATE CUP WINNERS/RUNNERS-UP

Qualifying Cup:

Season	Winners	Runners-Up
1926-27	Drumcondra	Cobh Ramblers
1927-28	Cork Bohemians	Strandville
1928-29	Richmond United	Fermoy
1929-30	Cahir Park	Glasnevin
1930-31	Cork Bohemians	Rossville

Intermediate Cup:

Season	Winners	Runners-Up
1931-32	Bohemians "B"	Cork "B"
1932-33	Shelbourne "B"	Cork Bohemians "B"
1933-34	Sligo Rovers	Tramore Rookies
1934-35	Tramore Rookies	Bohemians "B"
1935-36	B + I S.P. Co.	G.S. Railways (Cork)
1936-37	Longford Town	Fearons Athletic
1937-38	Terenure Athletic	Cork Bohemians
1938-39	Distillery	Cork Bohemians
1939-40	Distillery	Cobh Ramblers
1940-41	Distillery	Cork Bohemians
1941-42	Distillery	Cobh Ramblers
1942-43	No Competition	
1943-44	No Competition	
1944-45	U.C.D.	Cobh Ramblers
1945-46	Richmond Celtic (Cork)	Grangegorman
1946-47	Drumcondra "B"	Rockville (Cork)
1947-48	St. Patrick's Athletic	Cobh Ramblers
1948-49	St. Patrick's Athletic	Freebooters (Cork)
1949-50	Jacobs	St. Patricks Athletic
1950-51	St. James's Gate	Evergreen United
1951-52	A.O.H. (Cork)	Pike Rovers
1952-53	St. Patrick's Athletic "B"	Jacobs
1953-54	Albert Rovers	Jacobs
1954-55	Longford Town	Jacobs*
1955-56	Bray Wanderers	Workman's Club
1956-57	Workman's Club	A.O.H. (Cork)
1957-58	Bray Wanderers	Chapelizod
1958-59	Albert Rovers	Bray Wanderers
1959-60	Longford Town	Bray Wanderers
1960-61	Workman's Club	Jacobs
1961-62	Longford Town	Workman''s Club
1962-63	Home Farm	Limerick "B"
1963-64	Transport	T.E.K. United
1964-65	T.E.K. United	Glasheen

Season	Winners	Runners-Up
1965-66	Transport	Home Farm
1966-67	Home Farm	Tramore Athletic
1967-68	Home Farm	Athlone Town
1968-69	Longford Town	Transport
1969-70	Rialto	Home Farm
1970-71	Tullamore	Bluebell United
1971-72	C.Y.M. (Dublin)	T.E.K. United
1972-73	St. Brendans	Rialto
1973-74	Transport	T.E.K. United
1974-75	C.Y.M.	Belgrove
1975-76	Dalkey United	C.I.E. Transport
1976-77	Pegasus	Bray Wanderers
1977-78	Avondale United	A.I.B.
1978-79	Tramore Athletic	Swilly Rovers
1979-80	Cobh Ramblers	Tramore Athletic
1980-81	Tramore Athletic	Ballyfermot United
1981-82	Bluebell United	Tramore Athletic
1982-83	Cobh Ramblers	Bluebell United
1983-84	Ballyfermot United	Bank Rovers
1984-85	Bank Rovers	Hammond Lane
1985-86	Crofton Celtic	Everton
1986-87	Tramore Athletic	Bank Rovers
1987-88	Fanad United	Tramore Athletic
1988-89	T.E.K. United	St. James's Gate
1989-90	Bluebell United	Ballyfermot United
1990-91	Edenmore	St. Josephs Boys
1991-92	Pegasus	Bluebell United
1992-93	Bluebell United	Wayside Celtic
1993-94	Bluebell United	Cherry Orchard

* The 1954-55 Final was never played, Jacobs refusing to travel. Longford Town were awarded the Tophy. In its first five seasons the Intermediate Cup was known as the Qualifying Cup.

Summary of Winners

- **5** Longford Town,
- **4** Bluebell United, Distillery
- **3** Home Farm, Tramore Athletic, Transport,
- **2** Albert Rovers, Bray Wanderers, Cobh Ramblers, Cork Bohemians, CYM, Pegasus, St. Patrick's Athletic, TEK United, Workman's Club,
- **1** AOH, Avondale United, B & I, Ballyfermot United, Bank Rovers, Bohemians "B", Cahir Park, Crofton Celtic, Dalkey United, Drumcondra, Drumcondra "B", Edenmore, Fanad United, Jacobs, Rialto, Richmond Celtic, Richmond United, St. Brendan's, St. James's Gate, St. Patrick's Athletic "B", Shelbourne "B", Sligo Rovers, Terenure Athletic, Tramore Rookies, Tullamore, U.C.D.

"EVERPRESENTS" 1993/94
(Substitute appearances in brackets)

Athlone Town	27	*Frank Darby, Dave Dowling Chris Malone*
Bray Wanderers	27	*Alan Smith, Gavin Teehan*
Cobh Ramblers	34	*Stephen Henderson, Pakie Kelly, Ken O'Rourke*
Cork City	32	*Declan Daly, Stephen Napier*
Derry City	32	*Dermot O'Neill*
Drogheda United	32	*John Ryan, Colm Tresson*
Home Farm	27	*Karl Gannon (1)*
Kilkenny City	27	*Paul McDermott (1)*
Monaghan United	32	*Brian O'Shea*
St. Patrick's Athletic	32	*John McDonnell*
Shamrock Rovers	32	*Gino Brazil, Alan O'Neill*
Shelbourne	32	*Jody Byrne*
Sligo Rovers	27	*Mark McLean*
U.C.D.	27	*Seamus Kelly, Packie Lynch, Jonathan Treacy, Terry Palmer, Michael O'Byrne*

Everpresent in the past three seasons:

Dermot O'Neill (Derry City) 97 appearances

Everpresent in the past two seasons:

Frank Darby (Athlone Town) 54 appearances

Stephen Henderson (Cobh Ramblers) 61 appearances
(total includes 2 appearances for St. James's Gate)

Paul McDermott (Kilkenny City) 54 appearances (1)

Alan O'Neill (Shamrock Rovers) 64 appearances
(total includes 32 appearances for Dundalk)

Colm Tresson (Drogheda United) 64 appearances

Player Directory

Allen, Ronnie b. 3 Jun. 1968
St. Joseph's Boys to Shelbourne
　　　　　Sligo Rovers v **Shelbourne** (2-2) 23 Dec. '90
1990-91	Shelbourne	3	
Feb. '91	Limerick City (L)	7	(1)
1991-92	Athlone Town	20 + 1	
1992-93	St. Francis		
1993-94	Bray Wanderers	11 + 1	

Annand, Eddie b. Glasgow, 24 Mar. 1973
Oct. '92 Partick Thistle to Sligo Rovers (L)
　　　　　Sligo Rovers v Derry City (0-0) 25 Oct. '92
1992-93	Sligo Rovers	4	
Nov. '92	Partick Thistle		
1993-94	Sligo Rovers	22 + 2	(10)

Arkins, Vinny b. Dublin, 18 Sep. 1970
Oct. '89 Dundee United to Shamrock Rovers
　　　　　Shamrock R. v Bohemians (3-1) 15 Oct. '89
1990-91	Shamrock Rovers	25 + 2	(14)
1001 02	Shamrock Rovers	14	(5)
Nov. '91	St. Johnstone		
1993-94	Shelbourne	19	(7)

Arrigan, Brian b. Waterford, 9 Mar. 1974
Southend United (Waterford) to Waterford United
　　　　　Waterford U. v Drogheda U. (3-3) 20 Dec. '92
| 1992-93 | Waterford United | 17 | (3) |
| 1993-94 | Waterford United | 16 + 3 | (3) |

Ashton, Stuart b. Rochdale, 14 Oct. 1964
Summer '84 Rochdale to Cork City
　　　　　Dundalk v **Cork City** (1-0) 16 Sep. '84
1991-92	Cork City	2 + 1	
1992-93	Uxbridge (Eng.)		
1993-94	Cork City	0 + 1	

Askew, Billy b. Lumley (Eng.), 2 Oct. 1959
Jan. '94 to Waterford United
　　　　　Waterford U. v Longford T. (0-0) 30 Jan. '94
| 1993-94 | Waterford United | 3 | |

Bacon, John b. Dublin, 23 Mar. 1973
Jan. '92 Arsenal to Shamrock Rovers (L)
　　　　　Shamrock R. v Dundalk (1-1) 26 Jan. '92
1991-92	Shamrock Rovers	8 + 2	(3)
1992-93	Derry City (L)	12	(3)
1993-94	Shamrock Rovers	6 + 5	(1)

Baife, Eamonn
　　　　　St. James's G. v Finn Harps (0-0) 28 Feb. '93
| 1992-93 | St. James's Gate | 6 | |
| 1993-94 | St. James's Gate | 20 | |

Bannon, Paul b. Dublin, 15 Nov. 1956
Summer '89 Larissa (Greece) to Cork City
　　　　　Cork City v Drogheda U. (1-1) 3 Sep. '89
1990-91	Cork City	20	(1)
1991-92	Cork City	24	(3)
1992-93	Cork City	26 + 6	(4)
1993-94	Cobh Ramblers	30 + 1	(3)

Barden, Jimmy b. Waterford, 24 Nov. 1973
Summer '93 Southend United (Waterford) to Waterford United
　　　　　Waterford U. v Sligo Rovers (2-1) 3 Oct. '93
| 1993-94 | Waterford United | 14 + 7 | (1) |

Barrett, Séan
Milford United to Finn Harps
　　　　　Finn Harps v Waterford U. (2-0) 19 Sep. '93
| 1993-94 | Finn Harps | 25 + 2 | |

Barriscale, Joe b. Limerick, 4 May 1968
Vereker Clements to Limerick City
　　　　　Cork City v **Limerick City** (0-2) 26 Dec. '88
1991-92	Limerick City	3	
1992-93	Limerick	1 + 1	
1993-94	Limerick	11 + 1	

Barry, Alan b. Waterford, 10 May 1962
Aug. '89 Newcastlewest to Waterford United
1990-91	Waterford United	33	(1)
1991-92	Waterford United	25	(3)
1992-93	Waterford United	32	
1993-94	Waterford United	17	(1)

Barry, Brian b. Carrick-on-Suir, 8 Aug 1973
Aug. '89 Carrick F.C. to Waterford United
　　　　　Waterford U. v Home Farm (0-2) 3 Sep. '89
1990-91	Waterford United	16 + 5	
1991-92	Waterford United	20 + 2	(3)
1992-93	Waterford United	28 + 1	(2)
1993-94	Waterford United	15	

Barry, Dave b. Cork, 16 Sep. 1961
Summer '84 Everton (Cork) to Cork City
　　　　　Dundalk v **Cork City** (1-0) 16 Sep. '84
1990-91	Cork City	14	(1)
1991-92	Cork City	31	(4)
1992-93	Cork City	27 + 1	(6)
1993-94	Cork City	24 + 1	(6)

Bayly, Martin b. Dublin, 14 Sep. 1966
Summer '85 Coventry City to Sligo Rovers
1990-91	St. James's Gate	0 + 3	
Feb. '91	Athlone Town	7	(3)
1991-92	Monaghan United	24	(3)
1992-93	Shamrock Rovers	7 + 2	
Dec. '92	Home Farm	2	
Jan. '93	Linfield		
1993-94	Home Farm	24	

Benton, Steve b. Bristol, 20 Dec. 1973
Oct. '93 Bristol City to Cobh Ramblers (L)
    Cobh R. v Shamrock R. (1-3) 24 Oct. '93
1993-94   Cobh Ramblers   2
Nov. '93   Bristol City

Berry, Terry b. Leixlip, 4 Jan. 1974
Leixlip United to Shamrock Rovers
    Monaghan U. v Sham. R. (0-1) IG 19 Sep. '93
1993-94   Shamrock Rovers   3 + 1   (1)

Best, Conor b. 11 Aug. 1969
St. Patrick's Athletic to Kilkenny City
    St. Pat's A. v. Athlone T. (0-0) 27 Nov. '88
1990-91   Kilkenny City   17 + 4   (2)
1991-92   Bray Wanderers   11
1992-93   Monaghan United   -
    Bray Wanderers   1 + 4
1993-94   Bray Wanderers   21 + 1   (5)

Best, Robbie b. Dublin, 12 Sep. 1967
Nov. '90 St. Patrick's Athletic to Athlone Town (L)
    St. Pat's A v Athlone T (2-1) 10 Sep '89
1990-91   Athlone Town   22
1991-92   Bohemians   31
1992-93   Bohemians   37
1993-94   Bohemians   30

Blissett, Luther b. Jamaica, 1 Feb. 1958
Oct. '93 Bury to Derry City (L)
    Galway U. v Derry City (2-1) IG, 17 Oct. '93
1993-94   Derry City   4   (1)
Nov. '93   Bury

Blood, Ken b. Dublin, 20 Oct. 1972
    Bohemians v Shelbourne (2-1) 27 May '93
1992/93   Bohemians   0 + 1
1993-94   Bohemians   1   (1)

Bonner, Declan
Summer '91 Ardra Town to Finn Harps
    Monaghan U v Finn Harps (1-1) 6 Oct. '91
1991-92   Finn Harps   8 + 3
1992-93   Finn Harps   4   (1)
1993-94   Finn Harps   2

Bowes, Christian b. Dublin, 21 Aug. 1973
    Bray W. v Home Farm (2-0) 30 Dec. '90
1990-91   Home Farm   4 + 1
1991-92   Home Farm   22 + 1   (5)
1992-93   Shamrock Rovers   4 + 5
1993-94   Shamrock Rovers   1

Boyle, Declan b. Letterkenny, 12 Feb. 1974
Mar. '92 St. Catherines (K'begs) to Finn Harps
    Limerick C v Finn Harps (2-0) 15 Mar. '92
1991-92   Finn Harps   6
1992-93   Finn Harps   24 + 3   (2)
1993-94   Sligo Rovers   26   (1)

Boyle, Joe b. Leeds, 26 Sep. 1972
    Cobh Ramblers v Finn Harps (2-1) 7 Oct. '90
1990-91   Finn Harps   5
1991-92   Limerick City   -
Mar. '92   Finn Harps   2 + 1
1993-94   Home Farm   14 + 1

Brady, Austin b. Dublin, 17 Apr. 1955
Summer '90 Athlone Town to Drogheda United
1990-91   Drogheda United   20 + 1
1991-92   Monaghan United   25   (1)
1992-93   St. James's Gate   22
1993-94   Kilkenny City   0 + 2

Brady, Keith b. Dublin, 10 Oct. 1971
Summer '90 Belvedere to Bohemians
    Derry City v Bohemians (1-1) 2 Sep. '90
1990-91   Bohemians   27
1993-94   Longford Town   23 + 3

Brady, Kevin b. Dublin, 2 Dec. 1962
Summer '88 Shamrock Rovers to Derry City
    Bohemians v. Sligo R (1-1) 27 Dec. '81
1990-91   Derry City   30
1991-92   Shelbourne   14   (2)
1992-93   Shelbourne   27
1993-94   Shelbourne   15
Mar. '94   Ards

Brady, Paul b. Dublin, 25 Aug. 1970
Jul. '90 Shelbourne to Dundalk
1990-91   Dundalk   11 + 6
1991-92   Dundalk   8 + 8   (1)
1992-93   Bray Wanderers   19 + 3
1993-94   Athlone Town   25   (1)

Brazil, Gino b. Dublin, 28 Mar. 1968
Finn Harps to Shamrock Rovers
1990-91   Shamrock Rovers   1
1991-92   Shamrock Rovers   14
1992-93   Shamrock Rovers   31
1993-94   Shamrock Rovers   32   (1)

Brazil, Stephen b. Dublin, 15 Nov. 1974
    Kilkenny C. v. Home Farm (1-1) 31 Oct. '93
1993-94   Home Farm   0 + 1
Nov. '93   Bohemians   0 + 2

Brennan, Anthony "Anto" b. Dublin, 1 Dec. 1973
Huddersfield Town to Shelbourne
    Shelbourne v Bohemians (0-2) 11 Mar. '94
1993-94   Shelbourne   0 + 1

Brennan, John "Jumbo" b. London, 13 Dec. 1968
Summer '91 Salthill Devon to Galway United
    Drogheda U. v Galway U (0-0) 29 Sep. '91
1991-92   Galway United   23   (6)
1992-93   Galway United   20 + 2   (14)
1993-94   Galway United   28   (14)

Brett, Gordon b. Athlone, 6 Jul. 1974
St. Colman's to Athlone Town
    Bohemians v **Athlone T.** (2-0) 18 Oct. '91
1991-92	Athlone Town	6 + 5
1992-93	Athlone Town	8 + 3
1993-94	Athlone Town	2 + 3

Brien, Stephen b. Dublin, 26 Oct. 1973
Wolfe Tone Y.C. (Bray) to Bray Wanderers
    Home Farm v **Bray W.** (3-2) 5 Dec. '93
| 1993-94 | Bray Wanderers | 5 + 5 |

Britton, Matt b. Dublin, 29 Nov. 1973
Summer '92 St. Joseph's Boys to Dundalk
    Bohemians v **Dundalk** (0-1) 21 Feb. '93
| 1992-93 | Dundalk | 0 + 1 |
| 1993-94 | Dundalk | 9 + 9 | (1) |

Broughan, Donal b. Dublin, 28 Nov. 1972
Summer '91 Rivermount to Bohemians
    Galway U v **Bohemians** (3-2) 23 Feb. '92
1991-92	Bohemians	7 + 1	
1992-93	Bohemians	20 + 3	(1)
1993-94	Bohemians	23 + 2	(1)

Browne, Bobby b. Dublin, 9 Jun. 1962
Athlone Town to Shelbourne
1990-91	Shelbourne	21 + 6	(2)
1991-92	Shelbourne	22 + 6	(3)
1992-93	Shelbourne	25 + 9	(1)
1993-94	Shelbourne	5 + 4	
	Ards		

Browne, Mark b. Waterford, 10 Oct. 1967
Summer '88 Johnville to Cobh Ramblers
    Cobh R v. Bohemians (0-2) 4 Sep. '88
1990-91	Waterford United	14 + 2	
1991-92	Waterford United	5 + 2	
1992-93	St. Patrick's Athletic	19 + 6	(2)
1993-94	St. Patrick's Athletic	7	
Oct. '93	Waterford United	10 + 1	(3)

Buckley, Anthony b. Cork, 27 Dec. 1972
Jul '92 Peterborough United to Cork City
    Cork City v Waterford U. (1-0) 6 Dec. '92
| 1992-93 | Cork City | 15 | |
| 1993-94 | Cork City | 25 + 1 | (4) |

Buckley, Liam b. Dublin, 14 Apr. 1960
1991-92	Shamrock Rovers	5 + 5	(1)
1992-93	St. Patrick's Athletic	1	
1993-94	St. Patrick's Athletic	0 + 2	

Buckley, Martin
    Kilkenny C. v **Home Farm** (1-3) 14 Oct. '90
1990-91	Home Farm	24	
1991-92	Home Farm	26	
1992-93	Home Farm	24 + 1	(1)
1993-94	Home Farm	14 + 1	

Burke, Willie b. Dublin, 4 Sep. 1972
St. Joseph's Boys to Shamrock Rovers
    Shamrock R. v Waterford U. (4-0) 8 Nov. '92
| 1992-93 | Shamrock Rovers | 10 | |
| 1993-94 | Shamrock Rovers | 30 | (1) |

Burton, Paul b. Dublin, 23 May 1972
Blackrock College to U.C.D.
    Athlone Town v **U.C.D.** (1-2) 4 Oct. '92
| 1992-93 | U.C.D. | 13 + 5 | (2) |
| 1993-94 | U.C.D. | 12 + 2 | |

Butler, Michael b. Waterford, 29 Jun. 1976
Waterford Bohemians to Waterford United
    Waterford U. v Home Farm (4-2) 21 Nov.'93
| 1993-94 | Waterford United | 3 + 4 | |

Buttner, Stefan
Cherry Orchard to St. Patrick's Athletic
1991-92	Home Farm	3 + 14	(1)
1992-93	Home Farm	15 + 2	(2)
1993-94	U.S.A.		
Jan. '94	Kilkenny City	8 + 1	(1)

Byrne, Alan b. Dublin, 12 May 1969
Jul. '87 Lakelands to Bohemians
    Bohemians v Shamrock R. (1-4) 27 Sep. '87
1990-91	Bohemians	29	(1)
1991-92	Bohemians	28	(1)
1992-93	Bohemians	36	(1)
1993-94	Shamrock Rovers	28	(1)

Byrne, Gareth b. Dublin, 15 Apr. 1971
Summer '93 TEK United to St. Patrick's Athletic
    St. Pat's Ath. v Limerick (1-0) 25 Jan. '94
| 1993-94 | St. Patrick's Athletic | 1 + 1 | |

Byrne, Jason b. Dublin, 16 May 1972
Summer '91 Huddersfield Town to Bray Wanderers
    Bray W. v Shelbourne (0-1) 29 Sep. '91
1991-92	Bray Wanderers	26 + 1	(2)
1992-93	Bray Wanderers	27 + 1	(8)
1993-94	St. Patrick's Athletic	17 + 8	(7)

Byrne, John b. Dublin, 29 Aug. 1962
Jul. '90 Bohemians to Sligo Rovers
    St. Pat's Ath. v **Home Farm** (2-0) 22 Nov. '81
1990-91	Sligo Rovers	29	(3)
1991-92	Sligo Rovers	28	
1992-93	Sligo Rovers	27 + 3	(2)
1993-94	St. Patrick's Athletic	28 + 1	

Byrne, Joseph "Jody" b. Dublin, 30 Apr. 1963
Cambridge Boys to Dundalk
    Finn Harps v **Dundalk** (0-1) 13 Feb. '83
1990-91	Shelbourne	33	
1991-92	Shelbourne	33	
1992-93	Shelbourne	37	
1993-94	Shelbourne	32	(1)

Byrne, Keith
          St. James's G. v Waterford U. (1-2) 20 Feb.'94
1993-94   St. James's Gate   1

Byrne, Mick   b. Dublin, 14 Jan. 1960
Sep. '90 Huddersfield T. to Shamrock R.
          Home Farm v **Bohemians** (2-1) 25 Mar. '79
1990-91	Shamrock Rovers	15 + 1	(4)
1991-92 (Feb. '91)	Sligo Rovers	6	(1)
1991-92	Sligo Rovers	18 + 3	(3)
Jan. '92	Dundalk	1 + 2	
Mar. '92	Shelbourne	0 + 3	
1992-93	Monaghan United	28	(15)
1993-94	Monaghan United	30	(7)

Byrne, Pat   b. Dublin, 15 May 1956
Shamrock Rovers to Shelbourne
1990-91	Shelbourne	19 + 5	
1991-92	Shelbourne	4 + 5	(2)
1992-93	Shelbourne	1 + 1	
1993-94	Shelbourne	1	
Dec. '93	Cobh Ramblers	4	
Feb. '94	St. James's Gate	(Player/manager)	

Byrne, Paul   b. Dublin, 25 Nov. 1965
Jul. '90 Athlone Town to Bohemians
1990-91	Bohemians	25 + 3	(2)
1991-92	Bohemians	30 + 1	
1992-93	Bohemians	4 + 4	(1)
1993-94	Monaghan United	30 + 1	(4)

Byrne, Séan   b Dublin, 12 May 1971
          Galway U v. **Shamrock R** (1-2) 3 Dec. '89
1990-91	Shamrock Rovers	14 + 2	
1991-92	Shamrock Rovers	17 + 1	
1992-93	Drogheda United	13 + 2	(1)
1993-94	Drogheda United	21	(1)

Byrne, Tommy   b. Dublin, 30 Aug. 1969
Jan. '92 F.C. Boom (Belgium) to Bohemians (L)
          Bohemians v Dundalk (2-3) 7 Feb. '92
1991-92	Bohemians	9	
1992-93	Bohemians	16 + 2	(2)
1993-94	Bohemians	18 + 2	

Cairns, Adrian   b. Coventry, 15 Nov. 1963
1990-91	Bray Wanderers	18	
1991-92	Bray Wanderers	28 + 1	
1992-93	Bray Wanderers	13 + 1	
1993-94	Bray Wanderers	22 + 1	

Callaghan, Aaron   b. Dublin, 8 Oct. 1966
Dec. '93 Crewe Alexandra to Shelbourne
          St. Pat's. Ath. v **Shelbourne** (2-2) 5 Dec.'93
| 1993-94 | Shelbourne | 13 + 1 | (1) |

Campbell, Calum   b. Erskine, 7 Nov. 1965
Jan. '94 Kilmarnock to Sligo Rovers
          Bray W. v **Sligo Rovers** (0-3) 16 Jan. '94
| 1993-94 | Sligo Rovers | 2 | |

Campbell, Dave   b. Dublin, 13 Sep. 1969
Summer '92 Huddersfield Town to Shamrock Rovers
          St. Pat's Ath. v **Bohemians** (2-0) 1 Jan. '89
1992-93	Shamrock Rovers	3	(1)
Oct. '92	St. Patrick's Athletic	16	
1993-94	St. Patrick's Athletic	30	(4)

Campbell, Declan   b. Dublin, 3 Nov. 1970
'89 Belvedere to Drogheda United
          Shelbourne v **Drogheda U** (2-1) 22 Feb. '92
1991-92	Drogheda United	8	
1992-93	Drogheda United	5	
1993-94	Kilkenny City	20	

Campbell, Paul   b. Dublin, 15 Oct. 1969
Stella Maris to St. Patrick's Athletic
          Derry City v. **St. Pat's Ath.** (1-0) 1 Mar. '89
1990-91	St. Patrick's Athletic	0 + 1	
Oct. '90	Galway United (L)	17	(2)
1991-92	St. Patrick's Athletic	27 + 2	(4)
1992-93	St. Patrick's Athletic	20 + 5	(4)
1993-94	St. Patrick's Athletic	22 + 4	

Carlyle, Paul   b. Derry
Summer '86 Coleraine to Derry City
          Cobh R. v **Derry City** (0-1) 19 Oct. '86
1990-91	Derry City	33	(5)
1991-92	Derry City	24 + 3	(3)
1992-93	Derry City	27	(1)
1993-94	Derry City	8	
Oct. '93	Coleraine		

Carolan, Ray   b. Dublin, 14 Mar. 1973
Crumlin United to St. Patrick's Athletic
          St. Pat's Ath. v Cork City (2-4) 19 Jan. '92
1991-92	St. Patrick's Athletic	8 + 1	
1992-93	St. Patrick's Athletic	15 + 5	(1)
1993-92	St. Patrick's Athletic	5 + 3	

Carpenter, Peter   b. Galway, 29 Dec. 1967
'85 Southampton to Galway United
          Galway U. v Home Farm (2-1) 19 Oct. '86
1990-91	Galway United	11 + 1	
1991-92	Galway United	26	
1992-93	Galway United	19	(2)
1993-94	Galway United	24	(1)

Carr, Gerry   b. Coventry, 23 Dec. 1973
Summer '93 VS Rugby to Sligo Rovers
          Waterford U. v **Sligo R.** (2-1) 3 Oct. '93
| 1993-94 | Sligo Rovers | 21 + 2 | (1) |

Carr, Matthew b. Middlesbrough, 30 Oct. 1971
Summer '91 Northampton T. to Waterford United
          Waterford U v Home Farm (1-1) 6 Oct. '91
1991-92	Waterford United	8	(1)
1992-93	Waterford United	11 + 1	(1)
Dec. '92	Cork City	1	
1993-94	Cork City	-	
Oct. '93	Limerick (L)	7	

Carroll, John b. Dublin, 13 Oct. 1971
Summer '91 Liverpool to Shamrock Rovers
          Galway U v **Athlone T.** (1-0) 1 Dec. '91
1990-91	Shamrock Rovers	–	
Dec. '91	Athlone Town (L)	17	
1992-93	Drogheda United	25 + 1	
1993-94	Drogheda United	28 + 2	

Cashin, Paul b. New Ross, 16 Sep. 1967
Summer '89 Cobh Ramblers to Waterford United
          Shelbourne v **Waterford U** (0-2) 9 Mar. '86
1990-91	Waterford United	19	(3)
1991-92	Waterford United	26	(3)
1992-93	Shamrock Rovers	18 + 3	(2)
1993-94	Shamrock Rovers	5 + 2	(1)

Cassidy, Kevin b. Galway, 11 Jul. 1956
Our Ladys Boys to Galway Rovers
          Galway R. v Cork Alb (0-4) 11 Sep. '77
1990-91	Galway United	14 + 7	(1)
1991-92	Longford Town	15 + 1	(1)
Feb. '92	Galway United	3 + 2	
1992-93	Galway United	8 + 1	
1993-94	Galway United	3 + 3	

Caulfield, John b. New York, 11 Oct. 1964
Summer '86 Wembley to Cork City
          Home Farm v **Athlone T.** (2-2) 27 Oct. '85
1990-91	Cork City	30 + 3	(8)
1991-92	Cork City	33	(16)
1992-93	Cork City	25 + 6	(7)
1993-94	Cork City	25 + 5	(9)

Chapman, Danny b. Peckham, 21 Nov. 1974
Aug. '93 Millwall to Cobh Ramblers (L)
          Dundalk v **Cobh R.** (0-2) 5 Sep. '93
1993-94	Cobh Ramblers	4	
Sep. '93	Millwall		

Cleary, John b. Dublin, 7 Aug. 1958
1990-91	Dundalk	2	
Nov. '90	Galway United	20	(1)
1991-92	Galway United	27	(1)
1992-93	Galway United	–	
Dec. '92	Crusaders		
1993-94	Kilkenny City	9	

Clery, Billy b. Galway, 6 Nov. 1975
Belvedere to Galway United
          Drogheda U. v **Galway U.** (1-4)IG, 29 Aug. '93
1993-94	Galway United	3+2	(1)

Coady, John b. Dublin, 25 Aug. 1960
YMCA to Bohemians
          U.C.D. v **Shamrock R.** (2-2) 2G, 31 Oct. '82
1990-91	Derry City	16 + 4	(3)
1991-92	Derry City	30 + 1	(1)
1992-93	Shamrock Rovers	18 + 1	(1)
1993-94	Monaghan United	29	(1)

Coleman, Fergal b. Dublin, 21 Nov. 1972
'91 Leicester Celtic to U.C.D.
          U.C.D. v Finn Harps (0-0) 1 Nov. '92
1992-93	U.C.D.	1 + 4	
1993-94	U.C.D.	0+1	

Coll, James b. Glasgow, 28 Jun. 1962
Summer '89 Limerick City to Dundalk
1990-91	Dundalk	31	(3)
1991-92	Dundalk	31	(1)
1992-93	Dundalk	28	(2)
1993-94	Dundalk	27	(3)

Colwell, Jason b. Dublin, 31 Jan. 1974
Summer '91 Rangers YC to U.C.D.
          Cobh Ramblers v **U.C.D.** (1-1) 6 Oct. '91
1991-92	U.C.D.	20 + 6	(4)
1992-93	U.C.D.	26	(1)
1993-94	U.C.D.	22	(4)

Connell, Dave b. Dublin, 27 Nov. 1961
Aug. '89 to Shamrock Rovers
1990-91	Shamrock Rovers	30	
1991-92	Shamrock Rovers	32 + 1	(2)
1992-93	Shamrock Rovers	2	
Nov. '92	Ards		
1993-94	Drogheda United	19 + 6	(1)

Connolly, John b. Dublin, 28 Dec. 1971
Aug. '90 Cherry Orchard to Bohemians
          Limerick C. v **Bohemians** (0-2) 14 Oct. '90
1990-91	Bohemians	2	
1991-92	Bohemians	11	
1992-93	Bohemians	-	
1993-94	Bohemians	15 + 2	

Connor, James b. Twickenham, 22 Aug. 1974
Aug. '93 Millwall to Cobh Ramblers (L)
          Cobh R. v Shelbourne (1-1) 29 Aug. '93
1993-94	Cobh Ramblers	7	
Oct. '93	Millwall		

Conway, Tom b. Dublin, 7 Mar. 1959
Summer '77 Beggsboro to Athlone Town
          Athlone Town v Sligo Rovers (1-2) 23 Oct. '77
1990-91	Sligo Rovers	8 + 1	
1991-92	Sligo Rovers	14 + 2	(1)
1992-93	Sligo Rovers	1	
Nov. '92	Longford Town	17 + 1	(3)
1993-94	Longford Town	0 + 1	
Feb. '94	St. James's Gate	5	

Cooney, Stephen b. Birmingham, 17 Feb. 1971
Summer '93 St. Francis to Shelbourne
                Shelbourne v St. Pat's Ath. (1-0) 10 Sep. '93
1993-94   Shelbourne   15 + 8   (6)

Cooney, Wayne b. Birmingham, 23 Mar. 1968
Summer '88 Norwich City to Shamrock Rovers
                Shamrock R. v Athlone T. (0-1) 4 Sep. '88
1990-91   Shamrock Rovers   16
1991-92   Shamrock Rovers   18 + 2   (2)
1992-93   Dundalk   18 + 3   (3)
1993-94   Dundalk   11 + 2
Dec. '93   Bohemians   7   (2)

Corcoran, John
Crescent United to Galway United
                Cobh R. v **Galway U.** (0-2) 12. Sep. '93
1993-94   Galway United   0 + 2
               Crescent United

Costello, Greg b. Dublin, 5 Apr. 1970
Jan. '91 Swindon Town to Shelbourne
                Shelbourne v St. Pat's Ath. (1-2) 11 Jan. '91
1990-91   Shelbourne   10 + 1
1991-92   Shelbourne   23 + 1   (2)
1992-93   Shelbourne   30 + 3   (4)
1993-94   Shelbourne   28 + 2

Costello, Norman b. Galway
Salthill Devon to Galway United
                Galway U. v St. James's G. (4-0) 14 Mar. '93
1992-93   Galway United   2
1993-94   Finn Harps   9

Cotter, Cormac b. Cork, 14 Nov.1963
Summer '89 Crofton Celtic to Cork City
                Cork City v Drogheda U (1-1) 3 Sep. '89
1990-91   Cork City   27 + 5   (2)
1991-92   Cork City   25 + 3   (2)
1992-93   Cork City   26 + 8   (1)
1993-94   Cork City   9 + 7

Cousins, Tony b. Dublin , 25 Aug. 1969
                Waterford U. v **Dundalk** (1-1) 25 Sep. '88
1990-91   Dundalk   4   (3)
Sep. '90   Liverpool
1993-94   Bohemians   21 + 2   (8)

Coyle, Gary
From Home Farm Schoolboys
                Waterford U. v **Home. F.** (1-1)IG, 6 Oct. '91
1991-92   Home Farm   20 + 3   (4)
1992-93   Home Farm   14 + 4   (4)
1993-94   Home Farm   14 + 3   (2)

Coyle, Jason
                Home Farm v Limerick C. (0-0) 1 Mar. '92
1991-92   Home Farm   1
1992-93   Home Farm   7
1993-94   Home Farm   13 + 1

Coyle, Liam b. Derry, 21 May, 1968
Summer '93 Omagh Town to Derry City
                Derry City v Cobh R. (5-0) 6 Nov. '88
1993-94   Derry City   23   (8)

Coyle, Robert
Summer '93 Valeview Shankill to Bray Wanderers
                Longford T. v **Bray W.** (1-0) 19 Sep. '93
1993-94   Bray Wanderers   7 + 1

Craig, Stephen b. 14 Nov. 1957
Aug. '88 Bray Wanderers to Shamrock Rovers
                Waterford v **Home Farm** (7-2) 4 Jan. '76
1990-91   Shamrock Rovers   4
1991-92   Shamrock Rovers   0 + 2
Feb. '92   Athlone Town   1 + 2
1992-93   Limerick   31
1993-94   Limerick   29

Crawford, Jim b. Dublin, 1 May 1973
Aug. '91 Rangers YC to Bohemians
                Bray W v. **Bohemians** (1-0) 3 Nov. '91
1991-92   Bohemians   2 + 4
1992-93   Bohemians   9 + 7   (1)
1993-94   Bohemians   17 + 4   (1)

Creane, Adrian
                Finn Harps v Waterford U. (2-0) 19 Sep. '93
1993-94   Finn Harps   15 + 2

Cregoe, Tom b. Cobh, 21 Feb. 1972
Springfield to Cobh Ramblers
                Longford Town v **Cobh. R.** (3-1) 7 Apr. '91
1990-91   Cobh Ramblers   1 + 1
1991-92   Cobh Ramblers   12
1992-93   Cobh Ramblers   26
1993-94   Cobh Ramblers   18 + 3

Crolly, Trevor b. Dublin, 23 Apr. 1974
Summer '92 Belvedere to Drogheda United
                Shamrock R. v **Drogheda U.** (0-0) 30 Aug.'92
1992-93   Drogheda United   12 + 8
1993-94   Drogheda United   22 + 5   (2)

Crowley, Peter b. Waterford, 22 Oct. 1960
Summer '93 Waterford Bohemians to Waterford United
                Finn Harps v **Waterford U.** (2-0) 19 Sep. '93
1993-94   Waterford United   22

Cullen, Paul b. Bray, 5 Aug. 1968
Jul. '88 Bray Wanderers to U.C.D.
                Limerick City v **Bray W.** (0-0) 27 Sep. '88
1990-91   U.C.D.   27   (11)
1991-92   U.C.D.   27   (9)
1992-93   Shamrock Rovers   21 + 3   (6)
1993-94   Shamrock Rovers   4 + 4   (1)

Cummins, Dean
Summer '93 Neilstown Rangers to Kilkenny City
                Kilkenny C. v UCD (3-2) IG, 19 Sep. '93
1993-94   Kilkenny City   2 + 1   (1)

Cummins, Des
Longford T. v **Kilkenny C.** (1-0) 6 Oct. '91
1991-92	Kilkenny City	11 + 7	(4)
1992-93	Longford Town	0 + 3	
Nov. '92	St. James's Gate	11 + 2	(1)
1993-94	St. James's Gate	7 + 6	(1)

Cunningham, Ollie b. Castlebar, 27 Aug. 1966
Castlebar Celtic to Galway United
Galway U. v. Kilkenny City (2-1) 4 Oct. '92
1992-93	Galway United	25
1993-94	Galway United	5

Curran, Liam b. Derry, 10 Dec. 1972
Shelbourne v **Derry City** (0-5) 17 Mar. '92
1991-92	Derry City	0 + 1
1993-94	Derry City	2 + 4

Curran, Paul b. Derry, 5 Oct. 1966
Finn Harps to Derry City
Newcastle U v **Derry City** (1-1) 10 Nov. '85
1990-91	Derry City	31 + 2	(3)
1991-92	Derry City	32	(3)
1992-93	Derry City	32	(1)
1993-94	Derry City	31	(2)

Curran, Shane b. Tuam, 8 Apr. 1971
Sep. '91 Castlerea Celtic to Athlone Town
Athlone T. v Shelbourne (1-2) 26 Jan. '92
1991-92	Athlone Town	11
1992-93	Athlone Town	4
1993-94	Athlone Town	3

Daly, Declan b. Cork, 1 May 1966
St. Mary's (Cork) to Limerick City
Cork City v **Limerick City** (1-4) 26 Jan. '86
1990-91	Cork City	31
1991-92	Cork City	32
1992-93	Cork City	36 + 1
1993-94	Cork City	32

D'Ambrosio, Allessandro "Rossi"
Kilkenny C. v **St. James's G.** (2-0) 16 Jan.'94
1993-94	St. James's Gate	0 + 3

Darby, Frank b. Dublin, 23 Oct. '67
Summer '92 St. Columbans Boys to Athlone Town
Athlone Town v U.C.D. (1-2) 4 Oct. '92
1992-93	Athlone Town	27	(1)
1993-94	Athlone Town	27	(2)

Davis, Robbie
Crumlin United to St. James's Gate
St. James's G. v Waterford U. (1-1) 20 Feb. '94
1993-94	St. James's Gate	3 + 1

De Getrouwe, Elden b. Ghana
Jan. '94 Sparta Rotterdam to Dundalk (L)
Dundalk v Cobh R. (0-0) 23 Jan. '94
1993-94	Dundalk	3	(1)
Feb. '94	Raith Rovers		

De Khors, Red b. Dublin, 13 Dec. 1969
Bohemians to Shelbourne
Bohemians v Derry City (0-2) 11 Sep. 1988
1990-91	Shelbourne	18 + 3	(5)
1991-92	Athlone Town	28	(2)
1992-93	Sittingbourne (Eng.)		
1993-94	Athlone Town	5 + 5	

De Mange, Ken b. Dublin, 3 Sep. 1964
Summer '92 Hull City to Limerick
Athlone Town v **Home Farm** (1-1) 8 Nov. '81
1992-93	Limerick	28	(3)
1993-94	Ards		
Nov. '93	Bohemians	18 + 1	(1)

Devanney, Pierce b. Sligo, 1 May, 1972
'90 Local to Sligo Rovers
Derry C. v **Sligo R.** (0-0) 20 Oct. '91
1991-92	Sligo Rovers	4 + 7	(2)
1992-93	Sligo Rovers	6 + 6	(1)
1993-94	Sligo Rovers	5 + 7	(2)

Devereaux, Paul b. Waterford, 19 Oct. 1971
Aug. '88 Southend (Wford) to Waterford United
Shelbourne v **Waterford U.** (4-0) 14 Oct. '90
1990-91	Waterford United	9 + 3	
1991-92	Waterford United	22 + 2	(1)
1992-93	Waterford United	22 + 6	
1993-94	Waterford United	3 + 3	

Devlin, Mark b. Longford, 30 Jan.1969
Summer '91 St. Albans C. to Longford Town
1991-92	Longford Town	25	
1992-93	Bohemians	0 + 5	
Dec. '92	Galway United (L)	8 + 2	(1)
1993-94	Bohemians	2	
Oct. '93	Cobh Ramblers (L)	5 + 2	(1)
Dec. '93	Longford Town (L)	12	(2)

Dixon, Stephen
Bray W. v **Home Farm** (1-0) 26 Sep. '93
1993-94	Home Farm	3 + 4

Dodd, Alan b. Dublin, 13 Sep. 1969
Summer '93 Rathmichael Shankill to Shamrock Rovers
Bohemians v **Shamrock R.** (1-2) 6 Mar. '94
1993-94	Shamrock Rovers	3 + 3	(1)

Dodd, Declan b. Dublin
Home Farm v Monaghan U. (3-3) 9 Dec. '90
1990-91	Home Farm	10 + 1	
1992-93	Home Farm	14 + 2	(2)
1993-94	Home Farm	19 + 2	

Doherty, Adrian b. Strabane, 1 Jun. 1973
Summer '93 Manchester United to Derry City
Derry City v Cobh R. (2-0) IG, 21 Aug. '93
1993-94	Derry City	3	(1)

Doherty, Alan b. Drogheda, 24 Jul. 1973
Summer '92 Mellifont United to Dundalk
        Waterford United v **Dundalk** (5-4) 6 Sep. '92
1992-93   Dundalk   8 + 10 (1)
1993-94   Dundalk   7 + 3 (2)

Donnelly, Jimmy b. Kilkenny, 19 Apr. 1964
Waterford United to Shamrock Rovers
        Waterford U v St. Pat's Ath. (1-2) 16 Sep. '84
1990-91   Shamrock Rovers   2 + 4
Dec. '90   Kilkenny City (L)   8
Feb. '91   Drogheda United   8 (2)
1991-92   Drogheda United   25 + 1 (2)
1992-93   Kilkenny City   19 + 1 (3)
1993-94   Kilkenny City   20 + 1 (5)

Donnelly, Trevor b. Dublin, 12 Feb. 1974
        Home Farm v U.C.D. (0-1) 18 Oct. '92
1992-93   Home Farm   9 + 6
1993-94   Dundalk   6 + 10 (3)

Doohan, Mick b. Birmingham, 13 Jul. 1967
Summer '88 Dale United to Bray Wanderers
        Drogheda U. v **Bray W.** (2-1) 1G, 4 Sep. '88
1990-91   Bray Wanderers   26 (4)
1991-92   Bray Wanderers   30 (2)
1992-93   Bray Wanderers   32 (1)
1993-94   Dundalk   24 (4)

Doolin, Paul b. Dublin, 26 Mar ,1963
'80/81 St. John Bosco to Bohemians
        Sligo R. v **Bohemians** (0-2) 1G, 13 Sep. '81
1991-92   Shamrock Rovers   19 + 1 (1)
1992-93   Shelbourne   21 + 7 (6)
1993-94   Shelbourne   20 + 1 (1)
Feb. '94   Portadown

Douglas, Ian b. Dublin, 13 Feb. 1971
Summer '90 Drogheda United to Bohemians
        Cork City v **Drogheda U** (1-1) 3 Sep. '89
1990-91   Bohemians   31 (11)
1991-92   Bohemians   8 + 9 (1)
1992-93   Bray Wanderers   14 + 7
1993-94   Bray Wanderers   3
Nov. '93   Drogheda United   11 + 4 (1)

Dowling, David b. Athlone, 11 Feb. 1972
St. Peters to Athlone Town
        Athlone T. v. Shelbourne (0-2) 1 Sep. '91
1991-92   Athlone Town   7 + 3 (3)
1992-93   Athlone Town   19 + 1 (6)
1993-94   Athlone Town   27 (8)

Duffy, Ray b. Dublin, 5 Feb. 1964
Summer '89 Cherry Orchard to Shelbourne
        Shelbourne v. Galway U. (1-0) 3 Sep. '89
1990-91   Shelbourne   25 + 1 (1)
1991-92   Athlone Town (L)   7 + 2
Dec. '91   Monaghan United (L)   14 (1)
1992-93   Limerick   31
1993-94   Limerick   3
Aug. '93   Crusaders
Oct. '93   Limerick   11 + 1

Duggan, Pat b. Cork, 22 Aug. 1966
Aug. '88 Everton (MSL) to Cork City
        St. Pat's Ath. v **Cork City** (2-1) 4 Sep. '88
1990-91   Cork City   7 + 5
1991-92   Cobh Ramblers   24 + 1
1992-93   Cobh Ramblers   17 + 2
1993-94   Cobh Ramblers   0 + 1
Sep. '93   Everton (MSL)

Dully, Pádraig b. Athlone, 20 Apr. 1965
Summer '90 Athlone Town to Shelbourne
        Athlone Town v. Cork City (1-1) 20 Oct. '85
1990-91   Shelbourne   27 (9)
1991-92   Shelbourne   29 + 1 (10)
1992-93   Shelbourne   35 + 2 (14)
1993-94   Shelbourne   2

Dunleavy, Damien b. Sligo, 22 Jan. 1971
Local to Sligo Rovers
        Sligo R. v. Monaghan U. (0-1) 4 Sep. '88
1990-91   Sligo Rovers   17 + 3 (3)
Feb. '91   Raith Rovers
1991-92   Sligo Rovers (L)   3
1992-93   Derry City   11 + 2
1993-94   Finn Harps   20 + 2 (10)

Dunne, Derek b. Dublin, 14 Mar. 1967
Drogheda United to Home Farm
1990-91   Home Farm   **21 (1)
1991-92   St. Patrick's Athletic   4 + 5 (1)
1992-93   St. Patrick's Athletic   23 + 3 (1)
1993-94   St. Patrick's Athletic   30 + 1 (4)

Dunne, Liam b. Dublin, 1 Sep. 1971
Jul. '90 to Belvedere to Bohemians
        Derry City v. **Bohemians** (1-1) 2 Sep. '90
1990-91   Bohemians   12 + 12
May '91   St. Johnstone
1993-94   Bohemians   13 + 1 (4)

Dunne, Tommy b. Dublin, 27 Apr. 1972
        Home Farm v Longford T. (3-0) 25 Nov. '90
1990-91   Home Farm   4 + 1
Feb. '91   Dundalk   –
1991-92   Dundalk   11 + 3
1992-93   Dundalk   22 + 1 (1)
1993-94   Shelbourne   18 + 1

Dykes, Gavin b. Sligo, 2 Oct. 1967
Oct. '87 Local to Sligo Rovers
        Sligo Rovers v Cork City (0-2) 25 Oct. '87
1990-91   Sligo Rovers   30 (2)
1991-92   Sligo Rovers   29 + 2 (3)
1992-93   Sligo Rovers   30 (1)
1993-94   Sligo Rovers   24 (1)

Eccles, Peter b. Dublin, 24 Aug. 1962
1981 St.Brendan's to Shamrock Rovers
          Shamrock Rovers v U.C.D. (1-0) 18 Oct. '81
1990-91	Shamrock Rovers	26 + 2	(2)
1991-92	Shamrock Rovers	27	(3)
1992-93	Shamrock Rovers	25	
1993-94	Shamrock Rovers	29	(4)

Edward, Gareth
Shelbourne to St. James's Gate
          Bray W. v **St. James's G.** (0-0) 6 Mar. '94
1993-94	St. James's Gate	3

Eeles, Tony b. Chatham, 15 Nov. 1970
Nov. '93 Gillingham to Cork City (L)
          Cork City v Galway U. (1-2) 14 Nov. '93
1993-94	Cork City	2 + 2
Jan. '94	Gillingham	

Egan, Séan
Summer '91 Cherry Orchard to Longford Town
          Longford T. v Kilkenny City (1-0) 6 Oct. '91
1991-92	Longford Town	23 + 2	(2)
1992-93	Longford Town	6 + 1	
	CIE Ranch		
1993-94	Kilkenny City	24	

Ennis, Mark b. Dublin, 12 Feb.1964
'87 Shelbourne to St. Patrick's Athletic
          Shelbourne v Cobh R. (4-1) IG, 23 Nov. '86
1990-91	St. Patrick's Athletic	30	(12)
1991-92	St. Patrick's Athletic	32	(15)
1992-93	Derry City	29 + 1	(2)
1993-94	Derry City	6 + 3	(1)
Oct. '93	St. Patrick's Athletic	17 + 1	(6)

Ennis, Paul b. 15 Jun. 1963
Moyle Park College to St. James's Gate
1990-91	St. James's Gate	20 + 4	(6)
1991-92	Bray Wanderers	4 + 1	
Jan. '92	Finn Harps	7	(1)
1992-93	St. James' Gate	12	(3)
1993-94	Kilkenny City	19 + 3	(5)

Eviston, Terry b. Dublin, 17 Jul.1957
Summer '86 Athlone Town to Dundalk
1990-91	Dundalk	33	(10)
1991-92	Dundalk	31 + 1	(5)
1992-93	Dundalk	19 + 4	(1)
1993-94	Shamrock Rovers	25	(6)

Fagan, Peter b. Longford, 17 Feb. 1963
Local to Longford Town
1990-91	Longford Town	18 + 8	
1991-92	Longford Town	0 + 1	
1993-94	Longford Town	3 + 2	

Fallon, Thomas b. Dublin, 13 Aug. 1972
Summer '92 Dundalk to St. Patrick's Athletic
          St. Patrick's Ath. v Bray W. (1-1) 25 Oct. '92
1992-93	St. Patrick's Athletic	6 + 2
1993-94	St. Patrick's Athletic	0 + 1
Jan. '94	Athlone Town (L)	2

Fanning, Clem b. Waterford
Waterford Bohemians to Waterford United
          Finn Harps v **Waterford U.** (2-0) 19 Sep. '93
1993-94	Waterford United	19 + 2	(2)

Fanning, Colm b. Waterford
Southend (Waterford) to Waterford United
1992-93	Waterford United	2 + 2
1993-94	Waterford United	4

Farragher, Donnie b. Galway, 31 Aug. 1966
Summer '93 Mervue United to Galway United
          Bohemians v **Galway U.** (3-0) 20 Aug. '93
1993-94	Galway United	23 + 4	(13)

Farrell, Brian b. Waterford
Johnville to Waterford United
          Finn Harps v **Waterford U.** (2-0) 19 Sep. '93
1993-94	Waterford United	4 + 2

Farrell, Mark
Cherryfield to St. James's Gate
          St. James' Gate v Cobh R. (2-1) 4 Oct. '92
1992-93	St. James's Gate	9 + 9	(3)
1993-94	St. James's Gate	18 + 1	(3)

Farrell, Maurice b. 21 Nov. 1969
Summer '91 Elm Rovers to Bray Wanderers
          Bray W. v Galway United (2-0) 13 Oct. '91
1991-92	Bray Wanderers	7	
1992-93	Bray Wanderers	23 + 1	
1993-94	Bray Wanderers	20	

Fenlon, Pat b. Dublin, 15 Mar. 1969
Summer '87 Chelsea to St. Patrick's Athletic
          Shelbourne v **St Pat's A.** (1-0) 13 Sep. '87
1990-91	St. Patrick's Athletic	31 + 1	(12)
1991-92	Bohemians	31	(10)
1992-93	Bohemians	37	(15)
1993-94	Bohemians	20	(4)
Jan. '94	Linfield		

Finnan, Albert b. Limerick, 11 Nov. 1970
Janesboro to Limerick City
          Limerick City v St. Pat's Ath. (0-3) 28 Jan.'90
1990-91	Limerick City	14 + 9	(1)
1991-92	Limerick City	14 + 9	(1)
1992-93	Limerick	4 + 8	
1993-94	Limerick	17 + 4	(1)

Fitzgerald, Declan b Waterford, 22 Mar. 1974
Summer '92 Waterford Bohemians to U.C.D.
    Athlone Town v **U.C.D.** (1-2) 4 Oct. '92
| 1992-93 | U.C.D. | 10 + 2 | |
| 1993-94 | U.C.D. | 16 | (1) |

Fitzgerald, Paul b. Dublin, 14 Dec. 1966
Pegasus to St. Patrick's Athletic
    St. Patrick's Ath. v **U.C.D.** (2-0) 27 Oct. '85
| 1992-93 | St. Patrick's Athletic | 3 + 2 | |
| 1993-94 | Monaghan United | 6 | |

Fitzgerald, Shane b. Galway, 22 Dec. 1969
Salthill Devon to Galway United
    Bohemians v **Galway U.** (3-0) 20 Aug. '93
| 1993-94 | Galway United | 2 + 2 | |

Fitzgerald, Tommy b. Dublin, 2 Jan. 1970
Summer '89 Tottenham H. to Shelbourne
    Shelbourne v Galway U. (1-0) 3 Sep. '89
1990-91	Waterford United (L)	7	(2)
Dec. '90	Shelbourne	1	
Feb. '91	Limerick City (L)	9	(3)
1991-92	Limerick City	22 + 1	(11)
1992-93	Bohemians	18 + 3	(5)
1993-94	Bohemians	13 + 9	(2)

Flanagan, Robbie b. Dublin, 18 Sep. 1970
'89 Arsenal to Shelbourne
    Shelbourne v. Shamrock R. (1-2) 12 Nov. '89
1990-91	Limerick City (L)	13	
Dec. '90	Kilkenny City	16	
1991-92	Longford Town	19	
1992-93	Longford Town	8	
Dec. '92	Kilkenny City	13 + 2	
1993-94	Kilkenny City	3 + 1	
Feb. '94	St. James's Gate	6	

Flood, Brian b. Dublin, 22 Jun. 1971
Belvedere to Shelbourne
    Shelbourne v Galway U. (1-0) 3 Sep. '89
1990-91	Shelbourne	1 + 1	
1991-92	Shelbourne	12 + 6	(1)
1992-93	Shelbourne	20 + 6	
1993-94	Shelbourne	20	

Flynn, Paul b. Waterford
Summer '93 Waterford Bohemians to Waterford United
    Finn Harps v **Waterford U.** (2-0) 19 Sep. '93
| 1993-94 | Waterford United | 3 | |

Foster, David
Jul. '86 Stella Maris to U.C.D.
    Drogheda United v **U.C.D.** (0-2) 6 Dec. '87
| 1990-91 | U.C.D. | 3 + 3 | |
| 1993-94 | Home Farm | 6 + 1 | |

Francis, Séan b. Birmingham, 1 Aug. 1972
Sep. '91 Birmingham City to Cobh Ramblers (L)
    Cobh R. v U.C.D. (1-1) IG, 6 Oct. '91
1991-92	Cobh Ramblers	12	(5)
Dec. '91	Birmingham City Northampton Town		
1993-94	Cobh Ramblers	27	(9)

Frawley, Conor b. Athlone,. 20 Mar 1972
Willow Park to Athlone Town
    Galway U v. **Athlone Town** (0-2) 18 Nov.'90
1990-91	Athlone Town	11 + 4	(4)
1991-92	Athlone Town	22 + 3	(1)
1992-93	Athlone Town	25 + 1	(2)
1993-94	Athlone Town	26	(6)

Freyne, Patsy b. Cork, 6 Mar. 1964
Summer '86 Newcastlewest to Cork City
    Drogheda U. v **Newcastle U.** (2-0) 20 Oct. '85
1990-91	Cork City	15 + 2	(2)
1991-92	Cobh Ramblers	22 + 1	(2)
1992-93	Cobh Ramblers	22 + 1	(4)
1993-94	Cobh Ramblers	5 + 4	
Nov. '93	Avondale United		

Gabbiadini, Ricardo b. Newport, 11 Mar. 1970
Jan. '94 Frickley Athletic to Sligo Rovers
    Sligo R. v St. James's G. (3-1) 29 Jan. '94
| 1993-94 | Sligo Rovers | 8 | (2) |

Galbert, Derek b. Waterford, 16 Feb. 1974
Ferrybank to Waterford United
    Kilkenny C. v **Waterford U.** (0-1) 6 Mar. '94
| 1993-94 | Waterford United | 0+1 | |

Gallagher, John
Shamrock Rovers to St. James's Gate
1990-91	St. James's Gate	1	
1991-92	St. James's Gate	1 + 1	
1992-93	St. James's Gate	6 + 4	(1)
1993-94	St. James's Gate	5 + 3	(1)

Gallagher, Marty b. Derry
Jun. '92 Cauldaff to Finn Harps
    Finn Harps v Home Farm (3-2) 4 Oct. '92
| 1992-93 | Finn Harps | 16 + 7 | (1) |
| 1993-94 | Finn Harps | 24 + 2 | (4) |

Gannon, Karl b. Dublin, 11 Sep. 1974
Rivermount to Home Farm
    Waterford U. v **Home Farm** (1-1) 6 Oct. '91
1991-92	Home Farm	24	(6)
1992-93	Home Farm	16 + 2	(4)
1993-94	Home Farm	26 + 1	(16)

Gauld, Stuart b. Edinburgh, 26 Mar. 1964
Nov. '85 Hearts to Derry City
    Monaghan U v **Derry City** (0-2) 1 Dec. '85
1990-91	Derry City	31	(8)
1991-92	Derry City	31	(7)
1992-93	Derry City	30	(4)
1993-94	Derry City	24	(3)

Gavin, Fran b. Dublin, 16 Sep. 1960
Summer '90 Galway United to St.James's Gate
1990-91	St. James's Gate	21	
1991-92	St. James's Gate	22	
1992-93	St. James's Gate	21 + 2	(1)
1993-94	St. James's Gate	14 + 1	(1)

Gaynor, Tommy b. Limerick, 29 Jan. 1963
Summer '93 Millwall to Cork City
Limerick U. v Finn Harps (2-2) 13 Sep. '81
1993-94	Cork City	27 + 2	(11)

Geoghegan, Declan b. Dublin, 20 Aug. 1964
Jun. '88 Villa Park United to Drogheda United
1990-91	Drogheda United	8 + 3	
1991-92	Drogheda United	30	(1)
1992-93	Bohemians	28	
1993-94	Bohemians	0 + 1	
Oct. '93	Monaghan United	22	

Geoghegan, Stephen b. Dublin, 3 Jun. 1970
'88 Rivermount Boys to Drogheda United
1990-91	Drogheda United	27	(9)
1991-92	Drogheda United	3 + 1	
	Valley Park United		
1992-93	Shamrock Rovers	15 + 3	(7)
1993-94	Shamrock Rovers	30 + 1	(23)

Gibbons, John b. Dublin, 21 Sep. 1975
Summer '93 St. Kevin's Boys to U.C.D.
U.C.D. v Finn Harps (4-1) 26 Sep. '93
1993-94	U.C.D.	2 + 4	(1)

Giles, Chris b. Leeds, 26 Feb. 1973
Bromsgrove Rovers to Shamrock Rovers
Bohemians v Shamrock R. (2-1) 17 Jan. '93
1992-93	Shamrock Rovers	10	
1993-94	Shamrock Rovers	0 + 4	

Girvan, Mark b. Dublin, 24 Sep. 1968
'89 Kilkenny City to Drogheda United
1990-91	Drogheda United	27	
1991-92	Drogheda United	3 + 1	
Jan. '91	Longford Town (L)	12	
1992-93	Longford Town	26 + 1	
1993-94	Longford Town	23	

Glynn, Johnny b. Galway, 10 Oct.1966
Summer '84 Corrib Shamrocks to Galway United
Dundalk v Galway United (3-1) 14 Oct. '84
1990-91	Galway United	20 + 1	(6)
1991-92	Cork City	6 + 3	
1992-93	Cork City	33	(7)
1993-94	Cork City	24 + 5	(7)

Golden, Donal b. Roscrea, 22 Apr. 1972
Jul. '90 Killavilla United (Roscrea) to Athlone Town
Bray W. v Athlone Town (1-1) 8 Sep. '91
1991-92	Athlone Town	0 + 1	
1992-93	Athlone Town	7 + 5	(3)
1993-94	Athlone Town	16 + 5	(7)

Gorman, Mick b. Dublin, 14 Aug. 1961
Summer '89 Emfa to St. James's Gate
1990-91	St. James's Gate	21	(2)
1991-92	St. James's Gate	17 + 1	(1)
1992-93	St. James's Gate	24	(1)
1993-94	St. James's Gate	19	

Gormley, David
Shelbourne to St. James's Gate
St. James's G. v Waterford U. (1-1) 20 Feb. '94
1993-94	St. James's Gate	4 + 2	

Gormley, Eddie b. Dublin, 23 Oct. 1968
St. Joseph's Boys to Bray Wanderers
Derry City v Bray W. (0-0) 13 Sep. '87
Nov. '87	Tottenham Hotspur		
Jul. '90	Doncaster Rovers		
1993-94	Drogheda United	11 + 2	
Dec. '93	St. Patrick's Athletic	14	

Gormley, Philip b. Dublin
St. Joseph's Boys to Bray Wanderers
Bray W. v Longford Town (2-1) 28 Nov. '93
1993-94	Bray Wanderers	12 + 4	(1)

Gough, Alan b. Watford, 10 Mar. 1971
Sep. '93 Fulham to Galway United
Cobh R. v Galway United (0-2) 12 Sep. '93
1993-94	Galway United	27	

Gough, Derek b. 14 Jan. 1967
Bray Wanderers v Cork City (1-0) 19 Oct. '86
1990-91	Athlone Town (L)	3 + 1	
Dec. '90	Bray Wanderers	16 + 1	(8)
1991-92	Bray Wanderers	11 + 11	
1992-93	Bray Wanderers	3 + 2	
Nov. '92	Longford Town	18	(4)
1993-94	Longford Town	20 + 3	(2)

Grace, Jim b. Dublin, 17 Jul .1954
St. Patrick's Athletic to Athlone Town
Home F/Drums v Athlone T. (1-1) 3 Dec. '72
1990-91	Athlone Town	33	
1991-92	Bohemians	22	
1992-93	Drogheda United	27	
1993-94	Drogheda United	21	

Grace, John b. Dublin, 16 Feb. 1964
Kilkenny City to Limerick City
1990-91	Limerick City	30	
1991-92	Limerick City	24 + 1	
1992-93	Limerick	31	
1993-94	Limerick	2	
Aug. '93	Glentoran		

Greene, Ed. b. New York, 13 Apr. 1969
San Vitesse (Rome) to Shamrock Rovers
Shamrock R. v Derry City (3-0) 17 Mar.'94
1993-94	Shamrock Rovers	1 + 1	

Greene, Keith b. Waterford, 25 Jul. 1974
Johnville to Waterford United
    Waterford U. v Bray W. (0-0) 20 Mar. '94
1993-94   Waterford United   2 + 1   (1)

Greene, Shane b. Cobh, 2 Dec. 1975
Springfield to Cobh Ramblers
    Galway U. v **Cobh R.** (4-0) 5 Dec. '93
1993-94   Cobh Ramblers   1

Grehan, Gary
St. Patrick's Athletic to Longford Town
    Longford T. v St. James's G. (1-4) 14 Nov.'93
1993-94   Longford Town   1 + 1

Griffin, Robert b. Waterford 22 Dec. 1971
Jul. '90 Bolton (W/ford) to U.C.D.
    Longford Town v **U.C.D.** (0-2) 1G 7 Oct. '90
1990-91   U.C.D.   21 + 2   (5)
1991-92   U.C.D.   8 + 1   (3)
1992-93   U.C.D.   26   (10)
1993-94   U.C.D.   19 + 1   (4)

Hague, Paul b. Durham, 16 Sep. 1972
Jul. '93 Gillingham to Cork City (L)
    Cork City v Monaghan U. (1-0) 22 Aug.'93
1993-94   Cork City   5
Sep. '93   Gillingham

Hale, Richie b. Waterford, 9 Mar. 1972
Waterford Glass to Waterford United
    Derry C v **Waterford U** (6-2) 1G 16 Dec. '90
1990-91   Waterford United   2 + 7   (1)
1991-92   Waterford United   6 + 14   (3)
1992-93   Waterford United   8 + 4   (1)
1993-94   Waterford United   0 + 2

Halion, Eugene b. Tuam, 16 Apr. 1964
'88 Dynamo Blues to Galway United
    Cork City v **Galway U** (0-0) 11 Sep. '88
1990-91   Galway United   2 + 5
1991-92   Galway United   0 + 1
1992-93   Galway United   4 + 6
1993-94   Galway United   0 + 1

Hall, Paul
Summer '90 Harold's Cross Boys to St. James's Gate
    St. James's G. v U.C.D. (1-5) 2 Dec. '90
1990-91   St. James's Gate   0 + 5
1991-92   St. James's Gate   9
1992-93   St. James's Gate   27
1993-94   St. James's Gate   24

Hall, Richie
    Monaghan U. v **St.James's G.** (2-0) 21 Mar.'93
1992-93   St. James's Gate   4   (1)
1993-94   St. James's Gate   6 + 1   (1)

Hall, Stephen b. Hartlepool, 28 Oct. 1971
Nov. '92 Northampton Town to Waterford United
    Waterford U. v. Bohemians (1-0) 15 Nov. '92
1992-93   Waterford United   6 + 7
1993-94   Waterford United   10 + 1

Hanrahan, Joe b. Limerick, 21 Mar. 1964
Summer '90 Limerick City to Derry City
    Dundalk v **U.C.D.** (2-0) 10 Sep. '81
1990-91   Derry City   20 + 1   (2)
1991-92   Derry City   25 + 4   (3)
1992-93   Dundalk   18   (5)
1993-94   Dundalk   22 + 2   (1)

Hanrahan, Peter b. Limerick, 23 Feb. 1968
Summer '90 Limerick City to Dundalk
    Newcastlewest v **U.C.D.** (0-0) 19 Oct. '86
1990-91   Dundalk   32   (18)
1991-92   Dundalk   32   (6)
1992-93   Dundalk   31   (6)
1993-94   Dundalk   29   (8)

Harrington, Phil b. Bangor (Wales), 23 Nov. 1964
Summer' 88 Rhyl to Cork City
    St. Pat's Athletic v **Cork City** (2-1) 4 Sep. '88
1990-91   Cork City   30
1991-92   Cork City   29
1992-93   Cork City   31
1993-94   Cork City   29

Hastie, Will b. Melbourne, 7 Jan. 1973
Jan. '93 Kilmarnock to Sligo Rovers
    Sligo Rovers v. Shamrock R. (0-1) 3 Jan. '93
1992-93   Sligo Rovers   13   (1)
1993-94   Sligo Rovers   21   (3)

Heaney, Gary b. Derry, 18 Apr. 1972
    Derry City v St. Patrick's Ath. (1-0) 17 Feb. '91
1990-91   Derry City   2 + 2
1991-92   Derry City   0 + 2
1993-94   Derry City   5 + 3   (1)

Heery, Eoin
    Bray W. v **Kilkenny C.** (1-1) 21 Nov. '93
1993-94   Kilkenny City   12 + 4   (1)

Hegarty, Paul
    Derry City v Bray W. (0-0) 13 Sep. '87
1990-91   Derry City   22 + 5   (1)
1991-92   Derry City   12 + 1
1992-93   Derry City   3 + 2
Oct. '92   Finn Harps   20 + 1
1993-94   Finn Harps   24   (2)

Henderson, Dave b. Dublin. 11 Jun. 1960
    Home Farm v **Shamrock R.** (0-0) 25 Apr. '78
1990-91   St. Patrick's Athletic   23
1991-92   Shamrock Rovers   31
1992-93   Bohemians   38
1993-94   Bohemians   17

Henderson, Stephen
Summer '92 Distillery to St. James's Gate
                    Shelbourne v. Dundalk (0-3) 20 Oct. '85
1992-93   St. James's Gate   2
Oct. '92   Cobh Ramblers   25
1993-94   Cobh Ramblers   34

Herrick, Mark b. Cork, 10 Jun. 1973
Summer '93 Raith Rovers to Galway United
                    Bohemians v **Galway U.** (3-0) 20 Aug. '93
1993-94   Galway United   30 + 1   (6)

Hill, Ian b. Dublin, 9 May 1965
Sep. '88 Leicester City to Shelbourne
                    Shelbourne v Derry City (0-5) 30 Oct. '88
1990-91   Shelbourne   27 + 4
1991-92   Shelbourne   0 + 1
Nov. '91   Limerick City (L)   23
1992-93   St. Patrick's Athletic 32
1993-94   St. Patrick's Athletic 27

Hitchcock, Fran b. Dublin, 2 Dec. 1960
                    Thurles T. v **Shelbourne** (1-0) 7 Sep. '80
1990-91   Sligo Rovers   26 + 1   (2)
1991-92   Sligo Rovers   0 + 4
Oct. '91   Bohemians   9 + 9   (2)
1992-93   Sligo Rovers   18 + 3
1993-94   Cliftonville
Oct. '93   Limerick   16 + 1   (2)

Hogan, Eric b. Cork, 18 Dec. 1971
Summer '90 Rockmount to Cobh Ramblers
                    Cobh Ramblers v Finn Harps (2-1) 7 Oct. '90
1990-91   Cobh Ramblers   23 + 4   (5)
Aug. '91   Birmingham City
1991-92   Cobh Ramblers (L)   6
1992-93   Shamrock Rovers   11 + 1   (2)
1993-94   Cobh Ramblers   0 + 5

Honan, Brian b. Limerick, 8 Dec. 1973
U.C.D. to Bray Wanderers
                    Bray Wanderers v U.C.D. (0-2) 10 Oct. '93
1993-94   Bray Wanderers   9 + 5   (4)

Horan, Stephen b. Dublin
St. Joseph's Boys to Bray Wanderers
                    Bray W. v Home Farm (0-0) 30 Jan. '94
1993-94   Bray Wanderers   8

Houlahan, Ger b. Newry, 26 May 1965
Summer '93 Armagh City to Sligo Rovers
                    Home Farm v **Sligo Rovers** (0-1) 19 Sep.'93
1993-94   Sligo Rovers   11   (7)

Hutton, Peter b. Derry, 2 Mar. 1973
Bradford City to Derry City
                    Derry City v Cork City (1-3) 17 Mar. '91
1990-91   Derry City   1 + 1
1991-92   Derry City   26 + 5   (1)
1992-93   Derry City   22
1993-94   Derry City   28   (6)

Hyde, Declan b. Ennis, 28 Aug. 1963
Vereker Clements to Limerick City
                    Shamrock R. v **Limerick C.** (2-1) 19 Oct. '86
1990-91   Cork City   17 + 1   (2)
1991-92   Cork City   12   (3)
1993-94   Cork City   14 + 3   (2)

Irwin, Brian b. Dublin, 20 May 1971
Barnsley to Home Farm
                    Home Farm v Bray W. (1-0) 15 Dec. '88
1990-91   Home Farm   14 + 3   (7)
Mar. '91   Kilkenny City   3   (1)
1991-92   Dundalk   22 + 2   (8)
1992-93   Dundalk   13 + 7   (9)
1993-94   Dundalk   8 + 3   (3)

Istvan, Zoltan b. Baja (Hungary), 10 Feb. 1970
Jul. '89 Baja to U.C.D.
                    Bohemians v **U.C.D.** (3-0) 3 Sep. '89
1990-91   U.C.D.   24 + 2   (2)
1991-92   U.C.D.   7 + 3   (3)
1992-93   Monaghan United   10 + 5
1993-94   Home Farm   2

Izzi, Antonio (Tony) b. Dublin, 12 Nov. 1970
Summer '93 Cassino F.C. (Italy) to Shelbourne
                    Limerick v **Shelbourne** (0-0) 22 Aug. '93
1993-94   Shelbourne   4 + 11   (3)

Judge, Dermot b. Dublin
Oct. '90 Bray Wanderers to Shelbourne
                    Bray W. v Longford T. (0-1) 20 Oct. '85
1990-91   Shelbourne   18 + 2   (1)
1991-92   Bray Wanderers   18 + 3
1992-93   Bray Wanderers   21 + 1
1993-94   Bray Wanderers   20 + 1   (1)

Kaminsky, Jason b. Leicester, 3 Dec. 1973
Aug. '93 Nottingham Forest to Cobh Ramblers (L)
                    Cobh R. v Limerick (0-0) 25 Aug. '93
1993-94   Cobh Ramblers   2
Sep. '93   Nottingham Forest

Kane, Alan
Summer '91 Ballybrack Boys to St. Patrick's Athletic
                    St. Pats A v Drogheda U. (3-1) 8 Sep. '91
1991-92   St. Patrick's Athletic 31
1992-93   Shamrock Rovers   20
1993-94   Drogheda United   11

Kavanagh, Ciaran b. Newry, 28 Aug. 1972
Jul. '90 Bay United to U.C.D.
                    Longford Town v **U.C.D.** (0-2) 7 Oct. '90
1990-91   U.C.D.   23   (1)
1991-92   U.C.D.   20 + 3   (1)
1992-93   U.C.D.   27   (3)
1993-94   U.C.D.   21   (4)

Kavanagh, Colum b. Dublin, 8 Jan. 1959
Oct.'87 Drimnagh Dyn to St. James's Gate
 St. James's Gate v. Kilkenny C (1-2) 7 Oct. '90
1990-91 St. James's Gate 26 (10)
1991-92 St. James's Gate 25 (9)
1992-93 Kilkenny City 9 (2)
Dec. '92 St. James's Gate 8
1993-94 St. James's Gate 22 + 1 (10)

Kavanagh, Mick b. Dublin
Summer '90 U.C.D. to Dundalk
 U.C.D. v Galway United (1-2) 20 Oct. '85
1990-91 Dundalk 27 + 2 (1)
1991-92 Dundalk 9 + 4 (2)
1992-93 Dundalk 1
Nov. '92 Ards
1993-94 Ards
Nov. '93 Limerick 4 + 2

Kavanagh, Paul b. 17 Jul. 1967
Jul. '85 Trinity United to U.C.D.
 Bohemians v U.C.D. (2-0) 8 Dec. '85
1990-91 Shamrock Rovers 29
1991-92 Shamrock Rovers 2
1992-93 Shamrock Rovers 12
1993-94 Dundalk 13

Kealy, Dave "Dax" b. 9 Aug. 1965
Shamrock Rovers to Bray Wanderers
 Bohemians v Dundalk (0-0) 3 Nov. '85
1990-91 Bray Wanderers 7 + 6 (1)
1991-92 Bray Wanderers 2 + 5
1992-93 Bray Wanderers 2 + 5 (1)
1993-94 Longford Town 17 + 2 (3)

Kealy, Glenn b. Drogheda, 28 Feb. 1971
 St. Patrick's Ath. v Drogheda U. (4-1) 7 Nov. '93
1993-94 Drogheda United 0 + 1

Keane, Pascal b. Waterford, 5 Aug. 1967
Aug. '85 Dungarvan United to Waterford United
 Waterford U v Athlone T (5-1) 19 Oct. '86
1990-91 Waterford United 6 + 5
Jan. '91 Cobh Ramblers 4 + 2 (2)
1991-92 Waterford United 15 + 3 (5)
1992-93 Waterford United 32 + 1 (16)
1993-94 St. Patrick's Athletic 9 (2)
Oct. '93 Waterford United 10 + 3 (1)

Keane, Tommy b. Dublin, 16 Sep. 1968
Oct. '88 Colchester United to Galway United
 Cobh R v Galway United (0-0) 23 Oct. '88
1990-91 Galway United 25 + 2 (8)
1991-92 Sligo Rovers 7
Oct. '91 Galway United 15 (5)
1992-93 Finn Harps 23 + 4 (7)
1993-94 Athlone Town 25 (3)

Keddy, James b. Dublin, 26 Mar. 1973
St. Joseph's Boys to Home Farm
 Home Farm v Longford T. (0-3) 13 Oct. '91
1991-92 Home Farm 20 + 1 (5)
1992-93 Home Farm 24 + 1 (1)
1993-94 Home Farm 23 (3)

Keenan, Anthony b. Athlone, 12 May 1960
Athlone Town to Longford Town
 Home Farm v Athlone T. (0-3) 23 Dec. '79
1990-91 Longford Town 26
1991-92 Longford Town 10
Dec. '91 Cobh Ramblers 3
1992-93 Cobh Ramblers 2
Nov. '93 Athlone Town 23
1993-94 Athlone Town 24

Keenan, Val b. Dublin, 18 Feb. 1969
Summer' 88 St. Josephs Boy's to Shelbourne
1990-91 Shelbourne 10 + 6 (3)
1991-92 Athlone Town 23
1992-93 Athlone Town 27
1993-94 Athlone Town 26

Kehoe, Barry b. Drogheda, 12 Sep. 1962
 Home Farm v Dundalk (0-4) 29 Mar. '81
1990-91 Dundalk -
1991-92 Dundalk 0 + 1
1993-94 Dundalk -
Nov. '93 Drogheda United (L) 17 (1)

Kelch, Pat b. Dublin, 5 May 1966
'87 Home Farm to St. Patrick's Athletic
 Waterford U. v Home Farm (1-0) 20 Oct.'85
1990-91 St. Patrick's Athletic 29 (2)
1991-92 St. Patrick's Athletic 17 + 3 (1)
1992-93 St. Patrick's Athletic 24 (1)
1993-94 Bohemians 7

Kelly, Alan b. Waterford, 10 May 1962
Aug. '86 Carrick F.C. to Waterford United
1990-91 Waterford United 1 + 1
1991-92 Waterford United 13 + 6
1992-93 Waterford United 4
1993-94 Waterford United 4 + 1

Kelly, Colm b. Dublin, 26 Aug. 1975
Ballybrack Boys to Bray Wanderers
 Home Farm v Bray W. (3-2) 5 Dec. '93
1993-94 Bray Wanderers 10 + 1

Kelly, Darren b. Dublin, 20 Nov. 1973
Lorcan Celtic to Shelbourne
 Cork City v Shelbourne (3-1) 20 Mar. '94
1993-94 Shelbourne 2 + 2

Kelly, Gareth b. Dublin, 13 Jan. 1971
 Home Farm v Limerick C. (0-1) 20 Oct. '91
1991-92 Home Farm 15 (3)
Jan. '92 Shamrock Rovers 8 + 1
1992-93 Shamrock Rovers 15 + 3
1993-94 Shamrock Rovers 2 + 1

Kelly, Gary b. Dublin
summer '93 Ashtown Villa to Waterford United
　　　　　　　Waterford U. v Longford T. (2-2) 16 Sep. '93
1993-94　　　Waterford United　　　8

Kelly, Gerry b. Baillieston, 25 Nov. 1971
Oct. '92 Kilmarnock to Sligo Rovers (L)
　　　　　　　Shamrock R. v **Sligo R.** (0-0) 18 Oct. '92
1992-93　　　Sligo Rovers　　　6
　　　　　　　Kilmarnock
1993-94　　　Sligo Rovers　　　14 + 1　(1)

Kelly, Gerry
Summer '93 Shannon Town to Limerick
　　　　　　　Limerick v Shelbourne (0-0) 22 Aug. '93
1993-94　　　Limerick　　　3 + 7　(1)

Kelly, John b. Dublin, 15 Dec. 1963
1990-91　　　St. Patrick's Athletic　　　3 + 6　(3)
1991-92　　　Kilkenny City　　　25　(7)
1992-93　　　Kilkenny City　　　26　(8)
1993-94　　　Kilkenny City　　　18 + 1　(8)

Kelly, Kevin b. Basildon, 3 Aug. 1968
Dec. '87 Cardiff City to Waterford United
　　　　　　　Waterford U. v Derry City (0-0) 7 Feb. '88
1990-91　　　Waterford United　　　24
1991-92　　　Waterford United　　　25　(5)
1992-93　　　Waterford United　　　34　(6)
1992-93　　　Cobh Ramblers　　　20 + 4

Kelly, Liam
　　　　　　　Home Farm v Sligo Rovers (0+1) 19 Sep. '93
1993-94　　　Home Farm　　　6 + 2

Kelly, Packie b. Cobh, 25 Mar. 1968
Springfield to Cobh Ramblers
　　　　　　　Monaghan U. v **Cobh R.** (3-0) 15 Feb. '87
1990-91　　　Cobh Ramblers　　　22 + 1　(1)
1991-92　　　Cobh Ramblers　　　27　(1)
1992-93　　　Cobh Ramblers　　　25
1993-94　　　Cobh Ramblers　　　34　(1)

Kelly, Peter b. Dublin, 20 Nov. 1965
1991 Hamilton United to St.James's Gate
　　　　　　　St. James's G v Limerick C (0-0) 6 Oct. '91
1991-92　　　St. James's Gate　　　2 + 3
1992-93　　　St. James's Gate　　　27　(1)
1993-94　　　St. James's Gate　　　20 + 4

Kelly, Seamus b. Tullamore, 6 May 1974
Summer '93 Tullamore Town to U.C.D.
　　　　　　　Kilkenny City v **U.C.D.** (3-2) 19 Sep. '93
1993-94　　　U.C.D.　　　27

Kelly, Stephen b. Dublin, 19 Feb. 1971
Home Farm to Kilkenny City
　　　　　　　St. James's G v **Kilkenny C** (1-2) 7 Oct. '90
1990-91　　　Kilkenny City　　　6 + 1
Nov. '90　　　Limerick City (L)　　　2 + 1
　　　　　　　Brighton
Feb. '91　　　Longford Town　　　7　(2)
1991-92　　　Longford Town　　　25 + 2　(1)
1992-93　　　Longford Town　　　24　(6)
1993-94　　　Longford Town　　　8　(2)
Nov. '93　　　Dundalk　　　13 + 2　(3)

Kenneally, Anthony b. Cork, 4 Apr. 1971
Albert Rovers to Cork City
　　　　　　　Galway United v **Cork City** (2-1) 24 Sep. '89
1990-91　　　Cork City　　　1 + 2
1991-92　　　Cork City　　　7 + 8
1992-93　　　Cobh Ramblers　　　17 + 4　(2)
1993-94　　　Cobh Ramblers　　　21 + 4　(1)

Kennedy, Anto b. Dublin
Stella Maris to Home Farm
1990-91　　　Home Farm　　　10
1991-92　　　Home Farm　　　24
1992-93　　　Home Farm　　　4　(1)
1993-94　　　Bray Wanderers　　　15 + 1

Kenny, Johnny b. Riverstown, 31 Jul. 1970
Summer '92 Arrow Harps to Galway United
　　　　　　　Galway U. v Kilkenny C. (2-1) 4 Oct. '92
1992-93　　　Galway United　　　19 + 4　(6)
1993-94　　　Sligo Rovers　　　26　(8)

Kenny, Stephen
　　　　　　　Home Farm v Longford T. (3-2) 13 Mar. '94
1993-94　　　Home Farm　　　2 + 2

Keogh, Alan
St. Patrick's Athletic to St. James's Gate
　　　　　　　St. James's G. v Kilkenny C. (1-1) 4 Apr. '93
1992-93　　　St. James's Gate　　　2
1993-94　　　St. James's Gate　　　3

Keogh, Niall b. Dublin 2 Mar. 1973
Summer '91 Crumlin United to Shelbourne
　　　　　　　Bohemians v **Shelbourne** (2-1) 27 May '93
1992-93　　　Shelbourne　　　0 + 1
1993-94　　　Shelbourne　　　-
Oct. '93　　　Limerick (L)　　　22

Keogh, Robert b. Dublin, 16 Feb. 1973
'90 Verona Boys to U.C.D.
　　　　　　　U.C.D. v Monaghan United (1-0) 17 Mar. '91
1990-91　　　U.C.D.　　　2
1991-92　　　U.C.D　　　20 + 1
1992-93　　　U.C.D.　　　25 + 1
1993-94　　　U.C.D.　　　15 + 1　(1)

Kerley, Michael b. Limerick, 6 Jan.1971
Wembley Rovers to Limerick City
	Limerick C v St. Pat's Ath. (0-1) 3 Sep. '89
1990-91	Limerick City	24 + 2
1991-92	Limerick City	24	(1)
1992-93	Limerick	7
1993-94	Limerick	21	(1)

Kersham, Andrew b. Nenagh
Waterford R.T.C. to Waterford United
	Waterford U. v Bray W. (0-0) 20 Mar. '94
1993-94	Waterford United	3

Kiernan, Ian b. Athlone, 27 Sep. 1972
Jul. '89 Willow Park to Athlone Town
	Athlone Town v Galway U. (3-2) 8 Nov. '92
1992-93	Athlone Town	7
1993-94	Athlone Town	0 + 1

Killeen, Ronan b. Newry, 12 Apr. 1969
U.C.G. to Galway United
	Bohemians v Galway U. (5-3) 26 Oct. '86
1991-92	Galway United	23 + 4
1992-93	Galway United	16 + 1
1993-94	Galway United	18 + 2	(1)

King, Howard b. Dublin, 9 Sep. 1969
Shamrock Rovers to Bray Wanderers
	Shamrock R. v. Athlone T. (0-1) 4 Sep.'88
1990-91	Bray Wanderers	0 + 2
	Tolka Rovers
Nov. '91	Distillery
1992-93	Limerick	25 + 2	(5)
1993-94	Bohemians	14 + 6	(1)

King, Jason
Shelbourne to Home Farm
1992-93	Home Farm	24 + 1	(6)
1993-94	U.S.A.
Jan. '94	Kilkenny City	3 + 7

King, Lee b. Dublin, 11 Nov. 1969
Jul. '88 Rivermount to Bohemians
	Limerick C v Bohemians (3-1) 30 Oct. '88
1990-91	Bohemians	15 + 6	(1)
1991-92	Bohemians	21 + 3	(6)
1992-93	Bohemians	21 + 10	(1)
1993-94	Bohemians	-
Oct. '93	St. Patrick's Athletic	2 + 4	(1)
Jan. '94	Drogheda United	7 + 1	(7)

Kinnaird, Paul b. Glasgow, 11 Nov. 1966
Oct. '93 Partick Thistle to Derry City
	Galway U. v Derry City (2-1) 17 Oct. '93
1993-94	Derry City	20	(2)

Kinsella, Alan b. Dublin, 18 Jul. 1962
'80 Stella Maris to Bohemians
1990-91	Athlone Town	28
1991-92	Monaghan Town	23
1992-93	Monaghan United	29	(1)
1993-94	Monaghan United	28	(1)

Kinsella, Mick b. Dublin, 10 Dec. 1973
Summer '92 Belvedere to Drogheda United
1992-93	Drogheda United	5 + 5
1993-94	Drogheda United	6 + 3

Lacey, John b. Waterford, 19 Mar. 1975
Stoke City to Waterford United
	Kilkenny C. v Waterford U. (2-2) 17 Oct.'93
1993-94	Waterford United	9 + 4	(1)

Lafferty, Brian b. Ballybofey
Jun. '92 Bonaghee United to Finn Harps
	Longford Town v Finn Harps (1-1) 24 Jan. '88
1992-93	Finn Harps	19 + 1
1993-94	Finn Harps	11 + 3

Lafferty, Karl
	Finn Harps v U.C.D. (0-0) 5 Dec. '93
1993-94	Finn Harps	10

Lally, Stephen b. Galway, 11 Feb. 1964
'82 West United to Galway United
1990-91	Galway United	26 + 1	(2)
1991-92	Galway United	23 + 4	(2)
1992-93	Galway United	18 + 1	(1)
1993-94	Galway United	29	(1)

Lambert, Keith b. Dublin, 18 Jul. 1965
	St. Patrick's Ath. v U.C.D. (0-2) 22 Sep. '84
1991-92	Galway United	2
1992-93	Galway United	18	(1)
1993-94	Cobh Ramblers	-
Sep. '93	Galway United	26

Lawless, Christopher b. Dublin, 4 Oct. 1974
Rivermount Boys to Home Farm
	Bray W. v Home Farm (1-0) 26 Sep. '93
1993-94	Home Farm	6 + 1
Dec. '93	Sunderland

Lawless, Eugene "Gino" b. Dublin, 14 Jan. 1959
Cambridge Boys to Bohemians
	Cork Alberts v Bohemians (1-2) 10 Sep. '78
1990-91	Dundalk	28	(2)
1991-92	Dundalk	30	(2)
1992-93	Dundalk	28	(2)
1993-94	Dundalk	30	(1)

Lawless, Joe b. Dublin, 13 Feb. 1962
Bohemians to St. Patrick's Athletic
	Emfa v Bray Wanderers (1-1) 19 Jan. '86
1990-91	St. Patrick's Athletic	23	(4)
1991-92	Bohemians	31	(9)
1992-93	Bohemians	28 + 4	(3)
1993-94	Omagh Town (L)
Oct. '93	Derry City	17 + 1	(4)

Lawless, Thomas b. Dublin, 4 Oct. 1974
Rivermount Boys to Home Farm
	Finn Harps v Home Farm (1-1) 31 Jan. '93
1992-93	Home Farm	0 + 1
1993-94	Home Farm	7 + 3
Dec. '93	Bohemians	2 + 4

Lawlor, Dave   b. Limerick
Nov. '90 U.C.G. to Galway United
            Drogheda U. v **Galway U.** (0-0) 29 Sep. '91
1991-92   Galway United   3 + 2
1992-93   St. Michaels, Tipperary
1993-94   Limerick   9 + 2

Lawlor, Martin   b. Dublin, 1958
'76 Stella Maris to Dundalk
1990-91   Dundalk   29
1991-92   Shamrock Rovers   21
1992-93   Dundalk   21   (1)
1993-94   Dundalk   30

Lemon, Paul   b. Middlesbrough, 3 Jun. 1966
Aug. '93 Chesterfield to Derry City
            Shelbourne v **Derry City** (2-0) 5 Sep. '93
1993-94   Derry City   5

Lennon, Dermot   b. Athlone, 12 Aug. 1969
Jan. '92 St. Mary's (Athlone) to Longford Town
1991-92   Longford Town   4 + 3   (1)
1992-93   Galway United   -
Feb. '93   Athlone Town   1 + 2
1993-94   Athlone Town   4 + 1   (1)

Lennox, Gary   b. Kilwinning (Sco.), 6 Dec. 1969
Jul. '93 Falkirk to Derry City
            Derry City v Cobh Ramblers (2-0) 21 Aug.'93
1993-94   Derry City   7
Sep. '93   Ayr United

Lonergan, Darren   b. Clonmel, 28 Jan. 1974
Aug. '91 Tramore FC to Waterford United
            Longford T. v **Waterford U.** (1-1) 2 Feb. '92
1991-92   Waterford United   0 + 1
1992-93   Waterford United   30 + 1 (2)
1993-94   Waterford United   20 + 1 (4)

Long, Keith   b. Dublin, 14 Nov. 1973
Sep. '93 Stoke City to Dundalk
            Cork City v **Dundalk** (0-1) 17 Oct. '93
1993-94   Dundalk   9 + 3

Long, Philip   b. Cork, 3 Dec. 1961
Summer '86 St. Mary's to Cork City
            Bray Wanderers v **Cork City** (1-0) 19 Oct. '86
1990-91   Cork City   32   (2)
1991-92   Cork City   4
1992-93   Cork City   20 + 2
1993-94   Cobh Ramblers   23 + 2

Ludzik, Alek   b. Derby, 15 Jan. 1950
Nov. '69 Derby County to Cork Celtic
            Cork Hibs. v **Cork Celtic** (1-0) 30 Nov.' 69
1990-91   Cobh Ramblers   20
1991-92   Cork City   4
1992-93   Cork City   7
1993-94   Cork City   3 + 1

Lynch, Aaron   b. Dublin, 15 Nov. 1971
Aug. '90 Palmerstown Rgs to Home Farm
            Home Farm v Drogheda U (0-1) 7 Oct. '90
1990-91   Home Farm   9 + 3
1991-92   Home Farm   13 + 1 (1)
1992-93   Home Farm   18 + 4 (1)
1993-94   Home Farm   22 + 1

Lynch, Ger
1991-92   Home Farm   2 + 2
1992-93   Home Farm   2 + 3
1993-94   Home Farm   0 + 1

Lynch, Ian   b. London, 6 Feb. 1968
local to Sligo Rovers
            Galway U. v **Sligo Rovers** (5-1) 12 Jan. '92
1991-92   Sligo Rovers   0 + 2
1992-93   Sligo Rovers   -
1993-94   Sligo Rovers   12 + 6

Lynch, Jason   b. Cork, 17 Dec. 1970
Summer '90 to Rockmount to Cobh Ramblers
            Cobh Ramblers v Finn Harps (2-1) 7 Oct. '90
1990-91   Cobh Ramblers   26
1991-92   Cobh Ramblers   25
1992-93   Cobh Ramblers   25   (2)
1993-94   Cobh Ramblers   31   (1)

Lynch, John   b. Sligo, 1 Sep. 1962
local to Sligo Rovers
            Sligo Rovers v Athlone T. (1-1) 30 Nov. '86
1990-91   Sligo Rovers   1 + 1
1991-92   Sligo Rovers   -
1992-93   Sligo Rovers   -
1993-94   Sligo Rovers   0 + 1

Lynch, Patrick "Packie"   b. Dublin, 2 Jan. 1973
Jul. '90 St. Joseph's Boys to U.C.D.
            Longford Town v **U.C.D.** (0-2) 7 Oct. '90
1990-91   U.C.D.   24 + 1 (2)
1991-92   U.C.D.   23
1992-93   U.C.D.   22   (3)
1993-94   U.C.D.   27   (1)

Lyons, Julian   b. Limerick, 12 Dec. 1969
Newcastlewest to Limerick City
1990-91   Limerick City   17 + 4 (1)
1992-93   Limerick   6 + 5
1993-94   Limerick   5

McAvenue, Les
St. Patrick's Athletic to St. James's Gate
            St. James's G. v Athlone T. (0-2) 19 Sep. '93
1993-94   St. James's Gate   13

McCarron, Brian   b. Derry, 9 Dec. 1971
            Monaghan U. v **Derry City** (1-1) 26 Aug. '93
1993-94   Derry City   0 + 2

McCarthy, Kevin
Summer '93 Fairview Rangers to Limerick
    Limerick v Shelbourne (0-0) 22 Aug. '93
1993-94   Limerick   28 + 3 (8)

McCaul, Dermot b. Derry
Nov. '93 Coleraine to Finn Harps
1993-94   Finn Harps   3 + 1

McConnell, Ian b. Glasgow, 6 Jan. 1975
Sep. '93 Dundee United to Derry City (L)
    Derry City v Dundalk (1-4) 12 Sep. '93
1993-94   Derry City   0 + 1
Sep. '93   Dundee United

McCormack, Gary
Rush to Home Farm
    Longford T. v **Home Farm** (1-4) 22 Dec. '91
1991-92   Home Farm   3
1992-93   Home Farm   27
1993-94   Home Farm   25

McCormack, Mark b. Dublin, 30 Dec. 1972
Stella Maris to Shamrock Rovers
    Shamrock R. v Cork City (2-0) 3 Apr. '94
1993-94   Shamrock Rovers   0 + 1

McDermott, Dave b. Sligo, 23 Apr. 1977
local to Sligo Rovers
    Sligo Rovers v Kilkenny C. (3-0) 12 Mar. '94
1993-94   Sligo Rovers   0 + 1

McDermott, Paul b. Dublin, 7 Jul. 1961
Bluebell United to Shelbourne
1990-91   Shelbourne   6 + 6 (2)
Feb. '91   Limerick City (L)   7 (1)
1991-92   Bohemians   29 + 2 (1)
1992-93   Kilkenny City   27 (1)
1993-94   Kilkenny City   26 + 1

McDonald, Tommy b. Galway, 22 Feb. 1968
Summer '92 Salthill Devon to Galway United
    Galway U. v Kilkenny C. (2-1) 4 Oct. '92
1992-93   Galway United   0 + 1
1993-94   Galway United   1 + 2

McDonnell, Declan b. Dublin
1990-91   Home Farm   11 + 1
1991-92   Home Farm   5 + 7
1992-93   Home Farm   12 + 2
1993-94   Home Farm   1 + 1 (1)

McDonnell, John b. Dublin, 26 Mar. 1965
Drogheda United to St. Patrick's Athletic
1990-91   St. Patrick's Athletic   31
1991-92   Shamrock Rovers   27 (1)
1992-93   Shamrock Rovers   0 + 1
Nov. '92   St. Patrick's Athletic   18
1993-94   St. Patrick's Athletic   32 (2)

McDonnell, Martin b. Belfast, 8 May 1962
Galway United to Sligo Rovers
    Sligo Rovers v St. Pat's Ath. (1-2) 6 Apr. '80
1990-91   Sligo Rovers   14 + 1 (2)
1991-92   Sligo Rovers   25 + 2
1992-93   Sligo Rovers   27 + 1 (1)
1993-94   Sligo Rovers   20 + 2

McDonnell, Tony b. Dublin, 10 Feb. 1976
St. Kevin's Boys to U.C.D.
    Longford Town v **U.C.D.** (1-2) 27 Mar. '94
1993-94   U.C.D.   1

McElligott, Christy
Summer '91 Ballymun Town to St. Patrick's Athletic
    Sligo Rovers v **St. Pats Ath** (0-0) 1 Sep. '91
1991-92   St. Patrick's Athletic   17 + 5
1992-93   St. Patrick's Athletic   15 + 2 (1)
1993-94   St. Patrick's Athletic   10 + 2

McElroy, John b. Buncrana, 15 Dec. 1974
    Galway United v **Derry City** (2-1) 27 Mar. '94
1993-94   Derry City   2

McEnroe, David b. Dublin, 19 Aug. 1972
Jan. '94 Queens Park Rangers to St. Patrick's Athletic
    Drogheda U. v **St. Pat's A.** (2-0) 28 Jan. '94
1993-94   St. Patrick's Athletic   3 + 2 (1)

McGarvey, John b. Derry, 11 Sep. 1976
    Derry City v Dundalk (1-4) 12 Sep. '93
1993-94   Derry City   4 + 4

McGarvey, Scott b. Glasgow, 22 Apr. 1963
Sep. '93 Aris F.C. (Limassol, Cyprus) to Derry City
    Derry City v Drogheda U. (1-1) 26 Sep. '93
1993-94   Derry City   8 + 1

McGeever, Charlie
Jun. '92 Fanad United to Finn Harps
    Sligo R. v Shamrock R. (0-3) 7 Sep. '80
1992-93   Finn Harps   25 (4)
1993-94   Finn Harps   25 + 1 (2)

McGettigan, John Gerard b. Letterkenny, 29 Sep. 1967
Summer '85 Milford United to Finn Harps
    Finn Harps v Sligo Rovers (0-2) 20 Oct. '85
1990-91   Finn Harps   23 + 1 (1)
1991-92   Finn Harps   26 (3)
1992-93   Finn Harps   25 + 1 (3)
1993-94   Finn Harps   22 + 2 (3)

McGinley, Martin b. Glasgow, 11 Nov. 1972
Summer '92 Bradford City to Derry City
1992-93   Derry City   15 + 8
1993-94   Finn Harps   20 + 2 (2)

McGonnigle, Colm b. Donegal
Jun. '92 Fanad United to Finn Harps
    Finn Harps v St. Pat's Ath.. (2-1) 25 Jan. '81
1992-93   Finn Harps   22 + 3 (7)
1993-94   Finn Harps   16 + 9 (3)

McGrath, Derek b. Dublin, 21 Jan. 1972
Jan. '92 Brighton to Shamrock Rovers
    Bray W. v **Shamrock R.** (0-0) 19 Jan. '92
1991-92	Shamrock Rovers	7	
1992-93	Shamrock Rovers	29	(7)
1993-94	Shamrock Rovers	25 + 2	(7)

McGuinness, Stephen
    Home Farm v St. James's G. (3-1) 11 Oct. '92
1992-93	Home Farm	21	
1993-94	Home Farm	24	(4)

McIntyre, Declan b. Donegal, 28 Apr. 1960
Aug. '89 Derry City to Galway United
    Finn Harps v Drogheda U. (1-7) 24 Apr. '77
1990-91	Galway United.	28	
1991-92	Galway United	28	
1992-93	Sligo Rovers	4	
Oct. '92	Finn Harps	15	
1993-94	Finn Harps	15 + 1	

McIntyre, Emmet b. Derry, 6 Aug. 1972
    Derry City v Galway U. (1-1) 24 Mar. '94
1993-94	Derry City	0 + 2	

McKeever, Kevin b. Derry, 15 Sep. 1964
Nov. '93 Glentoran to Derry City
    Emfa v **Derry City** (1-1) 20 Oct. '85
1993-94	Derry City	16 + 3	(1)

McKenna, Brian b. Dublin, 30 Jan. 1972
Summer '91 Brighton to U.C.D.
    Cobh Ramblers v **U.C.D.** (1-1) 6 Oct. '91
1991-92	U.C.D.	15	
1992-93	U.C.D.	27	
1993-94	U.C.D.	-	
Nov. '93	Limerick	17	

McKenna, Jude
Summer '93 Longford Town to Kilkenny City
1993-94	Kilkenny City	10 + 3	

McLaughlin, Paul b. Birmingham, 8 Aug. 1965
Summer' 90 Derry City to Drogheda United
1990-91	Drogheda United.	23	(2)
1991-92	Drogheda United.	28	(3)
1992-93	Drogheda United	30	
1993-94	Drogheda United	23 + 2	

McLaughlin, Paul b. Johnstone (Sco.), 9 Dec. 1965
Jul. '93 Partick Thistle to Derry City
    Derry City v Cobh R. (2-0) 21 Aug. '93
1993-94	Derry City	27	(1)

McLean, Mark b. Paisley (Sco.), 30 Mar. 1972
Summer '93 Celtic to Sligo Rovers
    Home Farm v **Sligo Rovers** (0-1) 19 Sep. '93
1993-94	Sligo Rovers	27	

McMahon, Daithi b. Limerick, 25 Jul. 1973
Summer '91 Carew Park to Limerick City
    St James's G. v **Limerick City** (0-0) 6 Oct. '91
1991-92	Limerick City	8 + 5	(1)
1992-93	Limerick	7 + 8	(1)
1993-94	Limerick	21 + 9	(4)

McNab, Neil b. Greenock (Sco.), 4 Jun. 1957
Oct. '93 Tranmere Rovers to Derry City
    Galway United v **Derry City** (2-1) 17 Oct. '93
1993-94	Derry City	12 + 1	
Jan. '94	Witton Albion (Eng.)		

McNulty, Tom b. Hamilton (Sco.), 23 Feb. 1962
Summer '89 Finn Harps to Dundalk
    Dundalk v Cork City (1-0) 1G 16 Sep. '84
1990-91	Dundalk	32	(10)
1991-92	Dundalk	27	(8)
1992-93	Dundalk	28	(3)
1993-94	Dundalk	27	(1)

McStay, Willie b. Hamilton, 26 Nov. 1961
Oct. '92 Kilmarnock to Sligo Rovers
    Sligo R v Drogheda U. (0-0)11 Oct. '92
1992-93	Sligo Rovers	25	
1993-94	Sligo Rovers	23	

Madden, Dave
Shelbourne to Kilkenny City
    Waterford U v **Shelbourne** (0-0) 4 Sep. '88
1990-91	Kilkenny City	21 + 1	
1991-92	Kilkenny City	18	(1)
1992-93	Kilkenny City	9 + 2	(1)
1993-94	Kilkenny City	17	

Mahedy, Glen
    Kilkenny C. v **Longford T.** (3-1) 12 Dec. '93
1993-94	Longford Town	4 + 2	(1)

Malone, Chris b. Athlone, 24 Oct. 1971
Jul. '90 St. Mary's (Athlone) to Athlone Town
    Longford T. v **Athlone T.** (0-5) 11 Oct. '92
1992-93	Athlone Town	6 + 6	
1993-94	Athlone Town	27	(1)

Malone, Joey b. Dublin, 22 Jan. 1958
Aug. '90 Dundalk to Galway United
    Galway Rovers v **Bohemians** (0-0) 25 Sep. '77
1990-91	Galway United	14 + 3	
1991-92	Galway United	2 + 1	
Feb. '92	Longford Town	10	
1992-93	Longford Town	-	
Oct. '92	Waterford United	12	
Jan. '93	Monaghan United	8 + 1	
1993-94	Monaghan United	11 + 1	

Mannion, John b. Athlone, 29 Aug. 1960
Galway United to Shamrock Rovers
　　　　　　Dundalk v **Athlone T.** (3-0) 25 Jan. '79
1990-91　　　Shamrock Rovers　　15　　(2)
Dec. '90　　　Sligo Rovers　　　　7 + 2
1991-92　　　Derry City　　　　　25 + 4　(1)
1992-93　　　Galway United　　　22 + 1　(3)
1993-94　　　Galway United　　　24 + 1

Markovac, Robert b. Australia
Jan. '94 Hajduk Split to Waterford United
　　　　　　Waterford U. v Longford T. (0-0) 30 Jan. '94
1993-94　　　Waterford United　　4

Martin, Damien b. 21 Nov. 1971
Aug. '90 Rockmount to Cobh Ramblers
　　　　　　U.C.D. v **Cobh Ramblers** (0-0) 24 Feb. '91
1990-91　　　Cobh Ramblers　　　4 + 2
1991-92　　　Cobh Ramblers　　　1 + 6
1992-93　　　Cobh Ramblers　　　23 + 3　(7)
1993-94　　　Cobh Ramblers　　　6 + 5

Matthews, Alan b. Dublin, 27 Jun. 1965
Shelbourne to Galway United
1990-91　　　Galway United.　　　15 + 5
　　　　　　Bray Wanderers.　　　1
1991-92　　　Kilkenny City　　　　1
1992-93　　　Longford Town　　　9 + 1
1993-94　　　Longford Town　　　13 + 1

Meaney, Eddie b. Dublin, 26 Aug. 1970
Shamrock Rovers to Bray Wanderers
　　　　　　Longford T. v **Bray W.** (1-0) 19 Sep. '93
1993-94　　　Bray Wanderers　　　2 + 2

Melvin, Noel b. Ballina, 18 Dec. 1970
Summer '92 Donegal Town to Monaghan United
　　　　　　Cobh R. v **Monaghan U.** (2-2) 26 Oct. '92
1992-93　　　Monaghan United　　21 + 1　(6)
1993-94　　　Monaghan United　　22 + 6　(3)

Mernagh, Noel b. Galway, 11 Dec. 1963
'83 West United to Galway United
　　　　　　Galway Utd v Bohemians (0-1) 23 Oct. '83
1990-91　　　Galway United　　　29　　(5)
1991-92　　　Galway United.　　　30　　(9)
1992-93　　　Galway United　　　17 + 3　(3)
1993-94　　　Galway United　　　27　　(2)

Milne, Ralph b. Dundee, 13 May 1961
Oct. '93 Sing Tao F.C. (Hong Kong) to Derry City
　　　　　　Limerick v **Derry City** (0-1) 31 Oct. '93
1993-94　　　Derry City　　　　　1 + 1

Minihan, Dave b. Limerick, 15 Nov. 1973
Summer '91 Somerville Rovers to Limerick City
　　　　　　Limerick C. v Cobh Ramblers (1-2) 13 Oct. '91
1991-92　　　Limerick City　　　　6 + 11
1992-93　　　Limerick　　　　　　27
1993-94　　　Limerick　　　　　　25 + 1

Moody, Mick b. Wicklow, 24 Feb. 1960
Drogheda United to St. Patrick's Athletic
　　　　　　Limerick City v **Home Farm** (3-0) 16 Sep. '84
1990-91　　　St. Patrick's Athletic　30　　(1)
1991-92　　　Shamrock Rovers　　31 + 2　(1)
1992-93　　　Shamrock Rovers　　14 + 5　(1)
1993-94　　　Bohemians　　　　　19　　(1)

Mooney, Brian b. Dublin, 2 Feb. 1966
Summer '93 Sunderland to Shelbourne
　　　　　　Limerick v **Shelbourne** (0-0) 22 Aug. '93
1993-94　　　Shelbourne　　　　　30　　(6)

Mooney, Darren
St. Martins to St. James's Gate
　　　　　　St. James's G. v Waterford U. (0-0) 10 Oct. '93
1993-94　　　St. James's Gate　　 10 + 7

Moran, Joseph "Josh" b. Dublin, 8 Sep. 1966
Limerick City to Bray Wanderers
　　　　　　St. Pat's Ath. v Limerick U. (1-1) 20 Feb. '83
1990-91　　　Bray Wanderers　　　21
1991-92　　　Athlone Town　　　　22
1992-93　　　Bray Wanderers　　　19
1993-94　　　Bray Wanderers　　　17

Moran, Pádraig b. Athlone, 14 Jan. 1973
Jan. '93 Heart of Midlothian to Sligo Rovers
　　　　　　Sligo R. v St. Pat's Ath. (3-1) 24 Jan. '93
1992-93　　　Sligo Rovers　　　　10　　(1)
1993-94　　　Sligo Rovers　　　　14 + 3　(4)

Morley, Pat b. Cork, 18 May 1965
Sunshine George Cross (Australia) to Cork City
　　　　　　Finn Harps v **Waterford U** (1-4) 3G 25 Nov. '84
1990-91　　　Cork City　　　　　33　　(15)
1991-92　　　Cork City　　　　　33　　(11)
1992-93　　　Cork City　　　　　37　　(20)
1993-94　　　Cork City　　　　　31　　(15)

Morris-Burke, Johnny b. Newport Pagnell, 6 Dec. 1966
Aug. '90 Athlone Town to Galway United
　　　　　　Finn Harps v **Longford Town** (5-0) 11 Jan. '87
1990-91　　　Galway United　　　30　　(1)
1991-92　　　Galway United　　　12 + 8　(1)
1992-93　　　Athlone Town　　　 27　　(8)
1993-94　　　Athlone Town　　　 14 + 3　(1)

Morrisroe, Brian b. Dublin
Summer '93 Manortown United to St. Patrick's Athletic
　　　　　　Dundalk v **St. Pat's Ath.** (0-2) 26 Sep. '93
1993-94　　　St. Patrick's Athletic　0 + 4

Mullen, Eoin b. Dublin, 24 Jan. 1966
U.C.D. to Home Farm
　　　　　　U.C.D. v Sligo Rovers (1-1) 28 Oct. '84
1990-91　　　Home Farm　　　　12 + 3
1991-92　　　Home Farm　　　　27
1992-93　　　Home Farm　　　　27　　(2)
1993-94　　　Shamrock Rovers　　28 + 2　(3)

258

Mullen, Gerry b. Galway, 6 Jul. 1964
'81 Corrib Shamrocks to Galway United
               Limerick U. v **Galway U.** (2-0) 26 Sep. '81
1990-91   Galway United.   8 + 1   (1)
1991-92   Galway United   30 + 1   (8)
1992-93   Galway United   27   (11)
1993-94   Galway United   15 + 3   (1)

Murphy, Albert b. Dublin, 6 Nov. 1963
Oct. '87 Drogheda United to Athlone Town
1990-91   Athlone Town   27 + 1   (9)
1991-92   Athlone Town   22 + 3   (3)
1992-93   Drogheda United   17 + 1   (2)
1993-94   Drogheda United   3 + 2

Murphy, Barry b. 1 Apr. 1959
Summer '88 Bohemians to Shamrock Rovers
1990-91   Shamrock Rovers   28
1991-92   Kilkenny City   27   (2)
1992-93   Kilkenny City   20 + 3
1993-94   Athlone Town   26   (1)

Murphy, Liam b. Cork 20 Dec. 1961
Summer '80 Wilton United to Cork United
               Cork United v Dundalk (1-1) 7 Sep. '80
1990-91   Cork City   24
1991-92   Cork City   31 + 1
1992-93   Cork City   12 + 7   (1)
1993-94   Cork City   28 + 3

Murphy, Ronnie b. Dublin, 3 Sep. 1962
Summer '90 Bohemians to Dundalk
1990-91   Dundalk   32   (1)
1991-92   Dundalk   27
1992-93   Dundalk   30
1993-94   Monaghan United   27

Murray, Derek b. Dublin, 29 Nov. 1965
Jul. '87 Home Farm to Bohemians
1990-91   Bohemians   22 + 5   (2)
1991-92   Bohemians   1 + 4
Feb. '92   Monaghan United   5 + 2   (3)
1992-93   Monaghan United   19 + 1   (3)
1993-94   Monaghan United   26 + 2   (3)

Murray, Donal b. 1 Jan. 1972
Salthill Devon to Galway United
1992-93   Galway United   1 + 1
1993-94   Galway United   1 + 1

Murray, Matthew
Home Farm Schoolboys
               St. James's G. v **Home Farm** (0-2) 10 Nov '91
1991-92   Home Farm   18
1992-93   Home Farm   22   (1)
1993-94   Home Farm   21   (2)

Murray, Noel b. 8 May 1968
Oct. '92 Cromac Celtic (Belfast) to Derry City
               Drogheda U. v N'West (0-1) 13 Sep. '87
1992-93   Derry City   22 + 2
1993-94   Derry City   2
               Cormac Celtic

Myler, Andy b. Dublin, 2 Dec. 1975
St. Kevin's Boys to U.C.D.
               St. James's G. v **U.C.D.** (0-2) 9 Jan. '94
1993-94   U.C.D.   2 + 6   (1)

Napier, Stephen b. Clonmel, 27 Dec. 1972
Jul. '91 Middlesbrough to Cork City
               Cork City v Galway Utd (2-0) 31 Aug. '91
1991-92   Cork City   28 + 1   (1)
1992-93   Cork City   34 + 1
1993-94   Cork City   32   (1)

Neary, Ollie b. Galway, 9 Aug. 1968
Summer '93 Mervue United to Galway United
               Bohemians v **Galway U.** (3-0) 20 Aug. '93
1993-94   Galway United   13 + 6

Neville, Keith b. Dublin, 19 Apr. 1972
               Home Farm v. Monaghan United (3-3) 9 Dec. '90
1990-91   Home Farm   10 + 1
1991-92   Home Farm   9 + 1
1992-93   Home Farm   1
               Bohemians   1 + 1
1993-94   Monaghan United (L)   0 + 2
Jan. '94   Kilkenny City (L)   10   (1)

Neville, Mick b. Dublin, 25 Nov. 1960
Summer '90 Derry City to Shelbourne
1990-91   Shelbourne   30   (2)
1991-92   Shelbourne   27 + 3   (3)
1992-93   Shelbourne   37   (1)
1993-94   Shelbourne   30

Newe, Paul b. Dublin, 20 Apr. 1964
Summer '90   Dundalk to Shelbourne
               Shelbourne v Waterford U. (5-2) lg 3 Oct. '82
1990-91   Shelbourne   20 + 6   (14)
1991-92   Shelbourne   1
Nov. '91   Cobh Ramblers (L)   18   (9)
1992-93   St. Patrick's Athletic   16 + 7   (4)
1993-94   Monaghan United   22 + 2   (11)

Nixon, Mark b. Derry, 2 Dec. 1974
               Monaghan U. v **Derry C.** (1-1) 25 Aug. '93
1993-94   Derry City   1 + 1

Noctor, Alan
               Drogheda U. v **Bray W.** (1-0) 26 Jan. '92
1991-92   Bray Wanderers   0 + 1
1992-93   Bray Wanderers   2 + 8
1992-93   Bray Wanderers   5 + 2
               Cross Celtic

Nolan, Jimmy b. Galway, 6 Jan.1964
'82 Mervue to Galway United
               Dundalk v **Galway U** (1-0) 2 Oct. '83
1990-91   Galway United   25 + 2   (3)
1991-92   Galway United   14 + 3
1992-93   Galway United   14   (3)
1993-94   Galway United   5   (1)

Nolan, John b. Dublin, 16 Apr. 1964
Summer '90 Drogheda United to Sligo Rovers,
            Home Farm v **Shamrock Rov** (1-3) 14 Apr. '87
1990-91   Sligo Rovers   33   (1)
1991-92   Sligo Rovers   29
1992-93   Sligo Rovers   18
1993-94   Shamrock Rovers   12 + 2

Nolan, Peter b. Leeds, 18 Jun. 1971
Summer '90 Harold's Cross Boys to St. James's Gate
            St. James's G v Kilkenny C (1-2) 1G 7 Oct '90
1990-91   St. James's Gate   23 + 2   (2)
1991-92   St. James's Gate   26
1992-93   Kilkenny City   22 + 1   (1)
1993-94   St. James's Gate   22 + 1

Norris, Gerry
Summer '93 Carrick F.C. to Waterford United
            Finn Harps v **Waterford U.** (2-0) 19 Sep. '93
1993-94   Waterford United   1

Nugent, Martin b. Dublin, 7 May 1962
Summer '85 Usher Celtic to Bray Wanderers
            Newcastle U. v **Bray W.** (0-3) lg 27 Oct. '85
1990-91   Bray Wanderers   26   (4)
1991-92   Athlone Town   28 + 1   (3)
1992-93   Bray Wanderers   26   (7)
1993-94   Bray Wanderers   11 + 1   (1)
Jan. '94   St. Patrick's Athletic 8   (2)

O'Brien, Alan
            St. James's G. v Kilkenny C. (2-2) 7 Nov. '93
1993-94   St. James's Gate   1 + 4

O'Brien, Darren b. Dublin, 10 Nov. 1967
Jul. '86 Griffith Park Rangers to U.C.D.
            Newcastlewest v **U.C..D** (0-0) 19 Oct. '86
1990-91   U.C.D.   7 + 1   (1)
1991-92   U.C.D.   27   (9)
1992-93   U.C.D.   22 + 1   (11)
1993-94   U.C.D.   25 + 1   (13)

O'Brien, Donal b. Dublin, 10 Nov. 1967
Croatia (Australia) to Derry City
            Shelbourne v **Derry City** (1-0) 26 Oct. '90
1990-91   Derry City   7 + 2   (5)
1991-92   Derry City   18 + 8   (6)
1992-93   Derry City   29 + 2   (10)
            Woolongong Wolves (Australia)
1993-94   Derry City   16 + 1   (3)

O'Brien, Kieran b. Dublin, 29 Dec. 1972
Belvedere to St. Patrick's Athletic
            Sligo Rovers v **St Pats Ath** (0-0) 26 Jan. '92
1991-92   St. Patricks Ath   1
1992-93   St. Patrick's Athletic 9 + 1
1993-94   St. Patrick's Athletic 5 + 10

O'Brien, Mick b. Dublin, 28 Nov. 1970
Summer '92 Luton Town to Kilkenny City
            Kilkenny C. v Athlone T. (1-1) 1 Nov. '92
1992-93   Kilkenny City   20   (1)
1993-94   Longford Town   13 + 5   (2)

O'Brien, Pat b. Dublin, 12 Jun. 1971
Valeview, Shankill to Bray Wanderers
            Bray W. v St. James's G. (0-0) 17 Oct. '93
1993-94   Bray Wanderers   23

O'Byrne, Michael b. Dublin 15 Mar. 1975
Summer '93 Cherry Orchard to U.C.D.
            Kilkenny City v **U.C.D.** (3-2) 19 Sep. '93
1993-94   U.C.D.   27   (6)

O'Callaghan, Brendan b. Drogheda, 7 Jan. 1966
1990-91   Drogheda United   23 + 3   (5)
1991-92   Dundalk   3 + 5   (2)
1992-93   Cobh Ramblers   23   (10)
1993-94   Cobh Ramblers   22 + 5   (1)

O'Callaghan, James b. Dublin
Belvedere to Shelbourne
            Shelbourne v Cork City (0-1) 12 Apr. '92
1991-92   Shelbourne   1
1992-93   Sligo Rovers (L)   16
1993-94   Longford Town   26

O'Connell, Frank b. Dublin, 21 Apr. 1969
Summer '92 Ashtownvilla to Athlone Town
            Athlone Town v. U.C.D. (1-2) 4 Oct. '92
1992-93   Athlone Town   27
1993-94   Athlone Town   4 + 5

O'Connell, Patrick "PJ" b. Dublin, 7 Oct. 1973
            Drogheda U. v. **Home Farm** (2-1) 16 Dec.'90
1990-91   Home Farm   3   (1)
            to Leeds United
1992-93   St. Patrick's Athletic 3 + 1
1993-94   St. Patrick's Athletic 6 + 1   (2)
Jan. '94   Athlone Town (L)   8 + 1   (1)

O'Connor, Austin b. Cork, 7 Oct. 1969
Everton (M.S.L.) to Cobh Ramblers
            Cobh R. v Limerick (1-0) 30 Jan. '94
1993-94   Cobh Ramblers   0 + 6

O'Connor, Barry b. 17 Jun. 1972
Summer '89 Cherry Orchard to Shamrock Rovers
            Dundalk v **Shamrock Rvs** (1-0) 3 Sep. '89
1990-91   Shamrock Rovers   11 + 7   (7)
1991-92   Shamrock Roves   12 + 7
1992-93   Drogheda United   31 + 1   (10)
1993-94   Drogheda United   14   (5)
Nov. '93   Shelbourne   15 + 2   (8)

O'Connor, Derek b. Waterford, 8 Jan. 1971
Aug. '87 Tramore F.C. to Waterford United
        Cork City v **Waterford Utd** (3-0) 16 Jan. '89
1990-91	Waterford United	18 + 6	(3)
Feb. '91	Cobh Ramblers (L)	2	
1991-92	Waterford United	27	(7)
1992-93	Waterford United	9 + 1	
1993-94	Waterford United	4 + 1	

O'Connor, Michael b. Athlone, 8 Oct. 1960
Aug. '89 Dundalk to Athlone Town
        Athlone T v Drogheda (1-2) 4 Mar. '79
1990-91	Athlone Town	25 + 3	(2)
1991-92	Athlone Town	22 + 1	(11)
1992-93	Athlone Town	17 + 4	(9)
1993-94	Athlone Town	5 + 15	(2)

O'Connor, Tony b. Dublin, 15 Nov. 1966
Home Farm to St. Patrick's Athletic
        Galway U. v **Home Farm** (2-1) 19 Oct. '86
1990-91	St. Patrick's Athletic	28 + 2	(4)
1991-92	St. Patrick's Athletic	32 + 1	(1)
1992-93	Bohemians	30 + 1	(6)
1993-94	Bohemians	31	(2)

O'Doherty, Ken b. Dublin, 30 Mar. 1963
Jul. '92 Huddersfield Town to Shelbourne
        U.C.D. v Bohemians (1-2) 26 Oct. '80
| 1992-93 | Shelbourne | 31 + 3 | (4) |
| 1993-94 | Shelbourne | 22 + 2 | (3) |

O'Donoghue, Fergus b. Cork, 11 Oct. 1969
Summer '89 Tramore Athletic to Cork City
        Cork City v Bohemians (0-2) 16 Sep. '89
1990-91	Cork City	13	
Dec. '90	To Cambridge United		
1992-93	Cork City	36	
1993-94	Cork City	27	

O'Dowd, Greg b. Dublin, 16 Mar. 1973
Summer '92 Brighton H.A. to Longford Town
        Monaghan U. v **Longford T.** (5-0) 4 Oct. '92
| 1992-93 | Longford Town | 27 | (4) |
| 1993-94 | Dundalk | 27 | (2) |

O'Dowd, Tony b. Dublin, 6 Jul. 1970
Jan. '91 Leeds United to Kilkenny City (L)
        Shelbourne v Galway U. (1-0) 3 Sep. '90
1990-91	Kilkenny City	2	
1992-93	St. Patrick's Athletic	32	
1993-94	St. Patrick's Athletic	31	

O'Driscoll, Maurice b. Dublin, 2 Aug. 1966
        Longford T. v **Drogheda U.** (0-0) 19 Oct. '86
1990-91	St. Patrick's Athletic	23 + 6	
1991-92	St. Patrick's Athletic	28	
1992-93	Bohemians	36 + 1	(1)
1993-94	Bohemians	29	(1)

O'Flaherty, Ricky b. Liverpool, 1 Jan. 1966
| 1991-92 | Galway United | 2 | |
| 1993-94 | Galway United | 13 + 3 | (6) |

O'Halloran, Aidan
Young Munster (Rugby F.C.) to Limerick
        Limerick v Shelbourne (0-0) 22 Aug. '93
| 1993-94 | Limerick | 1 | |

O'Halloran, Christy b. Waterford, 22 Dec. 1966
Sep. '93 Waterford Glass to Waterford United
        Waterford U. v Longford T. (2-2) lg 26 Sep. '93
| 1993-94 | Waterford United | 13 + 4 | (3) |

O'Halloran, Ray b. Limerick, 6 Oct. 1969
Summer '87 Ballynanty Rovers to Limerick City
        Limerick City v Shamrock R (1-4) 13 Sep. '87
1990-91	Limerick City	32	(1)
1991-92	Sligo Rovers	27	(2)
1992-93	Limerick	31	(1)
1993-94	Limerick	30	(1)

O'Hanlon, George b. Dublin, 9 Dec. 1972
Nov. '93 Leyton Orient to Longford Town
        Bray W. v **Longford T.** (2-1) 28 Nov. '93
| 1993-94 | Longford Town | 17 | |

O'Leary, Willie
Home Farm to Bohemians
| 1993-94 | Monaghan United (L) | 0 + 1 | |
| Jan. '94 | Kilkenny City (L) | 4 + 1 | |

Olin, Billy b. Dublin, 24 Jan. 1963
Summer '91 St. Patrick's Athletic to Monaghan United
| 1991-92 | Monaghan United | 6 + 2 | (2) |
| 1993-94 | Monaghan United | 0 + 1 | |

Oliva Umberto
Oct. '93 Brighton & H.A. to Waterford United
        Waterford U. v Sligo Rovers (2-1) 3 Oct. '93
| 1993-94 | Waterford United | 3 | |

O'Neill, Alan b. Dublin, 2 Jul. 1957
Summer '85 U.C.D. to Dundalk
        Shamrock R v Cork Hibs (1-0) 28 Dec. '75
1990-91	Dundalk	33	
1991-92	Dundalk	29	
1992-93	Dundalk	32	
1993-94	Shamrock Rovers	32	

O'Neill, Alan b. Cork, 27 Aug. 1973
Summer '91 Cork City to Cobh Ramblers
        Cobh R. v Waterford U. (2-0) lg 17 Nov. '91
1991-92	Cobh Ramblers	8 + 3	(4)
Feb. '92	Birmingham City		
1993-94	Cobh Ramblers	9 + 1	(4)

O'Neill, Derek b. Dublin, 19 Jul. 1963
Jul. '90 Wollongong City (Australia) to Athlone Town
1990-91	Athlone Town	22 + 7	
1991-92	Kilkenny City	24	(7)
1992-93	Monaghan United	25 + 1	(3)
1993-94	Monaghan United	6 + 3	(1)

O'Neill, Dermot b. Dublin, 27 Nov. 1960
'81 Dundalk to Bohemians
        Sligo Rovers v **Bohemians** (0-2) 13 Sep. '81
1990-91	Bohemians	31	
1991-92	Derry City	33	
1992-93	Derry City	32	
1993-94	Derry City	32	

O'Neill, Mark b. Dublin, 4 Oct. 1972
Summer '93 Leyton Orient to St. Patrick's Athletic
        Drogheda U. v **St. Pat's A.** (1-1) 22 Aug. '93
| 1993-94 | St. Patrick's Athletic | 25 | (1) |

O'Reilly, Charlie b. Dublin, 6 Nov. 1962
Stella Maris to Home Farm
1990-91	Drogheda United	19 + 1	
1991-92	Drogheda United	26 + 2	(2)
1992-93	Home Farm	11	
1993-94	Kilkenny City	19 + 2	

Ormsby, Brendan b. Birmingham, 1 Oct. 1960
Summer '93 Scarborough to Waterford United (p-m)
        Finn Harps v **Waterford U.** (2-0) 19 Sep. '93
| 1993-94 | Waterford United | 23 | (2) |

O'Rourke, John b. Cobh, 14 Sep. 1970
KFC Tielt (Belgium) to Cobh Ramblers
        Cobh R. v Waterford U. (4-0) 28 Dec. '88
1990-91	Cobh Ramblers	2 + 4	(1)
1991-92	Cobh Ramblers	3 + 4	
1992-93	Cobh Ramblers	7 + 14	(2)
1993-94	Cobh Ramblers	5 + 7	(1)

O'Rourke, Ken b. Cobh, 29 Dec. 1972
Springfield to Cobh Ramblers
        U.C.D. v **Cobh Ramblers** (0-0) 14 Oct. '90
1990-91	Cobh Ramblers	11 + 3	(2)
1991-92	Cobh Ramblers	8 + 7	
1992-93	Cobh Ramblers	22 + 2	(3)
1993-94	Cobh Ramblers	34	(5)

Osam, Paul b. Dublin, 20 Dec. 1967
Summer '88 Mt. Merrion to St. Patrick's Athletic
        Limerick C v **St. Pat's Ath.** (0-1) 3 Sep. '89
1990-91	St. Patrick's Athletic	8 + 1	(1)
1991-92	St. Patrick's Athletic	30 + 1	(3)
1992-93	St. Patrick's Athletic	12 + 1	(2)
1993-94	Shamrock Rovers	18	(1)

O'Shea, Brian b. Dublin, 25 Feb. 1965
Summer '91 Newry Town to St. Patrick's Athletic
1991-92	St. Patrick's Athletic	2	
1992-93	St. Patrick's Athletic	-	
1993-94	Monaghan United	32	

O'Sullivan, Gary b. Dublin, 15 Feb. 1969
Jul. '86 Leicester Celtic to U.C.D.
        U.C.D. v Monaghan Utd (0-1) 16 Nov. '86
1990-91	U.C.D.	27	(2)
1991-92	U.C.D.	27	(2)
1992-93	Shamrock Rovers	15 + 5	
1993-94	Shamrock Rovers	-	
	Cobh Ramblers (L)	8 + 2	(2)

O'Sullivan, Tom b. Dublin, 31 Jul. 1973
Summer '92 Newbridge Town to Dundalk
        Drogheda U. v **Dundalk** (0-2) 20 Sep. '92
| 1992-93 | Dundalk | 11 + 2 | |
| 1993-94 | Dundalk | 3 + 10 | |

O'Toole, Pat b. Dublin, 2 Jan. 1965
Cherry Orchard to Shamrock Rovers
1993-94	Shrewsbury Town		
Dec. '93	Cobh Ramblers	5	
Jan. '94	Shamrock Rovers	2	

Palmer, Terry b. Dublin, 26 Apr. 1972
Jul. '90 Stella Maris to U.C.D.
        Drogheda Utd. v **U.C.D.** (2-0) 27 Jan. '91
1990-91	U.C.D.	8 + 1	
1991-92	U.C.D.	5 + 2	
1992-93	U.C.D.	17	
1993-94	U.C.D.	27	(1)

Parsons, Richie b. Dublin, 5 May 1970
1990-91	Bray Wanderers	10 + 8	(3)
1991-92	Athlone Town	15 + 9	(2)
1992-93	Monaghan United	0 + 3	
Nov. '92	Longford Town	19	(15)
1993-94	Longford Town	25	(11)

Patmore, Warren b. Kingsbury, 14 Aug. 1971
Aug. '93 Millwall to Cobh Ramblers (L)
        Cobh R. v Shelbourne (1-1) lg 29 Aug. '93
| 1993-94 | Cobh Ramblers | 8 | (3) |
| Oct. '93 | Millwall | | |

Peacock, John b. Glasgow, 17 Nov. 1973
Oct. '93 St. Mirren to Cobh Ramblers (L)
        Shamrock R. v **Cobh R.** (3-0) 31 Oct. '93
| 1993-94 | Cobh Ramblers | 4 | |
| Nov. '93 | St. Mirren | | |

Phillips, Colm b. Dublin, 5 Mar. 1957
Dunlaoghaire Celtic to Bray Wanderers
        Bray Wdrs. v Longford T. (0-1) 20 Oct. '85
1990-91	Bray Wanderers	14	
Jan. '91	Shamrock Rovers	2 + 3	
1991-92	Athlone Town	15 + 2	
1992-93	Bray Wanderers	18 + 1	
1993-94	Bray Wanderers	10	

Phillips, Justin b. Derby, 17 Dec. 1971
Nov. '93 Derby County to Cork City (L)
        Bohemians v **Cork City** (3-4) 26 Nov. '93
| 1993-94 | Cork City | 9 | (1) |
| Feb. '94 | Derby County | | |

Poutch, Neil b. Dublin, 27 Nov. 1969
Summer '90 Luton Town to Shamrock Rovers
        Shamrock R. v Athlone T (0-0) 2 Sep. '90
1990-91	Shamrock Rovers	27 + 2	(1)
1991-92	Athlone Town (L)	13	(1)
1992-93	Drogheda United	11 + 3	
1993-94	Drogheda United	2 + 1	

Power, John "Tramore" b. Waterford, 6 Feb. 1975
                Drogheda U. v. **Waterford U.** (1-0) 4 Oct. '92
1992-93   Waterford United   22 + 4   (2)
1993-94   Shamrock Rovers   1

Power, Mick
Summer '93 Belvedere to Drogheda United
                Drogheda U. v St. Pat's A. (1-1) 22 Aug. '93
1993-94   Drogheda United   0 + 2

Power, Philip b. Dublin, 22 Aug. 1967
Shelbourne to Sligo Rovers
                Shelbourne v Waterford U (0-2) 8 Nov. '87
1990-91   Sligo Rovers   15 + 9   (5)
1991-92   Athlone Town   4 + 5   (1)
Dec. '91   Monaghan United   18   (3)
1992-93   Monaghan United   22 + 2   (7)
1993-94   Monaghan United   17 + 9   (8)

Purdy, Richie b. Dublin, 12 Mar. 1972
                Home Farm v Emfa (0-1) 6 Nov. '88
Oct. '90 Home Farm to Dundalk
1990-91   Dundalk   2 + 1
1991-92   Dundalk   15 + 5
1992-93   Dundalk   28
1993-94   Dundalk   24 + 2   (2)

Quaid, Stafford b. Limerick, 14 Sep. 1974
Summer '93 Aisling Annacotty to U.C.D.
                U.C.D. v Finn Harps (4-1) 26 Sep. '93
1993-94   U.C.D.   0 + 2

Ralph, Stephen
WFTA to St. James's Gate
                St. James's G. v Cobh R. (2-1) 4 Oct. '92
1992-93   St. James's Gate   15 + 3
1993-94   St. James's Gate   8 + 2

Reddy, James "JJ" b. Dublin, 22 Apr. 1970
Summer '91 West Park to Longford Town
                Longford T. v Kilkenny C. (1-0) 6 Oct. '91
1991-92   Longford Town   8 + 7   (2)
1992-93   Longford Town   4 + 2
1993-94   Kilkenny City   17 + 7   (3)

Redmond, Pádraig
                Shamrock R. v Galway U. (2-5) 23 Jan. '94
1993-94   Shamrock Rovers   0 + 1

Reid, David b. Baillieston (Sco.), 17 Jan. 1974
Oct. '92 Kilmarnock to Sligo Rovers (L)
                Shamrock R. v **Sligo R.** (0-0) 18 Oct. '92
1992-93   Sligo Rovers   11   (2)
Dec. '92   Kilmarnock
1993-94   Sligo Rovers   17 + 2   (1)

Reid, John
                Dundalk v **St. Pat's Ath.** (0-0) 28 Aug. '92
1992-93   St. Patrick's Athletic   5 + 1
1993-94   Longford Town   23 + 1   (2)

Reid, Noel b. Dublin, 14 Mar. 1967
Summer '90 St. Patrick's Athletic to Athlone Town
                Bohemians v Galway U (5-3) IG 26 Oct. '86
1990-91   Athlone Town   18 + 9   (1)
1991-92   Athlone Town   28 + 1   (3)
1992-93   Drogheda United   27 + 2   (4)
1993-94   Drogheda United   20 + 3   (2)

Reid, Ollie
Curra Athletic to Finn Harps
                Finn Harps v Waterford U. (2-0) 19 Sep. '93
1993-94   Finn Harps   10   (1)

Reidy, Paul b. Galway, 9 Oct. 1968
Summer '92 Salthill Devon to Galway United
                Shelbourne v **Galway U.** (1-0) 3 Sep. '89
1992-93   Galway United   1 + 1
1993-94   Galway United   8 + 1

Reilly, Declan b. Dublin, 4 Apr. 1971
Summer '91 Iveagh Celtic to St. James's Gate
                Finn Harps v **St. James's G** (0-0) 20 Oct. '91
1991-92   St. James's Gate   15 + 3   (5)
1992-93   Kilkenny City   7
Dec. '92   St. James's Gate   17 + 1   (1)
1993-94   St. James's Gate   6 + 2

Reilly, James b. Dublin, 13 Sep. 1969
St. Francis to St. Patrick's Athletic
                St. Pat's A. v Monaghan U. (1-0) 9 Jan. '94
1993-94   St. Patrick's Athletic   4 + 2

Reynolds, Alan b. Waterford, 12 Jun. 1974
Sep. '91 Tramore F.C. to Waterford United
                Waterford U v Limerick C (1-1) 1 Dec. '91
1991-92   Waterford United   1 + 2
1992-93   Waterford United   30 + 2
1993-94   Waterford United   26   (1)

Reynolds, Joe b. Dublin 16 Mar. 1964
Shamrock Rovers to Shelbourne
1990-91   Shelbourne   27 + 1
1991-92   Drogheda United   32
1992-93   Drogheda United   30 + 1
1993-94   Drogheda United   19 + 3

Reynolds, Keith b. Athlone, 14 Oct. 1974
Jul. '92 St. Peter's (Athlone) To Athlone Town
                Athlone T. v. St. James's G. (0-1) 11 Apr. '93
1992-93   Athlone Town   1
1993-94   Athlone Town   1

Reynor, John b. Dublin, 25 Jul. 1964
1981 St. John Bosco to Bohemians
1991-92   Monaghan United   21   (1)
1992-93   Monaghan United   26
1993-94   Kilkenny City   22

Riordan, Séan b. Dublin, 28 Oct. 1972
                Monaghan U. v Home Farm (1-0) 10 Jan. '93
1992-93   Shelbourne   -
Jan. '93   Monaghan United (L)   13
1993-94   Shelbourne   2 + 2   (1)
Dec. '93   Limerick (L)   16   (1)

Robinson, Lee
Mar. '93 Stoke City to Dundalk (L)
Dundalk v St. Pat's A. (0-2) 31 Mar. '93
| 1993-94 | Dundalk | 1 | |

Robb, Wesley b. Dublin, 17 Aug. 1970
Nov. '90 St. Patrick's Athletic to Longford Town (L)
1990-91	Longford Town	11	(1)
Feb. '91	Athlone Town (L)	3 + 2	
1991-92	St. Patrick's Athletic	24 + 7	(1)
1992-93	St. Patrick's Athletic	3 + 1	
Oct. '92	Newry Town (L)		
1993-94	Home Farm	8 + 4	(2)

Roche, Darren
Athlone T. v **St. James's G.** (3-1) 28 Nov. '93
| 1993-94 | St. James's Gate | 0 + 1 | |

Roche, Declan b. Dublin, 9 Oct. 1970
Oct. '91 Partick Thistle to Cork City (L)
Cork City v Drogheda U (0-0) 20 Oct. '91
1991-92	Cork City	10	
Dec. '91	Shelbourne	10 + 3	(1)
1992-93	Derry City	7	
Oct. '92	Cork City	20 + 1	(5)
1993-94	Cork City	6 + 3	(2)
Dec. '93	Monaghan United		

Rogers, Derek b. Dublin, 6 Oct. 1967
'86 Shamrock Rovers to Galway United
Home Farm v Galway U (0-1) 3 Nov. '85
1990-91	Galway United	18 + 5	(2)
1991-92	Galway United	31	(1)
1992-93	Galway United	25	
1993-94	Galway United	25	

Rooney, Aidan b. Sligo, 31 Dec. 1971
local to Sligo Rovers
Bray W. v **Sligo Rovers** (0-3) 16 Jan. '94
| 1993-94 | Sligo Rovers | 0 + 1 | |

Rooney, Kieran b. Sligo
Sligo Rovers v Limerick C (1-1) 21 Oct. '90
1990-91	Sligo Rovers	3 + 4	(1)
1991-92	Sligo Rovers	8 + 8	
1992-93	Sligo Rovers	6 + 5	
1993-94	Finn Harps	22 + 5	(6)

Rushe, Stephen
Jun. '92 Culdaff to Finn Harps
Cobh Rmbs. v **Finn Harps** (2-1) 11 Oct. '92
| 1992-93 | Finn Harps | 19 | (3) |
| 1993-94 | Finn Harps | 11 + 1 | (1) |

Rutherford, Mark b. Birmingham, 25 Mar. 1972
Oct. '91 Birmingham City to Shelbourne (L)
Shelbourne v Sligo Rvs (1-0) IG 4 Oct. '91
1991-92	Shelbourne	26	(6)
1992-93	Shelbourne	37	(2)
1993-94	Shelbourne	25	(2)
Feb. '94	Shrewsbury Town (L)		

Ryan, Barry b. London, 5 Jan. 1971
Wembley Rovers to Limerick City
Limerick C v St. Pat's Ath. (0-1) 3 Sep. '89
1990-91	Limerick City	29	(3)
1991-92	Limerick City	27	(12)
1992-93	Limerick	23	
1993-94	Derry City	11 + 10	(2)

Ryan, Garrett
Summer '93 Ballynanty Rovers to Limerick
Limerick v Shelbourne (0-0) 22 Aug. '93
| 1993-94 | Limerick | 23 + 6 | (3) |

Ryan, John b. Dublin, 27 Feb. 1968
Dunboyne to St. Patrick's Athletic
St. Pats Ath. v Cork City (2-1) 4 Sep. '88
1990-91	Bray Wanderers	18	(6)
Feb. '91	St. Patrick's Athletic	2 + 5	(1)
1991-92	St. Patrick's Athletic	28 + 3	(6)
1992-93	St. Patrick's Athletic	25 + 4	(5)
1993-94	Drogheda United	32	(4)

Sandy, Dexter
U.S.A. to Finn Harps
Sligo R. v **Finn Harps** (4-1) 26 Dec. '93
| 1993-94 | Finn Harps | 2 | |

Savage, Dave b. Dublin, 30 Jul. 1973
Summer '90 Bromley to Kilkenny City
St. James's G. v **Kilkenny C.**(1-2) IG 7 Oct. '90
1990-91	Kilkenny City	3 + 5	(1)
Jan. '91	To Brighton H.A.		
1992-93	Longford Town	21 + 2	(2)
1993-94	Longford Town	24 + 1	(5)
May '94	Millwall		

Sayers, John
Summer '93 St. Francis to Derry City
Galway U. v **Shamrock R.** (0-1) 1 Apr. '91
1990-91	Shamrock Rovers	0 + 1	
	St. Francis		
1993-94	Derry City	8 + 1	

Scanlon, Trevor b. Sligo, 22 Sep. 1970
local to Sligo Rovers
Sligo R. v Finn Harps (4-1) 26 Dec. '93
| 1993-94 | Sligo Rovers | 0 + 2 | |

Seville, Colm b. Dublin, 8 Mar. 1966
St. Pat's Ath v Dundalk (2-1) 24 Sep. '89
1990-91	St. Patrick's Athletic	5 + 4	(1)
Feb. '91	Athlone Town	5 + 1	
1991-92	St. James's Gate	24	(6)
1992-93	Monaghan United	8 + 4	
1993-94	St. James's Gate	15 + 1	(1)

Shanahan, Alan b. Limerick,19 Jul. 1963
Fairview Rangers to Limerick City
1990-91	Limerick City	26	
1991-92	Limerick City	27	(2)
1992-93	Limerick	0 + 3	(1)
1993-94	Limerick	3 + 2	

Sheehy, Ciaran b. Dundalk, 30 Nov. 1970
 Derry City v **Dundalk** (2-0) 29 Mar. '92
1991-92 Dundalk 0 + 1
1992-93 Dundalk 3 + 3
1993-94 Dundalk 4 + 1

Shelley, Mick b. Dublin, 21 Jan. 1960
'85 Bohemians to Dundalk
1990-91 Dundalk 33 (1)
1991-92 Dundalk 28 (1)
1992-93 Dundalk 10 + 2
1993-94 Drogheda United 27

Sheridan, Barra b. Dublin
Home Farm to U.C.D.
 U.C.D. v Sligo Rovers (1-1) 14 Nov. '93
1993-94 U.C.D. 1

Sheridan, Davy
 Sligo R. v **Longford Town** (1-1) 10 Oct. '93
1993-94 Longford Town 1

Sheridan, Declan
 Finn Harps v Sligo R. (0-1) 17 Oct. 93
1993-94 Finn Harps 4 + 3

Sherlock, Eamonn b. Galway, 14 Dec. 1975
Salthill Devon to Galway United
 Cobh R. v **Galway U.** (0-0) 13 Dec. '92
1992-93 Galway United 1 + 2
1993-94 Galway United 2 + 1

Smith, Alan b. Dublin, 5 Jul. 1967
St. Josephs Boy's to Bray Wanderers
 Drogheda U. v **Bray W.** (2-1) 4 Sep. '88
1990-91 Bray Wanderers 26 (2)
1991-92 Bray Wanderers 29
1992-93 Bray Wanderers 27 + 2
1993-94 Bray Wanderers 27 (3)

Smith, Alan
1992-93 Home Farm 3 + 3 (1)
1993-94 Home Farm 1 + 2

Smith, Brett b. Gillingham, 20 Oct. 1974
Nov. '93 Millwall to Cobh Ramblers (L)
 Limerick v **Cobh R.** (1-5) 14 Nov. '93
1993-94 Cobh Ramblers 5
Dec. '93 Millwall

Smith, Dave
From Shelbourne youths
 Shelbourne v Shamrock R. (0-3) 25 Mar. '94
1993-94 Shelbourne 1

Smith, Declan b. Dublin, 19 Feb. 1969
Jul. '91 Bohemians to Monaghan United
 Waterford U. v **Monaghan U.** (1-0) 20 Oct.'91
1991-92 Monaghan United 3 + 1
1993-94 Monaghan United 0 + 2

Smith, Mike b. Liverpool, 28 Sep. 1973
Sep. '93 Tranmere Rovers to Derry City (L)
 Derry City v **Dundalk** (1-4) 12 Sep. '93
1993-94 Derry City 4
Oct. '93 Tranmere Rovers

Smyth, Aidan b. Dublin, 12 Jul. 1965
C.Y.M. to Home Farm
 Waterford U v **Home Farm** (0-2) 3 Sep. '89
1990-91 Home Farm 23
1991-92 Home Farm 24
1992-93 Longford Town 27
1993-94 Longford Town 10
Feb. '94 Kilkenny City 6

Smyth, Derek b. Dublin, 19 Jul. 1968
 Longford T. v **Bray W.** (2-1) 17 Mar. '91
1990-91 Bray Wanderers 2 + 3
1993-94 Monaghan United 1 + 2
 Bray Wanderers 12 + 5 (1)

Spence, Robert b. Helston, 28 Oct. 1972
Jan. '94 Torquay United to Sligo Rovers
 Sligo R. v St. James's G. (3-1) 29 Jan. '94
1993-94 Sligo Rovers 4

Staunton, David b. Dundalk, 16 Mar. 1967
1993-94 Drogheda United 2

Staunton, Thomas b. Dundalk, 20 Nov. 1973
 Dundalk v Bray W. (0-0) 22 Mar. '92
1991-92 Dundalk 1
1993-94 Dundalk 3

Stokes, Paul b. Dublin
Oct. '93 Bluebell United to Waterford United
 Bray W. v **Waterford U.** (1-1) IG 31 Oct. '93
1993-94 Waterford United 11 + 2 (7)

Sullivan, Joe b. Dublin
 Shelbourne v Cork City (0-1) 12 Apr. '92
1991-92 Shelbourne 1
1992-93 Longford Town (L) 14 + 2
1993-94 Longford Town 2 + 4
Feb. '94 St. James's Gate 4

Swan, Derek b. Dublin, 24 Oct. 1966
Nov. '90 Port Vale to Shamrock Rovers
1990-91 Shamrock Rovers 17 (10)
1991-92 Shamrock Rovers 23 + 2 (7)
1992-93 Shamrock Rovers 25 + 5 (8)
1993-94 Shamrock Rovers 2 + 1
Nov. '93 Glentoran
Jan. '94 Dundalk (L) 3

Sweeney, Liam
Jun. '92 Fanad United to Finn Harps
 Finn Harps v Athlone T. (0-5) 16 Sep. '84
1992-93 Finn Harps 26 + 1
1993-94 Finn Harps 6

Synnott, Eamonn b. Dublin, 5 Mar. 1970
Bohemians to Dundalk
　　　　　　　　Bohemians v Waterford U. (4-0) 3 Mar. '89
1990-91　　　Dundalk　　　　　　　3 + 12　(1)
1991-92　　　Dundalk　　　　　　　-
1992-93　　　St. Patrick's Athletic　-
Oct. '92　　　Newry Town (L)
Dec. '92　　　Kilkenny City　　　　13 + 1
1993-94　　　Longford Town　　　　9 + 5

Teehan, Gavin b. Cork
Ballybrack Boys to Bray Wanderers
　　　　　　　　Bray W. v Drogheda U. (0-0) 28 Oct. '90
1990-91　　　Bray Wanderers　　　6 + 3
1992-93　　　Bray Wanderers　　　23
1993-94　　　Bray Wanderers　　　27

Tilson, David b. Dublin, 17 May 1968
Jul. '89 U.C.D. to Bohemians
　　　　　　　　U.C.D. v Galway United (1-2) 20 Oct. '85
1990-91　　　Bohemians　　　　　24 + 2　(3)
1991-92　　　Bohemians　　　　　31　　　(10)
1992-93　　　Bohemians　　　　　27 + 1　(10)
1993-94　　　Bohemians　　　　　20 + 2　(5)

Timmons, Conor b. Dublin, 23 Nov. 1970
Jul. '88 Malahide United to U.C.D.
　　　　　　　　Bohemians v U.C.D. (3-0) 3 Sep. '89
1990-91　　　U.C.D.　　　　　　　19　　　(3)
1991-92　　　U.C.D.　　　　　　　26　　　(2)
1992-93　　　U.C.D.　　　　　　　27
1993-94　　　U.C.D.　　　　　　　26

Toal, John b. Dublin, 5 Nov. 1967
'89 Shamrock Rovers to Drogheda United
1990-91　　　Drogheda United　　25　　　(5)
1991-92　　　Drogheda United　　32　　　(2)
1992-93　　　Shamrock Rovers　　15 + 2　(1)
1993-94　　　Shamrock Rovers　　31

Toland, Maurice
1993-94　　　Finn Harps　　　　　16 + 1　(2)

Tracey, John b. Dublin, 16 Apr. 1959
St. Kevin's Boys to Bohemians
　　　　　　　　Bohemians vSt. Pat's Ath. (1-1) 20 Oct. '85
1990-91　　　St. Patrick's Athletic　32 + 1　(2)
1991-92　　　St. Patrick's Athletic　24 + 3　(1)
1992-93　　　St. Patrick's Athletic　23 + 1
1993-94　　　St. Patrick's Athletic　19 + 3

Trainor, Paul b. Belfast, 29 Nov. 1963
Oct. '92 Cromac Albion (Belfast) to Derry City
1992-93　　　Derry City　　　　　10 + 5　(2)
1993-94　　　Finn Harps　　　　　2
　　　　　　　Drogheda United　　4　　　　(1)

Treacy, Derek b. Dublin, 6 Apr. 1971
Howth Celtic to Shamrock Rovers
　　　　　　　　Shamrock R v Dundalk (0-0) 19 Nov. '89
1990-91　　　Shamrock Rovers　　23 + 1　(2)
1991-92　　　Shamrock Rovers　　19 + 8　(3)
1992-93　　　Shamrock Rovers　　16 + 2　(2)
1993-94　　　Shamrock Rovers　　2 + 6

Treacy, Jonathan b. Dublin, 26 Oct. 1971
Jul. '89 Home Farm to U.C.D.
　　　　　　　　U.C.D. v Galway United (1-0) 1 Apr. '90
1990-91　　　U.C.D.　　　　　　　23 + 1
1991-92　　　U.C.D.　　　　　　　27
1992-93　　　U.C.D.　　　　　　　24　　　(2)
1993-94　　　U.C.D.　　　　　　　27

Trehy, Pat b. Dublin, 5 Nov. 1971
Shamrock Rovers to St. James's Gate
　　　　　　　　Shamrock R v Shelbourne (2-3) 6 Apr. '90
1990-91　　　St. James's Gate　　1
1991-92　　　St. James's Gate　　1
1992-93　　　St. James's Gate　　25
1993-94　　　St. James's Gate　　21

Tresson, Colm b. Dublin, 29 Jun. 1971
St. Joseph's Boys to Bray Wanderers
　　　　　　　　Bray W. v Monaghan U. (2-0) 7 Oct. '90
1990-91　　　Bray Wanderers　　11 + 5　(3)
1991-92　　　Bray Wanderers　　16 + 4
1992-93　　　Drogheda United　32　　　(6)
1993-94　　　Drogheda United　32　　　(1)

Twomey, John b. Tralee
　　　　　　　　Shelbourne v Limerick (3-0) 5 Nov. '93
1993-94　　　Limerick　　　　　　2

Ussher, Paul
Shamrock Rovers to St. James's Gate
1990-91　　　St. James's Gate　　11 + 9　(2)
1991-92　　　St. James's Gate　　13 + 4
1992-93　　　St. James's Gate　　9 + 4
1993-94　　　St. James's Gate　　17 + 8　(2)

Van Boxtel, Eddie b. Amsterdam, 14 Aug. 1973
Leeds United to Dundalk
　　　　　　　　Dundalk v Bray W. (0-0) 22 Mar. '92
1991-92　　　Dundalk　　　　　　4
1993-94　　　Dundalk　　　　　　19

Vaudequin, Pascal b. Paris, 22 Sep. 1966
Summer '87 Dunkirke to Derry City
　　　　　　　　Derry City v Bray W. (0-0) 13 Sep. '87
1990-91　　　Derry City　　　　　27 + 3　(2)
　　　　　　　Rodez (France) (L)
1993-94　　　Derry City　　　　　20

Vaughan, Trevor
　　　　　　　　Athlone Town v Home Farm (1-1) 25 Oct. '92
1992-93　　　Home Farm　　　　0 + 2
1993-94　　　Home Farm　　　　14 + 1 ·　(3)

Wall, Shane b. Dublin
Summer '93 Greystones AFC to Bray Wanderers
　　　　　Bray W. v St. James's G. (0-0) 17 Oct. '93
1993-94　　Bray Wanderers　　0 + 3

Walsh, John b. 8 Mar. 1969
Summer '91 to Finn Harps
　　　　　Cobh Rmb. v **Finn Harps** (1-2) 19 Jan. '92
1991-92　　Finn Harps　　4
1992-93　　Finn Harps　　10
1993-94　　Finn Harps　　5

Walsh, Johnny b. Limerick, 8 Nov. 1957
Wembley Rovers to Limerick United
　　　　　Limerick v Bohemians (1-2) 3 Oct. '76
1990-91　　Limerick City　　32　　(1)
1991-92　　Limerick City　　22　　(5)
1992-93　　Limerick　　27 + 2　(1)
1993-94　　Limerick　　26 + 2　(1)

Walsh, Pierce b. Dublin, 16 Aug. 1964
Aug. '89 Athlone Town to Sligo Rovers
1990-91　　Sligo Rovers　　22 + 1
1991-92　　Sligo Rovers　　20 + 1　(1)
1992-93　　Sligo Rovers　　27
1993-94　　Longford Town　　23　　(5)

Warfield, Cathal
　　　　　Home Farm v Kilkenny C (1-1) 9 Jan. '94
1993-94　　Home Farm　　2

Weldrick, Alan b. Dublin, 8 Oct. 1971
Leicester City to St. Patrick's Athletic
　　　　　Kilkenny City v **Longford T** (0-0) 2 Dec. '90
1990-91　　St. Patrick's Athletic　　–
Dec. '90　　Longford Town (L)　　19　　(7)
1991-92　　Drogheda United　　29
1992-93　　Drogheda United　　19 + 8　(2)
1993-94　　Drogheda United　　0 + 2
Sep. '93　　Kilkenny City　　22 + 3　(6)

Whelan, 'Anto' b. Dublin, 23 Nov. 1959
Summer '88 Bray Wanderers to Shelbourne
　　　　　Finn Harps v **Bohemians** (0-2) 9 Sep. '79
1990-91　　Shelbourne　　28 + 2　(3)
1991-92　　Shelbourne　　26 + 4　(4)
1992-93　　Shelbourne　　16 + 1　(3)
1993-94　　Shelbourne　　30　　(2)

Whelan, Paul b. Dublin, 10 May 1964
Summer '84 Home Farm to Drogheda United
　　　　　Dundalk v **Home Farm** (2-0) 21 Nov. '82
1990-91　　Bohemians　　27
1991-92　　Bohemians　　30　　(3)
1992-93　　Bohemians　　31　　(2)
1993-94　　Bohemians　　15 + 1

Williams, Steve b. London, 12 Jul. 1958
Oct. '93 Exeter City to Derry City
　　　　　Derry City v Shamrock R. (0-0) 10 Oct. '93
1993-94　　Derry City　　2

Wilson, Karl b. Dublin, 9 Nov. 1973
Summer '93 Coventry City to Shelbourne
　　　　　Limerick v **Shelbourne** (0-0) 22 Aug. '93
1993-94　　Shelbourne　　3 + 2
　　　　　Ards (L)

Wilson, Mickey b. Monaghan
Summer '91 Dundalk to Monaghan United
　　　　　Monaghan U. v Finn Harps (1-1) lg 6 Oct '91
1991-92　　Monaghan United　　22　　(8)
1992-93　　Monaghan United　　24 + 2　(5)
1993-94　　Monaghan United　　14 + 12

Wilson, Willie b. South Shields, 21 Mar. 1963
Sep. '93　　Middlesborough to Derry City
　　　　　Bohemians v **Derry City** (2-0) 19 Sep. '93
1993-94　　Derry City　　3

Wogan, Terry b. 14 Dec. 1972
Jul. '91 Belvedere to Bohemians
　　　　　Bohemians v Drogheda U (1-1) 5 Apr. '92
1991-92　　Bohemians　　0 + 3
1992-93　　Longford Town　　2 + 2　(1)
1993-94　　Kilkenny City　　6

Woods, Billy b. Cork, 24 Nov 1973
Oct. '93 Coventry City to Cork City
　　　　　Shelbourne v **Cork City** (0-1) 8 Oct. '93
1993-94　　Cork City　　0 + 3

Woods, Ian b. Dublin, 24 Sep. 1967
Aug. '90 Kilkenny City to Athlone Town
　　　　　Waterford U. v **St. Pat's. Ath.** (2-1) 30 Nov. '86
1990-91　　Athlone Town　　21 + 6
1991-92　　Monaghan United　　23 + 2
1992-93　　Monaghan United　　27
1993-94　　Monaghan United　　29　　(2)

Wouters, Dominique b. Belgium
Nov. '93 RFC Liege to Waterford United
　　　　　Waterford U. v Home Farm (4-2) 21 Nov.'93
1993-94　　Waterford United　　13

267

AWARDS 1993/94

Soccer Writers Association of Ireland:
　　"**Personality of the Year**" Stephen Geoghegan (Shamrock Rovers)

Player of the Month Awards:

September:	Anthony Buckley	(Cork City)
October:	Stephen Geoghegan	(Shamrock Rovers)
November:	Alan Byrne	(Shamrock Rovers)
December:	Peter Hutton	(Derry City)
January:	John Brennan	(Galway United)
February:	John Kenny	(Sligo Rovers)
March:	Eoin Mullen	(Shamrock Rovers)
April:	Dermot O'Neill	(Derry City)
Special Award	Arnold O'Byrne	(Opel)

Professional Footballers Association of Ireland:

Player of the Year	Stephen Geoghegan	(Shamrock Rovers)
First Division Player of the Year:	John Kenny	(Sligo Rovers)
Young Player of the Year:	Jim Crawford	(Bohemians)
Special Merit Award:	Brendan McKenna	(Evening Press)

League of Ireland 'Legends' 1994:
Paddy Ambrose　(Shamrock Rovers)
Jack Fitzgerald　(Waterford)
Mick O'Flanagan　(Bohemians)

F.A.I./Opel Player of the Year Awards:

Senior	:	Stephen Staunton	(Aston Villa)
Young	:	Roy Keane	(Manchester United)
U21	:	Paul McCarthy	(Brighton & H.A.)
National League	:	Pat Morley	(Cork City)
Youth	:	Alan Moore	(Middlesbrough)
Junior	:	Cyril Conran	(Clonmel Town)
Ladies	:	Susan Ronan	(Welsox)
Schools	:	Anthony Scully	(Collinstown Park C.C./ Crystal Palace)
U/16	:	Stephen Carr	(Tottenham Hotspur)
U/15	:	Ross Darcy	(Stella Maris)
Hall of Fame	:	Noel Cantwell	
Special Merit	:	Frank O'Neill	
International Personality	:	Osvaldo Ardiles	

Previous Award Winners:

SWAI Personality of the Year:

1992-93	Pat Morley	(Cork City)
1991-92	Pat Byrne	(Shelbourne)
1990-91	Peter Hanrahan	(Dundalk)
1989-90	Damien Byrne	(St. Pats Ath)
1988-89	Jim McLaughlin	(Derry City)
1987-88	Terry Eviston	(Dundalk)
1986-87	Mick Byrne	(Shamrock R.)
1985-86	Liam O'Brien	(Shamrock R.)
1984-85	Pat Byrne	(Shamrock R.)
1983-84	Jim McLaughlin	(Shamrock R.)
1982-83	Noel Larkin	(Athlone Town)
1981-82	Tommy McConville	(Dundalk)
1980-81	Turlough O'Connor	(Athlone Town)
1979-80	Eoin Hand	(Limerick City)
1978-79	Jim McLaughlin	(Dundalk)
1977-78	Johnny Giles	(Shamrock R.)
1976-77	Mick Smyth	(Bohemians)
1975-76	Brendan Bradley	(Finn Harps)
1974-75	Johnny Fullam	(Bohemians)
1973-74	Paul O'Donovan	(Cork Celtic)
1972-73	Alfie Hale	(Waterford)
1971-72	Dave Bacuzzi	(Cork Hibs)
1970-71	Mick Meagan	(Drogheda)
1969-70	Peter Thomas	(Waterford)
1968-69	Mick Leech	(Shamrock R.)
1967-68	Johnny Fullam	(Shamrock R.)
1966-67	Al Finucane	(Limerick)
1965-66	Liam Tuohy	(Shamrock R.)
1964-65	Seán Thomas	(Bohemians)
1963-64	Joe Wickham	(FAI Secretary)
1962-63	Willie Browne	(Bohemians)
1962-63	Tommy Hamilton	(Shamrock R.)
1961-62	Dan McCaffery	(Drumcondra)

PFAI Player of the Year

1992-93	Donal O'Brien	(Derry City)
1991-92	Pat Fenlon	(Bohemians)
1990-91	Pat Morley	(Cork City)
1989-90	Mark Ennis	(St. Pats Ath.)
1988-89	Paul Doolin	(Derry City)
1987-88	Paddy Dillon	(St. Pats Ath.)
1986-87	Mick Byrne	(Shamrock R.)
1985-86	Paul Doolin	(Shamrock R.)
1984-85	Tommy Gaynor	(Limerick City)
1983-84	Pat Byrne	(Shamrock R.)
1982-83	Martin Murray	(Drogheda Utd.)
1981-82	Paul McGrath	(St. Pats Ath.)
1980-81	Padraig O'Connor	(Athlone Town)

PFAI First Div. Player of the Year

1992-93	Gerry Mullen	(Galway Utd)
1991-92	Barry Ryan	(Limerick City)
1990-91	John Toal	(Drogheda Utd.)
1989-90	John Ryan	(Bray Wanderers)
1988-89	Denis Cunningham	(Finn Harps)
1987-88	Fran Hitchcock	(Athlone T.)
1986-87	Alex Kristic	(Derry City)
1985-86	Owen DaGama	(Derry City)

PFAI Young Player of the Year:

1992-93	Richie Purdy	(Dundalk)
1991-92	Tony McCarthy	(Shelbourne)
1990-91	Barry Ryan	(Limerick City)
1989-90	Vinny Arkins & Tony Cousins	(Shamrock R.) (Dundalk)
1988-89	Liam Coyle	(Derry City)
1987-88	Paul McGee	(Bohemians)
1986-87	Martin Bayly	(Sligo Rovers)
1985-86	Liam O'Brien	(Shamrock R.)
1984-85	Peter Coyle	(Limerick City)

PFAI Special Merit Award:

1992-93	Phillip Greene (R.T.E.)
1991-92	Séan Thomas
1990-91	Tony Sheehan
1989-90	Charlie Walker
1988-89	Phillip Greene (R.T.E.)
1987-88	Harry Boland
1986-87	Liam Tuohy
1985-86	Harry McCue (Snr.)
1984-85	Derry Barrett
1983-84	George Goodson

Securicor Omega Express:

Fastest Goal of the season:
Mark Farrell   (St. James's Gate)
25 secs. v College Corinthians (FAI Cup 1st Rd.) 6/2/1994

Monthly Awards:

September:	John Toal	(Shamrock Rovers)
October:	Derek McGrath	(Shamrock Rovers)
November:	Donnie Farragher	(Galway United)
December:	Justin Phillips	(Cork City)
	Willie Hastie	(Sligo Rovers)
January:	Trevor Donnelly	(Dundalk)
	Maurice O'Driscoll	(Bohemians)
	Peter Eccles	(Shamrock Rovers)
February:	Mark Farrell	(St. James's Gate)
March:	Séan Francis	(Cobh Ramblers)
	Séan Riordan	(Limerick)

Bord Gais League of Ireland All-Stars

Alan Gough (Galway United), Declan Daly (Cork City), Peter Eccles (Shamrock Rovers), Ray O'Halloran (Limerick), John Coady (Monaghan United), Brian Mooney (Shelbourne), Alan Byrne (Shamrock Rovers), John Toal (Shamrock Rovers), Dave Tilson (Bohemians), Liam Coyle (Derry City), Stephen Geoghegan (Shamrock Rovers)

Honour Bound
Steve Staunton shows his Senior Player of the Year style (The Star)

Dublin Derby No. 2 *Bohemians v Shamrock Rovers*
151 games 1922/23 to 1993/94 (72 successive seasons!)

Bohemians v Shamrock Rovers

Bohemians: Wins : 41   **Shamrock Rovers:** Wins : 75   Draws : 35
Goals : 205   Goals : 310

Longest unbeaten sequence:
Shamrock Rovers (19 games)   Dec. '56 to Nov. '65

Season	22/23	23/24	24/25	25/26	26/27	27/28	28/29	29/30	30/31	31/32	32/33	33/34	34/35
Bohemians (H)	0-2	4-1	1-1	1-4	1-2	3-2	2-1	5-1	5-2	2-3	2-3	1-0	1-1
Shamrock Rovers (H)	2-0	2-0	1-1	0-2	4-0	0-0	2-2	0-1	3-3	2-0	2-2	2-3	2-5

Season	35/36	36/37	37/38	38/39	39/40	40/41	41/42	42/43	43/44	44/45	45/46	46/47	47/48
Bohemians (H)	5-2	2-5	2-3	1-3	1-4	2-2	1-1	1-1	3-2	1-1	1-5	1-3	0-1
Shamrock Rovers (H)	3-2	3-0	6-1	2-2	2-0	3-4	1-1	1-0	4-3	4-2	7-2	3-3	0-0

Season	48/49	49/50	50/51	51/52	52/53	53/54	54/55	55/56	56/57	57/58	58/59	59/60	60/61
Bohemians (H)	2-1	2-2	2-0	1-4	2-1	0-2	5-1	3-2	1-4	2-4	0-0	1-4	0-2
Shamrock Rovers (H)	2-2	7-2	4-1	1-0	1-0	1-0	7-0	4-0	6-0	6-0	4-1	5-0	1-1

Season	61/62	62/63	63/64	64/65	65/66	66/67	67/68	68/69	69/70	70/71	71/72	72/73	73/74
Bohemians (H)	2-3	0-0	1-2	1-2	2-4	0-2	1-2	0-3	1-2	1-0	2-2	3-2	0-1
Shamrock Rovers (H)	3-2	3-1	7-1	2-0	2-3	1-2	4-1	2-2	2-1	2-2	1-0	0-0	0-1

Season	74/75	75/76	76/77	77/78	78/79	79/80	80/81	81/82	82/83	83/84	84/85	85/86	86/87
Bohemians (H)	2-0	1-0	1-0	3-0	0-1	0-2	0-0	3-1	3-2	2-1	2-0	1-1	1-1
Shamrock Rovers (H)	1-2	1-0	1-2	0-0	0-1	1-2	2-2	2-1	3-0	1-1	2-0	3-0	3-2

Season	87/88	88/89	89/90	90/91	91/92	92/93	93/94
Bohemians (H)	1-4	2-2	1-2	2-3	1-1	2-1	2-0
	1-1			1-2	0-0		1-2
Shamrock Rovers (H)	1-1	3-1	3-1	0-2	1-3	0-1	2-1
		3-0	2-1				1-2

271

Transfer Trail

	From	To
Arrigan, Pat	Tycor Athletic	Waterford United
Blood, Ken	Bohemians	Monaghan United
Brady, Keith	Bohemians	Limerick
Brennan, John	Galway United	Sligo Rovers
Brennan, John	Sligo Rovers	Shamrock Rovers
Brett, Gordon	Athlone Town	Galway United
Broughan, Donal	Bohemians	Shelbourne
Brujos, Nick	Cliftonville	Sligo Rovers
Brunton, Robert	Stoke City	Sligo Rovers
Buckley, Anthony	Cork City	Boston College, USA
Buckley, Martin	Home Farm	Shamrock Rovers
Buttner, Stefan	Kilkenny City	Longford Town
Byrne, Alan	Shamrock Rovers	Shelbourne
Byrne, Brian	Glenmore Celtic	Dundalk
Byrne, Jody	Shelbourne	Dundalk
Byrne, Ray	Northampton Town	Shelbourne
Caffrey, Stephen	Cherry Orchard	Bohemians
Callaghan, Aaron	Shelbourne	Crusaders (L)
Carpenter, Peter	Galway United	St. Patrick's Athletic
Carter, Fran	Salthill Devon	Galway United
Cashin, Paul	Shamrock Rovers	Waterford United
Clarke, Paul	Dublin GAA	Shelbourne
Cleary, John	Kilkenny City	Monaghan United
Cleary, John	Monaghan United	Longford Town (p/m)
Coady, John	Monaghan United	Dundalk
Connell, Dave	Drogheda United	Limerick
Connolly, John	Bohemians	Shelbourne
Cooney, Stephen	Shelbourne	St. Patrick's Athletic
Corcoran, John	Galway United	Crescent United
Costelloe, Norman	Finn Harps	Galway United
Coughlin, Graham	Cherry Orchard	Waterford United
Cronin, Gareth	Sunderland	Cork City
Crowley, Danny	Home Farm	Limerick
Curtis, Len	Rotherham United	Shamrock Rovers
De Khors, Rod	Sittingbourne	Athlone Town
De Mange, Ken	Bohemians	Dundalk
Devanney, Pierce	Sligo Rovers	Finn Harps
Devereaux, Robbie	Colchester United	Shelbourne
Devlin, Mark	Bohemians	Athlone Town
Doherty, Alan	Dundalk	Finn Harps
Dominguez, Vitor	Lusitano De Evora (Port)	Waterford United
Doyle, Warren	Johnville	Waterford United
Donnelly, Trevor	Dundalk	Ballyclare Comerades (L)
Dully, Pádraig	Shelbourne	Cliftonville (L)
Dunne, Simon	Shamrock Rovers	St. Patrick's Athletic
Eccles, Peter	Shamrock Rovers	Crusaders
Elebert, Shaun	Shamrock Rovers	Longford Town

	From	To
Fallon, Thomas	St. Patrick's Athletic	Lusk United
Farragher, Donnie	Galway United	Mervue United
Farrell, Brian	Waterford United	Johnville
Fitzgerald, Tommy	Bohemians	Monaghan United
Flynn, Conor	Glenmore Celtic	Bohemians
Gannon, Karl	Home Farm	Shamrock Rovers
Garlick, Scott	San Diego University	Waterford United
Geoghegan, Stephen	Shamrock Rovers	Shelbourne
Geraghty, Graham	Kentstown Rovers	Bohemians (Trial)
Giltenan, Fergal	Wilton United	Cork City
Girvan, Mark	Longford Town	Kilkenny City
Glynn, Johnny	Cork City	St. Patrick's Athletic
Gough, Alan	Galway United	Shelbourne
Grace, Jim	Drogheda United	Longford Town
Grace, John	Glentoran	Drogheda United
Hale, Richie	Waterford United	Waterford Glass
Hall, Paul	St. James's Gate	Dundalk
Hall, Paul	Dundalk	Ballyclare Comerades (L)
Hanrahan, Peter	Dundalk	Bohemians
Hurta, Joan	Romania	Kilkenny City
Haxhiu, Gerd	Flamurtari Vlore (Albania)	Drogheda United
Healy, Stephen	Donaghmeade Celtic	St. Patrick's Athletic
Heary, Eoin	Kilkenny City	Home Farm
Heath, Seamus	Distillery	Derry City
Heffernan, Ger	Cherry Orchard	U.C.D.
Hogan, Eric	Cobh Ramblers	College Corinthians
Horgan, Joey	Local	Longford Town
Horgan, Robbie	Shelbourne	Shamrock Rovers
Izzi, Antonio	Shelbourne	St. Patrick's Athletic
Keddy, James	Home Farm	U.C.D.
Kelly, Ray	Athlone Town	Manchester City
Keogh, Niall	Shelbourne	St. James's Gate
King, Howie	Bohemians	Limerick
King, Lee	Drogheda United	Bohemians
King, Noel	Bohemians	Limerick
Kinnaird, Paul	Derry City	Bohemians
Kitson, Mark	Bristol City	Waterford United
Lally, Derek	Galway Hibernians	Galway United
Lawless, Gino	Dundalk	Bohemians
Lonergan, Darren	Waterford United	Oldham Athletic
Loughlin, Tony	Lincoln City	Dundalk
Lynch, Aaron	Home Farm	Shamrock Rovers
McCabe, Ultan	Newry Town	Drogheda United
McCarthy, Kevin	Limerick	Fairview Rangers
McCormack, Derek	Shamrock Rovers	Kilkenny City
McDonagh, Paddy	Oldham Athletic	St. Patrick's Athletic
McElligott, Christy	St. Patrick's Athletic	Monaghan United
McEnroe, David	St. Patrick's Athletic	Limerick
McGuinness, Ray	Bangor	Derry City
McKinlay, David	Middlesbrough	Cork City (L)
McStay, Willie	Sligo Rovers	Celtic (Coach)
Markey, Brendan	Cherry Orchard	Bohemians
Martindale, Dave	Tranmere Rovers	Derry City

	From	**To**
Mernagh, Noel	Galway United	St. Patrick's Athletic
Mooney, Stephen	Raith Rovers	Cobh Ramblers
Mooney, Wayne	Lansdowne Rangers	St. Patrick's Athletic
Moran, Danny	St. Joseph's Boys	St. Patrick's Athletic
Mullen, Gerry	Galway United	USA
Murray, Matthew	Home Farm	Bray Wanderers
Murray, Séan	Middlesbrough	St. Patrick's Athletic
Nolan, Peter	St. James's Gate	Cherry Orchard
Notaro, Colm	Cherry Orchard	St. Patrick's Athletic
O'Brien, Donal	Derry City	Glentoran
O'Brien, Kieran	St. Patrick's Athletic	Boston College, USA
O'Callaghan, Brendan	Cobh Ramblers	Drogheda United
O'Connor, Barry	Shelbourne	Drogheda United
O'Halloran, Christy	Waterford United	Waterford Glass
O'Halloran, Ray	Limerick	Galway United
O'Keeffe, Willie	U.C.C.	Cobh Ramblers
O'Neill, Derek	Monaghan United	Home Farm
Osam, Paul	Shamrock Rovers	Derry City
O'Sullivan, Tom	Dundalk	Drogheda United
O'Toole, Pat	Shamrock Rovers	Cobh Ramblers
O'Toole, Paul	Tycor Athletic	Waterford United
Parsons, Richie	Longford Town	Finn Harps
Patmore, Warren	Northampton Town	Dundalk
Power, Joey	Thermo King	Galway United
Power, Philip	Monaghan United	Home Farm
Pressmam, John	St. Malachy's	Bohemians
Quigley, James	Everton	Derry City
Quintongo, Jose	Estoril (Port.)	Waterford United
Reid, Mark	Stoke City	Sligo Rovers
Reid, Paddy	St. Malachy's	Bohemians
Reynolds, Joe	Drogheda United	Athlone Town
Riordan, Séan	Limerick	Shelbourne (R)
Rocastle, Steve	Fulham	Derry City
Romulus, Pop	Romania	Kilkenny City
Ryan, Barry	Derry City	Galway United
Saddington, James	Millwall	Shelbourne
Sanchez, Lawrie	Swindon Town	Sligo Rovers (P/M)
Sayers, John	Derry City	Ards
Scanlon, Trevor	Sligo Rovers	Finn Harps
Smith, Matthew	Plymouth Argyle	Cork City (L)
Stevenson, Ashley	Stoke City	Waterford United
Smyth, Gary	Donegal Celtic	Derry City
Trehy, Pat	St. James's Gate	Bray Wanderers
Vaughan, Trevor	Home Farm	Shelbourne
Voice, Scott	Wolverhampton Wanderers	Shelbourne
Walsh, Pierce	Longford Town	Limerick
Walsh, Pierce	Limerick	Monaghan United
Weldrick, Alan	Kilkenny City	Longford Town
Whelan, Anto	Shelbourne	Dundalk
Whelan, Paul	Bohemians	Shamrock Rovers
Woods, Ian	Monaghan United	St. Patrick's Athletic

L = Loan Transfer; PM = Player-Manager; R = Return from Loan

Final League Positions 1985/86 to 1993/94

Premier Division

	\ Season / Position								
	85/86	86/87	87/88	88/89	89/90	90/91	91/92	92/93	93/94
Athlone Town	8	12	-	6	10	10	11	-	-
Bohemians	4	3	3	5	6	9	5	2	6
Bray Wanderers	-	8	11	-	-	-	8	12	-
Cobh Ramblers	-	-	-	11	-	-	-	-	10
Cork City	10	7	7	8	5	2	3	1	2
Derry City	-	-	8	1	2	7	2	5	4
Drogheda United	-	-	-	-	11	-	10	9	12
Dundalk	3	2	1	2	3	1	4	4	8
Galway United	2	6	5	10	8	8	12	-	3
Home Farm	9	11	-	-	-	-	-	-	-
Limerick City / Limerick	7	10	9	3	9	12	-	6	11
Monaghan United	-	-	-	-	-	-	-	-	7
St. Patrick's Athletic	6	5	2	4	1	3	7	7	9
Shamrock Rovers	1	1	4	7	4	6	6	8	1
Shelbourne	11	-	10	9	7	4	1	3	5
Sligo Rovers	-	9	12	-	-	5	9	11	-
U.C.D.	12	-	-	-	12	-	-	-	-
Waterford United	5	4	6	12	-	11	-	10	-

First Division

	Season / Position								
	85/86	86/87	87/88	88/89	89/90	90/91	91/92	92/93	93/94
Athlone Town	-	-	1	-	-	-	-	6	2
Bray Wanderers	1	-	-	3	3	2	-	-	9
Cobh Ramblers	6	6	2	-	7	3	3	2	-
Derry City	4	1	-	-	-	-	-	-	-
Drogheda United	5	3	6	1	-	1	-	-	-
EMFA / Kilkenny City	10	9	10	9	4	7	8	9	8
Finn Harps	7	4	3	4	6	4	6	7	3
Galway United	-	-	-	-	-	-	-	1	-
Home Farm	-	-	4	5	5	8	9	8	6
Limerick City	-	-	-	-	-	-	1	-	-
Longford Town	3	10	7	8	8	9	10	5	5
Monaghan United	9	8	8	7	10	10	7	3	-
Newcastle United / N'West	8	7	9	6	9	*	*	*	*
St.James's Gate	*	*	*	*	*	5	5	10	10
Shelbourne	-	2	-	-	-	-	-	-	-
Sligo Rovers	2	-	-	10	2	-	-	-	1
U.C.D.	-	5	5	2	-	6	4	4	4
Waterford United	-	-	-	-	1	-	2	-	7

* Not L.O.I. Members

275

THE FRIENDLY SCENE

As we have come to expect in recent years the 1993/94 season proved to be yet another hectic one for National League sides on the friendlies front. Once again, particularly pre-season, home fans had ample opportunity to see at close quarters, a considerable array of English Premier League and Endsleigh Insurance League talent along with Scottish and Northern Irish sides.

Amongst the clubs which toured here were Leeds United, Tottenham Hotspur, Millwall, Bristol City, Cardiff City, Torquay United, Walsall, Raith Rovers, Kilmarnock, Cliftonville and Coleraine, whilst once-off visitors included Blackburn Rovers to Drogheda, Manchester City to Co. Louth neighbours Dundalk and Liverpool who took on Shelbourne. Indeed such was the interest in the latter game, the last of the big club friendlies, that many of those who made their way to Tolka Park failed to gain admission, sparking off strong criticism of 'Shels' handling of arrangements on the night.

Apart from meeting Irish club sides, Blackburn, Leeds and Liverpool also provided opposition for the Bord Gais National League selection who also took on the might of the RCS (Czechoslovakia) in a busy early season programme.

Another popular visitor during the season was Celtic, the Glasgow side being present to mark the re-opening of Richmond Park and the switching on of new floodlighting systems at Jackman Park, Limerick, and the Showgrounds in Sligo, all three welcome improvements to the local soccer scene.

As for the non-League boys, Ballinasloe Town once again flew the flag along with Ballyfermot side Cherry Orchard, whilst a Dalkey United selection which took on Mick McCarthy's Millwall was in fact almost exclusively composed of guesting National League players. Following recent tours which have seen them visit Norway and Florida, UCD once again took to the high seas with an ambitious visit to Australia. Showing good form the students were winners in all but one of their five encounters, losing only to a representative side from the Australia Capital Territories. Somewhat less ambitious was the visit north of the border by quite a few clubs to lock horns with their Irish League counterparts. Again this year results against our northern neighbours were a little disappointing, with a few notable exceptions.

Amongst the more impressive results achieved by home sides were wins for Kilkenny over Cardiff City, their third successive victory against English league opposition, St. Patrick's Athletic who trounced Scottish Premier outfit Raith Rovers and Derry City who enjoyed a fine win over Luton Town.

Well known international names who 'hit the net' in club friendlies this season included Shearer, Sheringham, Speed, Quinn, Dziekanowski, McStay, Vata, Rush etc. etc.

So then another very eventful year for friendlies on the home front with the return over a number of seasons by clubs like Leeds, Blackburn, Tottenham, Celtic and Millwall acknowledging the warmth of the reception afforded visitors by Irish fans. With a full itinerary of games again set for the coming '94/'95 season Irish fans should once more be spoilt for choice.

Friendlies 1993-94

Date	Teams	Score	Scorers
Jul. 16th	Shelbourne	(0) 2	(Gaynor 49, Cooney 82)
	Tottenham Hot.	(3) 4	(Flood o.g. 4, Turner 6, Sheringham 21, Barnby 53)
Jul. 18th	Drogheda Utd.	(0) 1	(Kinsella 66)
	Tottenham Hot.	(2) 3	(Sheringham 30, 35, Anderton 52)
	St. Patrick's Ath.	(2) 4	(Dunne 22, Keane 35, O'Connell 54, 80)
	Raith Rovers	(1) 1	(Dalziel (p) 41)
Jul. 20th	Shelbourne	(1) 3	(Costello 26, Izzi 54, Browne)
	Raith Rovers	(3) 4	(Dennis 33, Dair 38, McLeod 43, Dalziel 79)
Jul. 21st	Cork City	0	
	Leeds United	(2) 3	(Speed 13, Rocastle 18, Shutt 70)
	Galway United	0	
	Walsall	0	
Jul. 22nd	Drogheda Utd.	(0) 1	(Reid)
	Raith Rovers	(1) 1	(Dennis)
	Fermoy	(0) 1	(R. O'Connor 53)
	Walsall	(1) 3	(Dunne 17, Cecere 46, 55)
Jul. 23rd	Ballinasloe Town	1	
	Walsall	2	
	Athlone Town	0	
	Cardiff City	(2) 2	(Bird 21, Ramsey 41)
	Omagh Town	2	(Crilley, Paton)
	Sligo Rovers	2	(R. Rooney, Moran)
Jul. 25th	Cherry Orchard	0	
	Torquay United	3	(Kelly, Foster, Derby)
	Dalkey United	0	
	Millwall	(0) 1	(Allen 89)
	Derry City	(0) 1	(Dunleavy 66)
	Cardiff City	(0) 2	(Bird 60, Blake 67)
	Dundalk	(1) 1	(O'Sullivan 30)
	Manchester City	(2) 4	(Quinn 10, 51, Hill 36, Brightwell 46)
	Finn Harps	(1) 2	(Gallagher 27, McColgan 81)
	Bradford City	(2) 5	(McCarthy 2, Jewell, Oliver, Crawford)
	Glentorann	(1) 1	(McBride 2)
	Dundalk	0	
	Monaghan Utd.	0	
	Newry Town	(1) 4	(Staunton 12, 81, McCabe 49, McGee 65)
	Shelbourne	0	
	Portadown	(0) 1	(Cunningham 87)
Aug. 8th	Drogheda United	0	
	Blackburn Rov.	(0) 3	(Atkins 73, Shearer 83, 89)
	Sligo Rovers	(0) 1	(Hastie 66)
	Coleraine	0	
Aug. 11th	Cliftonville	0	
	Derry City	0	
Dec. 2nd	Derry City	3	(Hutton, Coyle, Heaney)
	Omagh Town	0	
Jan. 11th	Derry City	(1) 1	(Heaney 6)
	Luton Town	0	

U.C.D. Australian Tour

Date	Teams	Score	Scorers
Jul. 26th	Phoenix F.C. (NWS)	0	
	U.C.D.	1	(Quaid)
Jul. 29th	Gladesville (NWS)	0	
	U.C.D.	1	(Colwell)
Jul. 31st	Australian Capital Terr.	3	
	U.C.D.	0	
Aug. 4th	Deakin University	0	
	U.C.D.	5	(Burton 2, Griffin, Colwell, Lynch)
Aug. 7th	Essendon City	0	
	U.C.D.	4	(Quaid, Duffy (p), Colwell, Griffin)

Official switch on of Richmond Park Floodlights

Date	Teams	Score	Scorers
Jan. 12th	St. Patrick's Ath.	(1) 1	(Campbell 44)
	Celtic	(2) 4	(Biggins 13, 55, Byrne 31, McStay 50)
Jan. 26th	Derry City	(1) 1	(Kinnaird 26)
	Crystal Palace	(1) 2	(Gordon 34, Stewart 48)
	St. James's Gate	0	
	Walsall	(0) 1	(Lightbourne 88)
Jul. 26th	Bray Wanderers	(0) 2	(Smith 58, Nugent (p) 77)
	Torquay United	(1) 2	(Sale 10, Loram 53)

	Cobh Ramblers	(1) 1	*(Kelly 35)*
	Bristol City	(2) 3	*(Dziekanowski 10, Robinson 44, Brown 66)*
Jul. 27th	Derry City	(1) 1	*(Carlyle 19)*
	Partick Thistle	(2) 2	*(Cameron 23, 36)*
	Finn Harps	0	
	Kilmarnock	(0) 2	*(Browne 60, Mitchell 84)*
	Shelbourne	0	
	Millwall	(1) 4	*(Kerr 45, 48, 55, Dolby 90)*
Jul. 28th	Limerick	(1) 2	*(Hitchcock 28, Izzi 64)*
	Bristol City	(2) 3	*(Robinson 15, Baird 37, Morgan 85)*
Jul. 29th	Dundalk	0	
	Millwall	(2) 2	*(Dolby 9, Allen 39)*
	Kilkenny City	(0) 2	*(Wogan 52, Ennis 55)*
	Cardiff City	(0) 1	*(Blake 81)*
	Sligo Rovers	(0) 1	*(Houlahan)*
	Kilmarnock	(1) 1	*(Reilly)*
Jul. 30th	Galway United	0	
	Bristol City	(0) 1	*(Bent 73)*
Jul. 31st	Ballymoney Utd.	1	
	Shamrock Rovers	4	*(Nolan, Geoghegan, Swan 2)*
	Bohemians	(1) 1	*(Fenlon (p) 40)*
	Millwall	(1) 1	*(Kerr 5)*
	Derry City	(2) 4	*(Carlyle 7, Ryan 25, 87, P. Curran 89)*
	Ballymena Utd.	(1) 1	*(Johnston 26)*
	Monaghan Utd.	1	*(Wilson)*
	Cliftonville	3	*(Manley, Strang, O'Kane)*
Aug. 1st	Longford Town	0	
	Cliftonville	0	
Aug. 2nd	Carrick Rangers	1	
	Shamrock Rovers	1	*(McGrath)*

Terry Moore Testimonial

Aug. 4th	Glentoran	2	
	Derry City	1	*(Nixon)*

	Ballinamallard Utd.	0	
	Sligo Rovers	4	*(Devanney 3, Hastie (p))*
	Larne	0	
	Shamrock Rovers	2	*(Geoghegan, Burke)*
Aug. 7th	Derry City	(0) 1	*(Murray o.g. 84)*
	Crusaders	(1) 1	*(Turner 19)*
	Cliftonville	(0) 1	*(O'Kane)*
	Sligo Rovers	(2) 2	*(Moran, Shearer)*

	Finn Harps	(0) 1	*(Ewing o.g. 47)*
	Coleraine	(3) 4	*(Gaston 2, Cook, McNulty)*
Mar. 6th	Sligo Rovers	0	
	Celtic	(0) 1	*(Vata 70)*

Official switch on Jackman Park Floodlights

Mar. 8th	Limerick Select	0	
	Celtic	(1) 2	*(Gillespie 19, O'Neill 71)*

May 9th	Shelbourne	0	
	Liverpool	(0) 5	*(Hutchison 48, Rush 50, 51, Barnes 54, Redknapp 64)*

Hands off!
St. Pats' Eddie Gormley keeps Celtic's Rudi Vata at arms length (The Star)

Martin Nugent
Equalized for Bray v Torquay (St.P.A.)

NORTHERN IRELAND 1993-94

Smirnoff Irish League

	P	W	D	L	F	A	Pts.	GD.
Linfield	30	21	7	2	63	22	70	+41
Portadown	30	20	8	2	76	21	68	+55
Glenavon	30	21	5	4	69	29	68	+40
Crusaders	30	17	7	6	53	30	58	+23
Bangor	30	14	3	13	45	49	45	-4
Ards	30	13	2	15	59	55	41	+4
Distillery	30	11	8	11	41	40	41	+1
Cliftonville	30	11	10	9	41	32	40*	+9
Glentoran	30	10	7	13	46	43	37	+3
Coleraine	30	10	7	13	41	50	37	-9
Ballymena United	30	9	6	15	37	55	33	-18
Ballyclare Comrades	30	9	6	15	35	57	33	-22
Carrick Rangers	30	6	7	17	42	81	25	-39
Newry Town	30	5	9	16	26	52	24	-26
Larne	30	5	7	18	30	62	22	-32
Omagh Town	30	6	5	19	32	58	14+	-26

*Deducted 3 points for ineligible player; + deducted 9 points for ineligible player.

Top Scorer: (22) Darren Erskine *(Ards)* and Stephen McBride *(Glenavon)*

N.I. Soccer Writers Awards:
Player of the Year : Noel Bailie *(Linfield)*
Young Player of the Year : Declan Devine *(Omagh Town)*
Manager of the Year : Trevor Anderson *(Linfield)*

P.F.A. Awards:
Player of the Year : Glenn Ferguson *(Glenavon)*
Most Promising Newcomer : Peter Kennedy *(Glenavon)*

'Bass' Irish Cup Final:
7 May at *The Oval*
 Linfield (1) 2 *(Pebbles 45, Fenlon 90)*
 Bangor 0

Budweiser Cup Final:
21 Dec. at *The Oval*
 Linfield (1) 3 *(Doherty 26, Haylock 54, R. Campbell 56)*
 Ards 0

T.N.T. Overnite Gold Cup Final:
20 Nov. at *Windsor Park*
 Distillery (1) 3 *(Calvin 31, Cleland 79, Armstrong 115)*
 Bangor (1) 2 *(Glendinning 45, Spiers 52)* AET

Ulster Cup Final:
19 Oct. at *Windsor Park*
 Crusaders (1) 1 *(G. Hunter 30)*
 Bangor 0

Wilkinson Sword Irish League Cup Final:
26 Apr. at *The Oval*
 Linfield (0) 2 *(Peebles 57, R. Campbell 58)*
 Coleraine 0

Cawoods Co. Antrim Shield Final:
1 Feb. at *The Oval*
 Ards (1) 4 *(Browne 7, Wilson 55, Stranney 80, 89)*
 Crusaders (0) 2 *(K. Hunter 72, Collins 82)*

279

Irish League Clubs in Europe

Champions Cup Preliminary Round:

18 Aug.	Dinamo Tbilisi	(1) 2	*(S.Arveladze 8, Inalishvili 66)*
	Linfield	(0) 1	*(Johnston 56)*
1 Sep.	Linfield	(0) 1	*(Haylock 71)*
	Dinamo Tbilisi	(0) 1	*(S.Arveladze 46)* Agg. 2-3*

*Tbilisi dismissed after offering referee bribe in first leg

Champions Cup First Round:

16 Sep.	Linfield	(2) 3	*(Haylock 38, McConnell 42, Johnston 60)*
	FC Copenhagen	0	
29 Sep.	FC Copenhagen	(2) 4	*(Moller 4, M.Johansen 28, Hojer 90, Mikkelsen 105)*
	Linfield	0	Agg. 4-3 AET

Cup Winners' Cup Preliminary Round:

18 Aug.	Bangor	(1) 1	*(McEvoy 25)*
	Apoel Nicosia	(1) 1	*(Sotiriou 45)*
1 Sep.	Apoel Nicosia	(1) 2	*(Mihajlovic 16, Pounnas 69)*
	Bangor	(1) 1	*(Glendinning 4)* Agg. 3-2

UEFA Cup First Round:

14 Sep.	Crusaders	0	
	Servette	0	
28 Sep.	Servette	(0) 4	*(Andersen 57, Dunlop (og) 58, Giallanza 61, 70)*
	Crusaders	0	Agg 4-0

International Football

8 Sep. (WC)	Northern Ireland	(1) 2	*(Quinn 37, Gray 80)*
	Latvia	0	
13 Oct. (WC)	Denmark	(0) 1	*(B. Laudrup 84)*
	Northern Ireland	0	
17 Nov. (WC)	Northern Ireland	(0) 1	*(Quinn 73)*
	Rep.of Ireland	(0) 1	*(McLoughlin 76)*
23 Mar. (FR)	Northern Ireland	(1) 2	*(Morrow 42, Gray 49)*
	Romania		
20 Apr. (EC)	Northern Ireland	(3) 4	*(Quinn 4, 33, Lomas 25, Dowie 48)*
	Liechtenstein	(0) 1	*(Hasler 82)*
3 Jun. (Fr.)	Colombia	(2) 2	*(Perez 30, Valencia 44)*
	Northern Ireland	0	
11 Jun. (Fr.)	Mexico	(2) 3	*(Garcia 19 (pen), 31, Hermosillo 78)*
	Northern Ireland	0	

Statistics compiled by Marshall Gillespie. For further information on the Northern Ireland scene, readers are recommended to consult Marshalls super Northern Ireland Football Yearbook.

Cat and Mouse for Tom and Gerry
Tommy Coyne holds off Gerry Taggart at Lansdowne Road (EOH)

FIXTURES 1994-95

Premier Division Fixtures

Sunday, August 28th, 1994 - Series No. 1

Athlone Town	v	Sligo Rovers
Bohemians	v	Dundalk
Cobh Ramblers	v	Shamrock Rovers
Derry City	v	Shelbourne
Monaghan United	v	Galway United
St. Patrick's Athletic	v	Cork City

Wed./Thur. Aug. 31st/Sep.1st, 1994 - Series No. 2

Cork City	v	Bohemians
Dundalk	v	Monaghan United
Galway United	v	Athlone Town
Shamrock Rovers	v	St. Patrick's Athletic
Shelbourne	v	Cobh Ramblers
Sligo Rovers	v	Derry City

Sunday September 4th, 1994 – Series No. 3

Athlone Town	v	Monaghan United
Bohemians	v	Galway United
Cobh Ramblers	v	Cork City
Derry City	v	Shamrock Rovers
St. Patrick's Athletic	v	Dundalk
Sligo Rovers	v	Shelbourne

Sunday September 11th, 1994 – Series No. 4

Cork City	v	Derry City
Dundalk	v	Cobh Ramblers
Galway United	v	St. Patrick's Athletic
Monaghan United	v	Bohemians
Shamrock Rovers	v	Sligo Rovers
Shelbourne	v	Athlone Town

Sunday September 18th, 1994 – Series No. 5

Athlone Town	v	Shamrock Rovers
Cobh Ramblers	v	Monaghan United
Derry City	v	Galway United
St. Patrick's Athletic	v	Bohemians
Shelbourne	v	Cork City
Sligo Rovers	v	Dundalk

Sunday September 25th, 1994 – Series No. 6

Bohemians	v	Athlone Town
Cork City	v	Sligo Rovers
Dundalk	v	Derry City
Galway United	v	Cobh Ramblers
Monaghan United	v	St. Patrick's Athletic
Shamrock Rovers	v	Shelbourne

Dates for FAI Harp Lager Senior Cup 1994/95

1st Round
January 29th 1995

2nd Round
February 19th 1995

Quarter-Finals
March 12th 1995

Semi-Finals
April 2nd 1995

Final
April 30th 1995

N.B. it is advisable to check press for precise details as many clubs are switching games to Thursday, Friday or Saturday evenings. Kick-off times may also vary.

First Division Fixtures

Sunday September 25th, 1994 – Series No. 1

Finn Harps	v	Kilkenny City
Home Farm	v	Limerick F.C.
Longford Town	v	Drogheda United
UCD	v	Bray Wanderers
Waterford United	v	St. James's Gate

281

Sunday October 2nd, 1994 – Series No. 7
Athlone Town	v	Cork City
Cobh Ramblers	v	St. Patrick's Athletic
Derry City	v	Bohemians
Shamrock Rovers	v	Dundalk
Shelbourne	v	Galway United
Sligo Rovers	v	Monaghan United

Sunday October 2nd, 1994 – Series No. 2
Bray Wanderers	v	Finn Harps
Drogheda United	v	Waterford United
Kilkenny City	v	Longford Town
Limerick F.C.	v	U.C.D.
St. James's Gate	v	Home Farm

Sunday October 9th, 1994 – Series No. 8
Bohemians	v	Cobh Ramblers
Cork City	v	Shamrock Rovers
Dundalk	v	Shelbourne
Galway United	v	Sligo Rovers
Monaghan United	v	Derry City
St. Patrick's Athletic	v	Athlone Town

Sunday October 9th, 1994 – Series No. 3
Bray Wanderers	v	Limerick F.C.
Finn Harps	v	St. James's Gate
Kilkenny City	v	Drogheda United
Longford Town	v	Home Farm
U.C.D.	v	Waterford United

Sunday October 16th, 1994 – Series No. 9
Athlone Town	v	Cobh Ramblers
Cork City	v	Dundalk
Derry City	v	St. Patrick's Athletic
Shamrock Rovers	v	Galway United
Shelbourne	v	Monaghan United
Sligo Rovers	v	Bohemians

Sunday October 16th, 1994 – Series No. 4
Drogheda United	v	Finn Harps
Home Farm	v	U.C.D.
Limerick F.C.	v	Longford Town
St. James's Gate	v	Bray Wanderers
Waterford United	v	Kilkenny City

Sunday October 23rd, 1994 – Series No. 10
Bohemians	v	Shelbourne
Cobh Ramblers	v	Derry City
Dundalk	v	Athlone Town
Galway United	v	Cork City
Monaghan United	v	Shamrock Rovers
St. Patrick's Athletic	v	Sligo Rovers

Sunday October 23rd, 1994 – Series No. 5
Bray Wanderers	v	Drogheda United
Finn Harps	v	Home Farm
Kilkenny City	v	St. James's Gate
Limerick F.C.	v	Waterford United
U.C.D.	v	Longford Town

Sunday October 30th, 1994 – Series No. 11
Athlone Town	v	Derry City
Cork City	v	Monaghan United
Dundalk	v	Galway United
Shamrock Rovers	v	Bohemians
Shelbourne	v	St. Patrick's Athletic
Sligo Rovers	v	Cobh Ramblers

Sunday October 30th, 1994 – Series No. 6
Drogheda United	v	Limerick F.C.
Home Farm	v	Kilkenny City
Longford Town	v	Finn Harps
St. James's Gate	v	U.C.D.
Waterford United	v	Bray Wanderers

Sunday November 6th, 1994 – Series No. 12
Bohemians	v	Shamrock Rovers
Cobh Ramblers	v	Sligo Rovers
Derry City	v	Athlone Town
Galway United	v	Dundalk
Monaghan United	v	Cork City
St. Patrick's Athletic	v	Shelbourne

Sunday November 6th, 1994 – Series No. 7
Bray Wanderers	v	Longford Town
Drogheda United	v	Home Farm
Limerick F.C.	v	St. James's Gate
U.C.D.	v	Kilkenny City
Waterford United	v	Finn Harps

Sunday November 13th, 1994 – Series No. 13

Cork City	v	St. Patrick's Athletic
Dundalk	v	Bohemians
Galway United	v	Monaghan United
Shamrock Rovers	v	Cobh Ramblers
Shelbourne	v	Derry City
Sligo Rovers	v	Athlone Town

Sunday November 20th, 1994 – Series No. 14

Athlone Town	v	Galway United
Bohemians	v	Cork City
Cobh Ramblers	v	Shelbourne
Derry City	v	Sligo Rovers
Monaghan United	v	Dundalk
St. Patrick's Athletic	v	Shamrock Rovers

Sunday November 27th, 1994 – Series No. 15

Cork City	v	Cobh Ramblers
Dundalk	v	St. Patrick's Athletic
Galway United	v	Bohemians
Monaghan United	v	Athlone Town
Shamrock Rovers	v	Derry City
Shelbourne	v	Sligo Rovers

Sunday December 4th, 1994 – Series No. 16

Athlone Town	v	Shelbourne
Bohemians	v	Monaghan United
Cobh Ramblers	v	Dundalk
Derry City	v	Cork City
St. Patrick's Athletic	v	Galway United
Sligo Rovers	v	Shamrock Rovers

Sunday December 11th, 1994 – Series No. 17

Bohemians	v	St. Patrick's Athletic
Cork City	v	Shelbourne
Dundalk	v	Sligo Rovers
Galway United	v	Derry City
Monaghan United	v	Cobh Ramblers
Shamrock Rovers	v	Athlone Town

Sunday December 18th, 1994 – Series No. 18

Athlone Town	v	Bohemians
Cobh Ramblers	v	Galway United
Derry City	v	Dundalk
St. Patrick's Athletic	v	Monaghan United
Shelbourne	v	Shamrock Rovers
Sligo Rovers	v	Cork City

Mon./Tue. Dec. 26th/27th, 1995 – Series No. 19

Bohemians	v	Derry City
Cork City	v	Athlone Town
Dundalk	v	Shamrock Rovers
Galway United	v	Shelbourne
Monaghan United	v	Sligo Rovers
St. Patrick's Athletic	v	Cobh Ramblers

Sunday November 13th, 1994 – Series No. 8

Finn Harps	v	U.C.D.
Home Farm	v	Bray Wanderers
Kilkenny City	v	Limerick F.C.
Longford Town	v	Waterford United
St. James's Gate	v	Drogheda United

Sunday November 20th, 1994 – Series No. 9

Bray Wanderers	v	Kilkenny City
Drogheda United	v	U.C.D.
Limerick F.C.	v	Finn Harps
St. James's Gate	v	Longford Town
Waterford United	v	Home Farm

Sunday November 27th, 1994 – Series No. 10

Finn Harps	v	Limerick F.C.
Home Farm	v	Waterford United
Kilkenny City	v	Bray Wanderers
Longford Town	v	St. James's Gate
U.C.D.	v	Drogheda United

Sunday December 4th, 1994 – Series No. 11

Bray Wanderers	v	U.C.D.
Drogheda United	v	Longford Town
Kilkenny City	v	Finn Harps
Limerick F.C.	v	Home Farm
St. James's Gate	v	Waterford United

Sunday December 11th, 1994 – Series No. 12

Finn Harps	v	Bray Wanderers
Home Farm	v	St. James's Gate
Longford Town	v	Kilkenny City
U.C.D.	v	Limerick F.C.
Waterford United	v	Drogheda United

Sunday December 18th, 1994 – Series No. 13

Drogheda United	v	Kilkenny City
Home Farm	v	Longford Town
Limerick F.C.	v	Bray Wanderers
St. James's Gate	v	Finn Harps
Waterford United	v	U.C.D.

Mon./Tue. Dec. 26th/27th, 1994 – Series No. 14

Bray Wanderers	v	St. James's Gate
Finn Harps	v	Drogheda United
Kilkenny City	v	Waterford United
Longford Town	v	Limerick F.C.
U.C.D.	v	Home Farm

Sun./Mon. January 1st/2nd, 1995 – Series No. 20
Athlone Town	v	St. Patrick's Athletic
Cobh Ramblers	v	Bohemians
Derry City	v	Monaghan United
Shamrock Rovers	v	Cork City
Shelbourne	v	Dundalk
Sligo Rovers	v	Galway United

Sun./Mon. January 1st/2nd 1995 – Series No. 15
Drogheda United	v	Bray Wanderers
Home Farm	v	Finn Harps
Longford Town	v	U.C.D.
St. James's Gate	v	Kilkenny City
Waterford United	v	Limerick F.C.

Sunday January 8th, 1995 – Series No. 21
Bohemians	v	Sligo Rovers
Cobh Ramblers	v	Athlone Town
Dundalk	v	Cork City
Galway United	v	Shamrock Rovers
Monaghan United	v	Shelbourne
St. Patrick's Athletic	v	Derry City

Sunday January 8th, 1995 – Series No. 16
Bray Wanderers	v	Waterford United
Finn Harps	v	Longford Town
Kilkenny City	v	Home Farm
Limerick F.C.	v	Drogheda United
U.C.D.	v	St. James's Gate

Sunday January 15th, 1995 – Series No. 22
Athlone Town	v	Dundalk
Cork City	v	Galway United
Derry City	v	Cobh Ramblers
Shamrock Rovers	v	Monaghan United
Shelbourne	v	Bohemians
Sligo Rovers	v	St. Patrick's Athletic

Sunday January 15th, 1995 – Series No. 17
Finn Harps	v	Waterford United
Home Farm	v	Drogheda United
Kilkenny City	v	U.C.D.
Longford Town	v	Bray Wanderers
St. James's Gate	v	Limerick F.C.

Sunday January 22nd - Series No. 23
Athlone Town	v	Sligo Rovers
Bohemians	v	Dundalk
Cobh Ramblers	v	Shamrock Rovers
Derry City	v	Shelbourne
Monaghan United	v	Galway United
St. Patrick's Athletic	v	Cork City

Sunday January 22nd, 1995 – Series No. 18
Bray Wanderers	v	Home Farm
Drogheda United	v	St. James's Gate
Limerick F.C.	v	Kilkenny City
U.C.D.	v	Finn Harps
Waterford United	v	Longford Town

Sunday February 5, 1995 - Series No. 24
Cork City	v	Bohemians
Dundalk	v	Monaghan United
Galway United	v	Athlone Town
Shamrock Rovers	v	St. Patrick's Athletic
Shelbourne	v	Cobh Ramblers
Sligo Rovers	v	Derry City

Sunday February 5th, 1995 – Series No. 19
Finn Harps	v	Kilkenny City
Home Farm	v	Limerick F.C.
Longford Town	v	Drogheda United
U.C.D.	v	Bray Wanderers
Waterford United	v	St. James's Gate

Sunday February 12th, 1995 - Series No. 25
Athlone Town	v	Monaghan United
Bohemians	v	Galway United
Cobh Ramblers	v	Cork City
Derry City	v	Shamrock Rovers
St. Patrick's Athletic	v	Dundalk
Sligo Rovers	v	Shelbourne

Sunday February 12th, 1995 – Series No. 20
Bray Wanderers	v	Finn Harps
Drogheda United	v	Waterford United
Kilkenny City	v	Longford Town
Limerick F.C.	v	U.C.D.
St. James's Gate	v	Home Farm

Sunday February 26th, 195 - Series No. 26
Cork City	v	Derry City
Dundalk	v	Cobh Ramblers
Galway United	v	St. Patrick's Athletic
Monaghan United	v	Bohemians
Shamrock Rovers	v	Sligo Rovers
Shelbourne	v	Athlone Town

Sunday February 26th, 1995 – Series No. 21
Bray Wanderers	v	Limerick F.C.
Finn Harps	v	St. James's Gate
Kilkenny City	v	Drogheda United
Longford Town	v	Home Farm
U.C.D.	v	Waterford United

Sunday March 5th, 1995 - Series No. 27
Athlone Town	v	Shamrock Rovers
Cobh Ramblers	v	Monaghan United
Derry City	v	Galway United
St. Patrick's Athletic	v	Bohemians
Shelbourne	v	Cork City
Sligo Rovers	v	Dundalk

Friday March 17th, 1995 - Series No. 28
Bohemians	v	Athlone Town
Cork City	v	Sligo Rovers
Dundalk	v	Derry City
Galway United	v	Cobh Ramblers
Monaghan United	v	St. Patrick's Athletic
Shamrock Rovers	v	Shelbourne

Sunday March 19th, 1995 - Series No. 29
Athlone Town	v	Cork City
Cobh Ramblers	v	St. Patrick's Athletic
Derry City	v	Bohemians
Shamrock Rovers	v	Dundalk
Shelbourne	v	Galway United
Sligo Rovers	v	Monaghan United

Sunday March 26th, 1995 - Series No. 30
Bohemians	v	Cobh Ramblers
Cork City	v	Shamrock Rovers
Dundalk	v	Shelbourne
Galway United	v	Sligo Rovers
Monaghan United	v	Derry City
St. Patrick's Athletic	v	Athlone Town

Sunday April 9th, 1995 - Series No. 31
Athlone Town	v	Cobh Ramblers
Cork City	v	Dundalk
Derry City	v	St. Patrick's Athletic
Shamrock Rovers	v	Galway United
Shelbourne	v	Monaghan United
Sligo Rovers	v	Bohemians

Sunday April 16th, 1995 - Series No. 32
Bohemians	v	Shelbourne
Cobh Ramblers	v	Derry City
Dundalk	v	Athlone Town
Galway United	v	Cork City
Monaghan United	v	Shamrock Rovers
St. Patrick's Athletic	v	Sligo Rovers

Sunday April 23rd, 1995 - Series No. 33
Athlone Town	v	Derry City
Cork City	v	Monaghan United
Dundalk	v	Galway United
Shamrock Rovers	v	Bohemians
Shelbourne	v	St. Patrick's Athletic
Sligo Rovers	v	Cobh Ramblers

Sunday March 5th, 1995 – Series No. 22
Drogheda United	v	Finn Harps
Home Farm	v	U.C.D.
Limerick F.C.	v	Longford Town
St. James's Gate	v	Bray Wanderers
Waterford United	v	Kilkenny City

Sunday March 19th, 1995 – Series No. 23
Bray Wanderers	v	Drogheda United
Finn Harps	v	Home Farm
Kilkenny City	v	St. James's Gate
Limerick F.C.	v	Waterford United
U.C.D.	v	Longford Town

Sunday March 26th, 1995 – Series No. 24
Drogheda United	v	Limerick F.C.
Home Farm	v	Kilkenny City
Longford Town	v	Finn Harps
St. James's Gate	v	U.C.D.
Waterford United	v	Bray Wanderers

Thursday April 9th, 1995 – Series No. 25
Bray Wanderers	v	Longford Town
Drogheda United	v	Home Farm
Limerick F.C.	v	St. James's Gate
U.C.D.	v	Kilkenny City
Waterford United	v	Finn Harps

Sunday April 16th, 1995 – Series No. 26
Finn Harps	v	U.C.D.
Home Farm	v	Bray Wanderers
Kilkenny City	v	Limerick F.C.
Longford Town	v	Waterford United
St. James's Gate	v	Drogheda United

Sunday April 23rd, 1995 – Series No. 27
Bray Wanderers	v	Kilkenny City
Drogheda United	v	U.C.D.
Limerick F.C.	v	Finn Harps
St. James's Gate	v	Longford Town
Waterford United	v	Home Farm

285

Bibliography

Bass Sports Book of Irish Soccer (*Séan Ryan/Noel Dunne; Mercier 1975*)
Book of Irish Goalscorers (*Séan Ryan/Stephen Burke; Irish Soccer Co-op 1987*)
European Cups (*Ron Hockings; Kenneth Mason 1988*)
European Football Yearbook 1992/93 (*Ed. Mike Hammond; Sports Projects Ltd. 1992*)
Gillette Book of FAI Cup (*Séan Ryan/Terry O'Rourke; Irish Soccer Co-op 1985*)
Guinness European Soccer Who's Who (*Nich Hills/Tim Barrett; Guinness 1992*)
Guinness Record of World Soccer (*Guy Oliver; Guinness 1992*)
Guinness Soccer Who's Who (*Jack Rollin; Guinness, 7 editions*)
History of Athlone Town, the First 101 years (*Frank Lynch 1991*)
Hoops: A History of Shamrock Rovers (*Paul Doolan/Robert Goggins; Gill & Macmillan 1993*)
Ireland on the Ball (*Donal Cullen; ELO Publications 1993*)
100 years of Irish Football (*Malcolm Brodie; Blackstaff Press 1980*)
News of the World Football Annuals 1984-94 (*Invincible Press*)
Northern Ireland Football Yearbook 1993/94 (*Marshall Gillespie; Marshall Gillespie Publications 1993*) [*Formerly Irish Football Yearbook*]
Record of League of Ireland Football 1921/22-1984/85 (*plus supplements*) (*Niall MacSweeney; Assoc. of Football Statisticians 1985*)
Rothmans Football Yearbooks 1970-94 (*Queen Anne Press*)
Scottish Football League Review 1992-93 (*Sports Publications Ltd. 1992*)
Twenty Years of Irish Soccer (*Thomas Walsh; Sports Publicity Services 1941*)

Sources

Cork Constitution, Cork Examiner, 11-a-Side, Evening Echo, Evening Press, Irish Independent, Irish Press, Irish Soccer Magazine, Irish Times, Kerryman, Limerick Leader, Nationalist, Star, Sun, Sunday Independent, Sunday Press, Sunday Tribune, Sunday World, World Soccer.

Photographic Credits

(EB) Ebor Benson; (DC) Donal Cullen; (MD) Michael Duffy; EOH (Eddie O'Hare); (MG) Michael Geasley; (GU) Galway United; (CL) Catherine Levins; (PM) Peter Mulhall; (RN) Ray Nixon; The Star (Noel Gavin, Jim Walpole); (St.P.A.) St. Patrick's Athletic.